D1249605

Applied Organizational Communication

LEA'S COMMUNICATION SERIES

Jennings Bryant/Dolf Zillmann, General Editors

Applied Organizational Communication

Theory and Practice in a Global Environment

THIRD EDITION

Thomas E. Harris
University of Alabama

Mark D. Nelson
University of Alabama

Routledge
Taylor & Francis Group
New York   London

Cover design by Tonya Adams Nelson.

First Published by
Lawrence Erlbaum Associates
10 Industrial Avenue
Mahwah, New Jersey 07430

Reprinted 2008 by

Routledge
Taylor & Francis Group
270 Madison Avenue
New York, NY 10016

Routledge
Taylor & Francis Group
2 Park Square
Milton Park, Abingdon
Oxon OX14 4RN

© 2008 by Taylor & Francis Group, LLC

Printed in the United States of America on acid-free paper
10 9 8 7 6 5 4 3

International Standard Book Number-13: 978-0-8058-5941-6 (Softcover) 978-0-8058-5940-9 (Hardcover)

No part of this book may be reprinted, reproduced, transmitted, or utilized in any form by any electronic, mechanical, or other means, now known or hereafter invented, including photocopying, microfilming, and recording, or in any information storage or retrieval system, without written permission from the publishers.

Trademark Notice: Product or corporate names may be trademarks or registered trademarks, and are used only for identification and explanation without intent to infringe.

Library of Congress Cataloging-in-Publication Data

Harris, Thomas E., Ph. D.
   Applied organizational communication : theory and practice in a global environment / Thomas E. Harris and Mark D. Nelson. -- 3rd ed.
      p. cm. -- (LEA's communication series)
      ISBN-13: 978-0-8058-5941-6 (pbk. : alk. paper)
      ISBN-13: 978-0-8058-5940-9 (hardcover : alk. paper)

   1. Communication in organizations. I. Nelson, Mark D. II. Title.
   HD30.3.H372 2008   658.4′5--dc22   2007017210

Visit the Taylor & Francis Web site at
http://www.taylorandfrancis.com

To Shelia Harris, Tom's wife, for her support and insights regarding organizations and communication. Her sense of humor and perspective, endless patience, and love during the long hours required to write this book were remarkable. This book could not have been written without her assistance.

To Jean and Ed Harris, Tom's parents, for their unconditional love and lifelong curiosity.

To Anissa Whitten, Tom's daughter, for her willingness to embrace change while maintaining critical values and friendships.

To Tonya Adams Nelson, Mark's wife, for her love and laughter.

To Mark's parents, Delone and Jewel Nelson, for their steadfast support.

Contents

Preface

Organizational communication is a fascinating subject that is constantly evolving. The second edition of this book was published in 2002 and I noted that organizations had changed substantially from the first edition. This edition reflects the significant changes since 2002 while retaining the in-depth discussions of critical organizational communication concepts. In addition, Dr. Mark Nelson has agreed to co-author this edition, making the coverage even more complete. We have added important insights concerning critical perspectives and the reader will note extensive updates, revisions, and current examples. The majority of the original chapter titles have remained, because they allow the reader to quickly access specific information. In every chapter, change, diversity, and the digital age are examined.

In addition to providing extensive resources, this text reflects my own 35 years of experience as a teacher and an organizational consultant. In organizations ranging in size from Bristol Myers Squibb, Georgia Pacific, and IBM, to local and regional volunteer groups such as the Easter Seals, I have introduced, developed, and expanded the understanding and effective utilization of applied organizational communication concepts. As the reader discovers, each chapter presents an extensive analysis of selected topics, coupled with current and broad-based research. Hopefully, my own enthusiasm for a communication approach to understanding organizations shows in every chapter. Nelson's experiences reflect my own, and our combined research and experience are reflected throughout the text.

The book unfolds in the following manner.

The first three chapters are concerned with the perspectives necessary to understand the relationship between communication and organizations. Chapter 1 grounds the text in current and future changes, explains the transactional communication perceptive, and offers a systems perspective as a viable means for understanding organizations. Chapter 2 links perception with understanding communication and organizations. Chapter 3 provides an extensive discussion of the current organizational and management theories that have set the stage for the modern organization.

Organizational communication is a complex topic. Chapter 4, on verbal communication, presents an organization's eye view of how language functions and malfunctions. Chapter 5, on nonverbal communication, draws from the broad research available and applies the relevant information to organizations. Chapter 6 focuses on networks and channels, which are the means by which individuals, groups, and organizations connect. Symbolic behavior is examined in chapter 7, which develops the clear link between communication and organizations.

Chapter 8 is devoted to understanding listening. Chapter 9 explores interpersonal communication, and discusses transactions and problems including conflict and superior–subordinate relationships with new information on interpersonal skills development. Chapter 10 highlights how groups and teams are fundamental to any organization; this chapter has been updated to include a discussion of the contemporary approaches to group development. Chapter 11 offers the key concepts regarding leadership, including feminist perspectives on power and contemporary theories of leadership. As is fitting, new communication technologies are examined in chapter 12, which provides comprehensive insights into the benefits and challenges presented by new technologies at all levels in organizations.

This text is intended to be comprehensive, clear, interesting, current, and accessible. We have made a great effort to avoid a single, parochial view, because our consulting experiences have indicated clearly that a broad theoretical understanding is more useful to the individual and the organization. The most exciting aspect of our own careers has been the application of academic theories to actual organizational communication situations and returning to the classroom with examples to explain these theories. Throughout this text, we have tried to offer the same opportunity to the reader.

Acknowledgments

We would like to express our appreciation to the numerous organizations and individuals who have provided insights into the organizational communication processes as we have functioned as facilitators, change agents, consultants, and trainers.

In addition, we would like to thank the editorial staff at Taylor & Francis for its hard work, patience, and guidance in developing this third edition. Mark has added that he is indebted to Tom Harris for allowing him to be part of this project, remarking that Tom's guidance and generosity are beyond measure.

1
Adopting a Perspective

Realities

Anyone planning a career faces three realities. First, organizations permeate almost all aspects of our adult lives from providing careers to controlling our choices in goods and services. Even the smallest independent group of highly creative individuals must have some form of organization. We must interact with all sizes of organizations, ranging from Microsoft with its predominance in the electronic world to the local coffee, pizza, bagel, Internet café, or grocery store. This omnipresence in our postbaccalaureate careers means understanding organizations is synonymous with the pursuit of rewarding employment and achieving our goals. Except for the unusual and most likely unemployable individual, the need to operate effectively with and within organizations is as real a skill and an occupational necessity as knowing how to find a job or learn a vocation.

How we interact leads to the second reality. Later in this chapter and throughout this book, we demonstrate the importance of communication. For now, it is sufficient to state that communication is both a primary perspective for understanding how organizations function and a guide for how we should behave in organizations if we are to advance and enjoy our careers. Changing organizations are the third reality and we focus on these changes shortly.

The key concepts covered in this chapter include:

- The ever-changing world of organizational communication—the digital age, change, diversity
- Communication in organizations—importance to the organization, leaders, individuals
- Understanding organizational communication
- Perspectives—communication as process, transactional perspective
- Organizations as systems
- Complex systems—second-order change, learning organizations, sense-making, self-organizing

The Ever-Changing World of Organizational Communication

The changes impacting organizations are the third reality. As you will discover, organizing and communicating involve ongoing changes. "Change is

1

a ubiquitous phenomenon in organizations, and communication is a central process in planning and implementing change" (Jones, Watson, Gardner, & Gallios, 2004, p. 735). Although change has always existed, the speed, breadth, and impact of change are truly different as we travel through the new millennium. The Internet and globalization force innovation requiring organizations to be more efficient and "rewiring them for creativity and growth" (McGregor, 2006, p. 64). The dynamic nature of organizations is examined throughout this text. At this point, we will consider three forces—the digital age, speed of change, and diversity.

Digital Age

First, we are in the *digital age*. The massive growth in electronic communication has created a revolution easily as great as the Industrial Revolution that began in the late 1800s. The rivers of electronic 1s and 0s that computers create, move, process, store, retrieve, shape, and reshape are the basic elements of the postindustrial age. This *information revolution* reaches through innumerable circuits criss-crossing cyberspace. "In the 21st century, information technology will drive economic wealth. The innovations developed by the computing, telecommunications, consumer electronics, and electronic media industries will affect every business large and small—and dramatically change our home lives as well" (Katz, 1997, p. 1). Over the past 25 years, the Information Revolution has boosted productivity by almost 70% during that period (Mandel, 2005). The technology of information, or *infotech*, makes knowledge a vital commodity requiring the effective utilization of the distinctly human elements of an organization such as communication, culture, and leadership (Colvin, 1997). Google is so ubiquitous that it has become its own verb (Weise, 2005). In October 2005, for example, of the 5.1 billion Internet searches, 2.4 billion used Google, which, in many cases, "is taking the place of not only a trip to the library, but also a call to Mom, a recipe box, the phone book and neighborly advice" (Weise, 2005, p. 1D). However, as many individuals have found with the online Wikipedia, not all Internet information is correct because much of the available data is supplied by users who may not be experts on the topic (Weise, 2005). Another impact of the digital revolution is that we no longer depend on others to do many of our everyday tasks. "With digital cameras, we print our own photographs. With ATMs, we do the work bank-tellers used to do for us. We track online the packages we ship" (Toffler, 2006, p. 8). You can add numerous other web-oriented activities such as college registration, paying income taxes, doing searches, and so on.

This is a relatively new phenomenon. Integrated circuits have been around for about 40 years and microprocessors for a little more than 30 years. During those 30 years, microprocessors' performance has multiplied by a factor of more than 10,000. The first PC (1974) operated at 2 MHz and contained

256 bites of RAM. Today's newest PCs run at 500 MHz+ and have 3 million times as much RAM.

⟨Consumer electronics worldwide include 2 billion mobile phones; 1.5 billion TV sets; 820 million PCs; 190 million Game Boys; 70 million iPods; 50 million PDAs; and 3.2 million BlackBerrys (Conlin, 2006, p. 27). There are multibillions of microchips in coffee-makers, clock radios, calculators, cars, and computers and they are used to control airplanes, switch phone calls, watch weather systems, and track our bills or college grades. Computers control the power grids, the water plants, and a plethora of other utilities and public services that work seamlessly to keep homes and offices running. Last year more microchips were produced (and at a lower cost) than grains of rice (Conlin, 2006). As important as the internal combustion engine or the electric motor were as innovations, the microchip amplifies our intellect. Automobiles allow us to travel greater distances in less time with less strain. The computer and other digital devices free the mind, increase our ability to connect with others, and enhance our information resources.⟩

The *Internet*, originally created to enhance national security and academic research, is now a mainstay of life for many people and organizations and impacts every age bracket as shown by this breakdown of who is online: 19–29 = 88%; 20–49 = 84%; 50–64 = 71%; 65+ = 32% (Conlin, 2006). "The Internet has become ubiquitous, so companies can connect with talent anywhere in the blink of an eye, inside or outside the company. Open-source software can be plucked off the shelf to become the foundation of new software programs or Web sites (Hamm, 2005, p. 71). The *World Wide Web* (WWW) became a player in 1989. The Internet moves stand-alone computers from being text-processors and number-crunchers to communications devices, which change the way we use them, and begins "to alter in bold new ways how we work and live" (Spear, 2000, p. 90). "Technology has sped up economic and social life with inventions that take off with lives of their own, such as e-mail or gene manipulation" (Issak, 2005, p. 22). In fact, there are some legitimate misgivings regarding the digital impact. "The time for human communication is cut shorter; the means more homogeneous: the mode, cooler: Computer, fax and cell phone interactions replace face-to-face conversations and the charm and nuances of body language" (Issak, 2005, p. 27).

The *Y2K* (Year 2000) problem offers a clear example of computers' influence in most aspects of our lives. A great deal of time and energy was spent in the last few years of the old millennium attempting to correct the millennium bug, which had the potential to paralyze computers once January 1, 2000 arrived. Early programmers used only the last two digits of the year (e.g., 80 or 91) instead of all four numbers (e.g., 1980 or 1991) when designing the clocks that monitor and run computers. At the time, the memory required to store these additional two digits for all potential transactions would have been too expensive to commit or nonexistent. However, this meant that if the oversight was not corrected, January 1, 2000 (01.01.00) would be read by the computers used by banks, air traffic controllers, military defense or at home as 00 meaning it would be 1900 or the beginning of the last century. In theory, this could have shut down many organizations. The final cost of correcting this glitch surpassed $122 billion in the United States and $282 billion worldwide (International Data Corporation, 2000). As organizations rushed to correct Y2K, they discovered to their chagrin that billions of embedded microprocessors or microchips controlling factories, mixing fuel in automotive engines, automatically flushing some toilets, and operating digital televisions, smart phones, or video games could also create havoc. Even if an organization corrected its Y2K problems, it was still connected with numerous other computer-controlled devices that may not have been corrected by the year 2000. A programming decision made many years ago had the potential to impact almost everyone. For our purposes, Y2K underscores the wide-ranging impact of the digital age and the interdependency of organizational communication systems. We discuss interdependency later in this chapter and book.

By their very nature, electronics flatten corporate pyramids, change the competitive picture, redraw communication channels, and alter the traditional pathways for success (James, 1996). Electronic communication channels are overtaking memos and other written formats.

Internets, Intranets, CNN, and many other electronic media can connect almost all employed individuals. Students conduct information searches for papers, businesses seek competitive information, Web surfers visit chat rooms and discover unusual sites, and almost everyone in an organization can have digital connections. We have become an electronic global village. Organizations and organizational communication exist in a wired world. "Between 2000 and 2004, total global Internet usage grew 125%" (Friedman, 2005, p. 198). During the same time period, "Google went from processing roughly 150 millions searches per day to roughly one billion searches per day, with only a third coming from inside the United States" (Friedman, 2005, p. 198). However, these forms of digitized communication can be over-utilized. "Fully 25% of executives at large companies say their communications—voice mail, e-mail, and meetings—are nearly or completely unmanageable. That's according to a new McKinsey survey of more than 7,800 managers around the world. Nearly 40% spend a half to a full day per week on communications that are not valuable" (Mandel, 2005, p. 62). As the last observations support, the digital world has created significant forces for change, our next issue.

Change

Second, organizations are changing at a rate unforeseen only a few years ago. The question is no longer do organizations want to change, but how quickly can effective changes be inaugurated (Charan & Tichy, 1998). Corder (1999) reports the results of interviews with 100 senior executives in companies with

1,000 or more employees. "Change has become such a way of life that 73% of the executives in this survey said that their organizations have gone through tremendous transformations during the past 2 years" (p. 13).

The catastrophic events of September 11, 2001 involving the World Trade Center, the Pentagon, and airline highjacking provide previously unimaginable support for the impact of change on organizations. Predictions regarding future courses of actions, how to configure offices, and priorities concerning spending were forced to change. Struggling to survive, organizations responded by questioning their abilities to use information, downsizing, and reexamining how information and services are provided. For example, airlines and travel-related industries laid off massive numbers of employees, suffered significant losses, and began changing the way they conducted their business. Eastman Kodak, the world's largest photography company, reported a 77% drop in third-quarter earnings (2001) caused by the drop in leisure travel. Weyerhaeuser, the world's number one paper-maker, had profits fall 54% due to less demand for magazines and catalogues (Yen, 2001). Later in this chapter, you will have the opportunity to understand systems thinking; these events provide unquestionable support for the importance of considering the interdependence of systems. In addition, consider the following changes: information and service industries, downsizing, mergers, and globalization.

Information rich industries are creating a demand for knowledge workers and transforming the world economy from a dependence on manufacturing to services and technology-based organizations (Griffin, 2005). Knowledge workers require continued training to keep their skills from becoming obsolete. "It has been suggested, for example, that the 'half-life' of a technical education in engineering is three years" (Griffin, 2005, p. 464).

Currently, more than 75% of the jobs in the United States are service-related jobs accounting for well over half the United States gross domestic product (Colvin, 2005). Service means individuals are not engaged in making a product but instead they are providing services ranging from medical care to fast food restaurants. The shift away from a manufacturing-based economy means that knowledge and service work is replacing manual labor. In 1990, 1 out of 5 workers were employed in manual labor. "By 2010, no more than 1 in 10 workers will be engaged in making or moving things" (Boyett & Boyett, 1998, p. 321).

Change has not impacted all groups of workers equally. "The average hourly wage of rank-and-file workers—a group that makes up 80% of the work force—is slightly lower than it was four years ago, once inflation is taken into account" (Leonhardt, 2006, p. C12). Thomas, Cooper, and Blake (1999) estimate "that by the year 2020, a high-tech, well-to-do group will monopolize more than 60% of the income earned in the United States" (p. 184) but this group will hardly comprise the majority of workers. As an overview, "United States is in the midst of a transition from an industrial society ... to a brain-driven, knowledge-based economy. In other words, you create more value in the coming society through creative thinking and planning than in rote manufacturing" (Toffler, 2006, p. 7). By any measure, having a strong back and a willingness to work will not serve to guarantee a financially rewarding future.

Downsizing, which is purposely becoming smaller by reducing the size of the workforce or shedding entire divisions or businesses, continues with as "many as 25 percent of U.S. workers (being) affected by merger or acquisition in the 1990s while worldwide merger and acquisition activity grew to $3.5 trillion in 2000" (Pepper & Larson, 2006, p. 49). The overall impact has been job insecurity created by uncertainty over who will become unemployed. *Mergers* and *acquisitions* (M&A) are another major force contributing to downsizing. "In 2002, for example, over 6,900 M&A deals worth $458.7 billion were conducted in the United States; globally, over 23,500 deals worth $1.4 trillion were registered" (Cummings & Worley, 2005, p. 454). Among various strategic arguments, one important force for M&A is the cost savings generated by moving from two human resources or accounting departments, for example, to one central department. One consequence is the involuntary lay-off of personnel.

Major organizations are combining to form *international megacompanies*. This absorption of one organization by another includes almost all types of businesses. A cursory examination of the changing names for department stores, banks, and grocery chains offer ever-present proof. In every field, the large corporations are getting larger, reducing the potential for an upstart organization to enter a market. "Indeed, 300 multinational companies account for 25% of the world's assets" (Issak, 2005, p. 74).

Although larger organizations receive the brunt of attention, smaller companies provide the most job creation and opportunities. In the early 1970s, one in five American workers drew a paycheck from a Fortune 500 company. By the early 1990s, that ratio had fallen to 1 in 10. Of the 5.8 million U.S. employers, 89.1% are organizations with fewer than 20 workers. Only 0.3 percent have 500 or more (Mullins, 2003). The mid-1990s witnessed some 25 million Americans working as units of one, still highly dependent on the environment, but unencumbered by working with others in an organizational setting (Ussem, 1999). Companies with fewer than 500 employees "account for half the nation's economic output and 60 to 80% of all new jobs" (Lohr, 2006, p. E10).

Globalization impacts on every aspect of organizational life as organizations work with foreign subsidiaries, enter global markets, create international coalitions, and engage in multinational enterprises. The interconnectedness between economies has reached an unprecedented level. In the 1960s, only 6% of the U.S. economy was exposed to international competition. That percentage skyrocketed to more than 70% in the 1980s and continues to grow

(Rothwell, Prescott, & Taylor, 1999). For example, the best-managed firms venture into the international marketplace and routinely earn from 25% to nearly 100% of their total revenues by reaching beyond their national borders (McClenahen, 1998). Larger corporations often maintain foreign offices in more than 100 different countries. Most of us enjoy Colombian coffee; use Sony, Panasonic, or other Japanese equipment for entertainment, wear clothes sewn in an Asian country; or buy gas from BP (British Petroleum) or Shell (Dutch). Overseas, people recognize and enjoy Pepsi, Coca-Cola, Kentucky Fried Chicken, McDonald's, and purchase numerous U.S.-based products. For all practical purposes, Microsoft has defined how worldwide business will be conducted for many organizations. More specifically, "succeeding in today's economy requires fast reflexes and the ability to communicate and collaborate across the globe" (Mandel, 2005, p. 60).

The euro represents a dramatic example of interconnectedness. The January 1, 1999 adoption of this common currency by 12 countries changed the buying habits of 292 million residents. Only Britain, Denmark, Sweden, and Greece failed to adopt the new currency, although each country reserved the right to join later (Sancton, 1998). This represents "the biggest and most complex peacetime logistical operation in history" (Fairlamb, 2001, p. 48). These types of regional alliances have the potential to entirely reshape the competitive picture.

The digital revolution, mergers, and world competition forcing even greater demands for change in individual organizations spurn globalization's impact. Stewart (1993) concludes: "Paradox: Although it's hard to imagine a more macroeconomic subject, globalization is intensely parochial. Globalization's strongest effects are on companies" (p. 67) requiring organizations to embrace change, use different communication and distribution systems, and devote more attention to diversity. For the foreseeable future, organizational change or discontinuity will be normal and continuity will be abnormal (Cummings & Worley, 2005). Changes are occurring in every national and international aspect of business and organizations. One of the most significant issues is diversity.

Diversity

Finally, diversity within and between organizations presents significant challenges and opportunities. "Diversity exists in a group or organization when its members differ from one another along one or more important dimensions" including gender, ethnic origin, age, and many other factors (Denisi & Griffin, 2005, p. 509). The entire make-up of the organizational world has been changing and this will continue with substantial increases in participation by traditional minorities and dramatic changes in demographics, multicultural backgrounds, and interests. The growth in female, African American, Hispanic, and Asian workers means the end of the traditional dominance by white males. Clearly, diversity encompasses more than gender or ethnic background.

Age, physical characteristics, educational level, living arrangements (including single, traditional, dual-income, divorced, and same-sex), all provide an increasingly diverse organizational make-up (Cummings & Worley, 2005).

All workforce segments will increase as a percentage of the total workforce (except white males, whose numbers declined from 46.4% to 38.4% by 2005). There is a much greater likelihood we will be working with individuals who are not from the groups we traditionally associate with, than with such a group. Add the internationalization of many organizations and we are likely to be reporting to superiors, working with colleagues, and directing subordinates from different countries. This trend is unlikely to decrease because, nationally and internationally, "companies promote diversity primarily because it makes good business sense" (Bolman & Deal, 2003, p. 153).

The workforce changes are important. "For four decades, the number of women entering the workforce grew at a blistering pace, fostering a powerful cultural and economic transformation of American society" (Porter, 2006, p. A1). In 2000, "some 77% of women in the prime ages of 25 to 54 were in the workforce" (Porter, 2006, p. A1). However, there has been a leveling off of women in the workplace due to the increasing difficulty of balancing home- and family-related responsibilities with work demands (Porter, 2006).

By the year 2050, the U.S. population will increase by 50%, with immigration accounting for almost two thirds of that growth, which will create an increased need for multicultural understanding (Griffin, 2005). "By then, about half of all Americans will belong to what are now considered minority groups" according the U.S. Department of Labor's 1999 report (Associated Press, 1999, p. 5B). The 2000 census revealed that 3 in 10 people in the United States are minorities; 6.8 million people identified themselves as multiracial; Hispanics make up 12.5% of the population, exceeding the African American population of 12.1%; and Asian Americans make up 3.6% of the population (Kasindorf & El Nasser, 2001). "By 2050, 21% of Americans will be claiming mixed ancestry" (Kasindorf & El Nasser, 2001, p. 2A). A USA Today/CNN/Gallup Poll revealed that 64% of the 1,015 respondents felt it "would be good for the country to have more Americans thinking of themselves as multiracial rather than belonging to a single race" with 24% viewing this possibility as a bad outcome (Kasindorf & El Nasser, 2001, p. A1). Three quarters of the respondents in the 19–29-year-old age group greeted a multiracial country positively.

The new economy fostered by rapid change, globalization, and the digital age "favors workers who excel in manipulating information and solving problems. And, as it turns out, the biggest pool of workers with that skill set is women" (Farrell, 1999, p. 35). The Women's Research & Education Institute of Washington reports that U.S. women have been obtaining higher education degrees at a rapidly increasing rate and for the first time "the group of women between the ages of 25 and 35 have more education than their male counterparts" earning the majority of associate, bachelor's, and master's degrees

(Farrell, 1999, p. 35). However, these demographic increases are not reflected in promotions or positions. In 1998, members of minority groups represented only 12.4% of the officials and managers (Johnson, 1998). This is unfortunate, as an American Management Association and Business and Professional Women's Foundation study of more than 1,000 executives found that "management diversity is directly correlated with superior organizational performance" ("Diversity boosts," 1999, p. 5). Three key results of the study were: (1) Diversity breeds success because of the mixture of genders, ethnic backgrounds, and ages in senior management teams; (2) hiring diverse newcomers from the outside boosts performance; and (3) organizations that include senior managers under the age of 40 show a greater success pattern than those with *exclusively* older top executives.

Two-career families are becoming the norm, more individuals in the workforce are over 65 than in their teens, and women and people of color will outnumber the past majorities represented by white males. Once again, these shifts present new issues, challenges, and opportunities. "Today, in nearly four out of five couples—compared with one out of five in 1950—both partners are in the labor force, with women working nearly as many hours as men" (Hunter, 1999, p. 39). We have already indicated that some women are choosing not to work due to other commitments. However, the impact on couples where both are employed is undeniable.

Generation Y, numbering around 67 million and aged 20–29 (Fisher, 2006), comprise the second largest group of individuals to be entering the workforce. They are outnumbered only by the baby boomers who are discussed shortly. They seek flexibility, mobility, and different incentives than the security presented by earlier employment situations. An even more focused analysis includes the 42 million 16-to-25-year-olds who are also known as *millennials* or *echo boomers* (Jayson, 2006). This group shows great potential (having grown up with diversity and multiculturalism as facts of life), is more educated, faces fewer gender or ethnic barriers, and has a strong technological literacy. However, they have come of age in a globally competitive world where the path to the middle class is no longer a high school diploma (Jayson, 2006). In fact, "we live in a knowledge economy. *What* you know is beginning to count almost as much as *who* you know. Educational degrees are slowly becoming mere driver's licenses when looking for a job and moving from one job to the other. What you know and specialize beyond the credentials is what counts" (Issak, 2005, p. 214). Not everyone in this age group strives to be a high achiever.

Social scientists have identified an additional subgroup, *twixters*, who are adults who still live with their parents, feel free to job hop, and generally seem to be going nowhere (Grossman, 2005). "The percentage of 26-year-olds living with their parents has nearly doubled since 1970, from 11% to 20%" (Grossman, 2005, p. 44). Although this group may seem directionless, many sociologists attribute this apparent aimlessness to an attempt to choose the right path and to the willingness of family and society to accept the lifestyle. When contrasted with the same age bracket 40 years ago, "researchers found that by age 30, a much smaller percentage today (46% or women and 31% of men) have finished school, left home, gotten married, had a child or reached financial independence" (Jayson, 2006, p. 2D). For organizations depending on a youthful infusion, this technologically literate but somewhat unsettled group could present a challenge in terms of recruiting, retention, and motivation.

Sandwiched between these two groups are the 40 million *Generation Xers* (Fisher, 2006), which are the smallest group. As the first generation of "latch-key" kids with "no stay-at-home" moms, and with nearly 3 in 10 children being products of divorce, Gen-Xers' views regarding the role of work in their lives are different from their elders (Zemke, Raines, & Filipczak, 2000). Along with Gen Ys, they are technologically literate, well educated, and they accept change as part of everyday life. Known as the baby bust, Gen Xers "are unambiguously the smallest generation since the Great Depression" (Fisher, 2006, p. 49). Xers underscore that "work attitudes have shifted, and workers are more willing to leave jobs to gain time for leisure or family" (Denisi & Griffin, 2005, p. 516). Sixty-two percent of American workers say their job activities and responsibilities are increasing, many are foregoing their full vacation time, and they see no end in sight—it is no wonder that this group of workers might opt for a less stressful life (Schwartz, 2004).

At the other end of the age spectrum, there are 69 million workers aged 40 to 59 as of June 2006 (Fisher, 2006). As opposed to earlier predictions, 44% these baby boomers, born between 1946 and 1964, plan to work well past their 64th birthday (Fisher, 2006). To put this group in perspective, every "seven seconds, somebody becomes 60 in our country" (Willoughby, 2006, p. 1).

Gen Y and Gen X will face different challenges than the boomers. For example, a "young American today with at least two years of college can expect to change jobs at least 11 times before retirement" (Schwartz, 2004, p. 16A). Part of the reason might be the need "to put in your time" in some organizations. Another problem is a developing Gray Ceiling. Boomers are putting off their retirement, meaning many "twenty-, thirty-, and even forty-something managers are in trouble. In addition, The Society for Human Resource Management reports that 55% of big U.S. companies are "giving managers the tools to increase retention of baby boomers, including flexible or reduced schedules and retention bonuses" (Fisher, 2006, p. 50).

Essentially, the workforce includes the over-55 baby boomers, the time-squeezed midcareer employees, and the under-34 group (Dychtwald, Erickson, & Morison, 2006). As we have discovered, special considerations may well be necessary to adjust to this increased diversity in needs and attitudes (Dychtwald, Erickson, & Morison, 2006).

An intervening factor for many individuals is the increasing time demands that are creating strains on many families and individuals. The increase in knowledge-based occupations, where individuals take work home, respond to a 24/7 schedule, or worry about issues that have become a central part of their jobs, increases stress (Schwartz, 2004). In addition, business has moved away from traditional employment with 4 out of 10 Americans working on non-standard time (no more 9-to-5 workdays). The odd hours include evenings, nights, rotating shifts, and weekends to meet the demands of global supply chains and customers in every time-zone (Schwartz, 2004).

Stress, often created or increased by occupational demands, is a neutral concept. For example, it can motivate someone to study for an exam or do their best work. Stress "is a person's adaptive response to a stimulus that places excessive psychological or physical demands on him or her" (Denisi & Griffin, 2005, p. 492). Although negative stress can create numerous work related issues, "most stress-related health problems are a far cry from the phenomenon known in Japan as *karoshi*, or 'death from over-work'" (Schwartz, 2004, p. 16A). However, long hours or varying schedules, family pressures, increased technology, downsizing, rapid business expansion, and outsourcing and the other changes we have already discussed can lead to a sense of being out of control or stressed. In addition, all increase stress. Finally, complicated and creative work that cannot be easily reduced to a set of instructions is increasing, especially for the better educated employees (Farrell, 2005). Our point is that the ongoing diversification, combined with change and globalization, often leads to increased stress.

Race, gender, ethnicity, age, physical abilities, sexual orientation, social and economic class, access to education, disabilities, and other dimensions represent ongoing and significant areas of change (Reece & Brandt, 2005). With few exceptions, an enlightened and proactive approach to increasing diversity leads to excellent results (Denisi & Griffin, 2005; Reece & Brandt, 2005).

The digital age, change, and diversity underscore the importance of understanding organizational communication. The goal of this book is to provide an understanding that will be useful to you throughout your involvement with organizations. Although we could focus on managerial communication or leader-centered behavior, this unnecessarily limits your options as you choose and develop your career or careers. Different positions require different skills and understanding, and during your progression through any organization you will be alternatively both in charge and a relative newcomer. Therefore, your repertoire of knowledge and skills is more important than any one procedure. As you read the various chapters of this text, you will understand a great deal about managerial behavior, which leads you to be a better supervisor or manager. During this learning, you will also recognize the critical skills needed as a leader. Finally, you will understand how to use communication as a neophyte in a particular organization, during your transitions from one position to another and throughout the various organizational activities in which you will engage.

Communication in Organizations

Communication is one of the most dominant activities occurring in any work setting. The need to study, understand, and effectively use organizational communication has been, for many individuals, an after-the-fact enlightenment. As such, individuals in various occupations refer to the inability of others to communicate well, the lack of listening skills displayed by their colleagues, or the unwillingness of subordinates to follow instructions. At times, we all contend that other people fail to communicate and we are almost mystified that others do not hear us in the manner we intend. Over the years, experts in management theory have preached the need for improved communication. Unfortunately, being aware of the need for improved communication does not always translate into better understanding or use. A recent survey found that 14% of each 40-hour work week is wasted because of poor communication between staff and management, which equals a staggering number of seven work weeks of squandered productivity a year (Armour, 1998). The move to knowledge, information, and technology-dependent organizations spawned by the digital age only underscores the increasing importance of effective organizational communication (Jones et. al., 2004).

Importance of Communication to the Organization

Earlier in this chapter, we examined numerous changes impacting organizations. Chief Executive Officers (CEOs) of 531 U.S. organizations that had recently undergone change efforts were asked to identify one thing they would change about their efforts. Overwhelmingly, they pointed to the communication process (Larkin & Larkin, 1996). OfficeTeam, a leading staffing service, surveyed the Fortune 1000 firms and found that communication and people skills "will be subject to their severest test during the next millennium, thanks to the technological transformation of the workplace" ("The Challenges," 1999, p. 6). General Electric ("Survey: GE," 1984), in their study of 10,000 employees, found a direct link between good communication with the employee's immediate supervisor and job satisfaction in the specific categories of general problems, feedback, salary discussions, career counseling, and performance appraisal. Organizations listed in "The 100 Best Companies to Work for in 2006" see effective two-way communication as an underpinning to employees' motivation and the organizations' success (Colvin, 2006). "Look closely and you'll find that these companies (Best Small and Medium Companies to Work For) include their employees in the loop. They communicate well" (Pomeroy, 2004, p. 54).

For individuals, "the importance of communication skills for those who seek to gain employment or advance in their career fields is well documented"

(Kinnick & Parton, 2005, p. 431). But, many individuals enter the workplace ill-equipped to be effective organizational communicators. For example, "business schools have been criticized for not adequately teaching the communication skills and competencies needed in today's service-oriented, team-oriented, and decentralized environment" (Kinnick & Parton, 2005, p. 432). Reinsch and Shelby (1997) found that "management communication classes might be enhanced by giving significant attention to oral communication, particularly in dyadic, work group, team meeting, and presentation settings, and by giving significant attention to issues of conflict, of persuasion, and of interaction across organizational boundaries" (p. 21). The endorsements for more organizational and business communication training in higher education and the impetus for these observations are based on the impact of inadequate communication. "There is mounting evidence that poor communication between hospital staff and surgeons is the leading cause of avoidable surgical errors" (Landro, 2005, p. D1).

During my own consulting work with various companies, one of the tools used to determine the direction for training and development is a needs analysis given to members of the organization. The typical analysis involves 40 question areas, which are translated into 10 specific categories in need of additional training. In the last few years, the analysis has been given to one of the top 20 U.S. banking corporations, two plastic manufacturing companies, the headquarters of an international moving company, a steel manufacturing company, a large regional medical center, and several specialized companies. In every case, communication is ranked as first, or sometimes second, as the area in need of improvement within the organization. Invariably, the other top item is motivation, which also is discussed later in this text. These two items rank above many traditional organizational issues such as delegating, teamwork, time management, leadership, or job structure and planning. When people actually working are asked to decide where improvement needs to be made in an organization, they focus on communication. Boyett and Boyett (1998) conclude that inadequate information about organizations, customers, and individual performance is "the major cause of more than half of all problems with human performance. By improving the quality and timeliness of the information people receive, you can improve performance by as much as 20 to 50%" (p. 288).

Importance of Communication to Leaders

In addition to being important to organizations, communication is critical to the leader, manager, or supervisor (Bennis & Goldsmith, 1997; see chap. 11). Gardner (1995) concludes: "a key—perhaps the key—to leadership … is the effective communication of a story" (p. 37). O'Toole (1996) and Covey (1991) point to the ability to listen effectively as a key to leadership.

A shocking 40% of the people hired to be managers fail, according to a study by Manchester Partners International (Elliott, 1999). Of those, 82% leave because of their inability to build good relationships with peers and subordinates. A 20-year longitudinal study of Stanford MBA graduates showed communication to be an important part of their success in business and organizations and "a clear dominance in the importance of oral communication over written communication" (Harrell & Harrell, 1984). The Stanford study also indicated that a large number of the MBA students had chosen to become entrepreneurs or work with small businesses and found their communication abilities to be a significant asset in their success. Responding to an apparent lack of effective communication skills, MBA programs are increasingly requiring communication courses ("The Trouble," 2007).

Top executives, and those aspiring to become top executives, provide an equally important barometer of the need for better organizational communication. Any review of the top 10 best-selling, nonfiction books would include 2 or 3 dealing with the ingredients needed to be successful in business. These books almost universally draw the conclusion that behavior, which is manifested through communication with other members of an organization, is the key to executive success (Bennis & Goldsmith, 1997). The type of communication activity used by the excellent organizations and successful leaders is markedly different from the traditional types of managerial behavior.

Importance of Communication to the Individual

Not only is the ability to communicate effectively an important factor for organizations and leaders, it also is a vital skill for the individual (see chap. 9). From job interviews to relationships with coworkers or being promoted and becoming a leader, effective interpersonal communication stands out as a vital organizational skill (de Janasz, Dowd, & Schneider, 2002; Reece & Brandt, 2005). The continued growth in service, knowledge, and information jobs means that successful communication will dominate everyone's activities. At various times in everyone's career, the need to interview effectively, listen and gather information, lead others, work in groups and on teams, and respond to change makes effective communication skills a requirement for successful employment. At this point, we have established the importance of organizational communication.

Understanding Organizational Communication

In spite of the importance of communication in and to organizations, studying the subject seems to present a paradox for many individuals. On the surface, communication, especially in the nonprint areas, might seem to be too simple to really need to be carefully analyzed. After all, once we tell people that communication is important, and that "breakdowns" should be avoided, what else is there really to be studied? If employees should be listened to more often, then some type of general directive or meeting should make all the supervisors and managers aware of the problem, leaving little reason to try and examine something so obvious. In fact, a perusal of current management magazines yields a variety of articles on communication (ranging from effective language use, to listening, to using e-mail) and generally, the articles will be two to five pages in length. The suggestions for improvement are usually to the point, but the manager often learns that implementing the suggestions is not as surefire as the article makes them appear.

The more we become aware of the ineffective uses of communication in organizations, the more the concept seems to be all-inclusive and difficult to study. For example, the well-meaning manager, using an ongoing program of *Management by Wandering Around* (MBWA), which means visiting various parts of an organization or department with a casual, information-obtaining and relationship-improving motive. Done well, MBWA could create a strong sense of identification between management and employees. MBWA, one of the characteristics identified in studies of excellent companies, refers to the willingness of the management team to wander through various parts of the organization in order to listen to employees in an informal setting. The process is intended to develop relationships, gather information, and break down barriers (Peters & Austin, 1985). Although well intended, to the employees the manager might be seen as too intrusive or overbearing, merely using a gimmick, or simply increasing an unwanted "policing" tendency. If the employees have not previously seen the manager except during formal tours, why would they suddenly find her or his presence reassuring?

The more we learn about communication, the more we understand that all behavior is *potentially* communicative. In the communication process, each individual is both an actor and a reactor to the communication events. We introduce our own interpretation of events. We apply our own perceptual and interpretative lens to other's communication behaviors (see chap. 2). Because we simultaneously produce and respond to behaviors, the possible implications are truly astonishing. Each time we choose a particular behavior, the communication impact is highly dependent on a host of circumstances.

This seeming paradox can be resolved through a systematic study of organizational communication. For recent college graduates, for example, the merits of their job-related skills are often overshadowed by a lack of awareness of how to use communication in an organization, thereby slowing career development (Reinsch & Shelby, 1997).

Providing you with the knowledge necessary to be successful in your communication is the goal of this textbook and you will find this information useful to you throughout your career with any organization. This will be true in at least three circumstances. First, even when we are effective in our communication processes, we may lack the theoretical underpinnings to be able to explain why. When this happens, we cannot be certain of replicating our successes. Second, if we do not succeed, it is equally important to be able to examine the situation to identify and correct, if possible, those factors that caused the failure. Finally, when we face new or different situations, we need to be able to predict, with some degree of success, what communication behaviors will be likely to produce the results we would like to have. Because effective communication is fundamental to an individual's success, the systematic study of communication provided by this book gives you a significant advantage in your own career.

Perspectives

Two perspectives must be understood to develop our organizational communication skills: (1) communication is a process, and (2) organizations can be viewed most usefully as systems of behavior.

Communication as a Process

Identifying communication as a process is basic to developing our understanding of organizational communication activities. Early examinations attempted to provide models isolating the important factors in order to understand and quantify or qualify the impact of various communication behaviors. Three different stages can be identified in the model developing process.

The first models of communication were *linear* in nature and involved tracing a one-way flow of messages with the speaker or sender developing or encoding a message that would be sent over a channel or channels to be received by a listener or receiver. These models were simple in form and effective in drawing attention to certain aspects of the communication process while largely ignoring the importance of feedback.

As you probably can predict, this model is not very valuable in an organizational setting. If you cannot receive feedback regarding your communication, then you have no means for finding out if the message has been received correctly. In human communication, the idea that we can put something into a clear message that will be understood by other people is an ideal rather than an everyday reality.

The limitations of the linear model for depicting the communication process led to the *interactional* models of communication that took into account the critical importance of feedback and focused on the reciprocal message exchanges that occur between senders and receivers. From this perspective, feedback was any kind of signal or message that told the sender what was happening at the receiving end of the process. By accepting the importance of both participants in the eventual success or failure of the communication process, the interactional approaches were better able to explain the dynamic nature of human communication. The computer is based on this model. But, this model still assumes an interactive nature somewhat similar to a Ping-Pong game where the messages are exchanged rather than simultaneously shared.

Transactional Perspective

A fundamental problem with the linear and interactional models is that they lead to misnomers, and therefore misunderstandings, regarding the actual event called communication, presenting an incomplete explanation of the communication process. The simplest means of demonstrating the problem is to use a popular notion, the communication breakdown. When we fail to achieve our goals in an operation, procedure, or relationship, we frequently say that we have a "communication breakdown" or a "failure to communicate." This assumption is based on either a linear or a step-by-step depiction of communication. Somewhere in the process there is a breakdown. Naturally, if we could find the breakdown, we could correct the communication problem. The linear model would examine the sender's techniques or approaches. The interaction model would trace the sequence of events. Although both of these explanations have an appeal because of their simplicity, the *dynamics* of the communication process are not as easily explained. In the communication process, senders and receivers are simultaneously sending and receiving messages and neither person nor element in the communication activity can fail to communicate. This view of communication leads to the conclusion that *one cannot not communicate* once a transaction has occurred between individuals (Watzlawick, Beavin, & Jackson, 1967). This *does not mean that everything that happens is communication*, as is explained shortly.

Communication is a process where there is a mutual assignment of meaning, simultaneous responses by all persons in the transaction, ongoing giving and receiving of multiple messages, circularity, and numerous channels of communication (Berlo, 1960). Any form of human communication is an attempt to create meaning as long as it is purposeful. This view of communication as a transaction leads to three conclusions (Adler & Towne, 2003; Harris & Sherblom, 2005). First, the process is *complex and dynamic*. Transactions are contextual and therefore irreversible, unique, and unrepeatable. We interpret communication based on the circumstances and once it occurs that particular set of events cannot be repeated in the identical form. Second, as a process, *communication has no necessary beginning or end*, so labeling participants as senders and receivers is an arbitrary, although sometimes useful, distinction. We can assign the role of sender in a given situation, but almost all organizational communication occurs in the context of ongoing activities, relationships, and goals. Third, *everyone can be simultaneously affected and can affect every other member of the transaction*. In other words, we are sending and receiving at the same time. Consider for a moment how adopting a perspective that sees communication as complex, dynamic, irreversible, ongoing, contextual, and simultaneous can enhance your understanding of organizational communication.

Two important premises underlie these conclusions. First, human beings behave toward each other and, as living organisms, *cannot not behave* (Bateson, 1972). You might be concerned that this perspective leaves everything we do within the realm of communication and this issue has lead to some interesting academic debates.

However, the second premise is that the behavior, as we already have mentioned, *must be meaningful* to at least one of the participants. This is a powerful perspective. Clearly, it explains why seemingly innocent actions can elicit very negative responses. In addition, when we add this limitation, we free ourselves from including all behavior and we also free ourselves from the expectation that the intended message will be the one received.

Why would we opt for this broad-based, multiple behaviors perspective? A *transactional* approach can be a great asset for enhancing our understanding of communication (Adler & Towne, 2003). Difficulties arise in the communication process when there are incongruencies in the meanings in a transaction. You are probably familiar with the problem you have in responding to someone who gives different, and perhaps contradictory, messages. A classic example of this problem in an organization is the request by management for suggestions from employees regarding the organization. All too often, some suggestions are not responded to, met with indifference, or lost in some bureaucratic review process. Others are implemented. Employees are left with conflicting messages between management's stated desires and actions. Ironically, management often means a little, or a lot, of both messages and therefore continues the confusing behaviors.

Many organizations now refer to employees as associates, partners, team members, or consultants, to name a few, which can be a wise symbolic move. However, if this new title does not carry with it any more power, responsibility or decision making, employees might see a contradiction between the new title and the reality that nothing has really changed. Once again, the problem arises out of the confusion or incongruence within the transaction because the language and the actions contradict each other. Our earlier example of the manager who attempts to use management by walking around (MBWA) but finds the interpretation by employees is quite different from his or her intended meaning provides another illustration of this communication characteristic. It also could be that he or she lacks the *savoir-faire* or knowledge of how to effectively use the technique and it comes across as a stratagem or trick rather than a sincere attempt at better management.

Communication is based on the meaning attached to behavior by the participants. So, even when good intentions are behind certain activities ranging from soliciting suggestions to MBWA, we respond to the behaviors we can observe. To extend our example, the manager might react to employee cynicism by eliminating the practice of MBWA. However, the communication transaction already has begun, so the manager now will experience an important corollary to *one cannot not communicate*. Once a transaction has begun, although you *can stop giving expression, you cannot stop giving off expression because meaning can be attached to any change in behavior*. So, employees might be able to justify their initial distrust by observing the cessation of MBWA. The manager is not necessarily between the proverbial rock and a hard place in this example. With experience in using communication effectively, new behaviors need not come across as insincere.

In summary, communication is transactional. As an ongoing process, communication is the study of behaviors that elicit or produce meaning between and within individuals, groups, or organizations.

Organizations as Systems

Organizations are systems and subsystems or cosystems of behavior that are interrelated, interdependent, and interacting rather than chartable, linear, or static structures. You are familiar with the systems approach to understanding but may never have considered the reasoning. For example, the human body is a living system with numerous parts all interacting to maintain life within a larger ecosystem. In simple terms, a headache can influence many other parts of the body and hitting our funny bone or spraining an ankle makes the interconnected nature of our bodies all too apparent. This leads to the overall concept: *A system is composed of regularly interacting or interdependent groups of activities that form a whole*. A change in one aspect can affect change in other aspects.

Organizations are *dynamic, living entities* that have been put together to *accomplish some type of purpose—they are goal oriented*. The number and variety of parts to an organization can be truly astonishing. In an attempt to provide order, organizations establish many of the rules, roles, and behaviors that individuals follow to maintain their organizations. An organization's structure, tasks, and methods evolve out of the history of the organization's transactions with its changing members and environment. For our purposes, how these components work in relationship to each other is the vital question (Brache & Rummler, 1997). The arrangement of the interrelated parts creates the system.

The systems perspective is potentially seductive for looking at organizations because a "systemized pattern of behavior" is practically a synonym for the concept of organization. More properly, an organization should be viewed as a system because it is *the sum total of the various parts* and how those parts interact determine the output and growth of the process). Be warned, that "systems thinking generally requires a radical shift in how (organizational) members view the world: from seeing parts to seeing wholes; form seeing linear cause–effect chains to seeing interrelationships; from seeing static entities to seeing processes of change" (Cummings & Worley, 2005, p. 504). At the beginning of this part of the chapter, we mentioned the human body. As we engage in a fuller discussion, you might find using the human body as a relevant example of systems thinking. An obvious example could be the "freshman 15" weight gain that often occurs when students enter college, which reflects the impact of changing eating behaviors or input into the system.

First, the *organization as a system* is a perspective or framework toward organizations and not necessarily a theory (Katz & Kahn, 1978). Our consideration is with the integrated whole of the organization, which is made up of interacting and interrelated parts. Thus, the whole can range from individuals engaging in a business or interaction with others to Microsoft. Our goal is to understand the interacting parts of this system. The benefit of this view is it relieves us from looking at certain subgroups, such as managers, supervisors, marketing, operations, or sales, for understanding thereby preventing a myopic view of what actually occurs in the organization. To focus on a relationship with one colleague, for example, neglects the critical influences of other parts of the organization. The systems view of organizations provides a framework for looking at the organization as a whole in terms of process-related subsystems. Each subsystem in an organization—whether it is departments, job categorizations, or promotions—is separate and definable, but it is also interrelated and interdependent. All organizations are conglomerations of many subsystems, ranging from the annual company picnic organizing committee to the board of directors or trustees. If we are looking at an organization as part of an entire industry, we could have the *system* (the organization), the subsystems (components of the organization), and suprasystem or the industry as a whole (Farace, Monge, & Russell, 1977). For example, your university or college bookstore could comprise the system, the people working there would make up some of the *subsystems*, and the university or college would be the *suprasystem* because it owns the property and operates the overall higher education facility. You can add any number of other subsystems such as suppliers or textbook providers. When you frequent the bookstore, you become part of the system and customers are integral parts of the successful operating of any service industry. *Systems are arranged hierarchically*, so every system is a suprasystem for systems contained within it and a subsystem for systems containing it. In this case, the bookstore is a system to the college or university suprasystem.

The *Tragedy of the Commons* demonstrates the interrelated and interdependent nature of systems. In the 1800s in England, villages created a common grazing area in the middle of the village for everyone to use—this increased security for the livestock and convenience for the owners. Some villagers, seeking greater wealth or status, added to their livestock beginning a cycle where other villagers also added livestock. Soon the commons was overgrazed, making the commons unusable. Essentially, the villagers ignored the systems nature of the commons, the interconnectness of their futures, and focused on their individual success.

Interconnectedness of subsystems can be demonstrated by examining the current issue of global warming. Scientists noted the impact of global warming more than 10 years ago and the consensus among scientists regarding the reality of global warming has now solidified to rival the medical consensus on the dangers of smoking (Linden, 2006). "Precipitation patterns, the change of seasons, storm intensity, sea ice, glaciers, temperatures under tundras—all are in flux" as a result (Demos, 2006, p. 136).

Although public perception seems slower to respond, and political wrangling continues, "the last decades of the 20th century showed an unmistakable and extraordinary warming" (Linden, 2006, p. 248). From a systems perspective, changes in one part of the system in terms of emissions impacts other parts of the system as a result of interdependence.

Systems are composed of numerous constituencies. For example, there are other interests, perhaps an oil or coal producer, who do not wish to see a dramatic reduction in greenhouse gases for obvious reasons (Flannery, 2005). In some instances, government reports on the impact of gases have been altered by certain officials to lessen the impact of the evidence (Flannery, 2005). The journal *Science* concluded, after a review of the evidence, that unchecked global warming will lead to the destruction of our species (Hansen, 2005). Our point is the dramatic nature of a systems perspective. Rather than narrowly focusing on particular interests or demands, the systems perspective allows a broader view of the key issues and the impact of interactions.

In the past, many have seen our world as unidirectional leading to mental models that seek simple solutions to complex issues. Actually, we operate in a *complex system* with ongoing interconnection with intertwining loops of events and information, which are influenced by numerous parts of the organization (Senge et al., 1994). Remember our Y2K discussion at the beginning of this chapter. No single computer represented the entire problem, nor would fixing one subsystem guarantee an overall correction. We cannot simply focus on a single issue and assume that it is the cause for a particular event in an organization.

Second, all organizations exist within an environment and are both created and controlled by the environment. Organizations involve a pattern of recurrent activities of input, transformation, and output. Resources, or inputs (energy, matter, money, materials, personnel, or information) are imported from the environment. These are transformed or changed through various processes (means, methods, procedures, how-to-do-its, information, or techniques) in some fashion or another, and the resulting outputs (products, information, or services) are exported back into the environment. There are several important systems concepts worthy of additional discussion.

Openness

All human organizations function in varying states of openness or responsiveness to their environment, because their *boundaries are permeable and they constantly are engaged in interactions.* When the organization tends toward *isolation from its environment, it moves toward a closed status* (Bertlanffy, 1968). Actually, organizations cannot remain isolated for long because they are highly dependent on the consumer, supplier, and often government for their growth, stability, or survival. Inputs or resources such as money, materials, and information are provided by the environment, which, in turn, receives outputs from the organizations—these outputs can be products, services, and revised information. Because this is an ongoing process, to the degree that the outputs respond well to the inputs, the system will remain open and growth will occur. No living system is ever totally open (boundary-less) or totally closed, but successful organizations do not ignore input from their environments. In contrast with closed systems, which are best demonstrated by classical Newtonian physics, open systems maintain themselves with a constant interchange with the host environment, so there is a continual exchange of energy between the system and its environment. Specifically, all successful organizations seek and utilize customer input in order to remain open to the environment.

Thus, an *open system can be represented as a recurring cycle of input, transformation, and output.* Both the input and output characteristics of the open system keep the system in constant commerce with the environment, whereas the transformation process is contained within the system. An effective open system requires a balance among the three stages of the cycle, with the input taking into account both environmental demands and the capacity of the transformation cycle, and the transformation process absorbing the flow from the input and moving to the output stage. This system is a vital model for organizational life because it is concerned with the elements of the system; the structure of the system, the interdependency of the elements of the system, and the way the system is embedded in the environment.

At all levels of an organization from individuals within the organization to the environment surrounding the organization, communication is the process used to connect and coordinate the system and its subsystems (Rothman, 1972). As you already may have concluded, there is an excellent fit between the two perspectives presented in this chapter. Both communication and organizations can be understood best as open, living systems that are dynamic in nature. This is true for communication between individuals, within teams, departments, or groups, or throughout the organization.

Feedback

In order to maintain a steady state, an open system needs adaptive processes to receive information about its activities, which is called *feedback*. Feedback represents the ability of the system to generate and utilize evaluative information. Without such information, the system is blind to itself and the consequences of its actions. Ford Motor Company drastically reduced its production for the second half of 2006, after closing several plants and offering buy-outs to current employees, due to a lack of sales of sport utility vehicles (SUVs) and other vehicles. This situation was due, in a large part, to not paying attention to earlier customer trends or feedback (Carty, 2006). On a broader scale, the high failure rate for new businesses often is traced to the unwillingness of the entrepreneur to obtain information or follow advice, which is feedback, regarding how to operate (Hisrich, 1990).

Two types of feedback are possible. When the feedback reinforces, accentuates, or adds to the direction being taken by the system it is positive. The feedback is negative when it corrects a deviation (Senge et al., 1999). This is a somewhat different description of positive and negative feedback from the common notion that positive feedback equals a compliment. For a system, *feedback is the vital component that allows it to maintain a steady state.* Negative feedback decreases the difference between the desired results (*goal*) and the actual results. Positive feedback increases the differences. To illustrate these two types of feedback, remember our manager who is trying to follow the advice of organizational consultants by practicing MBWA. Managers can employ MBWA as a system-maintaining mechanism to receive information (*input*) in order to increase their understanding (*transformation*) of their interrelated subsystems or, in this case, the employees, in order to be more effective managers (*output*). Hopefully, employees will feel free to reinforce current managerial actions (negative feedback), explain why some procedures are not working well in helping the department meet its goals (negative feedback), or call for fewer work rules and greater freedom in individual actions (positive feedback). Although the call for less control is not necessarily system-maintaining, the insightful manager still can use this information to make some decisions regarding current practices toward employees and, if a change in work rules appears to be helpful to the organization, the information could become negative feedback.

The manager also has the opportunity during the wandering to use both types of feedback. If some behavior is out of line with the expectations, the manager might correct the subordinates about the work they are doing. This most likely would be considered negative feedback because it would be system-correcting. If the manager wanted greater innovation by a group of individuals, then positive feedback could be used to reinforce the changes where the manager removes some constraints.

Obviously, both types of feedback have an important role to play in an organization. Too much negative feedback creates a loss of initiative because employees soon learn that doing it "by the book" will create the least amount of difficulty. Organizations must maintain a steady state, however, so the manager, team, or leader must impose some system-maintaining behavior. Too much positive feedback could result in people doing their own thing with no coordination or direction. Eventually, the department would be unable to "organize" its actions and slowly work toward *entropy.* Finally, when the process of feedback is confined to the system itself, it would be considered closed, which, as we already have indicated, would be a destructive factor in an organization. When there is an interchange between the system and its environment through feedback, it is considered open (Senge et al., 1999). Essentially, a hotel that listens to customer comments would be open to feedback.

Entropy

Living systems tend toward entropy—disorganization, stagnation, or chaos. Human organizations are capable of resisting entropy because they can maintain and increase their supply of energy, information, and level of organization. In other words, disorganization can be resisted through the importing of external resources or providing addition support and structure to the existing subsystems. In addition, an organization must provide tangible and intangible outputs to its environment that enable it to receive the inputs necessary to its survival. Systems cannot survive in the absence of negative feedback or *information* (e.g., customer complaints) that enables them to detect deviations from course (e.g., excellent service). An organization maintains a *dynamic equilibrium* (steady state), which includes the basic "character" of the organization (manifested in recurring cycles of events). This steady state is highly stable even though the organization evolves over time in response to internal and environmental chances. Maintaining an organized structure is achieved through information processing. The processing is dependent on the *interpretation* (*coding process*) and how the information is filtered and passed on.

Organizational Subsystems

In all organizations, two internal subsystems continually operate. One consists of the *groups* within the organization and the other consists of the *dyadic or individual relationships*. The elements of these two subsystems are discussed in detail when we examine organizational communication concepts throughout the remainder of this text.

The system called the organization also has formal structure with definite lines of responsibility and authority. These often have been the basis for organizational charts, which define *the formal lines of authority and responsibility* within an organization. All organizations also have a much less easily defined informal structure, which includes emerging leaders, power politics, assumed authority, and so on. The formal structure outlines the authority, whereas the informal structure outlines the influence. At all times, these can be the same, different, or an interesting combination. The third-shift foreman or supervisor, for example, may have the authority to require the crew to skip their break time, but several recalcitrant members have the potential influence of voicing a grievance concerning the decision. If the recalcitrants are listened to, then temporary power or influence is shifted. What else comprises an organizational system?

Rational Objectives   Whenever people are gathered together in an organization, it is for some specific purpose. These objective goals, or "things to do," are established by the mandate behind the organization's existence and usually are divided into attainable subtasks or short-range targets. Within these subtasks are the specific tasks for each individual within the organization to accomplish. Frequently, these tasks are the reasons why someone was hired. Critically, all organizations have some rational objectives that provide the members with direction.

Methodology   Organizations also are structured around some ways of doing the tasks through training, tools, background, expertise, and procedures. This is, for all practical purposes, the definition of technology. In its narrowest sense, technology is the machinery—the physical things used ranging from cars to computers to cash registers for all occupations and organizations. But in its truest sense, the technological subsystem in an organization includes the way the tools are employed and how things get accomplished. These techniques are procedures developed from knowledge about and experience with the best ways to do a job at any particular point. The standard operating procedure establishes how a job is to be done and is part of the technological subsystem. When asked how something is accomplished in an organization, we are seeking information regarding the methodology.

Management/System Integraters   All organizations have a subsystem that organizes and controls the other subsystems, causing them to interact and resulting in increased effectiveness of the total organization. Although the term most often applied to this concept is *boss* or *supervisor*, in a real sense, managers are those individuals who integrate the system and subsystems for the goals of the organization. They are the ones that control the output. In the most basic terms, power, authority, decision-making, and coordination all represent this ability to manage. Whenever power and authority are being exercised, resources are affected, or someone is directing people in their efforts toward a common goal, that process represents the managerial structure.

Interdependence   All of these factors tell us that to make a change in one subsystem requires that some consideration be made regarding the implications for the other subsystems. By examining the level of interdependence, or asking what effect the change will have on other subsystems (environment, people, structure, objectives, technology, and management), it is possible to be aware of the values, or lack of value of the particular change. In our earlier discussion of communication, we offered the same observation that changes in one part of a relationship would create changes in other parts.

Two additional concepts complete this initial examination of organizations as systems.

Nonsummative The first concept is that the interactions between the systems in an organization are nonsummative, which means the whole is greater than the sum of its parts. Often, this concept is labeled *synergy* with the popular explanation that 1 + 1 never equals just 2. The interactions between the various components of the organization create synergy, or increased energy, to the system. The interactions between the various parts of the system result in the end-product being different from what each of the departments, individuals, or groups originally contributed to the process.

Equifinality In addition, a systems approach points to the principle of equifinality, which means the same end-product or outcome can be reached through a variety of conditions. In other words, there are numerous ways to accomplish the same goal or reach the same conclusion. This aspect of a systems approach explains why different organizations, departments, and individuals can achieve comparable successes without necessarily following the same route or process. One of the best examples of this concept lies in the development of general systems theory. The basic principles and elements of systems thinking were agreed on even though the scholars' backgrounds ranged from biology (Bertlanffy, 1968) to economics (Boulding, 1977).

Both nonsummativity or synergy and equifinality depend on communication between individuals and subsystems and are examples of the interlocking nature of communication and organizational systems. The perspectives of communication as a process and organizations as systems stem from the same philosophical base regarding living systems. As open systems, people and organizations are dynamic, ongoing, and ever-changing—not static entities. Our discussion of systems thinking up to this point has emphasized the concepts as they should function. Actually, organizations are complex systems with additional characteristics.

Complex Systems

Applied to a static example, a systems perspective obviously works. However, systems thinking and the dynamics involved provide a much more robust explanation regarding *the impact of change in complex systems—which includes all organizations*. Organizations are made up of various subsystems and units exhibiting mutual influence and interdependence. A change in one part of an organization or a department can impact on numerous other parts of the organization. Stata (1989) observes that "changes intended to improve performance in one part of the organization can affect other parts of the organization with surprising, often negative consequences" (p. 65). Essentially, the information used at a local level to make a change, which is often the only information available, can be counterproductive to the system as a whole.

Imagine an interstate highway as a dynamic and complex system. An accident during rush hour on any part of the interstate entering a metropolitan area creates a snowballing effect based on the limited information available and acted on by the individuals passing the accident. Perhaps there is needless "rubber-necking," lane changes, a ghoulish desire to see more, or debris on the road. The result will be a "domino effect" of slowed traffic that can take hours to resolve. Often, transformations occurring in an organization can be chaotic, uncertain, discontinuous, and disorderly for much the same reason. Add the dynamics of changes in the external environment ranging from natural disasters to shifting consumer preferences for a specific product or output and the importance of considering complex systems becomes apparent.

Second-Order or Quantum Change

Viable organizations are open to input from their environment and the internal subsystems. As parts of the organization interact, there are transformations. A *first-order change involves a simple, specific change in procedure or process as a result of a discussion or a problem-solving procedure.* Perhaps the department fails to schedule vacations effectively and a new method is developed. Because this is largely procedural, the department members or subsystems do not change themselves, their basic jobs, or the way they interact. Early attempts to apply systems thinking failed because they were trying to systematize or plot the organization to increase predictability and control rather than observing the interactions thereby focusing only on first order changes. Ironically, as we become more proficient at our jobs, we become less likely to consider second-order changes (Argyris, 1991). We impose the incorrect, but popular phrase, "If it ain't broke, don't fix it" which is the classic first-order, system-maintaining view. A popular expression is that the definition of insanity is doing the same thing over and over again and expecting different results.

A second-order or quantum change involves the organization's *context, process, or dynamic.* This is a fundamental change that impacts on how the organization functions. An obvious example is the shift by most high-performing organizations from controlling employees to treating everyone as a thinker and doer. Teamwork replaces rigid rules, isolated layers and structures are integrated in order to achieve synergy, and system openness occurs with the commensurate transformations.

Faced with important issues to resolve, groups and organizations attempt to adjust or fix what they are already doing *or* look for quantum changes. It is axiomatic in change that "more and more of the same will only provide more and more of the same." Returning to our earlier discussion of the digital present and future, organizations are becoming wired with information technology creating a more agile, virtual, global, and cybernetic system requiring entirely new ways of organizing and communicating. Accepting this input into the organization's operations promises second-order change.

What approaches are available to apply systems thinking to organizational communication and change? We examine three: learning organizations, sense-making, and self-organizing systems.

Learning Organizations

Senge (1991), among others, has forwarded the concept of learning organizations. Using systems thinking, Senge observes that organizations are constantly changing, as we noted earlier in this chapter. An organization must engage in self-renewal, questioning of processes, and sharing of information and meaning between people in order to remain viable. Unique to a learning organization is the capacity to think about what is being done as well as doing what must be done, which is called *double-loop learning* (DLL). Senge sees a clear link between communication processes, shared visions and meanings, and systems thinking.

When we learn a particular job or understand the procedures for doing something, we are engaging in single-loop learning (SLL), or adaptive learning. When we understand the principles behind a particular process, we are using DLL, or generative learning. Learning organizations, and living systems, can go beyond the routine and begin to develop creative and growth-producing processes. Effective DLL is concerned with how people think and reason about their behavior (Argyris, 1991). A simple analogy will demonstrate the difference between knowing how to do a job and knowing why we do a job, essentially the difference between skill and knowledge (Kim, 1993). A thermostat that automatically turns on the air conditioning when a room temperature goes above 75 degrees is a good example of single-loop learning (SLL). If the thermostat could ask "Why am I set at 75 degrees?" and then explore whether some other temperature might be more economically viable, it would be engaging in double-loop learning (DLL).

Similarly, students memorizing information for a test are engaging in SLL. If these students were asking how they could add to the information they have learned, or why is this is the best way to approach the subject, they would be engaging in DLL. Imagine an organization that allows its employees to constantly seek ways to improve the on going processes by engaging in understanding the "whys" as well as the "whats." DLL allows the organization to develop individuals and processes to resist entropy, create growth, and take advantage of change. Senge (1990) concludes: DLL "requires seeing the systems that control events. When we fail to grasp the systemic source of problems, we are left to 'push on' symptoms rather than eliminate underlying causes" (p. 8). Both second-order changes and double-loop learning offer insights into how organizations function as systems. People and organizations are adaptive, dynamic, ongoing, and ever-changing. Senge and his collaborators (1999) have collected diverse tales recounted by organizational change explorers based on a learning organization perspective. This applied approach includes initiating change, sustaining the transformation, and redesigning and rethinking during the process. This leads to a second important concept: *sense-making*.

Sense-Making

Organizations are complex and, for most individuals, not easily understood. Because we are not privy to the big picture, we engage in attempts to understand and make sense of our secular part of the organization (e.g., student, faculty, administration). To be sure, we often believe we understand because we are naïve about the organization. The chaotic and uncertain nature of the environment surrounding organizations, and the constantly changing subsystems within an organization, leads to a need to reduce uncertainty.

Weick (1979, 1995) provides important insights into a systems understanding of organizational behavior and the process of sense-making. Organizing, "the resolving of equivocality in an enacted environment by means of interlocked behaviors embedded in conditionally related processes," is constantly occurring (Weick, 1979, p. 91). Each of the concepts in his definition deserves discussion. First, a *system's behavior continually influences the environment it experiences.* We only experience being in a particular place because our own behavior led us there. Our being in that place and our past behaviors influence the nature of the place that we experience. Because of the mutual influence, there is circularity between the interactions of systems. The system's behavior continually influences the environment that it experiences. Practically speaking, when we join a conversation in progress, the influence is mutual between the original participants and the new entrant in the system.

Second, there is always equivocality, or uncertainty in the enacted environment, because the outside world is complex and changing. Time does not stand still. When relationships form (patterns of interlocking behaviors), organizing occurs that begins to reduce the uncertainty in the environment—*equivocality* reduction. Weick made an important point when he suggested that the term *organization* is static whereas living systems are continually in the ongoing process of organizing. If these processes of organizing stop, entropy takes over and the organization begins to disintegrate. Because we cannot control the external environment, we must continually engage in organizing to prevent our own irrelevance to it.

So, organization, Weick concludes, is information that has been produced by processes that reduce equivocality. Living systems continually are trying to increase their certainty about the world in which they reside. Attempts to reduce uncertainty occur through the communication processes, sense-making and meaning.

Self-Organizing

Increasingly, organizations are discovering that too much organization can be counterproductive to successfully dealing with change and chaos. Gates (1999) observes that previous economic eras have been marked by short periods of industry-wrenching change leading to *punctuated equilibrium.* "Today the forces of digital information are creating a business environment of constant change. Evolutionists would call this punctuated chaos—constant upheaval marked by brief respites" (Gates, 1999, pp. 411–412). In response, several theorists (Epstein & Axtell, 1996; Waldrop, 1993; Wheatley, 1992) have forwarded versions of *self-organizing systems thinking* and *chaos theory.* In a nutshell, these approaches argue that the machine metaphor that helped design the traditional organization makes the wrong assumptions. Collecting information, taking measurements, and setting goals, as means for imposing structure from above are outmoded approaches. Instead, employees should be turned loose to function as independent agents who can find meaning and purpose. Living entities, from large organizations to individuals, exist in relationship to the networks of interactions surrounding them. So, utilizing the information available from the environment optimizes the potential for growth.

Proponents of this perspective argue that people will self-organize and develop means for self-renewal if they are given the opportunity. For example, researchers in workplace learning found that workers organized themselves into "communities of practice" to accomplish jobs and they self-organized in ways that were invisible to supervisors and managers. In other words, a natural community was developed by workers without, or in spite of, any organizing from outside their group. Wenger (1991) explains: "Through exchanging questions, meeting in hallways, telling stories, negotiating the meaning of events, inventing and sharing new ways of doing things, conspiring, debating and recalling the past, they complement each other's information and together construct a shared understanding of their environment and work" (p. 7).

Perhaps the most obvious example of this self-organizing principle is the Internet. This highly decentralized set of agreements on ways to communicate developed without overarching controls. Order emerged out of chaos through the process of self-organizing. Not only does the Internet show how systems can self-organize, it also functions as an ongoing source for communication, renewal, decentralized decision-making, information, and connections with outside sources. The Internet is "a decentralized anarchy of a zillion computers, all acting (on a good day, anyway) as a single, well-oiled megamachine" ("The Website," 2001, p. 144). The fact that the Internet works demonstrates the holistic nature of systems.

Chaos theory, along with the various other approaches that fit within the same theoretical view, argues that the world will achieve organization without the extraordinary effort by a few members or entities. The underlying belief is that "relationships between many if not most naturally occurring phenomena demonstrate how small changes in the initial state of a system may lead to tremendously large differences in later states" (Coovert, Craiger, & Cannon-Bowers, 1995, p. 161). What appears to be disorderly can be fundamental in the process of determining the best order. The apparently chaotic process evolves and takes on complex patterns. The turbulence, movement, and change appear unpredictable but actually have rules of their own. So, the patterns of communication and behavior are more or less constructive and may not be caused by any particular economic condition, person, group, or product. Remember that a living system seeks messages and information about what is working and not working through feedback. If the organization or any of its subsystems close feedback off to prevent possible disorganization and chaos, they could also eliminate or reduce important feedback leading to atrophy and possible death. New meanings can lead to the spontaneous emergence of new ideas, behaviors, and concepts. As living systems "receive 'energy-rich' input from the environment, the level of stress within the system rises—the system becomes increasingly chaotic" (Kirk, 1999/2000, p. 3). The key for an organization is to balance chaos with organization so that vital, but apparently foreign meaning and information can enter and assist in creating better solutions to problems and planning for the present and future. "The boundaries of a balanced system are relatively permeable; there is a constant flood of new information coming into the corporation from the outside world" (Kirk, 1999/2000, p. 4).

The apparently chaotic pathways of foraging ants have been studied in order to improve various processes at companies including Procter & Gamble, Ford, Unilever, Boeing, Southwest Airlines, British Telecom, and Texas Instruments (Bios Group, 2000). Naturalists observed the food hunting process used by ants and found the initial scouts left a trail of chemicals called pheromones recognizable to the other ants. The first ant to successfully find food returns to the ant heap leaving the pheromones twice. This double marking signals the best and shortest route to the food supply for the remaining ants. The ants self-organize to optimize the food gathering process. Bios Group "is a pioneering Santa Fe company that applies biological solutions to business problems" (Bios Group, 2000, p. 232P). It has created software using ant algorithms—rules that imitate the movement of ants—and applied them to supply chain issues. In 1998, these ant algorithms were used to help optimize the routing of British Telecom's network and these same components have been applied to over 30 companies. Southwest Airlines, for example, redesigned its cargo operations based on the ant algorithms. "Bio's thesis, furthermore, holds that as connections proliferate in the new economy, it begins to resemble a living ecology" (Bios Group, 2000, p. 232T). In this case, a science-based adaptive scheduling process has been successfully designed from supposedly lowly ants to enhance the operations of major organizations. To repeat a basic premise: a living system seeks information through feedback in order to self-organize and sustain itself. Applying the ant algorithms based on this principle to organizational endeavors offered a new approach to serious problems.

Strange attractors describe the complex set of influences that underlie these patterns. Although the influences of the strange attractors are clear—the unexpected interactions that create important changes—the cause of the influences frequently remains unidentified or unknown. Chaos theory's much overused and clichéd analogy to describe the unknowability of the world's infinite interdependencies is: "A butterfly flaps its wing in Brazil; a stock market in Tokyo crumbles," or, our example of a tie-up on an interstate highway. In 1998, the El Nino weather system caused large increases in the bug population in the United States, creating a growth industry for termite protection companies. The Y2K crisis created new forms of international cooperation, provided unexpected efficiencies as a result of the upgrades used to resolve Y2K, and developed new skills for managing large, complex, computer-intensive projects (Maney, 2000).

In organizations, we are able to be more specific about the strange attractors and focus on the processes of influence rather than individual styles, pay rates, or other easily identified concepts that have little to do with the self-organizing process. Expanding our perspectives allows us to recognize the complexity of the interaction patterns, the communication processes, and systems operations. If this sounds abstract and somewhat fuzzy, you might be reacting with a linear need for clarity and structure. Chaos thinking is a deeper way of thinking about the communication and organizational processes. Fundamentally, self-organizing requires organizations to view the system and the ongoing processes such as communication as paramount to success. These three approaches—learning organizations, sense-making, and self-organizing—demonstrate the potential uses of systems thinking in the study of organizational communication. From these views, continuous change involving radical upheavals will force organizations to abandon long term planning in favor of developing effective processes (McKenna, 1997).

Systems as Cultures/Cultures as Systems

One of the most useful approaches for understanding the particular organizational system is to examine its culture. Every organization has a culture (Schein, 1990, 1999), which is based on the various interactions that occur or "the way we do things around here." The type of culture operating is dependent on the organization's environment and the interactions of the subsystems within the organization. The various communication activities are what keep the organization operating and provide the cultural foundation. These communication processes provide the behaviors that lead to " … a pattern of basic assumptions invented, discovered, or developed, by a given group (or organization) as it learns to cope with its problems of external adaptation and internal integration that has worked well enough to be considered valid and, therefore, to be taught to new members as the correct way to perceive, think, and feel in response to those problems" (Schein, 1985, p. 9). The assumptions include the values, style, written and unwritten rules of conduct, plus the history, structure, past and present leaders, mission, goals and objectives, and finances (Senn, 1986). The way individuals, groups, and subsystems communicate provides the "primary vehicle(s) for the active creation and maintenance of cultures" (Sypher, Applegate, & Sypher, 1985, p. 17).

The cultural perspective is developed more fully later (see chaps. 3 and 7). An organizational cultural approach, as defined by this text, incorporates the various disparate views of how and why organizations do what they do. When we combine the study of communication as an analysis of the process of behaviors or the "way we do things around here," with an understanding of the living systems nature of organizational cultures, we have an excellent basis for understanding how to develop our own organizational communication abilities. Rather than focus on isolated, although important factors, such as information or leadership, the cultural approach explains why behaviors become meaningful. Not only is there an interest in information, but we also can understand what happens to the information as it is processed by the various living systems in the organization ranging from individuals through departments to the organization as a whole.

Organizational communication is the study of meaningful behaviors within the system and subsystems of the organizational culture. These meaningful behaviors constitute the specific areas of study that we examine in this text.

Conclusion

We started this chapter by observing how important effective communication is to any organization. We then explained the dynamic changes occurring in every organization. Communication as a process and organizations as systems are derived from the same underpinning that focuses on processes not procedures. Communication is an ongoing, coactive process between individuals, groups, and systems. Organizations are interrelated systems of behavior that are interdependent. Both of these perspectives require further amplification through a specific discussion of the various communication processes in an organization, which is the focus of the remainder of this text. The organizational culture perspective is our means for unifying the two perspectives within the context of organizational behavior.

In chapter 2, we explain the impact perception and paradigms have on all the behavioral activities we engage in while we function in our job. Chapter 3 traces the development of management and organizations theories as a means of explaining current approaches to understanding organizations. Chapters 4 through 8 outline the principles that underlie communication in an organization, verbal, nonverbal, networks, channels, symbolic behavior, and listening. The titles of the chapters have been chosen arbitrarily to fit familiar categories in both the fields of communication and business and management. Each chapter, however, develops various approaches and insights to the general concept drawing from current research. Chapters 9 through 12 provide pragmatic application of these principles to those areas most likely to require additional understanding. These include interpersonal communication, group communication, leadership, and new communication technologies. In the end, you will have a proactive capacity to both understand and effectively use organizational communication. Because you will have established a broad-based perspective regarding perception, communication, and organizational behavior, and you will have developed a basic understanding of the underlying principles of organizational communication, you should be able to deal with new or different issues as they arise.

Study Questions

1. What are the major implications of the digital age? Change? Diversity? Can you identify situations where these three issues are not important? Why?
2. Why is communication important to organizations? Leaders? Individuals?
3. Do you agree that studying communication can appear to be paradoxical?
4. Can you think of examples where a communication problem or challenge seemed to have a simple answer that did not work?
5. Distinguish between studying communication as a linear, interactional, and transactional process. Explain the transactional process.
6. Outline the fundamental elements presented when we view organizations as systems.
7. What is demonstrated by the Tragedy of the Commons?
8. Differentiate between openness, feedback, and entropy.
9. What are the key elements in an organization subsystem?
10. What are the differences between first- and second-order change?
11. Explain learning organizations.
12. Why is sense-making important to studying organizational communication?
13. What are self-organizing and chaos theories and how do they relate to systems thinking?

2
Perception and Paradigms

Perception is the overriding influence surrounding our understanding of organizational communication. In organizations, the issues we pay attention to and the concepts we understand are based on what we perceive. The process of *perception is the selecting, organizing, and interpreting of sensory stimulations into a meaningful and coherent picture of the world.* We are constantly working to make sense of our surrounding environment as we make mental decisions, consciously or unconsciously, about events. These decisions represent an individual's or group's assessment or ideas about the real world. Once formed, perceptions are translated into *paradigms.* Paradigms are the working principles formed from our perceptions and past behaviors that we use to guide us as we respond to our surroundings, tackle problems, or deal with uncertainty.

The key concepts in this chapter:

- Perception
- Paradigms
- Our perceptual base
- Sensory and symbolic basis
- Psychological factors
- Globalization
- Organizational role constraints

Focusing on perception and paradigms is one of the advantages of a communication perspective for the study of organizations. Because the living system of an organization, by definition, includes a large number of variables, the behaviors we choose to "pay attention to" or select from the available data become the determining factors underlying our own behaviors within the organization. In a capsule, our view of reality, both in an organization and during our entire lives, is based on our perceptions. Perception and paradigms impact our judgment and subsequent actions dramatically. For example, medical malpractice suits represent a multibillion dollar expense added to American health care costs. The filing of a lawsuit is a clear indication that some aspect of the medical process was unsatisfactory to the patient. Studies indicate that patients who have been depersonalized, slighted, or treated abruptly are the ones that tend to sue (Bishop, 1994). On the other hand, patients treated with effective interpersonal skills including empathy and interest rarely sue. In other words, satisfaction with medical care has less to do with the doctor's credentials or the success of the treatment than the interpersonal treatment received (Bishop, 1994; Levy, 1997). We cannot trivialize the importance of good medical care nor the right of patients to expect adequate treatment. But, the quality of personalized care provided by the sued and nonsued doctors was based on the doctors' perception of their role with patients (i.e., their personal view of reality) and the resulting paradigms (i.e., their set of rules for responding) that determine their interpersonal role in the doctor–patient medical process. Stated bluntly, some doctor's paradigms toward patient care intentionally or unintentionally included ineffective interpersonal actions leading to patient dissatisfaction. In the studies reported, the nonsued doctors used more personalized care. Because both perception and paradigms are critical concepts, we discuss each one separately.

Perception

Gaining insights into the perception process is a foundational step in helping us become effective organizational communicators. *Perception is our interpretation of reality.* Our efforts to make sense out of the information and multiple inputs we receive are a prerequisite to knowing how to respond. This is an immensely complex procedure that is often synonymous with growing up, learning to make decisions, knowing how to act correctly and appropriately, plus a host of other behaviors we undertake in an organization. Consider the following three examples.

First, globalization presents a challenge in terms of how we view individuals with different cultures, upbringing, and backgrounds. "The journal *Science* finds that our stereotypes about different cultures, whether positive or negative, are just plain unreliable" concluding that there is about zero overlap between perception and reality (Weise, 2005, p. 9A). The *Science* study included 3,989 people in 49 different cultures worldwide. One useful example is a possible explanation for why Chinese and U.S. political leaders interpret events differently leading to fundamental differences in perception. In examining recent U.S. and Chinese dialogues and disagreements, Kuhn (2006) asked: "Why do China and America have such difficulty communicating?" His analysis concludes that, instead of fundamental differences over issues, "the cause of their at times cacophonous discourse could lie in something less obvious: the strikingly different academic training of their political leaders" (Kuhn, 2006, p. 33). The majority of U.S. national leaders have a legal background, whereas all nine of China's senior leaders are trained as engineers. "This is no small difference. Engineers strive for 'better,' while lawyers prepare for the worst" (Kuhn, 2006, p. 33). So, when U.S. and Chinese leaders attempt to understand each other's actions and motives, both parties are proceeding from fundamentally different educational, training, and problem solving backgrounds. We return to globalization later in this chapter.

Our second example allows us to examine health care for a second time, but with a different focus. Increasingly, organizations are facing significant financial demands in terms of health care costs and the effectiveness of programs promoting healthy living (Merx, 2005). A survey of 120 large- and medium-size companies revealed that "nearly two thirds didn't think their staffs were conscientious health care users or cared about making lifestyle changes that could lower health care costs" (Mehring, 2004, p. 28). "At the same time, 82% of workers believed they effectively used their health care benefits" (Mehring, 2004, p. 28). This impasse is largely caused by poor communication arising from each party making assumptions based on their perceptions of reality, according to Tower Perrin, a leading human resource giant, who conducted the survey (Mehring, 2004).

The last example also deals with medical issues from a personal perspective. When you receive medical samples or advice, how do you react? Surprisingly, "nearly 80% of blacks and 52% of whites believe they could be used as 'guinea pigs' for medical research" according to a survey of more than 500 blacks and 400 whites, randomly selected from across the United States (Fackelmann, 2002, p. 9D). In addition, "about 63% of African Americans and 38% of Whites said doctors often prescribe medication to experiment on people without their consent" (Fackelmann, 2002, p. 9D). In this survey, patients also expressed distrust regarding receiving a full explanation of the impact of research participation, thought doctors sometimes exposed them to unnecessary risks, and felt they were unable to fully question their doctor. At least two important insights developed from these results. First, there was no indication that the surveyed patients had any evidence to support their distrust, although African Americans often remember "the 1932–1972 Tuskegee study in which researchers denied treatment to nearly 400 black men with syphilis to see how the disease progressed" (Fackelmann, 2002, p. 9D). However, this does not explain the somewhat universal patient distrust. Second, we often misperceive what we do not fully understand.

There are two benefits to understanding the role of perception in organizations. First, we can adjust our own perceptual capacities to enhance our performances, and second, we can learn to better understand other people's actions and responses. We only can respond to behaviors by other people—knowing the underlying motives or reasons is rarely, if ever, possible. Therefore, the facts and knowledge we have about a situation are based on the process of our previous experiences, obtaining information and messages, imposing sequence and arbitrary order to the vast amount of potential data, and making choices regarding our willingness even to pay additional attention to particular information (Dobkin & Pace, 2006).

Our senses, including seeing, hearing, tasting, smelling, or touching, provide us with our interpretations of reality. This process of discrimination has the inherent by-product of never being "able to see it as it is," but only as we interpret it to be. *Reality, both within organizations and throughout our lives, is a function of the interpretation we assign to our own perceptions.* "There is only perceived reality, the way each of us chooses to perceive a communication, the value of a service, the value of a particular product feature, the quality of a product. The real is what we perceive" (Peters & Austin, 1985, p. 71). For example, one study concluded: "Our research uncovered one amazing fact: Almost 70 percent of the identifiable reasons customers left typical companies had nothing to do with product" (Whiteley, 1991, p. 9). Why did they leave? In most cases, they were disillusioned by poor customer service that can impact any organization (Hindo, 2006).

To bring this discussion into our context, why are you more concerned with organizational communication than acid rain? The answer, assuming that this is a correct assumption, lies in your response to a large number of stimuli from which you decided to pay attention to some input while excluding other available information.

Paradigms

Paradigms are our perceptual theories-in-use that influence our understanding of organizations and guide our actions. They explain how we should respond to our sensory experiences. As such, paradigms are a consequence of the perceptual processes we use in gathering and utilizing meaning and information. Paradigms, as originally highlighted by Kuhn (1962), explain how scientific researchers are influenced by their perception of the validity of certain concepts and theories. For the everyday practitioner, this means we make decisions not based on all the available information, but on our previous assumptions about reality. In recent years, the concept of paradigms has been expanded to include numerous other areas of human behavior. *Human action presupposes an associated paradigm*—we think and do things because we believe we have a reason.

Paradigms are the explanations organizational members accept as being more legitimate than others. These frameworks or constructs present a model, pattern, or a set of rules that define boundaries (e.g., rules, regulations, procedures, standards, or routines) and tell us how to be successful within those boundaries. Routines, habits, and other areas where we are not flexible (e.g., foods, music, or travel) are examples of our paradigms in action. Once the limitations of the operating paradigms are exposed, individuals can chose to shift to more functional appropriate interpretations of their perceptions to better meet our personal goals. Think back for a moment to the opening chapter of this text. When we began discussing systems or chaos theory, did you have some initial tendency to reject this information? If so, there is a probability these concepts might have seemed outside your paradigm for understanding organizational communication.

A paradigm can be any set of rules and regulations. When faced with uncertainty, we use a trial-and-error approach to find a suitable paradigm that will bring the appropriate results. Once we come upon a paradigm that seems to work, we stop the search. "Having identified paradigms with sufficient confidence to support action, individuals tend to be committed to what then amount to worldviews and their implied behaviors" (Choi, 1993, p. 7). Paradigms are extremely useful for focusing our attention, dismissing unnecessary information, increasing our confidence in problem solving, and concentrating our efforts. However, paradigms can blind us to important opportunities, unnecessarily limit our options for problem solving, distort information, and close our minds to creative alternatives.

Our *paradigms allow us to see some issues and ignore others.* If productivity is declining, some companies hire efficiency experts that concentrate on how employees use their time. After studying the organization, these experts might find that the methods used for job assignments must be revamped in order to decrease wasted time and increase productivity. Other variables, such as worker satisfaction, could be excluded because these issues do not deal directly with the efficient use of time.

For instance, the most obvious characteristic of "experts" is their ability to perceive certain things that other people do not necessarily notice. An art expert is someone who can tell the good from the bad or the authentic from the fake. And, as is always the case, this does not mean that other people cannot see the differences between the two. The art expert identifies the salient factors involved in the current paradigms regarding "art." As we specialize in an activity, we develop this ability to perceptually "hone" our view to the exclusion of unnecessary information. Because we have been successful in the past, we become seduced into believing we have the best paradigm for understanding specific problems. The tendency of the expert to see things that other people might not see and to do this at the necessary expense of other information is a working definition of paradigm.

Five Characteristics of Paradigms

To summarize, paradigms have five important characteristics and implications. First, in periods of uncertainty, we search for a suitable paradigm that will satisfactorily mitigate the uncertainty (i.e., provide some certainty) and latch onto that paradigm as soon as it is discovered. Second, because uncertainty leads to unpredictability, we are driven to locate a paradigm that can mitigate this issue. Third, precedents, past actions, or beliefs focus our attention toward certain solutions, which means we neglect what may be perfectly acceptable paradigms. In organizations, one readily available source of information is to observe how others have dealt with the same issue. However, past practices or responses may be misdirected, incorrect, or part of the problem.

Fourth, when we are uncertain, we imitate others as long as we find ourselves in a homogeneous group or believe that other individuals have adequate paradigms. Fifth, as long as the chosen paradigm is logically optimal, we continue pursuing a course of action that might be seriously flawed. Why would we pick a solution or course of action that was not the best? Human nature requires us to make some decision when faced with uncertainty. Therefore, an answer that allows us to take some action appears more desirable than inaction. Underlying our choice of paradigm is our need to make a decision to allow us to continue to function.

Change and Current Practices

Using a common concept, one person's trash is another person's treasure, or one manager's unnecessary coffee breaks are another's social gratification periods. In a tongue-in-cheek indictment of some investigations, cynics have observed that organizational research experts begin to know more and more about less and less until they know everything about nothing. Paradigms, which are based on perception gained through experience, always involve leaving out some details in favor of others. In fact, making selective decisions about which stimuli we will attend to is, by definition, creating the potential for exclusion of significant information.

The pressure for change forces us to attempt to increase innovation. But, innovation requires that we are open to alternative answers. Mattimore (1994) asks us to determine which of the following numbers is most different from the others:

1) Three
2) Thirteen
3) Thirty-three

Mattimore's answer appears later in this chapter. If you have the answer, or wish to face another challenge, proceed to Figure 2.1, which shows a popular exercise for outlining perceptual and paradigm blocks to innovation. Can you connect the nine dots by (a) using four straight lines and (b) not lifting your pencil or pen off of the page? You may cross a line, but retracing over an existing line counts as one of your four lines. Follow the instructions. We return to this example later in the chapter.

Understanding Our Perceptual Base

There are three primary sources for our perceptual base. These include our past experiences that provide us with a personal "reference file," our present organizational experiences or our "updating" of the file, and the actual physical limitations while obtaining the information.

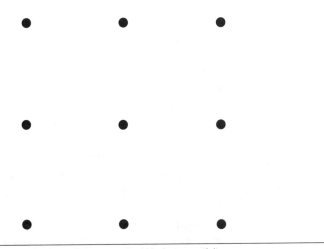

Figure 2.1 A popular exercise for outlining perceptual blocks to creativity.

Past Experiences

McLuhan and Fiore, (1967) communication commentators and philosophers, drew attention to our tendency to engage in *rear-view mirrorism* in our attempts to explain current events and changes. We drive toward the future looking in our rear-view mirror for direction and answers. In this process, "we march backwards into the future," because we tend to refer to the past to explain the present and the future (p. 26). Given the barrage of sensory material available to use, our attention tends to be based on those stimuli that have been significant to us in the past. The response people have to an event is not so much the reality of what is occurring, but which part of the event they are responding to often based on past experiences. As we process and remember information, we tend to regard information that seems familiar as valid creating an illusion of truth (Franklin, 2005). Past events can limit our abilities to process new information.

What we perceive is a combination of the event and our own perceptual system. Payer (1988), a medical journalist, provides a poignant example when he concludes that "Often all one must do to acquire a disease is to enter a country where the disease is recognized—leaving the country will either cure the malady or turn it into something else" (p. 25). Payer continues by pointing out that in France, where much of life is centered on the stomach, twice as many drugs for digestive disorders are available as in the United States—perhaps for good reason. Our past experiences orient us toward seeing particular illnesses and ignoring others.

Paradigms are utilized because we have taken a particular action in the past, can reference similar actions that have worked in the past, or are provided models from others regarding how they have handled such events (Choi, 1993). How often have you heard the timeworn medical advice to stay warm to avoid a cold, drink milk to ease ulcers, or suck out venom from snake bites? All three are based on years of misinformation (*American Health,* 1991). Experiments indicate that people left outdoors are no more likely to catch cold than those who stay warm indoors. Viruses cause colds. Milk is rich in protein, which stimulates acid production in the stomach and irritates an ulcer. Using your mouth to suck venom out is the worst thing you can do since the bacteria in your mouth multiply the risk of infection. But these folk medicine pearls of advice have been passed down from generation to generation and faced with snakebite, some of us might consider trying sucking out the venom. We have all been advised to stay warm to avoid a cold. For example, will you disregard past myths merely because you have received new and contradictory information? For many, when we receive medical advice based on medical research that deals with popular medical myths, our brains seem "to erode the memory of the (past) claim separately from its context–who said it, when, and other particulars, including the fact that the claim is not true" (Franklin, 2005, p. D5). In other words, the firmly held past beliefs often override perfectly valid current medical research.

Managers face similar perceptual challenges when they try to increase their staff's teamwork (Osburn, Moran, Musselwhite, & Zenger, 1990). For a moment, imagine you are a manager. Perhaps, for you, the success of the entire team is paramount and you focus on results. For some of the team members, individual achievement might be the prevailing issue so they expect individual recognition. For others, less group-oriented efforts might be desired because they prefer to work alone. Obviously, for others, there are a combination of factors operates. In addition, some members might have had good or bad experiences with teams and this influences their responses. Finally, in certain cases, individuals simply do not care about their jobs. Continuing with our earlier example revolving around customer service, organizations face difficult tasks because "[t]he individual [customer] perceives service in his or her own unique, idiosyncratic, human, emotional, end-of-the-day, irrational, erratic terms" (Peters & Austin, 1985, p. 71). Consider the last time you experienced poor customer service. Would most of your friends agree that the service was poor? Would the customer service provider agree with you? Often, the answers depend on our paradigm considering "good" service.

The increasing diversity in organizations requires us to become aware of our past beliefs as they pertain to other cultures and groups. Our backgrounds lead us to expect others to act in certain ways. In fact, many of us may not be prepared for living in an increasingly multinational world where, in the United States, "cultural diversification is a nationwide phenomenon" (Lustig & Koester, 2003, p. 7).

We do not need to look far to demonstrate that our understandings regarding other cultures remain limited. For example, a recent Harris poll reported that the average American believes 52% of the world speaks English, when the actual number is roughly 20% (Carey & Laird, 1999). Does this perception have consequences? Consider that "less than 1% of today's (USA) high school students are studying the languages likely to be the most important to the USA's future: Chinese, Arabic, Farsi, Korean, Japanese, Russia, and Urdu, according to the Education Department" (Lynch, 2006, p. 6B). Traditionally, the United States could focus on a traditional isolationism that has made some suspicious of foreign tongues and peoples. In addition, in the past, the United States's location as a continent surrounded by oceans and national prosperity has made some complacent. However, many feel the need to "address the USA's globalization Achilles' heel: Americans' lack of foreign language skills and general global awareness" (Lynch, 2006, p. 6B).

Even how we address someone has rules based on our cultural upbringing. North Americans value first names or nicknames, whereas other cultures believe in more formal forms of addressing people. In North America, there are important power codes in student–teacher, customer–waiter, or boss–subordinate situations. In Belgium, it is considered impolite to address someone in a jovial way that you do not know. Religious heritage determines how we observe holidays or recognize events. Jehovah's Witnesses, for example, do not observe Father's Day. In these cases, our perceptions are based on our own past experiences.

Back to Mattimore's number puzzle presented earlier. The number is 2—the only even number. If you picked correctly, you are in the minority. Because we have learned in the past to ignore items that are followed by ")" as part of the question or problem, we look right past 1), 2), and 3) and try and find important differences between 3, 13, and 33. We miss the point that there are five odd numbers and only one even number. Similarly, if you have connected the nine dots in Figure 2.1 while following the instructions, then you are the exception. The most common explanation for our inability to successfully connect the dots, as shown in Figure 2.2, is an unwillingness to go outside the artificial paradigm or "square" created by the dots. Hence, the expression that to solve some problems, we need to learn to think outside the box. The nine-dot exercise shows how quickly we approach a problem as it is presented creating a mental box based on our past experiences.

One last observation regarding past experiences. The *primacy effect* argues, essentially, that first impressions are lasting impressions. So, early experiences can frame subsequent events in positive or negative lights.

Present Organizational Experiences

When we enter the culture labeled "gainful employment," most of us recognize that our behavior must be adaptive in order to fit in and maintain our job. In most cases, we accept additional inputs into our own personal perceptual system in the form of instructions regarding the job requirements and performance, the rules and regulations regarding the culture, and the apparent

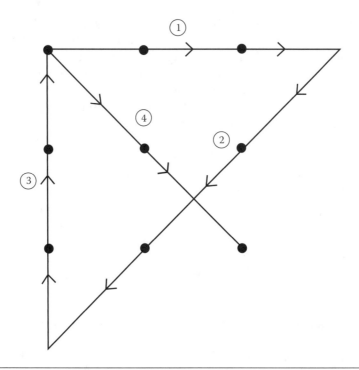

Figure 2.2 An example of the most common explanation for an inability to connect the dots.

interpersonal patterns. We slowly make "sense" of this new sensory data and, as we remain on the job, certain perceptions become permanently associated with the organization. These all become part of our orientation toward organizational behavior and our attitudes toward lunch hours, office location, or weekly staff meetings are all formed in the ongoing process of being part of the organizational system. We develop paradigms that tell us how to respond in particular situations or to particular tasks.

In a more general sense, our present experiences provide the information we have regarding the specific organizational culture. [Every organization, group, or department has a culture and each culture has its own attributes. Subcultures provide unique inputs to the organization's culture.] Marketing focuses on very different behaviors than shipping although both subsystems are concerned with the environment outside of the immediate office. Individually, we begin to form our own perceptual "realities" as we decide on an occupation, experience employment, or carry out numerous other organizationally related activities.

Earlier, we identified the primacy effect explaining how past impressions can influence our perceptions. A countering force is the *recency effect*. This explains how "the most recent information dominates our perception of others" (McShane & Von Glinow, 2000, p. 179). One obvious example would be customer service. A recent, horrible experience with a service provider can override past experiences. A second situation revolves around performance appraisals. Even though the superior about to provide the appraisal should include the 6-month or 1-year period, events that occur immediately preceding this important meeting tend to receive the most credence.

Actual Situational Limitations

We soon become aware that no one can be omnipresent in an organization. In fact, in many cases we are hired to do very specific tasks. Even those with extensive oversight responsibilities carry with their position physical limitations including what type of access they have to information, which parts of this information appear to them as being important, and how they will use that information to interpret the meaning. Each of these three factors can work to enhance or limit us in understanding particular issues within an organization. Our position, including the circumstances surrounding it, combined with all the other constraints—available information, resources, time, and so on—is always at work to control perception (Myers, 1991).

Past and present experiences, combined with situational limitations, influence practically all our decision-making activities. In an organization, for example, we look to past successes and failures with particular ideas and behaviors before making certain choices. Then we look to our present knowledge of the organization's structure to determine the best or most appropriate persons to approach regarding the issue. Finally, we incorporate past and present information to act on our choices.

In addition, our immediate surroundings can change our perception. One popular laboratory experiment has students take turns sitting in front of three pails of water—one hot, one at room temperature, and one cold (Cialdini, 1988). Each student is instructed to place one hand in cold water and one in hot water. Then the student is told to place both hands in the room-temperature water simultaneously. The student's face shows the effect. The hand that was in cold water now feels as if it is in hot water and the hand that was in hot water now feels that it is in cold water. "The point is that the same thing—in this instance, room-temperature water—can be made to seem very different depending on the nature of the event that precedes it" (Cialdini, 1988, p. 13).

Perceptual limitations have an impact on numerous issues in all organizations. Motivation (see chap. 11) is one of the most important and recurring problems organizations face. Managers have paradigms regarding how to motivate based on individual perceptions. One effective means of highlighting the different manager and employee perceptions regarding motivation is to ask each group to rank from 1 to 10 a list of items in order of their importance to the employee. The manager is asked to think of her or his employees and what is important to them, not the manager. The goal of the exercise is to highlight differences between those items employees think are important versus those

Table 2.1 Summary of Rankings by Employees and Management of 10 Items Important to Employees at Work

What Employees Say They Want from Their Jobs	What Managers Think Employees Want
1. Interesting work	1. Good pay
2. Full appreciation of work done	2. Job security
3. Feeling "in" on future developments	3. Promotion and career growth
4. Job security	4. Good working conditions
5. Good pay	5. Interesting work
6. Promotion and career growth	6. Tactful disciplining
7. Good working conditions	7. Management loyalty to workers
8. Management loyalty to workers	8. Help with personal problems
9. Help with personal problems	9. Full appreciation of work done
10. Tactful disciplining	10. Feeling "in" on future developments

that managers think are important for their employees. As Table 2.1 indicates, there are dramatic differences.

The explanation for the differences lies, to a large extent, in the managers' attempts to apply their own experiences and backgrounds to the employees' perceived needs and thereby attributing to the employees motives that simply do not apply. With little difficulty, we can see that the source of this misapplication lies in the three factors we discussed. The rankings reported in Table 2.1 are based on in-house training seminars conducted in 1995–2003. Regardless of where the exercise is used, there are substantial differences between the beliefs of managers and employees. When managers wonder why they have difficulties in motivating some of their subordinates, the first place they might look is their paradigms regarding what motivates their employees. The classic advice is: If you want to know how to motivate someone, ask them what they want. They may not know the answer, but they have to know better than you.

Sensory and Symbolic Basis for Perception

No matter how acute our own perceptual abilities might be, our reality is less than the actual event. A story about three baseball umpires comparing notes on how they do their job indicates the function of reality in perception. The first umpire stated: "I call them either balls or strikes!" The second umpire, in an attempt to sound like a better umpire, asserted: "I call them as I see them!" The third umpire, with what is probably the strongest statement about labeling and reality, declared: "They ain't nothing until I calls them!" For each of the umpires, their reality was based on their perception of their own role and their environment. In terms of perception, each of the umpires was correct. In the umpire story, no one disagreed that there was such a thing as a ball or a strike or that there was a need, for the benefit of the culture called baseball, to have someone call them. The issue was who would construct the reality.

In all cases, we are aided by a *group construct* concerning reality and this is especially important in an organizational culture. This construct is developed by placing boundaries that allow us to include certain characteristics or activities within a particular grouping while excluding others (Klyukanov, 2005). At work for example, we have a group definition of a "good" or "bad" worker. What constitutes a good or bad worker is essentially a group decision based on the combined past experiences each person brings to the job and the present environment. How about cheating? Although college students express concern over recent corporate scandals, with 84% believing the United States is having a business crisis in terms of ethics, "some 59% admit cheating on a test (66% men, 54% women) and only 19% say they would report a classmate who cheated (23% of men, but only 15% of women)" (Merritt, 2002, p. 8). In a survey of high school students, "74% said they had cheated on a test" (Zelizer, 2002, p. 15A). Perhaps even more telling, in a survey of 12,474 high school students, 43% of all respondents—and 41% of those bound for college—agreed with the statement "A person has to lie or cheat sometimes in order to succeed" (Marklein, 2003, p. 1D). From this survey, it would appear that the group construct seems to accept, and sometimes, endorse cheating. In addition, it would be reasonable to assume that past experiences and the present environment play large roles.

We also must realize that, as with the umpires, reality is always based on incomplete data. We cannot observe all the accompanying information to an event. This does not free us from having to form some type of perception because we must put the observed data in some context so that it makes sense to us. To do this, we abstract from reality and develop a symbolic construct. To us, this reality is no less valid than the one that would be based on all possible information. From a practical standpoint, meticulously gathering and evaluating all reports, advice, and communiques would prove impossible.

The final consequence of perception is the tendency of our perceived realities to "lock-in outcomes" that may result in stereotypes, presumptions, or other biases (Adler & Towne, 2003; Neuliep, 2000). Essentially, we tend to persevere in our judgments even when the evidence is overwhelming that they are wrong. If we have a particular image in a work situation, we often opt for perceptual consistency rather than accept contradictory information. Hence, once the perceptual image has been formed, we interpret subsequent events in light of the original perception and not the newly available. Our preconceived notion of reality becomes reality itself.

Our perceptions are also a function of the availability of reinforcement. Events are judged as likely or unlikely depending on the readiness to which they come to our mind. A communication professor observes to a friend: "Did you ever notice how many communication professors are chosen as the outstanding teacher at their universities? I'll bet it has to do with the way their background and education guide them in approaching their jobs." In spite of the apparent desirability of this claim, the basis for this observation probably has more to do with the likelihood of hearing about and noticing this particular phenomenon more than the activities of other professors in other disciplines. Many of the concepts held by individuals of where minorities, women, and older people fit into the workplace are based on traditional biases, which are reinforced by selective perception (Morrison & Von Glinow, 1990). *We make behavioral observations based on selecting information and cues that we have learned to pay attention to and use.*

Try this exercise to test your ability to rise above perceptual limitations. Many would argue that our language is biased toward the color white and against the color black. Table 2.2 challenges us to find positive black phrases and negative white phrases. Try to list 25 items in each category. In a moment, we offer some common answers. The problem is our past and current experiences do not include diversity-enhancing language so we do not use positive black and negative white as often as the opposite.

Reality is based, then, on our perceptions combined with the group and environmental data that we use to modify our original concepts. By definition, we use incomplete data in the process of forming an abstraction. This

Table 2.2 Language and Perception

The prejudice against the color black and for the color white permeates our language. A few examples:

Black-hearted	White magic
Black thoughts	Snow White
Black death (plague)	White Christmas
Black magic	

As a test of the strength of this phenomenon, try to think of words or phrases that use the color black in a positive way or the color white in a negative way. We'll get you started with "in the black" and "white as a ghost." Try to list at least 25 in each category.

POSITIVE BLACK	NEGATIVE WHITE
"in the black"	"white as a ghost"

symbolic representation tends to lock us into particular views of the world (Adler & Towne, 2003; Neuliep, 2000).

Psychological Factors in Perception

There are at least six psychological determinants of our perceptual abilities. In many cases, these categories influence each other and cross over.

Before we turn to these concepts, here are some responses to the exercise regarding language. Positive black could include: Black Beauty, black gold, black panther, black pearls, black pepper, black pride, black board, black coffee, or Black Flag. Negative white could include: white flag, white elephant, white water, men in white, white wash, white slavery, white supremacy, whitehead, or white as a sheet. You can augment these with a quick trip to the dictionary.

Attitude Set

An attitude is a learned predisposition to respond favorably or unfavorably to some person, object, idea, or event. They are "thoughts that you have accepted as true and that lead you to think, feel, or act positively or negatively toward a person, idea, or event" (Reece & Brandt, 2005, p. 128). This reaction tends to create a bias, which can be carried to the extreme and results in *tunnel vision* where we do not consider alternative viewpoints. In an organization, each of us has our own specialty that is more important to us than the others. Most individuals in sales, for example, argue that organizations cannot exist without sales because the cash flow generated by sales is the lifeblood of the company. Likewise, information and computer specialists make the same type of claim; only they refer to the mind, memory, and connecting power of the system.

The impact of attitude set can be observed in organizations doing business as usual even when there are multiple signs that this is an inadequate response to a changing environment (Bolman & Deal, 2003). The call for the "tried and true" processes is not incorrect, but taken to the extreme it eliminates system adaptation and innovation. We tend to place a great deal of faith in our attitude set. With little difficulty, we can see strong attitude sets toward religion, sexuality, and many other issues (Reece & Brandt, 2005).

Opening our perceptual systems is not always easy and this process is often the focus of training and development sessions. Before you proceed in your reading, look at Figure 2.3 and try counting the squares.

In training sessions, the responses range from 17 to 30 or more. You may have a different answer. In any case, our perceptual abilities are tested by this exercise because different individuals have a wide variety of answers. Normally, we put individuals into small groups to work out the correct answer in order to lead into a discussion of synergy and the importance of expanding perspectives. After lengthy discussion, each group usually will arrive at 30 squares as the correct answer. However, a few years ago, one group correctly pointed out that there were 32 squares in the illustration. Why? The word

Count The Squares

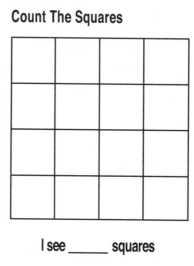

I see _____ squares

Figure 2.3 An exercise to test perceptual systems.

"squares" appears twice on the paper in addition to the actual squares. So, both answers of 30 and 32 are correct and underscore the importance of opening our perceptual systems.

Stereotypes and Self-Fulfilling Prophecies

Once we have an established attitude set, the application of that set can lead to stereotyping, which we have already discussed to some extent. As a general definition, *stereotyping is the tendency to lump all of a particular group of subsystems or systems into a particular characterization.* These are unreliable generalizations "based on a simplified image of a group" (Dobkin & Pace, 2006, p. 47). We are all familiar with the tendency to stereotype particular groups because they are different from us.

Group differences can be identified as cultural, functional, and historical (Pollar & Gonzalez, 1994). As you look at the categories, ask what types of stereotypes you or your group may hold toward others. The cultural differences include religion, age, ethnicity, immigrant status, and language capability. Functionally, we learn, think, respond to authority, and process information differently. Historically, we have different family compositions, intergroup relationships, and political views. Are you free from any stereotypes regarding these differences?

Stereotyping is almost second nature arising from advice similar to "don't talk to strangers" when we are young to personal beliefs regarding certain nonverbal attributes such as height or weight (see chap. 5). As a test, do you think the typical CEO (chief operating officer) would drive a passenger car,

SUV, luxury car costing over $70,000, or a pick-up truck? What do you believe is the average amount of money CEOs spend for their vehicles? When this question was asked in a national survey, 59% of the respondents believed a typical CEO owns a luxury vehicle. In fact, only 19% of the surveyed CEOs said they did. More than half drive a passenger car or SUV and 19% drive a pickup truck. Most respondents believed CEOs spent in excess of $70,000 for their primary cars, but CEOs actually spent an average of less than $25,000 ("Big Wheels," 2006).

Everyone engages in stereotyping because being able to focus requires the exclusion of some superfluous information. In organizations, *stereotyping* is becoming an increasingly important issue because traditional organizational demographics are being reworked by the rapid increase in the number of women, people of color, and other groups (McShane & Von Glinow, 2000). In our opening chapter, we examined the numerous changes occurring in organizations. Stereotyping our potential coworkers and colleagues can hamper our own success, satisfaction with our work, and our future advancement (Reece & Brandt, 2005).

In organizations, stereotyping can be identified using *allness, indiscrimination, and time-binding. Allness* is placing an entire group into one category. Consider the job interview process. Often credentials such as a college degree is seen as more important than other characteristics, so all applicants must have a degree. Interviewers' responses to body piercing, tattoos, or the interviewee's dress can determine the decision to hire (Hamilton, 2005). For others, the only good cars are American or imports. In these cases, the position includes the assumption of "all." Although we may be aware of the necessary caution that should be applied when speaking of minorities, such as all Latin men are passionate, all Gen Xers are materialistic, or all blondes are dumb, consider the manner in which we proceed to discuss other classifications such as supervisors, management, professors, unions, MBAs, high school dropouts, CEOs, today's youth, doctors, engineers, and many other job-related categories, and never pause to add the term "some." We would also be well advised to listen to the words of Dolly Parton when she was asked if she minded being called a dumb blonde. Her response: "I'm not dumb, and I'm certainly not a natural blonde." External appearances can mislead us.

As we become increasingly global, *ethnocentrism*, which is our tendency to *regard our own culture or nation as better or more correct than others*, can limit our perception (Reece & Brandt, 2005, p. 364). Extreme ethnocentrism means we reject the richness and knowledge of other cultures rather than applying *cultural relativism*, which accepts that different cultural backgrounds develop different communication behaviors. Our cultural conditioning can lead to making judgments regarding dissimilar groups that are based on superficial information rather than in-depth understanding. Note, once again, the very incomplete list in the last paragraph concerning "all." This leads to our second area.

Our second general category *is indiscriminate application of our limited perception*. With few actual exposures to an issue or idea, we generalize to all subsequent encounters based on these initial impressions. Remember the opening examples of perception. We do or do not like Japanese food, for example, after eating at one Japanese restaurant. Within a short period of time on the job, many individuals create concrete reactions to concepts such as unions (good or bad), work rules (very helpful or an insult to integrity), and many others depending on the particular occupation. Because categories are collections of subsystems, any attempt to apply an across-the-board statement will be less than accurate.

Finally, we *time-bind* events and individuals and fail to recognize that people, objects, events, and organizations change over time. Tom Wolfe coined the phrase "You can never go home again." His point was that home couldn't be time-bound because it always will evolve in some direction. As a living system, whoever or whatever it was that made up the concept of home would change and this same evolution will occur to any us who are away from home. If any of us worked at a McDonald's 10 years ago, there is little chance that our experiences would apply today. Yet, we are tempted to respond "been there, done that" as a means of time-binding.

As we seek to make sense out of our organizational environment, we must be cautious not to group people and concepts without carefully noting the inherent dangers.

Closure

For most individuals, knowing all the information regarding a situation is unlikely, perhaps unnecessary, and often impossible. Because we need a sense of completeness in a given situation, we employ closure. We fill in the vacuums with our versions of the appropriate information so that the event will make sense. In addition, if there is a gap in the story, individuals will provide the information in order to make the recollection of the event follow more coherently. Eyewitness accounts regarding accidents or crimes frequently incorporate this tendency toward closure in order to fill in the missing information. Consider the following situation.

> Your group had plans for after hours socializing. As you arrived at your destination, you spotted a man in uniform running home. The man suddenly noticed another man wearing a mask and holding a dreaded object. The first man turned around and ran back to the place he had come from.

Can you tell where the group members are? Do you have enough information to answer the question? We will discuss this situation in a moment.

Selectivity

In our presentation of perceptual biases, we indicated the impact our own attitudes and beliefs have on our perception. Selectivity is the tendency to interpret communication messages using those biases. As an unconscious filtering process, selectivity tends to exclude certain aspects, groups, or behaviors as we operate in an organization. We accept into our perceptual system certain facts or happenings that are consistent with our past experiences and beliefs. This occurs in three ways: exposure bias, selective retention, and similarity and liking.

Exposure Bias   We are more likely to attend to messages that are consistent with our existing beliefs and attitudes. If we buy a new car, we are suddenly surprised to see so many similar models on the road. Because we are now interested in a particular event, we focus our perception. This is an ongoing activity in which we attend to the same types of behaviors, and therefore meanings, with the result being a continual exposure to the same data. The manner in which we choose to read the different sections of a newspaper is an example of this bias. Choosing to read the *Wall Street Journal*, watch Fox news, or use any other source indicates a particular set regarding the type of information we are seeking.

In organizations, we tend to read e-mails and memos for information that applies directly to our own area of interest. If your particular area is marketing, there is little likelihood that you will be concerned with the decisions regarding the accounting department's interests.

Which leads us to the situation discussed earlier—did you conclude that there was insufficient information? Actually, the situation describes a baseball game. If you had difficulty in figuring out the situation, you probably were blocked by a desire for closure and your exposure bias.

Selective Retention   Not only do we notice particular messages but we also tend to remember those that are consistent with our needs, biases, and attitudes. In spite of the need to recognize the interrelatedness of each part of an organization, we perceive events that relate directly to the goals and activities we deem important to our success. Sometimes this represents *habituation,* which is "blocking out extraneous or unimportant messages in any situation" (Kreps, 1990, p. 30). Although we need to pay attention to those elements that have a direct hearing on our particular role, we do so at the expense of other information.

How well do we notice events and activities that surround us? Try the following test of information most of us should be able to provide.

What color stripe is directly under the blue field on the U.S. flag?
What building is on the $5 bill?

If quotation marks are considered as commas, is the first pair upside
down or right side up?

What color(s) is a yield right-of-way sign?

Each of these questions relates to easily available information that we perceive on a regular basis. However, many of us do not notice the color white,
the Lincoln Memorial, commas as upside down or yield right-of-way signs as
red, white, and black. Quotation marks, of course, appeared in the previous
paragraph.

Similarity and Likings   These are our tendencies to see positive attributes in
those individuals we like and negative ones in those we do not like. This can
be carried to an extreme in an organization and result in what is now popu-
larly known as *The Peter Principle* (Peter & Hull, 1969). This principle argues
in some organizations, those individuals who perform well at one level or in
one position will be promoted to the next level under the assumption that they
will perform well there also. One example would be promoting the best sales
person to being the sales manager. Based on this principle, the use of liking as
a means for making the decision is potentially disastrous, because the person
who is a competent salesperson might not want to be a manager, or might
lack the necessary skills to be an effective manager. Even more fundamentally,
doing one task well hardly indicates that the individual can do other tasks
with the same proficiency. The issue is one of using selective traits the person
provides to the job they are presently doing for the organization and general-
izing to all possible organizational activities.

Finally, when we allow someone's favorable or unfavorable traits to color
our opinion of them, we are employing the *halo effect* (DuBrin, 2000). Sometimes, the way someone dresses or their manner of speaking makes others like
or dislike them. Once again, in an increasingly global world, these differences
in behaving can lead to unfortunate decisions regarding how we view others.

Self-Concept

These three aspects of selectivity often are accentuated by each individual's
need to maintain their self-concept, which is a set of perceptions we have about
ourselves. Our need for a sense of cognitive consistency in which our own personal conceptual integrity is somehow held intact can be an important perceptual problem (Adler & Towne, 2003). We have certain beliefs, which lead
to a self-image that is an integral part of each of our make-ups. In many ways,
this self-concept requires that the incoming information be consistent with
the preconceived premise under which we operate. We carry an evaluative
frame of reference that predisposes us to respond to particular information in
a manner that maintains our own internal equilibrium between new information and the already accepted premises. In the process, we have the tendency
to maintain our own self-concept.

Our need to defend our self-concept has been most appropriately described by Gibb (1961) in his analysis of *defensive communication* (see chap. 8). Communication that is essentially evaluative will cause the receiver to become defensive, thereby inhibiting effective interactions because the individual will feel the need to defend his or her self-concept.

On the other side of the coin, if we are given supportive messages that are consistent with our self-image, there is a greater likelihood we will act on them in a manner befitting the situation. Simply put, we do not correctly perceive things we do not like or that threaten our self-concept as well as ones that fit neatly into our perceptual set.

Globalization

We will pause for a moment to discuss the impact on perception created by our increasingly global perspective. Throughout this chapter, we have used examples regarding global influences and characteristics. Too often, people allow *ethnocentrism*, or perceiving that "their own experiences, which are shaped by their own cultural forces, are natural, human, and universal" leading to the belief that they are superior to other cultures (Lustig & Koester, 2003). In our international working environments, we can all benefit from understanding the specific concepts underlying intercultural differences. To further clarify, we introduce five categories that are used to differentiate between types of cultures—individualism/collectivism, high/low power distances, uncertainty avoidance, masculinity/femininity, and high/low context (Klyukanov, 2005). We are not attempting to provide a full discussion of intercultural communication nor offering the key steps toward intercultural communication competence. As you have already noted in your own experiences, different cultural assumptions can create unnecessary perceptual difficulties.

Be reminded that "the relationship between national culture and organizational culture (see chaps. 1 and 7) is neither simple nor straightforward" (Stohl, 2001, p. 340). In other words, generalizations from the categories we provide should be applied very carefully because culture is learned not innate and organizational shareholders normally will adapt to the demands of their immediate.

Individualist and Collectivist.   These terms are fairly self-explanatory. Individualist cultures "emphasize individual achievements and rights, including the individual's right to make decisions for himself and herself" (Beamer & Varner, 2003, p. 70). There tends to be loose ties between individuals where we look after ourselves and families over the community at large. Work relationships tend to be defined by contracts and clearly stated expectations. Direct communication techniques are used more often.

If you are in a collectivist society, the interests of the group prevail over the individual. Strong, cohesive in-groups, which often continue throughout a lifetime, are protected by the participants. At work, the employer–employee relationship tends to be defined in more moral terms based on the ties to the group. Communication techniques are less direct.

As with other categories, these distinctions do not always hold true in any country or culture.

Power Distances   High-power distances are exhibited in cultures that accept inequalities in power distribution, as apparent in authoritarian and hierarchical cultures. For example, organizational cultures emphasizing rank (e.g., supervisor, manager, Corporal) are utilizing high-power distances. For several years, we trained U.S.-based Mercedes-Benz (Division of Daimler Chrysler) employees for their 2-week to 9-month training trips to Germany. Given the precision needed to assemble a Mercedes-Benz, training by the Daimler Chrysler experts in Germany was absolutely necessary. One area we examined is that Germans expect that supervisors and managers will be in charge. When communicating with subordinates, Germans tend to be blunt, clear, and precise, and expect the same behaviors in others. Input from subordinates is not considered important unless it is precisely focused on business concerns. Americans, on the other hand, are accustomed to a lower power distance where a collegial and egalitarian tone tends to govern superior–subordinate discussions. On the other side of the Atlantic, German supervisors were being trained on the power distance expectations for the incoming U.S. Mercedes-Benz employees. As a result, the high-culture supervisors/trainers (e.g., Germany) and the low-culture trainees (e.g., United States) were able to work together effectively.

When there is low-power distance operating, power is distributed as equally as possible. So, power is less hierarchical and authoritarian and participants feel they can question authority. As you have already surmised, power is very contextual because some U.S. companies are quite egalitarian and others are very hierarchical. In the United States, there are numerous examples of inequality at work ranging from pay and privileges to office setting to freedom to come and go without permission.

In organized settings, these distances can become very important. Later in this text (chaps. 10 and 11), we examine in more detail employee empowerment, self-directed work units, and power distribution.

Uncertainty Avoidance   If you find yourself seeking clear instructions, wanting to specialize, expecting professors to be the expert in the classroom and have all the answers, and find comfort in a strong set of rules, you exhibit the general characteristics of strong uncertainty avoidance. Often, these types of cultures depend on rules, laws, and enforcement to reduce uncertainty and there is a sense that there is only one correct way of operating. At work, there is a need for rules, precision, and punctuality.

When there is low uncertainty avoidance, the prevailing culture provides guidelines but few, if any, rules. Professors are seen as important, but not the source for all answers. There is more tolerance for behaviors and opinions that do not necessarily reflect other points of view. At work, employees work hard when needed, there are few formal rules, and punctuality is practiced when applicable.

Masculinity/Femininity When a culture emphasizes assertiveness, material success, and competitiveness, it is masculine. If collaboration, harmony, and nurturing are the key areas of emphasis, it is feminine. If you see specific roles for men and women, you are edging toward masculinity.

Context High-context cultures rely on the actual physical environment of communication or an internalized social context, or both, to convey a message's meaning. In these cultures, the information needed to understand messages has already been internalized by the individual. In other words, the "what and where" of our activities carries more meaning than the words we use, increasing the importance of nonverbal actions. China, many Latin American cultures, and some Mediterranean cultures such as Greece, Turkey, or Arab states are examples.

Low-context cultures expect messages to be more explicit. So, low-context cultures put their thoughts into words. As opposed to the heavy reliance on nonverbal messages in a high-context culture, low-context cultures believe thoughts need to be put into words to guarantee understanding. Information is more focused. Verbal messages tend to be more elaborate and verbal abilities are highly valued. Switzerland, Germany, and the United States are examples.

When we consider perception, these five elements can guide our own interpretation of events. Remember ethnocentrism, which we discussed earlier in this chapter—we believe our culture is superior to others. Our increasingly global community, especially in organizations, requires that we re-examine our presumptions when we work and communicate with dissimilar cultures.

Organizational Role Constraints

All positions impose limitations on exactly what we can perceive. These are real in the sense that we cannot be everywhere and certainly cannot observe all activities. In addition, there are those limitations imposed because we simply do not wish to wander out of the limitations that make good sense to us. We may choose to say something is genuinely "not my job," due to the reality that it is indeed not our job or because we do not want any additional responsibility. Even if we were free from all other perceptual limitations, the particular system we operate within still would put specific constraints on our ability to perceive all information. Two relevant examples feature superior–subordinate relationships.

Performance reviews, the semiannual or annual meeting between employees and their managers, offer a dramatic example of the differences created because of power and position differences. When asked if employees received feedback or advice on how to maximize their strengths, 49% of employees responded "yes," whereas 82% of managers responded "yes"—a 33% difference in opinion. When asked if employees receive sufficient feedback or advice on areas in which they need improvement, 57% of employees responded "yes," whereas 89% of managers responded "yes," creating a 32% gap in agreement (Haralson & Tian, 2003). The survey involved 1,818 employees and 1,814 managers at 278 companies. Because these are recurring events, not realizing the differences in effectiveness means the appraisal could be a waste of time or ineffective.

A more dramatic example would be medical operating rooms (ORs). "There is mounting evidence that poor communication between hospital staff and surgeons is the leading cause of avoidable surgical errors" (Landro, 2005, p. D1). The OR features an intense atmosphere "where surgeons are the captains of the ship, treated with deference because of their unique skills. As a result, nurses, prep technicians, and other aides can be afraid to speak up if they spot a problem" (Landro, 2005, p. D1). The OR can be difficult to change, because the surgeons' view of their role does not necessarily include listening to staff suggestions. "But in the OR, studies show that serious complications can arise from communication problems—such as nurses failing to notify a surgeon of a change in the patient's color or respiration. Earlier this year, VHA surveyed staff at 20 hospitals and found that as many as 60% of OR staffers agreed with the statement: In the ORs here, it is difficult to speak up if I perceive a problem with patient care (Landro, 2005, p. D4). Although nurses are quick to point to communication issues, the "VHA survey found that surgeons often don't perceive a problem with communication, while nurses do" (Landro, 2005, p. D4). Surgeons taking control of the operating room makes sense in terms of seniority but the lack of effective communication due to role differences could prove catastrophic.

At this point, you might be thinking that the entire discussion of perception and its impact on organizational communication is interesting and obviously important, but the problem should be easy to overcome simply by making this information available to active members of organizations. Unfortunately, the issue is too complex for a simple solution. Recall that we all operate within the organizational system as a whole while we also are operating within specific subsystems. Faced with the complexity of the entire system, we tend to concentrate on our own presentations of what we perceive to be effective roles. As we act out our roles within the system, we consciously and unconsciously neglect other factors within the organization. As guidelines, we have an overriding sense of what the culture will accept as proper, and we have the immediate influence of the subsystem, whether it is a department, a

Figure 2.4 The picture used to test perceptual constraints that may come into play in hiring practices.

specialty, or a goal on our ongoing behavior. The stimuli we choose to respond to will determine how we perceive a particular situation.

An extended program we used with one corporation's human resource directors regarding their own perceptual limitations in hiring practices demonstrates the issue. Human Resource directors are under a large number of constraints when they choose to interview candidates for possible employment. For example, most personnel directors have a list of questions they may not ask a candidate. The goal of the program was to demonstrate some of the significant perceptual constraints that come into play in spite of the general belief that hiring practices must be fair.

The group of about 30 was divided into six task forces to determine whether to hire a specific individual. The picture in Figure 2.4 was distributed with three of the task forces receiving a description of an older woman, at least 55 years of age, who had been a secretary for many years and was certain of how to do her job. Her attributes included confidence and the ability to follow through on work assignments. The other three received a description of a young woman, around 25 years of age, who had been to secretarial school and was very confident in her approach to her job. Although she had a flair for overdressing, she was a serious worker. Both candidates had excellent references. The rest of the description for both candidates was identical except for adjustments for the age of each person; the position to be filled required secretarial skills and the ability to manage 10 other members of the same office staff.

If you already have seen two individuals in the picture, congratulations. The members of the seminar did not fare as well. Being under tremendous constraints created by their own organizational roles, their apparent perception of potential peer pressure, and the immediate context of having to act out their abilities as personnel directors, each group went about the task as it was described. Those persons who initially advocated the existence of two faces, and there were surprisingly few, quickly dropped their observation in order to facilitate the group problem-solving process. The immediate task became the overriding issue.

Each group's deliberations regarding whether to hire the individual were recorded. At one point or another in the discussion, practically all of the perceptual limitations that we have predicted might occur in an organizational setting did occur in these groups. For example, in all six groups, age was an important issue with comments ranging from "older people make the best workers" or "experience is the best teacher" to "youthful enthusiasm is best for the changing workplace" or "schooling is the secret to present knowledge." Many of the individuals argued from their own experiences regarding past employees.

Because reality is also a group construct, there developed a consensus complete with attitude sets, stereotyping, closure, and selectivity. Each person also was concerned with maintaining their own self-concept within the group, which was evident in relation to their own positions as personnel directors. In reviewing the exercise for the participants, we were able to identify the perceptual issues we have discussed in this chapter as the major impediment to effective hiring practices.

The final step in this exercise was to ask each group to discuss their decision and the rationale for it. Each group was asked to choose a representative who then presented the findings. At this point, it should have been obvious that there were two faces in the picture. However, the perceptual set was so great that most of the groups refused to accept the other possibility. The group leaders became more concerned with their presentations and the maintaining of their own self-image. The leaders were also in a position of publicly forwarding the group's decision. These elements combined to create a highly defensive reaction to the challenges from the other perspectives. This type of study has been conducted for various other purposes with the same general result (Mulford, 1978). For this group, the hoped-for result was a greater understanding of the perceptual limitations with which we all work.

To test your own understanding of perception, examine Figure 2.5. The Arizona Public Service published a 21-page manual on ethical standards for its 7,000 employees with this logo on the front. Ten thousand copies were distributed to 25 different locations. Do you see anything wrong with the logo? Some workers refused to read the manual because the upside down star is a satanic symbol (Himelstein, 1994). Procter & Gamble had the same problem with the man-in-the-moon logo that was assailed by some religious leaders as

Figure 2.5 Arizona Public Service logo.

a sign of the devil. Both the Arizona Public Service and P&G abandoned their symbols. Perception is in the eye of the beholder.

The human resource managers also brought to my attention an important saying, which summarizes the apparent paradox regarding perception: "Always remember that you are absolutely unique, just like everyone else." This is the type of dilemma we face with perception. In order to sufficiently understand information as we receive it, we need to see it in groupings to make sense of the data. At the same time, this tendency to see things as being the same because they carry the general characteristics means that we miss the absolutely unique nature of each event. This chapter highlights the areas where we must work to resolve the apparent paradox. An awareness of the perceptual influence on our ability to communicate in an organization is the critical step. Often, we are limited in our ability to understand perception because "we are too close to be able to see it clearly" (Platt, 1970, p. 5).

Conclusion

Before we can effectively understand the various issues in organizational communication, we must appreciate the significant impact perception and paradigms have on all parts of an organization. Once we understand the impact, we can begin to overcome our own tendencies to be perceptually limited. In addition, we can understand the impact of perception on all the individuals we work with and the cultures of every organization. As we learn to more effectively select, organize, and interpret the various sensory stimulations in our organizational cultures, we will be more successful as organizational communicators.

Each of the remaining chapters in this textbook provides new information that assist you in expanding your personal reference file toward organizational communication. With increased sensitivity toward our perceptual blinders and sets, we become better able to correctly respond to the various behaviors occurring in an organization. Rather than depend on past experiences to explain current activities, we can interpret more accurately exactly what is occurring and respond in a more effective manner. Equally as important, we can become more effective in understanding other people. As you continue your organizational communication studies, carefully examine your assumptions in light of the new information being provided.

Study Questions

1. Why is it important to focus on perception and paradigms as we study organizational communication?
2. Provide three examples of paradigms you currently use, believe, or accept with regards to working, interviewing, or other work related activities. Explain.
3. What are the five characteristics of paradigms?
4. Provide an example of past experiences or rear-view mirrorism, present working experiences, and actual situational limitations from your own work experiences.
5. Explain the concept of organizational reality.
6. What are the key psychological factors in perception? Provide an example of each not covered in the text.
7. What are organizational role constraints? Provide an example from your own working experience.

3

Understanding Organizations

An Overview of Management and
Organizational Perspectives

The key concepts covered in this chapter include:

- Preindustrial society
- Evolution of organizational structure
- Scientific management
- Human relations management
- Human resource management
- Organizational cultures
- Understanding organizational cultures
- Critical perspectives
- Organizations—2000 and beyond
- Interpretations of organizational processes

Introduction

Organized activities have existed throughout recorded time. Papyrus records indicate that from 2052 BC to 1786 BC, the Middle Kingdom of Egypt's leaders introduced the subdivision of labor. In an early attempt to organize and communicate, around 59 BC, Julius Caesar used handwritten posters and sheets around Rome to keep people up-to-date. City states, villages, religions, and armies all required some type of organization.

The organizations we are familiar with have relatively recent origins. The past 100 years have spawned an amazing number of important advances, spurred by the Industrial Revolution, the development of large businesses, and the digital age, that have set the stage for the types of organizations we encounter.

Massive shifts in demographics have occurred. At the beginning of the 20th century, 40% of the U.S. population were involved in farming. In 1999, that number had been reduced to 3%. People moved from rural to urban to suburban life, from education for the elite to education for the masses, and from farm to factory to service and knowledge work. In addition, the working population is changing. By 2008, women and minorities will make up 70% of the incoming U.S. workforce according by 2008 (Armand-Delille, 2006). Single households in the United States now outnumber married couples with children. At the same time, only nine female CEOs ran Fortune 500 companies in 2005. Already boasting 300 million people, the United States is averaging one birth every 7 seconds, one death every 14 seconds, and one international migrant (net gain) every 26 seconds (Stuckey & Mullins, 2005).

This chapter develops chronologically. As you travel through this intentionally brief lesson, you may be wondering why it is important to return to examine the roots of the modern organization. As you will discover, each approach represents fundamental beliefs that directly influence organizational communication processes. Our stops include an examination of scientific management, humanistic management, human resource management, contingency theory, the cultural perspective, and the new organization. Two overviews are important. First, organizations must reach a balance between the need to accomplish tasks and the effective utilization of people. All organizations exist for some purpose and throughput is required to remain viable. Efforts to accommodate these two needs permeate organizational perspectives and practices. Second, paradigms regarding how to run an organization can lead to *trained incapacities*. When we discover a workable solution to a problem, we tend to overutilize the tried-and-true approach at the expense of other possible options. We become frozen in a particular paradigm that becomes a trained incapacity preventing us from seeing other viable solutions. Remember, each of the original approaches are likely to still be seen in practice in various forms so this is not so much a history lesson as an important briefing on why organizations do what they do.

Preindustrial Society

Placed in historical context, the modern organization is relatively new. For much of history, power and wealth were based on the ownership of property. The more land controlled by certain groups, the more power they possessed because they also controlled food, resources, and access to markets. Feudal monarchies, churches, armies, and rulers decided most people's fates and the sources of authority were based on long-standing institutions and procedures. Most individuals obeyed the ruling elite in accordance with traditional customs (Shani & Lau, 1996). Work, labor, and commerce were viewed by the ruling class in pre-industrial societies as something done by lower level classes or slaves. In fact, "until the scientific revolution began in the 17th century, virtually everyone lived on the verge of subsistence" (Colvin, 2005, p. 77).

From the 1760s to the 1830s, changes such as the Enlightenment, textile mills, and steam engines set the stage for the Industrial Revolution. Prior to the Industrial Revolution, most goods and services were generated within the family unit and most needs were met by the family itself, with the help of neighbors, or through bartering. Within larger families, management was mostly a matter of tradition. The state and the church represented organized authority and their dictates usually were followed because of compliance by decree or perhaps because of fear of retribution. In many cases, a certain sense of duty and devotion added to the ability of these large organizations to manage and govern. Around 1880 to 1930, mass production, electrical power, and different forms of democracy fueled a transformation in the way wealth was created. Power shifted from ownership of land to control of the means of production.

As we will restate at the end of this chapter, the eve of the 21st century showed a third power shift from means of production to the use and control of information. The instantaneous nature and the democratization of the information transfer process (i.e., anyone can copy a computer program, e-mail the boss, get online) is shifting power to speed, information, knowledge workers, and company members. The computer chip, it is important to remember, was invented in 1971 by Intel Corporation and the PC, or microcomputer, was created in 1975. Technology thrusts organizations into transformation.

Evolution of Organizational Structure

The Industrial Revolution caused dramatic changes as machine power became the major source of production, requiring the full-time attention of workers who shoveled coal into furnaces or fed raw materials to the machines. Managers operating the factories and assembly lines had to concern themselves with scheduling, coordinating, and rewards in terms of wages. The industrial revolution's technology advances soon outpaced the traditional management skills used in rural settings. Organized attempts at production by a large number of people needed clear management direction. In addition, many industries adopted multiple sites requiring coordination and means of transportation fueling the development of the railroads, telegraph, telephone, and numerous other means for connecting and coordinating. Migration to the cities to accommodate the demands for a large labor pool created a need for coordination in order to feed and house individuals unable to harvest their own food or barter with others. In addition, these new arrivals required transportation, housing, and numerous other services previously available in the countryside. Regardless of the virtues or vices of the 19th century, the beginning of the 20th century, driven by heavy industries such as steel, railroads, electricity, and oil, clearly presented new challenges requiring new theories and practices.

Scientific Management

When we are faced with a new situation, we search for an appropriate paradigm. *Scientific Management* provided the first clearly articulated and recognized approach to designing and running an organization. Three theorists stand out for their contributions to early management theory and practice. Taylor (1911) is the best-known advocate of scientific management and focused most of his attention on efficiency. We examine his approach to organizational design and then explain the important contributions of two other theorists,

Fayol (1949), an advocate for the classical approach to organizing, and Weber (1947), the promoter of bureaucracy.

Taylor and Efficiency

Early in the 20th century, Taylor (1911) looked at the typical production line and noticed there could be any number of workers performing the same job and that each one would be using a different method. He concluded that management would benefit greatly from studying these jobs, determining the best means for performing them, and then teaching all the employees with the same job the preferred method. Taylor became the *father of efficiency*. He believed that a manager's first duty was to analyze each job within the organization, find the right people for the jobs, and properly train them for the tasks.

This *assumption of managerial responsibility* for the worker's job underlies the concept of scientific management. In most cases, managers were responsible to owners for the profitable operation of the assembly line. So, managers were expected to educate the workers on the task and provide the proper tools for getting the job done. For the employees at the time, who were uneducated and relatively unskilled, the system seemed to work well. The phrase "hired hand" developed during this period because someone's "hands" were being hired to do a job. Taylor called for a clear job design by management for these unskilled workers. Work was divided into minute, repetitive, specialized, even mindless tasks and workers were instructed to repeat the same process in precisely the same manner (Hickman & Silva, 1987). This achieved predictability and control. Detractors have labeled this approach the lazy idiot theory because workers were expected to do exactly what the foreman told them to do and Taylor made it clear that he did not trust the worker to work without close supervision (Wind & Main, 1998, p. 9).

Taylor forwarded three basic assumptions. First, he believed that all individuals could be top performers if scientifically assigned to the correct task. Second, he believed performance was directly related to pay and the only real incentive needed for good work was fair pay. Finally, he advocated the use of clear-cut goals to enhance the potential for workers to perform well. The nicely mechanistic nature of this approach made his concepts quite popular. Scientific management did seem to fit the needs of organizations at the time it was introduced. Although scientific management frequently is associated with Taylor, Fayol and Weber deserve major credit for developing the premises of the classical theory of management.

Fayol and the Classical Approach to Organizing

Fayol (1949), a French coal-mining manager, wrote extensively about the nature of effective management based on his experience as a manager. He wanted a *classical, hierarchical pyramid of command* for each organization. At the top would be a chief executive, or at least a single executive authority, and at the bottom would be the online worker. Within this structure, there would be strict specialization and accountability. Levels of command and the sources for control would be clear at all times. With no exaggeration, the modern analogy would be a military operation during a time of strife. Management would be concerned with the planning, organizing, commanding, coordinating, and controlling of all aspects of the operation. Maximum efficiency would be accomplished through the most rational approach to management. Make no mistake; establishing the proper channels for determining who is in charge can be an important, and often essential, characteristic of any organization. Extensive organization charts used by many companies are examples of this desire.

One of the reasons Fayol was popular with business owners was his clearly stated argument that the goal of an organization, after all, was to develop material rewards for those in charge. His concepts, he argued, regarding the proper design of work based on certain principles of management would guarantee that result.

Fayol (1949) also recognized the need to go beyond the traditional structure in order to enhance coordination. Managers at the same level should be able to contact each other directly and discuss and coordinate their activities without going through a common boss at a higher level. This "gangplank" approach is known as *Fayol's Bridge*. At the time, the bridge was quite innovative as an approach to organizational structure, and it has had a useful impact on organizational theory. However, Fayol saw this moving between the direct chain of command as something that would be done in exceptional cases and not as a general rule. Although Taylor (1911) is known as the "Father of Scientific Management," Fayol's theories best clarify the concepts behind the classical approach to organizing.

Weber and Bureaucracy

Weber (1947), a great German sociologist, postulated the view that bureaucracy, or order through clear rules, was the best form of human organization. His approach was based on a belief that people respond to clear authority and that the best type of authority was free from tradition. In Europe, family structure, the church's and king's traditional authority, or the charisma of great leaders had been the basis for power and control. Weber believed that these traditions did not guarantee the best leaders or managers. Instead, organizations should have impersonal leadership that would be established through rule and regulations. In many ways, this is a logical extension of Smith's (1776/1937) concept of division of labor forwarded in *The Wealth of Nations*. Strict adherence to rules based on competence of individuals provides the ideal means of managing. Instead of making decisions based on favoritism, administrators would make all decisions according to specific rules, policies, regulations, and behaviors spelled out in a uniform manner.

A structure that chooses individuals based on their ability to do a specific job is certainly an improvement over the pre-1900 method of dispensing positions based on family ties or simple availability. Weber's (1947) *Theory of Bureaucracy* eliminated special privileges in hiring, promoting, or firing and therefore was concerned with the individual's technical competence. As long as individuals did their job to the specifications of the guidelines, they would be rewarded appropriately.

In practice, bureaucracy has not always fared as well as Weber might have hoped. A popular joke in Washington, DC, concerns a new missile, recently introduced by the Navy, which was causing problems: "It's called the civil service. It won't work and you can't fire it." In some cases, the very rigidity of the system tends to lead to excesses in impersonal behavior and lack of personal accountability.

Taken together, Taylor (1911), Fayol (1949), and Weber (1947) represent the basic tenets of scientific management. There are numerous other individuals who have contributed to the theory and implementation of the basic concepts of a clearly functional approach to management where purpose, and its corresponding form, personnel policy and procedures, are clearly defined through specific tasks, direct lines of authority, task training for personnel, and accountability. Their combined approach was straightforward and not laden with any ambiguities or paradoxes.

Given the choice, practically any manager at the beginning of the 20th century would choose the approach that provided clarity over ambiguity; thus, scientific management quickly became the predominant management mode. Henry Ford, one of the early users of scientific management for increased productivity through standardization, work simplification, motion studies, and clear controls, expressed the essence of the implementation of the scientific management philosophy. "All we ask of the men is that they do the work that is set before them" (Hall, 1965, p. 2). The method worked. In 1913 Ford started his moving assembly line, a major manufacturing innovation, in Highland Park, Michigan. Soon after introducing his new touring car for a record low price of $290.00 complete, half of the automobiles in the world were Model T Fords. Utilizing scientific management concepts, the labor needed to assemble a car dropped from 12 hours, 8 minutes to 2 hours, 35 minutes and continued to fall to 1 hour, 35 minutes by the following spring (Wind & Main, 1998). Numerous modern organizations still operate using Scientific Management's basic premises and the virtues of the classic corporation cannot be frivolously dismissed (Wind & Main, 1998). Ford also believed in paying employees well and his salaries of $5 a day were double the national average and sent shock waves through many other organizations. Unfortunately, he viewed individuals as extensions of his assembly line and, as a consequence, suffered enormously high levels of turnover.

A more current example of a traditionally bureaucratic and rules-driven organization would be the changing military. For example, "commanders once discouraged troops from starting a family while serving. Thus the old saying: 'If the Army wanted you to have a wife, it would have issued you one'" (Jelinek, 2006, p. 11A). In other words, the organization is correct and will set the rules of behavior. However, this inflexibility does not respond well to current military-related issues. The stress of the Afghanistan and Iraq wars on military families lead to more than 56,000 divorces between 2001 and the end of 2005. In response, the Army initially tried to explain how to pick a partner who would be able to handle the immense stress of a marriage that could result in death, life-altering injuries, or a spouse who was substantially changed after a wartime experience (Jelinek, 2006).

In spite of the apparent advantages of a rule-driven structure and a clear command and control operation, unbending paradigms were creating problems where the soldier might understand the need for direct control, but the family might have difficulties. Because the family represents a living system as described earlier, all parts of the system are impacted. The Army example brings us back to the potentially fundamental flaw of a purely scientific approach to structuring organizations.

With production and profit as the driving forces, treating employees as people was not a priority for many industrialists. During the 1892 steelworkers' strike at the Homestead Steel Works, 12 men were killed. Labor organizing and violence occurred at the railroads and mining in response to inhumane working conditions (Hammonds, Zellner, & Melcher, 1996). Often, a jolt such as union organizing or declining success is required to create new approaches.

Human Relations Management

As we discussed in the Introduction, one of the potential problems with any successful managerial approach is its overuse. A paradigm is established that works to solve the initial problems. Individuals and organizations have difficulty considering other approaches when different problems seem to surface. The human relations movement resulted, to a large extent, from the dramatic findings in what are now known as the Hawthorne Studies. Because these studies challenged some of the basic conclusions of the scientific management practitioners, we discuss them before outlining the major premises behind the human relations movement.

Hawthorne Studies, Attention and Recognition

Between 1927 and 1932, a series of studies were conducted at the Western Electric Company's Hawthorne Works (Roethisberger & Dickson, 1939). The original research was designed to discover the relationship between production and the level of lighting at the plant. The researchers' interest in working conditions was focused on determining which working conditions should be used to maximize worker productivity—a classic scientific management concern. Manipulating the level of illumination at the plant in order to make the employees more efficient and productive is the most famous of the various and extensive Hawthorne experiments. One group of workers was subjected to increased and decreased lighting to see if there was a correlation between lighting levels and the amount of work produced. The other group, functioning as a control group, received the same level of lighting at all times. To the surprise of the researchers, output rose regardless of the level of lighting. So, more or less lighting brought about increases in output. In addition, the control group began to respond to the new environment—they saw that they were picked for some reason—and their output also increased.

Researchers, at first baffled by these results, were forced to conclude that increased attention, a nonmaterialistic reward, was causing the changes. The experimenters had become *de facto* or surrogate managers because they had extensive contacts with employees, structured the workday in order to facilitate the experiment, and helped the group maintain contact with the organization. The workers interpreted this attention as an indication of the organization's interest in them. Prior to the studies, workers had predictable and impersonal jobs with a great deal of structure, numerous controls, and little individual attention.

The Harvard University researchers, headed by Mayo, interpreted the results as indicating the need for greater emphasis on human relations (Roethisberger & Dickson, 1939). By improving the social aspects of work, employees presumably would be more content with their jobs and therefore would be more productive. This explanation of the Hawthorne Studies called into question many of the major premises behind the scientific management view regarding a "day's pay for a day's work is all that was needed" and had a major impact on management practices. A large number of innovations were developed, which ranged from better break times and facilities to broader conveniences, such as air conditioning, not directly related to the strict scientific management approach (Clancy, 1989).

The Hawthorne Studies are important because they experimentally questioned the prevailing assumptions or paradigms about organizational management and design, and brought an awareness of the need for greater attention to human needs, motives, and relationships at work. Various scholars have offered alternative interpretations to explain the unexpected results of the studies. For example, in the original study, the supervisor assigned to the experimental group was one of the best in the plant, the workers were encouraged to develop a team effort, and there was a high degree of individual control in the workplace (Carey, 1967; Franke & Karl, 1978). Taken together, the studies and the various interpretations all point to the impact of social conditions on productivity. Mayo and his associates provided the groundwork for the humanistic movement.

During the first half of the 20th century, the service economy began to compete with industry. Organizations like Coca-Cola, Heinz Foods, Travelers

Insurance, and Sears became important parts of the U.S. economy and underscored the importance of employee satisfaction. "The information age probably began in the 1920s, when Walt Disney, Louis B. Mayer, and the rest of Hollywood began to build" businesses (Pearlstine, 1998, p. 72). People, more than strategy or structure began to emerge as an essential component of organizational effectiveness.

Goals in Conflict

A different slant on the difficulties organizations may experience when employing individuals was offered by Argyris (1957) who postulated that there were goals in conflict between the organization's needs and the worker's needs. His point is well taken. Traditionally, an organization's main goal has been producing throughput and accomplishing goals. To achieve these purposes, organizations perceived that they needed individuals who follow directions, accept supervision, and obey rules. Often, organizations have encouraged these behaviors creating employees who become submissive, passive, and dependent. In other words, they do as they are told. The best vehicle would be classical management techniques that focus on specific job requirements met through particular job skills and rewarded through material benefits. This clear "pay for performance" approach with control resting with the organization would provide the greatest predictability.

On the other hand, most individuals, according to Argyris, want to grow and develop and have some sense of self-control. Material benefits will meet the basic needs of individuals, but once these have been met, greater needs also must be addressed. Personal maturation and interpersonal competency, which often are thwarted by the organization's need for control and rationality, require development in order to achieve individual job satisfaction. These two sets of needs are bound to be in conflict.

Fundamentally, the "rational/legal bureaucratic" organization spawned by scientific management creates an atmosphere that is shortsighted and centered only on the organization. The system, through its tendency to try to evaluate and control individuals, creates a defensive attitude in people. This produces in the individual an infantile perspective because it uses fear, control, and dependence, causing behaviors characterized by indifference, irresponsibility, and passivity. These difficulties occur because the organization controls the workaday world, requires a single-job perspective, and encourages the perfection of a few skills for the good of the product (Argyris, 1957).

Argyris (1957) saw a vicious spiral because management will react to employees' attempts at independence with greater controls, as long as the scientific management perspective is maintained. Workers, of course, will escalate their own behavior and will retaliate with greater deviations and indifference. Employee thefts, for example, often are blamed on management's excessive concern for control. "Indeed, in enterprises of all sizes and shapes, from shoestring nonprofits to giant corporations, the scale of employee theft has soared" (Winter, 2000, p. 4D). Labrich (1994) concludes: "Understandably hostile workers rip apart and sink many a company whose top managers, whatever their public declarations, take that sort of narrow view (management control) of their employees" (p. 64). Strikes, hostilities, and industrial sabotage—especially when they are intended as statements of frustration—provide manifestations of Argyris' goals in conflict. Pragmatically, loyalty to organizations can be seriously undermined through management actions. A current joke is "the new definition of corporate loyalty is not looking for your next job on company time" (Labrich, 1994, p. 68).

To reiterate, organizations seeking efficiency, control, and profit place limits and controls on individuals to guarantee stability and predictability. Employees, seeking some sense of individuality, react to these controls leading to escalation in the organization's use of compliance creating controls. The vicious cycle created through this ongoing spiral of events creates turmoil, unrest, and ineffectiveness.

People-Oriented Management

Following the Hawthorne Studies and the various criticisms of scientific management numerous attempts were made to develop greater people-oriented management behavior. Rather than focusing only on production, supervisors and managers were told to make the individual worker feel more important in relation to the goals of the organization and the specific tasks required.

To decrease worker alienation, management strove to increase participation in various decisions and to treat the workers in a friendlier manner. Supervisors frequently were given "charm school" seminars to overcome the prevailing production orientation to ease the goals in conflict. Unfortunately, many managerial personnel saw this increased ability to influence employees as an opportunity to manipulate their employees into acceptance of management decisions (Rush, 1972). At its best, the human relations school created higher morale and undoubtedly made workers feel more appreciated while doing their jobs. However, just as the emphasis on productivity by scientific management had been excessive, depending on improved morale to cause high production was also an error. Happy people are not necessarily the best and most productive workers (Albanese, 1988). Some amazingly harsh criticism was directed at the human relations approach (Hertzberg, 1968). In reality, "The overwhelming failure of the human relations movement was precisely its failure to be seen as a balance to the excesses of the rational model, a failure ordained by its own equally silly excesses" (Peters & Waterman, 1982, p. 95). Or, as we predicted in the introduction, humanistic management became a trained incapacity.

In summary, in an effort to counteract the possible negative influence of managerial control, organizations moved in the direction of allowing petty issues to prevail. Comfort won out over consistency, personal indulgence over organizational perseverance, and so on, to the point that the humanistic approach allowed individual needs to supersede the needs of the organization. Top-down control used by the scientific management school was replaced by bottom-up control, and the results were a lack of productivity for organizations. As a consequence, the humanistic side of management became discredited and a large number of organizations reverted to scientific management techniques.

More subtle examples of organizational control operate widely. The use of time clocks or swipe ID cards, e-mail usage surveillance, piecework, bonus systems, and accountability with commensurate rewards and punishments provide control without some of the harsher attributes of a strictly scientific management approach. Organizations are driven by the concept that if you cannot measure it, you cannot control or improve it (Lawler, 1996). For example, with the increased use of computer terminals for many workers, more than one-third of the major U.S. organizations monitor voice mail, computer e-mail, Internet access, and individual strokes on the keyboard (Jones, 1998). Attempts by organizations to control employee's use of technology returns us to Argyris' goals in conflict arguments.

Summary: Scientific and Humanistic Management

Scientific management provided essential processes for the efficient and productive use of manpower after the Industrial Revolution. This concern for production remains one of the key variables in any managerial theory. However, the perspective was limited to enhancing productivity through job-centered activities that relied on clear and precise controls by the organization.

Mayo and the Harvard researchers discovered an equally important issue—people's needs—when they applied scientific management techniques to the issue of lighting at the Hawthorne Electric Works. The surprising increase in productivity regardless of the scientifically controlled variations led to the conclusion that the treatment of people was an equally important variable in increasing organizational success. As we predicted in the Introduction, concern for people is the other variable or issue in almost any approach for understanding how organizations operate effectively.

Humanistic management correctly noted the debilitating impact on individual performance and morale of relying solely on a production orientation. Argyris (1957) articulated the basic dilemma between the needs of the organization and the needs of the individual further explaining the dangers of a headlong pursuit of production goals on the individual's ability to work. Unfortunately, many of the attempts to apply humanistic management became equally manipulative and dishonest because they were really disguised attempts to pursue production goals at all costs. But the underlying premise behind the school of thought that workers must be treated as an important part of the organization, and must be dealt with as people, is an important tenet of organizational theory.

Human Resource Management

Human resource management recognizes that the extreme reliance on scientific management or human relations management will not provide an adequate approach to effectively managing people as a resource. Three assumptions underlie the human resources approach. First, the "people component" of an organization is an asset that can be developed in conjunction with an ongoing awareness of human needs. Second, one of the tools for achieving this development is a contingency approach to managing organizations, which observes that there rarely are simple answers. Finally, people are seen as problem-solving resources that work with other factors in an organization to achieve success. You should note the critical distinction between human relations and human resource approaches. Whereas human relations management concerned itself with treating people well to increase morale, human resources management sees people as vital resources that can contribute to the organization. Developing individuals and groups, it is reasoned, will increase the level of morale.

As with the first two views of management, human resource management was developed by a large number of theorists and practitioners. We discuss McGregor's (1960) Theory X–Theory Y and Likert's (1967) System 4 as cornerstone theories. Then we examine the premise behind the contingency theory—there is no one best way—and provide some specific applications of the contingency theory approach.

McGregor's Theory X and Theory Y

McGregor (1960) approached the general issues raised by Argyris (1957) with a different perspective. Rather than conflicting goals based on the tensions and conflicts between management and labor, the problems were based on how the manager views the workers, with the resulting assumptions or paradigms. The difference was between "the rigid, autocratic 'Theory X' company that whipped rebellious workers into line; and the enlightened 'Theory Y' corporation that nurtured people's natural instinct to contribute their best" (Wind & Main, 1998, p. 130). Two diverse patterns of thinking underlie these approaches.

Theory X thinking, according to McGregor, used erroneous assumptions regarding the kinds of employee motivations that operate on the job. *Theory X assumes that workers are motivated by extrinsic gratification* (e.g., work only for the money). At least five additional assumptions underlie the approach. *There is an inherent laziness on the part of individuals; a lack of ambition; an indifference to organizational needs; a built-in resistance to change; and a need for careful supervision.* Naturally, Theory X managers and organizations respond by being authoritarian and manipulative and relying on coercion, control, and possibly overt and covert threats. After all, if employees cannot be self-managing or reliant, what choice does a manager have except to control, distrust, and use money to motivate?

Theory Y, the alternative view, assumes humans will welcome the chance to work given the proper circumstances. Underlying Theory Y is a belief that people want meaningful work; will deliver the best possible effort when treated fairly; and can and should become self-actualized. Conflicts occurring at work can be mitigated because acceptable treatment will alleviate the problems. People will provide the input needed to make that work meaningful if they are given the chance. Fundamentally, McGregor pointed out that the personal beliefs of the manager determine their use of punishments and rewards as they deal with employees.

In sum, this dichotomy in managerial paradigms—workers must be controlled versus workers are a vital and developable asset—created a significant stir in almost all subsequent examinations of management processes. A Theory X manager treats people with disdain based on a distrust of employees' underlying motivations. A Theory Y manager sees people as an asset to be trusted and worthy of providing opportunities for personal growth and acceptable treatment. No fool, however, McGregor did not argue that all workers are responsive and productive.

Likert's System 4

The need to focus on Theory Y paradigms is one of the backbones of human resource management. Likert (1967) developed a more complex process for outlining the characteristics and consequences of the two contrasting management styles offered by McGregor. In *New Patterns of Management*, Likert (1961) certainly agreed with McGregor that there have been two contrasting styles of management—the scientific or production-oriented perspective and the humanistic or employee-oriented perspective. Rather than seeing the two styles as contrasting or inherently in conflict, Likert (1967) argued that employee-centered management with a clear task orientation will develop the most effective production team, thereby combining the best attributes of both views. This is his System 4 or participative process where group methods are used for decision making and supervision. System 4 demonstrates trust in subordinates. Based on this trust, decisions are decentralized and all employees exert considerable self-control over their activities. Supervisors and their teams are expected to set high performance goals. Likert's (1967) principle of supportive relationships provides some stern guidelines. He argued that the interactions and relationships must be supportive and capable of building the individual's sense of personal worth and importance. This is the job of "leadership and the other processes of the organization" (p. 103).

In System 4, communication is between groups and individuals rather than top to bottom. Supervisors serve as *linking pins* from one level in the organization to the next, all the way up and down the hierarchy. Each supervisor and his or her subordinates form a team or family group. At the same time the supervisor is a member of another team consisting of his or her peers and a superior. His linking pins—managers and supervisors—uphold the principle of supportive relationships as opposed to the traditional "we–they" stance between management and employees.

Likert (1967) also characterized three other systems with System 1 being exploitive authoritative (scientific) conforming to McGregor's (1960) Theory X, System 2 being benevolent authoritative run by a paternalistic despot, and System 3 being consultative at the lower levels with decision-making authority remaining concentrated at the upper levels. In studies of the four systems, Likert found the use of System 4 was most likely to lead to greater productivity. System 1, as the scientific management approach, tended to be the least effective.

McGregor (1960) and Likert (1967) offered an excellent transition from the human relations to the human resources approach. The human resources model values participation by members of the organization in decision making. Once individuals are part of the problem-solving process, they will become more committed to the overall success of the organization and realize greater personal growth and satisfaction. Organizational members become part of the solution rather than part of the problem. Although the human relations approach pays careful attention to individual needs and tries to make conditions in the work environment as positive as possible, the human resources model actively seeks greater input from members of the organization in decisions. Human relations overcame the depersonalized approach of scientific management, but it did not necessarily provide for individual fulfillment at work. As McGregor (1960) and Likert (1967) indicated, people have great potential for adding to the success of an organization and using people, as resources will enhance motivation and productivity. One important conclusion from *Industry Week*'s examination of the 100 best managed was that "a firm must be strongly committed to its employees" (Caudron, 1998, p. 98). The best know "they can't be successful without also paying attention to the hearts, minds, and lives of the people who make up their companies" (Caudron, 1998, p. 98). A useful example of how to combine a tight classical approach to efficiency with a human resources mindset is United Parcel Service (UPS) (Spain & Talbot, 1997). UPS constantly drives toward greater efficiency through the traditional time and motion studies. For example, they have determined that a delivery person should walk to a customer's door at a standard rate of 3 feet per second. Instead of wasting time searching for a doorbell, they should knock. Time is efficiency, which means more packages delivered, which translates into money. Simultaneously, UPS takes efforts to treat everyone with equality and dignity. Managers do not have their own parking places, they do their own photocopying, and they share the same cafeteria with everyone else. The CEO does not even have a personal secretary.

Mechanistic and Organic   As a means for summarizing these approaches to organizing, we will examine identified two polar characteristics—closed/stable/mechanistic and open/adaptive/organic (Kast & Rosenzweig, 1984). The first, *mechanistic*, is appropriate when the task is routine and unchanging because of a stable environment. All of the attributes of efficiency through procedural control work well in organizations where the jobs remained the same. In mechanistic organizations, managers rely on a command style "in which managers' instructions and decisions govern work operations. Communication tends to be one way, or top down, because managerial instructions dictate what subordinates do" (Courtright, Fairhurst, & Rogers, 1989, p. 172). Formalized job roles, hierarchies, information dissemination from the top down, and control operate in a mechanistic system. A visit to most government agencies, heavy manufacturing such as steel, or universities would reveal this design in operation.

The second, *organic*, recognizes that many modern organizations must respond to the turbulent, dynamic environment. This configuration tends to decrease rules and regulations in favor of innovation and development. Individuals become increasingly important to the organization rather than depending on the chain of command. The organic type of organization emphasizes communication, rapid processing of information, group decision making, self-control, and motivation. Team self-management, an issue we discuss at length in our chapter on small groups, is an example of an organic approach being embraced by many U.S. companies (Courtright et al., 1989). Table 3.1 further explains the differences in goals, technical, structural, psychological, and managerial subsystems. This dichotomy is useful for understanding but there is little reason to believe any organization is clearly mechanistic or organic at all levels, in all divisions, or at all times.

No One Best Way—Contingency Theories

The scientific and humanistic schools shared characteristics often valued when studying organizational performance. Both theories were universal, straightforward, and took a definite stand regarding which variables should be emphasized. Classical theorists wanted central control and management by a few whereas humanistic theorists wanted individual needs emphasized.

How can an organization combine the strengths of classical and human relations management without creating additional problems? Various theorists concluded that the best organizational structure and management style should vary from situation to situation. Contingency theories do not question many of the premises of the other approaches offered in this chapter. They merely tell us that additional variables must be considered before making a

Table 3.1 Descriptions of Organizational Cultures

	Polar Characteristics	
Systems	**Closed/Stable/Mechanistic**	**Open/Adaptive/Organic**
Environmental suprasystem general nature	Placid, certain, fixed, few participants, well-defined boundaries	Turbulent, uncertain, many participants, varied and not well-defined boundaries
Goals and values	Single goal, efficient performance, managerial hierarchy	Adapting, problem solving and innovation, extensive participation
Technical system	Repetitive tasks, homogeneous input, fixed output, programmed methods	Varied tasks, varied input and output, nonprogrammed methods
Structural system	Formalized organization, many rules and procedures, concentrated authority	Few written rules, informal enforcement, networks
Psychosocial system	Clearly defined status, based on hierarchy, use of extrinsic rewards, Theory X view, autocratic leadership, concentrated power	Status based on expertise, roles change with tasks, intrinsic rewards, Theory Y view, collaborative support
Managerial system	Hierarchical, autocratic decision making, fixed planning process, conflicts resolved by superiors	Network of control, participative decision making, reciprocal power, group conflict resolution

Note: Adapted from Kast and Rosenzweig (1984).

decision, designing an organization, and leading a group. This situational approach to management suggests that the tasks required and the environment surrounding the organization are critical variables.

Contingency theories offer the important conclusion that different organizational design and structures should be used for different tasks. There are no simple, surefire answers for how to run an organization. Because each set of circumstances has different contingencies, the methods of communication, decision-making processes, types of structure, and styles of leadership must be situational. The complexity of contingency theories has kept them from being as popular as some other methods of organizing and managing. After all, contingency theories argue that managers should become accustomed to aiming at a moving target. However, their very complexity tends to bring them closer to organizational realities.

Situational Leadership

Varying the leadership approach depending on the situation has been one important area for applying contingency theory. One of the best known theorists was Fiedler (1967). He hypothesized that the relationship between managerial style and a variety of organizational outcomes was mediated by an elaborate array of contingencies. His approach is instructive, for it sets the tone for many of the later developments (Fiedler, Chemers, & Mahar, 1978).

In theory, Fiedler argued, the manager can articulate the relevant contingency in a given situation and therefore can determine the effects of a particular leadership behavior on the situation's outcome. His emphasis is on the work group and he predicted that the group's effectiveness will be dependent on the leader's ability to match her or his style with the contingencies of the situation.

Contingency theory stresses the difference between leadership behavior and leadership style. Behaviors are the acts the leader performs while directing and coordinating the activities of group members. Fiedler (1967) postulated that "the effectiveness of a group is contingent upon the relationship between leadership style and the degree to which the group situation enables the leader to exert influence" (p. 15). Although there have been conflicting research results regarding his model, the situational nature of leadership has become an important tenet for additional research and management training (Kotter, 1990). The premise underlying this approach is important. Leaders must realize the impact of their particular style on group success.

Contingency thinking has been translated pragmatically into two approaches. The first, as we already have mentioned, observes that there is no single management style that is right for all organizations at all times. In fact, there are always a variety of possible approaches whose rightness is contingent on a particular situation. The second concludes that the results and performances wanted can be obtained with a careful linking of stimulus and response to behavior and reward in a chain of contingencies. Because individuals, organizations, and the multiple subsystems are constantly changing in response to the environment, each situation requires specific analysis. For many individuals in managerial positions, accepting uncertainty as a perspective is very uncomfortable. Ideally most persons in charge want some specific means for improving managerial performance even if they accept the general premise of the contingency approach. One of the attractions, after all, of the scientific approach is the certain prescriptions given to the leader.

These contingency approaches are the cornerstone of human resources management. The key is to combine the strengths of both the scientific and humanistic approaches to management. This is accomplished by recognizing the need for structured approaches to the development of individuals and groups within an organization. Using the premise that there are no simple, easy answers, contingency approaches have developed that call for an awareness of the players, situation, and environment before making any decisions or taking actions. Human resources management sees individuals as untapped resources that can be developed with the proper atmosphere. A mantra for many human resources managers is that people are the only asset an organization invests in that actually increases in value over time. Equipment, for example, depreciates quickly and requires replacement. People can become knowledgeable and skilled providing an almost untapped potential resource in many organizations. The conditions or contingencies surrounding an individual, and the managerial approach, will determine how well that person will develop.

Organizational Cultures

At this point, you should have a basic understanding of how various organization and management theories have developed. In spite of the chronological development, keep in mind that all three approaches we have outlined—scientific, human relations, and human resources/contingency—are widely utilized. Missing from the three previous schemes is the important impact of organizational cultures. This orientation demonstrates how the processes used by management and employees determine the behavior in organizations. All organizations have cultures and there is a symbiotic relationship between an organization's communication processes, culture, and environment. "Great companies create strong, positive company cultures that foster happy, engaged employees who feel empowered to make decisions in their daily work" (Pomeroy, 2004, pp. 46–47).

Revising Managerial Perspectives—The 1980s

Just as success breeds imitation by other organizations, as in the case of the scientific and humanistic management, waning prosperity brings a search for new alternatives. The late 1970s witnessed a decline in U.S. productivity and invited comparisons with other, more productive economies such as Japan (Wind & Main, 1998).

Prior to the 1980s, the Japanese were known as the producers of inferior products based, to a large extent, on imitation. American corporations had been remarkably successful and globally superior after World War II and the Korean War. Japanese dynamos like Sony and Toyota changed the landscape dramatically. In 1990, Lee Iacocca, then CEO of Chrysler, told *Fortune* magazine, "From 1980 to 1985, the products they were shipping weren't as good as they should have been … and the Japanese earned their right to say they build better quality cars …." (Healey & Kiley, 2001, p. 3B). Their cars lasted longer and their copying machines and integrated circuits proved more reliable and effective. Naturally, American businesspeople wanted to discover the secrets of Japanese manufacturing. Two important explanations were the 7-S Model and Theory Z.

The 7-S Model   A fundamental principle in organizations is you get what you pay attention to. Pascale and Anthos (1981) felt that Western organizations had placed a great deal of attention, faith, and effort into the three hard S's:

strategy, structure, and systems or scientific management. These lead to a fixation on individual glory and the joys of winning through intimidation.

In contrast, the four soft S's: *staff, skills, style, and superordinate goals* had received a relative lack of emphasis in Western organizations. These four skills provided the backbone of the successful Japanese corporation. The title of Pascale and Anthos' (1981) book, *The Art of Japanese Management*, nicely highlights the issues they discuss throughout their analysis. For a moment, consider the use of the word *art* at one end and the word *management* at the other. With little doubt, one of the greatest difficulties Western management seemed to have in adopting new tools such as soft management was that they did not consider management an art. They perceived management as a quantifiable science and art as a leisure activity. Hence, the number of organizations who incorporated the 7-S model in the United States was not great. Pascale and Anthos acknowledged that Westerners often find the concept "at best, remote, at worst, elusive" (p. 35), and that few American business leaders will mimic the Japanese style.

Theory Z The desire for more successful and productive organizations remained, and to satisfy this interest many organizations and managers turned to Ouchi's (1981) *Theory Z*. He presented characteristics of Japanese organizations and management that could be embraced by Western organizations. Theory Z is not Japanese management, but a homogenized version palatable to U.S. organizations. This was a wise approach because organizations are living systems and they will, for the most part, reject radical changes.

Ouchi (1981) observed that most Western firms were characterized by mutual distrust between employees and management, formal relationships, decision making only at the executive level, specialized training, narrow career paths, quick employee evaluation, and short-term employment. In contrast, the Theory Z style is characterized by mutual trust between employees and management, informal relationships, employee involvement in decision making, nonspecialized careers, slow evaluation process for employees, long-term employment, and flexibility and adaptation.

Effective managers, Ouchi (1981) argued, spend less time behind their desks and more time with subordinates and colleagues. This leads in turn to increased communication between supervisor and staff, better understanding by managers of employees and their job requirements, a fuller appreciation for work-related problems, and improved relations between supervisor and employees.

The pursuit of quality—the remaining heritage of the 1980s' efforts at incorporating Japanese management techniques—has become a cornerstone of practically every successful American organization (Griffin, 2005; Wind & Main, 1998). Many U.S. and international organizations use *kanban hoshiki* or just-in-time inventory control, *kaizen* or continuous improvement, and *poka-yoka*, which is Japanese for mistake-proofing involving a variety of devices to prevent inadvertent mistakes (Liker & Meier, 2006). As with every other system analyzed to this point, people remain a pivotal part of any success.

Understanding Organizational Cultures

When identifying a specific technique failed to make clear the reasons for Japanese successes, organizations broadened their perspectives and began to examine cultures. In a nutshell, *culture is an organization's shared beliefs and values—its distinct identity* (Harris, 1990). Culture is the "social glue holding the company together" (Baker, 1980, p. 8).

As groups and organizations learn to survive, adapt, and solve problems over a period of time, a culture emerges providing basic assumptions and beliefs that are "taken-for-granted" (Schein, 1990). The factors that constitute the culture include "the various rituals which members regularly or occasionally perform" (Paconowsky & O'Donnell-Trujillo, 1983, p. 136). Culture is the "way we do things around here" which can include any activities regularly engaged in by organizational members. Goffee and Jones (1998) concluded with culture is "the way things get done around here" (p. 9).

Perspectives on Studying Cultures

Prior to the early 1980s, organizational culture was recognized and studied by many organizational development experts but the concept had not gained mainstream recognition (Rothwell, Sullivan, & McLean, 1995). For example, J. D. Edwards & Co., the 24th largest software company in the world was founded in 1977 and had 1996 revenues of $478 million. Founder C. Edward McVaney wrote a 20-page document entitled "Corporate Culture" in 1981. In 1995, the company, realizing the importance of a dynamic culture free from political orientations, added injunctions against inter-office sarcasm, unprofessional attire, office politics, "backbiting, manipulation, negative behavior, and other divisive activities" that would be causes for termination (Jesitus, 1997, p. 18). Recognizing the continuing need for open communication, a "never surprise your boss" dictum was also included.

Functionalist and Interpretionist The expanding interest in cultures saw researchers pursue two different orientations that provide us with a useful nomenclature for labeling perspectives (Smircich, 1983). Naturally, many organizations were interested in the changes needed to make them successful. This *functionalist perspective is concerned with what an organization has that constitutes the culture.* If you examined the J. D. Edwards culture to see what elements could be adapted to your organization, then you would be utilizing a functionalist perspective. You would identify the current artifacts and activities that can be observed and possibly altered, reinforced, eliminated, or added to other cultures. The information produced by functionalistic research is used to create and sustain a system of beliefs for knowing and managing organizational experience. For many organizational leaders, these are the factors that must be worked with to enhance the ultimate success of the organization.

The interpretionist perspective focuses on the interactions that lead to a shared meaning. This perspective is more interested in understanding the process by which the culture is created and maintained (Bormann, 1983). At J. D. Edwards, the ongoing events would be examined in order to reach some conclusions regarding the shared meaning. The functionalist perspective is oriented toward making the cultural aspects of the organization as effective as possible in helping the organization obtain its goals, whereas the interpretionist perspective is interested in explaining the various processes that lead to shared meanings.

This division of the organizational culture concept is useful and both views reaffirm our need to attend to the behavioral aspects of organizational life. Organizational events include situations "where individuals assign symbolic meanings [through] stories, myths, rituals, ceremonies, and nonverbal objects of the organizational cultural inventory" (Putnam, 1982, p. 199). Once individuals assign meaning, they are more likely to act as if it is reality. Clearly a manager with a functionalist view would be wise to consider how he or she can have an impact on this shared reality. Students of organizational communication will find the interpretionist perspective their primary initial focus for understanding the issues creating and sustaining the shared reality. Put another way, if you chose a functionalist perspective, you will be an active learner of the expected behaviors so you eventually can use the knowledge to influence events. If you opt for an interpretionist perspective, you will gather information so you can understand the general impact of culturally shared meanings. Clearly, both perspectives have value.

Ethnographic and Clinical   Using a different approach, Schein (1985) made the distinction between ethnographic and clinical perspectives. "The ethnographer obtains concrete data in order to understand the culture he is interested in, presumably for intellectual and scientific reasons" (p. 13). The ethnographic perspective brings to the situation a set of presumptions that motivated the research in the first place. So, examining the impact of a particular type of culture on member satisfaction, for example, presumes that member satisfaction is important and should be tested.

On the surface, the clinical perspective is similar to the functionalist and is more interested in the ongoing factors in an organization that must be changed to enhance growth and development. The majority of organizational consultants take this perspective. However, they do not always establish a dichotomy between the functionalist and interpretative views of organizations. Instead, they discuss the level of cultural analysis.

Levels of Cultural Analysis Schein (1985) outlines three levels of culture. *Artifacts and creations*, Level 1, are the most visible. These elements constitute the physical and social environment, the overt behaviors, and the central values that provide the day-to-day operating procedures by which the members guide their behaviors.

Values, Level 2, provide normative or moral functions in guiding the organization or group members in dealing with certain key situations. These are the "ought to be" concepts as opposed to Level l's description of what actually is occurring. These values have been with organizations through the years and are reflected in statements like 3M's "never be responsible for killing an idea" or General Electric's "progress is our most important product." In studying America's most admired companies, Brown (1999) found in "every case, it's a matter of nurturing that unique, essential core" (p. 73). In the 1970s, British Airways was known as "Bloody Awful" or BA. The "epiphany" for British Airways, in addition to being privatized, was the realization that they were a service business and not a transportation business (Jesitus, 1997). Once British Airways changed its values toward being a service business, they enjoyed remarkable success. Disney does not exist to make cartoons for kids but to use their imagination to bring happiness to millions (Collins & Porras, 1994).

Assumptions, Level 3, are essentially the same as Argyris' (1976) theories-in-use, which are the implicit assumptions that actually guide behavior, and that tell group members how to perceive, think about, and feel about things (Argyris & Schon, 1974). These assumptions tend to be nonconfrontable and nondebatable. Wal-Mart's "exceed customer expectations" underlies all actions (Collins & Porras, 1994). So, having greeters at the door is something Wal-Mart does, but can change if there is a better way to exceed expectations. As you work to understand an organization's culture, each of these levels will be very useful. The divisions offered between functionalist and interpretive and ethnographic and clinician are helpful in focusing our attention on important issues.

Perhaps the most important point is each organization's culture is generally distinct, even though certain types of organizations tend to have a large number of similarities due to the environments in which they operate. However, just as there are cultural variations from the North and South and country to country, so do the attributes of various cultures vary from organization to organization and between the subsystems.

The cultural perspective's value is its ability to explain the behaviors of organizations instead of simply isolating types of leadership, products, or other specific artifacts. In a predominant number of cases, leaders come and go, product lines change, and artifacts are added or subtracted, but the organizations remain. So, we need to understand the cultural view of organizations in order to understand how organizations work.

Table 3.2 Types of Organizational Cultures

	Behavioral Characteristics		
	Authoritarian/ Bureaucratic	Compromise/ Supportive	Performance/ Innovative
Basis for decisions	Direct form authority	Discussion, agreement	Directions from within
Forms of control	Rules, laws, rewards, and punishments	Interpersonal/ group commitments	Actions aligned with self-concept
Sources of power	Superior	What "we" think and feel	What I think and feel
Desired end	Compliance	Consensus	Self-actualization
To be avoided	Deviation from authoritative direction	Failure to reach consensus	Not being "true to oneself"
Time perspective	Future	Near future	Now
Position relative to others	Hierarchical	Peer	Individual
Human relationships	Structured	Group oriented	Individually oriented
Basis for growth	Following the established order	Peer group	Acting on awareness of self

Differentiating Cultures

Two general approaches provide an opportunity to see the differences between general cultural attributes. The first applies the traditional labels of authoritarian, compromise, and performance. The second examines the impact of the variables of risk and feedback on corporate cultures.

Authoritarian, Compromise, and Performance The first is to divide them into three distinct types that reflect, to some extent, the previous discussion in this chapter of organizational and management theories. This categorization is popular because it is somewhat simplistic. All three cultures are more concerned with the way things occur in an organization than the particular managerial style being used, although organizational and managerial performance are always interdependent. Table 3.2 outlines the differences.

The *authoritarian culture* reflects many of the features of scientific management. Because the structure is extremely predictable, you should not be surprised to find many organizations operating with this orientation. Both the compromise and the performance cultures reflect some of the elements of the human relations model and most aspects of the human resources model.

The *compromise culture* is the nearest to the human resources model because it considers the group a fundamental strength for any actions. This approach requires a supportive atmosphere with a great deal of cultural backing. Attempts to introduce team-oriented innovations, such as QCs, will face serious obstacles unless they are supported by a compromise culture (see chap. 10). The compromise culture has many of the attributes of Likert's (1967) System 4 discussed earlier. McGregor's (1960) Theory Y manager would be required for this type of culture to be successful, but the dependence on group control is the prevailing feature.

The *performance culture* is highly dependent on self-motivation and personal growth. Sales-oriented organizations often strive for this type of culture. Once well established, this type of culture probably would use the human relations approach.

These categorizations of cultures explain how things are done. Simply realizing that managerial style is only a part of the overall culture would be of great help to you in understanding organizations. Any attempt, by a manager or anyone else, to impose an unacceptable behavior pattern into one of these cultures probably will lead to a rejection by the culture itself. This traditional, generic three-part division of organizational cultures provides us with a better understanding regarding how to use leadership, communication, groups, and numerous other activities.

Studying Successful Organizations   One of the earliest examinations of the elements behind successful organizations was *In Search of Excellence* (Peters & Waterman, 1982). This highly successful book has a decidedly functionalist perspective filled with important information for understanding successful cultures. The book identifies and discusses the qualities shared by these diverse organizations. In picking their sample, they chose ones that had excellent financial performance to support their "halo of esteem" in the business world. The organizations covered were measured by six long-term measures of superiority, which included growth and wealth creation over a 20-year period. They excluded banks because they traditionally have been too heavily regulated, preventing Peters and Waterman from applying their 20-year standard. Overall, their "major concern was and is how big companies stay alive, well, and innovative" (p. 4).

Eight different characteristics show fundamental distinctions between traditional organizations and the excellent companies. First, the excellent companies were *biased toward action* rather than being bound by paralysis by analysis. The phrase "read, fire, aim" summarizes the intent to act quickly rather than take a great deal of time. Second, they *stay close to the customer* and place the customer's needs over the internal organizational tendencies to worry about frills and the "sizzle not the steak." Third, *productivity through people* is championed over cost controls by controlling people. Efficiencies, quality, and budgetary limitations are obtained by training and developing people rather than adopting a Theory X approach that requires managers to see employees as the problem. Fourth, *autonomy and entrepreneurship* through the use of independent units and teams replaced top-down control. Fifth, the companies were *hands-on, value driven* instead of depending on remote control measures such as policy manuals. Sixth, they *stick to the knitting,* which means concentrating on their primary business or area of expertise rather than diversifying. Seventh, simple form and a lean staff with few administrative levels replace the tendency toward layering with a complex organizational structure. Finally, they exhibit *simultaneous loose–tight properties.* There is a belief in central values combined with a tolerance for differences in employees and actions. In general, structure and control by management existed in the traditional organizations whereas the excellent companies contrast sharply by being highly innovative, employee oriented, and dynamic. This 1982 analysis remains generally valid today with the important limitation that mimicry rarely yields the same results (Branch, 1999; Brown, 1999; Caudron, 1998; Fisher, 1998; Stewart, 1998).

In Search of Excellence provides an important set of information for individuals interested in organizational communication. Perhaps as instructive as the original study has been the mixed fate of the excellent companies since Peters and Waterman (1982) did their analysis. Fourteen of the companies changed their means of operating, varied on at least one of the eight operating principles, and ran into difficulties within 2 years of the book's publication ("Who's Excellent," 1984). Two outstanding failures were Peoples Express (airline) and Wang Labs (computer). In a constantly changing environment, few strategies can remain stagnant. In addition, the eight interacting principles indicate the interdependence of a large number of behaviors in the making of an organizational culture. By 1990, only 14 of the original companies still carried the excellence label (Pascale, 1990). The others stopped using one or more of the eight principles or failed to respond to a changing environment. In other words, the prevailing culture supported by numerous paradigms neglected the very aspects that created their excellence or were blinded to the impact of change.

Positive cultures emphasize the concepts of trust, shared values, closeness to customers, and hands-on use of technology permeate all these approaches. *Climate* is an important term for describing the daily feeling of working for an organization. Put another way, you can work for an excellent company but how you feel on a daily basis tends to depend on your closer set of colleagues or a particular superior.

Climates can range from nurturing or stultifying. In examinations, "The 100 Best Companies to Work For" show organizational cultures that support employees, encourage fun, offer flexibility, have excellent benefits, create an overarching sense of purpose, train and develop employees extensively, and cater to personal needs such as day care (Colvin, 2006; Fisher, 1998; Levering & Mozkowitz, 2006). "But here's the part that may surprise you: Nobody mentioned money" when asked why they found their company one of the 100 best (p. 70). The company's climate fulfilled important needs and made the work satisfying. "Pay being equal—most humans seem to need a better reason to get up in the morning" (Fisher, 1998, p. 70).

Organizational climate is an important term because many of the approaches to improving communication behavior in an organization are based on improving the climate. If the culture will support the behaviors, then working to maintain and improve the climate is an important task for all individuals in the organization. For the leader, it is the most important communication task for developing the company. Without a positive climate, there is little likelihood for an organization to effectively move toward excellence.

Critical Cultural Studies

Earlier, we indicated that organizational interpretations are shaped depending on the perspective used by the observer. Critical cultural studies proceed one step further and argue that organizations produce structure, rules, and procedures—theories in use—that may not be immediately recognized, but that provide employers power over individuals. For example, the ability to sanction or terminate someone is an overt use of power that can be recognized and confronted. Critical theory is more concerned with the covert use of power (Conrad, 1983) that is created through an organization's cultural practices (Conquergood, 1991). These taken-for-granted aspects that define organizational reality become the *ideology* controlling organizations (Deetz & Kersten, 1983). *Ideology* is never neutral because it reflects the interests of the dominant groups. The assumptions about how organizations and power relationships should function is reflected in the prevailing ideology. As we become and remain members of an organization, we assist in the manufacturing of consent where we willingly endorse our organization's use of power.

Wal-Mart provides a useful example of the power of ideology. Historically driven by promises to keep prices down, Wal-Mart has seemed to be blind to issues such as inadequate wages with an average associate living on $9.68 per hour or $17,600 a year or poor health care coverage, with fewer than half of Wal-Mart's employees insured (Gunter, 2006). In addition, "in a 2001 class-action suit, 1.6 million current and former female employees alleged that Wal-Mart systematically favored men over women in pay and promotion" (Gunter, 2006, p. 46). Wal-Mart counters that it has created more than 240,000 jobs from 2003 to 2006 and that three quarters of store management started in hourly positions. They also point out that they insure more than one million associates and their families. On gender discrimination, they point to initiatives to build a diverse supplier base, an Employment Advisory Panel, and public release of data on employment of women and minorities.

Why would Wal-Mart allow itself to be in these defensive positions? The critical observer would point out that in business, technical reasoning often overcomes the other forms of reasoning (Fischer, 1990; Habermas, 1987). In other words, working through a predetermined format may replace experiential understanding based on years of working. Perhaps more disturbing, organizational members might subordinate themselves because of a concern for security, finances, identity, or understanding as can be seen when organizational culture overcomes individual needs (Mumby, 1988).

In addition, organizations are inherently political and based on power distribution meaning that, by definition and design, some are in charge and others follow (Burrell & Morgan, 1997). Indeed, organizations drive their members toward *reification* where the actions of organizations are abstracted from their origin and become concrete and fixed—such as professor/student, doctor/patient, or manager/employee (Giddens, 1979). In addition, group-based interests can become treated as everyone's interests.

Most organizations have certain groups exercising a near-monopoly on power whereas others are denied any substantial power. As anyone who has worked for a traditionally oriented organization will attest, this point is difficult to dispute. People on production lines, manning call centers, or providing frontline customer service rarely have significant control or power. Critical theorists contend that this can alienate certain oppressed groups who can respond with a wide variety of active and passive behaviors to subvert the power structure. The lethargy demonstrated by many fast food employees makes this concept quite clear. The impact is also dramatic. "The annual turnover rate in the fast food industry is now about 300 to 400%. The typical fast food worker quits or is fired every 3 to 4 months" (Schlosser, 2002, p. 73).

Will teams, self-directed work groups, and empowerment overcome these inequities? On one level, they have a greater likelihood of succeeding because employees are provided a voice and some control. However, *concertive control*, where management places control in the hands of workers who collaborate to create rules and norms to control their behaviors, can actually reduce the employees' abilities to resist dominance because the employees now have a vested interest in fulfilling production, sales, or other goals (Barker & Cheney, 1994).

As has been discussed previously (see chaps. 1 and 3), the digital age with the variety of new technologies has lead to global organizations with flattening hierarchies, team-oriented structures, decentralization, and local decision-making. Because of the multiple locations, organizations are increasingly flexible and diverse.

At the same time, ideology makes responding to present demands difficult. "Professionals are still being managed as if they were in factories, in organizations designed to keep everyone siloed"(Mandel, 2005, p. 62). The "communications, coordination, and teamwork so essential for success these days is being superimposed on a corporate structure that has one leg still in its grey flannel suit" (Mandel, 2005, p. 62). Many professionals regularly put in more than 50 hours a week, wake up at 4 a.m. to call Europe, multitask, tie themselves to cell phones and other devices 24/7, and experience great frustration. Yet, the prevailing ideology in many organizations still resists telecommuting, flexhours, or other simple adjustments.

Feminist theory has had a profound impact on how people examine organizations and power relationships. We examine the concepts and insights when we analyze leadership (see chap. 12).

Organizations—2000 and Beyond

At the beginning of this chapter, we explained that organizational research and practices have developed along a continuum driven, for the most part, by a desire for speed, information, and efficiency. The stages appear to be somewhat predictable with one approach being modified or supplanted by another. At the same time, each of the organizational theories and management approaches discussed still exist. As you begin working with organizations, you are likely to encounter any of the types discussed. In reality, monumental changes are occurring that deserve our attention.

What types of changes are occurring? As introduced in chapter 1, changes include increased global competition; extremely rapid technological advances; profound demographic and work issues within the workplace; pressures from conflicting special-interest groups; confused, disillusioned, and cynical employees; and an unforgiving consumer (Grates, 1994). At the risk of endlessly repeating an important caveat, most organizations currently operating will continue using one or more of the theories already discussed in this chapter. We, however, need to be aware of the forces and changes impacting organizations.

Profile

Organizations will become more flexible in numerous ways. The classic command-and-control structure will be forced to change in part because of knowledge workers. Software engineers, for example, know more about the organization's product than their managers, creating a demand for effective two-way communication. Clearly, information and knowledge will have to flow freely in order to make certain it arrives where it is needed. Organizations will strive to improve service and lower costs while concentrating on specific core competencies or doing what they do best. Nine issues—knowledge, horizontal organizations, empowerment, information and digital processes, learning organizations, quality and customers, speed and time, focus, and communication—deserve further attention.

Knowledge

At all stages of organizational development, knowledge has played a key role. In the context of our discussion, *knowledge is the use of information to initiate and improve the organization's functioning.* Organizations attempt to apply the best available knowledge to their system to enhance throughput. Drucker (1993) argues that organizational knowledge has progressed through three stages. The first he labels the Industrial Revolution (1700–1880), which was the application of knowledge to doing things. *Drucker is unique in using this label for this time period*, but he is providing differentiation for the stages of knowledge use. During this time period, experience was converted into knowledge. What worked for individual crafts, occupation, or processes was studied. In a similar manner, the particular tools, processes, and products were examined in the first engineering, mining, and agricultural schools leading to a systematic set of information and knowledge about *how to do something.* Production techniques, developed from this accumulated knowledge, lead to factories causing a concentration of workers in central locations. Second, the Productivity Revolution (1881–Post World War II) saw the applying of knowledge to *improve work methods* as we discussed during our analysis of Scientific Management earlier in this chapter. During this time period, there was "practically no access to a middle-class income without a formal degree, which certifies to the acquisition of knowledge that can only be obtained systematically and in a school" (Drucker, 1993, p. 42). Finally, the Management Revolution (post-World War II–2020) is *seeing knowledge work rapidly replacing manual labor.* We have shifted from one set of knowledge about how to manage to a set of knowledges or disciplines. We moved from crafts to methodologies; ad hoc experiences to systems; anecdotes to information; and skills into concepts that can be taught and learned. In other words, we are completing the movement from manual to mental. This will force a rapid decentralization in order to innovate and take advantage of knowledge. Knowledge workers transform information into knowledge and wisdom to support decisions, actions, and outcomes.

Federalism is likely to become the optimum form with the various subunits, disciplines, or parts doing the creating while being supported by the center. This is not a hypothetical concept. ABB, a multinational organization of 20,000 employees, has a center (headquarters) of 150 people. We now examine the eight additional changes.

Horizontal Organizations

Organizations are becoming more horizontal and removing layers (Wind & Main, 1998). Ideally, this horizontal organization strives to remove the separation of people and place work into functional departments. Using a culture of collaboration with employees working together, cooperation between units is encouraged and the hierarchy is flattened (Ostaff, 1999). The need for speed, customer focus, innovation, and information require a greater dependence on networks rather than a hierarchy or chain of command forcing a horizontal approach. Flexibility in structure is becoming critical. Rather than being vertically integrated, organizations are becoming networked (Wind & Main, 1998).

The digital age will include work groups connected electronically even though they may be dispersed around the globe. Overnight delivery of content can now be replaced digitally by a keystroke and an attachment command on a computer. Virtualization will be used increasingly to determine outcomes without any need for our physical presence. Teams will solve problems, disband quickly and redeploy with a different mix of players to work on other issues. Informed workers with various roles will perform ad hoc tasks using input from many sources.

Empowerment

Allowing individuals to set their own work goals, make decisions, and solve problems is the basis for empowerment (see chaps. 10 and 11). Probably an overused term, the concept is on target. As we stated earlier, employees are an asset that can increase in value. But, that can only occur if they are allowed to use their minds. Employees are increasingly being viewed as an organization's most valuable assets (Branch, 1999; Caudron, 1998). They are being encouraged to initiate and participate in decision making through training, empowerment to take actions, and providing creative answers (Conner, 1998). In the old organization, the top levels were the thinkers and the lower levels were the doers. Empowerment, combined with a horizontal structure, allows everyone to be both a thinker and doer—the combined strengths lead to an empowered organization (Gates, 1999; Jasinowski & Hamin, 1995).

Information and Digital Processes

In the past, information tended to flow downward. In the future, information will move in all directions. As we indicated in chapter 1, capital and ownership of assets is being replaced by the power of information. "Though the term might sound cold, digital processes is about the empowerment of individuals. … A belief in empowerment is key to getting the most out of a digital nervous system" (Gates, 1999, p. 409). The impact is universal. "The Internet has become ubiquitous, so companies can connect with talent anywhere in the blink of an eye, inside or outside the company. Open-source software can be plucked off the shelf to become the foundation of new software programs or Web sites. Algorithms can be used to slice and dice market information and spot new trends" (Hamm, 2006, p. 71). We examine these trends more completely in chapter 12.

Learning Organizations

The dynamic nature of organizations underscores the critical impact of knowledge and learning. Informing and training is increasing in the highly competitive organizations (Branch, 1999). Rather than using a "need to know" philosophy where upper management hoards information from lower levels and, sometimes, each other, opportunities are created to increase understanding, involvement, and effectiveness. "A learning organization engages in a new way of communicating and interacting" (Barker & Camarata, 1998, p. 445; see chap. 1).

Quality and Customers

Most organizations understand the importance of quality. However, quality and customer satisfaction are moving targets because today's consumer has higher quality expectations (Cummings & Worley, 2005). Now, customers are being seen as allies, partners, and active participants in the creation and delivery of products and services and not a passive group that can be easily manipulated. Quality is such an underlying principle that for many organizations it is now an assumption or a fundamental part of doing business. Motorola announced its *six-sigma* standard in 1987. This amounts to no more than 3.4 mistakes per million parts. Although Motorola is unlikely to consistently meet this standard, it demonstrates how far quality has progressed. How significant is the six-sigma quality standard? If we have 99.9% defect-free work—much less than six sigma, 50 newborn babies in the United States would be dropped on the floor by a physician daily; 200,000 incorrect prescriptions would be filled each year; two planes would not land safely each hour at Atlanta's Hartsfield International Airport; we would be without electricity, heat, or water for 15 minutes each day; and 22,000 times an hour, banks would deduct the wrong check from someone else's account. In other words, "mistakes happen" is not an acceptable part of the customer's quality perspective.

Speed and Time

With the advent of new technologies, speed and time will remain at the forefront of organizational change. "Speed is emerging as the ultimate competitive weapon" (Hamm, 2006, p. 70). Speed to market, decrease in product development time, and higher efficiencies will remain cornerstones of organizations in the 21st century. Efforts at increasing efficiency will pick up because of technological advances, cost savings, and competition. "Competition is more intense than ever because of the rise of the Asian powerhouses and the spread of disruptive new Internet technologies and business models. Companies realize that all their attention to efficiency in the past decade was fine–but it's not nearly enough" (Hamm, 2006, p. 70).

Focus

Companies will concentrate on doing what they do best. For example, 3M wants to solve problems innovatively. The Girl Scouts of America strive to help a girl reach her highest potential. Hewlett-Packard wishes to make technical contributions for the advancement and welfare of humanity. Mary Kay Cosmetics wants to give unlimited opportunity to women. Walt Disney seeks to make people happy. In the list of the most admired companies in America,

"All ten companies on the top of our list have a single-minded focus" (Brown, 1999, p. 73). Wal-Mart moves merchandise effectively to its 3,000 stores, GE focuses on growth in shareholder value, Microsoft hires brilliant workers, and "Southwest Airlines promotes a culture that impels employees to deliver top-notch service on the ground and in the air" (Brown, 1999, p. 73).

Diversity

The entire workforce is changing as outlined earlier. By 2008, women and minorities will make up 70% of the incoming workforce. Single households in the United States now outnumber married couples with children (Armand-Delille, 2006). Even though the values of a diverse workforce are well documented, we face important challenges in making certain that differences are valued. There are important obstacles that continued advancement must overcome including changing the prevailing corporate culture to be more inclusive, increasing role models, actively working to alter stereotyping and preconceptions, and including marginalized groups into informal networks (Klimley, 1999). Needless to say, these are substantial challenges.

Global Perspective

As we indicated in chapter 1, few organizations operate within one national boundary. A 1999 earthquake in Taiwan shut down electronics factories around the world by interrupting supplies of semiconductors manufactured by just two companies in the same industrial part. One explosion at a chemical plant in Japan in 1992 cut off half the world's capacity for resin used to make computer chips—leading to a doubling of prices for memory chips increasing laptop prices by $100. A 10-day West Coast longshoremen's strike in 2002 cost the U.S. economy $20 billion in lost production when American factories were unable to import components. As we pass further into the new millennium, globalization will become a defining issue (Drucker, 1999). Not only are multinational organizations important, but few products we purchase originated in the United States. In addition, with 95% of the world's population not living in the United States, organizations would be foolish to ignore the world market. Ethnocentricity is assuming one's culture is best and using that assumption to respond to different cultures.

Communication

The link between these trends and success is communication. In 1993 the Wyatt Company surveyed 531 CEOs of U.S. organizations to find out what one thing should be changed about how they went about their change efforts. The answer: how they communicated with their employees about the change effort (Larkin & Larkin, 1996). As more companies move from hierarchies based on command and control to more consensal approach, team-building skills, problem-solving communication, networks, connections, and efficient message and information transfer will have to occur. "Ever since (Caesar), the greatness of leaders has been measured partly by their ability to communicate" (Stewart, 1999, p. 192). Organizational communication is seen as the key variable in almost all change efforts, diversity initiatives, and motivation as you will see in the remaining chapters in this text.

Interpretations of Organizational Processes

At this point, we have provided a background designed to explain the current state of organizations and their communication practices. We now offer a summary that places these concepts into four general approaches, paradigms, or perspectives.

By and large, this myriad of approaches fit under four broad and different frames of reference (Bolman & Deal, 2003). Three of the four frames you will recognize immediately from our earlier discussion—structural, human resources, and symbolic (cultural). The fourth, *political*, introduces the important areas of strategies, competition, and power discussed several times in this chapter and highlighted in the critical cultural section. This four-frame division is arbitrary for the purposes of explanation. Most individuals are oriented toward one of the frames, but use parts of the other three. Importantly, *each frame has its own vision of reality and presents significant, and quite different, views* regarding the maintenance and development of an organization.

Structural Frame

This frame is concerned with the goals, rules, and technology of the organization. So, this frame concentrates on the goal direction, structural clarity, and task accomplishment in an organization. It assumes that organizations exist to accomplish established goals and that a structure can be developed that is appropriate to these goals, the environment, technology, and the participants. Four principles underlie this frame: (1) a rational approach is the best; (2) specialization leads to better individual expertise and performance; (3) coordination and control are accomplished best through the exercise of authority and impersonal rules; and (4) structures can be systematically designed and implemented.

These principles lead to the important conclusion that organizational problems usually reflect inappropriate structure and can be resolved through redesign and reorganization. Structure itself is one of the central issues facing any organization. You may recognize the influence of Taylor (1911) and scientific management with his interest in breaking tasks into minute detail and retraining workers to get the greatest output. The work by Fayol (1949) falls into this frame because of his interest in a set of principles for managers regarding specialization, span of control, authority, and delegation of responsibility. Weber (1947) also fits in this frame.

In summary, this organizational framework has two axes: (a) differentiation (allocation of tasks and responsibilities across individuals and units), which creates a structure of roles, each with specified responsibilities and expectations; and (b) linkages (relationships between roles that create interdependence). Roles and interdependencies are coordinated vertically by authority and rules, and laterally through meetings, task forces, teams, and coordinates.

The structural frame helps create the more stable and formal aspects of human behavior in organizations. Activities and relationships are influenced by goals, roles, rules, and procedures. Any attempt to make people work well together requires some type of coordination. But, much of organizational life falls outside the jurisdiction of organization charts, policy, and formal authority.

Human Resources Frame

As we discussed earlier in this chapter, the human resources frame is concerned with individual needs, feelings, and prejudices with a strong underlying belief in the potential for development of each person. The human resources frame believes there exists a strong interdependence between the individual and the organization and that the search for collective purposes should underlie attempts to manage organizations. Whereas the structural frame is concerned with the way structure develops in response to an organization's task and environment, the human resource perspective adds the interplay between organization and people. From this perspective, people are the most critical resource in an organization and through their ideas, energy, skills, insights, and commitment the organization can be made or broken. Organizations can make a choice between being dehumanizing, alienating, and frustrating or energizing, exciting, and productive. The fit between the individual and the organization is of critical importance.

Maslow's (1970) hierarchy of needs, which range from the physiological to the final level of self-actualization, McGregor's (1960) concepts regarding managerial behavior, Argyris' (1957) analysis of goals in conflict, and Likert's (1967) System 4 fit within the human resources frame.

However, human resource theorists have had little to say about power and the allocation of scarce resources. "The works of Argyris, McGregor, and Likert devote much attention to concepts like communication, feedback, and leadership but rarely mention power," a criticism developed by the critical theorists examined in this chapter (Bolman & Deal, 1984, p. 105). Human resource theorists believe improvements will benefit employer and employee at the same time, therefore avoiding the problem of power.

From the structural frame, organizations are designed to be rationed systems where the central question is how to design the most effective system. The human resources frame also sees the organization as rational but finds mismatches between individual and organizational needs.

Political Frame

In many organizations, people compete, create boundaries and divisions, and pursue individually oriented goals. The political frame focuses on interest groups concerned with dividing perceived scarce resources. Coalitions are formed, often based on very different views of reality from other coalitions, with organizational goals emerging from ongoing processes of bargaining, negotiation, and jockeying for position between individuals and groups. The political frame assumes that there are inherently scarce resources making conflict and power central fixtures in organizational life. Organizations have an "undercurrent of bargaining, jockeying for position, and alliance formation" (Kanter, Stein, & Jick, 1992, p. 47). Although the human resources theorists see conflicts as open to a possible win/win resolution with enough time and effort by all parties, the political theorist is more likely to view divergent interests and conflicts over scarce resources as an enduring fact of life. When we push for our group's needs or forward our solutions as preferable to others, we are engaging in a political orientation. Power is an underpinning of this frame that was introduced with the critical theorists earlier (see chap. 11).

There are two major players in a politically oriented social system: authorities and partisans (Gamson, 1968). The authorities must exercise social control and the partisans may choose to challenge it and even overthrow it. So, the people seeking power use a variety of rewards to control individuals including authority, expertise, control of rewards, coercive power, and personal power (Kanter, 1977). Authorities have the exclusive access to power of position, but they are only one of many contenders for power. All contenders have access to different types of power ranging from sheer numbers to specialty forms such as information or expertise. You will recall that we made this observation in chapter 1 when we outlined the various parts of the system's perspective and discussed formal and informal power. Many of the barriers to equal employment opportunities evolve from this scarce resources perspective. Rather than welcoming differences, organizational subgroups cling to their prejudices defining others as those who are different in terms of race, religion, gender, or any other individual attribute (Rosen, 1991). Political savvy and skills in using symbols are of greater importance so doing a good job is not the issue, but appearing to do a good job is critical.

Both the structural and human relations schools downplay the existence of conflict. The political perspective does not worry about resolving conflict, but instead looks at the strategies and tactics of conflict. If you want to understand how organizations work, this frame argues, look at the natural pursuit of self-interest and how power is used to achieve personal interests.

Although carrying a certain amount of organizational reality, this perspective is likely to become a self-fulfilling prophecy. Without care, it can become overly cynical and pessimistic without seeking proactive, rational, and collaborative processes. Some political savvy is critical, but an overreliance on this perspective makes organizational life an ongoing game rather than a goal-oriented activity.

In sum, these three frames illuminate different beliefs and actions regarding organizations. The structural frame focuses on roles, relationships, and more formal ways of coordinating diverse efforts toward common directions. In the human resources frame, individual needs are central and the basic issue is how to design settings in which individual and organizational needs can be integrated. From the political perspective, organizations are networks of special interests: Coalitions, conflicts, and bargaining translate power into action. Groups that win the political battles are able to steer the organization in the directions they choose.

These frames are different, but they share some characteristics. They assume a world that is relatively certain—goals provide direction, effectiveness can be seen, needs can be identified, power can be understood, developed, and used. So, the *world is substantially rational*. Decisions are made by choosing the best alternative. People act rationally, as least judged by their own needs and beliefs. Groups behave rationally in attempting to further their own self-interests. Finally, the world is *relatively linear*. Goals are established to guide action, people determine what they want and take action to get it. Policies are developed through a sequential process of bargaining and conflict.

Symbolic Frame

The symbolic frame says that what is most important about any event is not what happened, but the meaning of what happened. The event's meaning is determined not only by the event itself, but by the ways humans interpret, or perceive, the event. We devote chapter 7 to a full discussion of symbolic behavior.

Many of the significant events and processes in organizations are substantially ambiguous or uncertain. Often it is difficult or impossible to know what happened, why it happened, or what will happen next. Unpredictability undermines rational approaches to analysis, problem solving, and decision making. To make sense out of this uncertainty, humans create symbols to reduce the ambiguity, resolve confusion, increase predictability, and provide direction. Events may remain illogical, random, fluid, and meaningless, but human symbols make them seem otherwise. As we discussed in chapter 1, the reduction of *equivocality* is a major driving force behind much of our organizational behavior (Weick, 1969).

The symbolic frame concentrates on the concepts of meaning, belief, and faith. Various methods are available for making organizational life more understandable. For example, myths provide explanations, reconcile contradictions, and resolve dilemmas. Metaphors make confusion comprehensible. Scenarios, stories, and symbolic actions provide direction in areas where the correct actions are not clear. This frame assumes that organizations are full of questions that cannot be answered, problems that cannot be solved, and events that cannot be understood or managed. Although traditional views see organizations as rational and objectively real, the symbolic frame counterpoises a set of concepts that emphasizes the complexity and ambiguity of organizational phenomena and the extent to which symbols mediate the meanings of organizational events and activities. Myths and stories provide drama, cohesiveness, clarity, and direction to events that are confusing and mysterious. Rituals and ceremonies provide ways of taking actions in the face of confusion, unpredictability, and threats.

In the end, we need some order, predictability, and meaning in organizations, which often seem to be filled with ambiguity and uncertainty. Rather than admit that we cannot solve these problems, we create symbolic solutions, organizational structures, and processes that serve as myths, rituals, and ceremonies that promote cohesion inside organizations and bond organizations to their environment. Each of the four frames emphasizes particular views of organizational reality.

Putting It Into Perspective

We also can put these four approaches to organization and management theory into perspective by examining two interacting variables—the type of actor and the type of system. Each perspective makes certain assumptions regarding the role of the action—either rational or social—and the type of system—either closed or open—in which the organization member will be operating. These interactions are based on the perspectives, paradigms, and theories used by management and leaders in the organization.

The earliest stage was based on a rational actor working with a closed system. The manager of a factory, for example, would make all the important decisions and set all the rules and regulations. This would be done through careful analysis of the job requirements and a strict adherence to certain standards of performance by workers. The primary reason for interactions between individuals was to get the job done as quickly and cheaply as possible while maintaining performance standards.

Humanistic management approached workers and their managers or supervisors as social actors and the primary job of the managerial staff was to initiate openness and a feeling of appreciation for the workers to establish a good work setting. Being cognizant of the workers' needs was of great importance and the work force used communication interactions to express those needs. The system remained closed, however, because the manager was still "in charge" and made all the production decisions without consulting the workers.

With the awareness that workers have a great deal of information that could be useful to the operation of an organization, human resources management moved back to a rational actor status but opened the system to worker input.

Decisions about how the operation should be carried out were opened up to the work force in general.

The final stage of theoretical development is represented by the more recent approaches to the managerial process. The work force is seen as a vital part of the open system and the manager is a social actor who works with the employees in an effort to forward the organization's goals. Using a cultural perspective, all factors are considered intertwined and the manager's job is to be part of the process. The open system, social actor view allows for a fuller understanding of the cultural perspective.

Merging Perspectives

Because organizations are a major factor in everyone's life, it is not surprising to find a large number of explanations for why they do what they do and numerous prescriptions made for how to manage them more effectively. Rather than assume that a particular approach is the most useful, organizational theories increasingly are becoming combinations of the various approaches we have discussed in this chapter. We must be careful not to assume that differences mean other perspectives are incorrect. For example, when attempts are made to divide cultural investigations into two approaches, we need to be aware that important issues and information are missed when one approach is assumed to be better than the other. There are very few absolute divisions when we consider organizational communication. Drucker (1999) provides one additional reason to learn how to manage ourselves rather than depending on organizations to manage us. Corporate life spans are growing shorter and we are living longer. This chapter arms you with a broad-based set of insights and tools to help you manage your own life.

Conclusion

We have examined the four major developments in organizational and managerial theory since the Industrial Revolution. Scientific management emphasized the importance of job design and efficiency. Management's key function was to effectively structure the work setting so that the organization's production goals were met. This structured, well-designed approach allowed top-down control of all the factors in the work setting.

With the Hawthorne Studies' conclusions challenging many of the premises behind scientific management, human relations management moved toward an emphasis on the work setting as a social force. Adding the importance of social interaction as a motivational tool is the major contribution of this perspective.

In an attempt to balance the excesses of the humanistic approach without returning to the strict control features of scientific management, human resources management approaches workers as human beings capable of self-direction if provided with the proper work setting and goals. People are a potential resource, who can be used effectively to enhance the organization's growth and productivity. Leadership is a critical variable in this approach and has led to a vast number of studies on contingency design and leadership style.

The final approach to organization and managerial theory takes an overview of the various approaches and looks at organizations as cultures. Based on serious criticisms of the present approaches to organizational development, the cultural approach offers us an excellent perspective for understanding the behavioral aspects of organizations. This view provides us with an important starting point for the full understanding of the power of organizational communication. The principles and pragmatic sections develop a further understanding of these concepts. As we demonstrated, the new managerial perspectives give a great deal of credibility to cultural studies, but include the other theories as part of the process of organizing.

All of this is changing at a rate unforeseen a few years ago. The modern organization will continue changing because of the environmental demands. Our systems perspective developed in chapter 1 is born out by this clear influence of external variables on internal operations.

This chapter is basic to your understanding of why organizations do what they do. Because each of the perspectives offered tells us about successful processes in management, you should understand the major contributions of scientific management, humanistic management, and human resources management. The important result of numerous studies indicating that there is "no one best way" tells us that the contingencies involved in organizational communication must be understood fully if we are going to be successful as members of organizations. Membership requires us to view organizations as cultures that have a large number of contingencies based on the factors making up the structure.

You probably are asking the logical question: If the new managerial perspectives are basically correct, then why worry about the other three views? There are at least two reasons. First, when we discussed cultures, we carefully included all four views. For example, the 7-S Model and Theory Z explain to us what ought to be important in the running of an organization. But when you first join an organization, adapting to it effectively will be more important than worrying about the validity of the type of managerial style. By adding cultures as a concept, you are also aware that the external environment greatly influences the type of culture operating.

Second, each of the views discussed works. In many cases, the manner in which the management perspective is employed is not as successful as it could be. However, you will see a large number of businesses, companies, and organizations successfully operating in spite of the type of management, or, in some cases, because of it.

What we have provided you are excellent maps of the territories you will be exploring and joining. With the information provided in the remainder of this book, you will have the tools needed for settling in effectively and productively. Few things can be more rewarding than learning to be successful at your chosen profession, and organizational communication is an important link in that success.

Study Questions

1. What are the major impacts of the Industrial Revolution on society and organizations?
2. Taylor, Fayol, and Weber are the individuals most often associated with scientific management. What are their similarities, or basic tenets, and what are the differences between these three men?
3. Why did the Hawthorne Studies change the way organizations viewed employees?
4. Explain the differences between human relations and human resources management approaches.
5. McGregor and Likert provided significant insights into managing people. What are their major contributions?
6. What is an organizational culture? How does understanding culture contribute to understanding organizational communication?
7. Explain the different approaches to studying and utilizing organizational cultures.
8. Provide examples of the difference between functionalist and interpretionist approaches. Are there similarities between these and Schein's ethnographic and clinical categories?
9. Define and provide examples of organizational climate.
10. Which change for organizations discussed at the end of this chapter surprised you most? Which one do you feel most adequate to respond to? Which one would provide the greatest challenge for you?

4
Verbal Communication

Verbal communication is a primary vehicle organizations use to maintain contact with their internal and external environments. Through the use of oral and written language, organizations—and all of their subsystems—coordinate, control, lead, and manage individual and group behavior. Verbal communication provides the tools needed to obtain, transfer, and store information and knowledge. "The competitive advantages achieved by those who use information well are formidable" (Wind & Main, 1998, p. 28). Although they are referring specifically to cutting-edge techniques and technology, the conclusion applies to everyone in an organization. Verbal communication has always been critical to organizations but the shifts toward service, information, and knowledge work combined with the increasing use of modern technology places an even greater emphasis on the use of language and symbols. Specifically, the digital age utilizes electronically transferred symbols increasing our reliance on various forms of written communication.

The key concepts in this chapter include:

- Verbal communication in organizations
- Understanding verbal communication—language and perception; language, culture, and discrimination; naming and understanding; denotative/connotative; jargon
- Semantic/symbolic analysis
- Verbal communication—organizational uses: stories and myths; transmitting values; metaphors; language and management; inconsistencies; humor
- Verbal communication and cultures

Organizations are affected by verbal communication in at least three ways. First, the environment provides extensive information to an organization through verbal communication. Second, individuals and teams use verbal communication to direct, manage, comprehend, and respond. This allows us to understand the organization's cultural expectations. Finally, knowledge conveyed through verbal communication is critical to individuals and organizations (Drucker, 1993). Verbal communication is the key means for obtaining, transferring, utilizing, and storing the information that underpins knowledge.

Verbal communication also allows us to understand the complex nature of communication in an organization because we are brought directly in touch with an apparent contradiction. On the one hand, clarity and directness are required to be effective in giving instructions, making assessments, and dealing with colleagues. On the other hand, language is powerful precisely because it is highly symbolic of much broader meanings. In a sense, language becomes almost magical when it reinforces and motivates, creates an *esprit de corps*, or enhances a company image (Kotter, 1990). This second category includes stories, myths, heroes, metaphors, and humor. Look at phrases like cube farms, idea hamsters, and ohnosecond—popular phrases in many leading organizations. A cube farm is an office filled with cubicles. Idea hamsters are people who always seem to have their idea generators running. An ohnosecond is the fraction of time in which you realize that you have just made a big mistake—taken from saying "oh no" when you hit the delete button by mistake. These phrases express a larger message than the words alone. Symbolically, they allow organizational members to talk, express frustrations, show respect, create a common bond, and display humor.

Two additional examples show the symbolic importance of language. Early in 1999, the New York City Transit Agency ordered its conductors to drop the word "please" as they ordered riders to "stand clear of the closing doors" as a time saving technique ("Conductors," 1999). Riders and commuters complained and the order was rescinded. Once again in the Big Apple, then-Mayor Rudy Giuliani said that officers should use "hello," "thank you," and similar polite terms during arrests and official duties in an effort to reduce "tensions between New York City police and the public" (Bacon, 1999, p. 8A).

We are making an arbitrary division between verbal and nonverbal communication in order to facilitate our analysis. However, these two factors are, for all practical purposes, not separable. By and large, organizational members, because of their organizational roles or personal preferences, learn to depend on particular means of communication for specific needs and outcomes, but the verbal and nonverbal aspects are always in play. Before discussing the functions of verbal communication, we examine its importance to organizations.

Verbal Communication in Organizations

Language, the underpinning of verbal communication, allows us to assign meaning to things. We are not just naming something. Instead, language "is core to the process of constituting indeterminate and ambiguous external world into specific objects" (Deetz, 2001, p. 6). We are capable of using language to make sense of the external world through drawing attention to specific objects. This allows us to distinguish between different objects.

As we assimilate into an organization, we create individual realities based on language so we can predict and control our own behavior. We are forced to decipher from a variety of clues what messages mean and which messages are important. As such, verbal communication provides the written and unwritten, spoken and unspoken rules and procedures. These lead to a common purpose, or a set of ground rules, which constitute the process of organizing the various subsystems. Understanding the nature of verbal communication can be difficult because "language is both commonplace and enigmatic, both superficially simple and infinitely complex" (Bowman & Targowski, 1987, p. 22). Gass and Seiter (1999) conclude: "Words are the primary means of persuasion. They not only affect our perceptions, attitudes, beliefs, and emotions, they create reality" (p. 144). Language has a major impact on all individuals and shapes their organizational reality. Verbal communication is written and oral.

Written Communication

Written messages have numerous organizational functions. These include mission statements, corporate goals and values, short and long range plans, job descriptions, work orders, e-mail, announcements, bulletins, informal notes, house magazines and organs, annual reports, handbooks, procedures, operation manuals, official guidelines, regulations, codes, contracts, performance appraisals, and meeting agendas and minutes to name a few. The organization's public statements, such as annual reports or press releases, provide a great deal of information about the type of culture an organization would like to project. No less important are the ongoing memos, e-mails, letters to an organization's customers and other interacting systems in the organization's environment, intranet and other electronic communications, and the written credos, sayings, and general culture forming messages surrounding the workplace. "The amount of text generated by office workers exceeds all other forms of printed matter. Original documents created by office workers are 80% of all documents" (Ward & Snider, 2000, p. 10D). The power of the written word is clear. For example, although oral praise is appreciated, putting it in writing often has a greater impact because the written form remains as a record that can be reviewed (Pell, 1995). A sarcastic comment made in passing becomes carved in stone when committed to the written page or sent by e-mail. Because it is virtually impossible to erase e-mail, great discretion should be used when responding to colleagues or copying others. Memos and electronic messaging are the most frequently used means of written communication.

If you review the last paragraph, you note that many of the examples of written communication focused on the more *formal* uses. However, "written communication is not as common as one might imagine, nor is it a mode of communication much respected by managers" (Griffin, 2005, p. 593). In fact, in one survey, managers "indicated that only 13% of the printed mail they received was of immediate use to them" (Griffin, 2005, p. 593). Even more disturbing, more than 80% responded to another survey by indicating that the written communication they received was of fair or poor quality (Buckley, 1999).

Current and future reliance on modern technology is leading to a highly interactive, instantaneous communication system with unlimited information storage possibilities. Although we discuss communication technologies throughout this text, we provide an extensive analysis in chapter 12.

Oral Communication

In chapter 1, we indicated the strong bias toward oral communication in organizations. Managers and supervisors prefer speaking to writing (Armour, 1998; Griffin, 2005). Oral communication is used in practically any activity requiring coordination. For example, interviewing, delegating, meetings, performance appraisals, giving and receiving orders, public statements, and instructing are primarily verbal. The less formal oral communication behaviors are just as important and include greetings, reinforcement, break time, and the ritualizing of particular informal, but expected behaviors.

Functions of Verbal Communication

Verbal communication is used in three ways. First, to enhance task accomplishments through task ordering; second, to make sense out of content with a process orientation; and third, to supply the bridge between myth and reality through narrative (Morris, 1971; Watzlawick, Beavin, & Jackson, 1967).

The first level, *task ordering*, involves cognitive meaning, which focuses on either/or choices. At this level, when given instructions, we either follow them, or we do not; understand them or not; or comprehend them or not. In many ways, contracts involve this level of meaning. This is a *task orientation*. Two examples are company rules and organizational charts. First, certain company rules are absolute. Prohibitions against the use of alcohol and drugs in most factories are, for example, clear cut statements regarding employee behavior that almost always lead to dismissal if ignored. Many safety violations simply will not be tolerated. Rules against sexual harassment, stealing, or plagiarism can be included. On a wider scale, organizational charts, which outline job functions and responsibilities, are efforts at task ordering.

Level two, *affective*, accepts the concepts of both/and, and isolates issues in terms of degrees of difference rather than absolute choices. Level two is a *process orientation*. When we think about content, we are in the process of sense-making. At this point, we are adding meaning to the hard reality of the language initially used and developing a more complex understanding of what is actually occurring. At this level, someone can be both a good worker and often late to work. This same worker can violate an important safety rule and still be worth retaining.

Two terms should make this second level clear. When we talk about leadership, many of us feel we have a relatively clear, recognizable cognitive definition. A leader is someone who leads, commands, or is in charge of others. Using the first-level task ordering, we say someone is or is not a good leader. In fact, excellent leaders quickly learn that simply being in command or in charge does not make for successful leadership (Kotter, 1990). Instead, a leader is someone who plans, organizes, sways, conjures, persuades, adapts, reprimands, and carries out many other functions (Bennis & Townsend, 1995; Blank, 1995). They are *leading* rather than just being the leader. The emphasis moves from simply being a good or bad leader to the process of leading. Excellent leadership can require almost paradoxical views of the job requirements. For example, managers are expected to produce harmony through healthy conflict, facilitate change by providing stability, draw strength from being vulnerable, and have fun while working (Bolman & Deal, 2003).

In the same vein, the word *organization* may be more appropriately labeled *organizing*. "Organizing is used to denote the processual, sequential, time varying nature of the behaviors of members in an organization" (Farace, Monge, & Russell, 1977, p. 19). Because organizations are simultaneously static and dynamic, predictable and chaotic, and understandable and mystical, they are not fixed or set simply because there is a particular label attached such as Southwest Airlines or IBM. Although their organizational charts outline the structure, the process of behavior more correctly explains what actually occurs.

This leads to the third level, *narrative*, which involves the combination of myth with reality. The things we say, for example, become both very real, in that we accept them as valid, yet they are based on a narrative form of proof. This level most accurately reflects how we actually think. At this point, we use metaphors, irony, humor, paradoxes, and the vast array of stories that fuel all organizational cultures. Great leaders or outstanding organizations are known because individuals pass on stories about them. Once these narrations are assigned credibility, we believe in the characterizations.

Concepts, at this third level, are *transformable, reversible, and simultaneously reality and myth*. These stories provide individuals with the understandable, shared reasons for why things occur. In every organization, stories exist to explain what leadership actually is supposed to be. Microsoft, Southwest Airlines, or Harvard become bigger than life because of their halo of esteem based on shared stories and myths.

The transformable nature of meaning can be demonstrated by seeing how consultants suggest organizations handle customer complaints. Virtually every customer service consultant argues that customer complaints should be viewed as an opportunity (Whiteley, 1991). By shifting the emphasis, the employee's reality concerning the complaining customer is altered from an adversary to a collaborator. In the same vein, organizations are encouraged to solicit employee suggestions and heed employee complaints. When we discussed the self-fulfilling prophecy earlier in this text, we indicated the dramatic shift that can occur when people use a different perspective to view a problem or issue.

This third level of language use is vital to an organization. In the extreme, plans are offered to make an organization appear to be on course and carefully structured. "Thus language trappings of organizations such as strategic plans are important components of the process of creating order. They hold events together long enough and tightly enough in people's heads so that they act in the belief that their actions will be influential and make sense" (Weick, 1987, p. 98). Organizational decisions often are "lucked into" through rational appearing processes. This becomes a backward decision-making process, where organizational members look back on a decision and see why it was rational. This process is used to make sense of complex, ever-changing situations, so that they can be managed (Conrad, 1985).

At first glance, delineating these three levels might appear unnecessarily complex. However, we need to understand the three ways we establish meaning through the use of language. The cognitive level involves the explicit choices we make. We either take a job, for example, or we do not. But the word *job* does not describe what we actually do. Chances are the affective level, where the job is both interesting and boring, or easy and hard, comes closer to describing our daily activities. The very nature of organizations leads us to the third level of narrative. Organizations often jerk, lurch, and slide into decisions and directions, and we are able to follow the organization because of the rich body of myths and stories that provide a guiding force for us.

Understanding Verbal Communication

The relationship between language and perception and the symbolic nature of language are two important aspects of verbal communication.

Language and Perception

Language, the basis for verbal communication, is the most logical place to bring our discussion. Language both facilitates and hinders our effectiveness in communication. Because we place a strong belief in the written word, as manifested in contracts, policy statements, and possible legal challenges, the impact of language in an organization can be one of the first communication processes we encounter. Our business and legal ethics mandate a dependence on language. To "get it in writing" or have the statement "signed" or "initialed" provides written proof of commitment. We also are guided in how to do our jobs by written and oral language. A large amount of operational information, or how to perform tasks, appears in writing and is explained verbally.

Language is an excellent paradigm to demonstrate the influence of perception on our understanding of reality. There is "the inescapable relation of language to the user's and the receiver's schemes of perception. To say things in a particular way is to advance a particular way of seeing—a way based on values" (Rentz & Debs, 1987, p. 38). Managers are counseled: "When planning an important communication, the focus should be on language, because it's language that governs thought, persuasion, and the perception of character, attitudes and values" (Blake, 1987, p. 43). Unfortunately, "some managers refuse to believe that the most important aspect of communication is not what is said or written, but the perception left by the communicator" (Barton, 1990, p. 32). Language does more than just relay facts.

The language used can determine a decision's outcome. In one study, managers who were told that a hypothetical business maneuver has an 80% chance of succeeding usually opted for the decision (McCormick, 1987). In a similar group, when told the decision had a 20% chance of failure, the overwhelming majority of managers decided not to accept the maneuver. "Decision-makers often allow a decision to be framed by the language or context it's presented in" (McCormick, 1987, p. 2). Killer statements, as shown in Table 4.1, often stop creative thinking because of the statements' ability to reframe an idea in a negative fashion.

Organizations frequently resist change because of the framing of the alternatives (Kehrer, 1989). In the 1980s, U.S. organizations held onto the concept that products made in Japan were inferior and provided no real competition in the marketplace (Nora, Rogers, & Stramy, 1986). With the spectacular successes by Japanese corporations in numerous arenas in the late 1980s, U.S. corporations recognized their incorrect framing and began focusing on increasing quality—the key ingredient in Japanese success. The dramatic increase in quality in the United States provides support for the critical premise that how we view and discuss an issue tends to determine how we think about that issue. Public opinion researchers refer to response bias to explain how the wording and context of a question can "trigger connotations or interpretations in the respondent's mind that can have a major effect on how a question is answered" (Jaroslovsky, 1988, p. 56). Language, or how the problem is described and framed, can influence our perception.

Language, Culture, and Discrimination

In subtle and not-so-subtle ways, our language use communicates messages about our background, education, and heritage. We utilize language to express our views of other groups. Recall in chapter 1, we outlined the rapidly changing workforce demographics.

One language-based difference often overlooked is *literacy*. "About one in 20 adults in the United States is not literate in English, meaning 11 million people lack the skills to handle everyday tasks" (Feller, 2005, p. 3A). Although recent immigrants "with limited or no English skills account for most of the group, the survey suggests that even the average adult has low skills" (Toppo, 2005, p. 1A). For example, the average adult group had difficulties interpreting a table on blood pressure, age, and physical activity or comparing per-ounce costs

Table 4.1 Killer Statements

1.	We tried that before.
2.	Our place is different.
3.	It costs too much.
4.	That's beyond our responsibility.
5.	That's not my job.
6.	We're all too busy to do that.
7.	It's too radical a change.
8.	We don't have enough time.
9.	Not enough help.
10.	That will make other equipment obsolete.
11.	Let's make a market research test of it first.
12.	Our office is too small for that.
13.	Not practical for operating people.
14.	The staff will never buy it.
15.	Bring it up again in 6 months.
16.	We've never done it before.
17.	It's against company policy.
18.	Runs up our overhead.
19.	We don't have the authority.
20.	That's too ivory tower.
21.	Let's get back to reality.
22.	That's not our problem.
23.	Why change it, it's still working OK.
24.	I don't like the idea.
25.	You're right, but…
26.	You're 2 years ahead of your time.
27.	We're not ready for that.
28.	We don't have the money, equipment, room, and/or personnel.
29.	It isn't in the budget.
30.	Can't teach an old dog new tricks.
31.	Good thought, but impractical.
32.	Let's hold it in abeyance.
33.	Let's give it more thought.
34.	Top management would never go for it.
35.	Let's put it in writing.
36.	We'll be the laughing stock.
37.	Not that again.
38.	We'd lose money in the long run.
39.	Where'd you dig that one up?
40.	We did all right without it.
41.	That's what we can expect from the staff.

(continued)

Table 4.1 (continued) Killer Statements

42. It's never been tried before.
43. Let's shelve it for the time being.
44. Let's form a committee.
45. Has anyone else ever tried it?
46. Customers won't like it.
47. I don't see the connection.
48. It won't work in our company.
49. What you are really saying is…
50. Maybe that will work in your department, but not in mine.
51. The Executive Committee will never go for it.
52. Don't you think we should look into it further before we act?
53. What do they do in our competitor's company?
54. It won't pay for itself.
55. It can't be done.
56. It's too much trouble to change.
57. I know a person who tried it.
58. It's impossible.
59. We've always done it this way.

of two cans of soup (Toppo, 2005). Immigrants account for obvious cultural differences in English proficiency, but low literacy also creates a subculture of individuals who are likely to be underemployed or destined for low-paying occupations. This analysis also underscores the importance of not assuming (see chap. 2) that your colleagues communicate with the same language proficiency. For example, "nearly half the 14.7 million undergraduates at 2- and 4-year institutions never receive degrees" to a large extent because they are ill prepared in basics such as reading and writing (Schemo, 2006, p. 8A). The 2006 ACT college entrance examine indicates that only 21% of students applying to 4-year institutions are ready for college-level work in all four areas tested: reading, writing, math, and biology (Schemo, 2006). Studies indicate that there is a "deep disconnection between what high school teachers think that their students need to know and what professors, even at 2-year colleges, expect them to know" (Schemo, 2006, p. 8A).

Within any country, there are subgroups whose cultural experiences provide unique language usages. "In addition to subgroups based on race, religion, or national origin, we are also experiencing an unprecedented growth in subgroup cultures and language communities associated with generation, social class, and political interest groups" (Verderber & Verderber, 2001, p. 111). So, language usage that appears to be quite clear to one individual can be equally murky to another because of significantly different literacy skills or cultural background.

Language can also reflect prejudice by labeling certain groups through *sexism, ageism, racism, classism, heterosexism, and tokenism.* These "isms" regard all members of a particular group as the same, which means we fail to see that within any categorization there are differences. For example, "racist terms are used by members of one culture to disparage members of other cultures—their customs or accomplishments. Racist language emphasizes differences" (DeVito, 2004, p. 173). Likewise, language that stereotypes any group is inherently prejudicial. *Political correctness* is an attempt to use inclusive speech through nonsexist, nonageist, and nonracist language (Hoover & Howard, 1995). We do have a choice regarding our language usage and verbal communication that excludes or marginalizes others creating unnecessary and potentially harmful divisions.

Different cultural backgrounds impact in all aspects of verbal communication. "Language is one of the most conspicuous stamps of a culture" (Sweeney & McFarlin, 2002, p. 379). Cultural characteristics are knowledge-based and provide a framework from which to understand more about a particular group but they do not define all members of the group (O'Mara, 1994). For example, Western languages focus on objects or referents and their logical relationships. Asian languages focus more on promoting and maintaining harmony. So, how something is said can be more important to Asians than the actual content of the message (Calloway-Thomas, Cooper, & Blake, 1999). In addition, whereas a word might translate easily, the interpretation can be quite different. A contract to a German, Scandinavian, American, Swiss, or British person is something to be signed and adhered to. Japanese, on the other hand, regard a contract as a starting document to be rewritten and modified as circumstances require. South Americans see a contract as an ideal unlikely to be achieved but necessary to avoid argument (Lewis, 1996). These differences are compounded by naive assumptions regarding other cultures. A 1999 Harris poll showed that the average American believes 52% of the world speaks English when actually it is about 20% (Carey & Laird, 1999). One of the ironies of language is that even the concept of English is not clear. As Table 4.2 shows, there are dramatic differences between English, as used in the British Isles, Australia, and American English. There are 74 countries where English is the primary language. Imagine, for a moment, all the possible differences between English speaking groups.

In the United States, misunderstandings based on language differences are becoming increasingly important. In medical facilities, dealing with the 50 million U.S. residents who speak a language other than English creates serious caregiving issues (Weise, 2006). For law enforcement officers, an inability to understand a victim or deal with someone under suspicion jeopardizes effectiveness (Taylor, 2006).

Few Americans speak foreign languages well ("Multilingualism," 2005). The gap can be seen when we realize that "in China, more than 200 million

Table 4.2 Do You Speak English?

England	United States
Dual carriageway	Divided highway
Ground floor	First floor
First floor	Second floor
Biscuits	Cookies
Dustman	Garbage collector
Carrier bag	Shopping bag
Flat	Apartment
Lift	Elevator
Underground	Subway
Queue	Waiting line
Way out	Exit
Sweet	Dessert

Australia	United States
Cheesed-off	Annoyed
Chook	Chicken
Cobber	Friend, mate
Crook	Sick
Fair go	A chance
Macca's	McDonald's
To get nicked	To get caught
On yer bike!	To get going
On ya! Good on ya!	Good for you. Good job.
Tinnie	Can of beer
Whinge	To complain
Yobbo	An uncultivated, uncivilized character

students study English. In the USA, just 24,000 American kids are studying Chinese" (Lynch, 2006, p. 6B). However, "in retooling for future global competition, the United States has a long way to go. Less than 1% of today's high school students are studying the languages likely to be among the most important to the USA's future: Chinese, Arabic, Farsi, Korean, Russian and Urdu, according the Education Department" (Lynch, 2006, p. 6B). Some companies are taking proactive steps. UPS, in 2002, "established a 'global trade curricula' for its more than 407,000 employees on the company website and seeks new hires who speak multiple languages" (Lynch, 2006, p. 6B). Not surprisingly, 61% of executives surveyed believe Spanish is the most useful second language in business (Yang & Lewis, 2005).

Some languages have hundreds of thousands more words than other languages, and others do not even have words for things that are commonly referred to in other languages (Rothwell, Sullivan, & McLean, 1995). In some Southeast Asian languages, there is no word for "no" and these languages lack an imperative verb form. What may seem logical, sensible, and reasonable to a person from one culture may seem irrational, stupid, and unimportant to a person from another culture. One source for this difficulty is that when we talk about other cultures, we tend to describe differences, not similarities and we may stereotype differences as negative and threatening. Verbal communication can reveal ethnocentrism or a refusal to value the differences between cultures.

Finally, there are gender differences in communication that are "the culturally determined behaviors and personality characteristics that are associated with, but not determined by, one's biological sex" (Verderber & Verderber, 2001, p. 124). In the workplace, female managers tend to be more positive, relational, facilitative, empowering, and cooperative when they communicate, whereas male managers tend to be more authoritative, directive, depersonalizing, and commanding (Byers, 1997; Gass & Seiter, 1999). Male-oriented language tends to be based on military and sports metaphors as a means for gaining acceptance (Harrangan, 1997; Rizzo & Mendez, 1990). You should note our use of the word *tend* before both the female and male generalizations.

Naming and Understanding

A fundamental characteristic of language is its capacity to name things as we explained in the Introduction. During the naming process, language necessarily provides *signification* to the item and excludes everything else from that particular category. This provides both *division* and *unity* because it excludes certain factors as it allows a common understanding of previously disparate ones (Burke, 1969). If someone is called a student, union leader, lawyer, or IBMer, this label provides a category that explains what the person is not as well as including what the person is. In the opening chapter, we discussed different generations, such as baby boomers or Gen Y, as if all generational members were somehow the same—that is clearly not possible.

 Perception, you recall from chapter 2, is the selecting, organizing, and interpreting of sensory stimulation into a meaningful and coherent picture of the world. Language is a primary mechanism used to accomplish this end. Imagine, for a moment, waiting to be introduced to your new manager and having one of your colleagues label the manager a "real stickler for detail." If you accept a job with the organization, you probably will be influenced by the initial description of the manager's biases. Although your job might entail a large variety of tasks, it will be difficult to not focus on paying attention to details as a major priority in everything you do.

Assigning a name or label allows us to make the item or activity more understandable. For example, the number of terms that have been added to business since the advent of the computer is remarkable. *Computerphobia* is the study of the 20% of adults or cyberphobes who have a fear of computers. A short list involving computers includes browser, bandwidth, CD-ROM, desktop, database, disk drive, DOS, download, e-mail, gigabyte, hard disk, and Internet. We intentionally stopped our list at the I's. You probably have thought of additional digital age, computer-related terms that easily fit into this list created by the Internet such as chat room, spam, and Web site. MySpace, for example, "is nothing short of a cultural phenomenon," which, in 2006 accounted for 82% of the traffic on social networking sites (Sellers, 2006, p. 68). In 2005, "it surpassed Google in terms of traffic, and now MySpace ranks second to Yahoo for page views, with one billion daily (Sellers, 2006, p. 68). In addition to the likelihood that you recognize MySpace, an arbitrary name designed to clarify the site's purpose, you also had no difficulty in identifying Google and Yahoo. If you had difficulties, you might have turned to Wikipedia.

However, naming also limits the application of the word because we now have a specific reference. Although we are certainly dependent on nonverbal and sensual messages, verbal communication provides a basic underpinning for how we will interpret our world. Because words are an arbitrary determination of a particular item, they can have an unpredictable impact when applied internationally. Coca-Cola in Chinese means "Bite the head of a dead tadpole." The Chevy Nova was *no va* in Spanish, which means "doesn't go." Broderbund, which means "brotherhood" in German, is a software-maker in California and a Ku Klux Klan-like group in South Africa. The Pepsi advertisement "Come alive with Pepsi" becomes "Come out of the grave with Pepsi" in German (Ferrell & Fraedrich, 1994). To prevent these misunderstandings, Sony's leaders chose the name for its ease of pronunciation in a variety of countries. Mercedes names its vehicles by letter and number (e.g., M-Class) to eliminate unintentional interpretations.

Finally, the boundary-setting nature of naming can create difficulties. One readily available example of how bureaucracies can limit adaptability to current and future needs is the National Asset Database that "is used by Homeland Security to divvy up the hundreds of millions of dollars in antiterrorism grants each year" (Lipton, 2006, p. 4A). Although New York City and Washington, DC, have seen their funds cut by 40%, the Old MacDonald's Petting Zoo, the Amish Country Popcorn factory, the Mule Day parade, Sweetwater Flea Market, Beach at the End of the Street, Nix's Check Cashing, and many other seemingly less than obvious terrorism targets are receiving antiterrorism grants (Lipton, 2006). The source of the problems appears to be definitions or standards tied to how the grants are defined. For example, under current definitions, the District of Columbia has half the monuments of Washington State.

Denotative/Connotative Meaning

One useful way to understand the impact of language is to distinguish between denotative and connotative meanings. With denotative meaning, there is no disagreement about what is meant because the reference is explicitly clear to everyone. On the surface, people should have little difficulty in clearly understanding each other. We use about 2,000 words in our daily conversations, which should facilitate shared meaning. But, the 500 most-used words have more than 14,000 dictionary definitions.

Connotative meanings depend on our own subjective reality and the immediate context. The emotional and affective responses that a word evokes from us are the connotative meanings. So, we have a fuller meaning for each word than its specific denotative intent (Locker, 1992). This is a powerful perceptual issue for organizations because it involves the impression or aura surrounding the word, based on experience instead of the prescribed meaning. So, words such as *strike, union, downsizing,* or *management* cause different reactions depending on who responds (Gould, 1996). For example, when a boss says "I'm empowering you to make that decision," employees may hear "You know exactly what I want you to do but I want you to feel good about it" or they may hear "I trust you to do the right thing so please follow your own best judgment."

Recognizing the impact of words, many organizations decided to abandon the term *employee* with its potential baggage regarding subservience or traditional working processes. The new titles include associates, team members, consultants, service providers, technicians, careholders, co-workers, employee-owners, job-owners, and partners. In addition to these general words, there are Microstrategists (Microsoft), Scitorians (Scitor), and AMSers (American Management Systems).

When you put ASAP (as soon as possible) on a request, you probably mean you want it as soon as possible and you are expressing a sense of urgency. Shipping departments in some organizations interpret ASAP as meaning whenever possible, so take your time. Responding to the overuse of the term, shipping departments simply strike back by disregarding the urgency through their own idiosyncratic interpretation of ASAP.

A very specific example of language interpretation is *sexual harassment,* which is defined as unwelcome sexual attention based as much on language as on physical actions. When one person "exhibits sexual approach behaviors and the other counters with sexual avoidance behaviors followed by continued sexual advance behaviors" there is sexual harassment (Stewart, Cooper, Stewart, & Friedley, 2003, p. 190). We need to remember that sexual harassment is a power issue not a gender issue and discussing illicit behaviors at work could easily offend someone (Fritz, Brown, Lunde, & Banset, 1999). Perception, once again, plays a role. In one survey, 75% of the men said they would be flattered by unwelcome sexual advances whereas 75% of women said they would be offended (Lubin, 1991). The issue of sexual harassment is much more complex than this brief discussion. Our point is that language need only be interpreted by one party to be communication and if that party claims to be offended it could be harassment.

Rednecks are not a protected class, leaving them open to organizational humor. One popular Internet message begins "you know the computer belongs to a Redneck if … (1) the mouse is referred to as a critter; (2) the keyboard is camouflaged; (3) there is a Skoal can in the CD-ROM drive," and continues through fifteen items. If you found these comments humorous, then you are supporting the connotative power of naming. However, if the intent of this joke was to diminish the importance of a colleague who happens to come from a Redneck background, then the power element of harassment emerges, although not legally. Put another way, the exact meaning of the word is not as important as the connotative meaning.

Connotative meaning also extends to a collective interpretation of a phrase, word, or concept that does not have to be explained. When an organization is described as being on the "cutting edge," people seem to understand the characterization even though it is unlikely that everyone knows what the phrase really means. The organizations studied in *In Search of Excellence* initially were chosen because of a halo of esteem (Peters & Waterman, 1982). General Electric and Coca-Cola frequently are listed among the most admired companies in annual surveys. Yet few individuals would agree on the specific reasons.

Jargon

Although increasingly part of everyone's communication, many terms such as *perks, just-in-time suppliers, VAM* (value added manufacturing), *CI* (continuous improvement), *robotics,* and *MBWA* originated in certain organizations. These terms began as jargon, which is the specialized or technical language used in an organization. It functions as a shorthand code comprehensible to coworkers. "A single word of jargon can identify an object, concept, or task that would require an elaborate explanation for someone outside the field. The special language of an occupation speeds communication within a closed fraternity of workers, while effectively excluding others" (Kunerth, 1983, p. 1). Each organizational culture develops specific terms for describing events.

Jargon serves to both include members of the profession and exclude outsiders. It can be wielded as an instrument of power, intimidation, and evasion. A physician might refer to *axilla bromidromsis* instead of an armpit's foul smelling odor and make the patient fearful of a problem that might simply be a long shower away from being cured. Legal terminology is often beyond the grasp of the uninitiated.

As the pressure for innovation continues, several increasingly popular examples of jargon are: circling the drain, meaning failing or about to go down the tube; mouse milking, which refers to a venture with maximum effort for minimal results; or fortune cookie, which is a witty way to refer to something

Table 4.3 Decoding Device for Letters of Reference and Performance Reviews

Code Words	Translation—May Really Mean
Careful thinker	Won't make a decision
Strong principles	Stubborn
Spends extra hours on the job	Miserable home life
Active socially	Drinks too much
Alert to company developments	Is a gossip
Average	Not too bright
Takes pride in work	Is conceited
Meticulous attention to detail	Nitpicker

you heard that is insightful. Have you encountered these examples of jargon? Probably not because jargon is organization-, task-, or industry-specific.

The government frequently uses terms such as revenue enhancement for tax increases and organizations use selective cutbacks to mean firings. The Department of Defense seems to be especially adept at using jargon to alter meaning. A hammer is called "a manually powered fastener driving impact device," a steel nut is a "hexiform rotatable surface compression unit," and a tent is a "frame supported tension structure" (Marklein, 1987, p. Dl). During military operations, civilian casualties become collateral damage, killing selected targets is neutralizing, and combat activities are peacekeeping. When discussing the Challenger tragedy, NASA called it an "anomaly," the astronauts' bodies "recovered components," and their coffins "crew transfer containers." An Air Force Cruise missile "terminated 5 minutes earlier than planned" because it "impacted with the ground prematurely."

Finally, one set of high school football players was just "deficient at a grading period" rather than failing their classes (Marklein, 1987, p. Dl). Chrysler received the 1989 English teachers' doublespeak award for telling AMC (American Motors Corporation) workers their new "career alternative enhancement program" meant they were fired. Although these euphemisms were used to obscure meaning, careful wording also can help prevent offending people. Officials at Expo 86 in Vancouver, British Columbia, proved to be masters at euphemisms by expecting "the occasional protein spill" from people on park rides, police were "security hosts," and rest rooms were "guest relations facilities." Using terminology that lessens or misdirects individuals is often termed *euphemisms*.

Letters of reference and written performance reviews can use carefully chosen terms to provide an insider's knowledge, which is for the individuals reviewing the application, of the possible meaning as shown in Table 4.3. Being obscure is a tactic that is not limited to the use of jargon.

Buzzwords are a special category of jargon. In a survey of the Fortune 1,000 vice presidents, buzzwords were seen as being inappropriate for formal reports, but useful for a variety of other business-related activities. "Most respondents feel that business slang can sometimes improve communication, make talking easier, make talking more comfortable, be amusing, or be the most precise and exact way to say a thing. Many also felt, however, that business slang expressions are boring, almost four fifths said they sometimes do not understand a given business slang expression" (Gilsdorf, 1983, p. 41). In organizations, being Dilberted is to be exploited or oppressed by your boss. Geeksploitation is taking advantage of your high-tech workers willing to work long hours if bolstered by junk food, flexible schedules, and no dress code. The I-way is the information superhighway. Prairie-dogging is popping up from your cubicle to glance around and see what your co-workers are doing. Uninstalled, a euphemism for being fired, augments the remarkable 1990s downsizing list including rationalizing, rightsizing, outsourcing, business process reengineering, slimming, forced reduction, release of resources, career change opportunity, or force management program. These all replace the earlier designations of being fired, sacked, canned, or laid off. We work in cube land, are wired to the web, and may have the bandwidth (ability) to handle a job. Jargon is a specialized form of verbal communication that occurs in all organizations and professions.

Before we leave this analysis, we have highlighted some current words and phrases in Table 4.4 that you should understand. Although these might not be familiar to you now, they are common concepts in most organizations.

Semantic/Symbolic Analysis

Semantics offers an explanation for why organizations can develop new names and why words are so open to multiple interpretations. Three principles underlie semantics.

First, *meaning is in people, not words*. Words do not mean, people mean. These two sentences are popular summations of the important principle that everyone has his or her own interpretation of reality (Craig, 1997).

Second, language is *representational*. As we already have seen, the word is not the thing. Words are symbolic representations of ideas or objects (Condon, 1975). We are free to create whatever words we choose, as we found out with jargon and buzzwords, and our only limitation is what other people interpret the word to mean. We can take a term and make it represent a reality, but the shared meaning is transactional.

Third, *both observations and inferences occur* when we use verbal communication. This semantic distortion needs to be identified, although there is little likelihood you would want to eliminate it. A statement of observation is factual, can be observed and verified, and is about the past or the present. Inferences can be made by anyone about anything in any time frame (Haney, 1967). As a consequence, inferences are much less reliable if we are interested

Table 4.4 Some Current Verbal Communication Concepts/Buzzwords

Benchmarking	Compares a business' activities to those of the best companies.
Collaborative workplace	Rejecting hierarchy, embracing teamwork.
Constant whitewater	Important and radical change will never end.
Core competencies	Build capabilities that customers will value and that competitors can't replicate.
Core management competencies	Managers with key skills including planning, communications, and leadership.
Customer satisfaction measurement	Focuses on identifying and meeting customer needs.
Delayering	Carving out a layer in the organization for elimination rather than downsizing all.
Derailment	Running afoul of some taboo. Getting off the career track.
Disconnect	A way to couch a disagreement or ineffective communication.
Empowerment	Pushing decision making as far down in the company as possible to be as close to the problem, decision, customer, or issue as possible.
Face time	Time spent in office. Often seen as an element in career success.
Growth strategies	Aim to lift profits by expanding revenues, not just cutting costs.
In alignment	Values and attitudes of employees compatible with the team, organization, leader.
In transition	Usually applies to executives out of work.
Mission and vision statements	Describe what the company will become and how it will get there.
Pay for performance	Ties compensation to reaching specific business goals.
Process-centered organization	Structuring around processes, not departments.
Reengineering	Radically redesigns business processes to improve productivity.
Six-sigma efficiency	Means being 99.997% perfect.
Strategic alliances	Create business partnerships among customers, suppliers, and even competitors.
Strategic planning	Develops a comprehensive program to position businesses for long-term success.
Thinking outside the box	Creating new processes.
Total quality management	Seeks to eliminate errors in order to reduce costs and better serve customers.
Value-based change	Emphasizing trust, candor, honesty, and integrity.

only in the facts. However, inferences comprise a substantial portion of organizational communication.

Organizations spend a great deal of time trying to prevent overly abstract instructions. In one organization, there is a large sign saying "never ASS-U-ME" anything is clear, unless both individuals can agree on the meaning. Too many errors occur because people assume they have been understood or that they understand and end up making the sign's message come true.

In conclusion, we have focused on three principles: Meaning is in people not words, language is representational, and there is an important distinction between observations and inferences.

Verbal Communication—Organizational Uses

First, all organizations use specific means for obtaining organizational goals, and language is one of the most important of these means. A sense of identification between the individual and an organization is vital. In essence, language outlines the goals and values important to our becoming a productive member of the organization. Even more fundamentally, "language is the primary vehicle in this process of identification, and the ways in which it is shaped and used by the individual often reveals his or her organizational personality—the extent to which the person has adopted the values of the organization" (Rentz & Debs, 1987, p. 44). We return to values shortly. Very little of this type of information is obtained through the cognitive level. In fact, organizations frequently operate at the affective level and myths become reality.

Stories and Myths

A tremendous amount of information is passed on to members of an organization through the telling of stories and myths (Sweeney & McFarlin, 2002). These explain "how the organization dealt with key competitors in the past, how it developed a new and exciting product, how it dealt with a valued employee, and so on, not only to spell out the basic mission and specific goals (and thereby reaffirming them) but also to reaffirm the organization's picture of itself, its own theory of how to get things done, and how to handle internal relationships" (Schein, 1985, p. 81). "Every leader tells a story. Forget bullet points and slide shows. The best leaders use stories to answer three simple questions: Who am I? Who are we? Where are we going?" (Weil, 1998, p. 38). In order to be a leader, we must understand that "a key—perhaps the key—to leadership ... is the effective communication of a story" (Gardner, 1995, p. 62). Although an organization's formal documents spell out the official statements of ideology, these informal means are what actually guide the organization. Stories provide a teachable point of view. Sony cofounder Akio Morito told this story to all of his salespeople: "Two shoe sales representatives find themselves in a rustic backwater of Africa. The first writes back, 'No prospect of sales. Natives do not wear shoes.' The second writes, 'No one wears shoes here. We can dominate the market. Send all possible stock.'"

This story could become simply another of the great salesperson stories that dominate all sales cultures. But, it takes on a mythical nature because it clearly spells out the need for optimism and opportunity hunting by Sony salespeople. Because it was delivered by the cofounder to all sales recruits, the story has an added dimension and significance. It becomes perceived reality for how a Sony salesperson must think and act.

All organizations have stories about past events. Of particular value to many organizations are the "stories recounting the histories of these visionary heroes (which) pass from generation to generation of managers" (Deal & Kennedy, 1982, p. 44). Hewlett-Packard's founders have used stories to underscore the company values. Cofounder "Dave Packard toured an HP factory, saw a cheap, thin prototype for a new product, twisted it into a mangled ball, and declared it 'a hunka junk.' It's a great lesson in prizing quality as well as cost" (Weil, 1998, p. 40). Tom Watson (IBM), Steve Jobs, William Kellogg, and Robert Welch (GE) all have extensive stories told about them that reinforce the importance of the individual. "In many firms stories are told about 'average' employees who became heroes by breaking dumb rules that contradicted firm values, or, conversely, by steadfastly sticking to practices that exemplified the culture" (Sweeney & McFarlin, 2002, p. 340). So, "through stories, parables, and other forms of oral and written history, an organization can communicate its ideology and basic assumptions—especially to newcomers, who need to know what is important not only in abstract terms but by means of concrete examples that can be emulated" (Schein, 1985, p. 82).

Because of the power of language, stories are not neutral (Mumby & Clair, 1997). By drawing attention to the interests of dominant groups, they reify structures, and reproduce power, they can create and maintain a culture of obedience (Witten, 1993). When organizational members are seeking guidance in making decisions, for example, stories offer easily remembered principles. If the principles are created by others who are interested in production and output over individual development, or unusual heroic efforts demanding unfair practices, or any other outcome that is not clearly in the interest of others, then a story can be an implement of power rather than simply a clarification of organizational values.

In organizations where the culture does not foster positive employee responses to management, heroes still emerge as the voices for the mistreated. Stories about these "counterculture" heroes also provide employees with rules, only these explain how to beat the system rather than support it. These stories, and other forms of verbal communication, become the backbone of symbolic resistance where the counterculture uses similar stories, values, and myths to take a stand against the prevailing norms.

Transmitting Values

The values "are the basic concepts of an organization; as such they form the heart of the corporate culture. Values define success in concrete terms for employees—'if you do this, you too will be a success'—and establish standards of achievement within the organization" (Deal & Kennedy, 1982, pp. 13–14). An organization that carries the message "never be responsible for making a mistake" (or at least getting caught) passes on a very different sense of values from the 3M Company, who states: "Never be responsible for killing an idea." The use of slogans and creeds allows companies to emphasize their organizational culture's particular emphasis, as shown in Table 4.5. If you would like to expand your list of slogans and creeds, almost any business-oriented magazine will have advertisements from the major organizations with an accompanying slogan.

Visions are used to express values in a clear and simple manner. The Girl Scouts of America want "to help a girl reach her highest potential." Merck Pharmaceuticals states: "To preserve and improve human life." "To give ordinary folk the chance to buy the same things as rich people" drives Wal-Mart. Walt Disney wants "to make people happy." Mary Kay Cosmetics states that

Table 4.5 Slogans, Creeds, and Shared Values

Company/ Organization	Slogan & Creed	Shared Values
Merrill Lynch	"A breed apart"	Expresses a concern for meeting customer needs
Toshiba	"In touch with tomorrow"	Product development
General Electric	"Progress is our most important product"	Product development
Honeywell	"Together, we can find the answers"	Teamwork and research
Dana Corp.	"Productivity through people"	Commitment to and from employees
Chubb Insurance Company	"Underwriting excellence"	Summation of goals
New York Stock Exchange	"The world puts its stock in us"	Placement of exchange
Cyrix	"The liberation of information"	Semiconductors' technology role
TIAA CREF	"Ensuring the future for those who shape it"	Summation of goals
Ontario, Canada	"The future right here"	Emphasizes desirability of area
Hewitt	"Improving business results through people"	Importance of people

it wants "to give unlimited opportunity to women." Nike concludes that its vision is to experience the emotion of competition, winning, and crushing competitors (Collins & Porres, 1996).

Heroes personify the values of the culture and act as role models for other employees to follow. All of this information is transmitted through the cultural network. As the primary (and informal) means of communication within an organization, this cultural network is the "carrier" of the corporate values and the heroic mythology. Storytellers, spies, priests, cabals, and whisperers form a hidden hierarchy of power within the company and can be powerful spokespeople.

Metaphors

Metaphors operate as verbal statements about the organizational culture and reflect the individual member's perception (Offstein & Nick, 2003). They function to symbolize something as if it were something else (Borman & Deal, 2003). When we say the world's a stage we conjure up an image of people putting on performances with the goal of gaining audience acceptance. "Metaphors play a critical role in the communication process. They are the best devices to use when describing abstract concepts and expressing emotions" (Johnson & Hackman, 1995, p. 100). Metaphors, like stories and myths, compress complicated issues into understandable images and allow members to make sense out of the organization, discuss and understand change, and bridge the known with the unknown (Putnam & Fairhurst, 2001). They affect our attitudes and actions. For example, a college president who sees the university as a research center will act differently from one who sees the university as a teaching organization (Bolman & Deal, 2003). "Metaphors, then, are unique because they trigger an individual's memory and sensory capacities ..." (Offstein & Neck, 2003, p. 24).

If an organization is perceived as a fighting unit (military metaphor based on war), a well-oiled machine (structural and mechanistic metaphor based on machines), or a winning team (a sports metaphor based on games), three entirely different assumptions of reality are being presented. For a moment, consider the strengths and weaknesses of these types of metaphors (Clancy, 1989). The strengths for a war metaphor include being goal-oriented, recognizing the difficulty of the process, and expecting strong and courageous leadership. At the same time, it emphasizes destroying the opponent in order to claim victory. In the pursuit of destruction, few sacrifices are too great. We go on "missions," "attack" the problem, are "outgunned," and can be "loose cannons." The machine metaphor emphasizes predictability, efficiency, goal direction, and sees itself as a serious wealth-producing tool. It is very clear. However, it treats people in an unfeeling way and overemphasizes rationality. Game metaphors stress goals, fun, teamwork, and leadership, but fail to recognize the complexity and ambiguity of business. Underneath the game metaphor is a naïve stress on winning because all games require opponents

Table 4.6 Metaphors

Our department or organization or group or project or boss is (something else) …

Big happy family	Police department	Cornucopia
Athletic team	Santa Claus	Volcano
Zoo	Military unit	Battlefield
Well-oiled machine	Disneyland	Insane asylum
Play pen	Circus	Garbage can
Penitentiary	Garden	Snake pit
Pyramid	Boiling cauldron	Steamroller
Circle	Dragon	Swamp
Windmill	Quick sand	Stage
First class	Explorers	Warriors
Black hole	Family	Savior

Active Metaphors—Compare a Situation With These Active Concepts

Cooking a meal	Piloting an aircraft	Sailing a yacht
Fishing	Watching a video	Jogging
Climbing a mountain	Playing tennis	Sunbathing
Getting married	Reading a novel	Blogging

Metaphors Applied to the Four Frames

Frame	Metaphor
Structural	Well-oiled machine
Human Relations	Big, happy family or team
Political	Chain of command, enemies, troops
Symbolic	Family, greater vision

and winners. This metaphor permeates many organizational discussions. We use "teamwork," celebrate a "slam dunk," "huddle" over an issue, and see issues or people as "out in left field." Both the war and game metaphors have tended to minimize women because they are not as likely to have had athletic or military experiences (Cleary & Packard, 1992).

Throughout this discussion of metaphors, the difference in gender usage has not been highlighted. Whereas males are likely to focus on war and sports metaphors, women are more likely to utilize metaphors dealing with stronger relationships.

Table 4.6 presents some commonly used metaphors and shows how the four frames presented in chapter 3 can be applied. "One of the best ways, for instance, to identify a manager's style of managing is to listen carefully for the metaphors he or she uses when referring to the company, the job, or to employees" (Redding, 1984, p. 105).

Language and Management

Managers and supervisors are encouraged to use language that makes people feel good about themselves and the job they are doing. This demand for the use of positive reinforcement through language shows a strong belief in the power of the spoken word (Redding, 1984). In addition, numerous suggestions have been made for managers to learn to use the right word at the right time to enhance employee motivation. The trick, or needed insight, for the manager is to choose the correct wording for the situation by accurately perceiving the needed symbolic message. For example, managers must be adept at giving less than positive feedback in order to correct problems without damaging the relationship.

Not only is verbal communication used to motivate, it also is used to predict, control, manage, coordinate, and perpetuate organizations. Managers and others in charge define for employees, subordinates, and colleagues what is expected of them in a given situation.

Inconsistencies

When faced with difficult verbal communication situations, organizational members may choose to present inconsistent statements to maintain the strategic advantage of being able to claim deniability. Negotiators of contracts may "deliberately use ambiguous or unclear language to avoid squabbles that might slow down or prevent a settlement" (Scott & Bain, 1987, p. 10). This same pressure often influences the manager who may say one thing and mean quite another. As Table 4.7 shows, the stated message actually has a much deeper meaning. The difference between these messages and euphemisms is that managers are monitored directly by subordinates who must implement the vague statements because some *strategic ambiguities* in organizations can maintain interpersonal relationships and supporting status distinctions (Eisenberg, 1984). There are times when the only way to deal with apparently impossible situations is to be unclear. We all have been faced with a situation where a compliment was required for something we did not think was well done. So, we issued an ambiguous comment like: "that's certainly different," or "you don't see many done that way anymore," or "only you would think to put those items together."

Paradoxes also can occur in the nature of commands, such as the manager who tells you "don't regard everything I say as an order, and that's an order," or the parent who tells the child "I've told you a million times, don't exaggerate!" To be told that all generalizations about organizations are incorrect also would appear to be paradoxical, although perhaps true (another paradox). The need for more employee creativity has become apparent to many organizations. In response, they have ordered employees to "be creative" which, as you probably

Table 4.7 How to Distinguish Between a Subordinate You Like and a Subordinate You Do Not Like

The one you like	The one you do not like
Is aggressive	Is pushy
Is good on detail	Is picky
Gets depressed from work pressures	Can't stand the heat
Is confident	Is conceited
Drinks because of excessive work pressures	Is a lush
Is a stern taskmaster	Is impossible to work with
Is enthusiastic	Is emotional
Follows through	Doesn't know when to quit
Stands firm	Is bullheaded
Has sound judgment	Has strong prejudices
Isn't afraid to say what he/she thinks	Is mouthy
Is close-mouthed	Is secretive
Exercises authority	Is tyrannical
Climbed the ladder of success	Married into the boss's family

already have noticed, is a *paradoxical injunction*. It often can be turned into a *double-bind* when there is a time limit placed on when the solution must be ready. So, if the employee takes the time to be creative, the answer will be late. If the answer is on time, it might not be very creative.

The *oxymoron* provides a nice example of the paradoxical phrase. "An oxymoron is two concepts that do not go together but are used together. It is the *bringing together of two contradictory terms*" (Blumenfeld, 1986, p. 36). For example, neat freak, near-miss, even odds, justifiably paranoid, almost candid, intense apathy, postal service, deliberate speed, qualified success, almost perfect, eloquent (or deafening) silence, negative benefit, original copy, routine emergency, same difference, minimum competency, functional illiterate, pure filth, a firm maybe, extensive briefing, awfully good, objective rating, second deadline, constant variable, pretty ugly, perfect misfit, and pure nonsense are oxymorons that appear in a variety of organizations and conversations (Blumenfeld, 1986, 1989). Although many of these are humorous, a large number of these terms are actually the strategic use of ambiguity. By saying something is a qualified success, the originator of the comment still can criticize the outcome because the praise is carefully hedged.

Humor

Humor is an excellent example of the importance of incongruences. A great deal of humor is based on paradoxes and incongruences (Bateson, 1972;

Duncan & Feisel, 1989). Although managing and work are supposed to be "serious business," humor provides organizational members with a means for coping with the various paradoxes and incongruences that are inherent in any organized activity (Lippitt, 1982). Sometimes laughter is the best medicine for tough organizational situations that are steeped in tension (Gibson, Ivancevich, & Donnelly, 1991, p. 253). "Surgical teams, cockpit crews, and many other groups have learned that joking and playful banter are an essential source of invention and team spirit. Humor releases tension and helps resolve issues" (Bolman & Deal, 2003, p. 293). Female middle managers often use humor as they confront a paradox of being in such a position, because they are expected to be both subordinate and controlling simultaneously (Martin, 2004). In fact, "it is less important to ask why people are humorous in organizations than to ask why they are so serious" (Bolman & Deal, 2003, p. 268). Southwest Airlines "encourages its associates to be themselves; have fun; and, above all, use their sense of humor" (Bolman & Deal, 2003, p. 401). When you fly on Southwest, do not be surprised to hear a comedy routine or singing as the flight attendants deliver the required FAA safety briefing. The result? Passengers tend to listen more carefully because of the humor and incongruence.

Humor has numerous organizational uses. It can: share messages, relieve stress, motivate employees, make a point in a strategic manner, relay interest, enhance group behavior, facilitate team-building, reduce personality conflicts and resistance to change, unmask power relations, and allow the discussion of delicate issues without requiring a full commitment (Bolman & Deal, 2003; Dwyer, 1991; Harris & Sherblom, 2005; McClane & Singer, 1991). Among its many uses, "humor integrates, expresses skepticism, contributes to flexibility and adaptiveness, and indicates status. Humor is a classic device for distancing but it can also be used to socialize, include, and convey membership. Humor can establish solidarity and promote face-saving" (Bolman & Deal, 1984, p. 164). One organization, demanding that supervisors improve the work climate, found a plaque appearing that stated "firings will continue until morale improves." Because the supervisors could not openly question the order, paradox and humor were used to partially alleviate the stress.

Organizations use humor to draw attention to specific issues. Consider some actual business signs around the United States. On an electrician's truck: "Let us remove your shorts." In a veterinarian's waiting room: "Be back in 5 minutes. Sit! Stay!" In a nonsmoking area: "If we see you smoking we will assume you are on fire and take appropriate action." Outside a radiator repair shop: "Best place in town to take a leak."

A professor once remarked that teaching would be a great job if it were not for the students. Although his comment was funny, the paradox he raises actually exists when it comes to customer service. The professor may simply have been overworked because of pressures to publish and serve on committees. Table 4.7, in addition to highlighting inconsistencies, also points to the errors managers may make when they evaluate subordinates. Because it overstates the potential biases, managers can simultaneously smile at the examples and identify their own tendencies to make incorrect judgments and couch them in carefully terminology.

Organizations can be characterized in a humorous fashion. The Dilbert cartoon strip has become a famous debunker of management fads. Organizations are portrayed as organized anarchies where problems, solutions, participants, and choice opportunities interact almost in a random fashion as the organization moves toward the future (March & Olsen, 1976). Ideas and possible solutions are tossed into the garbage can. After enough people sift through the contents, some type of decision emerges out of a process of interpretation (Robey, 1991). Both depictions debunk the concept and perception of a rational model of organizations or decision making.

These characterizations strike a cord of reality for organizational researchers, or practicing managers, who are trying to make sense out of certain organizational behaviors. Organizations rarely are "tightly run ships" that concern themselves with rational decision making. One obvious limitation relates to the size of an organization. A small family business will operate with a much smaller "trash can," and probably will be a little less monstrous and octopoid, simply because the store or business must open on a daily basis. In addition, the chaotic description carries more validity with upper level management, who are in charge of the planning functions, than with frontline supervisors or managers. However, in both of these examples, the individuals involved still must deal with the external environment replete with whatever octopoid tendencies it may possess (e.g., government regulations, incompetent bosses, late delivery of supplies).

This short discussion underlines that a "both/and" perspective is most likely to assist you in understanding organizations. Organizations are chaotic and predictable. Decisions are justified after the fact and also carefully planned. Both are true and the popularity of Murphy's Laws may be attributable to the unpredictable nature of organizations, as shown in Table 4.8.

We have discussed the impact of stories, myths, metaphors, inconsistencies, and humor in organizations. The particular type of culture operating also has an effect on the verbal communication. In turn, the verbal communication perpetuates the predominant culture.

Conclusion

Verbal communication is a critical part of every organization's behavior system. It acts as the link between the various groups, subsystems, and individuals in the organization. Both written and oral communication are important, although practicing managers and supervisors prefer oral communication.

Language has a direct impact on our perception of our organizational reality. That reality is cognitive, affective, and narrative and we continually

Table 4.8 Murphy's Laws

1.	If anything can go wrong, it will.
2.	Nothing is as simple as it seems.
3.	Everything takes longer than you expect.
4.	If there is a possibility of several things going wrong, the one that will go wrong first will be the one that will do the most damage.
5.	If you play with something long enough, you will surely break it.
6.	Left to themselves, things go from bad to worse.
7.	If everything seems to be going well, you have obviously overlooked something.
8.	If you see that there are four possible ways in which a procedure can go wrong, and then circumvent these, then a fifth way, unprepared for, will probably develop.
9.	Nature always sides with the hidden flaw.
10.	It is impossible to make anything foolproof, because fools are so ingenious.
11.	If a great deal of time has been expended seeking the answer to a problem with the only result being failure, the answer will be immediately obvious to the first unqualified person.
12.	The other line moves faster.

Murphy's Law and the College Experience

1.	During an exam, the pocket calculator battery will fail.
2.	Exams will always contain questions not discussed in class.
3.	All students who obtain a B will feel cheated out of an A.
4.	Campus sidewalks never exist as the straightest line between two points.
5.	At 5 minutes before the hour, a student will ask a question requiring a 10-minute response.
6.	When a student finally does a homework assignment, the instructor will not ask for it.
7.	If an instructor says "it's obvious," it isn't.
8.	If students have to study, they will claim the course is unfair.
9.	Students who obtain an A for a course will claim the instructor is a great teacher.
10.	Books and materials on reserve, aren't!

move between these three perspectives. Language allows us to label parts of our working environment and, in so doing, provide signification. By naming someone blue collar, white collar, pink collar, gray collar, or gold collar, we both include and exclude individuals. *Gold collar* is a term being applied by personnel directors to recent college graduates who expect to receive lucrative jobs immediately upon graduation. Denotative and connotative meaning occur every time we use verbal communication. Calling someone a "suit" has a connotative meaning that is much more important than the denotative description of a person's working attire.

Two approaches provide important information regarding verbal communication. The first, based on semantics, explains the tendency of language to move from the specific to the general. When instructions are considered, for example, it is in the best interest of all concerned to make the information clear. Jargon is an excellent example of the impact of naming an organizational reality.

The second approach deals with an organization's need to function in spite of ambiguity. Common cultural appeals provide a direction. In addition, the lack of clarity allows appeals to much loftier and more abstract concepts. In the use of metaphors, myths, stories, and humor lies the impact of cultures and the capacity to motivate. For you to be successful in understanding a particular organization, you must understand both levels of language use in verbal communication.

Study Questions

1. Outline the importance of verbal communication to organizations. Provide specific examples from your own experience where verbal communication was important to your work.
2. What are some examples of the use of written communication in organizations?
3. Provide examples of the three levels of verbal communication.
4. Why are killer statements useful examples of the relationship between verbal communication and perception?
5. How does language relate to discrimination?
6. Provide an example of the difference between denotative and connotative meaning.
7. What are the key points of semantics? Provide higher education or work related examples.
8. Discuss, with your own examples, the various organizational uses of verbal communication.
9. Explain the different types of inconsistencies. Provide higher education or work related examples for each one.
10. How does humor help or hinder an organization?

5
Nonverbal Communication

Key concepts in this chapter include:

- Verbal versus nonverbal communication
- Principles of nonverbal communication
- Facial display, eye contact, paralanguage
- Body language
- Clothing
- Proxemics
- Chronemics

Overview

"Actions speak louder than words," "People believe what you do and more than what you say," and "You should walk the talk" are three familiar admonitions that express clearly the importance of nonverbal communication in organizations. Nonverbal communication is vitally important to communication effectiveness (Anderson, 1999). Depending on the expert, nonverbal communication comprises from 93% (Mehrabian, 1981) to 68% (Birdwhistell, 1970) of a message's meaning. One summary concluded that nonverbal messages "can convey affiliation, positive regard, interest, dominance, credibility, or status; can reinforce or punish; (and can) affect what others learn, what attitudes develop, what approaches will be modeled, and what is expected" (Tresch, Pearson, Munter, Wyld, & Waltman, 1986, p. 78).

Nonverbal communication principles have wide organizational applications. Topics range from helping managers and leaders increase their effectiveness to improving office design, to understanding organizational cultures (Anderson, 1999; Schein, 1992). International communication success can hinge on culturally appropriate nonverbal actions and our increasing need to be able to work in diverse groups requires an appreciation for differences in nonverbal expectations and behaviors (Calloway-Thomas, Cooper, & Blake, 1999; Chung, 1997). Nonverbal communication has important consequences when organizations try to flatten the organization and treat everyone as equals. Traditionally, "in everyday workplace encounters, nonverbal communication announces and reinforces the differences in status that exist between members of an organization" (Remland, 2000, p. 350). Nonverbal communication includes office setting, dress, expressions, and artifacts. Most organizations go to great lengths to create the desired impression on visitors, clients, and employees through office and building design (Adler & Towne, 2003).

Because understanding nonverbal communication carries an implicit sense of power, some consultants are tempted to provide advice that goes well beyond the scope of nonverbal studies. For example, in reviewing audiotapes for the businessperson, Case (1987) concluded:

> It would be nice if these were the worst of a bad lot (of business tapes). But surely that honor has to go to *The Power of Subliminal Selling* by Ken Delmar. Delmar has so much advice for salespeople! Like, always look at the prospect so he can see both your ears. With certain kinds of prospects, sit close—but watch their blinks and if they blink too much, move back. Keep your hands in a "log cabin, fingers interlaced, and "lay your log cabin on your lap or hold it just above your lap. Now psychologically, "you are safe inside your log cabin." And Delmar is *serious* about this. (p. 22)

This chapter outlines the aspects of nonverbal communication that are generally predictable, gives you specific advice about certain behaviors, and stays away from unsupported "log cabin" generalizations. In addition, we have incorporated examples of intercultural differences in nonverbal behavior. With globalization and increased diversity, you need to remember that Western researchers have conducted the majority of the research we examine and you would be well advised to carefully study the cultural needs and expectations in multicultural settings through additional readings.

Verbal versus Nonverbal Communication

The first step in understanding nonverbal communication is to define the concept and delineate the differences between verbal and nonverbal communication. The four major differences between verbal and nonverbal communication will make this definition more clear.

First, the majority of nonverbal behaviors is *intuitive* and is based on *normative rules*. Except for behaviors such as good manners or etiquette, little formal training is provided for nonverbal communication. On the other hand, verbal communication is highly structured and reinforced through an extensive formal and informal learning process. There is no clear-cut linguistic structure for nonverbal communication even through researchers have found some consistencies in how people interpret nonverbal behaviors (Nelson, 2004). Although nonverbal communication has little or no formal structure, it does have a natural set of rules that are recognized through cultural norms. The vast number of changes in organizations and cultural norms remind us that "nonverbal communication is influenced by a number of factors, including cultural background, socioeconomic background, education, gender, age, and personal preferences and idiosyncrasies (Beamer & Varner, 2001, p. 160).

Second, verbal communication is confined to the use of language. *Nonverbal communication, then, is any part of communication that does not use words.* For the sake of analysis, this is a useful division. However, "nonverbal communication is so inextricably bound up with verbal aspects of the communication process that we can only separate them artificially. In actual practice, such separation does not occur" (Knapp, 1972, p. v). There are nonverbal behaviors that stand by themselves, such as a hitchhiker's thumb, but most nonverbal communication occurs in conjunction with some verbal act. For example, silence becomes a significant nonverbal act because it represents a break in the verbal aspects of a transaction.

The *Waiter Rule* offers a useful example of the interrelatedness of nonverbal and verbal communication. Essentially, the rule is that "you can tell a lot about a person by the way he or she treats a waiter" (Jones, 2006, p. 1B). In other words, we all know to act correctly when we are talking to a CEO or some other person with power. However, many of these power people watch how we treat people without a great deal of power, such as receptionists who are often asked about how job candidates acted toward them while waiting for an interview to begin. BMW North America President Tom Purves, contends that the Waiter Rule is true everywhere. If we are rude to people serving us, but courteous those we consider important, we are using a situational value system, which means we can turn on the charm when we believe it is in our best interests. "Be especially wary of those who are rude to people perceived to be in a subordinate role" (Jones, 2006, p. 2B). Being rude is both a verbal and nonverbal set of behaviors, although it is likely that the nonverbal aspects are clearer examples of violating the rule.

Nonverbal communication *operates in the present and is highly dependent on the context*, which provides a third distinction, and an important defining characteristic. In chapter 1, we introduced the concept that one cannot *not* communicate along with nothing never happens. Both of these phrases apply very specifically to nonverbal communication. "We form instantaneous impressions of people—favorable and unfavorable—based on their facial features, body shape, height, clothing, tone of voice, gaze behavior, use of space, facial expressions, and so on" (Remland, 2003, p. 368). During transactions, we use the first 30 seconds to make judgments about others (Hayes, 1996). This seemingly quick time frame makes sense because we must decide how to respond to the other person as the transaction proceeds. The cues provided during the initial moments provide essential data that help to frame our communication. All intentional and unintentional behavior is *potentially meaningful* and your communication is rich with nonverbal behaviors. Any nonverbal behavior one or both parties choose to assign meaning to becomes communication. This third distinction also means that we cannot stop nonverbal communication without actually removing ourselves from the context.

These three lead to the fourth distinction. The communicative capability of nonverbal behavior is *dependent on the potential for a behavioral response* or feedback (Burgoon & Saine, 1978). A great writer, or an ineffective memo, always can be read at a different time or place and have meaning. Some type of response must occur to nonverbal behavior when it happens for the behavior to carry meaning and have an impact on the transaction.

Based on these four distinctions, you probably have concluded that nonverbal communication is less rule-bound than verbal communication and is judged more by the situational variables than the absolute correctness of the behavior. This is a valid conclusion.

The remainder of this chapter provides two means for further understanding nonverbal communication. First, based on the research used in this chapter, 14 principles can be generalized that apply to nonverbal communication. These include eight guiding principles for all nonverbal communication and six principles governing nonverbal communication in an organizational setting.

Second, specific nonverbal behaviors relevant to organizations are presented. These allow you to understand the manner in which nonverbal communication operates in an organization and, with some caution, to generalize to other behaviors.

Principles of Nonverbal Communication

The eight guiding principles for all nonverbal communication are:

1. The *quality of relationships* is judged through nonverbal cues (Hickson & Stacks, 1985; Remland, 2003). When people try and determine if they have a good, bad, or mediocre relationship, nonverbal cues provide the supporting information that indicates the strength of the bond. For example, although handshakes are standard fare in business transactions, how the handshake is given, including other concurrent nonverbal behaviors, gives the participants information about the relationship.

2. Nonverbal communication is *more likely to be believed* than is verbal communication when there is an inconsistency or incongruence between the two message systems (Knapp, 1972; Malandro & Barker, 1983; Mehrabian, 1981). Members of organizations sometimes are criticized because they "talk the talk but don't walk the walk."

3. Nonverbal communication can be *assigned meaning if only one of the parties chooses to do so* (Remland, 2003). Perception is the key term, as we discussed in chapter 2. Inadvertent actions on the part of one person still can be very meaningful to the other person. With the complexity of most organizations, the increase in multicultural and diverse work forces, and constant changes, a vast potential for nonverbal behaviors to become meaningful exists even when there

is no intent on the part of an individual. Fortunately, the overriding parameters for our behaviors, provided by the cultural norms, prevent a large number of miscues.

4. Because *perception is the key variable*, forward leans, relaxed posture, decreased distance, increased touching (both real and symbolic), and enhanced attention all seem to provide positive messages in a transaction (Hackman & Johnson, 2000). By doing the opposite, negative messages are perceived.

5. The *rules* for nonverbal behavior *vary depending on the age, sex, and the various cultures* involved (Remland, 2003). These cultures can include group, regional, organizational, national, and international and all the possible combinations of these five cultures. Therefore, the nonverbal rules in a group or organization are likely to have some highly idiosyncratic behaviors.

6. The *context, social situation, and power* relationships help determine the rules and roles for nonverbal communication (Anderson, 1999; Henley, 1997; Remland, 2003). Where the behavior occurs and with whom it occurs are vital to interpreting the nonverbal communication.

7. *Females are generally more sensitive* to nonverbal cues and more accurate in sending nonverbal messages (Anderson, 1999; Knapp, 1972).

8. Although people can learn to interpret others' nonverbal cues more accurately, *greater success* will be achieved by concentrating on *our own nonverbal behavior* to make it consistent with our desired message(s) (Hackman & Johnson, 2000).

These eight principles apply to all nonverbal communication. For the purposes of understanding organizational communication, we provide six additional principles that apply more specifically to organizations:

9. Applying the eight guiding principles is *contingent on the specific cultural expectations* of the organization. So, in addition to the general concept in Principle 5, occupational role(s), group affiliation(s), and any subculture(s) or coculture (e.g., management vs. union, faculty vs. administration, engineers vs. production, computer designers vs. computer users, nurses vs. doctors) all further clarify and define the specific, acceptable behaviors. In addition, the multicultural nature of modern organizations reminds us that there are three cultural variations in nonverbal communication. First, "cultures differ in the specific repertoire of behaviors that are enacted" (Lustig & Koester, 2003, p. 180). In other words, although most individuals can enact almost all nonverbal activities, our specific cultural background focuses us on specific behaviors and discourages us from using other behaviors. Second, as in the United States, there are specific, often unspoken, rules for when and where nonverbal expressions are appropriate or

inappropriate. Finally, our personal background provides the guide-lines to interpret others' nonverbal activities not based on the value of the activity, but on how well it fits into our own expectations.

10. By and large, *organizational cultures will reward individuals* who adapt nonverbal behaviors to cultural expectations, and punish those who do not. Both the rewards and punishments tend to be subtle and reflected in actions such as promotions, type of office space, or inclu-sion in meetings.

11. *Organizational members learn and adapt* their own nonverbal cues intuitively as they become part of the culture. Individuals tend to reflect more and more of the occupational or group behaviors exhib-ited by other members of the organization.

12. *Business settings* provide individuals with an opportunity to *prove their abilities at culture adaptation* and thereby increase acceptance (e.g., dress, manners, addressing behavior, punctuality; Korda, 1975; Molloy, 1988; Seitz, 2000).

13. In organizations, *nonverbal communication is more important* than verbal communication in *informal settings* (Richmond, McCroskey, & Payne, 1987). Power and affiliation are shown through nonverbal behavior. As with all nonverbal communication, credibility, asser-tiveness, and awareness of others are transmitted nonverbally. "Even the most trivial action in a face-to-face encounter can say something about the balance of power in that relationship" (Remland, 2003, p. 340). When we show deference to another, we are in an asymmetrical relationship that is quite likely in more formal organizations.

14. Because most nonverbal communication can be *interpreted in a vari-ety of ways*, conservative, "safe" behavior and most fundamentally *culturally sanctioned actions* are the norm in most organizational cultures. Organizations that support deviations from traditional dress standards communicate their acceptance through the culture.

These 14 guiding principles are presented at the beginning of this chapter because most nonverbal experts agree on their importance in understand-ing and using nonverbal communication. Note this important caveat. As the digital revolution continues, globalization increases, and multicultural work-places become prevalent, some of these principles will change.

Finally, Table 5.1 presents the six specific nonverbal organizational com-munication functions.

In conclusion, there are 14 specific principles that can be applied to the gen-eral understanding of nonverbal communication. We now discuss facial dis-play, eye contact, paralanguage, body language, appearance, and proxemics.

Table 5.1 Functions of Nonverbal Communication

Functions	Explanation and Examples
Repetition	Reinforcing verbal messages with nonverbal behaviors. *Examples*: Supervisors moving their arms while giving instructions. Telling and showing someone how to do a task. Giving an O.K. signal or a pat on the back along with verbal praise.
Substitution	Using a nonverbal behavior in place of a verbal one. *Examples*: A head nod to indicate "yes," "a pat on the back," a "knowing glance," or a "thumbs up" for success. When the action is symbolic, it is called an *emblem*.
Accentuation	Nonverbal vocalizations can provide emphasis. *Examples*: The loudness of a person's voice often conveys the true strength of the message. A secret can be forecast by a whisper. A wink or furrowed brow *can* add to the impact of the verbal message. Distance *can* indicate seriousness.
Contradiction	The nonverbal and verbal messages are incongruent. *Examples*: A colleague's facial expression or vocal inflection gives a message opposite to the verbal one. *Sarcasm* is one of the best examples because the tone of voice provides a meaning that is quite different from the stated one. Making someone wait and then telling them they are important is an example. Someone asks what is wrong *because* of your appearance and you say, defensively, "nothing" is another example.
Regulation	Using nonverbal behaviors to initiate, continue, interrupt, or terminate interactions. *Examples*: Eye contact, gestures, nods, head motions, and numerous other behaviors indicate how the interaction should progress.
Complementing	Using nonverbal messages to supplement, expand, modify, or provide details to a verbal message. *Examples*: Looking confident while conducting a briefing enhances the quality of the presentation. Speaking softly while discussing delicate information.

Facial Display

Your face provides vital information regarding your own internal views about how things are going. "The face is the most extraordinary communicator, capable of accurately signaling emotion in the bare blink of a second, capable of concealing emotion equally well" (Blum, 1998, pp. 33–34).

With no formal training, observers of facial expressions can distinguish a varied range of emotions including interest/excitement, enjoyment/joy, surprise/startle, distress/anguish, shame/humiliation, anger/rage, contempt/disgust, and fear/terror. "Facial expressions are largely universal, products of biological imperatives" with six expressions—anger, fear, sadness, disgust, surprise, and happiness—that seem to be hardwired into our brains (Blum, 1998, p. 34). However, it is important to remember that the face can twist into 5,000 expressions ranging from a grin to a sneer making our interpretation of any facial expression open to challenge. One person's grin might be another person's grimace. Idiosyncrasies based on cultural backgrounds should encourage all of us to use great caution in believing we can read a person's facial display like a book. "Expressions aren't dictated by biology alone, however; they are deeply influenced by cultural attitudes" (Blum, 1998, p. 37).

In organizations, we tend to work toward less facial expression so that we can control the setting. Showing too much excitement, joy, rage, or humiliation is not considered professional in many settings. One consultant advises: "Your object should be to showcase your positive feelings and to disguise your negative feelings, unless letting them show will help you get something accomplished" (Gray, 1983, p. 28). We are quite adept at hiding our emotions, which is an expected behavior in most organizational cultures and in interpersonal relationships (Adler & Towne, 2003). This is enhanced by the lack of specific cues that directly correlate to internal feelings. "What scientists know for certain is that we are surprisingly bad at discerning the real emotions or intentions behind others' facial expressions" (Blum, 1998, p. 39).

Increased facial pleasantness enhanced an individual's persuasive success (Burgoon, Birk, & Pfau, 1990). In other words, stoic facial displays are not the key to motivating others. A practical interpretation of a pleasant perception is provided by the analysis of the "100 Best Companies to Work For," which has been featured every January in *Fortune* magazine. For the most part, these organizations encourage a fun-oriented setting that we can assume includes a decent number of happy and pleasant faces. However, each company has different expectations and cultural definitions regarding how fun should be displayed (Colvin, 2006; Levering & Moskowitz, 2006).

Three specific areas of facial display provide useful examples. They are smiles, hair, and makeup.

Smiles

The smile is illustrative of how the face is used. Although a smile can be indicative of a wide range of feelings ranging from happiness to nervousness, in the Western business world, smiles generally are considered positive communication behaviors. "Smiles are such an important part of communication that we can see them far more clearly than any other expression. We can pick up a smile at 300 feet—the length of a football field" (Blum, 1998, p. 34). Finally, a smile's message—along with feelings of anger, disgust, fear, happiness, sadness, and surprise, when expressed through facial changes—is internationally recognizable from simple photographs (Ekman & Friesen, 1987). The smile is the most recognizable signal in the world (Blum, 1998). You will want to take careful note of the fact that smiles are interpreted differently depending on the culture. In Western culture, smiles generally mean happiness or confidence, but in "Chinese society, a smile can disguise embarrassment, mask bereavement, or conceal rage" (Calloway-Thomas, et al., 1999, p. 165). "Germans smile, but not nearly as much as people in the United States. Koreans consider it inappropriate for adults to smile in public" (Beamer & Varner, 2001, pp. 164–165).

Several generalizations can be made regarding smiles and we concentrate on Western organizations. Smiling people are perceived as more intelligent and credible than those who do not smile (Gass & Seiter, 1999). Studies have shown that smiling and nodding increases waitresses' tips, increases positive impressions of job interviewees and helps them get jobs, and influences positively the student–teacher interaction (Gass & Seiter, 1999). However, as we already indicated with our discussion of Western versus Chinese smiles, correctly interpreting a smile's meaning can be difficult because smiles have at least 19 versions (Blum, 1998).

Smiles are controlled by the power relationships in an organization. A recent study "confirms that differences in power are manifested in facial display. The more powerful person, whether male or female, has the license to smile when he or she feels positively inclined and not to smile when he or she does not feel so inclined" (Hecht & LaFrance, 1998, p. 1343). People with less power are more obligated to smile whether they find the interchange to be valuable or not. How often have you displayed an appreciative smile or perhaps laughed at a professor's or superior's story regardless of its intrinsic value? Perhaps a more telling question is how often have you "wiped a smile off of your face" because to smile would have offended someone in power?

Increased smiling by the presenter resulted in greater compliance by the receivers to a persuasive attempt (Liss, Walker, Hazelton, & Cupach, 1993). Smiling, within the culturally approved parameters, is a worthwhile nonverbal facial gesture. In our increasingly multicultural settings, however, smiles do not always indicate the same feelings. How the smile and face are framed add to the nonverbal message. Our particular hairstyle is a good example.

Hair

As a general rule, organizations seek individuals who fit into their particular cultural expectations that establish the prevailing norms. The organization's culture and relationship with its environment (e.g., customers, clients) help determine the expectations regarding hair. Disneyland and Disney World strive for a clean-cut image, so they forbid moustaches and beards for men, whereas many digitally oriented companies have a different set of hair standards.

Changing our hair's style, length, location (e.g., beards), or amount are all examples of *body adaptors*. Body adaptors are different from the mostly reflexive movements called *adaptors*, such as scratching our head or drumming our fingers that are learned early in life. You will recall that the fifth general principle indicated that nonverbal rules vary depending on the age, sex, and cultures involved. This principle certainly applies to facial displays for men and women in organizations. To demonstrate this point, we consider a gender-specific issue for men and women that underscores the overall importance of understanding how nonverbal communication operates in organizations.

Emotions

The showing of emotions through overt actions, such as crying, stands as a clear violation of most organizational cultures: "The impact of tears depends on the field you're in, the company's culture and what's tolerated in a particular setting. In highly creative fields such as TV, public relations, and advertising, people aren't expected to be as much under control as in banking, law, accounting, and corporate business" (Edelson, 1987, p. D4). In addition, studies show that there is a double standard regarding crying at work based on the traditional "men don't cry but women do" bias (Adler & Towne, 2003; Butler, 1987; Edelson, 1987; O'Connell, 1991). Many males withhold overt emotion and simply strive to get even or dodge the bullet, whereas some females are more likely to cry to express anger or frustration (Plas & Hoover-Dempsey, 1989). Many organizational cultures are not oriented toward highly creative activities, so overly emotional displays, such as crying, simply are rejected as being inappropriate. In a survey of 8,033 *Working Women* readers, 78% said "crying in the office quashes professionalism" (Hellmich, 1988, p. D1). The point is, of course, that the behavior is examined in light of the expectations established by the cultural norms and not the legitimacy of the behavior itself.

The inherent link between emotions and nonverbal behaviors can be demonstrated by examining e-mail, a primarily verbal communication technology. *Emoticons*, the symbolic short cuts used to express certain feelings, are often added to replace the absence of nonverbals. For example, ;-) is winking (semicolon, dash, right parentheses); :-D is laughing (colon, dash, capital letter D); or >:-[is mad (right arrow, colon, dash, left bracket). These shortcuts are explained at www.chatlist.com but be warned—some of the emoticons are a bit racy. Most important is our apparent need to add nonverbal explanations to our verbal messages (also, see chap. 12). The impact of facial displays including smiles, hair adaptations, and emotions—underscores the general principles provided at the beginning of this chapter.

Eye Contact

Eyes have a special place in folklore and are often seen as an entryway to deeper meaning. People are accused of having shifty or evil eyes or observed as possessing bedroom or laughing eyes. Eye contact can express interest, attraction, intimacy, dominance, persuasiveness, aggressiveness, and credibility (Burgoon & Dillman, 1995).

Why do the eyes have such an impact? First, eye contact serves as *simultaneous communication* because it allows people to send and receive messages at the same time. This power to engage in an ongoing communication pattern may account for eye contact's popularity as a potential technique for increasing influence and judging the other's character. Direct eye contact is seen as an indication of honesty and credibility (Burgoon & Saine, 1978). In seminars we have conducted with professional interviewers, they are convinced that direct eye contact, which should be distinguished from staring, is an indication of self-confidence and forthrightness. Eye contact ranks second only to dress as an important nonverbal factor in an interview (Burgoon, Buller, & Woodall, 1996).

Too often, we attempt to determine if someone is being truthful by observing eye contact. "Three major statistical summaries of deception research show no statistically significant, overall relationship between eye contact and deception" (Anderson, 1999, p. 285). In fact, generally "the evidence linking eye contact and attributions of personality traits are correlational" meaning there is no direct link (Droney & Brooks, 1993, p. 715). In addition, individuals attempting to deceive others probably are aware of the importance of eye contact and studies have shown that deceivers may actually increase eye contact (Anderson, 1999).

Returning to our discussion on perceptual bias (chap. 2), an untrained or misinformed organizational member could misinterpret a lack of eye contact or an adverted gaze as an indication of dishonesty and act on their misperception. Perhaps even more important, diversity concerns and multinational changes require us to reexamine our view of eye contact. "…Chinese and Indonesians lower their eyes as a sign of respect. Prolonged eye contact is considered rude in Japan and the Philippines, but expected in Arab countries" (Calloway-Thomas et al., 1999, p. 166). Americans believe it is important to look someone in the eye, but in France, eye contact can be frequent and intense enough to intimidate some Americans (Calloway-Thomas et al., 1999). During listening, African Americans are more likely to make eye contact whereas Caucasian Americans tend to look away while listening (Gardenswartz & Rowe, 1993). If we firmly believe there is a direct link between another's eye contact and other behaviors, such as interest or listening, we are in danger of being incorrect in our multicultural organizational world.

How important are these distinctions and insights? Too often, advice is provided to managers based on shaky experiential observations. For example, in *Motivating People*, Heller (1998) concludes, "Confident eye contact is also important as a measure of motivation: demotivated people are less likely to look you straight in the eye" (p. 12). So much for that manager's brilliant and motivated Chinese computer whiz! In addition, what is confident eye contact? Even if Heller was correct in terms of a traditionally male-dominated white culture, his 1998 advice is dangerously out of touch with the modern diverse workplace and with research.

We can conclude that *status and power are shown through the use of eye contact*. In meetings, organizational members with the most power will be looked at more often (Duncan, 1975). Leaders can gaze more directly and with greater frequency than subordinates (Remland, 2003). Showing deference to power often is accomplished through diminished eye contact by subordinates putting further doubt on Heller's conclusions regarding eye contact.

Interestingly, speakers attribute more control and power to receivers who do not look at them (Burgoon & Saine, 1978). This may be due to the lack of simultaneous feedback. A total elimination of eye contact with reflective sunglasses creates a "Darth Vadar" effect that can cause fear and resentment in the receiver (Boyanowsky & Griffiths, 1982). Because all possibility for feedback is eliminated, receivers feel as if they have lost control of the transaction. Law enforcement groups attach importance to dark or one-way sunglasses. But once this artifact is positioned with the law enforcement culture's concern for control and power, their insistence on sunglasses makes sense.

You are seen as being more *honest and qualified* if you *gaze more* while speaking (Anderson, 1999). Dominant people gaze longer and advert their gaze less. However, once you achieve high status and power, you can choose not to use eye contact and this decision will have little impact, because the power differential is already known. This should not be taken as an endorsement for not using eye contact as you progress upward in an organization. Excellent leaders utilize strong interactive skills including eye contact (Anderson, 1999).

Eye contact also is used to *control interactions*. This regulating of the flow of the transactions can be simply failing to acknowledge someone's presence. Clearly, the potential for a response from someone is decreased if the amount of eye contact is minimal. Studies indicate eye contact is diminished during the telling of bad news or the providing of critical feedback. Eye contact is used to monitor feedback. Listeners and speakers tend to look away when a difficult subject is being discussed (Knapp, 1978; Remland, 2003).

In general, eye contact is a powerful means for establishing relationships and indicating an open, honest approach. Once you become more familiar with the specific cultural requirements, you can better judge how to use eye gestures. Certainly, it would appear to be a must in an interview situation. Any presentation will be assigned greater credibility if you use eye contact. Staring is not an acceptable norm in most organizations. Because we believe in the importance of eye gestures, we should pay attention to how they are used in a particular organizational setting.

Paralanguage

The manner in which something is said is *paralanguage,* which includes accents, emphases, vocal qualities, pitch, rate, pauses, silences, (a form of vocalic behavior), and anything that adds to the meaning we associate with the verbal (Anderson, 1999). *Paralanguage* includes a large group of behaviors such as pitch, time, rate, silence, and other vocal behaviors that add to the words. Sometimes referred to as *vocalics,* these behaviors provide information about emotions, reinforce meanings, and demonstrate understanding of the specific organizational communication skills expected. "Three emotions frequently experienced on the job—anger, boredom, and joy—can often be interpreted from voice quality" (DuBrin, 2000, p. 297). Paralanguage "affects not only (people's) credibility, but their ability to persuade as well" (Gass & Seiter, 1999, p. 177).

For example, the *rate of speech* affects credibility and attractiveness. Within reason, listeners judge a speaker as being more competent as the rate of speech increases (Street & Buddy, 1982). The same study found that listeners see a speaker as more attractive if he or she speaks at a more rapid rate. Conversely, the slowest rate of speaking is the least attractive. In fact, "people who spoke faster, louder, and more fluently and who varied their vocal frequency and intensity were perceived as more persuasive than those who did not" (Gass & Seiter, 1999, p. 177).

Voice quality illuminates the point. A person's accent or dialect, whether it is foreign, southern, general American speech, or any other, does have an impact on the initial impression, although the effect is short-term (Burgoon & Saine, 1978). A pleasing voice logically would make people more likely to listen to us. A conversational voice is seen as more attractive and as indicating a better education and a higher socioeconomic position than a dynamic voice (Pearce & Brommel, 1972; Pearce & Conklin, 1971).

Silence has at least two important uses. First, it can create interpersonal distance (Marlando & Barker, 1983; Remland, 2003). In response to a variety of emotions, individuals simply may choose to remain silent thereby symbolically withdrawing from active participation in the transaction. Interpreting another's silence is more complex because these emotions can range from fear to a desire to hurt someone. In a conflict situation, for example, remaining silent can be the wisest response available.

Second, silence is used in response to authority. Most individuals will allow the more powerful organizational member to speak and are willing to remain silent until the authority figure indicates they can respond (Burgoon, Buller, & Woodall, 1996). The communication impact of silence is not limited to showing respect. Defying authority by remaining silent also can send a strong message (Bruneau, 1973; Newman, 1982; Remland, 2003). In all cases, silence sends a message and knowing when to use silence is an important communication skill.

Paralanguage, those nonverbal attributes that add meaning to the language, are important in impression formation, credibility, and strategic avoidance of certain situations through the use of silence.

Body Language

Kinesics, or the study of body language, provides important information regarding behaviors in an organization. Without even using body movement, a person's height and physique send a message.

Physical Characteristics

Height seems to reflect a gender difference with greater height being a positive for males. "Height conveys status" (Remland, 2003, p. 341). For example, a male executive's height can be correlated to his job prospects and salary. In a study of 1,433 alumni of the University of Pittsburgh's Graduate School of Business, the average 6-ft tall man earns $6,000 a year more than does one who is 5 ft 4 in. tall (Olson & Frieze, 1987). Frieze, one of the study's authors, concluded that we subconsciously view taller men as being dominant and assertive.

These same biases were observed in a study of the hiring practices used for picking prospective high school principals (Bonuso, 1979). Roughly identical resumes were sent to New York State school superintendents with pictures that varied in body type from short/overweight to tall/ideal weight. The superintendents judged the tall, lean applicants as most qualified, and their ratings fell consistently with shorter, heavier applicants. Finally, a person's beginning salary is correlated to their height (Knapp, 1978). From a business perspective, a lack of height can be considered a sign of inferiority. We can fall short of a goal, think small, be shortsighted, or be looked down on. The Pittsburgh study revealed gender differences (Olson & Frieze, 1987). Of the 349 women surveyed, tall women were not significantly better paid than shorter ones. Although looks should have no impact on how well a person is paid, "the wage differential for attractive and ugly people is about 10% for both sexes" (Barro, 1998, p. 18).

Overweight individuals are vulnerable to job discrimination. "A team of Chicago psychologists reports that overweight job applicants, especially women, are highly susceptible to employment bias. Even moderately overweight is a minus" (Ianzito, 1995, p. 18). Employers discriminate against overweight people, especially women, when comes to hiring, firing, demotions, and pay levels. In fact, "weight discrimination is more common than discrimination based on other factors, including race and gender" ("Weight Discrimination," 1999, p. D1). The Pittsburgh Graduate School of Business survey (Olson & Frieze, 1987) cited earlier found men judged to be 20% or more overweight earned $4,000 less than men of average weight.

Being more physically fit probably does allow an individual to project greater self-confidence, which could work to a person's advantage in an organization (Cash, Winstead, & Janda, 1986). Height, attractiveness, and weight offer nonverbal messages, however inaccurate, to others. How we use our physical attributes also communicates.

Body Movement and Gestures

How individuals use their bodies provides messages to other organizational members. Specific characteristics include synchrony, gestures, and etiquette that offer useful insights into how organizations evaluate body movement and gestures.

Synchrony   Have you ever felt that you just clicked with someone else? Seemed to just get along from the very beginning? You may have been experiencing interpersonal synchrony. Establishing synchrony in interpersonal body movements is a basic characteristic of successful communication between equals and rhythm seems to be the fundamental glue by which cohesive discourse is maintained (Remland, 2003). This rhythmic *interactional synchrony* varies from culture to culture and job to job and may be critical to how well individuals communicate and work with others (Anderson, 1999). *Mirroring*, which is to imitate an individual subtly, can be used to achieve rapport (DuBrin, 2000). For example, adjusting your rate of speaking to the other person's rate can enhance rapport. Obviously, this must be done with some acumen or you will appear to be mocking someone. The goal is to get in sync to reduce possible nonverbal differences and possible barriers.

Numerous studies indicate that higher status individuals in an organization can have a more relaxed posture and greater movement so they are less likely to engage in synchrony with subordinates (Burgoon & Saine, 1978; Remland, 2003). Power can be asserted by not adapting to a subordinate's movements.

Gestures   Gestures in an organization tend to be evaluated based on how well the movements reinforce or challenge the existing relationships. Using the appropriate gestures for specific situations is important.

Power is reinforced through gestures (Henley, 1977; Remland, 2003). Subordinates are expected to display appropriate attention to superiors through correct facing behaviors, apt attention, and tightness of stance. Superiors can manipulate their body movements and gestures in order to enhance the quality of the interaction whereas subordinates are more likely to be expected to fit the cultural norm of subdued attendance. "The higher status person is always freer (in nonverbal movement) than the lower status person" (Henley, 1977, p. 103). "Sitting with one's leg over the arm of the chair, straddling a chair turned backwards, sitting with one's feet on one's desk, and leaving the jacket unbuttoned, hand in pocket (thumb out)—said to indicate superiority—can be seen as examples of relaxation gestures, which can be correlated to status" (p. 126).

Authority or dominant organizational members can point as a means of ordering others whereas subordinates would be violating cultural norms to direct superiors through pointing back (Seigel, Friedlander, & Heatherington, 1992).

In the United States, the palm of the hand seems to indicate openness, whereas the back of the hand has the opposite connotation. Being given the back of the hand means we are striking others—either figuratively or actually, and clenched fists or slicing movements carry very strong meanings. Most of us have been schooled not to point and this advice applies to organizational behavior as well. Pointing is a clear dominance behavior usually reserved for schoolteachers or the blaming process. So, you would be safe to conclude that movements indicating withdrawal or aggression should be avoided unless the circumstances clearly dictate them.

Hand gestures can indicate a wide array of meanings. *Illustrators*, movements that enhance the message by literally adding nonverbal reinforcement, are positive, are expected with dynamic individuals, and increase the likelihood of message acceptance (McGinley, LeFevre, & McGinley, 1965). *Adaptors*, which include various self-touching behaviors, are taken as indications of nervousness or quasi-courtship. Because nervousness and quasi-courtship behaviors challenge organizational norms, they provoke negative meanings and can reduce persuasiveness (Gass & Seiter, 1999). As we indicated earlier in this chapter, these adaptors are different from body adaptors, which are changes we make to our body's appearance.

In 2004, the president of Maspro Denkoh Corp., a Japanese electronics company, used *jankenpo* to decide whether Christie's or Sotheby's would sell his multimillion-dollar art collection (Crick, 2005). Known in the United States as Rock–Paper–Scissors (RPS), this apparently simple two person game where the opponents make a fist, count to three together, and expose one of three weapons—rock, paper, or scissors—provides a dramatic example of the power of overt gestures. The rules are clear: paper covers rock, rock blunts scissors, and scissors cut paper. The game can be traced to the Pacific Rim before it migrated to Europe in the 17th century as trade between the regions increased. Why use this approach? Although flipping a coin is a random approach, RPS involves an attempt to predict your opponent's intentions and keep your opponent from nonverbally predicting your moves. Thought-Works Inc., a Chicago-based IT services company allows its 700 employees to quickly break ties with RPS to keep the business moving forward. Kayak suppliers Harmony and Werner Paddles both named their new paddle Cascadia. Rather than going to court to decide who could use the name, they held a Kayak tug-of-war in a demo pool between Harmony's vice president and Werner's president (Hindo, 2004, p. 11). Harmony won and this nonverbal gesture saved time and prevented long-term resentments.

Globalization and increased diversity at the workplace requires some caution in using traditional U.S. gestures. Consider the following examples.

Raising our arms and moving the open hand back and forth in North America signals hello, goodbye or an attempt to get attention. In much of Europe this action signals "No!" Europeans raise their arms and bob their hand up and down in a basketball dribbling motion to signal hello or goodbye. The "OK" gesture made by forming a circle with the thumb and forefinger with the other three fingers pointing outward means "zero" or worthless in France, and is a profane gesture in parts of Europe and the world. "Thumbs up" in the United States means "good job" or "OK" —in Nigeria it is considered a rude gesture, in Japan it is used to count as the number 5, and in Germany it is used to count as the number 1 (Axtell, 1991). Gestures are vital nonverbal signals, but the interpretation is culturally bound.

Etiquette   Etiquette provides a good example of the impact of gestures. Although etiquette clearly includes verbal behaviors, such as correct introductions, titles, and addressing, good manners also demand close adherence to specific nonverbal expectations. Professionals are interested in etiquette because a great deal of executive business occurs in social settings (Beamer & Varner, 2001). A gaffe or *faux pas* may signal that the individual lacks the acumen to be granted credibility in forthcoming business dealings. In the commercial world, "bad manners might actually spoil a corporate image, hamper a deal, impede mobility" (Visser, 1991, p. 339). The U.S. Office of Consumer Affairs' study concluded that 91% of all customers would stop doing business with a company that offends them as a result of inappropriate etiquette (Rucker & Sellers, 1998).

During the job interviewing process, for example, candidates must accept that they are on stage and are being judged for the quality of their performance. "Employers want people who know how to live in a social world and interact in a business environment" (Forbes, 1990, p. C10). The judging process can be quite specific. J. C. Penney and Henry Ford based their management hiring decisions on whether or not candidates salted their food before tasting it (Sabath, 1990). Their reasoning, valid or not, was that someone who salts their food before tasting it implies they make decisions before checking all the facts—taste first, then season; or out of the force of habit—does not make the best decision, just the usual one. Although Penney and Ford may have been rash and their actions indicative of a perceptual bias (e.g., chap. 2), their preconceived notion of correct etiquette demonstrates how important actions can be in the organizational environment.

Organizations pay for employees to attend etiquette seminars. In return, individuals learn the following skills and reasons: Give clients the preferred seat in a restaurant—a power and deference move; keep jackets buttoned when standing, unbuttoned when seated—a willingness to accept cultural norms; place handbags and brief cases out of sight during meals—a statement that business will not be discussed before meals; and, do not drink alcohol or smoke unless the client does. Although all of this might sound obvious to you, organizations are attempting to reduce a *faux pas* that could damage a business relationship. These same general guidelines apply to individuals on a job interview, except interviewees should not drink hard liquor or smoke, even if invited to, or raise business matters before the host does (Mitchell, 1991). Company parties often act as opportunities for managers to prove they can demonstrate the correct behaviors, not drink too much, or draw too much negative attention (Raudsepp, 1983). Increasingly, business travelers are drinking less or choosing not to drink during business meals fearing they might say or do the wrong thing or give the wrong image (Nathan, 1999).

To a significant degree, properly performed etiquette goes unnoticed. Errors, as violations of expectations, can create unwanted attention to our lack of culture knowledge. Acceptable behavior is important and social occasions prove our acumen in this arena. On a broader scale, being socially awkward provides the wrong nonverbal impression in many organizational settings allowing us to be discredited.

Internationally, as you can well imagine, proper manners become even more complex. "Giving a gift seems simple. But in the tricky world of international business, this courtesy requires forethought. Otherwise, the giver risks a humiliating, deal-destroying blunder" (Speer, 1999, p. 3E). In some countries, give a gift that's too big or too pricey, and you run the risk of bribery charges. There are infamous gift-giving examples. A California construction company gave green baseball caps, intended as a friendly gesture underscoring a mutual enthusiasm for the sport, to top Taiwanese company executives at a meeting. Little did they realize that to traditional Taiwanese, green caps symbolize another pastime: adultery. The Americans unwittingly had accused their associates of having unfaithful wives. Even the process of accepting a gift varies. Americans, when handed a gift, open it immediately. Asians keep it low key, opening the present at the end of the meeting (Dunung, 1998).

Synchrony, gestures, and etiquette provide clear examples of the importance of movement. Surrounding these concepts is our clothing.

Clothing

Clothing or body covering is the single largest nonverbal cue we provide and it carries significant symbolic messages. What we wear tells others who we are, accurately or not, and/or who we want to be. The increasing adoption of Western dress in other parts of the industrial world signals one trend. Simultaneously, there is an adherence to traditional dress (e.g., the Japanese kimono, the African dashiki, the Amish black clothing) and coculture-specific dress standards. Every organization has written and/or unwritten codes regarding dress. Desiring to put the best image forward, organizations recognize that "clothing is a symbol interpreted by the perceiver in the process of impression formation, and it can influence perceptions of not only behavior, but intent" (Galin, 1990, p. 51).

Clothing and Messages

For a variety of reasons, clothing is very important to organizations. Regardless of the type of business, some dress requirements exist and the rationale is clear. Clothing communicates culture (Remland, 2003). "It is difficult to wear clothes without transmitting some type of message. Every costume tells a story, often a very subtle one, about its wearer. Even those people who insist they despise attention to clothing and dress as casually as possible, are making specific comments on their social roles and their attitudes towards the culture in which they live and work" (Morris, 1977, p. 213). So, if we indicate that we feel no need to conform to certain dress standards, we are revealing our own lack of awareness regarding the impact of clothing in organizations. Because "clothing is a potent—and highly visible—medium of communication" it "carries a flood of information about who a person is, who a person is not, and who a person would like to be. It is an important mediator of social life" (Morris, 1977, p. 216).

Casual Dress

A great deal changed in the 1990s regarding dress codes. IBM shed its dark suits and starched white shirts for men, and dresses and skirts for women (Berger, 1995). These changes in dress standards vary. "In some companies, it could mean a sport coat and colored shirt with a tie; in others, it could mean cutoff shorts and sandals. Corporate culture and customer preferences should dictate the style" (Hendricks, 1995, p. 81). Of the "100 Best Companies to Work for the America" in 1998, 75 have a casual dress policy every day. What started out in many companies as dress down or casual Fridays evolved into a casual day every day (Hendricks, 1996). A 1996 survey by Levi-Strauss found that "90% of employees have some casual days, and 83% are full-time casual" (Solomon, 1996, p. 51). Caggiano (1997) reported a 1997 survey that "revealed that casual or 'business casual' dress is standard at more than one third of the nation's fastest-growing privately held companies" (p. 148). "About 55% of employers allow casual dress once a week, down from 60% in 2001" (Armour, 2005, p. 1B). In fact, "the majority of people who work full time in an office setting have a dress code … with just 26% allowed to don casual work attire. Most—64%—work under a business casual requirement" (Armour, 2005, p. 1B).

When organizations feel dress standards are declining and potentially creating an image problem, they tend to impose specific requirements. For example, "the National Basketball Association now requires players to dress in business casual when on team or league business. The policy bans sleeveless shirts, shorts, and T-shirts and requires players on the bench and not in uniform to don a sports coat" (Armour, 2005, p. 1B). Other organizations are setting new dress rules, including no tight or revealing clothing, wearing suit jackets, dressing more formally, no jeans, and no sweats, shorts, or capri pants ("Dressing Smartly," 2003).

What is casual? In many cases, *dress down codes are just as restrictive as previous dress codes* and "corporate expectations can be as tough on grownups as peer pressure is for high school teens" (Peak, 1994, p. 31). You can still be out of "uniform" by dressing in an inappropriate manner. In response to perceived abuses in the casual dress unwritten code, "the number of companies permitting casual attire has declined for the first time since 1992" according to a 2000 Society for Human Resources Management poll (Armour, 2000, p. 1A). Reacting to the increase in tank tops, sweatshirts, and open-toed shoes in the workplace, "34% of the execs polled by Management Recruiters International" say "sloppy dressers are crossing the line" (Prasso, 2001, p. 8).

Finally, certain professions have not changed their dress standards dramatically. Studies of accounting firms, for example, observe an "equally important unwritten code ... that men must wear a suit and tie—not a sports jacket—every day. Women may wear pants suits" (Fortune et al., 1995, p. 41). Even when casual is accepted, "employers ... are realizing that they must look professional in order to build credibility with investors and clients" (Armour, 2000, p. 2A). Besides obvious comfort and fashion trends, what led to these changes in dress standards?

Casual Dress and Organizational Uses

Before you conclude that organizations are simply caving in to trends, we need to emphasize that organizations perceive clear benefits. Research generally indicates that when employees are allowed to dress more casually, their morale, as well as their productivity, increases significantly (Jones, 1996). In a 1997 survey, 85% of human resource managers said that casual wear improves productivity (Mannix, 1997). The casual dress trend is not just occurring in the United States.

In Japan, "strict conformity to the office dress code has been blamed for complacency and lack of imagination" (Terazono, 1995, p. 34). As a result, Hitachi has encouraged its employees to shed their coats and ties for polo shirts and slacks to stimulate creativity (Associated Press, 1999). They are also eliminating titles for personal names and abandoning the daily routine of morning calisthenics. Culture changes slowly. Many employees in Japan "do not believe that 'Fridaywear' will help them or the company discover new horizons, nor do they feel the need to find them" (Terazono, 1995, p. 34).

In a sense, dress standards are a work-in-progress because there is an equally strong trend toward uniforms. However, casual does not mean organizational members can wear whatever they please. "Business casual dress codes have spawned a multibillion dollar uniform industry" (Tsai, 2002, p. 1D).

Uniforms

Traditionally, organizations ranging from real estate to fast food to the military use uniforms. Increasingly, other organizations are providing uniforms for functional reasons and to save employee expenditures, provide a common front, and reduce dissent.

Uniforms serve at least two functions (Solomon, 1987; Tsai, 2002). First, they differentiate one class or group from another. A waiter or waitress, a priest, or an officer of the law can be singled out because of their uniform and they are treated differently. For the service industries, uniforms act as confidence boosters for customers because they indicate a "uniform" standard of performance. The type of uniform used can signal a service company's selling points, ranging from professionalism to simple good taste. So the "law and order" police officer, the efficient and professional rug cleaner, or the clean nurse all present a message to the outside. In addition, uniforms allow companies to recognize outsiders.

Second, uniforms provide a common sense of identification for the group wearing them. Members of the police force feel a certain kinship with other members when they are all in uniform (Remland, 2003). The same concept applies to putting uniforms on factory workers. Rather than divide between the blue, gray, and white collars, one unified outfit can provide common ground for the group. "Many organizations believe uniforms contribute to productivity and morale and ensure the workers are loyal to the organization's goals" (Solomon, 1987, p. 30). A uniform enhances the ability of an employee to identify with the company because they are living representations of the organization. An additional benefit is when a business pays for "clothing and accessories, the employee can spend more of his/her hard-earned money on other things" (Shaw, 1994, p. 24).

Mercedes-Benz (MBUSI) uses teamwear, "in which workers wear similar clothes, often associated with the company's name or logo emblazoned on them" (Tsai, 2002, p. 1D). MBUSI purchases five shirts and five pairs of pants annually for each employee. Normally, uniforms have names embroidered on them. At MBUSI, "it's part of a one-team concept—open communication going by the first name" (Tsai, 2002, p. 1D).

Traditionally, many Japanese corporations issued uniforms to all employees with only minor differences in style depending on the employee's position. Uniforms can create better organizations by allowing for a concentration on the tasks at hand and not on the obvious status differences pointed out by dress ("Egalitarian Rules," 1987; Ouchi, 1981). We have already noted the ongoing changes in dress standards in some Japanese organizations. At the same time, Toyota, Honda, and other Japanese-owned corporations have implemented dress codes in their American plants. Mercedes-Benz has common dress standards in its U.S. plant. In many team development efforts, matching shirts with the company logo are used to enhance identification with the team and organization.

On the other side of the coin, the leveling process brought about by a common uniform also can diminish an individual's sense of importance and achievement. Individual recognition for outstanding performance can be more difficult to observe because everyone looks alike. This can lead to resistance because it underscores the dramatic "tension that exists in this country (United States) between the need for affiliation and solidarity, on the one hand, and the need for autonomy and individuality on the other" (Shaw, 1994, p. 40). To the degree receiving personal acknowledgment is important, being dressed like everyone else can act as an individual demotivator.

Functions of Clothing

Clothing has four functions: comfort, safety, modesty, and cultural display. Comfort and, in particular, safety are subject to clearly defined rules in most organizations. Modesty is an expectation in most organizations and written and unwritten dress codes set the standards.

Cultural display includes statements regarding our willingness to accept the restrictions and requirements of an organization. For example, many stores and restaurants have signs saying "no shoes, no shirt, no service." We are expected to dress appropriately for many events. Some restaurants specify "tie required." According to Solomon (1987): "Ties are clearly cultural displays. The tie, like so many other details of costume, is unimportant either as a comfort device or as a modesty covering" (p. 20). The tie functions as a cultural badge that represents "the ancient use of clothing, preceding even its protective and modesty roles, and it remains today of supreme importance" (Solomon, 1986, p. 20). The manner in which different groups in an organization dress can communicate status differentiating high and low status organizational members (Remland, 2003).

Clothing demonstrates an understanding of the cultural requirements of the social situation—we are stating that we understand what is expected of us. A Gallup survey found that two thirds of working people want a dress code at work because the code clarifies the cultural expectations (Peterson, 1991).

Clothing and Perception

We make many decisions based on someone's clothing. Among the information inferred from dress are economic level and background, educational level and background, social position and social background, level of success, degree of sophistication, trustworthiness, and moral character (Thourlby, 1978). This is vital information because research shows that people form impressions and make judgments about others based on what they see within the first few moments of interaction (Armour, 2005). One study using college students as raters controlled the attractiveness of job candidates by altering the clothing (Mack, 1990). Well-dressed individuals were more successful than poorly dressed individuals with the same credentials. Tom Wolfe, a well-known author, made the following comment regarding blue suede shoes, which is very much on target: "1 love them and I wear them, even though you can't get a bank loan when you do" ("People," 1987, p. 4D).

In an initial job interview situation, the type of clothing is an important factor (Goodall & Goodall, 2006). During the interview, how the applicant looks ranks as the most important nonverbal cue. Other nonverbal factors include eye contact, facial expression, and gestures. But the willingness to mirror the dress of the interviewer shows an understanding of the cultural demands of the organization and increases acceptance by the interviewer. "The tendency for individuals to prefer those whose dress is similar to their own has been observed in several studies. The findings are consistent with the idea that perceived dissimilarities make people uncomfortable in work situations" (Galin, 1990, p. 51). The critical importance of *first impressions* in interviews has been recognized by innovative nonprofits helping disadvantaged women successfully interview for jobs (Weiss, 1995). In addition to dress, they focus on other image issues such as workplace etiquette, interview strategies, and advice regarding hair and makeup. Rather than gamble that an interviewee's first impression with a potential employer might be offsetting, these nonprofits work to remove this perceptual barrier. The most important lesson is that interviewers are quite susceptible to the nonverbal messages they receive from job applicants (Remland, 2003).

Just as dressing correctly for an interview is important, formal uniforms facilitate certain activities. For example, wearing a sheriff's or nurse's uniform leads to higher levels of contributions in law enforcement and health care campaigns versus attempts to obtain contributions while out of uniform (Lawrence & Watson, 1991). "A survey of 292 patients regarding doctors' clothing concluded: Appearance is an important aspect of the way doctors communicate with patients and doctors should pay attention to it. If doctors look good, they are taken seriously by their patients, and the patients believe they will be well taken care of" (Cope, 1987, p. 7). The study linked dress to the willingness of the patient to follow the doctor's advice (credibility), and to a sense of wellbeing instead of worry. The study, which was first reported in the *Archives of Internal Medicine*, found patients wanted their doctors to look like doctors. Carrying a stethoscope was a prime appearance (costume) factor expected by patients.

Dress and perception are intertwined and the style of dress influences interactions in a variety of circumstances. It is not always necessary to have expensive clothes because the situation often dictates the impact of clothing. For example, Hensley (1981) reported that in airports, well-dressed people were more persuasive, whereas, at bus stops, casually dressed people had greater success.

Molloy (1975, 1977, 1988) authored three books that have had a remarkable effect on the perception of correct business dress for professional occupations. Essentially, Molloy counseled everyone to dress conservatively, professionally, and seek authority-enhancing clothing as reflected in the titles *Dress for Success* (1975), *The Women's Dress for Success Book* (1977) and *Molloy's New Dress for Success* (1988). Molloy recommended darker attire because it demonstrated greater authority. Grays, dark blues, pinstripes, solid or diagonal ties, and so on were offered as guides for business success. Few clear directives were available at the time regarding dress standards so his books became guides that were accepted and followed—essentially any direction was preferable to no direction. Women were counseled to wear "the intimidation suit"—a dark, elegantly cut suit—by *Working Woman* magazine (Hellmich, 1988). Sixty-four percent of the 8,033 professions and managerial women responding to a survey by *Working Women* said a professional image was more important for women than men and 48% said they abide by the adage "dress for the position you aspire to" (Hellmich, 1988). "Despite a lack of supporting data, Molloy's claims are so widely read and quoted by the American business establishment that they have become guidelines that dictate U.S. business fashion" (Anderson, 1999, p. 307).

Regardless of the occupation, clothing does make a difference in how people are perceived. From the initial job interview to professional activities, correct attire is necessary to maintain the proper image with other people.

Clothing and Self-Perception

The clothing or "costume" we wear impacts on our self-perception. "The meanings transmitted by clothing profoundly affect the perception and thinking not only of the viewer, but of the wearer as well" (Molloy, 1988, pp. 38–39). You are already aware that when you feel appropriately dressed for an event, you are also likely to be more self-confident. "If you are proud of your clothing and mannerisms, you will project more self-confidence than if you are self-conscious about how you are dressed and act" (DuBrin, 2000, p. 94).

In one study, students on job interviews, who were dressed appropriately for the role, thought they had made a better impression on the interviewer than those not well dressed (Berry, 1987). Their enhanced self-image lead to a willingness to ask for a starting salary $4,000 higher than those individuals who were not well dressed. This confidence enhancing function also applies to our own role transformations as we undertake unfamiliar roles occurring because of promotions, new jobs, or different assignments. The importance of dress ultimately may be reduced to "a which came first, the chicken or the egg" type of analysis. Well-dressed people tend to project an image that is more likely to be accepted in the business world. The business world represents specific cultural interests that will be preserved by choosing individuals who do not threaten the organization. A major cue for the organization is an indication by the individual that he or she understands the "dress code." An inability to show an understanding of the underlying codes of conduct probably will lead to being rejected or provided less credibility. Cap these points with the fact that there is every reason to believe that individuals behave in a more confident manner when dressed for effect and we have a strong grasp of the relationship between dress and organizational inclusion.

One very interesting study found that employees dressed in company smocks and wearing nametags were more likely to be friendly toward customers than if they were simply well dressed. The researcher believed this "reflects the process of employees 'putting on' an organizational face when they put on their smock and nametag" (Fischman, 1988, p. 17). The uniforms seemed to act as cues for employees to follow company policy and smile, use eye contact, and thank customers. Given the importance of customer relations for service industries, the apparent relationship between uniforms and effective employee behavior is significant.

Clothing and Power

Once information is available that can be used to differentiate some groups from others, it can be used to establish power. Traditionally, people who wore the "suits" were management providing additional control. Ministers, professors, lawyers, and many other professions can use appropriate dress to indicate a superior position. The medical profession and law enforcement officers are two examples of where dress is used to create and maintain specific impressions.

Members of the medical profession often use dress to communicate power and status. The importance of dress to the patient already has been established and it is useful to differentiate doctors from other hospital staffers. We like our doctors to look like doctors and the medical profession likes being treated with all the respect due their profession. Clothing and appearance are primary means for achieving both these goals.

Uniformed police officers usually are treated as if they have power, so they do have power and can use it if they wish (DeVito, 2004). Organizations hire official-looking security guards for the deterrent effect and the acceptance of authority. The confrontational potential for law enforcement officers makes this group keenly aware of the power potential provided by dress.

Gender plays an important role in power dressing. Although casual dress seems to be a positive organizational improvement, some posit that "women are not taken seriously when dressing down," so it is recommended that "women adopt a conservative, authoritative, non-sexy" style (Mannix, 1997, p. 60). In fact, Neale and Norcraft (1990) observed that women find that regardless of the dress codes, "the corporate uniform—white shirt and blue suit—may be necessary at first to be taken seriously and to gain credibility and legitimacy" (p. 87).

Even the granting of casual dress requirements operates as a reminder of power relationships. First, the benefit is granted by management to the rest of the organization thereby reaffirming who is in charge. In addition, business casual is a no-cost benefit for the organization because the employee must invest in the new style of dress. In fact, informality "masks an increasingly hierarchical structure within companies" where the "typical American CEO makes 190 times the compensation of the typical worker; 20 years ago the multiple was only 40" (Weiser, 1996, p. 11).

Clothing, as exemplified through dress standards, uniforms, perception, and power is a vital aspect of nonverbal communication in organizations. Clothing speaks. At this point, we have discussed facial display, eye contact, paralanguage, body language, and appearance. These nonverbal characteristics focus primarily on the individual. The remainder of this chapter discusses *proxemics* and *chronemics*, which broaden our consideration of nonverbal communication.

Proxemics

We can manipulate space, the environment, and territoriality. *Proxemics* "is the study of how people differ in their use of personal space" (Lutig & Koester, 2003, p. 187). Hall (1966), the originator of the concept of proxemics, initially placed his emphasis on the unconscious structuring of space. Increasingly, individuals and organizations are aware of many of proxemics' ramifications and intentionally manipulate space.

Access and Control of Space

A subtle example of the relationship between territoriality and a person's place in the hierarchy is their freedom to use the space. First, if you have relatively free access to your territory, you are probably more powerful than many others in an organization. For example, high-level executives can arrive and leave with greater freedom, vary their lunch hours, use their telephone at their own leisure, lock their door, and so on.

Organizations let individuals know just what their capacity is in determining how much of their territory is really under their control. If some individuals wish to display pictures on their office walls, for example, they can. This discretion is not universally available. Office and cubicles often have "dress requirements" including the number and size of personal photographs that can be displayed. How much control individuals actually have over their use of space is a statement of status and power.

Second, if you have the ability to limit other people's access, you have a certain degree of status. In most organizations, the person with higher rank can enter freely a lower ranking person's territory whereas the lower ranking person must make special arrangements, such as an appointment, to enter the boss's territory (Anderson, 1999).

To make this discussion of territoriality clear, we discuss personal space and touch followed by office setup including offices, meeting arrangements, and buildings.

Personal Space

Your own cultural upbringing intuitively guides you in determining how far to stand from someone else. Hall (1959, 1966) identified four fairly distinct distances between individuals in the United States used to help define the relationship. Within these four distances are a close phase and a far phase that, when combined with the four distances, provide eight different spatial dimensions. The four identified distances are intimate, personal, social, and public. We examine how these distances are applied in the United States As with so many other nonverbal activities, distance is culturally defined so it can change dramatically from one country to the next. "How culture uses space is linked to its value system. For example, people from individualistic cultures require more space because they value privacy" (Calloway-Thomas et al., 1999, p. 164).

Intimate distance ranges from 0 to 18 in. with the close phase being actual touch and the far phase of 6 in. to 18 in. where we are fully aware of the other's presence. Physical contact and involvement are easy and activities, such as lovemaking and comforting, occur. In the far phase, individuals still can touch hands and tend to not use a great deal of verbalizations. Because of the closeness, this distance is not considered acceptable in organizations. We discuss touch more extensively once the four distances have been presented.

Personal distance ranges from 18 in. to 4 ft. We all have a *personal bubble* or protective space around us, which is an invisible boundary between others and ourselves. This bubble travels with each individual and expands and contracts under varying circumstances dictated by the elements of each transaction. At the close phase, which is 18 in. to 2 ft, we are comfortable in accepting our loved ones. In the far phase, we still can touch someone and can detect details about the other person. If an individual has sweat on their upper lip, dandruff on their shoulder, or severe halitosis, we detect it at this distance, which is between 2.5 ft and 4 ft.

In an organization, this far phase is used for personal business between very close colleagues. We still can touch or reach someone else, but only with conscious effort. Therefore, each individual has a certain amount of control over the interaction.

The vast majority of business transactions occur in the *social distance*. When two managers discuss company policy, they are likely to do so within social distance's close phase, which would be from 4 ft to 7 ft. In the close phase of social distance, individuals are able to conduct business and are fully aware of the other person's presence. An informal meeting at the water fountain, or conversing about information on a computer screen, could be conducted at this distance. In the far phase, which is 7 ft to 12 ft, business discussions become more formal. People become more dependent on the other nonverbal behaviors, such as eye contact and volume, to maintain the transaction. Social distance is 4 ft to 12 ft. The somewhat dramatic difference between 4 and 12 is reflected in the type of business transacted. Often the far phase of social distance is used to maintain contact without the need for constant interactions.

Once we are out of the arena of direct involvement with another individual, we are at a *public distance*. Any distance beyond 12 ft is considered public. The close phase is 12 ft to 15 ft. It allows us to understand the nature of someone else's actions, and we easily can defend ourselves or take the appropriate actions toward someone.

However, when people are in the far phase, which is more than 25 ft, there is no necessary recognition of individuals. People become part of the setting. A good example would be the president of a major corporation addressing all of the employees at a holiday party. In an almost automatic fashion, a distance of 25 ft would set up around the president. In addition, the president would be under no obligation to deal with any single individual. Often, briefings to large groups of employees occur at this distance.

There is substantial research suggesting the importance of distance to the attitudes held by the participants. People who are located in close proximity are seen as warmer, friendlier, and more understanding than are people located further away (Patterson, 1968). "The findings of a large number of studies collaborate one another and indicate that communicator–addressee distance is correlated with the degree of negative attitude communicated to and inferred by the addressee" (Mehrabian, 1969, p. 363).

Distance also reflects status and gender differences. Research indicates that status differences are emphasized by physical distance and minimized by greater closeness. "The higher the perceived status, the more space a person is given. Gender also has been shown to be a determining factor in the amount of space given or demanded. Men automatically receive more space than women" (Ray, 1999, p. 50).

In our gender-balanced and increasingly empowered working situations, leaders would be wise to consider how important distance can be to the success of a transaction. We can conclude that unless the situation calls for reinforcing differences in status through public distance, it would be wise to work toward reducing the distance between individuals to a level that is clearly consistent with the goals of the transaction.

Interpersonal distances include intimate, personal, social, and public. Within each of these categories are the close and far phases. Congruency between the distance used and the content of the transaction are vital.

Touch

Touch, in a business setting, is culturally regulated. Handshakes are a well-known mechanism for greetings, agreements, and farewells in many cultures. Interculturally, handshakes vary widely, with Americans and Germans preferring a firm handshake, the French a softer handshake, and Middle Easterners a handshake often combined with placing of their free hand on the other's forearm (Beamer & Varner, 2001). Other greetings include bowing or holding hands together. "Each gesture suggests openness and a clear sign that the greeter is not carrying a weapon" which many historians believe were the original purpose (Axtell, 1991, p. 21). For most U.S. males, a handshake that is too hard, long, "feminine" or flaccid can result in an impression not actually intended. In a survey of personnel managers at 30 companies, 90% indicated that a firm handshake by the applicant is important (Forbes, 1990).

Touch has a variety of other uses in an organizational setting. Depending on the relationship between individuals, touch can be used for consolation, support, and congratulations.

Power and dominance also are expressed through touching behavior. Henley (1995) observes that superiors can touch subordinates more frequently than the reverse. She also points to specific examples of when certain persons can put their arm on another's shoulder or put their hand on another's back because of their power (Henley, 1977). In the following dyads, you should have no difficulty in deciding who could put their hand on the other person with the greatest of ease, and with the least violation of cultural rules. The examples are manager and worker, teacher and student, doctor and patient, businessperson and secretary, and minister and parishioner. Because the first person in each dyad also has higher status, they could touch with greater ease. This freedom to touch acts, according to Henley, as a power and dominance behavior for men. When women use touch, she argued, it is interpreted in sexual rather than political or power-oriented ways.

Mehrabian (1981) explained touch in a different manner. Using the *immediacy principle*, he concluded that people are drawn toward persons and things they like, evaluate highly, and prefer, and they avoid or move away from things they dislike, evaluate negatively, or do not prefer. In this context, touching is a statement of liking more than power. Research on interpersonal attraction seems to support the concept that we touch people we like and avoid ones we do not like.

Somewhere between a Henley's political orientation and the interpersonal attraction studies would be the concept forwarded in some managerial literature that calls for a "pat on the back" of an employee after they have been disciplined (Blanchard & Johnson, 1982). This pat can be either actual or symbolic, but the impact is to reestablish trust and caring between the superior and the subordinate. In other words, I have told you of your errors (e.g., power) and I still want to maintain a close working relationship.

The organizational world uses the concept of touch in many symbolic ways, including out-of-touch, touching, bruising, touch base, keep in contact, stroking, rubbing the wrong way, and someone's a soft touch. In chapter 3, we mentioned the concept of a hired hand. We hand someone power; use hands-on or hands-off approaches; get a handle on a crisis; an agreement is at hand; organizations are handcuffed by rules; managers are heavy-handed; some people do not want to get their hands dirty; people are on hand; and numerous other terms using touch or hands to explain organizational processes.

Increasingly, actual touch is regulated in organizations. Part of the impetus stems from recent court cases regarding *sexual harassment*, which is unwanted sexually oriented behavior in the workplace. Clearly, unwelcome touch creates a hostile atmosphere so physical touching is limited, in many cases, to handshakes and sideways hugs (DuBrin, 1999). "Harassment—sexual or otherwise—is about power. Deliberate harassment is about other people showing that they have power over you" (Kearney & White, 1994, p. 111). At this point in your study of nonverbal communication, it probably is not a surprise to you that someone invading your personal bubble without your permission involves a significant use of power.

Stigmas and Powerless Stereotypes

Sometimes, individuals are seen as powerless. We maintain greater distances from individuals who have *stigmas*. According to Goffman (1963), these are individuals who are "possessing an attribute that makes him different from others in the category of persons available for him to be, and of a less desirable kind—in the extreme, a person who is thoroughly bad, or dangerous, or weak" (p. 3). In a very real sense, stigmas exist throughout the specialized cultures of various organizations. The discredited manager, the loud and complaining employee, the outlandish dresser, or the failed salesperson, for example, would seem to elicit greater distancing than people who accept or reflect the organizational norms. When you decide to leave one organization to work for another, do not be surprised if suddenly you are treated as an outsider who must prove yourself worthy before being invited to parties or involved in decisions.

When stigmatized individuals invade our personal space, they often are treated as nonpersons. When in a crowded elevator, most people simply try to ignore the presence of others by directing eye contact to the ceiling or the floor. Intrusions into our intimate space by an obnoxious or extremely outgoing person cause most individuals to treat the intruder as a nonperson or a "dummy" (Burgoon & Saine, 1978). These reactions allow people to deny that the invasion actually is occurring.

People who are seen as "unattractive, obese, short (men), dark-skinned, poorly dressed, baby-faced, and physically handicapped" (Remland, 2000, p. 335) become *powerless stereotypes*. In general, certain nonverbal characteristics allow groups and individuals to be stigmatized and therefore marginalized. Even the use of low-status behaviors such as looking down, giggling or smiling nervously, or speaking in high-pitched or nasal tones can lead to being stigmatized. "Numerous scientific studies demonstrate that we form all sorts of negative impressions of individuals simply because those individuals in some way communicate a low-status identity" (Remland, 2000, p. 335). Once someone is stigmatized, a vicious cycle begins because opportunities will diminish and additional stigmas can be applied. Stigmas and powerless stereotypes reinforce, once again, the pivotal nature of nonverbal communication in organizations.

In summary, the area around each individual that is used to regulate transactions with others is the first category of proxemics. Everyone has an invisible, flexible bubble surrounding them explaining why potential invasions have communication impact. Both distances and touch have specific rules of conduct that frequently are not stated, but are very real.

Territoriality

We have a biological tendency to own the space around us. Individuals literally extend out into the surrounding space and set up boundaries (Anderson, 1999). The various territories surrounding us, ranging from our car to our home to our parking spot, become part of who we are and we establish ownership. Markers are placed, such as leaving coats or books on chairs, to show our ownership.

For many of us, hospitals are foreign territories that provoke some misgivings. In discussing why patients and visitors might have this negative reaction, someone on the hospital staff might talk about GOMERS. The term stands for *Get Out Of My Emergency Room*. Emergency room doctors have a strong territorial perspective and resent anyone not truly ill invading their space. Their complaints about hypochondriacs and nuisance cases are so common, the phrase GOMER has been coined and in use for a long period of time.

Regardless of the organization, individuals will take over space around them. Supervisors or line managers will individualize their stations. Secretaries apply personal touches to their desks.

Understanding this natural tendency also explains why there is a *biological advantage* to the possessor of the space, and why there is a relationship between space and social hierarchies. In organizations, a person's office is set up in such a manner as to provide personal comfort, and therefore an advantage, in any transaction. Consultants frequently suggest that important issues be discussed away from anyone's own personal office. Labor union leaders and management representatives always seek neutral territory to discuss contracts.

Hall (1972) provided three dimensions for understanding how territoriality can be divided: *dynamic, semifixed, and fixed-feature.* Organizations have undergone significant variations on the original categories and we examine these changes.

Dynamic   Dynamic involves the use of space *as people communicate.* Each of Hall's (1959, 1966) four categories we outlined at the beginning of the discussion of proximity operate in the dynamic use of space. Organizations have found that the greater the interactions between individuals, the more likely there is to be a team or group orientation. Casual encounters before and after meetings, at breaks or meals, around the water cooler or computer terminal are vital communication events for an organization's culture.

Aware of the importance of casual interactions, at Procter & Gamble, "the corridors are deliberately wide and have couches where workers can stop for a quick chat. P&G equipped lunchrooms and lounges with electronic whiteboards that can convert scribblings to E-mail" (Hamilton, 1996, p. 112). Krohe (1993) observed that "the best conversations about the job happen not in the conference room, but in the snack room" (p. 18).

Controlling territoriality is another form of power. When people arrange furniture or other objects in their environment to control their transactions with other people, they are using the fixed feature process. This can include where we choose to sit at a meeting or how we arrange our office. Office design experts refer to *activity-based planning,* which is a method used to determine the appropriate mix of shared and individual workspaces that make up the workplace. This method incorporates the frequency, importance, and content of an individual's work activities to determine their appropriate spaces, both individually and in groups.

Semifixed   The possibilities for arranging furniture and seating patterns are practically endless. We discuss three aspects of the semifixed concept to demonstrate what the issues are—dyadic sitting positions, meeting arrangements, and office setup.

Dyadic Seating Positions   Several studies have been conducted that indicate that people will choose to sit in different positions depending on what they perceive are the goals of the transaction. Sommer (1969) reported four specific differences in where people will position themselves depending on the desired outcomes. Figure 5.1 shows the four positions.

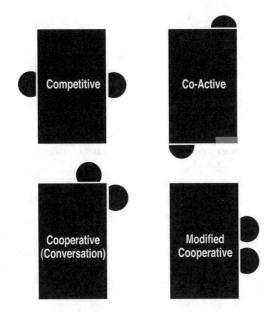

Figure 5.1 Four possible seating arrangements.

In *competitive* situations, individuals will sit across from one another. By facing an opponent, individuals can react to all of the possible moves or threats that might occur. People also feel safer because of the table. Finally, most competitive games are based on a "face-off" or "taking sides" so it makes sense that people would choose this positioning.

In our consulting experience, we have observed that this seating operates as a self-fulfilling prophecy because people became competitive even when there was no apparent reason. This positioning maximizes the potential for sending and receiving conflicting messages. It has the greatest interpersonal distance, which also helps explain the tendency toward combat rather than collaboration.

Sitting with a corner between the participants is called *cooperative* by some authors and conversation by others. The presence of the corner allows some protection of our personal bubble and still guarantees a concentration of the transaction because there is little personal distance. Information-gathering interviews often use this arrangement.

Sommer (1969) labeled sitting next to another person as *modified coopera-tive*. The side-by-side positioning allows the participants to concentrate on the task at hand. In organizations, individuals who are trying to work through the same task will adopt such a seating pattern. Because there is little interpersonal distance, or opportunities for conflicting nonverbal messages, individuals tend to concentrate on the job rather than on each other.

When distance is a desired element in the interaction, the *coactive* arrangement is used. In this situation, individuals can discuss specific issues without continually being in active verbal discourse. As Figure 5.1 shows, each of these positions provides different communication opportunities.

Meeting Arrangements   In meetings, sitting at the end of a rectangular table is a statement of leadership (Remland, 2003). Participants wanting to be considered part of the group frequently will choose the middle chairs.

Sometimes meetings provoke a King Arthur arrangement. As the myth is told, King Arthur used a round table to make certain no knight was given greater status over any other. As it turns out, the person sitting closest to the king was considered the "right-hand" man and still accorded the greatest status. In modern organizations, the king is ambidextrous because the positions to the left and the right on a rectangular table are considered power positions.

There are *power spots* around a table (Korda, 1986). At a rectangular table, the corner spots are the best for asserting power. When a circular table is used, the most powerful position is at 12 o'clock high, and the power decreases clockwise around the table from this spot.

At this point you might be concerned that the advice varies depending on the expert's personal perspective. Sitting at a meeting begins to look more like a game of musical chairs than an opportunity to engage in serious discussion. In many ways you would be correct. As you will recall from chapter 3, political perspectives regarding organizational behavior do lead to game playing.

So, where should you sit? A good question and a valid concern. The answer lies in returning to some of the earlier information regarding nonverbal communication. Because eye contact is one of the most powerful means of communication, placing yourself in a position where you can be in direct contact with those individuals you wish to focus on would seem to be the key. The King Arthur arrangement requires the lesser "knights" to look at you and the king. A power spot view focuses on the danger of being away from the *activity centers* at a table. A place at the table that is across from the leader provides an opportunity to directly challenge the king, but it could also leave the challenger out of the discussion if the leader demanded attention. Without invoking the political concepts, we still can predict that being outside the points of convergence of the discussion will isolate an individual. So, realistically, if you wish to be paid attention to, pick a high-profile spot.

As trite as some of this maneuvering may seem, power is a major concern in many organizations. Even if a political perspective, with its power orientation, is not the issue, we should worry about the seating arrangement. Where people sit, and whom they sit next to, does regulate individual participation.

Much of the expert advice centers on an individual's desire to lead or dominate a meeting. Although the advice by authorities differs, leadership clearly is established by sitting where an individual can control the transaction. As opposed to a dyadic meeting, where sitting across from someone can create conflict, having all eyes centered on a leadership position in a larger meeting obviously is desirable. Both ends of a rectangular table tend to be leadership positions. Various configurations are used to reduce power positioning with the oval-shaped table being one means that is gaining increased popularity.

Office Setup   The last aspect to examine is the office setup. Because territoriality always gives the advantage to the possessor, office holders can manipulate office setups to send messages and control transactions.

For many of us, creating the best possible climate, by minimizing power differentials, is our goal. In our work as consultants, we have found most managers eager to rearrange their offices to enhance the quality of interactions. Creating a neutral territory within the office, such as a sofa and chair or a small round table with two or three chairs, removes the desk as a barrier. An additional alternative is to seek a neutral meeting spot, such as a conference or break room. In addition, the "intention of future successful business is to create a working culture that is status-free, innovative, productive, founded on knowledge sharing, and based on work outputs instead of inputs" (Mackay & Maxwell, 1997, p. 45).

Increasing the ease of interactions between managers and subordinates has encouraged nontraditional arrangements—such as manager's desks among the troops—that increase the speed of communication while promoting team-building and fun environments (Meyer, 1997). At the Mercedes-Benz plant in Alabama, almost the entire administrative team had an open office setting, allowing any administrative team member to look across the entire floor. The president's office is located toward the middle near one side and the furniture is similar to all the other furniture. Teams are arranged in clusters, but team activities can be viewed by anyone looking around. For confidentiality purposes, or for team meetings that require a great deal of interactions, laptops, and whiteboards, there are conference rooms available.

Traditionally, in the United States, "the size of the office and its location are indicative of the business-person's success, importance, power, and status within the hierarchy" (Beamer & Varner, 2001, p. 175). Often high-ranking administrative personnel's offices have windows and are located on top floors.

The selection, display, and arrangement of objects also provide strong non-verbal messages. Diplomas, awards, and other artifacts emphasize expertise and background, whereas plants and other decorations might focus on comfort. The image that someone is too important to be dealing with a variety of trivial matters does seem powerful. Individuals expect some indications of expertise when they visit a doctor or lawyer's office. Although most lawyers do not constantly refer to the law books in their offices, it is highly reassuring to know the lawyer would be able to locate the necessary information, because of the displayed reading material. Ironically, with the advent of Lexus-Nexus and other legal referral systems, few attorneys consult their bound law books.

Fixed Feature

The fixed-feature arrangement includes "internal, culturally specific configuration, and external environmental arrangements such as architecture and space layout" (Hall, 1972, p. 210). The elements that go into the office, such as furniture, are fixed. These visible appurtenances do vary greatly depending on status, with larger offices, bigger desks, and no file cabinets indicative of the highest level of achievement. Fixtures that cannot be moved easily make the strongest statement. Decisions regarding office design and type, and who receives the best offices, fall into this last category.

The modern office building evolved through three major phases (Stone & Luchetti, 1985). The first phase was a row or military-like arrangement. In the early 1900s, office managers used the factory management procedures discussed in chapter 3 and put clerks into rows. According to Stone and Luchetti, "As organizations grew, many companies in which management preferred private, walled offices came to have depressingly long hallways lined with closed doors. Needless to say, in these places informal communication was discouraged" (1985, p. 104). This setup still exists. For example, the U.S. Postal Service mail distribution centers have clerks sitting in rows tapping out zip codes from letters. The major feature of this type of setting is a full concentration on individual work and little interaction with colleagues. This is a *structural* approach to organizational design.

The second phase came from the Quickborner team in Germany, who called for eliminating both the factory-like setting and the private cells. The criticism of offices includes observations such as: "It's supposed to be about open source (all information is available), but everywhere it's walls. We're told to work together, but our offices are designed for working alone" (Conlin, 2006, p. 100).

Instead, an *open setting* was used to encourage interaction. Placing everyone in a *commons* or open workspace is increasing in popularity. Predictions are that workers of tomorrow will immerse themselves as active team members and interact in company communities that are arranged like neighborhoods complete with busy intersections, commons, and quiet backyards (Gunn & Burroughs, 1996). Somewhat short of open settings is employing *social architecture* that is "creating offices for companies by mapping the informal networks in organizations and then structuring space around concepts such as who employees bounce ideas off of and who they like to hang out with" (Conlin, 2006, p. 101).

Edelman (1997) warns that for the open environments to work, executives and staff alike must value innovation and change more than comfort and prestige. Open spaces do leave people vulnerable to numerous distractions because of competing stimuli (Lieber, 1996). Many individuals need visual and acoustic space, as well as their own physical autonomy. For example, the capacity to conduct important, and often confidential, business is more difficult in an open setting, which was explained earlier in this chapter when we discussed Mercedes-Benz.

Critics say the main purpose of the open structure shift is not so much employee well-being as financial rationalism on the part of the company (Monk, 1997). It costs less to house everyone in a central location than to provide individual offices. "Corporations spend more on space than on anything else except people" (Conlin, 2006, p. 100). Next to salaries, office accommodation is the single biggest expense for many companies, representing between one tenth and one fifth of corporate budgets ("Re-engineering," 1995). Ten years ago, the typical office employee enjoyed 250 square feet of space, including a proportionate share of a building's lobby, corridors, and restrooms. Currently, companies moving into new offices are allocating only 200 square feet per person: a shrinkage of 20% (Carns, 1997). Earlier we discussed telecommuting. "Chances are that on any given day, up to 40% of your colleagues are not in the office" (Conlin, 2006, p. 100). So, the need for office space is diminishing.

An additional consideration is that many Americans are not fully comfortable with this totally open design. As a bridge between the closed doors and the open space, a landscaped partitioning process became popular and lead to *cubicleland*. This design allows individuals to feel as if they have privacy without erecting walls. People have their own territory within the open, but structured, design of the organization. For the organization, cubicles are inexpensive and easy to arrange and reconfigure. In addition, they provide hidden power to the manager to control employee behavior. "The mere possibility that a manager or employee will be engaging in some undesirable activity is sufficient to ensure that the corporation's standards are observed" in the cubicle arrangement (Gordon, 1998, p. 18).

But, employees still need places to meet. Panera Bread, a restaurant with more than 900 locations, caters to "the 23 million Americans in the Kinko's generation—they don't have an office. There is something like over 70% of our corporate society that are in cubes" (Shaich, 2006, p. 126). Panera's CEO sees providing a good, comfortable working environment encourages people to use his restaurant as a meeting place or a work space. Customers are welcome to stay as long as they like, meet with colleagues or customers, and enjoy a meal if they desire.

Where is the fixed, cubicle, and open environment leading? A 1998 study (Carey & Mullins) indicated that nearly a quarter of office workers has an office with a door and another 23% work in a cubicle without a door. So, in 1998, more than 50% were without offices or cubicles.

Caves and commons or *activity centers* are the third phase of office design and are being used with increased efficiency by various organizations. *Activ-*

ity-based planning, intended to respond to the actual space-related needs of employees, creates a unified team space that enables a combination of private and collaborative work. The goal is to provide the privacy needed for certain activities and still utilize open communication whenever possible. The terms are fully descriptive of the change in moving from workstations to activity centers. Different parts of an organization are set up for particular needs. So, specialized equipment can be scheduled for different groups at various times. Rather than expecting all activities to be conducted in a particular space, the individuals or groups move around from conference rooms to computer centers to other settings conducive to particular activities. The human expertise is movable providing the most efficient use of space.

Caves and commons allow for both small, quiet places (e.g., caves) for employees to work and team areas for spontaneous collaboration—commons (Bencivenga, 1998). Within the commons approach, rooms can be set aside for the duration of a project, instead of rooms scheduled hourly, to allow employees to keep brainstorming and development ideas posted as long as they wish that helps them to remain focused on the current project.

The dominant feature of the new office environment is the *central street or boulevard* that cuts through a variety of departments and must be used to reach coffee, vending machines, or cafeterias. The corridors create a place for spontaneous interaction between employees. Often these corridors are wider than other halls and lead to a work or team area with tables, wall rails for coffee cups, and whiteboards for writing or drawing (Bencivenga, 1998). Often, *enclaves*, which are enclosed areas for workers needing temporary privacy, are provided. Where offices are being eliminated, *hoteling* is being utilized. This "refers to the practice of having mobile employees dial up an office concierge and reserve space as needed rather than hogging prime real estate when they rarely make an appearance in the office" (Conlin, 2006, p. 101). Ernst & Young in Chicago coined this term to describe its program of not assigning offices to specific individuals on a permanent basis. Using an automated hotel-like reservation system, offices may be reserved in advance and assigned on a temporary basis (Hamilton, 1996).

Deciding between offices and cubicles provides grounds for a healthy debate. At Intel, cubicles are used, whereas at Microsoft in Redmond, Washington, the traditional office suite is in vogue. "Those who favor cubes claim they have better communication, less hierarchy, and a creative environment. But office-dwellers say they get more done by having a secluded lair for uninterrupted thought" (Dunkin, 1995, p. 106).

Focusing on workplace design is important. "A study of business decision-makers by the American Society of Interior Designers in Washington, DC, found that 90% think improvements in office design can boost productivity. And to help stay competitive, 68% said office design needs to be reviewed at least once every 5 years" (Dunkin, 1995, p. 106). "Buildings influence behavior by structuring relationships among members of the organization. They encourage some communication patterns and discourage others. They assign positions of importance to units of the organization. They do these things according to a plan that fits the company's strategic design, or to a nonplan that doesn't. They have effects on behavior, planned or not" (Seiler, 1984, p. 120). The use of rows, individualized offices, cubiclelands, caves and commons, or activity centers all help form certain behaviors by the employees.

Ergonomics is the field of study that concentrates on making a workplace as compatible as possible with the physical and psychological needs of the people who do the job (Gaines, 1987). The term is derived from the Greek, *ergo*, meaning work, and *nomics*, meaning management or law. With the increase in specialization, such as computers or robotics, semifixed equipment's design must be considered carefully for its impact on workers' comfort and productivity ("VDTs: Fitting," 1991). The external environmental control placed on organizations by the Occupational Health and Safety Administration, for example, has forced companies to install specific equipment for specialized tasks ranging from computer workstations to hazardous occupations.

Size and Location   Larger desks and offices and ones located higher up in buildings have traditionally been indicative of highest status. The number of barriers between an individual and a visitor also can be an indication of status. If a secretary answers someone's phone, or an appointment is necessary to meet with the person, this usually is taken as a power or status cue. The majority of high-ranking corporate leaders still limit access (Bennis, 1990).

We are in the midst of significant changes in this aspect of organizational functioning. In the past, individuals who wanted to increase their influence considered office placement as a significant factor and corner offices were most often the power spots (Korda, 1975). As we indicated earlier, offices are now moving to the middle. Raiford (1998) concludes that "the old adage that executives occupy offices along the perimeter wall and the staff occupies open-plan landscape on the inside has gone out of the window" (p. 46). In fact, "moving private offices into the interior of open plans is one example of how office cultures are changing to become more responsive to all employees" (p. 46). Korda's diagram of an office environment where power radiated from the corners has also changed with leadership migrating to the middle of the room (Stewart, 1997). The power office is passé also according to Stewart (1997). "The really fashionable housing for power players is a cubicle. Says Steelcase's CEO, Jim Hackett, who gave up a two-room suite with a marble fountain for the cylindrical phone-booth-like pod he inhabits today: 'People don't need to see me in a big fancy office to know that I'm the CEO'" (Stewart, 1997, p. 60).

Modern technology is also changing the impact of territoriality. The automobile, for example, provides a traveling office for numerous salespersons. For many organizations, employees are occupying *virtual offices*. Chiat/Day, the advertising agency, turned their shop into what may have been America's first virtual ad agency. Employees will work out of their homes or at clients' offices. "Chiat will provide everyone with personal computers and telephones, while keeping a few meeting rooms and study carrels for business that can't be handled outside" (Tilsner, 1993). Ernst & Young expects to save $40 million a year by moving employees into virtual offices. Consultants and auditors at Ernst & Young spend 50–80% of their time outside the office, so there is no perceived need for permanent space (Sprout, 1994).

The digital age has increased the number of *telecommuters,* where work is sent to the employees rather than expecting the employees to come to work. We have discussed telecommuting at several other points in this text with good reason. "A recent Boston Consulting Group study found that 85% of executives expect a big rise in the number of location-agnostic workers over the next 5 years" (Conlin, 2006, p. 100). Often, these telecommuters, or location-agnostic people, work at home with electronic equipment supplied by their company. Organizations report improvements in productivity of up to 50% (Dunkin, 1995). Three explanations for this remarkable increase are: individual control over goals and work design; freedom from distractions such as walk-ins and phone calls; and individual control over the environment. Because computer hookups make the actual location of the equipment a moot point, territoriality can be anywhere an individual telecommuter desires.

The international dimension of organizational communication clearly points to increased out-of-office employment. "With the global mobile workforce expected to grow by more than 20% in the next four years, some companies are already making radical changes" (Conlin, 2006, p. 101). Increasingly, "the professional class is going *bedouin*" (Conlin, 2006, p. 100). *Bedouin* means a nomadic Arabian, Syrian, or North African moving around the deserts or, for employees, home is where you can connect your electronic devices.

There are negatives to telecommuting. Employees miss out on spontaneous brainstorms and the synergistic possibilities provided by open office setups. Politically, by being out of sight, they could be out of mind and passed over for promotions. In addition, they are left out of the loop on official company business or office gossip. In addition, colleagues reporting to work daily resent telecommuters because they are not available to help handle emergencies (Dunkin, 1995). For many individuals, the satisfaction of interacting with colleagues makes telecommuting unattractive.

Space and territoriality impacts everyone. Ranging from zero proxemics through various configurations of an organizational setting, how a transaction is arranged influences the communication.

In summary, territoriality is a major nonverbal factor in organizations. The tendency to own space, the biological advantage afforded to the owner, and the status attributed to space all make territoriality a critical issue. Territoriality is manifested through the variations in the dynamic or interpersonal semifixed or office and meeting arrangements, and fixed feature factors.

Two approaches have predominated the allocation of space. The first, a military-like setting, is based on factory design, and a structural view of organizations. Offices in rows, structure, and everything in its proper place have characterized this type of space allocation. Allocating offices based on structural concerns increases the tendency toward political concerns because battles for office location and size tend to surface.

The second form of space allocation is the most predominant in the United States. Rather than the military rows, space use ranges from open spaces to the extensive use of partitions and cubicles. Moving into the 2000s, organizations are experimenting with creative office design. Activity centers are being forwarded in the modern organization. This use of design is work oriented. Numerous barriers exist to prevent the adoption of entirely open office configurations. For a large number of workers, their office is mobile or at home. In both cases, the impact of territoriality is shifted, but the importance is not diminished.

Finally, the actual functionality of a personal office is coming into question. We are as likely to be digitally connected as we are to occupy actual space.

Chronemics

Chronemics is the study of the use of time. Western cultures are very oriented to time as an important part of the workday. We say it flies, it's money, it's on our side, and it heals all wounds—all while waiting for no one. Factory workers are "on the clock," people receive "hourly wages," managers receive and give "annual" performance reviews, appointments are "on time," and so on. Time is how we measure and quantify work by using seconds, minutes, hours, days, weeks, months, seasons, and years. We are paid for our time and are congratulated for getting tasks completed ahead of schedule or on time. Time is money in Western cultures. With the Western hullabaloo over the new millennium, it is useful to remember that the year 2000 was 5758 in the Jewish calendar and 1419 in the Muslim calendar. Humans have measured time in one way or another since the beginning by observing the movement of the sun, moon, and stars. When we organize, time becomes a significant issue.

In organizations, the *powerful control time* (Remland, 2003). Powerful, dominant people talk more, communicate more frequently and longer in group settings, and interrupt more often (Anderson, 1999). In Western society in general, waiting time decreases as our power increases (Henley, 1977; Remland, 2003). One measure of our status is our control over our work schedule. Some form of "time clock" regulates hourly workers whereas managers can come and go as they set their own time. In the United States, managers work an average of 55–60 hours a week, but they can come in late, leave early, and rearrange their workday.

More telling is the *ability of others to control our time*. "Some people have the power to annex other people's time, and the more they annex, the more powerful they become; the more powerful they are, the more of others' time they can annex" (Henley, 1977, p. 49). In many organizations, *where you spend your time* indicates your status. So, time spent with your superiors is considered a sign of status. In other organizations, the type of assignment consuming your time can prove your power and status. So, if you are part of the strategic planning team you are likely to be judged more important than if you are on the annual company picnic committee. If the team members on either committee are high status people who are spending time with your group, then the group obtains additional power and prestige. Time allocation, a precious resource, speaks.

Punctuality is an important message. Being late for a job interview, for example, is tantamount to saying you are not interested in the position (Burgoon & Saine, 1978). People in high-power positions have the luxury of setting the meeting time for appointments *and* being late (Burgoon & Saine, 1978).

Waiting, the consequence of how time is used, has two functions (Levine, 1987). First, individuals measure someone's importance by how long they are willing to wait for them. The greater the person's prestige, the longer people will wait patiently. Anderson (1999) explains, "Like money and property, the rich, the powerful, and the dominant control time. By contrast, the lives of the less privileged are filled with waiting (and) waiting time decreases as status increases" (p. 321). How much prestige would you assign, for example, to a medical doctor that you did not have to wait to see? An empty waiting room, an assembly line approach, or easy access might make you somewhat suspicious about the doctor's reputation or credentials. In many cases, people value what they wait for and devalue what is given immediately.

The digital age has had a profound impact on the interconnectedness between our jobs and our own control of time. Traditionally, people worked 9-to-5, 5 days a week although individuals in management positions rarely saw a 40-hour workweek. Telecommuting, discussed earlier and spawned by the availability of home technology, altered the traditional workday. Now, 24–7 (24 hours–7 days a week) has become a familiar expression indicating that we can be reached through our wireless cell phones, laptops, and home electronic devices at all times in almost any location. We are wired. In addition, globalization has increased this likelihood of a never-ending workweek because other countries operate in significantly different time zones. As we move upward in an organization, it may become increasingly difficult to leave our work at our office.

Chronemics, then, is an important nonverbal communication mechanism. How time structures our lives indicates a great deal about our power and status. In a variety of ways, the manipulation of time sends messages.

Conclusion

Nonverbal communication is a fundamental part of organizational behavior. It differs from verbal communication because it: is based on normative rules; includes all behavior, not just verbal; operates in the present; allows all behavior to be meaningful; cannot be stopped; and is dependent on context.

Because nonverbal communication is so broad, 14 guiding principles should be applied. Eight of these principles apply to all nonverbal communication and 6 are applied specifically to organizations. As with all rules of human behavior, exceptions are clearly possible.

Specific nonverbal communication issues provide paradigms for understanding how organizations use and respond to behaviors. Facial display, eye contact, paralanguage, body language, and appearance are the five individual subjects. Proxemics and chronemics are concepts more dependent on external factors.

Facial display includes smiles, use of hair, and the display of emotions. The face is a major method for transmitting meaning. Eye contact is a powerful mechanism for controlling transactions and numerous messages are created through eye behavior. Paralanguage is the manipulation of various aspects of the voice that provides explanation for the verbal messages.

Body language is concerned with how the body is used to communicate. Height and physique give messages in organizations. The use of body movement and gestures explains how synchrony works. Specific gestures allow illustration and adaptation, and etiquette provides an example of how expectations exist in organizations regarding body language.

All organizations have specific appearance expectations or dress standards. Uniforms are the most obvious form of dress requirements and are used to enhance the quality of organizations. Clothing sends messages to other people and has specific functions for each individual. In addition, clothing affects other peoples' perception of our abilities and changes our self-perception. Dress influences a person's power. How an individual dresses makes a significant difference.

Proxemics is a broad concept explaining how people use space. Access and control of space are general issues underscoring an individual's position in an organization. Personal space, touch, stigmas, and territoriality are four additional issues in proxemics. Intimate, personal, social, and public are the four types of personal space. Touch is zero proxemics. Power, dominance, interpersonal liking, and effective management are all displayed through the use of touch. A stigmatized, or discredited, individual makes us withdraw touch.

In two-person positions in seating, where people sit can indicate a competitive, cooperative, modified cooperative, or coactive psychological set. When people gather for meetings, specific seating arrangements tend to create activity spots or power centers. Regardless of the perspective taken, where someone sits does make a difference in terms of how much they will actively participate and possibly lead.

Territoriality can be explained by examining dynamic, semifixed, and fixed features. Increasing experimentation with changing territorial design in organizations can be seen with commons, caves, and cubicles. In addition, the size and location of an office are important nonverbal messages. For many Americans, their car and home have become their offices.

Chronemics is the use of time. Because of the control aspects of organizational life, punctuality and waiting are clear nonverbal messages.

As indicated at the beginning of the chapter, all communication behavior is interrelated. So, although content, or the verbal aspects, is important, the form, or nonverbal conditions, also must be considered. We have risked belaboring our analysis of nonverbal communication because it is very important to our understanding of organizational communication. Too often, log cabin advice is given, and believed, instead of developing an in-depth understanding of the critical issues. Any attempt to explain organizational communication without fully examining nonverbal communication simply would be incomplete.

Study Questions

1. What are the four major differences between verbal and nonverbal communication? Provide examples of each from your own personal experience.
2. Which ones of the eight universal principles of nonverbal communication did you find most surprising? Provide your own examples for all eight.
3. There are six principles contingent on the organization's culture and expectations. Explain each one with specific examples.
4. What are the key elements of facial display?
5. How does eye contact function as a nonverbal means of communication?
6. Why is silence a form of paralanguage?
7. Discuss the different aspects of body language.
8. How does clothing function in an organization?
9. Explain the different aspects of space.
10. Distinguish between dynamic, semifixed, and fixed-feature designs.
11. Provide three examples from your own experience of chronemics.

6
Networks and Channels

Organizations are living systems with numerous subsystems exchanging energy, information, and meaning through a mirage of networks and channels. These pulsating veins carry the messages critical to the survival, operation, and success of the system. Dubbed *networks* and *channels*, there are important differences between these two concepts. Networks are similar to the pathways and roads that develop over time in any community whereas channels are closer to the well-planned and generally accepted routes. Networks can occur spontaneously. Channels usually are prescribed and restricted.

Key concepts in this chapter include:

- Networks
- Network properties
- Roles
- Network applications
- Grapevines
- Networks and change
- Channels
- Downward communication
- Upward communication
- Horizontal communication

A more formal distinction is in order. When the *patterns, flows, and pathways of communication interactions become regularized*—not just one-time chance encounters—they are labeled *networks* (Tichy, 1981). Networks are the observed patterns of organization manifested through communication (Nohria, 1998). *Channels* are *organizationally sanctioned* and are utilized to *structure the flow of information, messages, and possibly meaning*. Classical management and organizational structures controlled the information and messages creating expressions such as "follow the channels." Elaborate systems of vertical and horizontal communication channels developed as a result.

Internal and external information, knowledge, and communication are vital to organizations. Inadequate information is the major cause of more than half of all the problems in human competence in organizations according to some studies (Boyett & Boyett, 1998). Even in the most basic job, not knowing what to do or why you are doing it can lead to mistakes. Add a lack of feedback and the potential for incompetence skyrockets. Remember, to survive and prosper, a living system must be open to knowledge, information, and meaning. "Knowledge management is nothing more than managing information flow, getting the right information to the people who need it so they can act on it quickly" (Gates, 1999, p. 238). Our discussions earlier in this text remind us that when we are discussing organizational communication, *information and meaning are verbs not nouns and knowledge management is a means not an end.* "The end is to increase institutional intelligence or corporate IQ. ... Corporate IQ is a measure of how easily your company can share information broadly and how well people within your organization can build on each other's ideas" (Gates, 1999, p. 239).

Networks and channels have an interacting effect on each other. For the purposes of clarity, this chapter examines networks, or patterns of interaction first, then the channels of communication.

Networks

Networks permeate organizations connecting the vast array of internal and external systems and subsystems ranging from our colleagues to customers to resources. "All organizations are, in important respects, social networks and need to be addressed and analyzed as such" (Nohria, 1998, p. 290).

The central importance of networks has increased because of the multiple changes occurring internally and externally. Highly networked organizations operate well in fast-paced or chaotic environments because they receive extensive information and knowledge from their surroundings (Shani & Lau, 2000). The Internet and other mediated communication processes such as Intranet, or internal organizational computer message systems, provide obvious examples of networks. The more connected or interdependent an organization is with its surrounding environment, the more likely it is to need effective networking. "An organization's environment is properly seen as a network of other organizations" (Nohria, 1998, p. 290). A good example of external networking is the *network organization*, spawned by information technology. This is the "alliance of several organizations for the purpose of creating a product or serving a client" (McShane & Von Glinow, 2000, p. 13). Cisco Systems, the world's leading provider of business-to-business (B2B) computer networks, is "a constellation of suppliers, contract manufacturers, assemblers, and other partners connected through an intricate web of information technology" (McShane & Von Glinow, 2000, p. 13). Because 70% of the components and work in Cisco's product is outsourced, frequently no Cisco employee comes in contact with the actual product. In 2000, Cisco Systems was the world's second-most valuable technology company (Thurm, 2000). For Cisco Systems, the networking process becomes the organization.

B2B marketing provides a dynamic example of the power of the Internet. The business networks bought and sold $43 billion in goods and services in

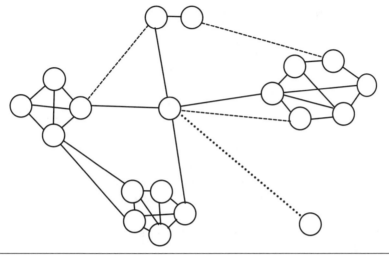

Figure 6.1 Typical network structure.

1999 and "by 2003, more than 90% of the $1.4 trillion in Internet commerce will be conducted between businesses" (Schonfeld, 1999, p. 67). Networks are central to internal and external organizational communication.

Defining Networks

Networks are the systems of interactions, both formalized and informalized, which are used in an organization and between organizations. They "are the patterns of contact between communication partners that are created by transmitting and exchanging messages through time and space" (Monge & Contractor, 2003, p. 440). Networks range from interpersonal to global.

In general, a network is *a web of freestanding participants linked or connected by one or more shared values.* These values may have a task or social orientation or both. Figure 6.1 indicates a typical network structure. At first glance, a network might appear to be a group. However, a network is distinct from a group in that it refers to a number of individuals (or other units) who persistently interact with one another in accordance with established patterns.

Finally, and perhaps most important, a network's operational definition is often a function of the investigator's specific area of interest. This means that if you are looking at the impact of telecommuting on stay-at-home employees, you will adopt a different definition of a network from someone who is studying top management teams. If you believe that friendship is a critical part of the success of teams, your network study will pay less attention to issues such as goal setting or task accomplishment. As with concepts such as communication and information, networks have multiple definitions.

Table 6.1 Functions and Activities of Networks

Function	Activities
Structure	Reflects the formal chart of the organization. This involves the passing of messages through the correct channels from the top to the bottom and back.
Information	Who actually controls the data that makes decisions.
Task expertise	The "how-to-do" information about processing a decision.
Status	Cliques of individuals who occupy the same type of organizational role.
Friendship	Based on interpersonal attraction and affiliation.
Social	Concerned primarily with the relationships with the ultimate goal being friendship or companionship.
Expertise	Concerned with obtaining necessary information and assistance in planning and organizing tasks.
Authority	Concerned with connecting the right power or authority individuals through various channels.

Each of these network functions will overlap, depending on the situation, individuals involved, or organizational culture.

Table 6.1 indicates some of the network functions discussed by researchers. Network types can range from electronic media (e.g., telemediated, computer-based, video screens, telephones) to a friendship network meeting over lunch. Network goals can include responding to specific occupational needs, meeting certain group needs, or providing information regarding job functions.

We belong to a variety of networks, which can operate independently or in conjunction with numerous other networks. How we do our jobs, complete tasks, work with other individuals and groups, or understand the organization depends, in large part, on messages delivered through networks. Networks offer insights into the strategic alliances, power and influence, and organizing efforts of an organization (Nohria, 1998). Because networks are microcosms of the patterns of communication in all organizations, they are complex and broad-based.

Networks perform a variety of important tasks because they connect people. In order to fully understand networks, we need to examine network properties.

Network Properties

There is a difference between classic organizational charts and networks. Charts outline who should communicate with whom. In networks, the ongoing patterns of influence are more dynamic. A great deal of communication is not formalized, does not travel in required directions, and may have little to do with authority (e.g., job roles, bosses, chain of command).

Both *prescribed and emergent* networks are important. A prescribed network indicates the direction for reporting and of influence and is similar to a channel. When we are assigned to a problem-solving group or placed in a team, we have been prescribed a means of communicating. An emergent network focuses on the flow of information, affective exchange, or actual influence. There can be considerable overlap between these networks. Two additional concepts—coupling and connectedness—need to be examined before we consider the various network roles.

Coupling The relationship process in networks is loosely or tightly coupled (Glassman, 1973; Weick, 1976). Coupling is related to *the amount of interdependence between subsystems. Loosely coupled subsystems* are related but *not highly interdependent.* When subsystems *are highly interdependent, they are tightly coupled.* In a tightly coupled situation, a change in one of the subsystems immediately affects or influences the other.

Loosely coupled relationships exist in a variety of organizations. Departments at a university, for example, tend to be loosely coupled. Although each department's activities and personnel need to be coordinated with the general university plans, there is little reason for constant interactions between departments.

When having a variety of subsystems pursuing their own agendas is not appropriate, tight coupling is necessary. Some types of organizations require an authoritarian form of control to maintain uniformity of standards. A Big Mac, one of McDonald's best-selling products, is supposed to taste the same in New York City as it does in Seattle. This is tightly coupled!

Do not mistake tight coupling as a synonym for classical management or top-down control. Coupling depends on the level of interdependence between the subsystems rather than the formal organizational structure. We are highly coupled when the other unit's actions impact directly or our activities or our actions impact on the other unit.

Autonomous units set up by organizations to research and develop new products often are *loosely coupled with the other organizational activities while exhibiting a high degree of coupling internally.* For example, *skunkworks* has become a much-used organizational term for a small, and often elite, clandestine team within a company. This somewhat less-than-endearing term is reserved for teams that create new products, solve difficult problems, or overcome major obstacles. "The term is a bastardization of 'skonk works,' the secret distillery in Al Capp's *Li'l Abner*" comic strip" (Carvell, 2000, p. 80). A Lockheed Martin engineer first used the term as a code for the company's—then Lockheed Aircraft—secret division for producing planes in World War II. Skunkworks "are the hallmark of innovative organizations" (Peters & Austin, 1985, p. 116). When GE decided to begin online auctions for their suppliers to bid on prices for parts, they set up "a skunkworks, a tiny laboratory that would hold experimental auctions and refine the process through trial and error" (Tully, 2000, p. 140). Now working throughout much of GE, some predictions are that this auctioning process could permanently revolutionize the $5 trillion marked for industrial parts.

Coupling is important as we strive to understand organizational communication. "The study of organizational communication should be less concerned with traditional distinctions between formal and informal communication and more concerned with identifying and understanding the coupling characteristics of organizational communication networks" (Daniels & Spiker, 1991, p. 104). Consider a final example. In most cases, students in a classroom are loosely coupled because everyone gathers simultaneously to examine the subject but there is little intermingling with many classmates after the class ends. Majors in the subject area, or study groups, could represent tightly coupled networks.

To conclude, in all organizations, there will be examples of loose and tight coupling within the general organizational structure. Some organizations encourage looser coupling whereas others demand strict adherence to specific rules or guidelines.

Connectedness   *Connectedness describes the extent to which network members identify with the goals of other members of their network.* When connectedness is related to a specific network, it is a measure of group cohesiveness (Pearce & David, 1983). At the one extreme are highly connected networks such as families with blood ties and a high level of integration of perspectives. Rural area farmers or coal miners' families are obvious examples where families have been forced to work together closely as support groups and for survival. There are infamous examples such as the Mafia. Family businesses, which pass from parents to children, are often highly connected networks. Somewhere shy of these are classmates, longtime friends, professional acquaintances, and family members who work together or who trade professional favors.

There are three advantages to a high degree of connectedness. First, increased connectedness among units leads to improved performance. Effective organizations have a high degree of employee identification with the basic goals because employees are well informed. "Too much secrecy and policies based on only a need to know restrict true participation to a small segment of the workforce. If employees lack data about costs, profits, losses, and business plans, they can't understand fully how they can contribute ideas for change and improvement" (Hickey & Casner-Lotto, 1998, p. 60). By connecting these estranged constituents, organizations can increase their chances for success.

Second, *intergroup connectedness* provides greater power to a group within an organization. If one unit is highly involved with another unit, the members of each unit have more power (Blau & Alba, 1982). Being connected means members of units have a greater opportunity for influencing other networks and increasing the cluster's resources.

Third, *highly connected networks increase information* because the members receive multiple inputs from a variety of sources. In addition, the information is more likely to be timely (Chae, Paradice, Koch, & Vo Van, Huy, 2005). With the continued dependence on technology in organizations, networks offer the means for making certain that people get the right information, at the right time, and in the right form (Penzias, 1989). Ford Motor Company's 350,000 blue- and white-collar workers are being provided with a Hewlett-Packard computer, a color printer, and unlimited Internet access for $5 a month in an effort to "boost technology skills, help with training and improve communications" (Eldridge & Armour, 2000, p. 1B). In addition to being an excellent employee perk, this connectedness should bring Ford employees closer together electronically on a 24/7 basis. Ford employees should become more comfortable with the Internet. Kerwin, Burrows, and Foust (2000) conclude, "Plugging hourly workers into the Net will also make it easier for Ford to communicate with employees worldwide" (p. 52). Delta Air Lines will provide similar opportunities to its 72,000 employees to boost productivity, increase computer and Internet skills, and assist in scheduling for pilots and engineers (Kerwin et al., 2000).

Both coupling and connectedness refer to the degree of interdependence between the subsystems or systems. Coupling is concerned with the structural interdependence whereas connectedness is concerned more with the psychological interdependence.

Weak Ties   High degrees of connectedness would seem to be advantageous. But wait, too much group like-mindedness can perpetuate problems because blind spots often are inevitable. The importance of *weak ties* enters at this point. Hiring a consultant to solve a particular problem in an organization is a good example of a weak tie. Rather than being part of the ongoing functioning of the organization, the outside expert brings different information, messages, and meaning. The expert's perspective is based on a particular set of knowledge regarding specific issues, or weak ties that "provide access to nonredundant information and novel knowledge" (Chae et al., 2005, p. 65). *Esprit de corps,* or strong cultures, are desirable attributes for departments, teams, or organizations, but being linked to information from outside sources is also vital to prevent errors and add new inputs. Groupthink provides us with powerful examples of the potential hazards of strong ties.

Groupthink   Janis (1972) was intrigued by the tendency of motivated, qualified, and informed groups to make poor decisions because of flawed judgments. He studied examples of disastrous decisions including the Cuban Missile Crisis, the Vietnam War, and the Watergate break-ins, and labeled this dysfunctional decision-making process *groupthink*. When groups or individuals become insulated from outside information, they are likely to perceive external inputs as a threat rather than as important information according to Janis. The group develops a likeness of thinking, or purpose, and rallies behind the group's leader thereby blinding them to important inputs—they move toward being a closed system. Janis counseled the establishment of weak ties in the forms of a devil's advocate, expanded resources, information, and improved decision-making processes to prevent the group from being closed.

There are numerous examples of the tragic results from groupthink. A careful analysis of the 1986 Challenger spacecraft disaster demonstrates that the pressure to launch the spacecraft led individuals to reject outside information and proceed with a deeply flawed decision (Gouran, Hirokawa, & Manz, 1986). The result was a needless loss of lives and a decrease in credibility for NASA. One author has labeled the process *freezethink*, because the commitment to launch was so great that the decision-makers stopped cold in their information gathering and solidified behind their erroneous course of action (Kruglanski, 1986). Studies of the Challenger disaster indicate that ample information was available to justify aborting the flight, but it was ignored, discredited, downplayed, or reframed to appear less ominous.

The Hubble Space Telescope fiasco offers a more complex story of how a highly talented group of individuals followed paths of flawed decision-making that were destined to failure (Capers & Lipton, 1993; Stein & Kanter, 1993). Hoping for a space exploration victory by putting a giant telescope in space, NASA and the supporting cast of engineers and designers at the Perkins-Elmer Corporation of Connecticut proceeded using numerous false assumptions regarding costs, design, and delivery time. Wanting to succeed blinded this group and left NASA with a telescope in space that did not work requiring subsequent and costly space flights to correct the errors.

NASA is hardly alone in providing current examples of groupthink. The University of Wisconsin-Madison apparently felt a need to illustrate a diverse student body on the cover of its fall 2000 admissions brochure (Wyatt, 2000). Unable to "find an authentic picture of diversity," they inserted the photo of an African-American male into a crowd of white football fans. The digitally altered cover was intended to convey an appearance of a diverse student body even though, as of fall 1999, fewer than 10% of the school's more than 41,000 students were non-white and 2.15% were black. The university instead made a decision that created national embarrassment and required the reprinting of all 106,000 copies at a cost of $63,000 to remove the picture (Wyatt, 2000, p. 5A). In 1996, Ford Motor Company removed the faces of Pakistani, Indian, and black employees and superimposed white faces (Parker-Pope, 1996). The photo was printed in newspapers worldwide and the employees whose faces had been changed reacted with shock. Ford, although embarrassed that the changes had been made, argued that the alterations reflected the ethnic makeup of Poland, which is almost entirely white and the photo was intended solely for that county. The pressure to appear diverse or to conform to a particular country's culture provides two current examples of the power of groupthink.

A much more tragic series of events put Ford in the news in 2000. The Bridgestone/Firestone ATX and Wilderness tires on the Ford Explorer were blamed for more than 100 deaths and numerous accidents (Dwyer, Carney, & Muller, 2000). Evidence appeared indicating that Bridgestone/Firestone had been aware of the problem since 1996 yet continued to supply the same tires. As the story unraveled, Ford appeared to have been aware of the problem but chose to discount its significance perhaps because the Explorer was the best-selling Ford vehicle and accounted for one fourth of Ford's sales (Healey & Nathan, 2000). In response to mounting pressures, 6.5 million tires were recalled in August 2000, Ford offered replacements through any tire dealership, and the inevitable lawsuits against Ford and Firestone began and settlements occurred in 2003 ("Bridgestone," 2005). When groups, teams, or organizations feel a threat from external sources, there can be a propensity to succumb to groupthink in a misguided attempt to protect their image or reputation. Often, this involves trying to retell or recast the issues in a more favorable way (Venette, Sellnow, & Lang, 2003).

These examples are important because we are examining well-qualified and highly motivated group members dealing with significant issues. The group process, however, was too tightly connected creating serious errors in judgment.

Overcoming the power of strong ties is not easy. Chen and Lawson (1996) report that in a laboratory study utilizing a survival exercise/game, the presence of a devil's advocate did not affect the amount of disagreements or the quality of decisions made. Their findings question the impact of a single solution to a group's tendency toward isolation. We have the tendency to band together when faced with an adversarial force rather than welcoming external messages. Remember, the harder we have worked as a group at arriving at a decision, the greater the tendency to stick to our decision. We now examine successful uses of weak ties to further clarify this point.

Using Weak Ties The tendency toward being closed to information and messages can be countered with the effective use of weak ties. Four examples should clarify this point.

Our first example, the 1983 Tylenol crisis, demonstrates how incorporating weak ties can assist in making effective decisions and handling a crisis. At the end of September 1983, seven deaths related to the ingestion of extra-strength Tylenol were reported in 2 days and Johnson and Johnson (J&J) had to decide how to respond to the crisis, including a major drop in sales, a potential public relations disaster, and additional deaths (Trujillo & Toth, 1987). The deaths were the result of cyanide poisoning and J&J correctly assumed that maintaining the public's trust was their most important task. Rather than relying on the public relations staff or a few key leaders, J&J immediately established a seven-member strategy team, communicated fully with the press, and integrated key organizational structures and functions (Trujillo & Toth, 1987). J&J's proactive approach to the crisis by seeking increased relations with the public and the press, and increased information regarding the best strategy, allowed the company to open up the system and utilize numerous weak ties—individuals and groups not normally part of the marketing or public relations process. Their handling of the crisis was so effective that they were able to increase their stock value and regain much of the lost pain reliever market within 5 months (Trujillo & Toth, 1987). Although this represents a public relations coup, it is even more dramatic as an example of the effective use of weak ties. J&J effectively opened up their organizational network, incorporated diverse opinions, and resolved the problem.

Second, most individuals use weak ties to enhance their own decision-making process. Choosing a college or university, for example, usually involves incorporating the opinions of close friends and family, or strong ties, and some outside reading and the advice of counselors and other sources, or weak ties. Perhaps your first contact with the school of your choice was through a mass mailing by the university.

Likewise, people outside your group of strong ties are a fertile source of information about employment opportunities (DuBrin, 1999). One study of professionals who had changed their jobs indicated the majority learned about the new position through sources to which they were weakly tied: "The thesis was that those to whom we are weakly tied move in different circles than we do and have different information than we do. The findings bore this out in that the vast majority of people who found new jobs through personal contacts were in touch with those contacts occasionally or rarely" (Roberts, 1984, p. 30). By networking, we can establish a set of ties that can increase our knowledge and potential for finding employment. "About 85% of job openings are found in the hidden job market" which includes jobs not advertised, registered with employment agencies, or listed with placement offices (DuBrin, 1999, p. 278). Expanding our immediate network makes intuitive sense. In fact, weak ties often provide information and perspectives not available otherwise. The problem, of course, is that we are most comfortable dealing with individuals and information familiar to us.

A third use of weak ties is regular, informal contacts, which function as *de facto* networks used by organizational members. As Mueller (1986) explained, "All large organizations have their interpersonal networks for exchanging favors on which much business depends. The very life of social systems has been dependent on the operation of informal networks" (p. 65). When information is sought, most professionals have a select group they call on for consulting, advice, or insight. Professionals have a list of individuals who are contacted for specialized information about certain issues.

Interorganizationally, there are *occupational communities* made up of individuals whose particular professions or areas of expertise develop their own networks (Chae et al., 2005; Van Maanen & Barley, 1984). These *communities of practice* often help set standards, develop operating procedures, and monitor certain activities (Wenger & Snyder, 2000). Lawyers, accountants, professors, human resource managers—the list is almost unlimited—create professional connections through associations that certify and provide credentials to members, provide important information, offer training and development opportunities, hold meetings, and take specific stances on issues. Organizations such as the National Association of Business Owners (NAWBO), Young Entrepreneur's Organization (YEO), TEC, or the Young President's Organization (YPO) provide company owners networks to gather information, offer insights and advice, and have fun (Greco, 1999). The companies that belong to TEC and YEO employ more than 1.5 million people and have combined sales exceeding $210 billion.

The Bridgestone/Firestone and Ford tire-separation SUV rollover lawsuits provide an example. Plaintiffs' attorneys, who bring tort lawsuits in product liability cases such as tobacco or faulty tires, are now forming coalitions of class-action law firms (France, 2001). "As a result of this unheralded management revolution, a sole practitioner based in a Buffalo strip mall can fight on equal terms with a company boasting bigger revenues than a Third World country" (France, 2001, p. 118). The Information Age, with the capacity to collect, store, and disseminate information to the coalition members, puts individual lawyers on an equal, and sometimes superior, footing with corporate attorneys. The AIEG (Attorneys' Information Exchange Group), founded in Birmingham, Alabama in 1980 and specializing in auto lawsuits, "began as an informal network of plaintiffs' attorneys with Ford Pinto cases. Fed up with the carmaker's hardball tactics, they began sharing internal corporate documents and trading tactical tips" (France, 2001, p. 118). To be sure, not everyone heralds these growing coalitions with favor including powerful corporate groups such as the American Management Association.

In addition, this professional networking process can be used to advance our careers and provide support and help. In turn, these professional associations must search out external input and information to "guard against using old ways of thinking and strategizing to interpret future trends and envision their implications" (Blaken & Liff, 1999, p. xvii). Weak ties in the form of external consultants, environmental scanning, and interorganizational information sharing are vital to maintain the health of any organization.

A fourth example of the power of weak ties is the *small world phenomenon*. Sociologist Stanley Milgram (1965) wanted to test the power of informal networks. He selected a volunteer person in Omaha, Nebraska, and a target person in Boston. The volunteer was sent the target's name and some information about the target and asked to send the target a packet. The volunteers did not know the target personally. So, the original source, or volunteer, was asked to find someone else who was also likely to know someone who could pass it on to the final target. Milgram repeated the study several times. The number of successful completions of this intercontinental task ranged from 12% to 33% with the number of links averaging from five to eight. He concluded that there are six degrees of separation. In other words, it took an average of only five intermediaries before the packet reached its recipient.

Six degrees of separation—how many people you can be away from the original source and still be connected—is a popular notion that became the theme of a play and the 1993 movie *Six Degrees of Separation*. These popularized the notion that a chain of six people or less can connect us all to each other. Consider the question, "Hey, do you know someone who …?" as you seek a job, connection, or problem solved. When you limit your inquiry to the friends of friends you are using two degrees of separation. When your friend knows someone who knows someone and so on you eventually arrive at six degrees of separation. The argument is that, at the six-degree point, the small world phenomenon begins to unravel. There are very practical organizational applications. "The small world model could be used to improve the operating efficiency of corporate giants like General Motors Corp., speed up transmissions over the Internet, and explain how infectious diseases spread and nerve impulses are coordinated in the brain" (Andreeva, 1998, p. 54). As organizations continue to become larger, as we discussed in chapter 1, creating small-worlds of problem solvers will be critical. "The key to turning a large world into a smaller, more efficient one is shortcuts: well-connected individuals or components that can cut across traditional boundaries in an organization" (Andreeva, 1998, p. 54). The Internet offers unlimited possibilities. For example, web communities are springing up that connect people of similar interests such as golf, neurosurgeons, or beekeepers allowing for a much broader link (Allbritton, 1998).

Responding that "It's a small world, isn't it!" is not an unusual occurrence. You may have been shocked in a conversation to find out that you both knew the same person or had worked for the same organization. What is not as surprising is to find out that you have an acquaintance that might know a particular person or work in the same organization as that person. If you were bent on getting a message to the target in the organization, you probably would be able to employ weak ties to deliver it. The Internet, with its capacity to quickly extend information sources, makes this type of search process even easier.

The strength of weak ties points to the importance of establishing broad, loosely constructed networks to enhance our functioning in an organization. All organizations depend on weak ties to accomplish their goals.

Clusters Connectedness has been classified further by looking at clusters, which are more richly connected, coupled, or tied than the general network.

In addition to the prescribed clusters, such as committees and work groups, there are coalitions and cliques.

A coalition is a perceived linkage among several individuals who believe that their ability to dominate organizational relationships is greater as a group than as individuals. So, coalitions tend to be temporary alliances with the goal being to control some type of activity. During reorganization, it is not unusual to find subgroups springing up to protect their traditional turf. In addition to domination, "coalitions often form when there are unusual or nonroutine demands, perhaps when firms develop new products or when the environment appears threatening" (Roberts, 1984, pp. 29–30). Special team efforts put together to complete projects or respond to outside threats that will be disbanded after the problem is resolved are examples of coalitions.

A *clique is a set of actors in a network who are connected to one another by strong relations.* Friendship networks are cliques. The more cohesive the group, and the more friendship ties that exist, the more active the process of communication. This, in turn, will lead to a greater uniformity of attitudes, opinions, and behaviors. Cliques will have frequent communication and information sharing and the linking between the members means the clique is tightly coupled and connected (Rogers & Agarwala-Rogers, 1976).

Roles

In theory, everyone is important to an organization and its communication processes. But, this assertion leaves the researcher with a monumental task. How and in what ways are they important? Network analysis points out that each individual in a network plays certain roles that can help and hinder the communication. Research has identified liaisons, gatekeepers, stars, bridges or linking pins, cosmopolites, and isolates as specific roles. As a catch-all category, individuals who have neither minimum nor maximum contact with others are referred to as members. The dynamics of any organization almost guarantees that group members perform different roles at different times fueled by the fundamental changes occurring in the modern organization. Our earlier discussion of living systems and communication makes it clear that merely being a member of the network creates the potential for messages. Now, we examine each of these roles. Along the way, you might consider which roles you have played during your professional and academic careers.

Liaisons   Liaisons are individuals who serve as intermediaries among various emergent work groups within a department or an organization. They provide the ties between the clusters and networks. Liaisons are not members of a cluster, but function as the link between two or more clusters. Liaisons are critical to the effective functioning of an organization (McShane & Von Glinow, 2000). Because liaisons are connected with various groups and are in contact with a variety of individuals, they receive more feedback and have more opportunities to deal with others.

Organizational liaisons include specialists (e.g., computer, health, safety, human resources) assigned either temporarily or permanently to work in units other than their own. Because of the importance of the linking process, a great deal of research has been conducted regarding liaisons. Among other findings, liaisons are more satisfied, hold higher official positions, and exercise greater influence because of their integrative role (Goldhaber, 1993). Liaisons have the potential for great influence in the organization because they transfer messages that they can alter, enhance, or diminish as they pass them along. "Most network studies find that 5 to 20% of an organization's members act as liaisons" (Tichy, 1981, p. 237). However, it would be incorrect to conclude that "once a liaison, always a liaison." In fact, research has not yet measured the stability of liaisons, so it is conceivable that the role passes between various network members. Based on what we know about the organization in 2000 and beyond, the liaison role would naturally move around a team or work group depending on the particular connecting needs.

For the purposes of clarity, remember that liaisons, bridges, and linking pins focus on slightly different connecting roles. The liaison does not belong to the different clusters, a bridge belongs to at least one, and the linking pin is involved in both.

Gatekeepers   A gatekeeper regulates the flow of information. This individual has the strategic capacity to decide what information will be forwarded to the other members of the clique. Gatekeeping has positive and negative effects in an organization.

One valuable attribute is that the person can prevent *information overload* by filtering and screening messages (Rogers & Agarwala-Rogers, 1976). Information, with its accompanying potential overload, is all too available today. For example, a weekday edition of *The New York Times* contains more information than the average person was likely to come across in a lifetime in 17th-century England (Wurman, 1987). The Internet has only served to exponentially expand the information being sent to all organizational members. The importance of the gatekeeping role should not be mistaken. The average business manager receives 190 messages per day (Labbs, 1999). Gatekeepers filter this massive number of messages.

The potential for screening out important messages is the most obvious problem with this role. When we discuss serial communication—which is communication that proceeds through a chain of individuals—later in this chapter, we further analyze this aspect of gatekeeping.

Two important factors to keep in mind at this point are (a) the messages the gatekeeper receives may or may not be forwarded, and (b) the messages may be filtered. The gatekeeper can make the decision to reduce, change, hold back, or push ahead one message over any other messages. This position's power lies in the control of access to messages and information.

For example, when you apply for a job, several gatekeepers may make important decisions regarding your qualifications before you ever have the opportunity to interview for the position. The actual decision-maker in the hiring process may not even see your resume if it does conform to the gatekeeper's notion of what the job entails. Finally, as we indicated with the "Waiter Rule," receptionists and secretaries frequently are asked about their impressions of a job applicant in terms of civility (see chap. 5). Their control of information regarding the applicant is a form of gatekeeping.

Stars   Stars are the focus of most communication within a group and they have many relationships with the other members. In an organization, stars tend to have "on the job" influence with most group members. Sometimes, this role is labeled the *opinion leader*, because the person is the center of network communication activity. Opinion leaders tend to be powerful, respected, and followed, without having any formal leadership role. Sometimes, these individuals are seen as "the invisible influencers in an organization–people who carry corporate clout but may not have an important job title" (Whitworth, 2006, p. 205).

Cosmopolites   A cosmopolite is an individual who has a relatively high degree of communication with the system's environment (Tichy, Tushman, & Fombrun, 1979). When they take on the role of providing information to the environment and bringing information back to the organization from the environment, they are called *boundary spanners*. These individuals link one organization with another.

Both boundary spanners and cosmopolites function as an interlocking element between the organization and its surroundings (Tichy et al., 1979). By bringing external information to the network, they help keep it alive by providing vital information to the network regarding the activities of the rest of the world.

Isolates   Isolates are decoupled from the network, removed from the regular flow of communication, and tend to be out of touch with the rest of the network. Determining how to apply the term *isolate* is relative.

First, someone can be an isolate with some decisions and deeply involved with others. Realistically, some group members tend to be isolated from certain decisions because they have nothing to add or are being ostracized.

Second, being removed from network activity can be by choice. For example, people doing fieldwork (e.g., linesman, sales, or deliveries), or a professor on sabbatical leave, are intentionally decoupled to enhance the individual's ability to work. Isolates report that their jobs are characterized by more autonomy and more identity than other roles.

In any case, being out of touch with the activities and decisions of the network has two important consequences. First, the information flow is restricted, either by a function of the individual's personality, or by choice. This lack of information can make it difficult for the network to maintain the isolate's commitment or coordinate the group's activities.

Second, by being on the fringe of the network, isolates develop some delimiting characteristics. Isolates can be less powerful, they may withhold information, they often perceive the system as closed to them, and therefore they would tend to be dissatisfied. In the end, the isolate cannot be an active part of the *esprit de corps* because few expressions of affect will take place. By staying at arm's reach from the ongoing political activities, isolates risk being passed over for important promotions or assignments. Out of sight is out of mind and influence often is a function of presence.

Enter the Digital Age   *Telecommuters* are dramatic examples of isolates, highlighting both the pros and cons (see chap. 12). Operating from home, these individuals connect with their organizations through machines connected to telephone lines creating a virtual organizational structure. The positive impact is that telecommuting allows individuals to work when and where they want, which should improve productivity. They tend to feel more motivated and more in control of their own lives. "Productivity gains of 10 to 40% and cost savings of $6,000 to $12,000 per year are common for employers" ("Virtual Offices," 2000). If there are responsibilities at home such as infant care, telecommuting could offer an additional benefit. International Data Corp., using market information on information technology, found that of "the 37.8 million households with dependent children, there are 11.6 million that have at least one parent who works from home" (Sharpe, 2000, p. 112). A survey in 2000 by the John J. Heldrich Center for Workforce Development found that 41% of employees say they can do their job away from the office with phone, fax, and Internet access (Carey & Mullins, 2000, p. 1B). Opportunities to increase productivity through electronics might be overlooked by organizations that insist on traditional work arrangements.

On the negative side, home responsibilities can complicate getting work done (Sharpe, 2000). Equally important, telecommuters often feel removed from the important political connections inherent with being physically at work. Human resource executives were asked if "employees who use telecommuting or virtual workplace programs help or hurt their careers" (Yang & Merrill, 2006, p. 1A). The responses were noticeably divided with 30% saying it helped, 25% saying it hurt, and 39% saying neither (Harris Interactive, 2006, p. 1A). An important concern regarding telecommuting is that it leaves you out of the loop—simply put, to be seen is to have influence and being available

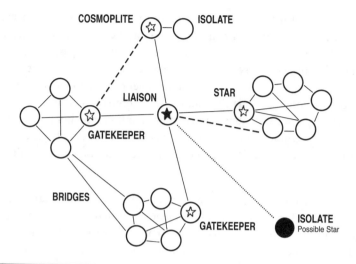

Figure 6.2 Various network roles.

to immediately engage in problem solving increases credibility. Visibility "increases with the amount of face-to-face contact rather than less personal forms of communication" (McShane & Von Glinow, 2000, p. 380). So, telecommuters may accomplish more work but feel isolated from their organizations. Finally, there is the social value of being with other individuals. In fact, "gossip is one of the things telecommuters miss most" (Fisher, 2005, p. 202).

Specific network roles include liaisons, gatekeepers, stars, cosmopolites, and isolates as shown in Figure 6.2. How these roles operate is even more apparent when we analyze the network types.

Intranets We devote an entire chapter to communication technologies (chap. 12). Intranets, or internal organizational websites, are a specialized form of digital communication deserving mention at this point. The new connecting power of intranets can change the entire hierarchical structure. Are intranets being utilized? A survey in 2000 revealed that companies are using intranets to enhance employee communication (78%), improve service to employees (59%), promote common corporate culture (45%), refocus human resources on strategic activities (29%), and reduce cost (28%) (Armour, 2000). Intranets may include access to employee phone directories, organizational charts, employee benefits, contracts, past employee publications, and videos of staff meetings (Holtz, 1996).

Because intranets also connect employees, they have the potential to bring employees together by fostering collaboration across physical and hierarchical boundaries (Scheider & Davis, 2000). The intranet "empowers employees and departments to become publishers and communication facilitators" (Holtz, 1996, p. 55). Intranets are a haven of organizational social knowledge allowing employees to feel more involved and more informed, connecting dispersed employees, and encouraging communication and collaboration (Scheider & Davis, 2000). In a recent survey at American Century Investments, 75% of the mutual firm's employees said they relied on the intranet for news about the company. Texas Instruments has an intranet program that gets new hires up to speed before they start their jobs. Other companies have concierge services that help plan vacations, information about competitors, or industry-specific news (Armour, 2000). Being connected is increasingly an electronic issue instead of the traditional gathering at the water fountain or talking to the right people.

Conclusion—Networks Networks accomplish three very important goals for their members. First, the relational influence created through transactions increases an individual's, group's, or department's power. Likewise, a team's, cluster's, or clique's involvement with other groups enhances its power. Second, they allow for the influx of information that might not occur if there were fewer external contacts. Finally, they offer affect- or friendship-oriented bonds.

Specialty networks, such as skunkworks or project management teams can be created for the very purpose of isolating the members from interactions with the rest of the organization. The goal is to enhance the quality of the single network away from the influence of the rest of the organization. These types of networks also overcome the apparent paradox between the need for teamwork and togetherness, as evident in successful organizations, and the dangers of groupthink.

Network Applications

To further understand the terminology, roles, and importance of networks, we will examine five concepts: network analysis, leadership use of networks, specialized networks, teamwork, and innovation. "Network analysis is capable of linking the micro and macro approaches to organizational behavior, and network concepts account for phenomena heretofore described only anecdotally or implicitly" (Tichy, 1981, p. 227). In other words, the small interpersonal relationships and the larger department, unit, and organizational interactions can be examined and understood in terms of networks.

Four examples show how networks aid organizations: using specialized structures, enhancing teamwork, allowing employees in the ownership of the organization, and having systematic management networks.

Specialized Networks Specialized networks are intended to make certain innovations occur by encouraging effective interactions between individuals and teams (Mohrman et al., 1995). We already have examined the effective use of networking. Examples such as skunkworks and the J&J Tylenol case demonstrate this process of making certain the right people get in touch with each other. Examinations of high performance organizations find that "the traditional hierarchy is dismantled" with teams and networks taking over many of the traditional responsibilities assigned to supervisors (Boyett & Boyett, 1998).

There are unlimited possibilities for the manipulations and configurations that can be used on the basic concepts presented by these examples. A more generic concept, based on effective networks, is teamwork.

Teamwork   Creating specialty networks is not always practical or applicable to particular tasks or organizations. In these cases, teamwork is used to maximize interactions (Bolman & Deal, 2003). Teamwork is virtually synonymous with organized activities and we devote an entire chapter to understanding groups and teams later in this text.

The secret to success is to effectively network as a team. Teams need to have leadership, member commitment, continued process development, and regular meetings (Mohrman, Cohen, & Mohrman, 1995). As such, *teams are ongoing, coordinated groups of individuals working together even when they are not in constant contact.* You will recall that networks are not small groups. Teams provide a specific justification for that conclusion. A team shares common boundaries, interdependent tasks, articulated purposes, and understood, owned, goals. As such, teams may start as coalitions, but in a short period of time they operate as a clique form of a network.

Employee Ownership and Incentive Programs   A number of companies are giving employees a real stake in the business through programs such as profit-sharing, gain-sharing or *employee stock ownership* plans (ESOPs). *Gain-sharing* "is designed to share the cost savings from productivity improvement with employees" (Denisi & Griffin, 2005, p. 392). Groups and teams attempt to lower costs, and otherwise improve productivity, and the resulting cost savings are quantified and translated into dollar values. As the name implies, ESOPs create stock ownership intended to increase employee motivation through involvement (Van de Vliet, 1997).

Systematic Management Networks   Individuals in charge do not and cannot operate alone. In particular, studies indicate that managers make extensive use of systematic networks. Kotter (1982) wanted to know what successful general managers (GMs) actually do so he observed 15 successful GMs over a 5-year period. He found that GMs establish broad networks with a variety of groups and individuals including their bosses, peers, and immediate subordinates. In addition, these managers had contact with financial sources, subordinates of subordinates, customers, suppliers, competitors, government, press, and the public. These networks included hundreds and sometimes thousands of people.

At one point or another we will all be in the position to be in charge of something. Regardless of your area of specialization, you will develop a variety of informal and systematic networks. You will learn who is most likely to be able to give good advice and who you must contact to accomplish specific activities. Within a short period of time, the informal and systematic networks probably will cross over each other. The post-2000 emerging organizational structure will continue to emphasize the importance of systematic networks where you will create interdependencies with a specific consultant, for example, and then extinguish it when the need is fulfilled.

Mentors provide another example of a systematic network. Mentoring is a process where an experienced employee helps a less experienced individual learn the ropes, anticipate possible problems, and take advantage of opportunities. As a neophyte, you might find it useful to find a mentor who will provide linking information to aid your entry, development, and advancement in the organization. These individuals can be wise to the workings of the organization thereby facilitating your entry into important networks (Ragins, 1997). When 4,561 respondents from 42 countries were asked in a recent survey, "How much of an impact does coaching or mentoring have on career success?" 46% responded great, 45% moderate, 8% small, and only 1% little or none (Yang & Gellers, 2006). Coaching is an interpersonal process between a superior and subordinate that focuses on behavior issues rather than overall issues covered in mentoring (Reece & Brandt, 2005). In many situations, these two terms are used intermittently.

Grapevines

Understanding our working environment is important so we actively seek information and meaning. One of the most important networks in any organization is the grapevine. When we need clarification, information, or feel powerless because we do not know enough about our futures or jobs, we tune into the grapevine (Bell & Smith, 1999). One survey indicated that "63% of U.S. employees get all or most of their information about their companies from 'water-cooler talk'" (Fisher, 2005, p. 202). Although many pundits dismiss the grapevine, or water-cooler talk, as gossip and rumor, this is a rash conclusion. In a recent nationwide poll by OfficeTeam, nearly 40% of executives huddled around the water cooler, or other common meeting place, said their discussions focused on business-related matters, 12% discussed sports, politics, and personal issues but only 9% comprised gossip (Salopek, 2000). This informal network is a vital part of the organizational communication process.

The term *grapevine* originated during the Civil War (Davis, 1953). The telegraph wires used to pass military intelligence were strung loosely from tree to tree, resembling a grapevine. This stringing procedure tended to cause the messages to be garbled. Grapevine is now applied to messages that travel through an organization with no apparent structure or clear direction (Davis,

1973; Gibson et al., 1991). Grapevine is an excellent metaphor for describing this networking process. Rather than moving in predictable directions, it travels where the ground is most senile; bears fruit in bunches (clusters), and heads in a variety of directions depending on the climate. The grapevine travels in all directions and operates overtly and covertly. We now examine the grapevine's functions and the process.

Functions of the Grapevine   The grapevine reflects the quality of the activities within the organization, fills an information void, and provides meaning to organizational activities.

First, the grapevine serves as a barometer providing vital feedback to management regarding the organization and its employees (Gibson et al., 1991). Although some managers try to stomp out the grapevine, most theorists feel the grapevine indicates the need people have to talk about their company and their jobs (Griffin, 2005). An active grapevine is indicative of the company's health and spirit and executives can learn a great deal by listening to it. Stories, whether passed through the grapevine or told in other settings, "say a lot about how employees believe the organization 'really' works" (Deetz, Tracy, & Simpson, 2000, p. 79).

Second, the grapevine functions as an important message source. The grapevine is most active when (a) there is great upheaval or change within the organization, (b) the information is new, (c) face-to-face communication is relatively easy, and (d) workers cluster along the vine.

Finally, the grapevine provides sense-making information to members of the organization. As messages travel through the grapevine, management's messages get translated into terminology that makes sense to workers. The grapevine helps interpret management for the employee, which makes it a vital aspect of organizational communication. Lussier (1999) makes an important observation: "When the grapevine allows employees to know about a management decision almost before it is made, management is doing something right" (p. 145).

So, the grapevine is an important source of messages and information for employees and for management. Does the grapevine perform these functions well?

Analysis of the Process   The grapevine indeed proves to be a vital tool for both employees and management. There are three specific attributes of the grapevine that make it important and useful. It is fast, accurate, and carries a great deal of information (Goldhaber, 1993). The grapevine's major disadvantage are rumors.

First, the grapevine is fast. We observed at the beginning of this chapter that networks are the express highways of an organization. This is certainly true of grapevines. In situations involving job security or layoffs, for example, numerous organizations have learned just how quickly the news spreads through the grapevine (Johns, 1988). Messages spread quickly as organizational members seek meaning.

Second, the grapevine is surprisingly accurate. Rather than being a source of unfounded gossip, the grapevine has an accuracy of 75% to 90% for noncontroversial information (Lussier, 1999). When errors do occur, they are generally in the area of incorrect emphasis based on incomplete information (Griffin, 2005). The grapevine is not always right, of course, because *being 75% to 90% accurate also means that the grapevine is inaccurate 10% to 25% of the time.*

Finally, the grapevine contains a significant amount of information. In addition to the messages regarding the organization's health or the employees' sentiments, the grapevine allows organizational members to vent messages that simply do not fit into the formal channels of communication. In the same vein, grapevines can carry socially oriented messages, which develop relationships and enhance a sense of belonging. In addition, the formal channels of communication often require reinterpretation so that the majority of employees can understand fully the meaning of the messages, which is accomplished through the grapevine (Timm & DeTienne, 1995). "Enlightened managers know that the more relevant and timely the information they provide to employees, the more likely the employees are to be highly motivated to do a better job, to advance their positions, and to further the goals of the organization itself" (Argenti & Forman, 2002, p. 155).

Rumors are the primary negative feature of the grapevine. These are based on unverified information communicated through the grapevine that lacks substantial supportive evidence. The greater the stress, importance, or ambiguity in the situation, the greater the likelihood for rumors. "Rumors often start when management disastrously tries to hide things from employees" (Lussier, 1999, p. 145). Rumors can take on a life of their own and threaten the organization (Light & Landler, 1990).

The activities of an organization's counterculture—ranging from dissenters to actual subversives—can be spread through the grapevine detailing reasons for these antimanagement positions. Lacking a proactive organizational communication process, rumors regarding these activities can spread through the grapevine supporting the rationale behind these anti-establishment activities.

Procter & Gamble's logo provides an excellent example of how rumors operate (O'Donnell, 2005). From 1981 to 1991 Procter & Gamble (P&G) fought the rumor that its corporate logo—which had a man in the moon against a field of 13 stars intended to stand for the original 13 colonies—was related to Satanism or some other anti-Christ symbol. At one point, P&G had to add employees to handle the 15,000 logo-related calls per month they were receiving on a nationwide toll-free consumers' line ("Company Still," 1988). P&G finally redesigned its symbol and eliminated the curly hairs in the man's beard that seemed to look like the number 6 ("P&G Logo," 1991). The number 666 is linked with the anti-Christ in the Book of Revelations in the *Bible*. Eventually, P&G changed its logo.

The Internet has added power to rumors. For example, one common rumor claimed that more than "25 companies ranging from Microsoft to Sony to Victoria's Secret were giving away money to anyone who forwarded promotional e-mails to friends" (O'Donnell, 2005, p. 3B). This simply does not happen. A disgruntled Marine claimed online that Starbucks did not support U.S. soldiers in Iraq because it refused to send free coffee to soldiers who asked for it. He later apologized, but no one knows the possible damage. Costco was accused online of being owned by China because the name stands for China Off Shore Trading Company. In truth, Costco is based in Washington State and is publicly traded. Sony and Target have also had to battle online rumors (O'Donnell, 2005).

Two rumors, or perhaps wishful thinking, seem to permeate colleges and universities. One is called the suicide rule: If your roommate commits suicide, you will receive straight As because your trauma will make it impossible to concentrate on your studies. Despite the prevalence of this rumor, researchers could not find a single campus without the rumor *or* with the rule (Brunvard, 1990). Likewise, most students will wait 10, 15, or 20 minutes for an instructor. After the expired time, the class will leave citing the "20-minute rule." Once again, researchers cannot find this rule in writing, but its acceptance makes it *de facto* policy on most campuses. This is not true for the suicide rule.

Rumors are powerful forms of grapevine communication because they offer explanations for events or offer hope for certain outcomes. Rumors also can reflect genuine fears held by organizational members. To minimize rumors, managers are counseled to keep employees informed, pay heed to the rumors, act promptly, and enlighten employees (Vickery, 1984). Essentially, feeding the grapevine with valid information is the secret to making this important channel of communication productive.

An entire field of study called *Urban Legends* relates to the widespread acceptance of stories that have no actual validity (Gillins, 1982). Starting with a phrase like, "It must be true, it happened to ...," these examples of modern folklore carry some type of poetic justice or moral about how to deal with certain situations. Organizations have similar legends regarding larger-than-life heroes who overcame difficult situations. These heroes provide operating information for other members of the organization on what to do. If morale is low, these anti-establishment heroes personify ways to beat the system. In either case, the rumors involve the organization's legends, folk stories, folk heroes, and villains.

The messages that pass through the grapevine are vital to the corporate culture. These stories about particular events become the legends of the organization. "Procedure manuals might have rules, but stories have morals." In fact, "A CEO can give all the rah rah speeches and hand out all the T-shirts she or he wants. But if the legends or the current desk-to-desk whispers are about actions she or he took that discredit her or his symbolic behavior, they may as well save their breath" (Waterman, 1987, p. 269).

Some managers find the grapevine useful when it passes information they like and they call it gossip and rumor when the information is unfavorable. This is a myopic view of communication. Whatever passes through the grapevine provides important information regarding the organization. One suggestion is rather than trying to control rumors, "get a few influential people and start your own rumors—accurate ones" (Fisher, 2005, p. 202). Increasingly, insightful organizations view the grapevine, whether person to person or electronic, to be a useful tool of communication of accurate and necessary information and messages (Griffin, 2005).

In conclusion, the grapevine is important, because it reflects the quality of the activities within the organization, fills an information void, and provides meaning to organizational activities. Contrary to popular assumptions, it is fast, accurate, and oriented toward information rather than gossip. In the absence of information, rumors occur to help explain events. Combating rumors requires a proactive approach to sharing information.

Networks and Change

The change process places the analysis of networks in perspective. All organizations must change by adapting to the environment, evolving to remain competitive or altering procedures and products simply to survive. The most admired companies, according to *Fortune* magazine, are those that are the most innovative (O'Reilly, 1997). In the period from 1995 to 2005, the 25 most innovative companies in the S&P (Standard & Poor) Global 1200 companies had a profit more than eight times greater than the less innovative companies and this success was largely due to innovation (Henry, 2006). Every organization will grow, diminish, gain and lose personnel, alter product lines, have new and different customers, and be influenced by a number of other environmental factors. To adapt to these changes, organizations engage in various processes of change.

Successfully managing change is very difficult (Cummings & Worley, 2005). Simply because a new procedure makes sense does not mean it will be accepted by members of the organization. "People resist change when they are uncertain about its consequences. Lack of adequate information fuels rumors and gossip and adds the anxiety generally associated with change" (Cummings & Worley, 2005, p. 159). Information about new or different products and procedures spreads through a process called *diffusion of innovation*. In numerous studies, excellent products or operating procedures can take 30 to 40 years before widespread dissemination (Rogers, 1983). Studies of new electronic technologies show, "It takes from 5 to 15 years before new electronic technologies catch on among consumers" ("New Technologies," 1999, p. 8). Portable electronic devices such as cell phones have proven that the adoption time can be significantly shortened when users perceive immediate values (see chap. 12).

When innovations are introduced, most of us do not use objective or scientific evaluations (Rogers, 1983). Instead, we depend mainly on the subjective evaluation conveyed to us from others we think are similar to ourselves. This dependence on the communicated experience of near peers suggests that the heart of the diffusion of the innovation process is the imitations by potential adopters of their network partners who have already adopted. "Study after study [that] Rogers reviewed reveals that (1) an innovation takes off only after interpersonal networks have become activated in spreading subjective evaluations and (2) success is related to the extent that the change agent or marketer worked through opinion leaders" (Peters, 1987, p. 241). Studies of successful change efforts support the importance of interpersonal and group networks that increase information exchange and support solutions to potential problems imposed by new technology (Tjosvold, 1995).

Our discussion of networks clearly does not incorporate all the specialized networks. As you become part of an organization, you will be engaged in a variety of digital and mediated networks such as e-mail, cell phones, computer conferencing networks, networking for specific goals, and various other links using personal computers, communication technology, and conference software. You will recall that a network can be almost any set of relationships an investigator chooses to isolate.

Conclusion—Networks

Before moving to a discussion of channels, consider what we now know about networks. Obviously, networks are critical to organizational functioning and we need a fuller understanding of them. First, networks are regularized patterns of interaction in an organization. Individuals belong to a variety of networks and depend on them for critical information, energy, and meaning.

Second, networks have properties including coupling, connectedness, and roles. Coupling is a reflection of the amount of interdependence between subsystems. The amount of identification by network members with the goals of the network is called connectedness. The strength of weak ties phenomenon is a good example of how networks function.

Groupthink and freezethink show the problem with overconnectedness. Organizations, as well as individuals, can use weak ties to overcome some of these problems.

Third, clusters can be divided into coalitions and cliques with specific roles. Coalitions are linkages for political or pragmatic purposes. A clique is created because of high connectedness.

There are numerous network roles. Research has identified liaisons, gate-keepers, stars, bridges or linking pins, cosmopolites, and isolates. Each role has a function in the network. In general, liaisons seem the most active and isolates are outside the network. However, different people play different roles at different times in a network.

Specific applications of networks include systematic management networks, specialized structures, teamwork, and employee ownership. Networks also provide a useful means for understanding the change process. The grapevine offers an excellent example of the institutionalization of a network.

At this point, you might be tempted to conclude that an understanding of networks would be sufficient as a perspective on communication flow in an organization. If our only concern were with influence, perhaps networks would suffice. However, channels are the sanctioned means of organizational communication so we need to understand them as well.

Channels

In all organizations, there is an intertwining of networks and channels. Although networks often operate in a *de facto* manner in the decision making process, most organizations assign significant *de jure power*, or sanctioned importance, to formal channels. These channels are downward, upward, or horizontal with accepted forms of restrictions that control these patterns. "The link between organizational structure and communication is a very basic and important one. Simply put, an organization's structure dictates who can or must communicate with whom. An organization's lines of authority show the pathways through which messages have to flow within organizations" (Greenberg, 1983, p. 319). If you have had an opportunity to work for an organization that believes in "following the channels," you have experienced the impact.

Channel Characteristics

Vertical channels—those flowing up and down the organization—have five characteristics. These include one-way or two-way communication, channels as organizational memories, channels as a managerial prerogative and responsibility, channel properties as intervening variables, and the different perspectives of the channel users.

One-Way or Two-Way Communication   At the most basic level, communication patterns can be analyzed as being primarily one-way or two-way. One-way is essentially top-down or "I talk and you listen." A traditional supervisor operating within the hierarchical, classical management structure gives or posts instructions, and expects no response beyond compliance from subordinates. In many organizations, managers assume that e-mailed directions or instructions can be sufficient to achieve successful communication. Two-way communication allows for questions, interactions, and discussion.

One-Way   When the tasks required are fairly straightforward, there may be little need for a response. Certain safety regulations, for example, are not open to question. Zero-tolerance policies, where the rules prevail regardless of the circumstances, are used by organizations with regards to sexual harassment or substance abuse to remove any doubts ("Preventing," 1999). You probably can generate several examples of one-way communication from your past employment or classroom experiences. Although we might consider this limited communication process suspect, if the sender and receiver have a good working relationship, are able to coordinate their activities without discussion, and the task is fairly straightforward, it might be a waste of time to engage in two-way communication.

Two-Way   In most cases, two-way communication is more successful. Clearly, organizational stakeholders need to feel that they have a say in the interaction. "To build morale, communication has to be two-way. At the 100 Best Companies, it's frequently positive" (Branch, 1999, p. 130). A large East Coast bank found that the "branches with two-way communication between people at all levels were 70% more profitable than branches with predominately one-way communication between managers and staff" (Moorehead & Griffin, 1998, p. 315). Training organizational members to understand, follow, and implement sexual harassment and substance abuse policies, for example, requires excellent two-way communication (Risser, 1999).

Channels as Organizational Memories   These message-processing systems are the data sources for the memory systems of an organization. Information, meanings, messages, and knowledge flow through these veins providing critical nutrients to feed the memory of the organization. McShane and Von Glinow (2000) offer a fairly obvious conclusion: "communication plays an important role in knowledge management" directly impacting the organizational memory (p. 233). In the opening chapter, we discussed how important knowledge is to the successful organization, and that management has the primary responsibility for providing information to enhance the quality and consistency of the memory.

Second, what we pay attention to and therefore accomplish in an organization is a function of the messages we receive regarding what the organization feels is important. Put another way, what appears in the channels draws attention to those concepts as being important. Hierarchies guard information within the management structure, whereas organizations working toward empowerment share information freely.

Channels as a Managerial Prerogative and Responsibility   Third, management has primary control of the vertical channels of communication. Employees are called to a meeting, asked for input, or issued a directive, and management usually decides the form, location, and time of these meetings.

Ironically, this sense of responsibility tends to lead to overcontrol by some managers when they attempt to guarantee communication success through careful guidance of the channels, especially in mechanistic, bureaucratic organizations (Cummings & Worley, 2005). Worried about miscommunication, managers might demand compliance without engaging in a two-way communication process or discussions. The leading organizations are increasing employee control over channels in an attempt to grow, take advantage of employee insights, and become even more competitive (Levering & Moskowitz, 2000).

Channel Properties as Intervening Variables   Channeling, timing, editing, and abstracting are four intervening variables that influence the sender's decision regarding the message. The consequence of messages traveling through intermediaries is explained through the concept of serial transmission. First, we consider the four intervening variables.

Channeling explains why messages are sent and others are withheld. In making a channeling decision, organizational members consider the perceived credibility that will be assigned to the source, the costs of communicating with that individual, the importance the receiver will place on the message, and the need for the information because of high connectedness or task interdependence.

Timing explains the rationale behind possible delays. Senders tend to delay messages until they are certain the receiver will pay attention. "This might not be the best time for this information or message" is a fairly common observation. For example, the climate or atmosphere might be wrong or the message may not be important to the sender when compared to other information currently being handled. So, the transmission is delayed. Finally, the number of links involved in the process also impacts timing. More links increase the likelihood that one of the links will delay the transmission.

Editing involves modifying the message. If the sender believes changing the message will increase its chances for acceptance, then distortion can occur. The message's format can be changed and the ambiguity of the original information provides a powerful opportunity. Finally, message receivers tend to edit the content depending on the amount of credibility they assign to the original source.

Abstracting occurs when we try and simplify or shorten the original message. Upper level management tends to want the "bottom line" or "key issues." Once again, we tend to simplify messages in the hope that we will increase their acceptance or understanding. All four of these concepts should be clear to anyone who has tried to alter a message to make certain it was more acceptable or modified a message to make it clearer.

Table 6.2 Serial Transmission

That's No Eclipse—It's a Blackout.
Chain of Command, J5 Directorate, to All Officers from J5

Director: Gentlemen, tomorrow at 1315 hours there will be a total eclipse of the sun. This is a rare phenomena and I would like the officers of J5 to internalize this experience in order to broaden their cognitive awareness. All personnel will fall out on the parking area and I will explain the circumstances which cause eclipses of the sun and moon. Should there be inclement weather, we will not be able to see the eclipse, but I will speak to all personnel in the J5 conference room.

Deputy Director: Gentlemen, by order of the director, there will be an eclipse of the sun. If it rains, you won't be able to see it from the parking lot, so the eclipse will take place in the J5 conference room. This is a rare phenomenon which does much to enhance the individual officer's internalization of broad awareness.

Ch. M. Sgt.: Tomorrow, the director and the deputy director will eclipse the sun. If it rains or snows, this'll take place in the conference room. If not, it'll happen outside.

Ch. P&S: My officers don't need an eclipse of the sun.

Ch. Plans: Let's include this in our insurgency prevention plan.

Ch. Weapons: Can you eat an eclipse?

Action Officer: It looks as though the J5 Directorate will be eclipsed tomorrow. It is a shame that this doesn't occur every day.

Serial transmission is the sending of messages along a chain of people or links. The popular child's game, telephone, where one person whispers a message to another, who then proceeds to pass it on to another, until the last person states the message they received, illustrates this problem. For children, this experience is funny because the final message form is always very different from the original. When this same process is illustrated to managers, they are surprised. In any organization, there are numerous links through which messages must travel.

Messages will become distorted. Table 6.2 shows a humorous, and widely used, example of the possible distortions in downward communication. Various aspects of serial transmission operated to change the message substantially from the first version to the second.

Three characteristics of serial transmission create the principal problems. They are condensation, closure, and expectations. *Condensation* is caused when individuals use fewer words or details as they pass the message along. When we are given a message to pass along to someone else, we might assume some aspects are irrelevant or redundant so we simplify the message. In the process, vital information can be lost. *Closure* occurs because we tend to have a low tolerance for ambiguity. Relayers of messages fill in the missing information as they repeat it so that the message makes more sense. When the relayers add meaning to a message based on their *own expectations*, we have the third type of serial transmission problem. All three of these serial transmission problems are important because the changes are not a result of willful distortion. They are, instead, attempts to make sense of a message as it is passed along.

So what? Actually, the consequences are quite serious. Regardless of the intent of the message initiator, the individuals or groups receiving the message will not be privy to the same meanings. The new millennium demands highly adaptive organizations able to quickly utilize knowledge and information. To accomplish this task, superiors and subordinates will need to understand and utilize much of the same information. If the quality of transmission is suspect, so are the actions.

Different Perspectives   Finally, superiors and subordinates frequently have different information needs situated in different responsibilities and activities. In a traditional organization, different levels of an organization worked with different problems, stakeholders, and issues. Managers did not run machinery and sales people rarely packed products. "The information requirements of superior and subordinates are not symmetrical. What the superior wants to know is often not what the subordinate wants to tell him; what the subordinate wants to know is not necessarily the message the superior wants to send" (Katz & Kahn, 1966, p. 239). So, even when the other channel characteristics are working to enhance effective communication, different perspectives existed. This use of the past tense does not mean that the majority of organizations have overcome this compartmentalization of jobs, groups, and functions. However, it is becoming increasingly apparent that integration of activities is much more important than separation.

A remarkably simple but tragic example of different perspectives was demonstrated in the last week of September 1999 when NASA lost its $125 million Mars Climate Orbiter as it approached Mars' surface (Hoversten, 1999). The 9-month trip through space was for naught because the crucial calculation by two geographically separated teams for the orbiter's thrust as it approached Mars was incorrect. The Lockheed Martin team in Denver used English measurements with their equation relying on pounds and feet whereas NASA's Jet Propulsion Laboratory in Pasadena, California, assumed the calculations were in metric terms based on kilograms and meters. The error caused the craft to veer to within 37 miles of the Martian surface leaving it well below the minimum of 53 miles for staying outside the gravitational pull. Although the technical transmission through channels was fine, the human equation failed.

In summary, channel characteristics are: (1) one-way or two-way, (2) providers of important information about the organization's memory, (3) primarily a managerial prerogative, (4) subject to numerous intervening variables, and (5) affected by different perspectives.

We can add even more clarification to channels by examining vertical and horizontal communication. Vertical communication is downward and upward.

Downward Communication

Downward communication reinforces the hierarchical nature of organizations. When superiors communicate with subordinates, they are exercising implicit or explicit control. This form of communication is vitally important and done well helps establish a positive climate (Hiam, 1999). The Hudson Institute, an internationally recognized public policy organization, surveyed more than 3,000 employees from a broad spectrum of U.S. organizations and found that one in three employees have no commitment to their employer and only 45% feel a strong commitment to their organization (Walker Information, 2000). The study, *Halfway Out the Door*, concluded: "An employee's commitment is generated from their daily interactions with the company and its policies" (Walker Information, 2000, p. 13). Of primary importance was the extent to which "employees have access to information and whether or not employees are satisfied with the way it is communicated" (Walker Information, 2000, p. 13).

Functions of Downward Communication

The five most prevalent functions are: (1) giving job instructions; (2) providing job rationale; (3) explaining procedures, policies, and practices; (4) furnishing performance feedback; and (5) transmitting information regarding the organization's mission and goals (Katz & Kahn, 1966).

Job Instructions   Employee tasks, as explained in directives, contracts, operating manuals, union contracts, and job descriptions, are all part of the job instructions. The goal of the oral and/or written communication is to let employees know what they are supposed to do and how they are supposed to do it.

For example, training new employees how to accomplish specific tasks falls to a supervisor. Outlining the expectations for neophytes is vital. Another example is the demand for continual growth and development of all organizational members that often involves new and altered job expectations.

Job Rationale   We need to know why we do what we do. Letting employees know how their job and tasks relate to other individuals, positions, tasks, and overall objectives is an important function of downward communication. Providing the why or big picture for an organization's activities is the goal behind many orientation, or perhaps more appropriately, indoctrination programs (Bolman & Deal, 2003).

Procedures, Policies, and Practices   The various policies, benefits, customs, processes, and rules are explained, and often reaffirmed later, with downward communication. Bulletin boards, memos, and meetings are often forums and employee handbooks tend to spell out the expected behaviors. Training manuals explain procedures, employee handbooks outline policies, and operating manuals present practices.

Performance Feedback   Ironically, in many organizations, continued employment—still having a job—is feedback (i.e., if you are not fired, you must be doing a satisfactory job). When feedback does occur, it is when a specific task is not being accomplished well or a specific job requirement, such as being on time, is not met. Unfortunately, many managers practice *management by exception* where the only recognition or feedback occurs when something is wrong or needs to be corrected.

Performance evaluation is a critical part of a manager's job. Employees need to know if they are doing a good job, how to correct inadequacies, and where they are lacking (Benton, 1995). In too many organizations, the annual performance appraisal is the primary tool for providing this critical feedback (Newton, 2001). Ironically, this annual event often is doomed to failure because of the perceptual differences between superiors and subordinates caused by a lack of ongoing feedback. In *Abolishing Performance Appraisals*, Coens and Jenkins observe that "80% of people think of themselves as being in the top quarter of all performers" (quoted in: Newton, 2001, p. 5B). In other words, when we come to our once-a-year review, our own perception of our performance is likely to be out of line with where we rank in relation to other performers. Even if our superior is attempting to provide important and candid performance information, our self-perception regarding performance might be remarkably off track. The key is a performance appraisal system that is constant, specific, related to performance, and designed to improve the subordinate (Peters, 1987). Peter Block, considered by many as the most quotable consultant, defined performance appraisals as "your annual reminder that someone else owns you" (Lee, 1999, p. 34).

Knowing when to provide feedback—timing—can be tricky. Many employees do not need or want constant supervision. When it is appropriate to leave an employee alone, the phrase management by wandering around is changed to management by wandering *away*. We return to feedback in the next chapter.

Information Regarding the Organization's Missions and Goals   Becoming familiar with the organization's ideological perspective is important. Employees need to know why an organization does what it does and the excellent companies need to make certain every employee can identify the specific goals of the organization (Levering & Moskowitz, 2000). In designing the high-performing organizations, employees are aware of what managers know, understand threats to their organization, realize the implications of their own decision-making—good and bad—on the organization, see the need for better technical skills, develop strong social skills, and understand customer expectations (Pasmore, 1996). Increasing the information flow downward is a critical variable in organizational success (Wind & Main, 1998).

This acculturation process that aims at the effective integration of employees into the overarching goals and objectives can be started in the orientation and training sessions. Southwest Airlines, Disney, and FedEx are examples of companies that go to great lengths to clarify the uniqueness of their organizations (Peters, 1987).

All five downward communication processes are important. Consultants continuously hammer home the importance of having a well-informed workforce and urge managers to spend their time "trying to catch people doing something right"—rather than using management by exception.

Analysis of Downward Communication

Unfortunately, the downward communication process is not always successful (Bolman & Deal, 2003). One possible answer would be that organizations do not know how to communicate downward effectively even though many try. A 1994 survey of more than 90,000 employees by the IRS and National Treasury Employees Union found that "only 29% say upper management officials communicate honestly with employees" (Herman, 1994, p. A1). In times of change and uncertainty, the best organizations increase their use of downward communication through a wide variety of techniques including posting financial information on bulletin boards, holding meetings with individuals and groups, better utilizing office space to increase interactions, and having more openness (Armour, 2001).

Downward communication is important and needs to be more effective. What prevents superiors from more effectively communicating information downward? In addition to the problems with serial transmission discussed earlier, certain specific issues deserve further elaboration.

Barriers to Downward Communication   First, there is a problem deciding the type (e.g., financial data, management concerns, employee issues) or content (e.g., amount of detail, specifics) of downward communication. At the risk of sounding like heretics, one national consulting firm argues that management should tell employees everything! Their point, of course, is that current management practices tend to filter information and decide what employees need to know, making the organizational knowledge level remain low. As we already have discussed, control of the channels and the content is primarily in the hands of management. There is little likelihood that employees and management will share the same goals (what) or channel preference (how), so the information passed on to employees often can lack relevance. Some filtering may be important because not all information is valuable to employees. But few managers are omnipotent, so vitally important information might be withheld. Because managers and employees do not do the same job, their information needs are frequently dissimilar.

The second downward communication problem, then, is the relevancy of the information. Simply providing more information does not mean that people will be better informed. The information must be useful to employees and this is where there is likely to be a problem. When information has little application, any efforts in communicating it are largely wasted and may discredit the source. If there is an unlimited, or perhaps unending, amount of downward communication, there will be overload.

To handle this overload, employees filter the messages and decide which ones are the most important. This filtering can range from employees incorrectly using the information, to disregarding it, to removing themselves from the information flow. Obviously, none of these is a desirable outcome for the manager, supervisor, or organization.

This information adequacy versus information overload creates an apparent paradox. Just providing information is not sufficient to satisfy the needs of employees. The issue is how to effectively choose what information to provide to employees, rather than the volume. Enlightened management can bypass the dilemma by using genuine team development techniques where subordinates are an integral part of the information system (Rees, 1991). The advantages of a strong organizational culture also minimize the information dissemination problem. Finally, the increased use of Intranets might minimize the filtering by managers while increasing access to employees.

Providing the appropriate information to employees is important. Numerous examples exist of the importance of a well-informed and involved work force (Osburn, Moran, Musselwhite, & Zenger, 1990). Downward communication, to be effective, must deal with what is communicated, how it is communicated, and if it should be communicated at all. In addition, excellent downward communication will be assigned the greatest credibility if upward communication works well.

Upward Communication

Few managers or leaders would take the position that they did not want to hear from subordinates. Communication from the lower levels to the upper levels is upward communication. As we already have established, the very process of passing information through channels creates some problems and these apply to upward as well as downward communication.

Functions of Upward Communication

Upward communication provides four types of messages: (1) suggestions, (2) what subordinates are doing, (3) unsolved work problems, and (4) how subordinates feel about each other and the job (Katz & Kahn, 1966).

Suggestions for Improvement   Organizations have come to realize that the person actually doing the job is an important resource for organizations. Frontline individuals are most directly in contact with the equipment, processes, and customers so they can make suggestions regarding the various work processes. An employee suggestion system is a "formal program to solicit, evaluate, implement, and reward employees for their ideas to improve certain aspects of the organization" (Myers, 1998, p. 980). Eastman Kodak Corporation, the oldest, continuous suggestion system in the United States, began when an employee was awarded $2 for suggesting that the windows in the production department be washed in order to improve the lighting (Mathis & Jackson, 1994).

How effective are suggestion systems? Most great corporate innovations come from frontline workers, not managers. In fact, 75% of product-improving and money-saving ideas come from workers who deal with the products and problems every day. The reasoning is simple—the individual closest to the problem or operation is most likely to recognize the symptoms and see possible solutions. The best companies worldwide are getting at least 50 ideas per employee per year. Dana Corp.'s 48,500 employees submit an average of 1.22 ideas a month or "666,120 nuggets of labor-saving, cost-cutting, productivity-increasing wisdom" (Teitelbaum, 1997, p. 168). At Dana, some 70% of all suggestions are used. Southwest Airlines' employee suggestion system, IdeAAs in Action, has almost 50,000 suggestions annually. In 1991, the $58.5 million savings produced by the program generated enough to pay for a new Boeing 757 (Mathis & Jackson, 1994).

Success depends on the follow-through on suggestions, which should be a matter of days, not months. Employees will offer many ideas if they know their ideas will receive a fair, timely hearing and that the good ones will be implemented quickly ("Ideas," 1999). Virtually every organization has experimented with some type of suggestion box. Too often, the box symbolizes empty offers by management to open channels of upward communication. In the companies that are serious about nurturing this upward communication process, suggestion systems are implemented using idea forms, complete with numbers to track the source of the suggestion, and professional managers to encourage and collect suggestions. "A survey of 6,000 companies by the Fairfax, Virginia-based Employee Involvement Association shows that the responding businesses have saved an average of just over $6,000 for each suggestion used" (Allerton, 2000, p. 80).

Obtaining suggestions from employees has two obvious benefits. First, suggestions provide valuable information regarding the organization's procedures and practices leading to cost savings, revenue generation, improved quality, better safety, and increased customer satisfaction ("Building World," 1998). Second, a well-functioning suggestion system serves as proof positive that the organization listens to employees thereby enhancing employees' belief in the communication process and the organization.

Subordinates' Activities   Superiors need to be aware of the success or failures of their subordinates. Upward communication provides information about the progress on a particular job, including the subordinates' achievements and problems. At the least, upward communication is a means of giving feedback on how accurately downward messages have been received. Regardless of the management system being used, some type of upward communication of information about the subordinates' activities is necessary. Supervisors must check the effectiveness of instructions, progress, and ongoing activities.

Unsolved Work Problems   If there are problems in completing the work, supervisors need to know. Issues ranging from equipment breakdowns to ergonomic problems can cause frustration that in turn can decrease motivation and productivity. When employees decide to expose unethical or illegal organizational activities it is often because upward channels of communication are not open. These *whistleblowers* normally feel thwarted in their attempts to change blatant examples of waste, fraud, or corruption, so they go public to gain satisfaction (Glazer & Glazer, 1986). Although their motivations differ depending on the specific example, their activities demonstrate a failure in the upward communication process (Donnelly, 1991). For example, the whistleblower that reported his company for selling faulty helicopter engines to the U.S. Coast Guard did so because he felt something had to be done ("Whistle Blower," 1990). At the time he was not aware that he would also end up receiving $2.7 million under the False Claims Act, an 1863 Civil War era law that gives private citizens a direct financial stake in exposing government fraud (Smart & Schine, 1991). In spite of the potential financial bonanza from reporting fraud in governmental contracts, the driving force behind whistleblowing remains frustration with the upward communication process (Hamilton, 1991).

How Subordinates Feel About Each Other and Their Job   Issues such as inequities in treatment, real and imagined grievances, harassment, and safety problems require effective communication opportunities between superiors and subordinates. Two extremely serious problems are sexual harassment and violence. For example, "according to various estimates, about one quarter of U.S. and Canadian women have been sexually harassed at work" (McShane & Von Glinow, 2000, p. 140). More than 2 million individuals experience some form of violence at work every year and it is largely unreported (Lardner, 1998).

Do employees speak up? In general, unless there is a high degree of trust, most employees do not. Being able to deal with employee problems before they become unmanageable is in the best interest of any organization. In a study of successful customer service organizations, Berry (1999) discovered that trust in the approachability of leaders was critical to increasing upward communication.

Analysis of the Process   Universally, organizational communication experts see the upward communication process as less effective than downward communication. There are at least two reasons.

First, procedures for encouraging upward communication are inadequate. Few U.S. companies and institutions have broad, explicit structures for dealing with employee concerns. Even if employees are willing to go over the supervisor's or manager's head, they might find themselves in an *Alice in Wonderland*-like situation, with few rules and less direction.

Second, control by management over workers is a presumption of many organizational systems. Although the importance of open communication is frequently discussed, many employees learn early on that comments, complaints, and suggestions are viewed as "rocking the boat." Never criticize or complain become the watch-words. The Japanese have an expression that summarizes this fear: "The nail that stands up is the one that gets hammered down."

In many organizations, these factors are changing. Through the various processes of downsizing, flattening the structure so there are fewer layers, and implementation of teamwork processes, organizations are lessening the debilitating effect of organizational structure on upward communication. However, there are four specific barriers.

Barriers to Upward Communication   There are many reasons why employees do not utilize the upward communication process. Are employees reluctant to report bad news to their supervisors? From 1991 to 1995, only 50% of employees felt that management encouraged the reporting of bad news to supervisors. From 2001 to 2005, that increased to 65% ("Bad News," 2005, p. 1D). Four prominent reasons are risk, distortion, manager's use of information, and personal restrictions.

Risk   There are three types of risk involved in the upward communication. First, when employees admit they are having trouble with a particular task, they also are exposing themselves to being seen as incompetent (Dansereau & Markham, 1987). They become vulnerable. The critical intervening variable is the amount of trust between the employee and the supervisor (Boyett & Boyett, 1998). Obviously, if employees were not happy at work, speaking to the boss would be a wise decision. However, if the message is taken as one by a malcontent, the manager's response could include lost credibility for the employee. This is not a new phenomenon. The Persian Messenger Syndrome—killing the bearer of bad news—originated in ancient Greece and Sophocles' tragedy *Antigone*. A messenger fears for his life because he knows Creon, the king of Thebes, will be unhappy with the news he brings and kill him for being the bearer of bad tidings. General Motors has a company joke that says, "At GM, we not only shoot the messenger, we bayonet the stretcher carrier." Kill the messenger is such a well-accepted concept that it is part of most corporate dialogues. Ryder Truck executives have a solution for "shooting the messenger—Shoot the guy who shoots the messenger" (Waterman, 1987, p. 107).

A second risk issue is the fear of reprisal. Especially if the individual plans to take the issue up the ranks past the immediate supervisor (e.g., fails to follow the designated chain of command), there is the fear that in the immediate future, or in the long run, the bypassed supervisor or manager will be able to even the score. Many supervisors have been encouraged to develop a middle-management macho ethic where they are told to handle problems on their own (Rowe & Baker, 1984). Employees' complaints can be viewed as undercutting this expertise. Even the most secure managers will not be pleased to see a continual stream of subordinates "going over their heads" with issues, problems, or suggestions.

A very subtle example of reprisal and risk is the "you raised it, you solve it" tendency in organizations. Often, when individuals bring problems to the attention of their superiors, they are assigned the task of finding the solution. In addition to being a form of reprisal, subordinates quickly learn that opening a "can of worms" that could lead to unexpected outcomes may not be a wise strategy. Hence, silence becomes golden—or at least very secure. In some cases, delegation of a problem can be the manager's ultimate revenge. A more severe form of reprisal is to eliminate the source of the message.

These three risk factors mitigate against upward communication. When it does occur, it frequently is distorted.

Distortion is the second issue. We already have established the problem with serial transmission. In upward communication, extensive evidence exists that each person distorts information passed upward in the hierarchy. In the extreme, a gatekeeper may simply reroute, or refuse to pass on, some messages.

A more prevalent distortion takes the form of exaggerating favorable and minimizing unfavorable information as it pertains to the person sending the message (Huber & Daft, 1987). As with risk, the first barrier, trust between the superior and subordinate determines the degree of distortion.

Second, employees might believe it is pointless to utilize the channels: "Employees at all levels often think that it's useless to complain about certain kinds of problems" (Rowe & Baker, 1984, p. 130). In some cases, such as highly technical issues, an employee might feel inadequate to raise the issue. In other cases, such as disagreements with co-workers, the issue might seem too trivial or bizarre. Raising the issue could lead to a worsening of the working environment. So, the known, even when it is less than perfect, can appear more comfortable than the unknown.

Finally, employees might not communicate upward because of an overriding sense of loyalty, a lack of belief in the system, or a fear of the possible changes a message might create. These barriers are important because they could supersede efforts by management or the organization to encourage upward communication.

In conclusion, effective downward communication enhances the willingness of employees to communicate upward. When subordinates are convinced their supervisors are withholding information, they will follow suit (Danseareau & Markham, 1987). This reciprocal relationship between the two forms of communication underscores the importance of formulating an overall communication policy rather than just a few, isolated efforts.

Horizontal Communication

Teamwork, cross-functional work units, skunk works, interdepartmental cooperation, and just getting the right people together to solve problems are all examples of horizontal communication. When the process is largely informal, it represents a network. As collaboration between subunits becomes more formalized, it evolves into channels.

Functions of Horizontal Communication   Horizontal communication accomplishes five functions. These are task coordination, problem solving, sharing information, conflict resolution, and building rapport. Horizontal communication is a valuable asset in many cases for getting the work done effectively. Allowing people at the same level to communicate regarding ongoing issues increases their ability to resolve potential conflicts. The cooperation increases job satisfaction and can increase efficiency because issues can be resolved at the level they occur.

Analysis of Horizontal Communication   Coordination between units, rather than through vertical channels, is imperative in many cases. A horizontal design flattens hierarchies, integrates the many different tasks of a business, and focuses attention on the customer creating a more effective organization (Ostaff, 1999). "In the past, it took a lot of middle people to accomplish a transaction" including pass-throughs of information from one unit to another, transfer and control points, distribution centers, and storage and access points (McLagan, 1999, p. 22). "But, technology, new communication services, express delivery, and business models" make it possible to work directly with other units (p. 22). At the same time, research indicates that the virtual organizations where individuals are connected primarily through computer networks will move from decentralization to some form of a centralized hierarchy to enhance access to experts and create more efficient communication (Aluja & Carley, 1998). In an organization, knowledge, information, and access to resources can be powerful motivating forces.

Faced with the challenges of the 21st century, what would prevent increased horizontal communication? Empire building, specialization, and a lack of rewards tend to keep subunits isolated from each other.

The armed forces provide a useful example of *empire building*. During the 1987 Grenada invasion by American troops, an Army unit found itself pinned down by enemy fire. The soldiers wanted to call in a fire mission from the Navy ship offshore. However, the soldiers could not communicate with the ship because the Army and Navy did not share codes. So, an Army "officer crawled to a pay phone, made a credit card call to the operations officer in his home base in Georgia; he in turn called the Navy at the Pentagon, which in turn radioed the ship to order the fire mission" (Wagman, 1991, p. A5). During Operation Desert Storm in Kuwait and Iraq in 1991, Air Force commanders could not communicate directly with the Navy computers on board ship to send daily targeting information for the Navy aircraft, so they "resorted to hand delivering floppy disks to each carrier every night" (Wagman, 1991, p. A5). Although not as dramatic as combat, many organizations find their subunits engaged in turf battles, information hurtling, and needless duplication.

Specialization is part of the modern organization. You are already familiar with the "over the wall" problem between units. Kodak provides a useful example. When it first developed the disposable camera, the marketing department created the concept. Then the engineering department created the design. Next tooling prepared the plant for production. Finally, manufacturing made it. After making it for a short time, manufacturing discovered a less expensive way to make the camera and the camera went back to the drawing board (Jones, 1999). The problem? Each part of the organization focused on its specialization and not the entire process. A lack of rewards for cooperating may keep subunits from working together. If there are no rewards for cooperation, why should subunits devote time and energy to the task?

In conclusion, horizontal communication is increasingly critical to organizations. Because it is not fully sanctioned within an organizational structure, many of the potential benefits are not fully realized.

The channels of communication are the sanctioned and recognized means for sending messages. Downward communication is the most used means and upward communication is potentially one of the most effective means. These vertical channels are the most accepted in traditional organizational structures. Horizontal communication is vital as a means for coordination. Without exception, excellent organizations strive to enhance the effectiveness of these three channels. Table 6.3 highlights some of the most used channels and networks in organizations. To conform to our earlier analysis, they are divided into upward, downward, and horizontal. Specific network types are

Table 6.3 Organizational Communication Networks and Channels

Upward Communication

Brown bag lunch (informal lunch with superiors)

Communication audit (analysis of communication process)

E-mail

Employee opinion surveys

Family day/picnics

FAX

Focus groups

Grapevine

Group/team meetings

Intercom systems

Letters

Management by wandering around (unvarnished listening)

Needs analysis for training

Ombudsman (representative to mediate differences)

Participative decision making (teams, projects)

Performance appraisals

Small group opportunities to speak up

Subordinate evaluation of superior

Superior/subordinate meetings

Teleconferencing

Telephone

Voice mail

Written messages

Downward Communication

Annual report

Awards and recognition

Brochures

Company magazines

Corporate mission, values, philosophy

Daily/weekly briefings

Electronic bulletin board

E-mail

Family day/picnics

FAX

Grapevine

Handbooks

Help/information telephone lines

Hotline

Intercom systems

Job descriptions

Letters

Management feedback programs

Mass meetings

Memos and reports

Mentoring

New employee orientation

Newsletters

Policy manuals

Posters

Superior/subordinate meetings

Teleconferencing

Training

Video/audio information

Horizontal Communication

Directory of departments and functions

Cross functional work units

E-mail

Family day/picnics

Grapevine

Kudos programs (colleagues nominate colleagues for recognition)

Letters

Mass meetings/gatherings

Meetings with team, peers, other managers, work groups

Memos and reports

Peer evaluation programs

Problem solving groups

Task forces

Teleconferencing

Water cooler/informal gatherings

also included. Organizations use idiosyncratic communication processes so the variations on this list are almost limitless.

Conclusion

Our examination of networks and channels might seem exhausting. However, with communication effectiveness remaining a key issue in organizational and individual success, how we connect, receive, and deliver messages in organizations may be the key to success. In all organizations, networks and channels are the methods used for exchanging messages, information, meaning, and connecting. Networks represent the regularized communication interactions. Channels are the sanctioned means of communicating.

Networks can be both formal and informal means of communicating. As we have discovered, networks can configure in a vast number of ways. Coupling explains the degree of interdependence between subsystems. Organizations tend to have both loose and tight coupling. Connectedness is the term used to describe the degree of interdependence in a network. Highly connected networks offer advantages to organizations. The digital age has created numerous additional examples and opportunities for networks.

The strength of weak ties explains how independent, or loosely connected sources, can influence individuals and groups. Groupthink explains the dangers in a closed decision-making process. Information can be obtained by using weak ties, which can be used effectively in a variety of decision-making situations.

Connectedness is clarified further by looking at clusters, which are the highly coupled groups within the organizational networks. Coalitions and cliques are the two types of clusters. Coalitions are created to influence organizational relationships. Cliques are connected by strong relations between the members.

Individuals have various roles in a network. In addition to being members, the most predominate roles are liaisons, gatekeepers, stars, bridges or linking pins, cosmopolites, and isolates. Each of these roles has specific characteristics that determine the individual's impact on the network. Network members may have different roles at different times.

There are different types of networks. Specific applications of networks include network analysis, systematic management networks, specialized networks, teamwork, and innovation. These are examples of the many different applications of networks in organizations. The concept of loose coupling within the larger organizational framework helps explain how the change process operates.

The grapevine is one of the best-known types of networks. As a constant force in all organizations, grapevines provide excellent examples of how networks operate.

Channels are vertical and horizontal. Vertical channels have five characteristics. These include one-way or two-way communication, channels as organizational memories, channels as a managerial prerogative and responsibility, channel properties as intervening variables, and the different perspectives of the channel users. Vertical channels include downward and upward communication.

Downward communication has five functions in an organization. As vital as downward communication is to the effective functioning of an organization, the process is ineffective. Information is filtered as it passes downward. Upward communication passes information from the lower levels of the organization through the hierarchy. There are four functions of upward communication. Unfortunately, this process is also ineffective. Little encouragement is offered for upward communication and management is in control of the process. Barriers include risk, distortion, and a self-imposed gag by the employee. Horizontal communication is the flow of messages between function areas at a specific level in an organization.

Study Questions

1. Describe the concept of networks from your own work experience. Were you central to the process? Can you label your role?
2. Why are networks important to organizations?
3. Distinguish between coupling and connectedness. Provide examples of loosely and tightly coupled and connected networks.
4. How do managers use networks?
5. Distinguish between downward, upward, and horizontal communication. Describe the processes and functions. Are there limitations? What are they?
6. What is the grapevine and how does it work?

Symbolic Behavior

The power of communication to create and maintain meaning that is shared by members of an organization is a theme that has permeated this text. In the introductory chapter, we established that communication functions as the lifeblood, and sometimes the embalming fluid, for all organizations. This chapter places in context the most human part of organizations—symbolic behavior that results in various degrees of shared meaning and values between organizational members.

The following topics are explored:

- Seven basic propositions—Symbolic behavior
    1. Organizational complexity creates a reliance on symbolic messages
    2. Uncertainty promotes a continual process of organizing
    3. Symbolic behavior creates and maintains organizational cultures
    4. Symbols constitute the basis for interpersonal reality
    5. Groups reaffirm the importance of symbolic behavior
    6. Leadership requires effective symbolic behavior
    7. Incongruencies and paradoxes are managed through acculturation
- Tools of symbolic behavior
- Six limitations of symbolic behavior
- Performances—Roles, front, dramatic realization, mystification, rituals
- Complexity

Symbols allow individuals, groups, and organizations to engage in the complex behaviors required to work together. "Symbolic action includes all the behaviors we engage in that are meaningful—that is, that come to represent to others our attitudes, beliefs, or intentions" ranging from language to nonverbal acts to group phenomena (Cooper & Nothstine, 1992, pp. 2–3). Symbols stand for something else so they can be used to explain past behavior, respond based on past experience, use accumulated knowledge, cope with the present and the future, and create unity and division. They allow us to make sense of our organizational environment.

Symbolic behavior's impact is evident at the organizational, group, and individual levels. This is hardly an insight at this point in our examination of organizational communication, because you are well versed in the importance of symbolic behavior. Throughout the first six chapters, you have been provided numerous examples of symbolic behavior in organizations, their cultures, and the various subcultures. This chapter takes these pieces of the jigsaw puzzle, which have appeared at the appropriate points in our discussion of other issues, adds the remaining pieces, and provides a comprehensive picture of symbolic behavior. Although the justifications for a symbolic perspective are strong, you already were forewarned in the beginning of this text that selected views of organizations, including symbolic, could be parochial and myopic.

With this disclaimer in mind, this chapter begins the analysis by presenting seven propositions underscoring the symbolic perspective. Then, verbal and nonverbal communications, as the delivery mechanisms for symbolic behavior, are examined. Five important limitations to symbolic behavior are provided to make certain our understanding is well situated. Finally, we examine the concept of performance as it relates to organizations.

Basic Propositions—Symbolic Behavior

Overview

The symbolic behavior perspective argues that organizational reality is socially constructed through communication (Cheney & Christensen, 2000; Putnam, Phillips, & Chapman, 1996). Because of uncertainty, individuals constantly are organizing themselves by creating and responding to a group based reality (Weick, 1995). These processes and interactions create, maintain, and transform the organizational structures. This collective sense-making means there can be multiple realities produced through the various cycles of human interactions. "Symbolic behavior refers to a person's capacity to respond to or use a system of significant symbols" (Faules & Alexander, 1978, p. 5). The following issues, which are examined as propositions, are intertwined with symbolic behavior: complexity, uncertainty, cultural creation and maintenance, interpersonal reality, group behavior, leadership, and the management of incongruences.

Complexity

Proposition 1: Organizational complexity creates a reliance on symbolic messages. Most organizations are too vast, unpredictable, and complex for easy understanding. When we enter the experience called "work," we are faced with uncertainty regarding the goals, power structure, road to success, or even how to get the work accomplished. This complexity is compounded by the multitude of ongoing behaviors including transactions between individuals, individuals to groups, groups to groups, groups to organizations, organizations to organizations, and organizations to public behaviors. "In many ways the crisis in business today is a crisis in meaning. ... Those who would aspire to leadership roles in this new environment must not underestimate the depth of this human need for meaning. It is a most fundamental human craving, an appetite that will not go away" (Albrecht, 1994, p. 22). In other words, the maze of interactions requires some symbolic clarity.

As a consequence, our world of work is an interpretative experience. "As for the present, each member of an organization has directly experienced only a 'sliver' of the nonsymbolic; each member's overall picture is but a construct provided by the symbol systems of words, numbers, and nomenclatures. Refusing to see or acknowledge the dominating role of symbolicity in shaping notions of 'reality' is to cling 'to a kind of naive verbal realism'" (Tompkins, 1987, p. 85). Organizations are subjective realities rather than objective phenomena (Pacanowsky & O'Donnell-Trujillo, 1983).

Symbolic messages allow members to make sense out of their environment creating a social reality (Faules & Alexander, 1978; Mills, 2002). For example, few individuals can comprehend a behemoth like IBM with its international realm or a large university's sphere. Being unable to grasp the entire scope of an organization, we respond to the organization's essence as it is presented symbolically. Highly bureaucratic organizations, such as schools, colleges and universities, business conglomerates, research and development organizations, political campaign organizations, and government bureaus have been labeled *organized anarchies* (Cameron, 1980). Within these organizations, there are ambiguous connections between structure and expected activities. Therefore, subunits carry out their parochial activities based on their own interpretations of the organization's purposes, goals, and consequences for performance. Clarity for individuals and groups is more localized.

Most individuals are disconnected from the underlying strategies or top management planning so the overall purpose of the organization is clarified primarily through symbolic messages ranging from language usage to parking arrangements to formal and informal dress standards. "A critical task in organizations is creating and evolving shared understanding, a kind of sensemaking that is basic to creative leadership" (Palus & Horth, 1998, p. 2). These "basic assumptions provide a map by which we engage in our organizational lives" (Keyton, 2005, p. 26).

Even the smallest business must respond to bureaucratic restraints, such as tax and building codes. Although individuals may be their own bosses, they still are subject to the labyrinth of rules, regulations, and conflicting advice (e.g., "make a profit" and "always place the customer first"). Complexity and incongruity can leave us feeling helpless but the lifeline is our ability to identify with symbolic images (Boulding, 1961).

Organizations develop a standardized set of meanings through microcultural verbal and nonverbal symbols. The mechanisms chosen for delivering the messages— verbal and written channels, nonverbal communication, networks, interpersonally, in groups, by leaders, and electronically—carry significant symbolic consequences, which are created and maintained by the organization or subsystem within which we function. Note that even posted rules like no running, no talking, no eating, no cheating, and no smoking provide us with symbolic clarification. At the beginning of this text, we noted that Ford Motor Company has provided a home computer for all employees and access to the Internet. Although the increased communication is important, the symbolic importance is even more revealing.

Uncertainty and Organizing

Proposition 2: Uncertainty promotes a continual process of organizing. The symbolic interpretation of organizational reality deals with the process of sense-making. In other words, we are constantly organizing our shared experience. "Organizing is defined as a consensually validated grammar for reducing equivocality by means of sensible interlocked behaviors" (Weick, 1979, p. 3). Because organizing is complex, meaning is provided through symbols. This meaning is negotiated between individuals, within groups, and during an individual's passage through an organization (Eisenberg & Riley, 1988). Organizational members make sense out of the everyday events through a set of shared symbols (Brown, 1986). The complexity and vastness of most organizations means the different subcultures create a multitude of potentially different stories, explanations, and interpretations of reality (Boje, 1995).

An organization's "reality is socially constructed through the words, symbols, and behaviors of its members" (Putnam, 1983, p. 35). In fact, this common ground is a prerequisite to effective organizational functioning. "One of the important defining characteristics of organizations is that within an organization, there are consensually shared perceptions and definitions of the world" (Pfeffer, 1981, p. 12). Medtronic, the company that invented the battery-powered pacemaker in 1957 "so dominates the pacemaker, neurostimulators, and stents market that you'll often hear it referred to as the Microsoft of the medical-device industry" (Whitford, 2001, p. 110). It is also one of the 100 best places to work, according to the 2000 study, and it connects its 22,000 employees together "by corporate culture—the stew of rules, mores, and traditions that says something about what it means to work at this company and not some other" (Whitford, 2001, p. 110). New hires are presented their Medtronic medallions inscribed with "Alleviate Pain, Restore Health, and Extend Life" extracted from the mission statement. Even its folklore adds to Medtronic's mission. Bakken, the founder, became interested in the potential for electricity and medical care when he watched the 1931 film version of *Frankenstein*. This would be interesting trivia if the story did not remind all employees of Medtronic's life sustaining mission and their responsibility to help others. As a result, "86% of Medtronic employees (in the survey for the 100 Best) said their work had special meaning, 94% felt pride in what they accomplished" (Whitford, 2001, p. 111). The social construction of the Medtronic experience creates fulfillment for its employees.

The *symbolic-interactionism* perspective pays heed to the symbolic reaction people have to their organizations. Employees, it is argued, form their organization-specific concept of self as a result of their ongoing interactions with other parts of the organization, ranging from individuals, subordinates, and superiors to work rules and architecture. The work environment presents us with an elaborate code of values, attitudes, roles, and norms of behavior that are appropriate to the organization (Wood, 1999). Our role definitions and responses to situations are indications of the symbolic importance we have assigned to ongoing communication events. One Federal Express (FedEx) folk tale is about a delivery person who had been given the wrong key to a FedEx drop box. So he loaded it into his truck and took it back to the station, where they were able to pry it open and get the contents to their destination the following day. At FedEx, this employee is remembered as a hero who maintained the on-time, overnight goal. If you wonder just how powerful this type of lesson is, imagine what would happen at the U.S. Postal Service (USPS) if someone uprooted a mailbox from a sidewalk. They would be considered unbalanced and probably charged and dismissed for damaging property. Both reactions by the organizational members are a result of the processes of organizing and sense-making.

Organizational cultures prescribe the ways members react symbolically to organizational phenomena by presenting them with culturally approved explanations, shared perceptions, and a mutual sense of social order. This collective interpretation of social reality is vital to the effective functioning of an organization.

Cultural Creation and Maintenance

Proposition 3: Symbolic behavior creates and maintains organizational cultures. All organizations have cultures that are learned, shared, and transmitted. The cultural perspective represents a process orientation to organizational reality (Pacanowsky & O'Donnell-Trujillo, 1983). "Organizational culture is socially acquired and shared knowledge that is embodied in specific and general organizational frames of reference" (Wilkins & Dyer, 1988, p. 513). For example, the metaphors—ranging from machines (people are merely part of the production process) to brains (information and intelligence processing) to psychic prisons (toe the company line, bound by golden handcuffs, working in a difficult environment) to voyages (adventure requiring teamwork)—used to characterize organizations set the stage for acceptable and unacceptable activities. If you were told you would become entangled in a psychic prison, you certainly would react differently than if you were invited to join one big, happy family (Clancy, 1989).

Culture is the shadow side of the formal organization as reflected by its unique character, style, energy, commitment, and way of doing things. It provides the glue for cohesion and the oil for lubrication. As people perform their culturally sanctioned behaviors, their actions assist in creating and maintaining the organization. In addition, culture prescribes how we are to respond to a variety of situations with culturally specific rewards and penalties possible depending on our performance. "Culture has a pervasive influence on how an organization functions" (Sanchez, 2006, p. 33). Rewards, punishments, interaction with the business environment, work processes, patterns of social interaction, customer service, and numerous other attributes are directed by the culture.

The earlier Medtronic discussion provides one useful example. At Microsoft, also one of the 100 best places to work, employees believe "that Microsoft is different from other places (and) ... that they themselves are different from other people" (Gimein, 2001, p. 126). A common theme among Microsoft employees when asked to describe their experiences makes the point. Gimein (2001) relates a story told to him over and over that he labels the *secret garden*. "Once I was lost, they said; I did not fit in; then I found the key to the magical garden of Microsoft, where I belonged in the first place" (p. 126).

Aligning employees through symbolic processes including culture can create awesome power. Medtronic, Microsoft, and a remarkable number of other organizations use culture to achieve this alignment. The changes associated with the new millennium require this aligning process. "In this emerging new era when so many people can work for whomever and from wherever they like, coalescing around shared values becomes a logical, effective organizing principle for a business enterprise. Creating, articulating, and sustaining the organization's values thus become one of management's most important jobs" (Colvin, 2000, p. F-9). In providing advice on how to move an organization forward, many experts focus on culture enhancements or changes (Galpin, 1996; Schein, 1994). In general, organizations should shift from being goal-directed to vision-directed; price-focused to value-focused; product-driven to customer-driven; rigid to flexible; and hierarchical to flat and empowered (Wind & Main, 1998). Most organizational members accept these general goals even though the content behind the changes is never quite as clear.

In truth, most organizations could not operate if a strict, rational response was required as a basis for every action or behavior. So, cultures provide direction through the shared assumptions, values, and meanings. If nothing else, people have a reason for committing time, personnel, and resources to a particular activity. The culture, whether fully understood or simply accepted, provides useful, overriding rationale for activities that otherwise might seem meaningless. We need to emphasize that not all employees grasp the full impact of an organization's culture. When asked, "Do you agree that your company has a widely embraced and understood corporate culture?" only 44% of employees sampled (1,281 nationwide) responded yes, 37% responded not sure, and 19% said no (Yang & Gonzalez, 2005).

Meetings provide a useful example. In most organizations, people are spending more and more time in meetings. Surveys of participants indicate that more than 50% of the meeting time is wasted due, in large part, to poor planning, meeting format, and ineffective leadership (Dressler, 1995; Mosvick & Nelson, 1987). From a structural, time-and-motion perspective, bad meetings can be expensive. If there are eight people at the meeting averaging $40,000 a year in salary and benefits, the "cost is $320 an hour, including salary and benefits, or $6 a minute" (Dressler, 1995, p. 6B).

But, what if the real value in meetings arises from the ritual itself and not output or time spent? From a symbolic perspective, taking part in the "ritual of decision-making," by attending meetings and making the right comments, can be as important as actually making a decision. These activities can reaffirm the importance of the organization, goals and visions, certain issues, or the individuals in attendance. For example, our reasoning might be that this meeting, be it weekly, specially called, or task-based, must be significant if this many prestigious members are willing to commit their time and energy. The status or expertise indirectly assigned to the participants by being included in this important meeting also reaffirms that the organization carefully deliberates important issues. Even the seating format or the use of an agenda versus a somewhat free-for-all setting, speaks to the culturally accepted values and beliefs. So, two-day retreats, often isolated from the day-to-day pressures, provide a vital refurbishing of the *esprit de corps* by setting goals agreed upon during the retreat that may never be acted on. In fact, having some direction is rational and spending time sorting through conflicting agendas, dealing with different personalities, or stabilizing working habits provides a potentially worthwhile symbolic and pragmatic justification.

Symbolically important activities offer an excellent opportunity for change. Galpin (1996) calls for a change in the way we do things around here to connect culture to the change process. As examples, he offers replacing written memos with face-to-face weekly meetings, establishing ceremonies and events that reinforce the new way of doing things including award or recognition ceremonies, and using new ways to deliver communication including multiple channels. Rather than indicting bureaucracy and advocating a need for quicker decisions in order to be more customer friendly, Kotter (1996) suggests using metaphors, analogies, and examples as the following sentence reflects: "We need to become less like an elephant and more like a customer-friendly Tyrannosaurus Rex" (p. 92).

In the more successful organizations, cultures act as reinforcers for productive behaviors. They assist members in coping with environmental uncertainties and in coordinating activities. Cultural maps, made up of general and specific frames of reference, allow individuals to define situations they encounter and develop an appropriate response" (Wilkins & Dyer, 1988, p. 523). Our symbolic frame of reference defines "aspects of the culture such as general definitions of roles, relevant groupings of individuals, relationships between groups and the whole, relationships between the organization and

Table 7.1

Match the following organizations with their vision:

1.	Girl Scouts	A.	People working more effectively
2.	3M	B.	Boundryless, speed, & stretch
3.	Steelcase	C.	Self-confident and self-respecting young women
4.	Domino's Pizza	D.	Respect for individual initiative
5.	FedEx	E.	Fun and creative self-expression
6.	General Electric	F.	Responsiveness, on time with no excuses
7.	Crayola Crayon	G.	Products & services when consumers want them

Note. Correct matches: 1–C; 2–D; 3–A; 4–G; 5–F; 6–B; 7–E.

outside groups, ideological orientations about the nature of humans, the kind of work that needs doing, repair strategies when things go awry, and so forth" (Wilkins & Dyer, 1988, p. 523). When Ford says, "quality is job one" (Q1), Pepsi simply demands "Beat Coke," or any organization states "the customer is always right," the slogan provides a *master symbol*, which establishes that goal as paramount and easily understood.

Mottoes, visions, and mission statements add to an organization's ability to shape its own culture. In 1912, the following words were inscribed on the New York City Post Office: "Neither snow nor rain not heat nor gloom of night stays these couriers from the swift completion of their appointed rounds." This pledge was never intended to be the official motto of the U.S. Postal Service (Burrell, 1997). Stamps (1999) observes: "And yet, such is the power of words to shape belief that millions of Americans still take this pledge to be the motto of the Postal Service and imbue the words with an almost sacred trust" (p. 45). Table 7.1 presents a sample of mission statements used by well-known organizations. See if you can correctly match the statement with the organization.

We are familiar with broad missions and values such as "In God We Trust" (United States), "Live Free or Die" (New Hampshire), and "Manly Deeds, Womanly Words" (Maryland). Famous leaders use statements to provide clarity of purpose. For example, Malcolm X resolved: "I believe in the brotherhood of men, all men, but I don't believe in brotherhood with anyone who doesn't want brotherhood with me ...." (quoted in Stamps, 1999, p. 46). We are the makers "of meanings in the world that sometimes seems without meaning. Few things help us find meaning more than a cause to believe in, better yet, about which to get excited" (Waterman, 1987, p. 11). This overriding ideology allows members "to take their lead from the organization's own vision"

(Mitzberg, 1991, p. 62). One organization boasted "the difficult we do immediately, the impossible takes a little longer." Contrast the power of that group image with a popular sign seen in some small businesses that shows several figures bent over in laughter saying "you want it when?"

Cultural scenes outline the relevant times, settings, issues set forth to justify switching from one organizational frame to another (Wilkins & Dyer, 1988). For example, moving from a management meeting to an interaction with a customer changes the cultural scene. Working with a customer who has a long-term relationship with your organization presents different demands than a one-time encounter (Gutek, 1995). Individuals face different scenes, different skills, and a commensurate different set of role expectations in order to correctly respond to the scene. Understanding the implicit rules governing these role expectations can be vital to our own successful responses.

There are pluses and minuses regarding organizational cultures. Organizational cultures provide guidelines regarding the expected practices and communication functions as the choice individuals use when responding to the symbolic reality. As you are well aware at this point, cultures provide meaning, help organizations capture and direct the collective will, create distinctive norms, promote values, and encourage high performance. At the same time, cultures can create dysfunctional norms, groupthink, and counterproductive behaviors. A cynic might observe that even the psychic prison provides meaning, albeit unpleasant, in an uncertain setting. As you are already aware from our earlier discussions, cultures provide values, assumptions, informal ideologies, attitudes, myths, symbols, rituals, language, jargon, rumors, prejudices, stereotypes, social etiquette, dress, and appropriate demeanor. "Symbolism, in short, creates organizational environments as well the motives of those who act" (Tompkins, 1987, p. 83).

The first analysis of *The 100 Best Companies to Work for in America* concluded: "The 100 best offer an added benefit of such value that it's difficult to place on the same scale: a working life for thousands of people really worth living and worth looking forward to every waking day" (Levering, Moshowitz, & Katz, 1985, p. xiv). The now-annual 100 best rankings confirm this critical attribute of the best companies—a potpourri of programs, actions, and accommodations that make an individual's time at work satisfying.

Interpersonal Reality

Proposition 4: Symbols constitute the basis for interpersonal reality. The stimuli to which we assign meaning create and maintain our own reality. As Frank and Brownell (1989) put it, "The concept of symbol is at the heart of human communication" (p. 199). There is a symbiotic process whereby we communicate with symbols and symbols create the meaning we are responding to (Burke, 1969). Therefore, all "communication processes can be seen as ways in which any organization attains personal meaning for its employees. From talk designed to accomplish tasks to talk designed to spread gossip, communication processes are the lifeblood of any company, because they allow the company to do what it does" (Wilson, Goodall, & Waagen, 1986, p. 107).

Roles, symbols, and interaction deserve further attention. Our roles, constructed by our perceptions of organizational situations, are defined socially through communication (Duncan, 1962; Petrelle, Slaughter, & Jorgensen, 1988). Our idiosyncratic definitions of the workplace based on the symbolic experiences point us toward certain actions that we present through our role behavior. Role-taking, or role performance, does not represent a false persona. Instead, we are attempting to respond to the demands presented by the situation.

Verbal and nonverbal symbols allow us to formulate an understanding of what otherwise would likely seem unclear given the nature of organizational experience. There is *symbolic interaction* through the communication of significant symbols (Duncan, 1968). Working becomes a *negotiated experience* whereby we participate in creating organizational meaning based on our interpretation of the significant symbols. Our interpretation is reaffirmed or challenged by other organizational members who co-construct dialogues with us (Pacanowsky & O'Donnell-Trujillo, 1983). Effective role understanding and performance requires an understanding of the culture's meaning.

Finally, symbols clarify the *proscriptive norms* in an organization. Most organizational norms are proscriptive rather than prescriptive because they specify whether a behavior is appropriate, not which behavior is appropriate. The historical practices, rituals, activities, and events of the organization provide the broad outline of meaning that allows us to act accordingly (Blumer, 1969, Giddens, 1984). Dressing conservatively, listening to employees, or providing excellent customer service are examples of proscriptive expectations based on a particular cultural setting, rather than specified means for carrying out the activity. Group expectations and sanctions bind individual activity, which brings us to the fifth proposition.

Group Behavior

Proposition 5: Groups reaffirm the importance of symbolic behavior. In the end, individuals identify most with the subculture, or group, to which they belong. This community, unit, work group, or department allows us to see that culture "can be understood as a set of solutions devised by a group of people to meet specific problems posed by the situations they face in common" (Ting-Toomey, 1985, p. 74). These solutions, or "the way we do things in this group around here," occur in every small group. Group activities, ranging from break time to regularly scheduled meetings to levels of cooperation, represent highly symbolic behaviors.

Because groups develop their own cultural identities, there can be three types of subcultures. An *enhancing culture* embraces the dominant cultures' values, a *counterculture* challenges the values, and an *orthogonal culture* accepts the values of the dominant culture as well as its own (Duncan, 1989). The excellent companies represent the first type of culture where employees begin to see themselves as stakeholders who wish to help the organization succeed because they feel enculturated. The companies view the stakeholders as assets to be protected and developed.

Countercultures evolve for a variety of reasons. For example, a *mutually exploitative* setting might occur where alienated employees resist control and unfair wages and "give as little labor as possible for as high a wage as possible" (Anderson & Englehart, 2001, p. 12). Parts of an organization may become isolated or feel neglected creating a bond between the alienated group members.

Subcultures created through certain professional ties or interests can develop. Nurses and doctors present excellent examples of orthogonal cultures since their professional affiliations and standards provide specific group-based norms within the context of a particular medical setting. Diversity of the organization's members, based on the various divisions already discussed, provides numerous additional examples of the potential discontinuities between a group's values and the organization's (Gardenswartz & Rowe, 1993; Harris, 1997; Zemke, Raines, & Filipczak, 2000). The various cultural levels in any organization can create divisions (Deetz, Tracy, & Simpson, 2000). Organization-specific examples include different departments or job functions (e.g., shipping, sales, production), locations (e.g., plant, headquarters, region), and subgroup membership (e.g., union, management, exempt, nonexempt, new, fully acculturated) can create these three types of subcultures. Inevitably, leaders are called on to coordinate interpersonal and group activities and leaders also rely on symbolic behavior.

Leadership

Proposition 6: Leadership requires effective symbolic behavior. We have already linked leadership to symbols and cultures earlier in this chapter. A useful distinction can be drawn between management—as the process of planning, organizing, leading, and controlling—and leadership (Wind & Main, 1998). In order to provide legitimacy to the practice of management, quantifiable approaches, based on careful planning, often are used. However, "few people doubt that managers traffic in images and more often act as evangelists or psychologists than accountants or engineers" (Duncan, 1989, p. 229). Effective leaders know how to use symbolic behavior and act as facilitators. At the highest level, "executive behavior is mostly talk. It is more symbol intensive than labor intensive, requiring the creation of meaning for those doing the direct work" (Jonas, Fry, & Srivastra, 1989, p. 205). We have devoted an entire chapter later in this text to the numerous issues regarding leadership in organizations. For now, we concentrate on symbolic leadership.

Two attributes underlie symbolic leadership. First, symbolic leadership is the vital link between organizational needs and employees' understanding.

Second, the organizational culture explains to the leader how the role is to be enacted. Accepting that leadership requires excellent management skills, successful leaders have symbolic, as well as rational, political, and human resource impact. Wise leaders utilize symbolic behaviors. "All business is show business. All leadership is show business. All management is show business. That doesn't mean tap dancing; it means shaping values, symbolizing attention—and it is the opposite of 'administration' and especially, 'professional management'" (Peters & Austin, 1985, p. 265). Actions speak louder than words in many cases. "Visible management attention, rather than management exhortation, gets things done. Action may start with the words, but it has to be backed by symbolic behavior that makes those words come alive" (Waterman, 1987, p. 11). This reminds us that those leaders using empty symbolic messages will be discredited quickly. Waterman (1987) continues, "most managers rely too heavily on language and not enough on the great wealth of other symbols available to them" (p. 265).

Symbolic management concentrates on manipulating and developing values, beliefs, and commitments in order to maintain or change organizational cultures (Kotter, 1988). Leaders, then, influence the culture by paying attention to certain behaviors, attributes, and outcomes (Schein, 1985). National consultants hammer away at the premise: What a leader rewards through symbolic attention is what the leader gets (Kerr & Slocum, 1987; Peters, 1989). Managers, vice presidents, or presidents who visit the hot or unpleasant parts of a plant in the middle of summer, drop by training sessions, or spend time inquiring about particularly difficult jobs are operating on the principle that physical presence is more effective than lip service. Leaders walk the talk by symbolically demonstrating their meanings (Keyton, 2005). When leaders, managers, and employees attempt to use the advice provided by cultural messages, they are confronted with the complexities of the world of work.

Managing Incongruences

Proposition 7: Incongruences and paradoxes are managed through acculturation. In chapter 3, we discussed the inherent conflict between joining an organization in order to gain the benefits and the desire for individual freedom. We face the irony that in order to enjoy our freedom, we must surrender some of it to earn a living. If we want to advance, we quickly learn the value of ascribing to the cultural expectations. For most of us, this is a relatively easy dilemma to negotiate because rules, roles, and requirements have been placed on us throughout our lives.

Although uncertainty requires continual organizing, and working requires surrendering some freedoms, incongruences and paradoxes require some action. Paradoxes, dilemmas, and contradictions are part of organizational life. The most successful companies can hold paradoxical views including being conservative at the core but progressive toward the community and employees or pursue high quality at the lowest possible cost (Collins & Porras, 1994). You were introduced to paradoxes and double binds in chapter 4, "Verbal Communication." Symbols can reduce ambiguity and tension by providing shared values. Does trying to develop a consistent culture result in certainty? When asked, "Do you agree that your company has a widely embraced and understood corporate culture?" 44% answered yes, 19% responded no, and 37% were not sure (Yang & Gonzalez, 2005). The issue becomes even clearer when we examine mergers and acquisitions. These often fail because of the clash between the organizations' cultures (Pepper & Larson, 2006). About 50% of these mergers and acquisitions fail to meet their financial projections and "as much as 85% of that failure is attributable to the failure to manage the practical challenges of cultural integration (Pepper & Larson, 2006, p. 49). Returning to our point, uncertainty and incongruencies are important organizational issues.

A closer examination of managers, employees, and ethics underscores the importance of a symbolic lifeboat.

Managers/Leaders Managers are faced with conflicting demands regarding how they should act. After examining the current literature on leadership, a manager could conclude that appropriate behavior includes being enthusiastic but calm, very friendly and approachable but always keeping a distance, candid but a very quiet and deep thinker, firm but flexible, tough but compassionate, and very serious while having a great sense of humor. As if these expectations were not difficult enough to reconcile, organizations pursuing a path of renewal and growth expect managers to spearhead teamwork and entrepreneurship, which are processes requiring more of a hands-off approach. How can managers fulfill these apparently contradictory behaviors? The answer, for many, is by accepting the symbolic norms of the job, department, and organization. In some cases, the norms call for control over collaboration (e.g., bureaucracies). In others, anarchy over discipline (e.g., highly creative firms) prevails. Excellent organizations have discovered that harmony can be produced through healthy conflict, managers can manage best by learning from frontline employees, listening—not talking—is power, deviance can be a productive norm, strength can be drawn from vulnerability, change can be facilitated though stability, and work can be fun. Managers can draw on the myths, stories, and organizational history to form rough guidelines for their behavior. Because leaders can be expected to be evangelists or psychologists, as well as organizers of work, trafficking in images as a means for resolving paradoxes is a viable, and much used, response (Duncan 1989, p. 229). Telling stories to help make sense for organizational members is one leadership tool. Gardner (1995) argues that "a key—perhaps the key—to leadership … is the effective communication of a story" (p. 62). He concludes that stories are a "fundamental part of the leader's vocation" (p. 43).

In certain situations, leaders can overwhelm subordinates. For example, in the intense atmosphere of operating rooms (ORs), surgeons "are the captains of the ship, treated with deference because of their unique skills. As a result, nurses, prep technicians, and other aides can be afraid to speak up if they spot a problem" (Landro, 2005, p. D1). Because "doing a better job of preventing errors in critical areas of hospital care" (Landro, 2005, p. D4), is perceived as most important, other important issues can receive less attention. "There is mounting evidence that poor communication between hospital staff and surgeons is the leading cause of avoidable surgical errors" (Landro, 2005, p. D1). Is this important? "In the OR, studies show that serious complications can arise from communication problems—such as nurses failing to notify a surgeon of a change in the patient's color or respiration. Earlier this year, VHA surveyed staff at 20 hospitals and found that as many as 60% of OR staffers agreed with the statement: "In the ORs here, it is difficult to speak up if I perceive a problem with patient care" (Landro, 2005, p. D4). Note that the responsibilities placed on the surgeon may force choices between task orientation and control over developing a team atmosphere that encourages more open communication. As we have noted earlier in this text, many medical facilities are moving toward teambuilding and team care (Appleby & Davis, 2001; Caroll, 2002).

Employees   For organizational members the entire organizing process is filled with paradoxes (Poole & Van De Ven, 1989). Organizational cultures direct individuals toward the solution. Most people do not ponder and are not privy to the organization's plan of action. Instead they are guided by the symbolic messages sent by the culture, manager, or work group.

There are situations where a generalized response would be inappropriate. *Strategic ambiguity* allows for multiple interpretations by individuals in an organization of the prevailing culture (Eisenberg, 1984). For example, service can be an overriding goal, but the individual can determine the means for fulfilling this mandate. Many hospitals have rigid structures and hierarchies with clear job functions outlined and a top down control orientation designed to control costs. At the same time, everyone is called on to perform excellent, individualized patient care. Depending on the quality of the symbolic messages, which is critically tied to the ongoing reinforcement, hospital employees may be able to negotiate this difficult dilemma. Strategic ambiguity does not suggest that misleading or lying are useful strategies. Instead, not providing clarification might offer employees sufficient maneuverability with various issues to make their conflicting demands negotiable.

Concepts such as "less is more" when it comes to writing a memo or revising a report, or K.I.S.S. (Keep it Simple, Stupid) when giving instructions or training a new associate, seem paradoxical unless the cultural messages consistently are reinforcing the expected behavior. Our earlier discussion of whistle-blowing or glorifying the announcing of mistakes demonstrates how organizational members' attempt to resolve conflicting demands can be helped or hindered. Whistle-blowing, in particular, brings us to our third area of interest.

Ethics The organizational culture can assist us in resolving uncertainty regarding ethics. Ethics are our standards of moral conduct or judgments about whether our actions, values, or decisions are right or wrong (Gabriel, Fineman, & Sims, 2000; Johannesen, 1996). The world of work is filled with ethical decision-making moments ranging from using the company phone or e-mail for personal business to discrimination to allowing potentially dangerous products to be sold. To resolve apparently paradoxical issues, such as make a profit but do not sell any product that could be dangerous, organizations must have a proactive culture. Barbara Toffler, head of Arthur Andersen's Ethics & Responsible Business practices group, concluded:

> A company with a culture where leadership is serious about ethics, where employees feel fairly treated, and where the culture values and rewards ethical behavior, is far less likely to encounter ethics/compliance problems than a company whose culture demands unthinking obedience to authority, focuses solely on punishing bad behavior, and whose leadership gives only lip service to ethics. ("Beware," p. 5)

Many organizations and business people are highly ethical whereas others seem to provide lip service. Regardless, members can be faced with serious ethical dilemmas. Examples abound. Not reporting health and safety violations or hoping a warranty will run out before an identifiable problem becomes too severe are tempting routes for some business people. Ford Motor Company and Bridgestone/Firestone tires were forced to reveal prior knowledge of serious tire defects that caused Ford Explorers to go out of control and, in some cases, rollovers resulting in more than 100 deaths (Healey & Nathan, 2000). Companies, such as Union Carbide and USX, have underreported injuries to avoid Occupational Safety and Health Administration (OSHA) inspections. Information based equipment, such as computer terminals, may be causing serious ergonomic problems for the operators. The E. F. Hutton Group received a $7 million fine for check kiting, which is the practice of issuing checks in excess of the signer's bank balance with the expectation of making deposits in time to cover the checks. General Electric was fined $1.04 million for defrauding the Air Force of $800,000 (Dresang, 1986). "Eastman Chemical and Archer Daniels Midland Co. recently admitted that they engaged in price fixing—colluding with other companies in order to keep prices above competitive levels" (McShane & Von Glinow, 2000, p. 14).

Racial- and gender-based discrimination has denied equal access to service in public accommodations where famous names like Shoney's and Denny's became synonymous with racism (Faircloth, 1998; Harris, 1997). Corporations restricted access and mobility to women and minorities (Labich, 1999; Moorhead & Griffin, 1998). Texaco became infamous as the embodiment of racism where taped conversations of executives included racist language and talk of destroying key evidence resulting in a $175 million settlement (Labich, 1999; Roberts, 1998). The Center for Women's Policy Studies found that "women of color in corporate America doubt their employers' commitment to diversity, according to a survey of more than 1,500 women of color at 16 Fortune 500 companies" ("Women of," 1999, p. 5). Whereas the three previous corporate examples were based on reported activities, this survey reports the perceptions of this critical group who must respond to the daily issues.

Making a profit, remaining in business, or dodging a potentially serious legal issue can provide convenient rationalizations for questionable ethics such as not reporting violations. "Four in 10 workers say they know of ethical or legal violations at their company in the past 2 years" according to a survey by Walker Information (Carey & Jerding, 1998, p. B1). These included sexual harassment (19%); lying on reports/records (16%); conflict of interest (15%); stealing/lying (15%); lying to supervisor (15%); bias—race, age, and so on (15%); and drug/alcohol abuse (12%). A fourth of workers responding to a 1999 Yankelovich survey reported that they have been asked to do something against their ethical standards and 41% complied (Hall & Tian, 1999). In the same survey, 40% said they would try to resolve the ethical dilemma without losing their job. If the ethical guidelines appear to be in place merely to protect management from blame, they breed cynicism and actually promote unethical behavior according to Anderson's survey of more than 2,800 employees in six large U.S. companies with ethics/compliance programs in place ("Beware," 1999).

Employees face ethical decisions when deciding whether to accept gifts from vendors, pad expense accounts, surf the Net, or make personal phone calls at work. Some critics argue that business ethics is an oxymoron because winning is always rewarded and winning is defined as making a profit. When organizational members have to decide between the ethical and the profitable, clear symbolic messages supported by a rich cultural heritage can provide help (Peters & Austin, 1985). *Thematics*, "the organizational descriptions and stories members tell themselves in order to make sense of what they do," offer guidelines for how to behave (Anderson & Englehardt, 2001, p. 151). For example, customer service individuals can be faced with a set of mixed messages including do everything you can to please the customer *and* keep your costs down, or give attention to each individual *but* keep moving from customer to customer so no one waits. Excellent customer service organizations make it clear that customer satisfaction should be the paramount concern (Albrecht, 1988). Too often, organizations call for excellent customer service from the frontline employees and managers, but people evaluating the performance of a work unit focus on cost control measures (Cone, 1989).

On important ethical issues, *stories* can offer guides to the "right ways of thinking in a particular arena of action. They are, therefore, not just interesting stories, but stories that have consequences, that tell us right from wrong" (Andersen & Englehardt, 2001, p. 154). When we do not know what to do, these guidelines to successful solutions in the past outline culturally accepted responses. Of course, these stories can also "conceal, disguise, and gloss over" critical issues because highlighting certain issues means they do not highlight other critical issues (Andersen & Englehardt, 2001, p. 155). Shoney's, Denny's, and Texaco have changed their corporate cultures to embrace equality (Faircloth, 1998; Labich, 1999). Make no mistake, the issues have not disappeared but an emphasis by corporate leaders on symbolic behaviors is one key to guiding ethical decisions by organizational members (Wentling & Palma-Rivas, 1998).

These seven propositions provide a backdrop for understanding symbolic behavior. We now examine the means used to carry out symbolic activities. We are providing a brushstroke approach because many of the functions of symbolic behavior have been examined repeatedly in our earlier discussions.

Tools of Symbolic Behavior

Anything that provides symbolic meaning to people can be considered a tool. Not only is this consistent with our perspective and definition of organizational communication, it also explains why the manipulation of symbols can be difficult. Examples of the use of symbolic tools have been peppered throughout the first six chapters. Let us return to verbal and nonverbal communication. Specifically, we examine stories, titles, slogans, attention, dress standards, and priorities.

Verbal and nonverbal communications provide symbolic meaning. The values of the culture are underscored by the vocabulary because what is talked about receives attention. As Deetz (1982) put it, "The conceptual distinctions in an organization are inscribed in the system of speaking and writing" (p. 135). A partial list of verbal behaviors includes stories, myths, rituals, fantasies, ceremonies, titles, and jokes (e.g., see chap. 4). Nonverbal behavior and objects create an additional set of symbolic actions through events, activities, and surroundings (e.g., see chap. 5).

We already pointed to the power of *stories* when we discussed ethical considerations. As you read the following discussion of stories, note the highlighted uses and values. Stories allow the organization to *coordinate action* at a distance. As they are told and retold, people are reminded of key values. Not only is a common thread provided, but during the sharing process general guidelines develop and are reinforced allowing organizational members to customize diagnoses and solutions to local problems. According to Weick (1988), "Stories are important, not just because they coordinate, but also because they register, summarize, and *allow reconstruction of scenarios that are too complex for logical linear summaries to preserve* [italics added]" (p. 31).

Stories *provide guidance* to individuals in all organizations. In addition to setting the rules, they can serve "as metaphors for the bureaucracy-busting essential to vitalization of a decentralized company. Bill Hewlett, cofounder of Hewlett Packard, visited a plant on Saturday and discovered a lab stock area locked. He wanted scientists to have access to labs when they wanted. So, he went to maintenance, grabbed a bolt cutter, and cut the padlock off the lab stock door. He left a note asking them never to bolt the door again signed 'Thanks, Bill'" (Waterman, 1987, p. 267). The story, as it is told and retold, promotes action underscoring changes in the culture, supports innovation, and deals with employees in a personal manner.

Numerous organizations pay attention to the symbolic importance of *titles*. In moving from a traditional bank to a merchant bank, Bankers Trust renamed front senior vice presidents *partners* and loan officers *associates*. According to Waterman (1987), " ... paying attention to the messages embedded in titles and rewards (communicates) to everyone that there were ... significant changes in 'the way we do things around here'" (p. 268). Other companies refer to employees as partners, customer service representatives, technicians, or associates.

Slogans and brute attention focus employee interest. Waterman (1987) suggested, "Use symbols to strengthen what you communicate verbally about your priorities. There's nothing like a well-placed slogan or an unexpected bit of adventure to kick off a new priority. It's amazing how much T-shirts and coffee mugs can do to help focus attention that 'something's changed around here'" (p. 255).

Dress standards are another pervasive example. Traditionally, upper management dressed up more than lower level employees. Remland (2000) reminds us that "clothing communicates culture" (p. 123). Trends including uniforms for everyone from management on down to casual dress diminish these differences. In other professions—for example, UPS deliverymen, nurses, priests, airline pilots, or firefighters—crisp, professional uniforms provide assurance to the wearers and observers of competence. Earlier, in our discussion of nonverbal communication, we provided an extensive analysis of dress standards.

Finally, the *priorities* placed on daily activities in organizations carry enormous symbolic impact. The top officers at FedEx spend an inordinate amount of time on minor personnel grievances as symbolic proof of their people orientation. The senior vice president of personnel at FedEx observed: "The president and chairman are dead serious about making sure employees are treated fairly. So they spend time on it. If they spend 3 or 4 hours a week on grievances, it is a good symbol" (Levering et al., 1985, pp. 110–111). Many managers would respond, "Where can I find the time?" FedEx managers underscore the point that time ultimately is saved when people identify with the organization.

These examples might lead you to believe that strong organizations and effective leadership should be centered on symbolic behavior. As we have emphasized throughout this text, rarely can we focus on a single strategy. The complexity of the organizational communication world requires an understanding of a variety of approaches. In addition, there are significant drawbacks.

Limitations of Symbolic Behavior

Earlier in this text, we demonstrated how human relations were overused following the Hawthorne Studies. Likewise, an over-reliance on symbolic activities can lead to significant problems. These include unethical manipulation, empty or meaningless actions, omnipresence, divisions, and unexpected interpretations. We begin by underscoring the point that using symbolic activities to achieve goals is more difficult than it might appear.

Easier Said Than Done

Excellent and socially responsible social missions, enlightened leadership, and progressive practices are clearly the paths organizations should follow. The advice is widely forthcoming with organizational investigators arguing for more democracy, increased empowerment, and greater profit sharing. Philosophically, there can be little question but that given the power of the modern corporation, these goals should be pursued.

Sound simple? It isn't. Robert Hass became the leader of Levi Strauss & Co. in 1996. He was well known for his enlightened management practices that included doing more than "dressing the world in riveted denim; he was intent on showing that a company driven by social values could outperform a company hostage to profits alone" (Munk, 1999, p. 83). He argued that "Levi's wasn't just a garment company committed to social responsibility. It was a politically correct organization that happened to be in the garment business" (Munk, 1999, p. 86). It was an outstanding position for any organization but the mission never translated into action. Instead of uniting everyone under this banner, people split between holding onto the old way of doing things and following Hass. Innovation stagnated. Employees were faced with incongruences that were not resolved by mission statements alone. In 1998, Levi changed its mission statement from "To sustain responsible commercial success" to "To be the casual apparel authority." From a symbolic perspective, we should applaud the initial goals and question why the implementation was unsuccessful. In the end, the words were not enough.

Do not misunderstand—Levi's goals were outstanding. But the implementation created confusion, disorientation, and threatened the future of the organization. Without the requisite skills, simply calling for change is not enough. There are five additional problems with symbolic actions.

Unethical Manipulation

Second, it can be unethical. Symbolic actions are a means to an end. The judgment regarding ethics lies in the motives of users as well as the ends produced. As Waterman (1987) put it, "Because symbolism is such a potent source of influence, it can be used to manipulate people. We all know of the ways it has been put to use in the past" (p. 271). False promises, pie-in-the-sky approaches, and dangerous work assignments are good examples. Skipping over the abuses by some evangelists and used car dealers, employees and managers can be misled. The use of gimmickry, using superficial pleasantness to cover up dishonest activities or intentions, providing misleading or incorrect advice regarding safety, or providing untrue explanations for behaviors are means used by unethical organizations, managers, or coworkers in order to obtain some advantage.

Full of Sound and Fury, Signifying Nothing

Third, symbolic behavior can be used in place of substance. Waterman (1987) explains that on the organizational level. "Symbolic behavior can be a substitute for doing what you are supposed to do. It can convincingly give the appearance that you are going along with written or unwritten rules and norms, while all along you are undercutting them" (p. 271).

The U.S. Navy, when they began the Polaris submarine project in the 1950s, used a management center, weekly meetings, and the PERT (Performance, Evaluation, and Review Technique) to demonstrate to observers the care being taken in making decisions. In fact, these three factors, although providing an excellent facade, were not very influential in the outcome. PERT, for example, provided an excellent image. As Deal and Kennedy (1982) explained, "PERT's real value was in convincing the outside world that this project was important" (p. 70).

Organizations invest large amounts of time and money to develop teamwork, yet they may not know what the end product should look like and often assume that a lack of "unsportsmanlike conduct" means teamwork is occurring. Therefore the efforts can be misspent. In 210 BC, Pertonius Arbiter observed: "We trained hard, but it seemed that every time we were beginning to form into teams, we would be reorganized. I was to learn later in life that we tend to meet any new situation by reorganizing, and what a wonderful method it can be for creating the illusion of progress while producing confusion, inefficiency, and demoralization."

Individuals also can be co-opted by symbolism over substance. Leaders can develop a vested interest in preserving the corporate mythologies. As Zaleznik (1989) put it, "Leadership believes in and passes on and acculturates new groups in ... these myths, thereby creating a loss of leadership. People at the top become ill-prepared to lead in the direction of change" (p. 14).

Although myths are important, leaders must be careful not to be pulled into a fantasy. Zaleznik continues, leaders "must remain highly objective and have the capacity to look at the world as it is" (p. 14). If leaders are crippled or blinded by an outdated mythology or supported by an incorrect ethnocentrism, they will misunderstand the real nature of the world in which they live (Dalziel & Schoonover, 1988). Myths are helpful in dealing with paradoxes, but they can be counterproductive when responses to a changing environment are required. People actually may believe the myths and forget the allegorical nature of the stories and heroes.

Finally, symbolic behavior can replace accomplishment. Without meaning to, we can get caught up in the *activity trap,* where style gets substituted for substance (Robbins, 1980). Diversity efforts are criticized for focusing more on comparative statistics generated by sporadic efforts and less on the nature of the issues and clearly thought-out strategic solutions (Harris, 1997). In some organizations, the pressure to be productive can be so overbearing that individuals make certain they look busy even when there is nothing to do. Adding to the problem is the tendency toward *chronic externalitis.* This is the term given to the obsession some managers have in creating a successful image of themselves in the minds of others (Strasser & Loebs, 1985).

Omnipresence

The symbolic messages can prevent effective change or realistic responses to environmental demands. Hackman and Johnson (2000) observe: "Change is difficult because cultures are organized around deeply rooted assumptions and values that affect every aspect of organizational life" (p. 239). *Esprit de corps,* for example, also create *trained incapacities* leading to a discounting of external information or influence (Folger & Poole, 1984). Texaco, groupthink, and collective perceptions regarding diversity are examples we have already analyzed. Because cultures create identification and unity (Tompkins & Cheney, 1983), these *trained incapacities* can occur when values are strong or the culture's influence is too pervasive. Specifically, obsolescence, resistance to change, and inconsistency are the three risks posed by strong values (Deal & Kennedy, 1982). It is not difficult to find examples. In the 1980s, American auto manufacturers operated as if Japanese competition was unimportant. Retailing giants disregarded the impact of discount stores such as Wal-Mart.

Sears and Roebuck provides a familiar example encompassing all three problems. For years a leader in selling to Middle American customers, Sears failed to recognize the changing expectations of its clientele (Deal & Kennedy, 1982; Kelly, 1990). Faced with lagging sales, Sears tried to go upscale with its product line. This shift left the original consumers behind. More fundamentally, Sears employees—who sold highly functional if not very glamorous merchandise for years—were poorly trained to sell Macy's type products. In an attempt to overcome this malady, Sears reversed itself and slashed prices to appeal to the K-Mart (a.k.a. Big K) and Wal-Mart loyalists (Diamond, 1991). The results from these maneuvers demonstrate the potential problems with strong values. The original Sears organization was stale and riddled with obsolescent, albeit strong, values. When the organization was recast, employees were resistant to change and customers were not interested in a new Sears (Kelly, 1990). More recently, Sears has revamped its reward system for managers moving away from an entitlement mentality where salaries were guaranteed to a performance-based salary (Chandler, 1998). Twenty percent of a manager's salary is based on customer and subordinate satisfaction. Unless these changes are well communicated and clearly followed, the overriding cultural values will prevail over any changes.

Strong cultures dictate roles and performances meaning individuals can be co-opted by the culture and its messages (Conrad, 1985). Although strict adherence to cultural expectations can be vital, such as in the military during combat, there are numerous examples where this can create tunnel vision. Gabriel et al. (2000) conclude: "Rules can become the opium of bureaucratic officials" (p. 31). A culture that is bound by an overriding tradition can stifle.

The power of an organization's culture often emerges during a crisis. For example, after the American Red Cross admitted mishandling contributions after the September 11 attacks, it promised to reform its operating procedures. However, the Red Cross' Hurricane Katrina response was equally inadequate even though internal documents show the leadership was warned that internal disputes could result in a repeat of the 9/11 failures. Senator Charles Grassley, who as Finance Committee chairman who oversees charitable organizations concluded: "This type of culture, a culture that discourages people from coming forward, management that does not want to hear the bad news, and are more concerned about good press than good results, is a theme I am hearing too often" (Associated Press, 2005, p. 3A). Although the American Red Cross' goals are worthwhile, the prevailing culture has limited needed reforms.

We already discussed ethics. Police psychologists argue the alienation between many law enforcement officers and the public is the result of a sick police subculture determined to maintain the "thin blue line" between their own subculture and the outside (Meredith, 1984). Other researchers argue that police must react effectively in life and death situations, control their emotional reactions to potentially bizarre, disturbing, and stressful situations while presenting a front to the surrounding community that broadcasts safety, authority, and control (Waldron & Krone, 1991). They develop an internalized identity that allows them to deal with their group membership. Regardless of the explanation, the officers' subculture demands a we–they, good guys–bad guys perspective that can prevent good judgment. In the process of "learning the ropes" idealistic young officers begin to mimic the posture and activities, buttressed by the cultural messages contained in police policies, procedures, and actions, and soon respond to issues of law and order based on actions sanctioned by the subculture.

One consequence of this tradition is that police forces have remained predominately male. Only 12% of the police officers in the United States are female and of "the nation's 17,000 police departments, only 123 have women chiefs (Johnson, 1998). By and large, this culture designed to negotiate police pressures in this "tough" men's work has placed barriers meaning the "nation's policewomen are facing a bullet-proof glass ceiling" (Johnson, 1998, p. 1A). The strong police subculture, supported by the very real life-threatening situations, emotional strain, and pressure from the public, creates a single-mindedness that can be counterproductive. We can begin a list of professions where assumptions are made regarding who can and cannot handle the work or would present the wrong image. Would you expect to see a male or female in the following occupations: Auto repair, clerical support, bank teller, grade school teacher, or fireman (you get the point)? Earlier, we pointed to cultures as effective means for directing individuals during paradoxical situations. Clearly, this direction can lead to errors in organizational and individual behavior.

Fosters Divisions

The schism between police officers and the public supports the fourth problem with symbols. Symbols can create great divisions in an organization. Culture provides both division and unity, and the symbols used to reinforce the organization can create powerful alienation between individuals and groups. Subcultures develop between managers and workers, blue and white collars, or factory and sales creating the potential for a "them versus us" environment.

These divisions inevitably enable or privilege some while restraining or subjugating others. Titles and rank, as indications of advancement and accomplishment, also reinforce differences between individuals and provide a potential for we–they thinking and acting. The impact of parking spaces, time clocks, and numerous other nonverbal artifacts on the organization's members was discussed earlier. When problems occur, *scapegoating* the other group becomes all too tempting. The stronger the symbolic division, the greater the likelihood that the blame will be placed externally (Gabriel et al., 2000). Competition between divisions, shifts, or members of management within an organization are classic examples. Mistakes are the fault of the technical people or accounting or lazy sales forces or poor supervision. Often a stereotypical negative label such as "traitor," "trouble-makers," "over-the-hill," or "just don't care" allows this division to become generalized from an event to a group.

Unexpected Interpretations

Finally, symbolism can be unpredictable. Because individuals respond to symbolic behavior through their own frame of reference, attempts to use symbolism can have unintended results. As Waterman (1987) observed, "When Ford Motor wanted to emphasize quality back in 1979, it put a bunch of Japanese cars in the plant to show employees what you could do if you really put your mind to quality. The result was that employees went out and bought Japanese cars" (p. 270). Rather than accept quality as a goal, Ford employees accepted Japanese cars as better cars.

In other cases, when there is a powerful "management versus employee" climate, employees go to great effort to never be labeled a "company man or woman." The bizarre behaviors of true believers, often misguided by their own interpretations of strong symbolic messages, have occurred throughout history. Placed in the context of an organization trying to establish a common theme, our conclusion must be that a judicious use of symbols is necessary or the wrong action based on the right intent can occur. A powerful sense of organizational pride can lead to dysfunctional responses by employees and managers.

This is not to suggest that unethical manipulation, empty or meaningless actions, omnipresence, divisions, and unexpected interpretations are the only troublesome outcomes from symbolic actions. As a means of highlighting the possible problems, these five issues are instructive. We now consider the logistics of presenting symbolic messages.

Performances

The stage or drama metaphor provides a useful means for understanding how symbolic behavior is carried out through individual role performance and rituals. A dramatistic perspective views individuals as actors "who creatively play, improvise, interpret, and re-present roles and scripts" (Conquergood, 1991, p. 187). We can test the performance premise by examining our own consumer behaviors. For example, why is the experience involved with drinking a cup of latte in the entertaining environment of a local Starbucks or other coffee dispensing eatery worth four dollars? Because the set of intangible activities that support the actual service itself provide a satisfying experience or a performance worth an increased financial burden (Pine & Gilmore, 1999). A steak is, fundamentally, a steak. But the culinary experience is surrounded by a series of events that are staged to engage us in some manner. A well-performed drama replete with accomplished performers including the waiters, ambiance, and supporting cast will determine how we judge the time we have spent. If poorly performed the event will be discredited.

Role Performance

Learning to act out appropriate roles is a fundamental aspect of human development and important to our organizational success. In a *theatrical* sense, role performance means portraying someone else. The *dramatistic* perspective refers, instead, to an individual's behavior in society. As we learn to recognize and define social situations, we develop appropriate roles for others and ourselves. In a play, we are expected to learn and deliver specific lines. In organizational performances, we must be situationally relevant and vary our communication to the surrounding events. Therefore, roles are *co-constructed* dialogues rather than monologues (Pacanowsky & O'Donnell-Trujillo, 1983). The enactments occurring provide us with important information regarding the social situation and mold our own performances. Roles involve doing the work that can range from specific assigned tasks to practices that are carried out because they fill the needed requirements of the job as expected by the culture. There is more to an effective role performance.

They are *historically constrained*. Our behaviors in an organization, if they are to be assigned credibility, are not impromptu events. As a UPS driver, you cannot simply choose not to wear the famous brown uniform nor change in any dramatic manner how a package is delivered (Pine & Gilmore, 1999). At Disney, the cast members, as all employees are called, are required to perform in very specific ways. The various theme parks are master examples of a set of roles presented to create a positive experience.

Roles are not counterfeit acts, but behaviors that maintain social stability by facilitating predictability in human interaction (Faules & Alexander, 1978). Roles constitute those behaviors necessary to be accepted by others as a colleague, boss, manager, leader, or organizational member. The better the presentation, the higher the credibility assigned, leading to the bestowing of status, position, office, or acceptance. Finally, roles facilitate the creation, maintenance, and transformation of the organizational meaning. Southwest Airlines, for example, encourages its flight attendants and gate attendants to use one-liners. When employees tell the one-liners, they are furthering the corporate driven culture. So, these acts are not neutral but are, instead, *politically driven*—there are motives behind the acts (Deetz, 1995; Mumby, 1988). By supporting the culture through enacted performances, the actors come together to further support the organization's culture. In the same manner, acts conducted to subvert the culture through insurgencies, rule violations, or malcontents are politically driven.

Three elements in a presentation are an appropriate front, dramatic realization, and mystification (Goffman, 1959). We make choices about how we want to present our role, which constitutes role enactment.

Appropriate Front Putting on an appropriate front (e.g., choice of clothes, language, facial expressions, excellent customer service) provides messages to support the role. Returning to the nonverbal chapter, a plethora of other artifacts and actions also comprise our front. In theory, we decide to engage in a drama to an audience, which can be a consumer, a manager, or a colleague. As

Goffman (1974) put it, "Indeed, it seems that we spend most of our time not engaged in giving information, but in giving shows" (p. 508).

Some individuals seem more adept at saying and doing the right thing at the right time, thereby avoiding malapropisms with some regularity. Individual and group role abilities often determine the acceptability of the act (Pacanowsky & O'Donnell-Trujillo, 1983). According to Boulding (1961), "If the role is occupied by individuals who do not have the requisite skills, the image of the role is profoundly modified by all those with whom they come in contact" (p. 105).

We are assisted by the numerous cues offered by "the culture of the organization (that) provides the background in which specific situations arise. It establishes broad parameters for acting" (Conrad, 1985, p. 201). We learn to establish credibility through making the appropriate choices. Normative criteria, based on relative, situational data allow us to understand the role expectations. It must be remembered that role performance is episodic, co-created, and often improvised, so acting a role is not always easy.

Dramatic Realization   Using verbal and nonverbal symbols to fulfill the requirements of the role leads to *dramatic realization*. The term *performance* brings with it several important concepts. We have already indicated that performances are contextual, and are based on immediacy and the cultural fit. Customer service provides an example. If we are partaking of a relationship-oriented service (e.g., relationship developed over time), we expect the provider to act quite differently from one-time interactions or encounter-oriented services (Gutek, 1995). We have high expectations for the importance of the relationship developed over time and expect that the co-created history will impact on how we are treated. An encounter-oriented situation (e.g., drive-through restaurant) carries little or no long-term impact, so the moment is just a moment.

So it goes with any presentation. Employees being corrected for poor performance should seem contrite and a hospital should not lose medical records. Partaking in *scripts* to reaffirm the culture occurs in almost all settings. For example, although most surgeons would agree that germs are destroyed in about 30 seconds, they scrub down for about 7 minutes before an operation (Deal & Kennedy, 1982). Why the extra 6 minutes? Surgeons are schooled to scrub 7 minutes so to scrub less would be to violate cultural expectations, make one appear ill-prepared for the operation, and risk informal censure for not being conscientious. Appropriateness to the culture's rules or scripts is the measuring rod for the appropriate front and achieving dramatic realization.

Image presentation and impression management are popular concepts for these efforts (Lord & Maher, 1991). Although there may be legitimate concerns regarding unethical impression management, it is a useful tool "to secure leadership positions and to achieve … goals" (Hackman & Johnson, 2000, p.

24). Ingratiating, "an attempt by individuals to increase their attractiveness in the eyes of others" (Liden & Mitchell, 1988, p. 573), is a part of impression management that occurs when the actor feels the audience controls significant rewards. Much of the emphasis on image presentation can be seen as the realization that some roles require skills that might not be developed fully, and using the stage metaphor draws attention to the role of the audience.

Mystification   To this point, we have focused on fitting in. In addition, a certain amount of mystification is required to put distance between the actor and the audience. You can draw on the verbal and nonverbal chapters for examples of mystification ranging from the outfitting of an office to the language used by certain professions. An interesting case in point is provided by the tests frequently administered during pre-employment and advancement sessions. Personality tests represent a desire for scientific rigor/and underscore American expectations for rationality in making decisions (Trice & Beyer, 1985). This science of selection is questionable "because many studies reveal that devices such as selection interviews and personality tests have modest to poor reliability and validity, or predictive value" (Gabriel et al., 2000, p. 13). Many organizations put applicants through numerous interviews, difficult questioning, and a waiting period. Microsoft is famous, or infamous, for how it interviews (Gimein, 2001). One question inevitably asked is "Why are manhole covers round?" Another is "How many piano tuners are there in the world?" The answers are not a matter of technical ability, but simply reasoning under pressure. The covers are round because any other shape would fall in. There are as many piano tuners as there are (1) pianos to be tuned where the (2) owners can afford to purchase the service.

Because the results of the evaluation procedures or the insiders' actions are rarely shared with the test-taker, there is mystification in the hiring or promotion process. Imagine the difference between being hired immediately—you'll do as a "warm body," versus having to wait for 2 weeks to know if you have the job after a rigorous written examination and interview schedule. Subaru-Isuzu is willing to take as long as 6 months to hire and the "fastest hire took 9 weeks" (Pfeffer, 2000, p. 499).

Not all companies are interested in hiring the best and the brightest. Enterprise Rent-A-Car is the largest rental company in the United States and it has expanded at a rate of 25–30% a year for over a decade. Almost all Enterprise's people are college graduates who are hired for their sales skills and personality. The chief operating officer, Dennis Ross, commented: "We hire from the half of the college class that makes the upper half possible. ...We want athletes, fraternity types" (Pfeffer, 2000, p. 497). Enterprise wants individuals who can work with customers. Amazon.com tells the temp agencies to "send us your freaks" (Hof, 1998, p. 108). Because the employees work in warehouses filling orders, looks and dress are less important than a willingness to work.

Rituals

Once roles become systematized, they are regarded as rituals. Rituals are acted out by the performances and encompass all repeated activities. Acting correctly, scrubbing down, and being professional are examples of individual rituals. Rituals provide for organizational reality. For our purposes, it is helpful to focus on the rituals of arrival, belonging, and exclusion (Wood, 2004).

Rituals of Arrival   At some point everyone is a newcomer. The rituals of arrival include those processes that explain what we must learn in order to be a bonafide member of the organization. For starters, neophytes rarely are afforded full privileges to use equipment, park close, leave their station, arrange their lunch time, pick their desks, and so on. Even gaining entry to parts of the organization can be difficult.

Socialization is the process of indoctrinating new employees to a company's policies. New members find that "taken-for-granted ways no longer fit; the familiar customs and practices of the previous job or role are inappropriate" (Gabriel et al., 2000, p. 16). Strong cultures make the salient expectations clear. Disney puts all employees, now called actors, through their scripted training program. Southwest Airlines uses orientation and training to both teach culture and let new employees know how fortunate they are to have been hired (Pfeffer, 2000). We can learn what is expected of us from a more formalized, organizationally sponsored socialization process (e.g., orientation). In many cases, we learn informally through the people we meet and with whom we work. If policies regarding breaks, lunch, use of the computer, or personal calls are not explained by the organization, we quickly learn from others. Not knowing is not an option for most individuals.

Many organizations have adopted a clear acculturation process to guarantee successful socialization (Harris, 1990). Clear does not necessarily mean easy. "The IBMs and Procter and Gambles of the world present new recruits with a series of specific hurdles to jump—surviving punishing working hours, performing very basic work to remind them of their humble status, ... sacrificing domestic and leisure time for the company" (Gabriel et al., 2000, p. 17).

Rituals of Belonging and Exclusion   Once you are part of an organization, there are rituals of belonging and exclusion. *Belonging rituals* are indications that you are being accepted within the organization and/or work group. Being invited by colleagues to certain meetings, out for a meal, or into a project can show belonging. At the same time, some groups make it clear that you are excluded.

For example, in numerous organizations, being promoted to supervisor from the ranks also means losing a large number of contacts. You literally are excluded from the hourly ranks. Knowing how to act in a period of individual advancement can offer a difficult test. In one study of workers being promoted to managers, the individuals were required to alter successfully their body, dress, and social communication to act managerial although not changing to the point of losing credibility with their co-workers (Caudill, Durden, & Lambert, 1985). This is a tricky issue because failing to change creates a credibility problem with other managers, and being a "company person" will hurt in the process of managing friends and colleagues.

Social dramas occur in every group and reinforce the belonging rituals. The drama is processional and occurs when there is a *breach of the symbolic system*. Dramas are likely to follow four phases: breach, crisis, redressive action, and reintegration or recognition of the schism (Turner, 1980). In a miniform, an employee talking back to a manager in front of other employees is a breach of etiquette, roles, and rules. The turbulence can be handled in a variety of ways, but a crisis has occurred. Perhaps the employee is suspended; or the manager chooses to dress the individual down in front of everyone else; or the traditional "in my office now!" or the employee is asked to explain the point further. If someone must apologize, a redressive action has taken place. The same point would be true if management decided the employee was correct, there was recognition of the schism, and reintegration develops with new guidelines regarding employee feedback. The drama acts as a means for reaffirming, negotiating, and/or transforming the cultural standards. Critically, these breaches or shocks are moments of sensemaking that put the taken-for-granted organizational practices into question (Weick, 1995).

This discussion provides the final, essential issue to a dramatic presentation. As the performance unfolds, the audience must remain front stage. *Backstage* is the region reserved for members of the cast and a correctly staged act does not allow the audience to gain access. If they do, they might discredit the performance. As the show is put on, dramatic realization requires that the audience not get behind the scene, discover flaws in the act or front, and discredit the performance (Harris, 1984).

Goffman (1959) observed, "All roles require a certain degree of skill in the performance of the role as well as an image of the note itself" (p. 216). Impressions are formed based on very little information. A façade, even if it is an organizationally sanctioned one, must be maintained or it invites the loss of credibility. Guarding the backstage is important during the entire presentation process, from interviewing to participating in the rituals of arrival, to the period of belonging. "The struggles, politics, negotiations, anguish, and actual joys of organizing remain, for the most part, invisible to the consumer: they are backstage. When they are revealed, showing how precarious the organization can be, it can come of something of a shock…" (Gabriel et al., 2000, p. 5).

Letting the role take over your entire persona is equally destructive. Although the play is the thing, the trick, it would seem, is never letting the act overcome the person. So, congruency, fulfilling of expectations and coordination among actors (team members) is required. If the concept of backstage is still unclear, consider our earlier discussion of the hiring process.

Consider a second example: Being a team player and effectively creating a successful team are positive attributes. But, according to Frank and Brown (1989), "no one knows exactly what it means to coordinate work groups. Therefore, rituals or specific procedures are developed in the hope that coordination will result" (p. 216).

The list is almost endless. When you are asked to act like a leader, you seek symbolic manifestations of the correct actions that will make you appear to be a leader with an image of ability and confidence. We coordinate and plan without a clear notion of exactly what these two activities mean. Expected behavior can be tautological when it takes the form of "we know we have good teamwork when everyone is working well together" or "good leaders get things done" or "if it ain't broke, don't fix it."

No one should assume that careful hiring practices are incorrect. Nor should teamwork be discounted or leadership underrated. The point is simply that we try to act correctly, based on past and current symbolic reinforcements, for dramatic realization. It may very well be that we also achieve excellent leadership and teamwork and hire the correct people.

Organizational rites are "planned activities that have both practical and expressive consequences. When this definition is applied to corporate life, such diverse activities as personnel testing, organizational development programs, and collective bargaining can be seen as rites that have not only practical consequences but also express important cultural meanings" (Trice & Beyer, 1985, pp. 372–373).

So, presentation, image, consistency, and all the other activities so important to a well-staged performance for individuals and groups, applies to organizations. Performances are a useful place to end our discussion of symbolic behavior. As much as we might like to believe that individuals and organizations can control performances, we also are aware that one cannot not communicate. Regardless of the staging, individuals often can see behind an invalid act and discover flaws.

Conclusion

For many individuals studying organizational communication, symbolic behavior is the obvious focal point. Because we are symbol users, and symbol abusers, this attention is well deserved.

Seven propositions outline the power of symbolic behavior in an organization. The following issues are intertwined with symbolic behavior: complexity, uncertainty, cultural creation and maintenance, interpersonal reality, group behavior, leadership, and the management of incongruences.

Tools of symbolic behavior can be identified through various types of verbal and nonverbal communication. What we say and do provides significant symbolic messages.

But symbolic behavior also can lead to extremely negative outcomes. These include unethical manipulation, empty or meaningless actions, trained incapacities, divisions, and unexpected interpretations.

Finally, performances highlight the ongoing role of symbolic behavior in organizations. This dramatistic perspective also draws attention to the danger of believing that acting is the same as performing a useful, justified role in an organization.

At this point, we have examined the perspectives regarding organizational communication in the first three chapters, and then provided an in-depth analysis of the principles of organizational communication in chapters 4 through 8. The remaining chapters offer specific insights into the pragmatics of organizational communication.

Study Questions

1. Find an example of each of the basic symbolic behavior propositions. Which one is the easiest to find? Which one is the most difficult? Why the difference?
2. What is the importance of uncertainty and/or incongruity?
3. Outline the elements in organizational cultures.
4. What is a negotiated experience? Provide an example.
5. Explain each of the limits of symbolic behavior.
6. Why are ethics a serious concern?
7. Provide a diagram for performances.
8. Explain dramatic realization and mystification.
9. Differentiate between the different rituals. Use your own college or university experiences as examples.

8
Listening

Listening is a critical part of the organizational communication process. The accurate perception and interpretation of messages is vital for effective organizational communication transactions to take place. To enhance our understanding of the role of listening in organizational communication, this chapter unfolds in the following manner. First, we examine the current status of organizational listening. Second, the four stages of listening—sensing, interpreting, evaluating, and responding—are analyzed. Third, active, passive, deliberative, and empathetic listening are addressed. Fourth, the special requirements of organizational listening are developed; feedback constitutes the fifth issue. Finally defensive and supportive climates are presented. This analysis concentrates on the following issues:

- Importance of listening
- Costs of poor listening
- Current status of organizational listening
- Difficulties in delineation
- Four listening stages
- Types of listening
- Feedback
- Defensive and supportive climates

Importance of Listening

In a sense, this should be an obvious point. We cannot communicate successfully with someone unless the message is received and understood. The case for the importance of listening is significant, as we now discover.

Benefits of Effective Listening

The advantages of effective listening are almost endless. Listening has been shown to be a vital skill for successful managers, supervisors, and professional employees occupying more than 60% of their average day on the job (Cooper, 1997; Wolvin & Coakley, 1996). Oral communication, as exhibited through the four skills of listening, following instructions, conversing and giving feedback, "was consistently identified as the most important competency in evaluating entry-level candidates" (Maes, Weldy, & Icenogle, 1996, p. 78). A survey of The American Society of Personnel Directors ranked listening as a critical communication competency for successful job performance (Curtis, Winsor, & Stephens, 1989). Misunderstandings are reduced, innovation increases, and morale improves at the workplace as a result of effective listening (Yukl, 1994).

Bone (1998) links effective listening with learning, building relationships, being entertained, making intelligent decisions, saving time, enjoying conversations, settling disagreements, getting the best value, preventing accidents and mistakes, asking intelligent questions, and making accurate evaluations. In addition, it paves the way toward better personnel relationships, fewer mistakes and errors, more successful meetings, shared viewpoints and perspectives, a stronger culture, and a greater organizational cohesiveness (Wolvin & Coakley, 1996). Good listening is essential to business success (Goby & Lewis, 2000).

Listening and the Communication Process

Listening is the most used channel of communication. We spend up to 70% of our waking day communicating (Osborn & Osborn, 1994). Of this 70%, from 42 to 60% (or more) is spent listening (Purdy, 1996). In organizations, the percentage is frequently greater. Executives spend between 45% and 93% of their day listening (Wolvin & Coakley, 1996). Covey (1989), in his perennial *Business Week* best seller, *The Seven Habits of Highly Effective People*, identifies Habit 5 as "seek first to understand, then to be understood" (p. 235). He argues that we must listen with the intent to fully, deeply understand the other person emotionally and intellectually before we offer advice or prescribe action (Covey, 1991). Table 8.1 further supports Covey's conclusion.

Research indicates, however, that although about half of our communication time is spent listening (Johnson, 1996), most of us are not very good listeners (Alessandra & Hunsaker, 1993). The average college student listens effectively to only about 50% of what is said and remembers only 25% of that

Table 8.1

A story illustrates the danger of the leader always being in charge and refusing to listen.

NAVY:	Please divert your course 15 degrees to the north to avoid a collision.
CIVILIAN:	Recommend you divert YOUR course 15 degrees to the south to avoid a collision.
NAVY:	This is the captain of a U.S. Navy ship. I say again, divert YOUR course.
CIVILIAN:	No, I say again, you divert YOUR course.
NAVY:	THIS IS THE AIRCRAFT CARRIER ENTERPRISE, WE ARE A LARGE WARSHIP OF THE U.S. NAVY. DIVERT YOUR COURSE NOW!
CIVILIAN:	This is a lighthouse. Your call.

content after 2 days (Wolvin & Coackley, 1996). In medical situations, where accurate diagnosis would seem critical, many physicians do not listen carefully enough to their patients' stories (Nyquist, 1996).

Measured by its ramifications, or by the percentage of communicating time consumed, listening is important. This importance is underscored by examining organizations, our third point.

Listening in Organizations

Listening plays a role in almost any occupation or business. For example, negotiating is a prized skill in many organizations. Fisher and Ertel (1995) conclude that "Regardless of intentions or favored tactics, listening to the other side, so that you can then make good choices about what to do and how to do it, is universally important" in negotiations (p. 77). High performance teams have "an open communication structure that allows all members to participate. Individuals are listened to regardless of their age, title, sex, race, ethnicity, profession, or other status characteristics" (Wheelan, 1999, p. 42). Increasing employee involvement through the shift from vertical to horizontal communication, as discussed earlier, requires a free flow of information between colleagues where mutual understanding is the responsibility of the participants and not just a reliance on vertical communication. Cohen & Fink (2001) add, "the skills required of employees— teamwork, conflict resolution, initiative, openness—are increasingly likely to be required of all employees and will enable organizational development not yet imagined" (p. 44). Building relationships, especially in a digitally driven, knowledge-based economy is a skill based on effective listening.

Earlier we outlined the shifts in organizations toward service and information processing. Customer contact is the sine qua non for service organizations (Albrecht, 1988; Boyle, 1999). CRSS, one of the world's premier architectural firms specializing in construction management and managing power cogeneration plants, sees listening as a cornerstone of its organization. Peters (1992) explains. "CRSS's remarkable record includes designing some of the world's most complex projects. Its approach to working with its clients is what sets the company apart. Amazingly, CRSS architects established, and then maintained for over four decades, preeminence and competitive advantage via one 'simple' tactic—taking listening seriously. CRSS builds on listening, worries about listening, works ceaselessly at improving its listening skills. CRSS' technology of listening turns out to be a benchmark knowledge-management saga" (p. 399). Procter & Gamble (P&G), makers of products such as Bold, Crest, Cover Girl, and more than 300 others (with 98% of all households in the United States using at least one of their products), employs a variety of techniques to remain one of the 10 most-admired U.S. companies for 8 consecutive years. P&G believes the customer is most important, and lists 99 rules for its employees to pursue. Rules 4 and 5 encourage employees to find out what the customer wants and does not want. Rule 6 admonishes to "listen carefully. It's easy to misunderstand the consumer." Rule 7 counsels to "Keep listening after the sale is made" (Decker, 1998).

Listening to employees is equally important. Merck, chosen by *Working Mother* as one of the 10 best places to work in America, "invests in people by listening to them" (Caudron, 1998, p. 102). Industries where individuals communicate primarily through digital processes, such as information acquisition and utilization, have found an increased importance for the role of face-to-face communication (Zuboff, 1988). Dependence on computers decreases interpersonal contact. Electronic mail, individual computer workstations, and specific task assignments isolate individuals from interactions. Hollingshead and McGrath (1995) conclude that all "forms of computer mediation, to some degree, place limits and structure on the communication process itself, necessarily limiting the channels and modalities by which members can communicate with each other ... " (p. 31), meaning each interpersonal listening opportunity takes on even greater importance. The problem is that decreased interpersonal contacts create fewer opportunities to double check listening accuracy to make certain an error has not occurred. In addition, as digitized workplaces allow more individuals to pursue full or part-time work at home via a computer modem linked to the office system, casual, ongoing work contacts become fewer and fewer. Colvin (2000), reviewing the promises of 21st-century organizations, concludes, "But we make a foolish and ancient error if we forget that quirky humans still very much need interaction, recognition, and relationship," which require excellent listening skills (p. F-9).

For all organizations, effective listening is important (Deal & Kennedy, 1999). Service industries, now comprising more than 70% of jobs in the United States (see chap. 1), maintain and improve customer satisfaction through effective listening. In information-based industries, opportunities to communicate interpersonally are diminished, making each listening event potentially more important. Quality can be achieved only through coordination between individuals and subunits, which requires excellent listening.

Managers and Leaders   For leaders, listening is often the most important skill (Ray, 1999). When 1,000 human resources professionals were asked to rank the number-one skill of effective managers, they listed effective listening (Windsor, Curtis, & Stephens, 1997). In another survey of personnel directors in 300 businesses and industries, listening was ranked as the most important skill for becoming a manager (Whetten & Cameron, 1991). Leaders need to "solicit feedback from others. Listening that accurately interprets verbal and nonverbal messages is a primary linking skill" (Hackman & Johnson, 2000).

Listening helps in discovering emerging problems, dealing with hostile employees, managing interpersonal conflicts, enhancing employee morale, and adding to the manager's professional image (Morgan & Baker, 1985).

Bosses are admonished to "develop formal and informal devices aimed at spurring intense, proactive listening" (Peters, 1987, p. 304). The managerial functions of exchanging job information, receiving and giving directions, seeking and providing information for decisions, coaching and counseling, meetings and conference participation, performance reviews, interviews, and negotiating all require effective listening skills. In the article, "Leaders Thrive on Practical Listening," Hart (1998) explains: "Patience is the key to good listening. This is a fast-paced world, both personal and professional. Many studies confirm that the single greatest reason for conflict is misunderstanding. Misunderstandings are universally prevented if you slow down, listen, and understand what the other person is saying" (p. 49A). O'Toole (1996) concludes that a value-based leader must listen to dissenting opinions in order to test ideas, without being a prisoner of public opinion.

Subordinates   An examination of 24 different studies found effective listening to be the most important skill for persons in entry-level positions (DiSalvo, Larson, & Seiler, 1976). Once hired, listening is critical to learning, understanding, and participating in communication (Burley-Allen, 2001; Hamilton, 2005).

Costs of Poor Listening

Second, ineffective listening is expensive. For example, a simple $10 mistake, if made by 100 million workers in this country, would cost more than a billion dollars. Usually, our mistakes have a multiplier effect because they must be corrected or redone, doubling the time used. If the error is passed onto a customer, there might be additional costs in terms of future business. If the error requires the involvement of others, then the costs skyrocket. Disregarding the dollar cost, "those little mistakes waste time, cause embarrassment, irritate customers, alienate employees, and, ultimately, affect profits" (Wakin, 1984, p. 45). Poor listening can lead to numerous problems. "On average, people are only about 35% efficient in listening. This lack of effective listening often results in missed opportunities to avoid misunderstandings, conflict, poor decision-making, or a crisis because a problem wasn't identified in time" (Burley-Allen, 2001, p. 119). So, although we may hear important information, our efficiency in processing and utilizing the input is poor. In conclusion, "the list of problems caused by ineffective listening is endless, and the exact cost is incalculable" (Gibbs, Hewing, Hulbert, Ramsey, & Smith, 1985, p. 30).

Current Status of Organizational Listening

Based on this universal agreement regarding the importance of listening, you might assume that effective listening is practiced in most organizational settings. Consider several studies and reports that call that conclusion into question.

Training and development managers feel listening is one of the most important problems leading to ineffective performance or low productivity (Hunt & Cusella, 1983). Retaining staff is a critical issue for many organizations (Hudson Institute, 2000). A Linkage, Inc. survey which questioned "655 employees about their willingness and intentions to stay with their current employers found that the managers and organizations who actively listen to employees' input ranked very high" ("Survey says," 2001, p. 8). Trust was the most important issue (Hudson Institute, 2000).

Many individuals and organizations seem immune to the evidence and continue to neglect listening. Individually, we seem unaware of our deficiencies. Fuller (1991) observes that "there are few people with IQ's above room temperature who wouldn't say they were good listeners" (p. 54). He goes on to point out that this confidence is not supported by the listening effectiveness research. Donaldson and Donaldson (1996) add, "The reason most people don't listen more effectively is that they don't want to listen. They just want to talk. You must decide listening is worth doing; then you must do it" (p. 118).

We have risked belaboring the point regarding listening because the case for improved listening would seem to be too great to ignore. If our premise is correct, why is listening not dealt with more effectively by organizations and, in many cases, textbooks on organizational communication?

Difficulties in Delineation

Three factors cause listening to be a difficult topic to cover. First, listening often falls prey to the same type of reasoning preventing a fuller understanding of organizational communication in general. Either listening is so obvious that we all should be asked simply to be better listeners, or it is too complex to be easily understood (Burley-Allen, 2001). If you feel a sense of *deja vu* regarding this possible dilemma, you would be correct because we confronted the same issue in chapter 1 regarding the study of organizational communication.

Second, for all practical purposes, listening cannot be separated from other organizational communication skills. For example, our verbal communication is meaningless unless someone else listens, and being able to respond effectively to verbal communication is contingent on effective listening. In addition, listening to the nonverbal aspects of a message is critical to understanding.

Third, organizational members conceptualize effective listening by others based on nonverbal and verbal responses during the process (Hunt & Cusella, 1983). We are judged to be effective listeners, in other words, by how nonverbally and verbally responsive we seem to be during the transaction (Lewis & Reinsch, 1988). A listener's overt messages are perceived as an important component of their listening behavior. So, questions, praise, advice, and thanks are positive listening behaviors, along with nonverbal behaviors such as eye contact (Hackman & Johnson, 2000). There are gender differences in listening styles that impact how individuals behave in transactions (Brownell, 2002). In the United States, "feminine communicators are more likely than masculine ones to show they are listening by nodding, keeping eye contact, and gesturing in response to messages" (Wood, 2000, p. 68). Put another way, women communicate in an effort to build rapport whereas men tend to communicate to report (Tannen, 1990).

Globalization draws increased attention to listening because there are "general cultural tendencies in regards to listening that can create misunderstandings" (Hall, 2002). Learned behaviors such as eye contact, (see chap. 5) occur simultaneously while we listen and unaccustomed actions, such as reduced eye contact, might make us believe someone is not listening (DeVito, 2004).

In conclusion, effective listening is vital to organizational health. Although listening's role seems obvious, organizations often overlook listening precisely because it appears too apparent to require highlighting. Next we examine the four listening stages and the listening behaviors most important to organizations.

Four Listening Stages

The four listening stages are sensing, interpreting, evaluating, and responding. In most cases, these four stages occur in rapid succession with little awareness on our part. Because listening is a complex process, understanding each of the stages, and the possible barriers, will enhance our abilities to listen. In most cases, improving our own listening abilities will bring greater rewards than trying to force others to be better listeners. An important exception to this generalization is the power of feedback, which is discussed later in this chapter.

Sensing

Good listening begins with sensing the message. There is a difference between simply hearing and listening with understanding. Hearing involves the biological senses that provide for reception of the message through sensory channels (Verderber & Verderber, 2001). In addition to the auditory senses, we depend on our visual senses, which sometimes are called our *third ear* (Berko, Wolvin, & Wolvin, 1996). Nonverbal communication cues provide a great deal of what we sense as we listen to others. Finally, there are physical barriers in organizations, such as distance or loud background noise, which prevent listening.

There are numerous perceptual barriers that may alter or screen the messages we receive (see chap. 2). The specific organizational barriers we discuss include external noise, internal noise, organizational distance, and selective attention.

External Noise In many organizations, sound levels, distracting stimuli, and competing messages can prevent effective sensing. Many manufacturing plants have noise levels, for example, that make listening difficult and workplaces have numerous ongoing activities. Multitasking, an increasingly apparent external distraction in many organizations, requires dividing attention (see chap. 12). Poor acoustics, other ongoing activities, or street sounds can inhibit the listening process. Noise and distractions generated by the environment can distract from listening (DeVito, 2004).

Internal Noise Internal noise, or interference created by the listener, occurs when we are preoccupied, under pressure, or have other priorities. Sometimes this is referred to as *nonhearing*, because we may be physically present but not processing any messages (Tracey, 1988). We can all be primary candidates as we focus on other issues (e.g., hungry, tired, defensive, other tasks or job pressures, external issues). Referred to as an *internal monologue*, the receiver does not give full attention to the task of sensing the message (Howell, 1982). Even the time of day can make a difference regarding our listening effectiveness because it influences attentiveness and overall motivation (Wolvin & Coakley, 1996). In addition, the amount of time a person has to engage in the listening process also will affect the outcome.

We may *prejudge* the sender. Deciding the individual lacks credibility, is not worth paying attention to, or reminds us of someone we were sorry we listened to at some earlier point will prevent us from being effective listeners. More general forms of stereotyping can prevent us from seeing beyond a sender's outward label of management, union, professor, tall, old, young, or any other characteristic. The potential distrust brought on by stereotyping can prevent a valid sensing of the message.

If the message is *not assigned significance*, it is likely to be ignored. Frequently, messages about safety or work rules "go in one ear and out the other," according to people who are in charge of safety. A good example is provided by the story of a worker in a chocolate factory who fell into a vat of chocolate. She began yelling: "Fire! Fire!" Immediately several fellow workers came to the rescue. After they pulled her out, they asked, "Why did you yell, 'fire!'" She answered, "Would you have come if I had yelled 'chocolate?'" Her fellow workers needed a message to which they would assign significance.

Finally, a listener may be so *apathetic or hostile* that he or she does not even pick up on the message (Tracey, 1988). For subordinates, and superiors for that matter, ineffective listening can be a useful form of self-protection (Timm & DeTinne, 1995). In order *not to be changed*, embarrassed, or hurt, we simply do not listen accurately. The multiple changes impacting on organizational members require developing new skills and knowledge. A *fear of failure* created by difficult material or procedures also can create poor listening (Floyd, 1985). These three factors of apathy, fear of change, and fear of failure can operate throughout the listening process.

Organizational Distance

The inherent organizational distance between the various job classifications (boss–employee, doctor–staff, professor–student) can create perceptual differences. In the past, subordinates were expected to listen and superiors were supposed to talk. Bosses provided answers with little input from sub-ordinates. This century requires changes in these traditional behavioral role expectations.

At a different level, superiors and subordinates have very different per-ceptions of organizational reality. Although a manager might be "fired-up" about a proposed change in procedure, a subordinate might be wondering what additional job responsibilities would be involved. Finally, verbal and nonverbal differences may exist because of culture, educational backgrounds, or occupational activities, making comprehension difficult.

Selective Attention

To be effective, a listener must fully sense the message. Four explanations are offered to explain why selective attention is given to one particular message over another. First, there are automatic, unconscious rules, such as focusing on a sender who states our name or mentions a subject important to us. Our chocolate factory story is a good example. Second, we make conscious decisions about which messages we are likely to accept. If there are multiple messages, we unconsciously prioritize our listening activities. Choosing to concentrate on the boss's message, rather than a co-worker's simultaneous message, is a normal occurrence in organizations. Third, we may be put off by the difficulty of the mental task, because complex tasks require more concentration and energy. Fourth, we have a strong need for consistency. When messages con-trast with our preconceived notions, we may dismiss them. Roadblocks exist even as we are receiving the message, which can detour the listening process. Listening is the process of becoming aware, to the degree possible, of all the cues that another party emits (Van Slyke, 1999).

In summary, we have examined how external and internal noise, organiza-tional distance, and selective attention prevent effective sensing of the message.

Interpreting

Hearing a message, and then attending to it, are two vital aspects of effective listening. However, the listener must interpret or assign meaning to the mes-sage. This is an immensely complex process because we are taking messages and deciding in which category the message belongs.

A quick review of some of the issues we have covered so far in this text will underscore the complexity. When we discussed language, for example, we observed that words have numerous meanings and various levels of inter-pretation. When you started reading this text, some words did not fit into previously developed categories—you lacked a clear means of interpreting the information. Perception and paradigms act as additional filters or limiting factors in organizational communication. And so it goes through each of the topics we have covered.

Understanding occurs when the listener fully comprehends the other person's frame of reference, point of view, and feelings regarding a subject. The expression "I know you believe that you understand what you think I said, but I am not sure you realize that what you heard is not what I meant" speaks to the importance of understanding.

A frequently told story regarding the original TAB commercial revolves around the jingle "Let's taste new TAB." A fourth-grader wrote to Coca-Cola and explained that it came over the radio as "Less taste, new TAB." Coca-Cola immediately changed the ad.

Finally, consider the following story. A boy is involved in a serious automobile accident. His father was driving the car and was killed instantly. The boy was rushed to the hospital in critical condition. The doctor in the emergency room took one look at the boy and screamed: "Oh my God, it's my son!" What is going on in the story? Some individuals are confused because the father was killed in the accident. The answer, of course, is the doctor is the boy's mother. Interpretation, because of preset assumptions, can be inaccurate. This story leads into the third part of the listening process.

Evaluation   The third stage is evaluation. At this point, we make judgments regarding our acceptance of the messages (DeVito, 2004). These decisions to accept, alter, or reject the messages are based on the receiver's own knowledge or opinions. In theory, this is an important quality control step. We decide if the message supports the point being made, or if the individual and the message have credibility. This stage can be used too quickly, resulting in messages being accepted or rejected without any real justification. Effective listeners are careful to evaluate the message by weighing the evidence, and sorting fact from opinion, as they strive to make this a useful stage.

Thought Speed   During the interpreting and evaluating stages, listeners can capitalize on thought speed to sort through messages. Senders have a normal speaking rate of 125–150 words per min. On average, we can understand approximately 300 words per min (Wood, 2004). This differential can be used to enhance listening.

Role Requirements   Role requirements can lead to incorrect evaluations. As Callerman and McCartney (1985) explain, "A supervisor must believe subordinates have experience, ideas, problems, and solutions to contribute to the organization and must demonstrate that belief through active listening so that subordinates will gain greater respect for themselves as individuals and for their supervisors" (p. 39). Traditionally, subordinates have been expected to show interest in their superiors' communication without providing any real feedback (Bormann, Howell, Nichols, & Shapiro, 1980). So, in addition to the organizational distance discussed under sensing, role requirements often impede interpretation and evaluation. Managers can increase their listening effectiveness in the judgment stage by listening for what is not said, considering the other person's emotions and background, and allowing criticisms of a manager's "brilliant" policies (Peters, 1987). The evaluation stage provides us with the opportunity to judge a message's quality (Verderber & Verderber, 2001). Thought speed allows for strong analysis. However, role requirements can lead to a lack of credibility by managers to a subordinate's ideas.

Responding

This final stage involves the various types of feedback. In some ways, compliance—doing what we are told—can be seen as a form of responding. More likely we expect some type of response in most listening situations. This final stage provides data to the sender for judging the success of the communication process. Research indicates that effective listeners provide and use more feedback than do ineffective listeners (Lewis & Reinsche, 1988). Studies of listening in organizations indicate that listeners are expected to make some type of overt response, whether it be verbal or nonverbal, to be judged a good listener (Tracey, 1988). This admonition becomes somewhat complex when we introduce the importance of silence. In negotiating or conflict management training, participants are reminded that "it is better to remain silent and appear to be a fool than to open your mouth and remove all doubt." Silence encourages the other person to continue just to fill in your silence, which can be a key skill for organizational members (Blair, 1999). If you choose silence as a strategy out of respect, humility, self-defense, or for some other reason, remember the importance of some form of nonverbal attention (e.g., head nods, eye contact).

These four stages explain the listening process. Although we have discussed each one in detail, in the listening process these stages occur rapidly. The examination of each one highlights many of the factors that can limit effective listening. In addition to the listening stages, there are specific types of listening behaviors, which we now explain.

Types of Listening

Listening behaviors can be divided between passive and active listening, and deliberative and empathetic listening.

Active Listening

When we assume that listening only requires the receiver to be in attendance, we are referring to passive listening. This is listening without directing the speaker verbally or nonverbally. Some individuals are quite adept at pretending to listen, and others simply assume that being present is the same as actually listening (DeVito, 1989).

Active listening is a process where the listener sends back to the sender signals indicating what the listener thinks the sender meant (Harris, 1997). The receiver becomes part of the transaction and takes an active responsibility for understanding the feelings of the other person. Donaldson and Donaldson (1996) observe that "listening is something you *do*—not something that gets done to you" (p. 117). Understanding the sender's total message, including both verbal and nonverbal information, along with the content and feelings expressed, is the receiver's responsibility. Active listening enables receivers to check on the accuracy of their understanding of what a sender said, express acceptance of feelings, and stimulate senders to explore more fully their thoughts and feelings (Wilson, Hantz, & Hanna, 1989). Listening is "building rapport and relationship rather than simply receiving the speaker's words accurately" (Harris, 1997, p. 9).

Learning to listen rather than be in control can be difficult. "There is a common thread to difficult doctors: most have problems talking to, or listening to patients" (Kolata, 2005, p. A16). One suggestion provided for doctors to become better listeners is rather than immediately offering advice, say "uh huh" three times. So, if the patient says he or she is having chest pains, simply say "uh huh." Then the patient says, I've also been having headaches." "Uh huh." The patient finally says, "It all started when my brother died of an aneurysm in the brain. I wonder if it's related?" By holding off and listening, the doctor discovers the potential root cause of the problems (Kolata, 2005).

Three techniques for developing your active listening skills are *paraphrasing, expressing understanding, and asking questions.* Paraphrasing is stating in your own words what you think the sender meant. This is not part of the interpretative stage. Instead, you really are providing the sender with your summary of the content of her or his message. This allows you to check the accuracy of your perception of the message. By using objective descriptions, you are responding to the verbal and nonverbal signals given by the sender.

Fighting the tendency to *daydream* or focusing on other issues can be especially difficult (Kreitner, 2005; Verderber & Verderber, 2001). One means of fighting daydreaming is to paraphrase actively. Paraphrasing also works well in emotionally charged situations. If another confronts you in an angry manner, an excellent defense is to acknowledge the issue as you paraphrase. Statements like "before we go any further, let me make certain I understand," followed by a paraphrase takes the issue from emotion to content. The other person will be responding that you are correct, or incorrect, in the paraphrasing but both parties are now discussing issues, not emotions.

We must heed an important word of caution regarding paraphrasing. It can be redundant and annoying if it is simply trading words. The goal is to restate the same meaning presented by the sender, but in a different form. This allows the sender to verify, modify, or reject the listener's interpretation. So, if it seems to be simply parroting the sender, paraphrasing becomes extremely awkward.

When you echo the *feelings of the sender*, you are using the second technique—*expressing understanding*. This restatement of the feelings that you hear from the sender as correctly as possible allows the receiver to check more accurately on how well the sender's feelings have been perceived and understood. Additionally, your expressed understanding might allow a sender to view her or his feelings more objectively.

Finally, *asking questions* designed to encourage the sender to express the feelings he or she wants to express is important. By allowing the senders to explain fully their thoughts and feelings, we encourage senders to provide additional information. Questions help to clarify areas of uncertainty. Remember that questions designed to make us look like debaters or lawyers are not appropriate. For years, professionals have cautioned against questions poising false dilemmas such as "Do you still beat your wife, husband, child, or companion?" Regardless of how you answer, you are guilty of currently engaging the objectionable behavior—you answer "yes," or having done it in the past by answering "no." In organizations, these types of questions might include "Do you still cheat on your travel expense vouchers?"; "Do you still come in late every morning?"; or "You don't still believe that stupid plan will work, do you?"

Deliberative versus Empathetic

Some authorities divide organizational listening into the two categories of deliberative and empathetic (Koehler, Anatol, & Applebaum, 1981). *Deliberative listening* focuses on the listener's capacity to hear, analyze, recall, and draw valid conclusions from information presented. Because reducing mistakes and increasing task coordination often are organizational priorities, a large number of training programs and listening tests are concerned with deliberative listening (Cooper, 1997). When the goal is to be an *efficient* listener who listens accurately, this approach works. Although being accurate in receiving messages is important, there is more to being an effective listener in today's organization.

Empathy is putting ourselves into the other person's "shoes." Many authorities see empathy, or the ability to see an idea or concept from the other's perspective, as the key to effective listening (DeVito, 2004). *Empathetic listening* concentrates on the feeling part of the sender's message. The listener's goal is to relate to what the other person is thinking or feeling regardless of the content. For this to work, you must be nonevaluative in the listening process. The listener should not interrupt the speaker, nor present a threatening environment. Increased diversity changes, with all the potential advantages for organizational success, demand an even stronger capacity to be an empathetic listener. Different backgrounds guarantee a different set of expectations regarding work. A colleague, for example, who is suddenly thrust into caring for an aging or ailing parent needs to be listened to with a sympathetic ear.

Empathy is easier to describe than to actually use. How, for example, can a manager really understand what it means to deal with angry customers everyday? How can a first-year employee relate to the trials and tribulations of a senior-level executive? The answer lies in truly suspending judgment and accepting, for the moment, that the messages carry validity.

Differentiating Organizational Listening

The majority of the early research on listening was conducted in classroom settings. The results indicated that good listening habits were tied to mental set, skills and habits, general intelligence, and some specific intelligence-related traits (Nichols, 1962). With an educational setting as the paradigm, it is no surprise that the focus was on how well the audience could be trained to receive the message (Lewis & Reinsch, 1988). The major impediments to listening were identified, and methods were offered to overcome these barriers to listening. Classroom listening research has been oriented primarily to gaining information.

Organizations expect a greater use of job-oriented listening behaviors. Effective organizational listening is based on the relational aspects of the communication process. Specifically, it is related to active listening including empathy and receiving skills, verbal and nonverbal behavior, relationships, and managerial style. When we are interested in organizational effectiveness, we should remember that "listening skills cannot be separated from other communication concerns within the organizations" (Lewis & Reinsch, 1988, p. 49). Our verbal and nonverbal skills are tied to listening effectiveness. Table 8.2 provides a humorous, tongue-in-cheek, list of listening behaviors typical of poor listening by managers. Ironically, this management style also limits the manager's effectiveness as we noted, in addition to their own limited listening profiles. Reverse each statement in Table 8.2 and you have a useful guide for effective leadership listening.

We have outlined values and types of listening. Our final concern is with the use of feedback and the impact of climate in the listening process.

Feedback

In the simplest of terms, feedback is the receiver's verbal and nonverbal response to a sender's communication. Feedback is an ongoing part of the relational process. Because we cannot not communicate, verbal and nonverbal feedback are occurring at all times during a communication transaction. So, no overt response is still a response. At various points in this book, we discuss feedback.

Positive and Negative Feedback

When we first encountered positive and negative feedback in chapter 1, we presented the systems thinking perspective that positive feedback was a message to continue deviating or perhaps even accentuate the deviation. Negative

Table 8.2 20 Listening Habits Designed to Help You Irritate Your Subordinates

1. When they come in with a problem, you do all the talking.
2. Don't fail to interrupt them when they talk.
3. Don't look at them when they talk—that way they can't tell if you're listening or not.
4. Make them feel they're wasting their time—that way they won't come back.
5. Continually shuffle papers or play with a pencil or pen.
6. Pace around the room while they talk.
7. Use your best poker face to keep them wondering if you understand them.
8. Ignore them to take incoming phone calls—be sure not to have your secretary hold your calls or ask anyone to call back later.
9. Don't ever smile—this makes them afraid to talk to you.
10. Ask questions about everything they say—this will let them know you doubt everything they say.
11. Get them off the subject by asking questions and making comments that don't pertain to the subject at hand.
12. Keep them on their toes by putting them on the defensive when they make a suggestion about improving things.
13. Embarrass them by answering their questions *with* a question—one you're sure they can't answer, of course.
14. Continually take notes while they're talking. This will get them so worried about what you're writing, they'll forget what it is they want to say.
15. Let them know you're doing them a favor by listening to them.
16. Never do today what can be put off until tomorrow—tell them: "we'll have to think about it."
17. If other people are in the room, be sure to ask the employee some personal questions.
18. If they happen to have a good idea, be sure to let them know you've been thinking about that too.
19. Every couple of minutes look at your watch or the clock while they're talking.
20. Keep on using your computer, don't lift up your gaze from the screen, and assure them: "Just keep on talking, I'm listening."

feedback called for a return to the earlier protocol of the system thereby decreasing the deviation.

For most of us, the more common connotations for the term *positive* means "supportive" and the term *negative* means "modify," "change," "alter," or "correct the source" or the source's messages (Benton, 1995). For example, head nods and smiles might encourage us to continue telling a story, whereas frowns or yawning might discourage us. In organizations, this is too simple an approach. For our purposes, *feedback is the vital process of developing individuals and organizations toward improved performance*. We now consider several issues.

First, honest feedback regarding job performance is a requirement for individuals looking for opportunities for self-understanding and for sustaining job satisfaction (DuBrin, 1999). People like to know how well they are doing. A survey of nearly 1,500 customer service representatives and call-center mangers found that "timely feedback can contribute to a positive call-center environment" (Salopek, 1999, p. 16). Organizations providing feedback that includes recognition and job performance measurements enjoy higher levels of job satisfaction among their employees. The Gallup Organization and Carlson Marketing Group found a strong correlation between employee satisfaction and increased company profits, according to their nationwide survey of U.S. workers ("Recognition," 1999). "Employees indicated that they favor recognition from managers and supervisors by a margin of 2–1 over recognition from coworkers or other sources. And nearly seven out of 10 (69%) employees say nonmonetary forms of recognition provide the best motivation" ("Recognition," 1999, p. 5).

Second, feedback involves more than individuals. McIntyre and Salas (1995) explain: "Teamwork implies that members provide feedback to and accept it from one another" (p. 24). As we have already indicated, organizations seeking improvement need rigorous feedback (Collins & Porras, 1994). Successful organizations that retain employees and develop excellent morale provide formal feedback opportunities for employees including surveys (Buckingham & Coffman, 1999).

Honest should not be confused with brutal or destructive feedback. Harsh criticism is a useful example. In a study of 108 managers and white-collar workers, the poor use of criticism was one of the five most openly mentioned causes of conflict at work (Karp, 1987). One source of destructive feedback is the tendency to *manage by exception*, which is limiting feedback to others to situations where something has gone wrong. In this type of environment, we hear little or no comments regarding our performance until a mistake is made. Managers forsake their responsibility to develop people and people assume that no news is good news. When the criticism arrives, it appears to be abrupt, out of context, and harsh.

A more productive approach is to spend sufficient time reinforcing positive actions, so that any criticism is interpreted as part of an effective coaching and development process between the superior and subordinate. For example, some companies encourage subordinates to reveal mistakes in order to open up the communication channels by creating a positive feedback process. Temps & Co. offers to pay employees $250 for describing an interesting mistake (Levinson, 1987). Although $250 may seem extremely supportive, employees must explain how the mistake happened to their peers in order to prevent repeating the problem. The reward encourages an early detection of potentially serious problems. So rather than hiding the problem as a means to avoid criticism, Temps & Co. has developed a process that proactively tackles problems and develops solutions.

To further understand feedback, we discuss defensive and supportive climates and then effective feedback techniques.

Supportive and Defensive Climates

One of the most widely used concepts in the teaching of communication is *defensive communication*. In his classic article, Gibb (1961) outlined the different consequences from feeling defensive and feeling understood. Gibb's article "is the most requested communication article in the history of the field" (Weick & Browning, 1991, p. 9). Essentially, he argues that we have a choice in how we offer feedback to others. Defensive producing messages focus on the other as a person, whereas supportive messages focus on behavior or the problem. Naturally, we become defensive when someone blames us. Consistent with our view throughout this text, both verbal and nonverbal behaviors tend to produce supportive and defensive climates (Wolvin & Coackley, 1996). Gibb (1961) contrasted six defensive and supportive climates in the following manner. When we provide feedback, we have a choice between *evaluating* or *describing* an issue. Evaluation judges and looks for blame, whereas description offers neutral statement of fact. Contrast trying to change someone's attitude or to influence how they act through *control* with the use of a *problem orientation*, which attempts to change the problem, not the person. A third contrast is between *strategic* communication where we manipulate or use gimmicks instead of being *spontaneous* by being honest and open. An additional issue is the contrast between being *neutral* and showing *empathy*. If someone is indifferent to us, we tend to become defensive. Fifth, making it clear that we are *superior* to someone else, including the ability to exercise power, will make him or her defensive. The contrasting behavior, *equality*, forecasts a willingness to work together and is clearly a desired stance in today's organization. Finally, being dogmatic, or a know-it-all unwilling to change, is indicative of *certainty*. The supportive contrast is *provisionalism* where we offer tentative conclusions open to discussion and change.

The consequences of these two types of feedback responses in organizations are significant. Defensive producing feedback impedes effective communication (Sweeney & McFarlin, 2002). On the other end of the continuum, empathetic understanding promotes greater job satisfaction, lower job turnover among subordinates, and greater mobility within the organization (Gordon, 1988).

Effective Feedback Techniques

Judgments should be reworded in order to be descriptive. The key is to have some objective measure that compares actual behavior with some standard, and a nonevaluative means of providing the feedback. Table 8.3 outlines the

Table 8.3 Guidelines for Effective Feedback

Feedback should be...

1. Descriptive rather than evaluative.
2. Specific rather than general.
3. Appropriate, taking into account the needs of the sender, receiver, and situation.
4. Directed toward behavior that the receiver can do something about.
5. Well timed. Usually, the more immediate the feedback, the more effective. There are the wrong times also.
6. Honest rather than manipulative.
7. Understood by both parties. Additional input is sought, if needed, to enhance and clarify the process.
8. Proactive and coactive. When it requires changes in past behaviors, specific directions should be provided for the expected change. Both parties should agree on the need for change and the remedy.
9. Never "dump" past grievances on an individual. It should be a natural process in the ongoing relationship between superior and subordinate, co-workers, or any subsystem in the organization.

basic steps and issues in using effective feedback. Most feedback, in an organizational setting, should deal in specifics, focus on actions, not attitudes, determine the appropriate time and place, and refrain from inappropriately including other issues (Karp, 1987).

The underlying power of feedback lies in its capacity to validate the assumptions, constructs, and ideas we have about other people's actions. Before offering performance feedback, consider asking permission. By predicating our feedback with an offer to the other person along the lines of "Do you want to hear my position or opinion?" we share the power of feedback rather than imposing it. Similarly, being aware of the importance of good timing, being positive, taking responsibility through "I" statements, and being direct, allow the feedback to be toward helping someone rather than criticizing them. The constructive use of feedback, coupled with a supportive climate, allows individuals and groups to move toward clearer interpersonal understanding. So, in addition to listening to an individual, adding the dimension of feedback allows both parties to respond to the intended meaning of a message. Although we are presenting feedback as a separate issue, we always are providing feedback. The key is to make certain the feedback is supportive to enhance the quality of the transaction.

Conclusion

Listening is a major communication factor in organizations. Not only is listening important to organizations and individuals, ineffective listening is costly.

The current status of organizational listening is not strong. A major reason for this weakness lies in the difficulty in delineating listening factors from the overall communication patterns. In fact, focusing on listening is the most important contribution of this chapter. By being aware of the lack of emphasis, we can be more effective in understanding and using listening.

Examining the four stages of the listening process allows us to focus on the numerous factors that can prevent effective listening. Each stage—sensing, interpreting, evaluating, and responding—is significant in the listening process.

Active listening is designed to enhance the ability of the sender to successfully complete the message. Organizations make different uses of deliberative and empathetic listening. Most important, research indicates that active participation by the listener in the communication process is important.

Feedback and climate are the final areas of concern. In organizations, feedback is vital. However, the transaction can be supported or limited depending on the type of climate. Defensive producing climates limit the willingness of the sender to participate in the transaction. So, effective feedback must be provided to enhance the listening process.

At the very least, this chapter should provide some important information regarding the relative lack of effective listening in organizations. In spite of overwhelming evidence for the need for better listening, it often is ignored as an important issue. To enhance our own effectiveness, we should concentrate on making our listening behaviors more effective. By and large, good listening encourages others also to listen more effectively.

Study Questions

1. When is listening difficult for you? Do you feel there are times when others do not listen to you? Can you draw some general conclusions regarding the barriers to listening?
2. Why is listening important? Be specific in terms of roles and the organization.
3. What is the difference between deliberative and emphatic listening? What type would you prefer others to use?
4. Explain the four stages of listening.
5. Develop an example of how to use paraphrasing.
6. Explain the rationale behind the concepts of defensive and supportive climates.

9
Effective Interpersonal Communication in Organizations

Key concepts in this chapter include:

- Functions of interpersonal communication in organizations
- Defining interpersonal communication—component, situational, developmental
- Differences in perspectives regarding transactions
- How humans process information
- Interpersonal communication effectiveness—interactive and humanistic management
- Superior–subordinate relationships

Interpersonal communication is the process of transacting meaning between individuals. It is a major component of organizational behavior at every level (Maes, Weldly, & Icenogle, 1997). Interpersonal communication is fundamental to obtaining employment, succeeding on the job, and being an effective colleague, subordinate, or manager.

In the past, organizational members learned to work with a fairly predictable set of colleagues. Now, the workplace is becoming a series of hellos and good-byes. The "average employee will stay at their organization 3.6 years and have 13 to 15 jobs over the course of their lifetime" (Hudson Institute, 2000, p. 11). With this level of mobility, knowing how to adapt to new cultures and colleagues is important.

Friendships are important to company performance. A recent Gallup study of 400 companies found that employees' ability to form close friendships at work was among 12 indicators of a highly productive workplace (Shellenbarger, 2000). But, developing friendships can be difficult. A survey conducted by the management consulting firm of Moran, Stahl, and Boyer found that 2,000 survey-takers who had been relocated or promoted said they needed roughly 8 months to adjust to their new situation and "get up to speed" ("Relocation Adjustment," 1987). A good deal of the adjustment time was spent in learning particulars about the new position or job *and* adapting their interpersonal communication skills to the new situation. For example, a remarkable 40% of new managers fail (Elliot, 1999). Manchester Partners International surveyed 826 human resources managers to discover why so many new managers flamed out. "The failure to build good relationships with peers and subordinates is the culprit an overwhelming 82% of the time" (Fisher, 1998, p. 160). Fisher (1998) continues: "Hordes of consultants, coaches, and other gurus of various stripes have been studying the reason new managers fail, and their unanimous conclusion is that personal chemistry and cultural compatibility—the soft, people-skills stuff that makes up that old black magic called fit—are all-important" (p. 160).

The forces of change, discussed throughout this text, require us to recognize "the mushrooming variety of modern life" (Wood, 2000, p. 122). We are becoming "saturated by widely diverse views, goals, and values that seep into our own perspectives" (Wood, 2000, p. 123). On the positive side, these rapid changes allow us to experience diversity. But, without an understanding of interpersonal communication, we are likely to find the challenge daunting.

You will use interpersonal communication when you (1) interview for a job, (2) learn about specific duties, (3) operate on a day-to-day basis, (4) lead and manage others, (5) go to company-sponsored social events, (6) participate in the mentoring, (7) sell, (8) take part in numerous specialized issues and events (e.g., performance appraisals, coaching sessions), and (9) eat your meals or enjoy social events with your colleagues—to name a few. In addition, organization specific tasks include informal talks, planned appointments, telephone calls, gathering around the copy machine, visiting customers and clients, working on task forces, and so on.

Interpersonal communication is a vital part of innovation. DrugCorp found that "interpersonal communication provided researchers with their most important channels of access to information and stimulation of new ideas" (Zuboff, 1988, p. 363). One study determined that personal communication was the crucial factor in 8,070 of the cases of innovation (Zuboff, 1989).

Task Orientation

Interpersonal communication in organizations is similar to our everyday friendships, but two task-oriented characteristics differentiate it. First, organizations are *goal–oriented,* with their chief concern being output (e.g., goods, services, information, public relations, throughput; see chap. 1). In other words, we are hired to accomplish something and assist in achieving specific and general goals. Organizations are purposeful and the expectations are that employees will work toward common goals.

Second, organizations require a *co-orientation* of behavior, which "involves the elicitation of behavioral coordination among communicators for the accomplishment of commonly recognized goals" (Kreps, 1990, p. 149). Organizational membership means more restrictions on our behaviors. Essentially, we are giving up the freedom to do whatever we want in order to be rewarded in some fashion for doing what the organization wants. This requires an ability to predict what other organizational members will do. Miller (1990) explains: "When people communicate with others, they make predictions about the probable outcomes, or consequences, of differing message strategies, or alternative message selections" (p. 97). Therefore, we are *striving to reduce uncertainty*. In organizations, the higher the level of predictability between colleagues, the greater sense of comfort everyone is likely to feel about working together. The corollary to this statement also holds. The more your co-workers can depend on you, the greater the trust and comfort between the staff. Dahle (1998) passes on the observation that "probably 95% of firings are a result of failing to fit into a company's culture. If people don't know you, they can't trust you" (p. 185). Goal orientation and reliance on others are important concepts for clarifying the role of interpersonal communication in organizations.

Defining Interpersonal Communication

Interpersonal communication can be explained through a componential, situational, and developmental definition.

Componential

Many examinations of communication present models. Most transactional models (see chap. 1) accept that communication is: (1) A process involving (2) both purposive and expressive messages (3) composed of multiunit and (4) multilevel signals that (5) depend on the context for their meanings (6) interpreted by the interactants (Haworth & Savage, 1989). In all interpersonal communication situations, there are certain universals that are present (e.g., two participants, channels, context, verbal and nonverbal communication) and a model offers us a means for appreciating the complexity of the transaction process, outlining of areas of potential communication difficulties, and isolating variables (DeVito, 1989). The graphic display of components allows us to identify factors and understand more fully the issues involved in communication. At the same time, in examining the model, you are probably struck with the feeling that there must be more to interpersonal communication.

Situational

The interdependence created by a dyad is the most obvious characteristic of interpersonal communication. Organizations establish these *interpenetrative* and interlocking relationships to coordinate work. "The dyad begins to function when there is the possibility of the actions of each person affecting the other" (Wilmot, 1979, p. 9). So, superior–subordinate relationships, colleagues, project team members, or any other working combination are, by definition, examples of interpersonal communication.

This *codependence* is a critical factor in many working situations. You cannot refuse to work with someone just because you do not want to be their friend, and you must cooperate with other people to accomplish many of your assigned tasks. Working effectively with coworkers, bosses, customers, and subordinates will be directly related to your own personal success. The inability to get along with others is the number-two reason for employees getting fired ("Personnel Problems," 1990). The others are incompetence (first), dishonesty (third), negative attitude (fourth), and lack of motivation (fifth). On the other side of the coin, the ability to get along with others is the second most important attribute for getting ahead according to *The Wall Street Journal* (Nirenberg, 1989). Integrity is the first. Supporting codependence, it would seem, is a prerequisite to keeping a job and advancing.

Developmental

Many relationships evolve from work-related interdependence to genuine friendships. This *developmental perspective* focuses on interpersonal communication in organizations as it progresses from first introductions onto the numerous paths any dyad may travel (Miller, 1990). Friendships depend on social penetration or a willingness to go beyond superficial exchanges regarding the weather, time, or sports. Habitual and routine dyadic experiences (e.g., greetings, leave-taking, meeting attendance) remain at a superficial level (Benton, 1995). Even though the situation is between individuals, the relationship is impersonal.

A relationship is likely to become interpersonal if physical proximity, attitude similarity, and need complementarily exist (Miller, 1990). In a nutshell, we are more likely to become friends with someone when (a) we interact with them, (b) we hold somewhat similar attitudes toward social, political, and economic issues, and (c) they somehow meet certain of our psychological needs.

When we first start working with someone, *physical proximity* is automatic. Attitude similarity and need complementarily become known during the initial stages of the relationship, as we focus on *uncertainty reduction*. We seek information that will help us communicate more effectively. In other words, we want to know what to say after we say hello. Verbal and nonverbal clues, offered during these initial meetings, allow the participants to apply structure, predictability, and meaning. As you are already aware, our judgments are somewhat faulty (see chap. 2), but they still provide us with some predictability regarding future interactions. Next time you meet someone, monitor your efforts as you paint a mental picture about the other person. You also are making decisions regarding future interactions. As you work to ingratiate yourself, you also are seeking additional insights to see if there is a similarity of attitudes or to discover any capacity by the other person to meet some of your psychological needs. Communicating is the only way to find out whether we are willing to proceed to an interpersonal relationship from the initial impersonal one. The relationship develops its own set of rules rather than depending on socially established ones.

A relatively new approach to understanding how we know and manage our own and others' emotions is *emotional intelligence* (EI). This differs from cognitive intelligence (IQ). People with a high level of EI are able to respond effectively to others' emotional cues, discriminate among these emotions, and use the information to guide their thoughts and actions toward others (Goleman, 1996; Greenspan, 1997). Goleman (1996) sees two sets of competencies: personal competencies, or the ability to manage yourself, and social competencies, or the ability to handle relationships. EI has attracted both a popular and an academic following and it may offer some useful insights regarding how we succeed in the developmental process.

Differences in Perspectives

As you become familiar with the literature on organizations, you will find the terms communication, information, messages, and meaning freely substituted. Part of the complexity in terminology usage comes with the expansion in uses and meanings of the term information.

Types of Information

Everyone agrees that creating meaning is the ultimate goal of communication. To be fully comfortable with the concept of information, it is useful to divide it into information theory, information technology, and human information processing.

Information Theory   Information theory rests on the concept of probability and it permits us to quantify and measure certain aspects of communication (Shannon & Weaver, 1949). Essentially, we ask "is this new?" if this is something we did not know before. If we respond "yes," we have information. This binary decision is one of the critical attributes of the modem computer (Kidder, 1981). For example, a word processor's spell-check only tags words that are "new"—they do not appear in the computer's memory, leaving the conclusion that they are not correct spellings. Computer programs are written in languages that are based simply on endless variations of four words: "yes," "no," "if," and "what?" Combine them and you have: "If yes, what?" "If no, what?" These combinations lead to computer reports that can be divided into information gathering, analysis, and decision-making.

Information Technology   Information technology deals with information transmission. We discussed the impact of information technology at the beginning of this text. Regardless of how we frame the analysis, the information technologies' pervasiveness is clear. Technology increases integration and dependencies across organizational functions. Previously isolated activities, such as the sales and shipping departments, are tied to the rest of the organization. Sometimes in nanoseconds, increased speed occurs, along with greater interdependence. Mistakes become more costly.

Organizations communicate more easily across time and distance, more rapidly to targeted groups, more reliably in terms of communication events, and more selectively through control of access with a combination of technologies (Huber, 1990; see chap. 12). Some examples are computer-assisted communication (e.g., electronic mail, image transmission devices, computer conferencing, videoconferencing) and decision-making technologies (e.g., expert systems, decision support systems, online management information systems, external information retrieval systems). Just as the telegraph became the primary technology for the railroads, the calculator for brokerage houses, and the radio for armies, computer technology is having a significant impact on organizations. A walk through most modern factories will provide a complex display of computer technology designed to enhance tasks ranging from inventory control to quality. As Turnage (1990) explained, "New office automation has transformed organizational communication in many ways through videoconferencing, teleconferencing, computer conferencing, and electronic mail" (p. 172).

Technology's capacity to produce information also has created an information glut. For many executives, wading through the memos, e-mails, and numbers is like trying to get a drink of water from a fire hydrant (Rothfeder & Bartimo, 1990). This information explosion is very real. "The total volume of information generated worldwide annually equals about 1.5 exabytes of data—a stack of 1 trillion floppy disks that could reach to the moon and back four times" (Ward & Snider, 2000, p. 10D). To put this in context, "five exabytes would equal all the words spoken by humans in the history of the world" (Ward & Snider, 2000, p. 10D). As a point of reference, a byte is a single character, a kilobyte a very short story, a megabyte a small novel or floppy disk, a gigabyte a pickup truck filled with paper, and a terabyte all the X-ray film in a large hospital. As a specific example, e-mail carried somewhere between 610 billion and 1.1 trillion messages in 2000 (Ward & Snider, 2000, p. 10D).

There is a critical distinction between the capacity to *automate* and *informate* (Zuboff, 1989; see chap. 12). Reducing dependency on human skills, such as keeping track of inventory, is a type of automation. If you own a phone that can do dozens of tricks, you are already familiar with how technology can outpace immediate human usefulness. When we go beyond replacing human activities and develop strategic advantages we are *informating*. Until we reach this phase, we are merely substituting an efficient electronic process for a more cumbersome and perhaps physically impossible task.

On the positive side, information technology offers significant opportunities to enhance information gathering and use. Communication processes are changed inherently when information technology is added. Increased information processing, transfer, and storage, however, does not necessarily lead to better organizational communication.

Human Information Processing   Human information processing concentrates on *information when it becomes meaning.* We process the data and through cognition develop some knowledge regarding the information. To examine this process, answer the following question: A hobo can make one whole cigar from every five cigar butts that he finds. How many cigars can be made if he finds 25 cigar butts? The answer is not five (Bartlett, 1979). At first, you might find this story confusing. After all, 25 butts divided by 5 must equal 5. Although a binary reduction might provide the answer, you are more likely to have an "ah, ha" recognition of the correct answer. Regardless of the number of times you apply the criteria of "what's new?" your quest will not be satisfied. As you add reasoning or meaning, you begin to manipulate the information. Each time the hobo smokes a cigar, he is left with a butt. So, the answer is ... (we confirm your correct answer later in this chapter).

Humans are decision-making experts when they develop a combination of knowledge, experience, and intuition. We chunk many small fragments of information into a few, significant issues. By identifying relevant patterns, and being able to dismiss unimportant details, experts (e.g., medical doctors, consultants, technicians) can see patterns that lead to the correct response (Lord & Maher, 1990). The importance of balancing hard data and intuitive skills is increasingly clear to a large number of executives. In one poll, 43% of the 349 executives surveyed said they relied on intuitive, "gut feelings" when making tough decisions (Pinnacle Group, 1987). Another survey of the senior managers of the 1,200 largest industry and service companies in the United States indicated that 61% of the 300 respondents wanted to be less dependent on numbers and more dependent on intuition (Learning International, 1986). "Information is no substitute for thinking and thinking is no substitute for information" (Naisbitt & Aburdene, 1985, p. 149). By the way, the answer to the cigar problem is six.

How Humans Process Information

Information is a critical tool for operating in an organization. We now know that there are three different types of information in organizations. You also should be aware that there is some disagreement regarding human information processing. In an extensive analysis of management and psychological literature, Lord and Maher (1990) found four predominant taxonomic systems for information processing models. The models are rational, limited capacity, expert, and cybernetic.

Rational Models

Rational models assume that people operate in a controlled processing mode using analytic procedures. These models are data-based, bottom-up patterns, which assume people can process thoroughly all relevant information to come to a valid outcome. Assigning probability and utility values in an effort to come to a rational solution is how individuals reach decisions, according to this model. But, Lord and Maher caution, "the Achilles' heel of such models is that they are not descriptively accurate" (p. 12). People rarely have enough information to behave optimally. To be truly rational, we would have to be omniscient or possess extensive knowledge. These models are counterintuitive because they demand some rigor in the information processing. But, few of us actually consider all possible alternatives or have access to all the information. In fact, we often make impressionist decisions based on a sorting process designed to eliminate bad choices.

Limited Capacity Models

The limited capacity models, in contrast to the rational models, show how people simplify information processing. These models accept that we are unlikely to process all possible information before we make a decision. The *satisficing model*, for example, assumes that information processing stops when the first acceptable alternative is identified (Simon, 1955; see chap. 2). By using cognitive heuristics and simplified knowledge structures, we work within very limited conceptualization of the problems we are dealing with and consider only a few of all possible alternatives. In many social situations, we are likely to use this model because we cannot wait to accumulate all the information we need. In hunting for a job, we are likely to accept the one that satisfies most of our criteria (i.e., salary, location, working conditions). Note that this sounds like the intuition perspective discussed earlier. However, when a person has been making a judgment for a long period of time, they actually are processing information using the expert model.

Expert Models

Expert models are also dependent on limited capacity, heuristic driven methods, but we are no longer examining novices dealing with decisions. For example, although anyone can guess at a chess move, the chess master has approximately 50,000 chunks, or familiar chess patterns, in mind (Simon, 1987). Experts process information very differently. Studies consistently show those experts "recognize immediately what novices require great effort to discover. However, it should be stressed that experts are not superior information processors in the general sense; rather, they perform better only within their specific domain of expertise" (Lord & Maher, 1990, p. 14). All three of these models are featured in management literature as means for understanding information processing. Because you already are versed in a systems perspective and a process orientation, you probably are thinking there must be more to how people utilize information. You are correct.

Cybernetic Models

Finally, the cybernetic models argue that information is processed over time rather than in a single, static event. So, "behavior, learning, and the nature of the cognitive processes themselves may be altered by feedback" (Lord & Maher, 1990, p. 15). These models consider the future, the present, and the past. Through learning and adaptation, the cybernetic model allows a heuristic answer to be considered and applied over time. A systems approach, learning organizations, and double-loop learning fit with the cybernetic model (see chap. 1). This process orientation distinguishes the cybernetic models from the other three.

The four models provide a different explanation for information processing in typical work situations. To make certain our point is clear, consider how you decided on which college to attend or made your last major buying decision. Although ample resources are available for making rational choices (e.g., college evaluation books, *Consumer Reports*), you may not have taken the time or made the effort. Maybe you wanted to "get on with the decision" and picked the first college that seemed to fit your needs—the limited capacity model. Perhaps you turned to individuals you respect—experts—to provide information regarding your choices. Or, you could take numerous college level courses over the span of many years and become an expert. Finally, you might have changed college choices and, even more likely, you might have changed your major once you entered college. This cybernetic approach would seem optimal. But, we do not always have the luxury, interest, ability, or time for changing cars or colleges as we proceed through the double-loop learning process. These discussions of information processing highlights that we are not rational decision-makers in many organizational situations (Lord & Maher, 1990). An astounding example of how poor we can be as decision-makers involves Americans who earn less than $35,000 a year (Abundis & Lynn, 2000). In a recent poll, 40% believed they would be able to accumulate a nest egg by winning a lottery or sweepstakes whereas only 30% saw savings or investing as a solution. Because the odds are 1 in 80 million for winning the Powerball type of lottery, this would not seem to be a carefully considered plan of action. To return to our original point, the word information has many meanings.

Interpersonal Communication Effectiveness

Effective interpersonal communication requires a repertoire of skills with which we perform the appropriate acts in response to the situation. *Our organizational setting frames the range and types of acts available to us.*

To be effective, the performance we present must be consistent with the image desired in the interpersonal encounter. In a job interview, for example, we somehow must put forth a desire to be hired, a sense of confidence in our abilities, and some humility regarding our preparedness at this moment in our careers. In so doing, we need to convey a willingness to learn as well as the ability to contribute. The trick, of course, is to know when to show strength and when to show vulnerability. Learning to understand and adapt to the demands of the situation will make us more effective.

Advice on being effective interpersonally is not difficult to find. We know that the interpersonal behaviors must be situationally appropriate, fit within the cultural expectations, and be relationally appropriate (Redmond, 2000). These criteria become even more relevant considering the changing workforce, organizational structure, and international involvement. An appropriate interpersonal act in the United States can be a serious *faux pas* in another country (Axtell, 1991). The massive changes in the U.S. population demonstrated in the 2000 census require even greater attention to our interpersonal communication.

In an attempt to organize the various interpersonal effectiveness models DeVito (1989) developed two general perspectives or approaches. They are not mutually exclusive, but they do draw attention to different aspects of dyadic behavior. If success is the desired outcome, you probably will be most interested in an interactive management model. If you are primarily interested in fostering meaningful and satisfying interactions, the humanistic model may be the best direction. Often, these two approaches complement each other. "In general, the more complex a required work relationship tends to be, the wider the range of interaction styles needed by the individuals in that relationship" (Cohen, Fink, Gadon, & Willits, 2001, p. 216). Our division is for clarity's sake.

The Interactive Management Model

The interactive management model is pragmatically based, focusing on interpersonal communication competence. "Being interpersonally competent, able to make effective relationships, is indeed a skill that an organization member should have" (Cohen et al., 2001, p. 203). Communication competence is clearly situational and, more often than not, dependent on the abilities of both individuals. The most obvious organizational measure is the bottom-line performance.

A widely used management training approach, which divides individuals into four categories of interpersonal effectiveness, provides an excellent overview. The categories are conscious-competent, conscious-incompetent, unconscious-incompetent, and unconscious-competent. One of the goals for studying organizational communication is to become conscious-competents.

Conscious-competents, the first group, are individuals who are aware of the reasons for their competence. They can replicate their successes, can consciously adapt to changing circumstances, and correct their failures. *Conscious-incompetents* are individuals who are not yet professionals, but they have the advantage of knowing they have to learn. This awareness allows them to experience growth and development. *Unconscious-incompetents* assume effective interpersonal communication is easy, comes naturally, and therefore does not take a great deal of work. This group is likely to reach their level of incompetence early in their organizational careers. Finally, *unconscious-competents* are very good at many of the things they try, but they do not know why. So, when it comes time to replicate particular behaviors, they are not certain what caused the success in the first place. In addition, when these individuals fail, they cannot identify the reasons. Although these four categories are not exclusive, they do draw attention to the pragmatic side of interpersonal communication effectiveness. Being conscious of the needs for development versus "flying by the seat of your pants" is preferable.

Interpersonal communicators pursing an *interactive management approach* utilize five qualities: confidence, immediacy, interaction management, expressiveness, and other orientation (DeVito, 1989).

Confidence   When we are able to handle ourselves with apparent ease, we are judged as being competent. Organizations encourage managers to take Dale Carnegie Courses, join Toastmasters, and/or attend management development seminars. Some of the desirable features include being relaxed in posture, communicating a sense of confidence, and using a degree of flexibility in our voice and body movement. Controlling how we appear makes people believe we are confident. When we seem comfortable, at ease, and not shy, we are more likely to be interpersonally successful. For managers, this is the capacity to share power, delegate important work, and involve employees (Moorehead & Griffin, 1998).

Immediacy   Creating a sense of closeness by showing a sense of interest and attention leads others to judge us as competent and persuasive (Anderson, 1999). There are various aspects of immediacy. For example, using the other person's name when discussing a job instead of simply saying "I feel ..." or referring to "our" needs and how "we" will get it done—using joint references instead of you—provides a sense of togetherness. Feedback directed at the other person's remarks and reinforcing the other person draws individuals closer together. Rather than going through the motions of working with someone else, we show an interest in working with them. Encouraging leaders to manage by walking around and to listen carefully to feedback employ the principle of immediacy.

Interaction Management   To satisfy both parties during the transaction, each should feel as if they are contributing to the interchange. Managers, for example, must let the subordinates know they are being listened to. According to DuBrin, Ireland, and Williams (1989), "An effective leader has the ability to read people and situations" in order to do the right things at the right time (p. 338). The effective interaction manager is both a sender and listener who provides appropriate verbal and nonverbal feedback. Questions we can ask regarding interaction management include: "Do you create an atmosphere that encourages people to ask questions, get involved, and trust you?" or "Are you aware of the total impression you are making when you talk to people?" (Matejka, 1989). Effective interaction managers tend to be proactive by taking the initiative and responsibility for what occurs, instead of reacting to circumstances or events (Covey, 1989). Earlier we discussed Emotional Intelligence (EI), which is one measure of self-monitoring.

Expressiveness   Genuine involvement in the interaction is a sign of expressiveness. Providing verbal and nonverbal actions that indicate engagement with the other person, conveying interest in the interaction, and encouraging openness in others are all attributes of expressiveness (DeVito, 1989). Active listening provides a good example (see chap. 8).

Other-Orientation   Effective other-orientation refers to our ability to adapt to the other person. We perceive the other person's viewpoint. We display empathy, interest, and attentiveness through verbal and nonverbal means. Asking for someone's input, confirming the other person's views or perspectives, and asking questions designed to further your own understanding are examples of verbal other-orientation. One of the harshest comments that can be made about people is "they are totally wrapped up in themselves." Constantly talking about ourselves, focusing on our own problems or successes, and doing most of the talking are examples of a "me-orientation." An overly political or strategic orientation to organizational membership based on a we–they viewpoint broadcasts a me-orientation.

These five characteristics—confidence, immediacy, interaction management, expressiveness, and other-orientation—make up the pragmatic model of interpersonal effectiveness. For many of us, opting for a pragmatic perspective might not be completely satisfying. As we already discussed, many business relationships develop into excellent interpersonal friendships, which often are a vital part of job satisfaction. The humanistic approach presents those attributes needed to enhance bonding between individuals. At the risk of being overly repetitious, these two approaches are not opposites. They do represent two different ways of defining and approaching interpersonal communication effectiveness.

The Humanistic Model

The humanistic model takes its cue from writers who have sought to define superior human relationships. Five general qualities form this model: openness, empathy, supportiveness, positiveness, and equality (DeVito, 1989).

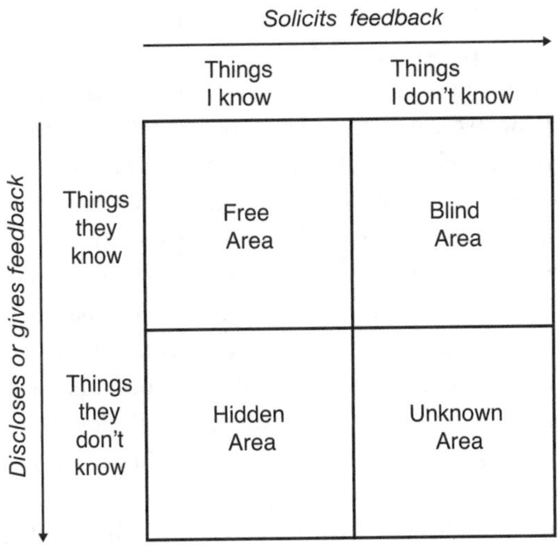

Figure 9.1 The Johari window.

Openness   The amount of interaction we are willing to have with other people is called *openness*. As apparent as this concept might seem, we make conscious and unconscious decisions about just how much information we will share with other people, how reciprocal the openness is, how honestly we react to incoming messages, and how willing we are to "own" our own feelings (DeVito, 1989). This somewhat complex process is called *self-disclosure*, which is the intentional sharing of personal information (Redmond, 2000). Wilmot (1979) asserted that, "'No other communication behavior is so closely linked to close relationships as being open—engaging in self-disclosure" (p. 236). When we let someone know something about ourselves that they do not already know, it creates vulnerability, indicates trust, helps build a foundation or closeness, and it is a requirement for relationship enhancement. But, it is not a requirement for many of our professional, productive, and healthy relationships (Wilmot, 1979). In organizations, we would be unwise to disclose the same information to our new supervisor that we provide to our close friends.

Johari's window is a useful way of envisioning self-disclosure. Johari was derived from the first names of the two persons who developed the model, Joseph Luft and Harry Ingham (Joe-Harry). Window refers to the four quadrants or selves that are open, blind, hidden, and unknown. The four quadrants are dependent on the information known to self, not known to self, known to others, and not known to others, as shown in Figure 9.1. As one quadrant gets larger or smaller, it affects the other three. The model underscores that the different aspects of self are not separate pieces but part of the whole person. According to DeVito (1990), "Like the model of interpersonal communication, this model of self is a transactional one in which each part is intimately dependent on each other part" (p. 53).

The *open self* includes all information known to self and to others. In a professional setting, we are likely to withhold information for a variety of reasons ranging from a lack of trust to a need for privacy to inappropriateness. If the people we work with know little about us, they have no reason to trust us. With the increase in interdependency in most organizations, successfully getting along with other people requires some disclosure of personal information. Often, this includes information such as age, background, interests, family background, and education. As you become more comfortable with the cultural setting in a particular subunit of the organization, you will open up more of this quadrant. Our willingness to self-disclose is, to a large extent, learned behavior. So, simply being told to provide more personal insights might not help you in the self-disclosing process.

The *blind self* represents those things about yourself that other people know that you do not. Dubbed the "dandruff on the collar" or "bad breath" quadrant, issues in the blind self can range from the trivial to the significant. For example, if every time you are expected to make an important sales call, you get sick or snap at people, you are exposing your blind self. Many times, management errors (e.g., not returning critical phone calls, being late, setting the wrong priorities or goals) are readily apparent to your co-workers, but not to you.

The *hidden self* includes all the information you know about yourself, but you choose not to disclose. At work, the list of issues that you might not want to make available to other people can be quite extensive. Usually, personal problems are not appropriate for company time. Some fears or recognition of your own shortcomings may be kept to yourself. An initial feeling that you are "in way over your head" probably will be kept hidden until you are more certain about how well you can work through the problem.

The *unknown self* represents truths that neither you nor others know. To the degree that we open up some of our hidden self, and allow some feedback on our blind self, we can expand the open self and reduce the unknown self.

In theory, appropriate self-disclosure enhances relationships. Obviously, you cannot trust someone you do not know beyond the obvious messages provided by their front. In general, self-disclosure is appropriate when it meets the following six criteria, as outlined by DeVito (1990) and Wilmot (1979):

1. It is motivated by a desire to improve the relationship, rather than for selfish purposes. Imposing guilt, for example, is not likely to enhance the relationship. It takes into account the effect disclosure will have on the other person so if the self-disclosure will create undue burdens on the other person, it might not be appropriate.
2. It fits the communication situation. Disclosing to the wrong person, or at the wrong time, or in the wrong setting only will lead to

problems. To be effective, self-disclosure should be a function of an ongoing relationship. The other person should be in a position to provide an open and honest response to the self-disclosure. In addition, it must be well-timed and fitting to current events.

3. There must be opportunities for the other person to reciprocate.
4. The focus should be on the here and now rather than the past. It should concern what is going on between and within persons in the present.
5. It moves in relatively small increments.
6. It is confirmable by the other person.

From a humanistic perspective, self-disclosure is a must for effective relationships. In organizations it is important—to be sure—but there must be judicious use for it to be effective. Not being trusted by our superiors, subordinates, or colleagues, means we are in for a very difficult time. In an organization, incremental self-disclosure would seem to be the key. Cohen et al. (2001) conclude, "The greater the extent of self-disclosure and feedback, the greater will be the resulting level of trust." They also warn, "The greater the level of openness that is required, the greater the level of risk experienced" (p. 239). Opening ourselves to others is a requirement to be trusted but there always will be some level of risk.

Empathy The capacity to feel what someone else feels is at the core of the human communication process. Earlier, when we examined listening, empathy was introduced. Regardless of the researcher, empathy is "centrally associated with connectedness, mutuality, relatedness, and the sharing of meaning among people" (Bruneau, 1989, p. 1). By "putting yourself in the other person's shoes," you are better able to understand and communicate (Lussier, 1999).

Supportiveness A supportive climate is fostered when we describe rather than evaluate and are provisional rather than certain (see chap. 8). In providing feedback, one of the key goals should be to create a supportive atmosphere where what is being done is discussed rather than the individual doing it. Focusing on behavior rather than attitude is fundamental to letting people in an organization know we are discussing the situation, not them. "A relationship that makes each person feel supported, adequate, and worthy will generally lead to mutual feelings of closeness, warmth, and trust" (Cohen et al., 2001, p. 234).

When we are provisional, we display an open-minded, tentative attitude. By and large, we are willing to listen to opposing points of view and change our own if it is warranted. In other words, we enter the transaction willing to hear and support the other person's perspective.

Positiveness Although it may appear to be a Pollyanna approach at first, presenting a positive perspective regarding other people is important. Seeing the bright side of things is an appealing characteristic. In order to do this, we must have positive self-concept and communicate positively. *Self-concept* is a sum total of numerous social transactions throughout our lives (Wilmot, 1979). If you have experienced a large number of successes, or can change goals when you have faced insurmountable barriers, you are likely to have a good self-concept.

The simplest way to explain positiveness is to examine negative behaviors. When a colleague continually "nay says" your ideas, or disapproves of your work, or considers your efforts a waste of time, your natural reaction is to shy away from him or her. People who constantly criticize your behavior or find fault with how you handle yourself exhibit negativeness. Because interpersonal relationships develop incrementally over time, the types of messages we send along the way determine the structure and content of the relationships. If we want a productive interpersonal relationship, positive messages seem to be more effective.

Equality   All relationships have some inequality (Watzlawick, Beavin, & Jackson, 1967). A dyad is considered symmetrical when the communicants perceive themselves as equals. A complementary relationship is where there is a hierarchy in which one person is superior to the other in some sense. Both equality and superiority can be slippery concepts. If someone works for you and controls information you need, they will have little difficulty establishing a complementary relationship (and probably you will have little difficulty accepting it) as they brief you. When the office breaks for lunch, you might want the relationships to be more symmetrical so everyone can enjoy the break. If you are the person in charge and you announce it is time to return to work, this complementary statement probably will be taken as a command, rather than just a friendly reminder.

So, what is equality? At work, or in any other interpersonal relationship, accepting someone is the real meaning of equality. The issue is atmosphere, not actual equality. When disagreements occur, problem solving is utilized rather than putting the other person down or correcting them.

The humanistic model has much to offer for interpersonal effectiveness. For certain, some of your colleagues will become friends. Some of these friendships will turn into long-term relationships. With the increasing time spent at work and the increase in women working, organizational romances are inevitable. In fact, "the odds are 4 in 10 that a marriage or an enduring relationship will result from an office romance—and the odds will rise as more women go to work" (Ciabattari, 1999, p. 25). Most office romances have little negative impact on the participants or the workplace (Dillard, Hale, & Segrin, 1994). In fact, employees may improve their work performance in order to impress their romantic partner, overcome possible negative perceptions, or compensate for potential biases from other organizational members (Dillard & Miller, 1988).

Because there is the potential for co-worker jealousy and the possibility that you will not be perceived in the best professional light, handling workplace romance within the cultural expectations of the organization is important (Lowndes, 1993).

At numerous times we have discussed the importance of a pleasant working environment. From the 100 best places to work studies to examinations of excellent organizational cultures, working with people we view as friends is important.

Specific Applications

You will be judged competent as a communicator if your behaviors are appropriate, which is demonstrated by doing the right thing at the right time. This still leaves a somewhat perplexing question regarding what guidelines can be established. There is no shortage of advice. Almost all national consulting organizations have their favorite, and often copyrighted, approaches to developing effectiveness. In a moment, we examine one example that demonstrates how we can focus our interpersonal communication improvement efforts. Numerous other options exist ranging from the Myers-Briggs Style Indicator (1976), probably the most widely used set of tests, to very specific approaches that concentrate on leadership or listening or team building. The majority of tests that concentrate on personal styles are based on the work of Carl Jung (1923). Briefly, Jung argued that introversion and extroversion were the two predominant attitudes. These interact with the four functions of thinking, feeling, sensing, and intuiting. Research indicates that how we communicate impacts on our leadership (see chap. 11) and interpersonal effectiveness (Fitzgerald & Kirby, 1997).

Social Styles

One measure of our behavioral preferences is our social style. Byrum (1986) wrote, "Social style is defined as patterns of behavior that others can observe and respond to" (p. 213). It reflects the pervasive communication patterns we have become comfortable with and use habitually. As we learn to cope with others during our formative years, we develop our social style. This becomes somewhat habitual and manifests itself in current, interactive behavior (Merrill & Reid, 1981). Certain styles are perceived as being more favorable than others in certain situations (Snavely, 1981). When used as a learning tool, social styles tests, exercises, and seminars train individuals to adapt well to the demands of the situation and the individuals involved (Hunsaker & Alessandra, 1982). Social style training is based on the values of accepting the differences in others and willingness to adapt to them. Forwarding the premise that people perform best in positive relationships, and that many working relationships can be improved, social style approaches argue that knowing yourself and understanding others can help (Byrum, 1986).

There are three basic issues underlying the social style concept—assertiveness, responsiveness, and appropriateness. *Assertiveness* is our willingness to ask or tell and influence or be influenced by others. *Responsiveness* is how much we emote or control our feelings. In other words, do we display openly or withhold expressing emotion (Byrum, 1986)? These two behaviors interact to form four styles—driver, expressive, amiable, and analytical. Each of the styles has specific behaviors that lead to increased likelihood of success in certain situations and with particular individuals and the same behavior can be problematic with other individuals. By and large, we are most comfortable with people who have the same style, and can experience some tension in dealing with people whose styles have nothing in common with our own (Byrum, 1986).

Drivers prefer to take charge, complete tasks, and solve problems—doers and command specialists. These individuals are high in assertiveness and low in responsiveness. Their communication tends toward moving quickly, speaking faster, using direct eye contact, and trying to control others. The drivers' positive attributes include being practical, independent, decisive, and efficient. When overused, drivers can become pushy, dominating, harsh, and tough.

Analytics are nonassertive and nonresponsive. They are thinkers and technical specialists. Their communication tends toward slower speaking, fewer statements, and the use of facts and data. Habitually, analytics are cautious and make a maximum effort to organize. The analytics' positive attributes include being industrious, orderly, exacting, and orderly. When overused, analytics can be critical, indecisive, picky, and moralistic.

Expressives are assertive and responsive. They are intuitive and social recognition specialists. Their communication tends toward faster speaking, more statements and feeling, and animated with direct eye contact. Expressives try to involve everyone, worry about the future, and are impulsive. The expressives' positive attributes include being ambitious, enthusiastic, dramatic, and friendly. When overused, expressives can become manipulative, undisciplined, reactive, and egotistical.

Amiables are nonassertive and responsive. They are relationship specialists. Their communication tends toward slower speaking, focus on people, fewer statements, and use of stories and opinions. They tend to be unhurried, relate to others, and search for cooperation. The amiables' positive attributes include being supportive, respectable, dependable, and willing. When overused, amiables can become conforming, pliable, dependent, and unsure.

Interpersonal communication assumes some sense of concern for the "other." This is where social styles approaches are used by most organizations. What is our ability to be adaptable, resourceful, or competent? This is our *versatility*. If we are inflexible or rigid, we rank low on versatility, and being adaptable and resourceful provides for a higher ranking. The effective interpersonal communicator develops style flexibility in light of the demands of the situation (Goodall, 1990). This versatility is our response to the other person's social style. We do not change our basic message; we change how we communicate in order to overcome potential style clashes. Someone's style of communicating gives you the information you need to proceed in a transaction (Norton, 1983). Their actions, as you perceive them, *limit* your choices as you attempt to effectively adapt. We need to be very cognizant that knowing ourselves is critical to this ability to adapt. In addition, we would not go to great lengths to adapt if the relationship was not important.

The goal is to reduce unnecessary style clashes. For example, if you are dealing with a driver, you should explain *what* first, proceed rapidly, support the other person's results, talk about immediate action, provide freedom, be businesslike, time-conscious, and factual (Byrum, 1986). That makes sense because the driver wants to move forward and take action. If, however, your primary social style is amiable, you would prefer talking about positive, people oriented issues. In many cases, this would diminish your success with a driver because your approach doesn't fit the driver's communication needs. For the expressive, explain *who* first, proceed enthusiastically, support the other person's intentions, talk about people and opinions, provide discipline, be stimulating, open, and flexible. The amiable should be adapted to by explaining *why* first, proceeding softly, supporting the other person, talking about personal life, providing initiative, being gentle, specific, and harmonious. The analytical style should be approached by explaining *how* first, proceeding deliberately, supporting the other person's principles, talking about documented facts, providing deadlines, being patient, organized, and logical.

On the surface, the social styles approach might appear naive or even manipulative. However, most of us have learned to adapt to circumstances and individuals in order to be successful. If we are to be interpersonally competent, we need to be able to adapt appropriately to situational or environmental variations ranging from colleagues to customers.

A final application of the styles approach is worth noting. There is a possibility that you have prejudices for or against certain types of behaviors. If this is the case, you are likely to attribute your prejudices to the other person's personality or character. In reality, you are responding to the other's behavior (Goodall, 1990). The styles approach offers us the ability to control our responses and to manage our own behaviors. If you become adept at enhancing your social style, and understanding why you have not been successful with certain people, you are on the road to being a conscious-competent communicator. A second measure of our behavioral choices is how we manage conflicts.

Conflict Management

Conflict is an inherent and ubiquitous part of organizational life (Yeung, 1997). For example, executives spend "18% of their time—more than 9 weeks a year—resolving employee personality clashes" ("Managing employee," 1996,

p. 16). These represent *emotional, or nonrealistic, conflicts* arising from the need to release tensions or aggressive impulses. Anger, distrust, fear, resentment, or personality clashes can erupt in many forms from "going postal" to withdrawing to becoming verbally aggressive. When people are unable to work together or groups are continually at odds with others, there is *dysfunctional or destructive conflict.*

Substantive, or realistic, conflicts occur over the allocation of resources, job assignments, work processes, change, or the distribution of rewards. Anytime a group works together, disagreements over goals, direction, and process will occur (see chap. 10). These conflicts occur over disagreements about tasks (what), processes (how), allocation of resources (with what), goals (why), or power (who). Toyota credits "lots of conflict" over how they produce their cars as a major contributor to their enviable position as a quality producer (Ward, 1998).

Functional or constructive conflicts are vital to an organization (Amason, 1996). The task-related confrontations help organizations become more creative (Chambers, 1998). As we learn to work through conflicts we improve our working relationships and increase our commitment to the group, team, and organization (Kindler, 1996). Conflicts bring hidden problems to the surface and allow individuals and group members to focus on the important issues (Amazon & Sapienza, 1997). As a matter of fact, a recent study of 500 successful companies revealed that performance and productivity had much less to do with traditional organizational procedures and processes than with how well conflict and situations of potential conflict were handled at all levels in the organization. Conflicts occur at different levels as shown in Table 9.1.

Conflict Resolution Styles   Our own conflict resolution preferences also complicate conflicts. For some, conflicts are defined in terms of winning, which means someone must lose (Levine, 1998). Others would prefer to retain the relationship rather than win. There is an adage in customer relations: "win the argument and lose the customer." If we successfully show customers that they are wrong, they can shop elsewhere. In organizational settings where we are interdependent, winning or defeating others carries the potential resentment and wrath of the losers or perhaps a future lack of cooperation.

There are five possible responses to conflict based on our *assertiveness or concern for self* and our *cooperativeness or interest in satisfying others* (Killman & Thomas, 1997). The difference is between a motivation to satisfy our own interests versus a motivation to satisfy others. These are not necessarily opposites.

Collaborating is being assertive about your own goals, yet having a high concern for the other's goals while being assertive about your own. *Competing* is insisting that your goals prevail showing little concern for others. *Avoiding* is physically or psychologically abandoning your own goals and allowing others to prevail. *Compromising* is meeting somewhere in the middle, which means knowingly settling for less. *Accommodating* is allowing the goals of the other

Table 9.1 Types of Conflicts

Intrapersonal	Internal conflict over goals or cognition created because of inconsistencies in our thoughts. When we feel dissonance between our thoughts and actions, two or more goals, or two or more values, we will experience intrapersonal conflict.
Interpersonal	Conflict between two or more people. This can be a personality, task, or a combined conflict.
Intragroup	Conflict within the group over the task (substantive conflict) and interpersonal relations (affective conflict). Teams, task forces, and small groups must experience some types of conflict or they will "go along to get along."
Intergroup or department	Conflict due to competition between groups over achieving goals or over department issues such as power, status, and resources.
Intraorganizational	Conflict between levels such as supervisors/subordinates, line staff (people who have direct responsibility for some organizational function and the staff that advises them), role conflict and role ambiguity (unclear tasks make the job difficult), horizontal conflict (between departments at the same level in the organization).
Interorganizational	Conflict due to competition between two or more organizations. Although organizational, this is a positive mechanism for producing creative alternatives and innovation. Resources, however, can sometimes be diverted to this battle and away from other, critical organizational needs.

parties to take precedent while you remain in the situation. Table 9.2 explains the five styles and indicates when each is most likely to be successful.

Even a cursory review of the five choices would lead us to conclude that we should vary our responses depending on the circumstances. However, when we find ourselves in the middle of a conflict, it is difficult to think rationally enough to analyze the conflict and then apply the appropriate response to the situation. Therefore we must "stay alert for the moment a conversation turns from a routine or harmless discussion into a crucial one" (Patterson, Grenny, McMillan, & Switzler, 2002, p. 48). To do this requires skill, determination, and often the ability to go against our habitual, behavioral tendencies. Most of us have more than 20 years of practice at being who we are now—obviously we need to practice to develop new patterns of behavior. Table 9.3 outlines some useful strategies that, when practiced, can lead to more successful, high-stakes encounters with others.

Table 9.2 Conflict Management Styles

Competitive	Win/lose, zero sum where the other person must lose for you to win. Power, dominance, and submission of the other. *Behavioral characteristics:* Uncooperative but assertive. *Descriptors:* Tough battler, coercive, we–they, I'm OK/you're not OK *When to use:* Quick, decisive action needed (e.g., emergency) or unpopular, but necessary action must be followed (e.g., safety rules). When the issue is ethically important, you must take a stand, and you cannot use collaboration. *When not to use:* When conversion is needed as opposed to compliance. No other alternative strategies will work.
Compromise	Split the difference resulting in a lose/lose outcome because an optimum solution is not reached. Majority rule, acting for the common good, finding "acceptable solutions." *Behavioral characteristics:* Moderately cooperative and assertive. *Descriptors:* Conciliator, negotiation, policy enforcer. *When to use:* When a balance of power has been reached and no other alternatives are available. If there are relatively unimportant issues. The long term resolution is not worth the effort. *When not to use:* If it is becoming the resolution for all conflicts. When both parties cannot afford to yield. When a significant problem exists.
Accommodating	Forego our own goals to satisfy the relationship. Generosity, self-sacrifice, and yielding to the other's point of view. *Behavioral characteristics:* Cooperative but unassertive. *Descriptors:* Friendly helper, suppression, smoothing over, harmony, I'm not OK/you're OK. *When to use:* When harmony, future good will, or the relationship are more important. When you are wrong on the issue or your timing. If it is an organizational rule (e.g., come to work at 8 a.m., no shorts). *When not to use:* When the outcome impacts on important issues. If your insights need to be heard.
Avoiding	Sidestepping, denying, postponing, or withdrawing. Let "fate" decide. Physically or mentally withdrawing from the conflict. *Behavioral characteristics:* Uncooperative and unassertive. *Descriptors:* Impersonal complier, denial, lose, and leave, I'm not OK/you're OK. *When to use:* When the timing is wrong, you are wrong, a cooling off period is needed. You need more information. *When not to use:* When it indicates that you do not care. When you cannot afford not to be involved.
Collaboration	Win/win strategy where everyone's concerns and needs are considered. Problem-solving. *Behavioral characteristics:* Both cooperative and assertive. *Descriptors:* Integrator, coactive, I'm OK/you're OK. *When to use:* When individuals and groups will commit the time and energy needed to solve a problem. Any important issue. *When not to use:* When two people cannot work together. When issue does not deserve the energy. Lack of time. Issue not open for collaboration.

Table 9.3 Strategies for Crucial Conversations

Principle	Skill	Crucial Questions
1. Start with heart	Focus on what you really want.	What am I acting like I really want? What do I really want? • For me? • For Others? • For the relationship? How would I behave if I really did want this?
	Refuse the sucker's choice.	What do I not want? How should I go about getting what I really want and avoiding what I don't want?
2. Learn to look	Look for when the conversation becomes crucial. Look for safety problems. Look for our own [communication] style under stress.	Am I going to silence (masking, avoiding, withdrawing) or violence (controlling, labeling, attacking)? Are others going to silence or violence?
3. Make it safe	Apologize when appropriate. Contrast to fix misunderstanding.	Why is safety at risk? • Have I established mutual purpose? • Am I maintaining mutual respect? What will I do to rebuild safety?
4. Master my stories	Retrace my path to action. Separate fact from story. Tell the rest of the story.	What is my story? What am I pretending not to know about my role in the problem? Why would a reasonable, rational, and decent person do this? What should I do right now to move toward what I really want?
5. State my path	Share your facts. Tell your story. Ask for other' paths. Talk tentatively. Encourage testing.	Am I really open to others' views? Am I talking about the real issue? Am I confidently expressing my own views?
6. Explore others' paths	Ask Mirror Paraphrase Prime Agree Build Compare	Am I actively exploring others' views? Am I avoiding unnecessary disagreement?
7. Move to action	Decide how you'll decide. Document decisions and follow up.	How will we make decisions? Who will do what by when? How will we follow up?

Note. From K. Patterson, J. Grenny, R. McMillan, and A. Switzler (2002), *Crucial Conversations: Tools for Talking When the Stakes are High.* Copyright 2002 by the McGraw-Hill Companies. Reproduced with permission.

Additionally, we often develop *trained incapacities*, or a dependence on a limited number of choices, early in life that tend to be self-reinforcing (Folger & Poole, 1984). When our conflict management style choice works, we attribute our success to our strategy. When we fail, we tend to fault the other party or group (Groder, 1989). Our internal reasoning usually follows a pattern such as the following: We received the promotion because we fought for it (or laid back, or befriended the boss), but we lost the promotion because we were outgunned (or the other side was crooked, or the evaluation process was biased). Success is attributed to our choice but failure is attributed to the other party. Essentially, our responses make sense to us at the time (Hocker & Wilmot, 1985). The boss who explodes (necessary to relieve tension; keeps employees on their toes), the subordinate who calls in sick (cannot face another failure; it's a terrible job anyway; everyone's doing it), or the student who cuts class (too much work for 3-hour credit; the professor is unfair; the material is too hard) are using a conflict management style that makes sense to them.

As organizational diversity and multicultural changes continue, examining our habits is important. Research shows that generally females prefer indirect tactics for conflict resolution as opposed to more assertive methods preferred by their male counterparts (Ohbuchi, Fukushima, & Tedeschi, 1999). They are more interested in maintaining the relationship and are more motivated by a justice goal (to achieve or restore social fairness). Some attribute a lack of female representation at upper levels of management as a question of style (see chap. 10). However, "new studies find that female managers outshine their male counterparts in almost every measure" (Sharpe, 2000, p. 75). One explanation is that "women think through decisions better than men, are more collaborative, and seek less personal glory" (Sharpe, 2000, p. 75).

Internationally, individualistic cultures (e.g., United States, Canada, Australia) prefer active, assertive, and confrontational tactics for resolving conflicts (Ohbuchi et al., 1999). Collectivist cultures (e.g., Japan, Venezuela, Chile) prefer passive, collaborative, and avoiding tactics in order to maintain the relationship. Coming from different cultures means we can find ourselves in disagreement over the basic conflict resolution strategy.

A *contingency approach*—doing the right thing at the right time based on the circumstances—becomes particularly useful in organizations where you will encounter difficult people, aloof colleagues, and a myriad of other personalities. Before doing what comes naturally, we should decide which style is most likely to create a positive outcome. Not everyone wants to or can collaborate. In an irrational situation, rationality might not work. The old fable about the scorpion and the frog may help clarify this issue. The scorpion, unable to swim, asked the frog to carry him across the stream, but the frog resisted on the grounds that the scorpion would sting him to death. "Look," said the scorpion, "use your head. If I sting you while we're in the stream, we both die." A reassured frog finally agreed. Of course, when they reached the deepest part of the stream, the scorpion stung the frog. As the frog was dying, he cried: "Why? Now we both die." To which the scorpion replied, "Once a scorpion, always a scorpion. It's my nature." The scorpion was willing to use counterproductive behavior because it made sense to him. Moral to the story—worry more about changing your approach to conflicts than hoping others will change.

Organizations are expecting the results of collaboration so we need to learn to work with others and increasingly operate in teams (Shani & Lau, 2000). There are multiple justifications. A collaborative style is clearly related to enhanced interpersonal and performance rewards. Organizational members are more likely to realize their personal and work goals (Weider-Hatfield & Hatfield, 1996). Teams are more successful in a multitude of situations (see chap. 10). The alternative strategies, accommodating and compromising, when employed by a superior to a subordinate, do not affect task completion or compliance and they decrease the subordinate's willingness to communicate openly in an upward fashion. They also lead the subordinates to view conflict management as less effective. Avoiding strategies are positively correlated to conflict (Weider-Hatfield & Hatfield, 1995).

Superior–Subordinate Relationships

The most important work-related communication relationships in an organization have traditionally been between supervisors and subordinates (Eisenberg, Monge, & Farace, 1984). "In interviews with 2 million employees at 700 companies, Gallup found that how long employees stay at companies and how productive they are is determined by their relationship with their immediate supervisor" (Zipkin, 2000, p. 1A). As we observed at the beginning of this chapter, interpersonal communication plays an important role from our job interviews to our leaving. In between, there is an entire spectrum of transactions between employees and bosses that span daily work, specific assignments, raises, problems, successes, and social life.

One, often overlooked, aspect of organizational life is the friendship relationships between employees and supervisors. These relationships may come about as a result of friends being promoted into supervisory positions over other friends or as a natural result of spending 40 or more hours together during the workweek. Whatever the circumstance, these relationships, both romantic and nonromantic, often cause what Zorn (1995) has described as dialectical tensions in friendships between supervisors and subordinates. Table 9.4 outlines these dialectical tensions in more detail.

Superiors and subordinates, however, may differ in their perceptions of a wide variety of organizational matters. One research summary found differences between superiors and subordinates on the superior's leadership style and the subordinate's: performance and obstacles to goal performance, skills and abilities, concern over pay, and authority. In addition, these two groups

Table 9.4 Dialectical Tensions in Friendships between Supervisors and Subordinates

Connection/Autonomy	Friendships are generally characterized by closeness and connection. Supervisors and subordinates, on the other hand, usually experience a degree of distance and autonomy encouraged by organizational hierarchies.
Openness/Closedness	Openness and the free sharing of information generally characterize friendships. Supervisors and subordinates, on the other hand, often withhold information from one another because of confidentiality issues or power issues related to status differences.
Novelty/Predictability	Novelty is not uncommon among friends at work, however, it is often characterized as a source of stress. Therefore, as a way to preserve these awkward and unequal relationships, predictability is often sought.
Equality/Superiority	Equality and the downplaying of factors that might indicate superiority generally characterize friendships. Supervisors and subordinates, on the other hand, are often confronted with issues that highlight status differences making it difficult for some on-the-job-friends to engage in typical supervisor–subordinate roles.
Privilege/Uniformity	Friendships are generally characterized by privileges both tangible and intangible. Supervisors, however, must act in more uniform ways to ensure equal treatment for all employees.

Source: Zorn, 1995.

differed over how much time a job takes to learn and how subordinates should allocate their time (Johns, 1988).

Supervisory Communication Behavior

Effective managers and leaders are skilled at human relations, develop others, make decisions, provide role models, use humor, understand language, use positive nonverbal behavior, develop networks and encourage upward and downward communication, listen effectively, develop strong symbolic messages, and apply power effectively—this is a prodigious set of expectations for any manager, tempting some to concentrate on task requirements over people issues.

In meeting these expectations, supervisors would be well advised to engage in positive, open, and receptive communication (Pace & Faules, 1994). Various research studies have found that superiors spend from one third to two thirds of their time communicating with subordinates (Jablin, 1985). The key skills include empathy, approachability, openness, sensitivity, information-sharing, and an ability to ask rather than tell (Redding, 1972). Superior–subordinate communication does not occur in a vacuum so climate, culture, task, group size, gender, and occupational type all function as intervening variables. The type of communication we use in interviewing, coaching, or performance appraisals needs to be appropriate to that particular task.

Bolman and Deal (1991) put interpersonal communication in perspective when they concluded: "Individual differences and interpersonal dynamics continue to spawn organizational muddles. ... In organizations, as in the rest of life, many of the greatest joys and most intense sorrows, the highest peaks and deepest valleys, occur in relationships with others" (p. 134). Understanding the dynamics of interpersonal communication, and learning to alter how we behave with others, will allow us to operate more effectively in any organization.

Conclusion

Dyadic relationships are a major influence in most aspects of organizational behavior. This chapter has focused the concept of interpersonal communication so you will be better able to understand, adjust, and adapt. The functions of interpersonal communication in organizations range from coordinating tasks and maintenance functions to developing interpersonal relationships. By understanding the three definitions of interpersonal communication, you will be able to analyze why different groups and people perceive the issue differently. In fact, all three are of value.

The difference in perspectives regarding interpersonal transactions also provides useful insights regarding individual preferences. Information, and information processing, are cutting edge issues because the impact of information will continue to grow.

Deciding what is effective interpersonally is difficult. With this in mind, we discussed ten attributes that lead to being successful. By approaching the issue from an interactive management and humanistic view, we are able to pull together a fuller understanding. Superior–subordinate communication offers a useful example. One of the true insights a communication perspective brings to organizations is the capacity to improve interpersonal communication. This chapter should assist your pursuit of that important goal.

Study Questions

1. Develop a definition of interpersonal communication. Justify your approach.
2. What are the three types of approaches to information?
3. Which of the four information-processing approaches do you use most often? Provide examples of all four from your personal experience.
4. Which characteristic of the interaction management model do you consider least important? Most important? Why?

5. Which characteristic of the humanistic model do you consider least important? Most important? Why?
6. Differentiate between the four social styles.
7. Explain the importance of a contingency approach to conflict management.
8. What is the role of supervisory communication behavior?

10
Small Group and Team Communication

Small groups and teams are the cornerstones of organized behavior, operate at all levels of an organization, and play a major role in informal and formal activities. More than 70% of all U.S. companies of 100 or more employees have employees working in teams (Sweeney & McFarlin, 2002). "Teams are a favorite way to organize employees, to get work done, and to facilitate workplace learning" ("Industry Report," 1995). Increasingly, organizations are using groups to fuel improvements, develop new ideas, and motivate employees. The key concepts in this chapter are:

- Scope of groups and teams
- Definition and types of groups
- Groups as subcultures
- Group cohesiveness, norms, and roles
- Group development
- Advantages and disadvantages
- Employee involvement
- Teams and teamwork
- Limitations to team building
- Self-managing work teams

Examples of great groups are Walt Disney's animators; Lockheed Martin Skunk Works, whose engineers produced the stealth fighter; and the Manhattan Project, makers of hot, iridescent oblivion—the atomic bomb (Bennis & Beiderman, 1997). Groups and teams shine in a variety of settings. At Suburban Hospital in Bethesda, Maryland, teams are credited with "reducing errors, shortening the amount of time patients spend in its 12-bed ICU (intensive care unit), and improving communication between families and medical staff" (Appleby & Davis, 2001, p. B1). The speed of advances in modern medicine makes it difficult for individuals to keep up to date. Suburban Hospital uses teams to overcome this problem. Like the ICU, "in high-pressure workplaces, such as nuclear plants, aircraft cockpits, or the military, teamwork is essential to survival" (Appleby & Davis, 2001, p. B2). Whole Foods Market, based in Austin, Texas, with 183 locations in North America and the United Kingdom, recently ranked 15th on *Fortune* magazine's annual list of the "100 Best Companies to Work For" (Colvin, 2006). Their success is based on self-managing work teams that are responsible and accountable for their own performance. "The central idea is giving a group responsibility for a meaningful whole—a product, sub-assembly, or complete service—with ample autonomy and resources and collective responsibility for results" (Bolman & Deal, 2003, p. 149). The teams at Whole Foods Markets have the authority to hire, fire, determine pay rates, specify work methods, and manage inventory. At the University of California–Irvine, teams were able to make the purchasing of parking permits easier and faster saving students and staff time and the university more than $1 million (Woodyard, 1998). The president of Wes-Tex Printing in Brownville, Texas, "turned the task of speeding up production to his 130 employees. That led to the formation of interdisciplinary teams, the kind of cooperation on the plant floor that lead Wes-Tex to being named winner of the 2001 RIT/USA Today Quality Cup for small business" (Woodyard, 2001, p. 3B). The teams identified delays in the production process, readjusted work schedules and dramatically reduced delivery times resulting in an expected "5% increase in its more than $7 million in annual revenue" in 2001 similar to the increase it first realized after the team process in 2000 (Woodyard, 2001, p. 3B).

"At Minretek Systems, a Falls Church, Virginia, nonprofit organization that conducts scientific research in such weighty areas as counterterrorism, criminal justice, and the environment—tapping the collective insights of employees through effective teamwork is a key part of the business" (Pomeroy, 2004, p. 50). Teams are at the heart of the new organization. Rather than focusing on functional activities, teams learn to truly collaborate, create high levels of dependency, and communicate extensively (Hope & Hope, 1997).

Small groups and teams are successful in a wide variety of settings and situations. The importance of small groups makes sense because the vast majority of tasks accomplished by organizations requires more than two people. A group develops interdependence among the members as a means to accomplishing goals. On a broader scale, the more an organization tries to achieve, the greater the need to subdivide the work into smaller units that can concentrate on specific problems, issues, and solutions.

The first half of this chapter examines small group and team behavior in general, and the second half explains the use of teams to increase productivity through employee involvement. Before we extend our discussion concerning the interesting and important uses of groups, we need to lay the groundwork by understanding the scope, definition, types, characteristics, norms, cohesiveness, roles, and meetings.

Scope of Groups and Teams

Because of their central importance to organizations, groups influence decisions, problem-solving effectiveness, individual self-identity and self-concept, power allocation and application, and symbolic information such as values, justifications, and frames of reference. An organization's cultural rules and ongoing procedures are sanctioned by the various groups of individuals forming the immediate work groups. The immediate group, team, or unit will carry out our indoctrination into an organization. Organizational cultures depend on small group activities to reinforce their rites and rituals. You will be a member of a primary work team consisting of your colleagues, supervisors, subordinates, and assigned activities. In addition, you will be a part of long-standing work teams, project and development teams, advice units such as committees, and one-time teams put together to solve problems. Understanding the importance of groups and teams is a vital aspect of our success in organizations. Survey results titled: "Unwanted: Solo Artists" report what 150 executives told Accutemps, a staffing firm, was most likely to hurt a person's chances for getting ahead. Poor team-player skills received 57% of the responses, complacency received 21%, excessive complaining received 14%, and defensiveness received 6% ("By the Numbers," 1995). In other words, not knowing the importance of teams or lacking teamwork skills limits our success.

Dependence on groups will expand as organizations attempt to increase productivity and solve problems through team building and specialized task forces. This is a wise choice. In an examination of some 50 years of studies on cooperative decision-making, the *Review of Educational Research* found that groups are more effective at solving problems than individuals (Berko, 1996). Even if a solution is not forthcoming, group "meetings frequently serve as the focal point for boosting group morale and motivating workers to higher productivity levels" (Cragan & Wright, 1991, p. 239). Groups offer an excellent format for obtaining and reinforcing consensus.

Establishing a small group and successfully using the process are two different things. Your own experiences with small groups at school, work, or socially will probably confirm that observation. Committees, conferences, and meetings have fostered many tongue-in-cheek comments. A sampling includes: "A meeting brings together a group of the unfit, appointed by the unwilling, to do the unnecessary"; "A camel is a horse designed by a committee"; "A conference is a meeting of people who by themselves can do nothing, but who collectively agree that nothing can be done"; and "A conference is a meeting to decide when the next meeting will be held." David Ogilvy is credited with the observation: "Search all your parks in all your cities—You'll find no statues to committees."

The remainder of this chapter is devoted to providing you with a broad understanding of how groups are utilized in organizations. This chapter progresses in the following fashion: definitions of small groups, types of small groups, characteristics of small groups, group cohesiveness, group norms, roles, group leadership, group development, advantages and disadvantages of groups, tailored group techniques, employee involvement, traditional problem-solving groups, and semi-autonomous work units. First, what are small groups?

Definition of Small Groups

In keeping with our definition of interpersonal communication, we can define small group communication as the process of transacting meaning between three or more individuals. Throughout this chapter, we integrate the concepts of groups and teams. *However, it is important to remember that groups tend to have a much shorter organizational lifespan than teams.* How do groups differ from interpersonal communication?

Nine elements make up our working definition. Small groups include: (1) face-to-face communication, (2) among a small group of people (3–20 depending on the researcher), (3) who share a common purpose or goal, (4) perceive a sense of belonging to the group, (5) have interdependence, (6) create and enforce norms and shared standards, (7) exert influence on one another, (8) over a period of time, (9) through some structured patterns (Harris & Sherblom, 2005). In other words, the fate(s) of the participants are linked together intentionally in the pursuit of some common goal(s) employing some accepted standards.

In organizations, groups are utilized in a much broader fashion and roam in numerous directions not covered by many traditional definitions. As Jablin and Sussman (1983) put it, "An organizational group is a collection of three or more organizational members who interact (more or less regularly) over time, are psychologically cognizant of one another, perceive themselves as a group, and, most important, are embedded within a network of interlocking tasks, roles, and expectations" (p. 12). This expanded perspective allows us to include work teams, quality circles, project teams, special research units, semiautonomous work units, and digitally connected teams.

Differentiating Small Groups

A small group is not just a collection of dyads in one place. With interpersonal communication, "the loss of one is the loss of all" (Wilmot, 1987, p. 19), because the capacity to carry on the relationship has been dissolved. Small groups significantly change the number of interactions possible and alter the interdependence. As we add colleagues to our small group, we change the potential communication between members. We also shift the capacity of some members to contribute, change the potential for creative thinking, and adjust the possible satisfaction obtained by each individual. Small groups increase the number of interactions, and a group can survive (and sometimes flourish) with the departure of any individual or the addition of another.

When we discussed networks (see chap. 6), we reached the conclusion that all groups are networks, but not all networks are groups. A network can involve two people or it can extend throughout an entire organization. Our analysis of networks provides you with a great deal of background regarding groups. Of specific interest are the concepts of coupling and connectedness. When subsystems (e.g., members of a department, research and development team) become highly interdependent, they are tightly coupled. Most small groups experience tight coupling when they are concentrating on the task or the social interaction. If your company encourages independent actions by small groups within the corporate structure, it is using loose coupling.

Connectedness describes the extent to which network members identify with the goals of other members of their network. We established that increased connectedness enhances employee performance, provides greater power to the group, and offers increased information. As we proceed with our analysis of small groups, you will want to recall the concomitant impact of networks. Effective groups are tightly coupled and highly connected within the group itself. When we examine the use of employee involvement procedures (e.g., suggestions, quality circles, self-managing work teams) later in this chapter, you will see the importance of these concepts.

A further analysis of the types of groups operating in organizations is in order.

Types of Groups

For the purpose of clarification, groups can be viewed as informal and formal. Informal groups do not appear on the organizational chart and are not part of the operating blueprint. Formal groups are sanctioned by the organization and appear on charts, planning documents, or calendars.

Informal Groups

An informal group emerges naturally from the interaction of members and may or may not have goals related to the organization's goals. These groups structure themselves, develop some type of implicit or explicit membership requirements, maintain themselves because they have useful social and business purposes, and have tremendous power in shaping attitudes and behavior, which ultimately affects production.

Informal groups will develop if the elements of physical proximity, attitude similarity, and need complementarily occur, as is the case with interpersonal relationships (Miller, 1990). For example, groups of middle managers, secretaries, or shipping clerks often have complementary needs and their attitudes can be quite similar because of organizational roles. As with interpersonal communication, doing the same type of work can provide an initial bridge between individuals and group members. Groups also will develop if they can facilitate goal accomplishment for the members. A complementary need and an attitude similarity are likely if the task simply is too large for any one individual. This is not hypothetical. Developing a new computer or designing a different manufacturing process usually takes more than one person. At Apple, the Mac team, headed by Steve Jobs, "operated like a superstealth startup within the company. Holed up in an ascetic, two-story building near a gas station dubbed the 'Texaco Towers,' the team was intensely competitive with other Apple divisions, such as the Lisa computer." Their voracious commitment to teamwork and "renegade spirit" fueled the team through long hours and low pay. And it paid off—the Mac sold faster than any PC that came before and marked a turning point in the history of the PC (*Fortune*, 2006). At the Mayo Clinic, one of the premier medical operations in the world, "specialists don't just visit a patient; they swarm the patient with an integrated team, diagnosing a complex problem, proposing treatment—and often slotting the patient for surgery within 24 hours of the diagnosis" (Roberts, 1999, p. 150). Teamwork is part of the Mayo Clinic's culture and it "is built into the treatment of patients, and it's integrated into the clinic's fabric of governance" (Roberts, 1999, p. 153).

Formal Groups

Formal groups are sanctioned by the organization. Their primary function is the attainment of organizational goals (e.g., productivity, sales, market strategy). Two broad groupings are functional groups and task (or project) groups. *Functional groups* are specified by the structure of the organization and define the relationship between a supervisor and subordinates. These groups are permanent or quasi-permanent (e.g., advertising department, top management team, the data processing group, the maintenance crew). The first group you automatically will be a member of in an organization is your primary work team.

When employees are brought together for the purpose of accomplishing a specific task (e.g., solve a production problem, create a new credo), they become a *task or project group* (e.g., problem-solving, quality circles, committees, task forces, planning teams). These groups can operate for a short- or long-term period and they are designed to enhance coordination, communication, innovation, interaction, and productivity. Although the functional group will remain until there is a reorganization of the structure, task or project groups are intended to self-destruct after they have accomplished their specific goals.

As you already have realized, we have made several arbitrary divisions for the sake of clarification. In most organizations, groups encompass a wide variety of activities. They can range from informal groups created by a job-related, mutual interdependence (e.g., human resources department and the rest of the organization), shipping and sales departments, loan officers throughout a bank) to those who interact frequently to issue-specific task forces (e.g., reorganization task force, new facilities committee).

Adding to the complexity of understanding groups, organizational scholars are focusing more on work units and work teams (Cummings & Worley, 2005). We carefully outline the role of work teams later in this chapter. For now, you should understand that work units are composed of individuals placed in situations with high task interdependence (e.g., traditional assembly line, a specific office), and work teams are individuals involved in mutual goal accomplishment (e.g., self-managing work teams, task forces, quality circles, committees). Now that we have defined and differentiated small groups, it is important to examine small groups as subcultures.

Groups as Subcultures

Small groups function as subcultures with their own networks, channels, and degrees of effectiveness. From the *symbolic perspective*, "each group develops a history of shared experiences that influences present and future performance" (Frank & Brownell, 1989, p. 224). Small groups provide the rules, roles, and concepts required for understanding the organization. This is essentially a provincial, group-based definition of the structural, human resources, and political frames. When an individual joins an organization, the initial influence comes from coworkers who form the immediate group. The informational/sense-making function at the employee's early stages of involvement is substantial, although it diminishes as we are with an organization for a longer period of time. During the metamorphosis to a full-fledged member, employees become less dependent on the interpretations of the members of the group and more reliant on their own perceptions and interpretations of reality (McShane & Von Glinow, 2000). As newcomers we cannot be fully aware of the group's expectations or standard operating procedures. The *socialization process* is a time for learning about expectations, politics, people, standard operating procedures, and values that evolve from our interactions, to a great extent, with our immediate group.

Groups are living systems, so as new members are being assimilated the transactional nature of the group means that the other members will need to change by adapting attitudes and behaviors to accommodate the newcomers. Given the increasingly diverse nature of organizations, group survival might well depend on how well the group can accept different individuals and develop strong relationships (Brown-Johnson, 2004; Crabtree, 2004; *New Zealand Herald*, 2006; Zemke, Raines, & Filiczak, 2000). Living systems also have their own self-sustaining features, so the group will also require or influence the newcomer to fit into the existing norms. The amount of group cohesiveness, length of time people have worked together, and number of newcomers entering the group all have an impact on the flexibility of the group and the likelihood that rules can be altered by the new member (see chap. 9). Some adaptation is increasingly necessary. For example, retention of employees is a significant issue in many organizations, with employees staying at a particular job 3.7 years on average. Although the group might attempt to exclude newcomers who are different, the very survival of the group can depend on the capacity to adapt.

As you join an organization you need information regarding "what's going on and how it's done." Nike, who continues to build running shoes that are innovative and appealing to customers, provides a good example (Yang

& Buderi, 1990). The 1990 "Air 180" featured a large urethane window that afforded a 180-degree view of the heel air bag. This was an extension of the Visible Air line, which was introduced in 1987. These shoes sported a tiny window in the heel and allowed Nike to overtake Reebok in running shoes sales of $2.2 billion with profits of $243 million. This research effort was carried out behind a cage-like door guarded by a stuffed gorilla. Why? Because the research team was called APEs—advanced products engineers—who were headed by a "King of the APEs." This team has designed the multisport "cross-trainer" shoe, the "aqua sock" widely used by swimmers, and, for diversity, Batman's boots and the self-tying sneakers that Michael J. Fox wore in the movie *Back to the Future II*. The new product engineers were provided a vast number of cues regarding the team spirit, the sense of uniqueness held by the team, and the sense of humor regarding job titles. All of which underscores the importance of creativity and product development over rules, regulations, and simply getting along. If you join an organized anarchy that, you recall from chapter 7, involves enormous organizations that are beyond our comprehension, the cues provided by your immediate work group will provide you with the information needed to "make sense of it all." Groups offer rites, rituals, routine, and regime to organizational members.

Sense-Making Functions of Small Groups   You were introduced to the sense-making function of symbolic messages (see chap. 7). Because the world of work is largely an interpretative experience, small groups provide a primary sense-making service (Bolman & Deal, 2003). Groups employ sanctions, develop procedures and processes, and establish shared norms. As the chapter on symbolic behavior explained, you cannot know everything about an organization and what you know is filtered and processed through your organizational experiences.

This *socialization* is the way in which newcomers are transformed from outsiders into effective group members. Four influences by groups are worth highlighting (Cohen & Fink, 2001). First, groups offer explanations regarding the nuances behind the events, rules, procedures, and regulations in every organization. As a newcomer, you will need to know who to turn to for specific advice, what rules are "on the books" but not enforced, and what to avoid at all costs. As you are included in these informal networks, the organization begins to make more sense. What cues, messages, and nuances are presented? Consider the next three points.

Second, joining a new organization is stressful and loaded with uncertainties. The work group provides a predictable and stable backdrop for comprehending the processes. On gaining entrance to the creative advertising department, for example, you quickly become aware of how things are done on a daily basis, who you can approach with questions, and which person or persons are in charge. The computer development organizations in Silicon

Valley encourage bureaucracy-busting behavior to encourage creativity. This can lead to strange hours, and apparently bizarre group activities (e.g., Nike). Other organizations that are tied into a more rigid set of behaviors (e.g., banks, government, hospitals) make it clear that specific actions are endorsed and others are prohibited. A fairly obvious example of specific expectations would be prescribed dress standards. Almost all financial institutions, such as banks, expect employees to avoid jeans, cut-offs, and so on because of their expectation that employees will forward a professional image. Once your initial indoctrination with the organization is over, your group ties will increase your understanding of the operating rules and procedures. Your group provides a variety of sources for information that facilitates your own capacity to understand the workplace.

Third, the work-related attitudes of the group provide a set of norms for the newcomer. If breaks always extend an extra 5 minutes or everyone engages in the personal use of a computer or telephone, you are receiving messages regarding how the group feels about the company and the job. The actual job performance of newcomers often is based on modeling the work behaviors and methods of peers. Group members often are aware of their power over the neophyte. Sometimes, "conversations are staged—half consciously—to educate the new employee, and fellow employees volunteer advice about appropriate behavior" (Huber, 1986, p. 159).

Finally, we learn the fundamentals of group membership by modeling ourselves after other members of our work group. Standard operating procedures (SOPs) are almost always different from one organization to another, from the college classroom to a job, and between groups.

Group Cohesiveness

Groups vary greatly in their effectiveness. One characteristic of effective groups is a high level of cohesiveness, which can be defined as *unity of purpose and action*. Many authorities consider this closeness as a primary component of effective groups that should be pursued (*Fortune*, 2006). At the same time, it "is difficult to draw definitive conclusions in this area, but it appears that when the team is well trained, has confidence in its abilities, and is goal-oriented, the effects of cohesion will only serve to strengthen team effectiveness" (Cannon-Bowers, Tannenbaum, Salas, & Volpe, 1995, p. 355).

Unity of purpose is achieved by establishing goals. The expression "every time you aim nowhere, that's where you get" describes one of the reasons groups flounder. Unity of action, or group cohesion, is based on individuals liking each other, the desirability of group membership, and trust. Although we can assign someone to a department, team, or group, unless he or she also values group membership there may be little group cohesion.

A note of caution is required. Merely being committed to the team might not lead to effective performance. More important, "a cohesive team is likely to perform effectively only if its members are committed to the organization within which the team functions" (Cannon-Bowers et al., 1995, p. 355). This makes a great deal of sense. Being committed to other team members establishes a social contract of sorts but it does not mean the team will accomplish its work-related goals. To provide a further understanding, we examine group climate, group talk, group ideology, groupthink revisited, and feedback. Group climate is an excellent place to begin.

Group Climate

How group members feel toward each other and the group process can be gauged by examining the group climate. A highly integrative climate tends to create a high performance group or team. Wheelan (1999) observes: "High performance teams have an open communication structure that allows all members to participate. Individuals are listened to regardless of their age, title, sex, race, ethnicity, profession, or other status characteristics. This enhances productivity because all ideas and suggestions are heard" (p. 42).

Member satisfaction increases to the extent that *leadership style* allows for participation and equal distribution of control across participants. When leaders facilitate the development of shared understandings and interpretations of reality among group members, the climate remains positive. In addition, leaders help to direct the group, encourage full participation, and manage external relationships by removing obstacles to team performance and development (Cummings & Worley, 2005). If we feel that our group respects our viewpoint, clarifies our role in the group, and accepts us, we are likely to find membership a rewarding experience.

Consensus is a process designed to create a decision in which all members of a group agree on the results. The outcome might not be everyone's first choice. But, during the process, everyone has been heard, all relevant ideas have been considered, and everyone is willing to live with the final decision. Although there are no guarantees, extensive research supports the importance of (a) active participation, (b) increased group cohesiveness, (c) managing conflicts by dealing with the issues not the personalities, and (d) communication intended to clarify and share information in achieving consensus. Inherent in the positive use of consensus is the assumption that in successful teams members "have a common goal but bring different knowledge and skills to team subtasks" (Ilgen, Major, Hollenbeck, & Sego, 1995, p. 123).

Group Talk

How do we actually talk in a group? Four approaches, labeled *group talk*, have been identified—problem-solving, role, consciousness-raising, and/or encounter approaches (Cragan & Wright, 1991). Problem-solving and role discussions are basic to team functioning.

Team problem solving and role understanding issues are important for groups and teams. At Lucent Technologies's supply chain networks division, and numerous other companies ranging from Motorola to NASA, a paperplanes program intended to foster team-building, increase intra-office communication, and improve client relations is used. During the session, managers are assigned jobs like wing cutter, gluer, or test pilot. Managers form assembly lines to build the planes and learn in the process how complex the coordination process can be. In addition, the facilitator can change specs at any time forcing teams to learn to adapt to the customer needs instructor ("The Plane Truth," 2001). In addition to seeing the problems associated with any assembly line process where the plans are unclear and the roles not well established, team members also gain insights into the communication issues and the need to develop a common vision and purpose.

Consciousness-raising and encounter approaches might seem to be outside the realm of organizational behavior, but they are used in numerous ways. Management teams use retreats and outdoor problem-solving activities to foster teamwork skills. As team pride works to overcome individual orientations, people become better able to orient themselves to the entire group. Bolman and Deal (2003) argue that managers "can serve a deeper, more powerful, and more durable function when they recognize that team building at its heart is a spiritual undertaking. It is the creation of a community of believers, united by shared faith and shared culture" (p. 44).

Team building is used to create a common symbolic identity. A sense of oneness is formed, which leads to *group fantasies* (Bormann, 1975). A group fantasy puts "in each of its members a feeling he (or she) has entered a new realm of reality—a world of heroes, villains, saints, and enemies—a drama" (Bales, 1970, p. 152). In other words, the same process that leads to a cultural identity discussed earlier (e.g., chaps. 3 & 7) creates a team spirit that helps explain events and guide behavior. Employees may pass on stories of extraordinary efforts that led to great successes as a team. Southwest Airlines, for example, touts the 20 minutes turnaround for its incoming and departing flights as a major component for its success (Freiberg, 1996). This process was developed out of necessity by the Southwest Airlines management team because they were forced to sell one of their four planes during their early years in order to remain in business. They had to maintain all of their air routes and schedules with one less plane and the 20 minutes turnaround accomplished that goal. Now, this crisis-oriented team success story permeates Southwest Airlines' culture.

At other times, fantasies present a we–they explanation for events. As team members, we might relate how management (they) prevented the team (us) from succeeding, providing the essence of a heroes and villains drama. Competition between work units, such as sales and delivery or manufacturing and engineering, provides fodder for the fantasy cannon. Recognizing the potential dangers of negative fantasies on reaching the group's goals can be extremely useful. Positive fantasies offer direction, clarity, and enjoyment as the group works toward being a cohesive unit.

Group Ideology

Group differentiation occurs when there is polarization and stereotyping of the opposition (McShane & Von Glinow, 2000). This tendency of groups to utilize the "other" groups as a rallying point has been observed for years by sociologists. In fact, the fine line between *esprit de corps* and a hardening of the group's perceptions toward other groups has disturbed many leaders of diverse subunits. Groups develop *ideologies*, which are "the beliefs the group holds about the 'structure of action' in the social system and about itself and other groups" (Putnam & Poole, 1987, p. 580). Obviously, when the group members hold a similar ideology, they are more likely to act as a unit. As a means for developing substantive organizational issues such as quality production, customer service, or efficiency, this likeness of mind is clearly useful. To the degree that the process leads to a fortress mentality, subversion of cooperative intergroup behavior, or a we–they perspective (e.g., employee–manager, union–company, student–teacher), it can be counterproductive. Groups can become so absorbed by their own ideology that they begin to make bad decisions.

The Federal Bureau of Investigation (FBI) received unwanted attention when it disclosed that it had withheld more than 3,000 pages of documents from Timothy McVeigh's defense attorneys in the Oklahoma City bombing trial (Johnson, 2001). For many observers, this was the latest in a series of situations where the FBI made decisions using a perspective that depreciated the importance of other groups. These include: Ruby Ridge—an incident wherein an unarmed woman holding a baby was killed and evidence about the incident was withheld; Waco—a standoff ending in massive fire and dozens of deaths; FBI Crime Lab—a flawed scientific experiment which led to inaccurate testimony in numerous cases; Wen Ho Lee—a nuclear scientist who was charged with 59 criminal counts, but the case fell apart leaving only one charge; and Robert Hanssen—a top FBI counterintelligence officer who sold secrets to Russia for a decade ("FBI's Repeat," 2001). We might be tempted to point to incompetence, but a more likely culprit is an overdependence on in-group ideology. Federal prosecutor Ronald Woods concluded, "the problem with the FBI is that they think they know better than prosecutors and judges. That's a mindset that's existed within the FBI for years, and that needs to be changed. It's arrogance" (quoted in Johnson, 2001, p. 3A). Sen. Chuck Grassley, R-Iowa, "blamed the missteps in the Oklahoma City case on a 'cowboy culture' within the bureau" (quoted in Johnson, 2001, p. 3A). Earlier in this text, we discussed groupthink and the FBI examples may have reminded you of the concept. We now examine it once again in light of its influence on groups.

Groupthink, Balkanization, Risky Shift, and Group Polarization

An excessive amount of peer pressure, often combined with a powerful leader, encourages group members to go along to get along. Small, highly cohesive groups can unconsciously undermine their basic mission in order to preserve the cohesive social structure of the group (Aldage & Riggs-Fuller, 1993). Since its initial publication (Janis, 1972), the theory of groupthink has been one of the most widely cited contributions to the study of decision-making. Interpersonal attractiveness and cohesion are positively related to the development of groupthink (Street, 1997). There is less proof that task cohesion, by itself, will create groupthink.

Yahoo!, one of the early success stories on the Internet, suffered from poor decision-making by its top management team. In 2000, they committed "a series of blunders that would downgrade the No. 1 Internet portal from powerhouse to Milquetoast" (Elgin, 2001, p. 115). The top management team failed to respond to a changing economy and the purchase by America Online, Inc. of old-media giant Time Warner, Inc. That deal rearranged "the planets of the media universe—and rock(ed) Yahoo's world" (Elgin, 2001, p. 115). Rather than reconfiguring Yahoo to respond, "consensus management in gridlock" and "corner-office intrigue" controlled the team leading to a paralysis. The "Three Amigos"—the nickname for the top team—"felt invincible and had little incentive to seek talent or advice outside their brain trust" (Elgin, 2001, p. 118). Yahoo's market cap, or the sum value of Yahoo's stocks and bonds that are outstanding, fell from $110 billion in 2000 to $11 billion in 2001.

The potential for disastrous decisions is significant. "Persons individually smart, when put into groups, have arrived at decisions fabulously dumb: Quaker Oats' decision to acquire Snapple, Xerox's decision not to exploit the fax machine, which it was first to market" to name a few (Farnum, 1997, p. 150). On a smaller scale, Our Lady of Elms College in Massachusetts decided to raise $1 million for student financial aid by publishing a cookbook ("School Burned," 1988). You can imagine the deliberations leading up to this decision (e.g., everyone loves our recipes; people are seeking ways to give money to our college). The group's enthusiasm led to the ordering of 100,000 cookbooks, which cost $400,000 to print. They were left with 94,000 copies of the cookbook and an enormous debt. Their inflated expectations of success (e.g., selling 100,000 books for a $1 million profit) combined with the importance of helping students put the group on the road to groupthink. Ironically, they initially had ordered 200,000 but were talked down by the printer.

Likewise, groups often form intragroup rivalries that can lead to feelings of indifference or hostility toward other groups. This behavior is known as *balkanization*. And, like groupthink, balkanization is the enemy of collaboration, innovation, and change. A recent Pricewaterhouse Coopers survey of large, multinational organizations revealed that 90% of them had experienced "moderate" to "a great deal" of change during the past 2 to 3 years—another 90% foresaw continued change for the future of their organizations (McClenahen, 2006). Together, groupthink and balkanization can limit the access to and the consideration of different perspectives within a group or organization which can be devastating in today's culture of change in organizations.

Groupthink can be understood further by looking at how the framing of information during the decision-making process can influence the outcome. *Framing* describes how the information is presented. In a study reported in the *New England Journal of Medicine*, 44% of the people questioned were prepared to accept a risky treatment for lung cancer if told it would give them a 68% chance of surviving. When the same treatment was described as having a 32% chance of dying, only 18% said they would undergo the treatment ("Safety Risk," 1989). Two theories explain what can happen in groups.

The *risky shift phenomenon* argues that groups are more prone to taking a chance than individuals. Given the choice between certain loss and a risky alternative, the vast majority of groups will take the chance (Whyte, 1989). Imagine the group discussions preceding the establishment of a position titled "Manager of Competitive Assessment" (e.g., industrial espionage). Given the immense competition from other firms and the enormous costs of product development, many American corporations now accept, or at least engage in, spying. Yes, we just framed the issue in a manner that makes the spying concept palatable. In fact, the Society of Competitor Intelligence Professionals, a 1,400-member group, is an organization of corporate spies whose sole purpose is helping companies gather information about other company products ("Corporate Snooping," 1990). The Futures Group is a consulting company that helps corporations design, develop, and operate their own intelligence organizations. Futures' vice president added fuel to the fire by concluding, "The Japanese are professionals. They're the ones who started it. They do it almost by second nature" ("Corporate Snooping," 1990, p. 7E). Given "their" sins, what choices do American corporations have but to follow suit? And, while they are at it, they might as well spy on each other (after all, everyone is doing it, so we had better also). Although corporations probably have engaged in spying for a long time, framing the decision by providing a certain loss (e.g., product knowledge, competitive advantage, Japanese threat, plant closing) compared to a viable alternative, practically guarantees many groups will opt for endorsing snooping, sans the midnight break-ins or bugging and the cloaks and daggers.

A different picture is painted by the *group polarization phenomenon theory*. Sometimes groups make less risky decisions. Supported by more than 200 studies, it argues that people can become more extreme in their decisions when they are part of a group because of their own propensities. Gass and Seiter (1991) conclude: "If you are predisposed to making a slightly risky decision, being in a group might cause you to make a riskier decision; if you are predisposed to make a conservative decision, being in a group may cause you to make an even more conservative decision" (p. 137). If the group leans toward risk, and you are already a risk prone individual, you are likely to become even more extreme or willing to act. The same is true for being conservative.

The influence of groups on decision making is positive when the proper prerequisites, training, climate, and processes are in place. Otherwise, there is a possibility for poor decisions because of undue group influence.

Group Norms

The behavioral expectations for group members are called *norms*. Norms are the standards or rules of behavior that provide order, allow understanding of the group's activities, and ensure that we will orient ourselves toward the group's performance. "They are social inventions which help the group to control and regulate its activities, and to express its identity and values" (Gabriel, Fineman, & Sims, 2000, p. 331). We learn "the set of assumptions or expectations by members of a group or organizations concerning what kind of behavior is right or wrong, good or bad, appropriate or inappropriate, allowed or not allowed" (Schein, 1969, p. 59). Norms can range from where people sit to who speaks to dress codes to the behaviors needed to retain a job.

Not all norms apply to every group member with the same intensity. New members, for example, might be expected to be attentive and reserved. In other cases, the group expects the newcomer to go through some hazing in order to prove their willingness to accept the group's standards. Although hazing is well known in college Greek societies, being assigned grunt work—a phrase derived from military service where the menial jobs require only a grunt during acceptance and performance—or completing an assignment nobody wants, are important rites of passage for the newcomers as we join the group.

Types of Norms

Norms are crucial or peripheral. *Crucial norms* help the group survive, and a violation of these will lead to censure. *Peripheral norms*, when violated or ignored, represent more of an indiscretion than a transgression. In prison, a fink (e.g., stoolie, stool pigeon) violates a crucial norm regarding inmate behavior and punishment, when the violation is discovered, is quick and certain. Codes of behavior exist in almost any group and can be articulated with pejorative labels (e.g., teacher's pet, company man, double-dealer, Judas, Brutus, snake in the grass, squealer, cop-out, back-stabber). Jealousy over a new colleague's success probably would suggest that a peripheral norm (e.g., don't rock the boat or reduce other group member's credibility) is close to being violated. Fear that a younger, healthier, or more energetic group member might "break the curve" or "create new work standards" can bring strong group sanctions ranging from statements about the behavior to warnings about the implications of continuing to surpass production quotas or shine too bright as an individual performer. In an organization where everyone is expected to spend long hours working toward the organization's success, not working hard would represent a violation of the crucial norms.

Norms also are expressed explicitly or implicitly understood (Daniels & Spiker, 1991). *Explicit norms* are standards such as policies, and *implicit norms* are learned by observing the group in action. To repeat an earlier observation, these shared expectations arise from the external culture (e.g., organization) and the group itself, and conformity is expected in most cases.

Sanctions   Group members have a large number of actions they can take to alter norm violations by nonconformists. For example, verbal threats, criticisms, and ridicule can be directed at the individual. Gossip and rumors can be spread behind the person's back to discredit him or her. Exclusion from social gatherings (e.g., lunch, after-hour social gatherings) and unfriendliness at work can be used to intimidate the individual. Work tools, memos, personal items, and important records can be misplaced to make life difficult. Although it might seem bizarre to have such activities occur at work, the determining factor is the importance placed on the norm by group members as a survival factor. On the flip side of this picture, the group can take significant actions to reward individuals who conform and support group norms (Cohen & Fink, 2001). How individuals carry out the perceived norms is called *roles.*

Roles

The way we act in a group or team is a role. Whereas norms are expectations regarding behaviors for everyone, roles suggest that members may be expected also to act differently from each other. As Johns (1988) said, "Roles are 'packages' of norms that apply to particular group members" (p. 246). There are two ways of examining roles. The first is a *deterministic* view where roles are assigned to an individual (Offerman & Gowing, 1990). Depending on the group, we may be expected to act as a secretary, chairperson, researcher, or passive participant. These assigned roles are based on normative standards.

Emergent roles occur through the dynamics of the group process. For example, you can be assigned the role of leader, but in many groups the actual leader emerges as the discussion carries forward. One of the complexities of fulfilling a role is the difference between how we perceive the role, how we are expected to act out the role, and how we actually perform, or enact, the role. For example, on the surface the role of student should be fairly straightforward—someone who studies. In reality, the role is enacted in a vast variety of ways.

For many years, group researchers have utilized a set of group roles based on the group task, the group building and maintenance, and individual roles. *Group task behaviors* include initiating, elaborating, coordinating, summarizing, recording, evaluating, and seeking or giving information. If group members focus on encouraging, harmonizing, enhancing communication channels, observing processes, following others, and setting standards, they are using *group maintenance behaviors*. Although both task and maintenance behaviors are needed for a team to succeed, a third category involves *self-oriented behaviors*. These include blocking the group from reaching consensus, being aggressive, withdrawing, dominating, and being a special interest leader. None of these categories are necessarily exclusive, but an appreciation for the variety of individual behaviors in a group allows us to understand the complexity of roles.

Role assumption occurs when you take on the expected behaviors outlined by your team, department, or group. Although a particular role may seem quite simple "on paper," the actual acceptance and acting out of the role can be very difficult. Demographic studies indicate, for example, that today's youth are less willing to accept restrictive roles if the only rationale is that they must "pay their dues" (Zemke et al., 2000). When the expectations are unclear, there is considerable *role ambiguity*. Being told to be assertive, innovative, patient, and a team player would seem to be a call for a set of actions filled with ambiguities and potential conflicts. *Role conflict* occurs when we are faced with incompatible role expectations (McGrath, 1984). New supervisors who have come up through the ranks often find difficulty when they become a supervisor or manager and maintaining their friendships with their new subordinates (former colleagues).

Group Leadership   We devote an entire chapter later in this text to leadership. Groups and teams vary widely in their make-up, purposes, and responsibilities. In some cases, leaders simply direct the work group toward specific goals or tasks. In other cases, leaders back away from the process in order to develop self-directed work groups, which we analyze shortly.

Team leadership makes a difference in team performance (McIntyre & Salas, 1995). To be effective, leaders are expected to "know their stuff," listen to other team members who have special expertise, serve as models of teamwork, provide feedback, and build respect from members (McIntyre & Salas, 1995).

To maximize success, the leader must be able to adapt to the situation (Harris & Sherblom, 2005). Every group, as a living system, is unique because of the differing membership, task, and environment (Bolman & Deal, 2003). Most groups also have a history that establishes expectations regarding the leader's behavior.

Group Development

As living systems, groups develop as the members interact. Based on a broad range of research, a fairly predictable pattern emerges. Fisher (1970) outlined four stages: orientation, conflict, emergence, and reinforcement. Tuckman (1965) offered his own four stages: forming, storming. norming, and

Table 10.1 The Phasic Model of Group Development

Stage/Phase	Description
Orientation/ Forming	During this phase, group members are uncertain about the other members or the actual group process. So, communication tends to be tentative with a great deal of agreeing. Members attempt to clarify by asking questions. Getting to know one another, developing a direction, initiating some types of plans, and obtaining information are important to this phase.
Conflict/ Storming	This is the most complex phase. Members are trying out for various roles, including leadership, and often find they are avoiding the inevitable conflicts over ideas or individual roles. This phase is critical to group and team success because it allows the airing and clarifying of significant issues.
Emergence/ Norming	Group cohesion begins to occur. This phase is where team members begin to understand that "there is no I in team." Members begin to enjoy the team process and maintaining the relationships fought for in the second phase.
Reinforcement/ Performing	At this point, group members emphasize consensus regarding the decision and the group is mobilized to follow through. Solutions and problem solving predominate during this phase.

performing. Later, a fifth phase of adjourning was added (Tuckman, 1977). For both of these models, the process involves four or five stages that occur in sequence. As neat a package as this appears, most groups are likely to cover these steps, but not necessarily in the order found in Table 10.1.

For most organizations, understanding that groups and teams must proceed through some fairly well defined steps is useful. Too often, organizations expect immediate results. In fact, teams must experience all four phases. Few groups, however, will proceed as neatly as we have described. Consequently, the phase or sequence models are often incomplete in describing the complexities involved in group development.

Multiple Sequence Model

Poole (1983) was instrumental in changing the predominate paradigm of group development. Poole's work helps us to understand when and why groups depart from the traditional phases offered by Fisher and Tuckman. As such, Poole (1983) offered a multiple sequence model of group decision development. The model portrays a more complex understanding of group decision making involving activity tracks and breakpoints.

Group activity tracks are at the core of understanding the multiple sequence model. Poole (1983) suggested that, minimally, descriptions of group decision-making involve three activity tracks: task, relationship, and topic. *Task-process activities* are those activities related to task management and decision-making, such as: problem analysis, orientation, group process reflection, and a variety of issues related to the group solution (e.g., guidelines, design, evaluation, and selection). *Relational activities* are those activities related to the management of relationships or social activities related to the group's work. These activities involve four relational issues: work-focused relationships, such as focused work with no criticism and critical work through criticism and repartee; conflict relationships, such as idea opposition and conflict resolution approaches; integration issues; and ambiguity issues related to relationships. *Topical activities* represent the final track in Poole's model. These activities are related to specific issues and deliberations related to the group's discussion. As such, these activities will vary from group to group.

The activity tracks are useful in distinguishing the multiple sequence model from the phasic model. When the activity tracks develop in a coordinated manner, the phases identified by Fisher and Tuckman are easily identified. But, when task and relational activities evolve at different times, the phasic model is inadequate at describing such behavior.

Breakpoints are important transitions in the development process that help us to understand how groups evolve beyond the smooth transitions implied by the phasic model. Breakpoints may take the form of *delays*, due to a group's tendency to recycle through an issue of activity; *disruptions*, in the form of conflicts or group failure; and other *normal breakpoints*, such as topic shifts or meeting adjournment. When breakpoints occur in all three tracks at the same time, the phasic model holds true. When a breakpoint interrupts only one of the tracks, however, the group may spend more time on that activity than the others; indicating that the three tracks may operate independently.

Punctuated Equilibrium Model

Gersick (1988, 1989, 1990), drawing on concepts from the field of natural history, proposed a model of group development known as *punctuated equilibrium*. This model has two phases separated by a transition point. The first phase is characterized by stable but inertial movement until the midpoint of the group's lifespan. Halfway between the group's first meeting and the group's official deadline for task completion, a major transition occurs. This transition leads to the second phase wherein group members work together in new and accelerated ways to accomplish the group's goals.

The punctuated equilibrium model suggests that regardless of the amount of time a group has to accomplish its task, group members will pace themselves until the midpoint period. On recognizing that they are at midpoint, group members reevaluate their roles and task behaviors for a more coordinated and urgent effort toward goal achievement.

Advantages

There is a large number of advantages to using groups (Applebaum & Batt, 1993; Harris & Sherblom, 2005; Lewis, 1998; Katzenback & Smith, 1993). First, they provide a broader perspective and input regarding issues. As such, groups generate more and better solutions when synergy is in action. The diversity of opinion and the possibility of focusing the group's energy on a particular issue can lead to excellent results. For a manager or supervisor, the group can allow insights not available through interpersonal discussions.

A second advantage, for the leader, is the work group learns more about the issues behind the decision-making process, which should enhance understanding. Even when making an excellent decision, managers can leave subordinates feeling confused or resistant simply because the rationale is not clear.

Making good decisions is a third advantage. Groups allow for a testing of a large number of options. Increased creativity can occur, along with some excellent "piggy-backing" by group members on ideas already formulated by the organization and the manager.

Fourth, groups create a scenario for collaboration and commitment. Whether it be a new operating procedure, different working hours, or altered dress codes, it pays to let the group examine the needs and come up with a solution. This group-generated solution adds information during planning, and credence to the solution meaning a greater likelihood of group enforcement (remember our discussion on sanctions at the beginning of this chapter). For the other organizational members, a peer group mechanism for explaining the rules has been developed rather than a decision handed down from management.

Increased morale is a fifth reason for using groups. Meeting your colleagues in a group setting can help lower interpersonal barriers, enhance team spirit, and provide for common goals. Groups also allow you the opportunity to develop networks of people to call on at different times for other purposes.

Finally, groups allow individuals a chance to demonstrate personal value to the organization. Assuming you are making contributions to the meeting, a variety of individuals will be able to form an impression regarding your abilities and talents.

Disadvantages

Not all groups work well. Increasingly, group work is a mainstay of our education system. For most of us, some of the experiences are positive and others we would prefer to avoid. Evidence indicates that the biggest problems are a lack of training in how to use groups and the failure to allow adequate implementation time in order to work through the group process leading to significant problems (Katzenback & Smith, 1993; Lewis, 1998).

There are additional impediments. First, corporate culture and management style set the tone. When the company's first priority is "Never make a mistake," groups become an arena for placing blame. Who would openly commit organizational suicide by admitting that they were responsible for the recent losses because of poor judgment, cost overruns, or stupidity? Groups can allow individuals to spread the blame if something goes wrong. "This mind-set comes partly from having people tell us that the world is highly competitive, even cutthroat. It's a dog-eat-dog world, we're told, in which nice guys finish last. So when we are asked to cooperate in a team, this runs counter to everything we have been taught to do to survive in this world" (Lewis, 1998, p. 73).

Second, successful groups consume an enormous amount of time. Taking the time away from other activities is fine as long as the group is productive. Quick decisions rarely justify the use of groups unless "signing off" (e.g., covering one's posterior, forcing agreement, requiring public acceptance) is desired. Organizations tend to want answers rather than respecting the importance of time in developing a successful group process. So, participants rush to the solution.

You are already familiar with the third problem, the possibility of groupthink or balkanization. Overly homogeneous groups will avoid healthy conflicts, or intergroup rivalries flourish, which diminishes the possibility for a strong solution to many problems.

Finally, groups require excellent planning, leadership, and facilitating skills, which some managers do not have. Committing an organization to extensive training in effective behaviors is an obvious solution. But, many managers do not see the need.

These five advantages and four disadvantages to groups provide you with some insights into the group process. Table 10.2 provides you with a comparison of effective and ineffective groups on a variety of characteristics. This summary places much of the preceding analysis in perspective. The dramatic differences between the two types reflect, in a large part, the changes occurring in the more successful organizations in terms of structure, format, individual development, and innovation.

Small groups, when used correctly, are extremely important. Although they cannot resolve the limitations imposed by an organization's culture, they do provide significant advantages. Even the stiffest, most formalized, leader-controlled group can include employees in an organizational activity. The remainder of this chapter is spent examining the concept of employee involvement, the use of parallel structures, and semiautonomous work units.

Employee Involvement

You probably have reached the conclusion, by this point in your analysis of organizational communication, that informing and involving individuals in the organization's ongoing activities is vital. All employee involvement (EI)

Table 10.2 Comparison of Effective and Ineffective Groups

Effective Groups	Ineffective Groups
Goals are clarified and changed to that the best possible match between individual goals and the group's goals may be achieved; goals are cooperatively structured.	Members accept **imposed goals**; goals create internal competition.
Communication is **two-way**, and the open and accurate expression of both ideas and feelings is emphasized.	Communication is **one-way** and only ideas are expressed; feelings are suppressed or ignored.
Participation and leadership are **distributed** among all group members; goal accomplishment, internal maintenance, and developmental change are underscored.	Leadership is **delegated based on authority**; membership participation is unequal, with high-authority members dominating; only goal accomplishment is emphasized.
Ability and information determine **influence and power**; contracts/agreements are built to make sure individual goals and needs are fulfilled; **power is shared**.	Position determines influence and power; power is concentrated in the authority positions; **obedience** to authority is the rule.
Controversy and conflict are seen as a **positive** key to members' involvement, the quality and originality of decisions, and the continuance of the group is a good working condition.	Controversy and conflict are **ignored, denied**, avoided, or suppressed.
Decision-making procedures are matched with the situation; different methods are used at different times; **consensus** is sought for important decisions; involvement and group discussions are encouraged.	Decisions are always **made by the highest authority**; there is little group discussion; members' involvement is minimal.
Interpersonal, group, and intergroup **behavior** are stressed; cohesion is advanced through high levels of inclusion, affection, acceptance, support, and trust. **Individuality** is endorsed.	The **functions** performed by members are emphasized; cohesion is ignored and members are controlled by force. Rigid **conformity** is promoted.
Problem-solving competence is **high**.	Problem-solving competence is **low**.
Members **evaluate** the effectiveness of the group and decide how to improve its functioning; goal accomplishment, internal maintenance, and development are all considered important.	The **highest authority** evaluates the group's effectiveness and decides how goal accomplishment may be improved; internal maintenance and development are ignored as much as possible; stability is affirmed.
Interpersonal effectiveness, self-actualization, and **innovation** are encouraged.	"**Organizational persons**" who desire order, **stability**, and structure are encouraged.

programs are efforts to include employees in the information gathering, decision-making, and/or implementation stages (Moorehead & Griffin, 1998). These efforts are designed to create and enhance high performance (Applebaum & Batt, 1993). In successful organizations, teams are used to achieve greater creativity, improve quality, and increase employee involvement (Abbott, 1990; Deetz, Tracy, & Simpson, 2000). As a leader, manager, or group member, you will have to make some important decisions regarding the techniques you employ when involving subordinates, colleagues, and superiors. Actively involving employees in an organization is a vital component in any developmental effort (Applebaum & Batt, 1993; Lewis, 1998; Manz & Sims, 1993). EI programs enlist various degrees of participation in the management process ranging from making suggestions to semiautonomous work units.

Scope of Employee Involvement Programs

These programs already exist in the majority of organizations. Most U.S. firms report one or more forms of EI, but many are approaches (such as a suggestion box or quality circle) that do not fundamentally change the level of decision-making to include the lower levels (Bolman & Deal, 2003, p. 150). The General Accounting Office categorized EI programs ranging from suggestion systems, which have the lowest amount of active employee participation, to self-autonomous work units (GAO, 1989). Others include labor-management committees, quality circles, quality of work-life programs, task forces, incentive plans, and employee communication programs. Sixty-eight percent of these companies use self-managed or high-performance teams (Dumaine, 1994). The EI formats most used, such as suggestion systems, are the least effective based on the GAO study.

There are dramatic examples of successful teamwork (e.g., FedEx, GE Appliance, Kodak, Eli Lilly, Xerox, Corning, Motorola, Ritz-Carlton Hotels, Marriott, Wal-Mart, Nordstroms), but only 10% of workers are in *high-performance* teams (Dumaine, 1994; Fortune, 2006).

At any one time, Federal Express has more than 1,000 quality action teams (QATs) working on problem solving (Golightly, 1993). QATs are 4- to 10-member problem-solving teams, often comprised of both management and hourly employees, who identify problems, pinpoint root causes, develop and implement action plans, and track the effectiveness of solutions.

Teams and Teamwork

Teams are ongoing, coordinated groups of individuals working together even when they are not in constant contact. In organizations, the term is used loosely, as you can see in Table 10.3. Groups put together to solve a specific problem are often labeled *teams*, but in most instances organizational teams are characterized by continuous working relationships.

Table 10.3 Types Of Teams

Work groups	Involves the normal workflow.
	Individuals who normally interact in completing tasks.
Project work teams	Individuals from one or more functional areas.
	Selection based on background and expertise.
	Solve a specific problem or set of problems and then disband.
	Management assigns team members and tasks
	Usually involves weekly or biweekly problem-solving sessions.
Improvement teams	Recommends changes in organizational process.
	Created for specific problems.
	Disband once resolved.
High-involvement work team performance	Manager/supervisor still present.
	Manager/supervisor handles traditional tasks such as scheduling, reviews, discipline, coordination with other departments, administrative duties, attending management meetings.
	Team members begin to learn one another's jobs.
	Problem-solving initiative is shifted to team members.
	Conflict management is shifted to team members.
Self-directed work teams	Members are multiskilled and flexible.
	Former manager/supervisor focuses on planning, product development, increasing market share.
	Team members schedule work, perform appraisals, coordinate with other departments, make job assignments, select new members, monitor equipment and process, attend management meetings.
	Peer reviews, hiring and firing, interacting with external customers, preparing budgets, handling disciplinary situations, and operating as a business unit become team responsibilities.
	Former manager/supervisor becomes a coach. They are multiskilled and flexible.
Integrating teams	Coordinate work across departments and the organization.
	Often focus on shared issues (technology, customer).

Importance of Teams

The importance of teams and teamwork is obvious to anyone working with organizations (Applebaum & Batt, 1993; McShane & Von Glinow, 2000). Likewise, "the importance of team building is well established, and its high use is expected to continue in the coming years" (Cummings & Worley, 2005, p. 230). Examples of the power of teamwork to assist in transforming organizations are provided in practically any discussion of renewal and change (Dalziel & Schoonover, 1988; Nora, Rogers, & Stramy, 1986; Wellins, Byham, & Wilson, 1991). Team-building represents the most widely used form of organizational development because it offers a systematic method for improving the interpersonal and task aspects of regular work groups. As Naisbitt and Aburdene (1985) put it, "Fast, flexible, loaded with talent, the small team model is the most popular and widespread alternative to bureaucratic organization" (p. 38). Being involved in the initiation of ideas and processes creates understanding, shared vision, a collaboratively developed team strategy, and buy-in to the final plan (Lewis, 1998). As manufacturing and service technologies continue to develop—for example, just-in-time inventory systems, lean manufacturing, robotics, and service quality concepts—there is increasing pressure on organizations to implement team-based work designs" (Cummings & Worley, 2005, p. 230). "In high pressure workplaces, such as nuclear plants, aircraft cockpits, or the military, teamwork is essential to survival" (Appleby & Davis, 2001, p. B2). Medical teams are now seen as important additions to successful hospital treatment. In many hospitals "medical decisions are often dictated by phone or scribbled into charts as doctors dash to and fro. Yet in an ICU (intensive care unit), poor communication can be deadly" (Appleby & Davis, 2001, p. 1B). The Suburban Hospital in Bethesda, Maryland, "credits team care with reducing errors, shortening the amount of time patients spend in its 12-bed ICU, and improving communication between families and medical staff" (Appleby & Davis, 2001, p. 1B).

For our purposes, teams are divided into groups seeking solutions to particular problems (e.g., task forces, specialized work groups, quality circles), and the semi-autonomous, self-directed, or *self-managing work teams* (SMWT). Although both approaches represent important attempts to involve employees in the problem identification and solution processes, the SMWT encompasses participative management.

We cover four issues regarding teams. First, the role of problem-solving groups as parallel organizational structures is examined. Quality circles provide us a useful example of the successes and limitations of parallel problem-solving groups. Second, three inherent limitations to the use of parallel problem-solving groups are provided. Third, we examine the successes of SMWT. Fourth, the concepts behind the SMWT are outlined.

Problem-Solving Groups

Parallel organizational structures, such quality circles, teams, labor-management cooperation committees, and other issue-specific employee participation groups, are commonly utilized approaches for increasing EI. These groups are different, however, from the ongoing informal groups or your department, office, team, or crew membership. Parallel groups are assigned the tasks of investigating and providing solutions to issues and problems. However, the ultimate decision on implementation remains with another part of the organization (e.g., boss, committee, other departments). They are given the *responsibility without the authority*. To clarify this point, we examine quality circles.

Quality Circles   In the 21st century, quality is an assumed value, a driving force for competitive advantage, and often appears as part of an organization's mission. EI is an "integral part of quality management because quality is the responsibility of all employees in everything they do" (McShane & Von Glinow, 2000, p. 321). This was not always so.

In the 1980s, American businesses were stung by the quality gaps between their products and those produced by the Japanese. In searching for an answer, organizations focused on the Japanese use of *quality circles* (QC). American businesses rushed to adopt QC approaches, with 80% of the Fortune 500 companies having some type of QC and 44% of all companies with more than 500 employees using QC (Dumaine, 1994; Lawler & Mohrman, 1985).

QC provide us with a good opening for our discussion of parallel approaches. QC are "voluntary groups of employees who work on similar tasks or share some area of responsibility, and who agree to meet on a regular basis to discuss—and perhaps solve—key problems related to their work" (Baron, 1983, p. 558). The groups have 6 to 12 members who focus on specific issues to resolve a quality problem. Usually they meet once a week to analyze these work-related problems and to propose solutions to them. Typically, a QC has little or no authority to spend organizational resources and no direct control over the acceptance or implementation of the solution. Most QC are limited to making an analysis and providing recommendations for improvement to management.

There are numerous documented examples of QC successes (Johns, 1988), especially in specific quality areas, and in the general area of morale building (Baron, 1983). A sample of the Fortune 1,000 companies indicated that 68% of the companies had some form of QC (Jacobs, 1982; Marks, 1986). These companies reported a 69% success in productivity improvement and a 72% success in quality improvement (*Employee Involvement in America*, 1989).

This rush also led to a failure rate "in more than 60% of the American organizations in which they have been tried" (Marks, 1986, p. 38). Many organizations abandoned their QC program within a year (DuBrin, Ireland, & Williams, 1989). This lack of success can be attributed to a variety of causes. For example, a demand for quick answers, union objections, time away from the job by employees, unrealistic expectations, threat of change, inadequate QC participant training, or the misuse of QC for solving certain problems doomed many of the efforts. Managers were not adequately trained in how to accept and utilize the QC answers (Karp, 1983; Marks, 1986). In addition, consulting firms seem to have marketed QC effectively without actually adapting the concept to specific organizational needs (Wood, Hull, & Azumi, 1983). In addition to this list of reasons, there are inherent limitations to parallel problem-solving team building efforts.

Limitations to Team-Building Efforts

As organizations attempt to capture the potential power of EI, parallel efforts will encounter three very specific problems. These are individual rewards, inappropriate management style, and segmentalism (Kanter, 1983). Because these barriers can be countered by SMWT, they warrant further analysis.

Individual Rewards

Traditionally, organizations have rewarded the best customer service provider, the employee with perfect attendance, or the highest producer in sales (Gabriel et al., 2000). Individuals, departments, shifts, or divisions are pitted against each other in various forms of internal competition where success is defined as being superior to another component of the organization (e.g., maintenance vs. production, 1st shift vs. 2nd shift, East Coast sales vs. South). Our educational system is replete with an emphasis on individual rewards ranging from grades to class ranking to recognition of other individual achievements.

In addition, competition seems to be part of our culture. Neuborne (1997), when considering the impediments to teams makes the following observation. "People in the United States are individualistic. We like competition—individual competition. ... The idea of interdependence is not part of our culture" (p. 2B).

This reliance on individual rewards is counterproductive to team-building (Crocker, Charney, & Chui, 1984; "Work Incentives," 1994). Because there is little reason to work with the team, individuals tend to focus on WIIFM (What's in it for me?). Teams begin to experience intrateam conflict over perceived scarce resources such as who will be the leader, what assignments will be given to different individuals, and what rewards can be expected (Lefton, 1988). In a recent survey by the Hay Group, only 41% of the companies are satisfied with the method for paying teams (Neuborne, 1997). "Employees are stuck with an old-fashioned pay scale that was set up to reward hierarchy. ... About 30% of team failures are based on the lack of a team-based salary structure (Neuborne, 1997, p. 2B). In a nutshell, looking out for number one is an impediment to many team-building efforts.

Inappropriate Management Style

Even when supervisors and managers believe in team efforts, they may not be prepared to undertake the necessary actions. This is true for two reasons.

Loss of Power   Many organizations emphasize the importance of titles, status, and job position. Managers and supervisors can view employee involvement in the decision-making process as a threat to their own power and authority

(Manz & Sims, 1998; Meyer & Stott, 1985). This perceived loss of power often drove first line supervisors to resist QC and team efforts (Klein, 1984). One study, based on interviews, small group meetings, and reviews of corporate information, concludes that current corporate bureaucracies establish the counterproductive norms of good management behavior (defined as behavior leading to advancement and job security), which include ignoring the long term, avoiding responsibility, concentrating on appearances rather than reality, hypocrisy, and slavish acceptance of current dogma (Jackall, 1983).

Managing versus Leading Later in this text, we discuss leadership at length. Research into effective leadership draws several differences between managing and leading. Generally, managers do things right, act as strategists, are commanders, and function as architects of the work place system. Leaders do the right things, act as visionaries, move from commanders to storytellers, and abandon being an architect in order to be a change agent (Albrecht, 1994; Bennis, 1994; Blank, 1995; Katzenback et al., 1998). Managing is required to plan, budget, organize, and control. Overuse of these managerial tools tends to sabotage EI programs. Leaders empower individuals and teams by strengthening the control individuals and groups have throughout the decision-making process.

Instead of being the boss, reward dispenser, and coordinator, managers and supervisors become liaisons, linking pins, and facilitators. Without proper training, managers and supervisors will conduct business as usual rather than deal with the uncertainties inherent in employee involvement through teams.

Segmentalism Breaking an organization into separate units with their own budgets and design, leads to *segmentalism*, which is the tendency of units to be indifferent to, or actually compete with each other in order to protect and expand their turf. According to Egan (1988), "Isolationism and empire-building instead of system enhancing integration of the subunits of a corporation or institution constitute one of the main forms of corporate irrationality" (p. 146). Building empires, guarding turf, and preventing loss of control are powerful deterrents to effective team building (Kanter, 1983). What manager would willingly assign a subordinate to a cross-disciplinary team when someone else might claim the rewards?

In organizations, managers control the allocation of resources. If teams are formed without considering these three inherent limitations, the process will be less than a great success. Parallel teams, including QC, do help involve employees, enhance morale, and gather excellent information. In addition, individuals learn how to work with others more effectively.

Choosing the Best Fit

Our QC analysis introduced the concept that the *right type of team must be used for the right job*. Texas Instruments, considered a forerunner in the use of teams, has only 5% of its workforce in self-directed teams. The remaining 95% are members of project teams that can last as little as two weeks. Even this limited move to teams "improved annual revenue per employee from $142,000 to $227,000 in two years" (Neuborne, 1997, p. 2B). When it comes to teams, one size does not fit all.

At the same time, the full potential of EI cannot be realized in teams that have limited power in problem-solving or taking actions. Table 10.4 shows the differences between traditional management, parallel structures, and SMWT.

Bud Sutter, President of Employees Claim Management, paints an interesting picture in describing the difference between a traditional approach to managing and an increased use of employee involvement. Imagine two types of boat races. In one, you are a crewmember of a sculling team. These are the long, thin, lightweight boats used by various universities, educational institutions, and clubs. The primary skills are rowing in unison following the direction of the team leader. Continuity is the key as all the oars—in the successful boats—move as one. In the other, you are part of a sailing crew competing in a race in high winds. In this case, there is chaos as each member completes their work and helps the other members at a moment's notice. The captain cannot possibly direct each individual so excellent cross-training, teamwork, individual responsibility, and skill development are needed prior to the event. Discontinuity is the norm because the upcoming demands are unpredictable. For employees, Sutter argues, past organizations have focused on the first type of team—regimented, predictable, and controlled. Increasing EI requires us to become comfortable with the second format. Part of the challenge is to develop both employees and managers toward a new mindset that allows increased responsibility to be placed on the team.

Self-Managing Work Teams

SMWT are self-regulating. This independence from outside authority represents a significant movement from problem-solving groups to a more participative management system (Torres & Spiegel, 1990). After sufficient training and experience, SMWT members *work together as one to complete a total job*. As the teams develop, they increase the group's knowledge and understanding and gradually take shared responsibility for planning, organizing, decision-making, controlling, scheduling, and goal-setting. SMWT work toward continuous improvement in the performance of their work unit. These high performance teams can increase productivity, improve quality, reduce conflict, reduce turnover and absenteeism, realize cost savings of 30% to 70%, increase innovation, and enhance employee quality of work life (Boyett & Boyett,

Table 10.4 Three Employee Involvement Stages

From ...

(1) Manager
Solves
Problems

   To ...

   (2) Employees Help
   Identify and Solve
   Problems

      To ...

      (3) Problem-Solving
      Part of Employees'
      Job—Can Take
      Action

In Traditional Organizations
Directed, Top-down

Parallel Teams
Quality Circles
Task Forces

Self-Managing
Work Teams
(SMWT)

1998; Manz & Sims, 1993). Edy's Grand Ice Cream in Fort Wayne, Indiana, embarked on the SMWT process and over 5 years saw an 83% reduction in scrap, 57% increase in productivity, and 39% drop in cost (Woods, 1997). Although the anecdotal evidence for team effectiveness is overwhelming, the Texas Center for Productivity and Quality of Work Life conducted a "most revealing scientific study of the bottom-line effect of teams." This "study is one of the first rigorous scientific efforts that shows the clear financial effect of the team approach in dozens of organizations" (Manz & Sims, 2000, p. 189).

Successfully introducing and implementing SMWT requires selection, training, and direction for everyone involved from the team members to the former supervisors, now coaches and facilitators and management.

Concepts Underpinning Self-Managing Work Teams

SMWT represent a structural and procedural change in traditional organizational operations (Rees, 1991; Torres & Spiegel, 1990). Rather than operating as a parallel structure, the problem-solving group becomes a fundamental work unit. The supervisor and employees work together as one to complete a total job. With experience and training, team members gradually take shared responsibility for planning, organizing, decision-making, controlling, scheduling, goal setting, and in general, regulating continuous improvement in the performance of their work unit. For example, in the past a typical employee response to a production problem in a traditional organization would be to sit down and wait for a foreman, supervisor, or manager. In SMWT, employees take the responsibility to solve the problem. They do so because their knowledge, involvement, power, and responsibilities are expanded. Table 10.5 outlines the differences between traditional, transitional, and self-directed organizations.

Traditional Organizational Approaches

The goal is to move *from control* by management *to commitment* by the team members. Earlier in this text (see chaps. 1 and 3) we discussed the evolving nature of organizations. As a short refresher, in the traditional orientation, controls are imposed to increase efficiency that usually involves seven elements. In sum, it

1. separates planning from implementing;
2. uses standards for minimum acceptance performance;
3. applies a management structure based on specialization and top-down control;
4. has management prerogatives and authority;
5. establishes status symbols for rank and importance;
6. provides compensation based on a fair day's pay for a fair day's work;

Table 10.5 Evolution of Employee Involvement

Traditional	Transition	Semiautonomous
"Not my job"; see my supervisor; control by management	Supervisor with some team participation; employee input sought	Each team's job is the daily work; internal control by team
Solve problems based on supervisor's guidance and instructions	Investigate problems; suggest solutions	Accurately predict problems and develop workable controls for them
Few, well-trained specialists	Some people trained	All people trained
Work to meet predetermined standards; external control	Problem-solving; no power to implement	Continuous improvement based on team's own analysis
Narrow-based jobs	Some team activity	Broad-based jobs
Task focus	Function focus	Business focus
Little information given to employees	Limited information given to problem-solving groups	Full information
Specialized functions	Specific problem focus	Integrated functions
Single-skilled jobs	Focus on production, morale, or quality issue	Multiskilled jobs
Performed by supervisor	Controlled and judged by superiors	Performed by team

7. encourages an adversarial relationship between worker and employer or management and union.

Moving from traditional management to SMWT often requires a transition through the use of problem-solving groups (e.g., project teams, QC), as was discussed earlier. During this phase, management style must shift toward increased EI. Because old habits die hard a problem-solving group can be used to set the stage for the expanded use of EI through SMWT.

Characteristics of the SMWT

Commitment by employees to higher performance is the key ingredient in the success of the SMWT. Eight characteristics make the SMWT different. They are:

1. broader, more flexible job design—broad-based jobs;
2. planning and implementation combined in one unit—increased autonomy and integration;
3. ambitious performance expectations replacing work standards—self-management;

4. compensation given for learning and teamwork—pay for knowledge and performance;
5. strong employee/team member voice—greater involvement;
6. union–management or employee–organization relations tending toward mutuality;
7. employee assurances of a secure future;
8. leaner, more flexible management flat structure.

In sum, a team is not just a group. Although problem-solving groups are important, a team shares common boundaries, interdependent tasks, articulated purpose, and understood, owned goals. In addition, SMWT have a greater likelihood of overcoming the three barriers faced by many problem-solving groups.

SMWT and the Traditional Barriers to Team-Building

First, SMWT help overcome the impact of individualized rewards because SMWT are designed to create member interaction and *interdependence*. As a team unit, rewards are given based on the group success not individual achievement. Rather than viewing colleagues as competitors for scarce resources, the team learns that working together can maximize success. SMWT provide for group identification and increased job satisfaction. Task excellence is achieved because members identify with the issues and the solutions. Because they design the solution, individual team members feel a greater obligation to guarantee successful implementation (Applebaum & Batt, 1993; Katzenbach & Smith, 1993; Wellins et al., 1991). Migrating geese face enormous obstacles. A popular handout in team training sessions, shown in Table 10.6, explains the key team techniques used by geese and relates their actions to effective team behaviors.

Second, the role of managers and supervisors is dramatically different in SMWT. In traditional organizations, the manager has the decision-making power, the information, the rewards, and in many cases, the expertise. The impact of this approach already has been discussed. The manager tells people what to do and becomes an administrator rather than a leader. In SMWT, shared responsibility and control take the place of the traditional manager carrying the responsibilities and burdens of managing performance alone. The primary role of the manager is that of a coach. This coaching role includes setting high standards, forwarding all necessary information and knowledge, working with the team members, acting as a liaison with other parts of the organization, being the team's champion, obtaining resources, delegating responsibility, and inspiring increased collaborate efforts. The SMWT leader constantly asks: "How can each problem be solved in a way that further develops my subordinates'/team members' commitment and capabilities?" This process includes empowering others, moving decisions to the proper lev-

Table 10.6 Teamwork Lessons from Geese

- As each goose flaps it wings, it creates an uplift for others behind. There is 71% more flying range in a V formation than there is flying alone.
  Lesson: People who share a common direction and sense of purpose can get
  there quicker.
- Whenever a goose flies out of formation, it quickly feels the drag and tries to get back into position.
  Lesson: It's harder to do some things alone than together.
- When the lead goose gets tired, it rotates back into the formation and another goose flies at the head.
  Lesson: Shared leadership and interdependence give us each a chance to lead as well as opportunities to rest.
- The geese in formation honk from behind to encourage those in front to keep up their speed.
  Lesson: We need to make sure our "honking" is encouraging and not discouraging.
- When a goose gets sick or wounded and falls, two geese fall out and stay with it until it revives or dies. Then they catch up or join another flock.
  Lesson: Stand by your colleagues in difficult times as well as in good.

els, providing a vision and communicating it, and building trust and openness. These leaders must be comfortable with resolving conflicts, removing fear from the workplace, dealing with unacceptable behavior, creating an environment where the team takes initiatives and chances, providing information, and not rushing for results (Hultman, 1998).

Third, SMWT overcome segmentalism. Because the team and the former manager are now interested in problem solving, they learn to look beyond their limited area of responsibility. Collaboration with other units is critical to minimizing or resolving most problems. With the former manager as a liaison, champion, and resource obtainer, the team can concentrate on the issues at hand such as quality, customer satisfaction, safety, or production.

Finally, the appropriate introduction of SMWT includes adequate training. Given the tendency for people to look out for number one, this is no small task. Table 10.7 provides a summary of the skills and knowledge needed to make any self-directed unit succeed. This list also provides you with a useful measure on how successful almost any team effort will be. Although all the categories might not apply, the general thrust regarding the critical factors and skills for team success have been developed combining years of group and team research.

Table 10.7 Critical Factors/Skills for Successful Teams

1. **Communication**
   Listening
   Face-to-face communication
   Diverse people and viewpoints for creative synergy
   Removal of we/them perspectives to open up boundaries
   Trust
   Consulting with others
   Ability to influence other members

2. **Collaboration**
   Input from others
   Removal of tunnel vision
   Shared leadership, goals, vision, rewards, responsibility, skills, information, enthusiasm, and mental framework

3. **Conflict**
   Explicit conflict to clarify misunderstandings
   Used to enhance relationships
   Must be managed well
   Assertiveness

4. **Customer satisfaction**
   Everyone team deals with can be a customer
   Ask customers what they want and do it
   Accept customers' priorities, not team's

5. **Equality**
   Power differentials must be reduced or eliminated
   Status differences must be negotiated or downplayed
   An egalitarian philosophy must prevail

6. **Training and development**
   Must be continuous learning
   Time and experience working together is needed
   Training allows focus on critical skills

7. **Shared vision**
   Team members have common understandings
   Compatible views of the internal and external environments

8. **Feedback and monitoring**
   Team members provide task-clarifying feedback
   Constructive feedback regarding performance, errors, and improvement

(continued)

Table 10.7 (continued) Critical Factors/Skills for Successful Teams

---

9. **Decision making**
   Problem solving
   Planning
   Gather, share, and use information effectively
   Shared resources
10. **Leadership**
    Coordinate activities
    Assess performance and correct if necessary
    Focus on mutual goals and interests
    Deal with conflict
    Remove or control cliques
    Eliminate fear
    Worry about process, not just results
    Share information

Note: Adapted from Beyerlein (1993), Cannon-Bowers et al. (1995), Dumaine (1994), and Hultman (1998).

The Benefits and Costs of SMWT

A review of the various studies of SMWT reveals an impressive array of success stories. When introduced and supported well, SMWT: (1) improve work methods and procedures, (2) increase productivity, (3) increase staffing flexibility; (4) help attract and retain employees, (5) enhance employee quality of life, (6) reduce conflict, (7) enhance the quality of decision making, (8) increase innovation, (9) realize cost savings from 30% to 70%, (10) improve product or service quality, (11) foster innovation, and (12) reduce the need for a large supervisory staff (Boyett & Boyett, 1998; Wellins et al., 1991; Woodyard, 2001).

SMWT set the production goals, which tend to be higher. Feedback is employed effectively to improve performance. Cross-training enhances the ability of team members to help out and replace each other. The SMWT do their own set-up, thereby eliminating the need for supervisory assistance.

If this sounds too good to be true, the various analyses of SMWT also highlight some significant impediments. If SMWT programs are to be implemented successfully, these factors must be considered carefully.

Five *costs* occurring in many programs are: (1) increased training costs, including the use of staff or outside consultants to facilitate the implementation; (2) unmet expectations for organizational change; (3) conflicts between participants and nonparticipants in the SMWT process can occur if only a few teams are formed; (4) time lost in team meetings and slower decisions as teams learn to use a consensus approach; and (5) resistance to the change by some staff support groups.

There are seven *pitfalls* in these programs. They are: (1) insufficient or too late training for the teams, (2) management too impatient for results, (3) failure to acknowledge that people will test the system, (4) trying to implement when the technology for a particular change is insufficiently known, (5) inadequate time allowed for the experience to gel before it is evaluated, (6) inappropriate boundaries chosen for team membership or responsibilities, and (7) a corporate culture radically counter to the self-managing team philosophy.

SMWT require a substantial investment in time and forethought in order to be successful. A large number of traditional assumptions concerning organizational structure must be challenged and changed. Implementation can be difficult, but the successes of SMWT make this approach to EI and organizational transformation exciting and important.

Placing EI and SMWT in Perspective

EI programs provide a significant means for involving employees in the various stages of decision making. They represent a fundamental awareness that individuals are valued assets. Given the current pressure on organizations to increase competitiveness and transform into more productive entities, EI's more successful approaches would seem to be required.

Faced with increasing costs, uncertainty, complexity, and the pace of change, many organizations have turned to teamwork, and team-building as a solution. Because teamwork represents one of the best means of EI, efforts in this direction are extremely useful. There is a difference between creating parallel problem-solving structures and empowering a team by making it self-managing.

You will be asked, at many points in your organizational career(s), to solve problems, enhance teamwork, and use groups effectively. We have risked belaboring our discussion of teams and semiautonomous work units to explain the actual impediments and the rewards you should consider as you organize the communication processes in your groups.

In this section, we have discussed five issues. First, the role of problem-solving groups as parallel organizational structures was presented using QC as an example. The successes and limitations of parallel problem-solving groups, as represented by QC, offer insights into the use of teams. Second, three inherent limitations to the use of parallel problem-solving groups suggested a need for an alternative. When well-trained, teams work. The most successful examples are SWMT. Because SMWT are a significant structural and psychological change, the basic concepts behind SMWT were outlined.

Too often, organizations have rewarded values such as "If it ain't broke, don't fix it." The less effective EI programs tend to be superficial and lack credibility with employees. By passing managerial power to employees, new values can be encouraged, such as "If it ain't broke, fix it anyway"—continuous improvement. The goal is to create work environments where power, knowledge, information, and rewards are shared. By assuming more responsibility for quality and continuous improvement, employees ultimately become self-managing through their work teams. Although implementation is difficult, the rewards can be remarkable for the organization and its members.

Conclusion

Depending on the expertise of a particular organizational researcher, different factors will be seen as the most important part of an organization. So, for one group, networks and channels are critical. Others point to a particular theory, leadership, or motivation and the important knowledge areas. Still others look to the one-to-one relationship as the key factor. However, one area where the interests of scholars converge is small groups. As we stated in the introduction, groups are the gears and inner workings of an organization. Regardless of the organization you join, the coordination, complexity, and working of small groups will be important to you.

This chapter has provided you with a definition of small groups that explains why the scope is so broad. We further explained small groups by outlining the types and characteristics.

Groups are subcultures that experience varying degrees of cohesiveness and develop their own climate and ideology. All groups develop norms of behavior that are enforced by group members. Part of the process of fitting into a group is understanding these roles and group leadership patterns. Groups also have their own patterns of development.

The last part of this chapter provides you with an extensive analysis of how employee involvement, teams, and semiautonomous work units are used. A careful reading of these concepts provides you with an in-depth understanding of how organizations actually employ the group process.

Study Questions

1. Provide examples of the different types of groups.
2. What are group talk and group ideology?
3. Provide examples of norms and roles.
4. Do you believe the disadvantages of groups outweigh the advantages? Why?
5. How do parallel groups differ from self-managing groups?
6. What are the primary concepts underlying self-managing work teams?
7. Explain the traditional barriers to team building.
8. What are the major advantages of employee involvement?

11
Effective Leadership in Organizations

Although observers and authorities differ regarding the specific actions needed to create and maintain a successful organization, they all agree that leadership plays a pivotal role (Bennis, 1994; Hackman & Johnson, 2000; Kotter, 1988; Kouzes & Posner, 1987; O'Toole, 1996; Peters, 1987). There are literally thousands of books describing leaders or giving advice on what it takes to be a leader. History provides a laundry list of legendary military, political, and religious heroes that are often seen as great leaders. Anecdotal material abounds regarding specific organizational leaders such as Lee Iaccoca (Chrysler), Mary Kay (Cosmetics), Walt Disney, Sam Walton (Wal-Mart), Jack Welch (G.E.) or Bill Gates (Microsoft). The less known founders or leaders of the Hondas, IBMs, Subways, and many local and regional organizations have been key forces in shaping their organizations. Remember Howard Schultz? He was the CEO of Starbucks, a coffee chain so successful that it is flourishing even during the downturns of the early 2000s (Schwartz, 2001). The average, loyal Starbucks customer visits 18 times in a month—for a cup of "special" coffee! When the company becomes a success story, investigators discover that the leadership activities were a key factor. The key concepts covered in this chapter include:

- Definition of leadership
- Leadership characteristics
- Leadership and management
- Power
- Leadership theories
- Motivation
- Conflict management
- Leadership direction

This chapter provides a systematic examination of leadership. You are already privy to a great deal of leadership information. Our goal here is to collect our understanding of leadership in one chapter. This is accomplished by following these steps. First, we explain the seven key leadership attributes as a means for defining the concept. Second, a differentiation between management and leadership is provided. Because communication is vital to leadership, the third part of this chapter explains this link. Fourth, several major behavioral approaches to understanding leadership are examined. Fifth, the link between leadership and motivation is presented. Next, conflict management techniques are introduced. Finally, the chapter offers some firm leadership direction.

Definition of Leadership

Being an effective leader is an admired attribute and a sought-after skill. But, what is leadership? For a moment, stop reading and think about your last experience as the leader of a group or team. Answer the following questions about your leadership experience:

- Did you emerge as the group's leader or were you appointed?
- Did your leadership involve maintaining the status quo, or were you responsible for significant change within the group or team?
- How did you influence the behaviors of your team members?
- How did the team members respond to you?
- What was the most challenging part of your role as leader?
- What do your answers tell you about your current leadership?

Now that you have taken a moment to do some self-analysis, let's turn our focus to the leadership of others. Once again, stop reading and make a list of 10 leaders. Answer the following questions about your leaders:

- What do they have in common?
- Do you have some criteria for calling someone a leader?
- Is your list composed of famous and infamous—but well-known—individuals?
- Did effectiveness in a particular activity make them a good leader?
- Were they successful in every leadership activity they tried?
- How do you know these individuals were good leaders?
- Did they have good press or are there examples of good deeds?
- Now, compare your list of leaders with someone else's list.

For most of us, these two exercises raise as many questions as they answer. Leadership is "a process whereby an individual influences a group of individuals to achieve a common goal" (Northhouse, 2004, p. 3). Hackman and Johnson (2000) devote the better part of a chapter defining leadership. Practically every perspective provides part of the picture on leadership in organizations. Like democracy, goodness, or other terms we all use frequently, leadership is a concept best defined by examining its seven general characteristics.

Leadership Characteristics

Seven concepts—vision, willing followers, influence, emotional intelligence, information seeking, situational adaptability, and communication—appear in the majority of leadership examinations. We offer these not as a complete picture, but as the underpinnings of effective leadership.

Leaders forward a *vision* that clarifies direction, provides meaning, and motivates followers (Bennis, 1994; Cybert, 1990; Wheatley, 1994). Bennis and Nanus (1997) state: "We cannot exaggerate the significance of a strong determination to achieve a goal or realize a vision—a conviction, even a passion" (p. xi). This sense of direction provides meaning. "More and more organizations and their people are in a crisis of meaning. ... Those who would aspire to leadership roles in this new environment must not underestimate the depth of this human need for meaning" (Albrecht, 1994, p. 22). Getting people to commit to common values and objectives within an organization is the foundation of corporate culture (Drucker, 1998).

Second, leaders have *willing followers* (Blank, 1995; Miller, 1997). This places the *relationship* between leaders and followers as the pivotal issue. Leadership is interpersonal more than it is personal and is used to create "the interacting ebb and flow between leader and follower" (Blank, 1995, p. 31). This relationship will be further developed when we examine emotional intelligence. Leadership clearly depends on responsive followers "in a process involving the direction and maintenance of collective activity" (Hollander & Offermann, 1990, p. 179). Leadership is more likely to occur in groups (Northhouse, 2004), but it is equally important in interpersonal contexts (Buckingham & Coffman, 1999).

A third major attribute is *influence* (Yukl, 1994). One operational definition of leadership is "any attempt to influence the behavior of another individual or group" (Hersey, 1984, p. 14). Although style and actions may differ, leaders are able to sway others to join in an action. *Influence is the capacity to set priorities and goals.* As Cybert (1990) observed, "Leadership is the ability to get participants in an organization to focus their attention on the problems that the leader considers significant" (p. 29). Often, the leader's optimism toward an issue or problem enrolls people in her or his vision (Bennis & Nanus, 1997). A plaque at Epcot in Orlando, Florida, states "If you can dream it, you can do it.—Walt Disney."

Fourth, leadership involves emotional intelligence (see chap. 9). "Leaders have always played a primordial emotional role. No doubt humankind's original leaders—whether they be chieftains or shamans—earned their place, in large part, because their leadership was emotionally compelling" (Goleman, Boyatzis, & McKee, 2002, p. 5). Evidence suggests that leaders who can create environments that are emotionally positive reap the benefits of long-term business success. And, although you may have used words such as vision, powerful, strategy, and intellect to describe the leaders whom you identified in the exercise at the beginning of this chapter, Goleman (2002) suggests that, "great leadership works through our emotions" (p. 5).

Fifth, leaders *seek information* and encourage others to do the same. Leaders are often called on to make rapid decisions. However, effective leaders know that important decisions require a thorough understanding of the alternatives, consequences, and internal and external influences. Likewise, most problem-solving models include "information-gathering" as a vital stage in the process. Effective leaders are more likely than their ineffective counterparts to seek a wide range of information before making decisions. But, what is equally as important to note is the impact of such a leader on his or her followers. Leaders who are perceived to possess the transformational qualities, as we examine later in the chapter, actually influence their subordinates to engage in information-seeking behaviors more often than other associates (Madzar, 2001).

Sixth, leadership is *situational.* The activity called leadership is defined by what an individual does in the context of the situation. A war hero may fail miserably in running a local bakery. As Clark and Clark (1990) put it, "Leaders deserve to be so-called only when they have been the key players in acts of leadership" (p. 20). Individuals do not always become leaders because the situation often determines our roles. Perhaps the best explanation for how leaders operate is to note that "Effective leadership, research suggests, is remarkably chameleon-like. ... [It] is a function of the situation in which it is found" (Kotter, 1988, p. 21).

Leaders practice situational leadership by adapting to the circumstances. Jones (2000) draws an interesting analogy. "Like piano players, leaders also need to be adept improvisers, willing to set aside their scripts and listen for signals, follow their instincts, and imagine a future that has not yet arrived" (p. 2).

Seventh, *communication* is central to successful leadership activities (Bennis & Nanus, 1997; Clemes & Mayer, 1987; Drucker, 1998; Hackman & Johnson, 2000; Miller, 1997). "In writings on leadership and in business people's accounts of their own leadership crises, the ability to communicate effectively emerges repeatedly as the most important skill to cultivate" (Barrier, 1999, p. 28). Creating and using symbolic behaviors—walking the talk—is a key (Kotter, 1995). What leaders do and how they direct their attention allows followers to *trust* and understand (Buckingham & Coffman, 1999; Miller, 1997). In many ways, leaders shape actions by telling stories. Gardner (1995) concludes: "a key—perhaps the key—to leadership ... is the effective communication of a story" (p. 62). Effective interpersonal communication skills (see chap. 9) allow the leader to mold and direct interactions. "This can involve the leader using various symbols—language, strong images, metaphors, physical settings—to influence the way people see their worlds; the leader 'manages their meanings'" (Gabriel, Fineman, & Sims, 2000, p. 321). Leaders use symbolic activities to direct their followers (see chap. 7).

Communication also includes the effective use of listening, feedback, two-way processes, and recognition (Domerer, 1998). Finally, "inadequate information is the major cause of more than half of all problems with human performance. By improving the quality and timeliness of the information people receive, you can improve performance by as much as 20 to 50%" (Boyett & Boyett, 1998, p. 288). We have already seen the impact of information under the fifth leadership characteristic.

These are seven general leadership characteristics. Be warned that there is no "single comprehensive list of leadership qualities and ... no single path to leadership" (Clark & Clark, 1990, p. 70). We now investigate leadership approaches.

Leadership and Management

In an effort to clarify the importance of leadership, traditional management practices have been placed in juxtaposition with leadership (Bennis & Nanus, 1995; Kotter, 1990; Kouzes & Posner, 1987; Zaleznik, 1989). Assuming the existing management paradigms were partially at fault for a lack of organizational change, these authors denigrated management and ennobled leadership (Rost, 1998). In fact, although there are important differences in perspectives, they are not opposites.

Management is defined as the process of getting work done through others. Management involves the four broad functions of planning, organizing, leading, and controlling, which are critical to getting the work done. *Leadership,* as we just indicated, involves *vision, willing followers, influence, situational appropriateness, emotional intelligence, information, and communication.* Make no mistake, people operating under the mantra manager exhibit numerous leadership characteristics and leaders often must manage.

Different Perspectives

Perhaps the cleanest distinction between the two perspectives is that managers are people who *do things right* and leaders are people who *do the right things* (Bennis & Nanus, 1995). Other important differences in perspectives include leaders focus on innovation, change, and dealing with turbulence whereas managers create stability, harmony, and constancy (Anderson & Anderson, 2001; Kouzes & Posner, 1987; O'Toole, 1996). Leaders use influence and managers rely on authority (Rost, 1998).

Because a manager's job traditionally has been to bring stability and predictability, they maintained the status quo instead of responding to changing circumstances (Kotter, 1990). The flood of books and studies critical of managerial behaviors observe that in situations requiring leadership (e.g., internal and external change, competition, quality, customer service, loyalty), managers are relying on well-tuned, time-honored, and control-centered managerial responses. Much like symphony conductors, managers try to keep everyone strictly within the prescribed music. With the turbulence and change we discussed in the opening chapter, leaders are like contributing members of an improvisational jazz group. The musicians carefully listen to each other and use the interplay to create new directions. The leader helps coordinate and shares the spotlight (DePree, 1993; Lambert, 1995). Given the important changes in diversity, organizational structure, and global influences, this comparison usefully highlights the perspectives (Yearout, Miles, & Koonce, 2000).

Power

Power is the capacity of a person, team, organization, or culture to influence others (Pfeffer, 1997). Being able to get other people to voluntarily do something we want done is the essence of leadership. Traditionally, managers have relied on *positional power* and the organization's rules whereas leaders tend to rely on *influence*. All relationships are based on various components of power and, implicitly or explicitly, the granting of power is reciprocal. That does not mean it will be equal or the same for all parties (Anderson & Englehardt, 2001).

Power runs deeper. At the organizational level, when we accept employment or membership in an organization, we explicitly or implicitly agree to abide by certain operating procedures. Power is exercised by a relatively straightforward deal that offers wages and other compensation for our willingness to give up some of our freedoms (e.g., control of time, specific work, choice of colleagues). Traditional managers have accepted this institutional power resulting in important consequences.

Powerlessness

Traditional hierarchies created and maintained a power structure where managers made decisions, passed judgments, gave assignments, and determined success or failure (French, Bell, & Zawacki, 2000). Bureaucracy, structure, and Tayloristic work practices produce powerlessness in subordinates because superiors make the major decisions. Establishing rules to achieve predictability also means imposing control, using power, and rewarding or punishing. The consequence is a loss of critical employee input, commitment, and motivation especially given the changing workforce (Chambers, 1998).

These are numerous examples of the *taken-for-granted assumptions* (e.g., the way we do things around here) that create a hidden power called *hegemony*. When we accept the governing power structure as legitimate, we are controlled. One of the tactics in teaching innovation and creativity is to encourage participants to break the basic accepted rules of the first grade (e.g., hegemony) including "always raise your hand before you speak," "color inside the lines," and "don't cheat." These hidden rules, however, can lead to subordinates—and often middle level management—feeling powerless.

For managers who feel getting the work done within certain guidelines is all-important, giving up power is analogous to chaos. "All this talk about what you need to be a great leader—listening to your team, serving your employees, caring about the customer—it's enough to make General Patton skip his next reincarnation" ("How can," 2001, p. 28). Patton is a fabled U.S. commander in World Wars I and II who made it abundantly clear that his word was the only word.

The unequal distribution of power found in many organizations leads to the *marginalization* of less powerful groups and individuals. For example, because most Western organizations have been created and controlled by European American males, many of the accepted rules do not afford less powerful organizational members the opportunities for success (Gentile, 1996). Race and/or gender have limited the upward mobility of individuals and groups (Bell, Denton, & Nkomo, 1993). A corporate culture based on the assumptions that the current ways of operating are correct will be inhospitable to marginalized groups as they attempt to advance upward in the organization (Ragins, Townsend, & Mattis, 1998). In addition, when certain groups are looked at as being the "other" or "not like us," *homophily* comes into play. This is our tendency to prefer to work or interact with people who are similar (see chap. 9). As individuals in power search for subordinates to promote, they gravitate toward certain groups that traditionally have not included those marginalized.

How significant are these barriers of homophily and hegemony? Texaco issued a $175 million check in 1996 to settle a racial discrimination lawsuit. The evidence against Texaco included "dicey taped discussion among company executives that included racist language" (Labich, 1999, p. 206). Black employees were called "black jelly beans"—in addition to more racist statements—and there was talk of destroying documents (Fisher, 1998b, p. 186). Widespread institutional racism (e.g., hegemony, homophily), underpaying hundreds of minority employees, and consistent racist and sexist comments forced Texaco to come to the expensive settlement. Evidence included "the vile occasion when a White employee stopped outside the coveted two-window office inhabited by an African-American woman and said, 'Jesus Christ, I never thought I'd see the day when a Black woman had an office at Texaco'" (Labich, 1999, p. 206). Texaco also agreed to change (Labich, 1999). In 1998, minorities accounted for 4 in 10 new hires, and more than 20% of the promotions. Texaco spend 15% of its overall budget on minority- and women-owned vendors. Diversity training for all employees and a direct link between the successful implementing of new diversity initiatives and the career advancement of middle and top executives created momentum. The vision-driven process has made a difference. At the same time, "company officials caution that transforming their culture is an ongoing process," which offers a useful example of leadership (Labich, 1999, p. 212).

To return to our basic point, homophily, like hegemony, becomes a form of power used in conscious and unconscious ways to limit access to positions of power and prestige. Managers, as the monitors of the status quo, use the existing power differentials.

Empowerment

Leaders attempting to engage organizational members reorient these taken-for-granted perspectives toward *empowerment*, which is *enabling subordinates to make decisions, solve problems, and set work goals* (Belasco & Stayer, 1994). The people closest to the work are given more control and choice. "Empowerment refers to a feeling of control and self-efficacy that emerges when people are given power in a previously powerless situation" (McShane & Von Glinow, 2000, p. 116). Jan Carlson, CEO of Scandinavian Airline Systems (SAS), consistently one of the 100 best companies to work for in the annual *Fortune* survey, encourages responsibility, empowerment, decentralized authority, and trust by letting employees discover the problem and the solution within themselves (Heifetz & Laurie, 1997). To be effective, employees must be given significant tasks and control over how these tasks are pursued (Liden & Arad, 1996). "The paradox is that all too often management says the right words—'let workers be empowered'—but doesn't share real power. Power doesn't corrupt, powerlessness does" (Fisher, 1999, p. 10). Self-directed work units (see chap. 10) are excellent examples of empowerment (Barnard, 1999; see chap. 10).

Stories that surface in organizations demonstrate empowerment and often define leadership. For example, at Procter & Gamble, an hourly employee noticed that the labels on Jiffy peanut butter in the store were off-center. He bought all the bottles assuming that P&G would pay him back. They did, of course, and he became a hero and a leader in the pursuit of quality (Peters & Austin, 1985). A Domino's Pizza truck driver was passing a home where there had been a bad fire. The owners were sifting through the damage. He took the initiative to return to his store, explain the situation to the manager, and return with two pizzas. One of the owners acted perplexed and pointed out that, with the fire, they certainly were not ordering pizza. The driver replied that he knew that, but figured they must be really hungry. The pizzas were on the house—and the driver offered to take them back if they were the wrong kind! Now that's empowerment—and a new, confirmed Domino's customer (Hart, Heskett, & Sasser, 1990–1991).

Marriott Hotels have been leaders in empowering employees. At the Minneapolis Marriott City Center, employees are authorized to spend $10 at their discretion to satisfy guests. In one case, a guest complained about not finding a particular book in the hotel gift shop. The cashier, at the end of her shift, walked to a local bookstore and purchased the book with her $10. The guest was astonished, and likely a firm Marriott customer for life (Hart et al., 1990–1991, p. 16). W. L. Gore & Associates, with more than 5,000 employees, has no titles or hierarchy (Shipper & Manz, 1992). They use a team approach without formally, designated teams—they form themselves based on the needs. There are no bosses or managers, but many leaders. Chevron Chemical's "Bringing Out the Best" program includes 3,400 employees in the United States who—

with no input from management or even a nomination process—decide who should be recognized for their contributions at work resulting in rewards and recognition (Vesepej, 1998). These examples demonstrate empowerment where leadership *enables others* to do the right thing at the right time based on their own perception regarding the situation.

Employee empowerment is the most widespread and proven way to be a winner in today's harshly competitive environment (Jasinowski & Hamrin, 1995). *Industry Weeks'* survey of the 100 best-managed companies concluded that companies had to invest "in the activities that make empowerment a reality. These include trust, teamwork, training, decentralization, and linking employee performance to measurable business results" (McClenahan, 1998, p. 101). Because of this, "companies that invest in employee empowerment also invest a lot in employee communication" (p. 102). This investment allows a company to identify conditions that create powerlessness and remove them through formal organizational practices and informal information-providing techniques (Conger & Kanungo, 1998). "Federal Express has institutionalized employee involvement by guaranteeing employees access to the senior management meeting held each Wednesday" (French et al., 2000, p. 480). IBM uses a corporate ombudsman who represents employees' viewpoints to top management. Amoco allows subordinates to have input regarding their superiors' effectiveness. "PepsiCo has involved and empowered all employees by announcing profit-sharing for all" (French et al., 2000, p. 480).

The road to empowerment is long and complex. Leaders must be committed to the process, willing to share and give up power, and win the trust of their followers (Thorlakson & Murray, 1996). Decision-making, team-building, and communication skills must be strengthened throughout the organization. Leaders accomplish these ends by applying effective interpersonal skills, creating meaning, articulating a vision, using symbols to clarify visions, and inspiring followers. "By managing meaning and using power to create the perception that organizational and employee interests converge, empowerment programs reduce the necessity of having to use more visible or coercive forms of power to ensure organizational goals are met and to quell resistance" (Hardy & Leiba-O'Sullivan, 1998, p. 461).

As leaders pursue organizational development, they have seven types of traditional power they can exercise, as shown in Table 11.1. These powers also exist in followers and enlightened leadership works to incorporate power sources into proactive developments.

Feminist Conceptualizations of Power

Although power has been described as "the currency of leadership" (Bennis & Nanus, 1985), many people are uncomfortable when it comes to discussing or exercising power (Kouzes & Posner, 1993). Perhaps this is true because we hear, all too often, about the misuse of power. Likewise, our traditional

Table 11.1 Sources of Power

Expert power	Based on the person not the position; special knowledge or expertise.
Reward power	Ability to deliver something of value to others. Discretion to dispense rewards.
Coercive power	Force compliance; ability to administer punishment.
Legitimate power	Based on position rather than person. Granted the right to use power and control.
Referent power	Respect, liking, or a feeling that power holder can provide rewards or advancement. Admired person is a role model.
Connection power	Interpersonal or network linkages provide importance.
Information power	Possesses needed information. In digital society, information is power.

Sources: Bolman & Deal, 1991; French & Raven, 1959; Hocker & Wilmot, 1985.

understanding of power (as illustrated in Table 11.1) is related to exercising control "over" others. In contrast, feminist theory suggests a more facilitative use of power where power is "manifested through someone" (Dunlap & Goldman, 1991, p. 13). Such a conceptualization has lead to four major feminist tenets related to power as described by Smith (1997).

1. Power is viewed as dynamism and strength versus authority and control.
2. Power is developed and manifested with others versus over others.
3. Power is shared through teamwork and interdependence versus competition and domination.
4. Power is developed through information sharing versus information as a source of power.

These tenets help us to view power through a relational lens rather than our traditional, hierarchical lens (Maier, Ferguson, & Shivastava, 1992). "Sharing power and information … gives employees and coworkers the wherewithal to reach conclusions, solve problems, and see the justification for decisions" (Rosener, 1990, p. 123).

On your journey to understanding leadership, it is important to examine the key theories. What creates and maintains a leader?

Leadership Theories

Practically every leadership analysis offers a theory or a set of guidelines for success. These fall into several specific categories and our review allows you to examine your own beliefs about leadership.

Trait Theories

According to the trait approaches, effective leadership is best understood in terms of certain traits, or specific personal characteristics possessed by leaders. During the early part of the 20th century, numerous studies concluded that certain psychological and physical characteristics predisposed individuals toward leadership positions (Hackman & Johnson, 2000). Attempts at compiling these characteristics can take two forms. One is the *great person theory*, which focuses on past heroes, leaders, or successful individuals. Although it is interesting and intuitively appealing to discover characteristics common to various leaders, researchers have had little success in developing a profile of physical or psychological traits held by the majority of leaders.

The psychological testing movement, also emerging during the early part of the 20th century, attempted to establish certain traits. Stodgill (1974) reviewed these studies and concluded that leaders have a strong drive for responsibility and task completion; are adventuresome and original; exercise initiative in social situations; have self-confidence; accept consequences of decisions and actions; can influence behavior; tolerate stress, frustration, and delay; and structure social situations to the issues at hand. This established a *leadership type* concept. Table 11.2 provides a summary of attempts to develop common leadership traits.

Personality type, as an indicator of leadership potential, has long been of interest to organizational investigators. To date, there is an absence of measures of leadership personality (Clark & Clark, 1990). This has not deterred the use of personality measures, such as the Myers-Briggs Type indicator (MBTI), to try and determine the factors that make leaders successful. The MBTI seems to be a useful test for an individual's preferences for a particular occupation and for self-awareness, but there is less support for using the MBTI as a predictor of leadership success or job performance (Gardner & Martinko, 1996; Zemke, 1992).

Another prominent leadership trait, especially important when the leader must evoke loyalty and trust, is charisma. Originally, this meant leadership based on emotional appeal (see emotional intelligence in chaps. 9 and 11). Charisma, a Greek word, means "divine gift," and early researchers saw such a leader as having considerable power over followers, especially in times of crisis (Hollander & Offermann, 1990). Now, charismatic leadership involves (a) articulation of a strategic vision, (b) inspiration and empowerment of followers, and (c) superior articulation and impression management skills (Conger, Kanungo, & Associates, 1998). Charisma is an attribution made by followers based on what they observe of the leader's behaviors. When successful, charismatic leadership works because it ties the self-concepts of the followers with the organization's vision, goals, identity, and purpose (Shamir, House, & Arthur, 1993). Examples of charismatic leadership make it clear that it is

Table 11.2 Key Leadership Characteristics

Global viewpoint
Strong **communication** skills, listening, empathy, can persuade others
Stimulator with the ability to **create** enthusiasm and **drama**
Trust of employees, integrity, relates and creates bonds, mutual support
Treat people **fairly and honestly** to create loyalty, capitalize on relationships
Ability to **develop people**, understand individual differences
Must be a good **teacher**, develop chains of **followership**
Develop **participation by employees** rather than control by managers
Drive, willingness to work hard, take initiative
Believe in their company and ability to instill that belief in others
Use **influence** to cause actions
Innovate, be an idea generator, knowledge, intelligence, adventuresome, original
Relentless in **pursuing excellence**
Focus on **enduring values**, positive thinker
Talented to shape **action plans** in terms of **customer** needs, can take charge
Gives **equal attention to all stakeholders**—customers, employees, and community; builds a network of acquaintances
Courage to be scrutinized, held to a higher standard, **integrity**
Tolerate stress, frustration, and delay

Sources: Buckingham & Coffman, 1999—reviews of 80,000 managers' actions; Katzenback & Locke, 1991—key traits; Miller, 1997—interviews with CEOs of top five international companies; Stodgill, 1974—pioneering attempt to identify common denominators. Additional sources are found in the reference section.

"a product of communication" (Hackman & Johnson, 2000, p. 118). As such, it can be an important component of transformational leadership, which we discuss shortly.

Bennis (1997) raises an important challenge to charismatic leadership. He asks what makes a leader and concludes that "many leaders, however, couldn't be described as particularly charismatic, but nevertheless manage to inspire an enviable trust and loyalty among their followers. Through their abilities to get people on their side, they make changes in the culture of their organization and make their visions of the future real. How do they do it? When I ask them, they talk to me about human values: empathy, trust, mutual respect—courage" (p. 107).

There is a dark side to charisma. "The attractiveness of the charismatic leader makes it easy to overlook critical weaknesses" (Clark & Clark, 1990, p. 50). Be warned, "Charisma is a tricky thing. Jack Kennedy oozed it, but so did Hitler and Charles Manson. Con artists, charlatans, and megalomaniacs can make it their instrument as effectively as the best CEOs, entertainers, and presidents. Used wisely, it's a blessing. Indulged, it can be a curse" (Sellers, 1996, p. 68).

Three examples are the Highly Likeable Floater, *Hommes de Resentment,* and Narcissists (Hogan, Raskin, & Fazzini, 1990). *Highly Likeable Floaters* are positive, facilitate individuals and meetings, and make no enemies. As such, they float up in the organization without any agenda or performance. But, they do not know how to lead. *Hommes de Resentment* are able to be charming with great social skills. But, below this surface is an independent set of resentful tendencies based on a passive-aggressive personality. So, on the surface everyone likes this individual. But no one knows this person and cannot trust or follow him or her through the change process. Finally, *Narcissists* carry feelings of entitlement, expectation of special privileges, omnipotence, and self-centeredness. Why are these people charismatic? Apparently, they come across with a great deal of self-composure, assertiveness, and self-confidence. Their external picture of leadership is hiding a true willingness to exploit subordinates, curry favor with superiors, and use any measure necessary to self-promote.

Ethical charismatic leaders focus on their followers. They convert followers into leaders, make them confident, powerful, and capable, and help them develop a set of internal standards to guide their actions and behaviors (Gardner & Avolio, 1998). "They create transformations in their organizations so that members are motivated to follow them and seek organization objectives not simply because they are ordered to do so … because they voluntarily identify with the organization, its standards of conduct, and willingly seek to fulfill its purpose" (Gardner & Avolio, 1998, p. 394).

Recent studies regarding managerial effectiveness also highlight gender differences. "New studies show that female managers outshine their male counterparts in almost every measure" (Sharpe, 2000, p. 75). A summary of the results indicates that women executives, when rated by their peers, underlings, and bosses, score higher than their male counterparts on motivating others, producing high-quality work, listening to others, and fostering communication. They tie with males on strategic planning and analyzing issues (Neuborne, 1996; Sharpe, 2000). These recent findings are provocative. Past research has suggested that women receive lower evaluations when they occupy traditionally male-dominated positions that, in a somewhat bizarre manner, supports the concept of traits—at least people's reactions to stereotypical traits (Eagly, Karau, & Makhajani, 1995; Heilman & Block, 1995). An additional measure is pay. Female management occupations earn 71.7 cents on the dollar compared to men, whereas female chief executives earn only 69.9 cents on the dollar compared to men. These statistics mirror the wage gap nationally. Our earlier discussion of homophily further explains why females and minorities can receive lower evaluations as leaders even when they are doing a good job.

Does this support a female–male dichotomy regarding leadership? "Leaders perceived as transformational, whether male or female, exhibit gender balance—displaying characteristics traditionally regarded as masculine and feminine" (Hackman & Johnson, 2000, p. 327). Put another way, successful leaders in the 21st century will utilize specific skills shown to be effective by either gender (Witherspoon, 1997). This makes the task of being an effective organizational leader even more challenging.

Finally, we can misunderstand the importance of our own leadership traits. In the vast majority of cases, our success is due to our followers. Any coach will tell you that "if you don't have the horses, you can't run the race." Unfortunately, if something has worked in the past when we were in leadership situations, we can be tempted to keep on using and, perhaps, abusing that particular trait (e.g., charisma, empathy, control). Waldroop and Butler (1998) warn that "it is hard for managers to understand that the traits that won them promotions may no longer be desirable in their present, swollen form" (p. 293).

Pointing to physical and psychological attributes can appear overly simplistic, but no examination of leadership theory would be complete without some understanding of how variables such as personal characteristics contribute to effectiveness. Certain traits clearly contribute to the ability or inability to lead (see Table 11.2).

Process Theories

A different means to understanding leadership is to examine the process. We include two-dimensional models, the Blake Mouton leadership grid, contingency and situational approaches including Fiedler's contingency theory, Vroom Yetton, and situational leadership. Each of these has been tested with varying success. They also remind us of the numerous explanations available for effective leadership.

Two-Dimensional Models

Studies at Ohio State University and the University of Michigan after World War II found two interacting variables—people and tasks—that impact leader effectiveness. At Ohio State University, investigators used a questionnaire approach and found a set of nine key factors that characterize the nature of leadership behavior (Stodgill & Coons, 1957). With a factor analysis, two dimensions of leadership emerged—consideration of others and initiating structure. The University of Michigan's Institute for Social Research tried to identify styles of leadership behavior that would result in increased workgroup performance and satisfaction. Although these studies have been criticized as being naive in their attempts to offer simple conclusions for very complex issues, they highlighted the difference between employee-oriented and production-oriented communication (Katz, Macoby, & Morse, 1950). Employee orientation included an emphasis on delegation of responsibility and a concern for employee welfare, needs, advancement, and personal growth. Production orientation included close supervision, legitimate and coercive power, work performance, and meeting schedules and deadlines. These initial studies established the groundwork for follow-up studies showing that leaders should use both concerns to be effective. Production and employee concerns are not dichotomies, but descriptions of how a leader behaves.

Blake and Mouton's Managerial Grid   Using two axes—concern for people and concern for production—Blake and Mouton (1985) offered several possible leadership postures. Their contribution to understanding leadership was to draw attention to the interacting nature of a leader's choices regarding people and production. Numerous alterations have occurred to keep their approach current (McKee & Carlson, 1999).

In all variations, they argue that a high concern for people and a high concern for production yield the best possible outcome. On their grid, they assign a 1 to 9 for the 2 axes. So, team management receives a 9,9 because it employs a collaborative approach seeking to maximize the success of both axes. If a leader is not concerned with production (1) but focuses only on people (9), country club leadership (1,9) is being used where accommodating individuals' personal needs is all important and production falls by the wayside.

When production is most important (9) and people's needs are largely ignored (1), authority is being exercised through controlling actions (9,1). Followers are not encouraged to participate in the decision-making process. Some leaders try to balance production (5) with an equal concern for people (5) by making certain they do not rock the boat thereby producing adequate results. This maintains the status quo or middle-of-the-road (5,5) for the type of leader who will obtain mediocre success. Finally, when there is a low concern for production (1) and a low concern for people (1), we have indifferent or impoverished (1,1) leadership.

The Managerial Grid allows us to visualize the interactive patterns created by the two dimensions. In reality, leaders are often faced with balancing these two demands. However, this approach is open to the criticism of arguing for the "one best way" that can be openly questioned in terms of situational adaptation. Proponents of the Grid respond that there are certain principles that should not be sacrificed (Blake & McCanse, 1991). The collaborative (9,9) approach where employees will grow, become autonomous, and find satisfaction is an ideal objective. However, there are situations where a high concern for people and a high concern for task might not be useful.

Contingency and Situational Approaches

The search for heroes as models for leadership highlights an important issue. Different individuals succeed in different leadership situations. The skills needed to save a company or to invent a new product may not be the same leadership skills needed to work with a mature organization. Although you may make a great Little League coach, you may not be able to create a 5-year vision for an organization. But, winning the Little League title still is heralded as an example of exemplary leadership. Right? The most important leadership activities are those that are appropriate to the situation. In other words, the environment is as important as a particular style.

Contingency Theory   This theory speaks to this concept. Fiedler's (1972) theory is that a leader's effectiveness in achieving high group performance is contingent on (a) the need of the leader for a relationship or task orientation, and (b) the degree to which the leader has control and influence over a particular situation. He argued that changing leadership behavior is difficult, so it would be better to change the circumstances. Leaders who are task-oriented belong in situations that are very favorable or unfavorable, whereas people-oriented leaders perform best in situations that are intermediate in terms of favorableness. His theory has been most useful for determining if a leader is task- or people-oriented. To be optimally effective, subordinates would have to be selected to fit the leader's predisposition. Although this is unrealistic, the emphasis on the interdependence between a large number of variables (e.g., subordinates, leaders, situation, task) is an important perspective toward understanding the impact of the environment on leadership effectiveness. Because of "the myriad of leader, follower, and situational factors that affect the leadership process," any single theory will be somewhat inadequate (Hughes, Ginnett, & Curphy, 1998, p. 150).

Path-Goal Theory   This theory points to the leader's job in developing more desire by subordinates to achieve organizational goals (House & Mitchell, 1974). At the same time, leaders are expected to help their subordinates find satisfaction in their work. At times, the leader will improve the motivation of employees by making the rewards for productivity more attractive (e.g., recognition, raises, promotions). Sometimes the employees' work is poorly defined and the leader will respond by clarifying the job structure or task requirements (e.g., general setting, training, supportive supervision). At other times, the work is highly structured. In this case the leader would strive to meet the personal needs of the subordinate (e.g., praise, understanding). The leader develops the path that will help the subordinate reach the appropriate goal. The bond between leaders and followers occurs because of the leader's ability to grip subordinates with a program of action involving a goal, with a path to achieve it.

Vroom–Yetton Model   This model points to the important leadership variable of decision style. It requires the leader to choose a style on a continuum from autocratic to democratic, depending on the problem and its contingencies (Vroom & Yago, 1988). This is the position taken by most contingency theorists, which directly challenges the assumptions that democratic approaches, or any "one best way," always should be pursued.

Putting the leader's behavior into the context of the environment provides a reality that is not as apparent from two-dimensional approaches. To the degree possible, leaders should choose their actions based on research concerning the situation.

Situational Leadership Theory   Arguing that there is no one best way, Hersey and Blanchard's (1988) Situational Leadership Theory is based on the premise that different leadership approaches should be used depending on the requirements of the situation. LEAD uses the traditional divisions of task-oriented and relationship-oriented behaviors, but focuses on the subordinate's ability and willingness to do a particular activity. This "task maturity" is recognized by Hersey and Blanchard as a catch-all for several variables the leader must be able personally to take into account given the particular employee or task. A leader should use: (1) telling (high-task orientation in order to teach the subordinate); (2) selling (high-task orientation and high-relationship orientation in order to motivate the subordinate); (3) participating (high-relationship and low-task orientations because the subordinate is capable, but needs support); and (4) delegating (low-task and relationship orientations because the subordinate is prepared to complete the work).

There is little evidence to show LEAD actually results in better subordinate development. "Nevertheless, Situational Leadership Theory is a useful way to get leaders to think about how leadership effectiveness may depend somewhat on being flexible with different subordinates, not on acting the same way toward them all" (Hughes et al., 1998, p. 145).

Transactional Leadership

Many of the day-to-day activities between leaders and subordinates consist of a *transactional* exchange of rewards for services where a superior offers something (e.g., promotions, fulfilling promises, granting favors, continued employment) in exchange for a subordinate's actions. Transactional leadership manages and helps organizations achieve their current objectives by initiating and clarifying what is required of subordinates (e.g., Path Goal). The two factors of initiating structure (task) and consideration (people) are emphasized as means for determining how to lead various individuals (e.g., contingency, situational). These approaches will work for the ongoing leadership process but they will fall short when major change is required. "Ironically, by focusing on performing for someone else's approval, corporations create the very conditions that predestine them to mediocre performance" (Senge, 1990, p. 7).

A transactional leader can direct employees to change but they are likely to resist.

Contemporary Leadership Theories

The leadership models associated with the trait and early process theories are all "leader-oriented" approaches. That is to say, these theories focus on the leader's attitudes and actions. Some of them reference subordinates; however, the central figure in all of them remains the leader. Several contemporary approaches to leadership, however, address more fully the relationship between the leader and the follower. Some of these theories, which have had a considerable impact on the field, include transformational leadership, culture as leadership, and moral leadership.

Transformational Leadership   The term *transformational leadership* was first used by Downton (1973) and was later incorporated into contemporary leadership theory by Burns (1978), in his Pulitzer Prize-winning book, *Leadership*. According to Burns, transformational leadership occurs when "one or more persons engage with others in such a way that leaders and followers raise one another to higher levels of motivation and morality" (p. 20). Bass (1985) suggests that whereas transactional leadership can affect "first-order changes" (e.g., employees working harder to achieve a promised reward); transformational leadership can affect "second-order changes" (e.g., unique changes in attitudes beliefs, values, motivation, and performance; see chap. 1). Both approaches can impact and improve performance; however, transformational leadership is likely to produce more dramatic results. Transformational leadership motivates employees to go beyond what is expected (Bass, 1996), to provide new ways of training leaders (Avolio & Bass, 1991), and to more fully recognize the importance of leader–follower interaction processes (Northhouse, 2004).

Consequently, Yukl (1998) argues that followers of a transformational leader feel "trust, admiration, loyalty, and respect toward the leader, and they are motivated to do more than they originally expected to do" (p. 325). This is accomplished because the transformational leader "looks for potential motives in followers, seeks to satisfy higher level needs, and engages the full person of the follower. The result ... [is] a relationship of mutual stimulation and elevation" (Konnert & Augenstein, 1990, p. 68).

According to Bass (1985), much of the research that has been conducted with regard to transformational leadership theory shows that effective leaders use a combination of transactional and transformational behaviors. Bass's (1985) model of transformational and transactional leadership incorporates seven different factors. These factors are summarized in Table 11.3. The seven factors work together to provide a "process" rather than a "trait" viewpoint of leadership.

Table 11.3 Bass's Model of Transactional and Transformational Behaviors

Transformational Factors

1. Idealized influence (also called ethical charisma)

    Building trust, role modeling, and providing vision and direction

2. Inspirational motivation

    Use of symbols to focus followers' efforts, communicating high expectations, motivating, and modeling ethical behaviors

3. Intellectual stimulation

    Encouraging creative problem solving and motivating subordinates to develop and consider new approaches to organizational issues

4. Individualized consideration

    Treating organizational members with respect, listening to needs, coaching and effectively using delegation to challenge and develop employees

Transactional Factors

5. Contingent reward

    Clarifying expectations for outcomes and using incentives to reward effort

6. Management-by-exception

    Using negative reinforcement such as corrective actions, punishments, and negative evaluations in order to improve performance

Absence of Leadership

7. Laissez-faire

    Relinquishing leadership responsibility, ignoring problems, avoiding contact and organizational planning

Additionally, Bass (1985) indicates that the transformational leader uses three methods to transform and motivate followers: (1) helping them to become more aware of the importance of the task outcomes, (2) encouraging them to rise above their own self-interest for the sake of the group, and (3) triggering what Maslow (1954) called their higher order needs. Moreover, many authors (Conger, 1989; Kouzes & Posner, 1987; Peters & Austin, 1985; Trice & Beyer, 1993) suggest that certain guidelines may aid leaders in their quest to become transformational. These guidelines, articulated by Yukl (1994, pp. 368–373), are outlined in Table 11.4.

And, finally, as Bass (1994) explains:

Unlike the transactional leader who indicates how current needs of followers can be fulfilled, the transformational leader sharply arouses or alters the strength of needs which may have lain dormant. ...It is

Table 11.4 Guidelines for Transformational Leadership

1. Develop a clear and appealing vision
2. Develop a strategy for attaining that vision
3. Articulate and promote the vision
4. Act confident and optimistic
5. Express confidence in followers
6. Use early success in small steps to build confidence
7. Celebrate successes
8. Use dramatic, symbolic actions to emphasize key values
9. Lead by example
10. Create, modify, or eliminate cultural forms
11. Use rites of transition to help people through the change

leadership that is transformational that can bring about the big differences and big changes in groups, organizations, and societies. (p. 17)

Culture as Leadership   Perhaps one of the most interesting and elusive forms of leadership is the culture as leadership model (see chap. 7). Schein (1998) is noted as being one of the leading contributors to the study of organizational culture as it relates to leadership. Proponents assert that the culture of an organization drives the structure of the organization and that all corrective action goes back to the culture. The shared belief systems and assumptions held by the members of the organization help to define an organization's culture (Schein, 1992). Moreover, Schein (1994) defines organizational culture as "a pattern of shared basic assumptions that have been invented, discovered, and/or developed by a group as it learns to cope with problems of external adaptation and internal integration" (p. 247). And, as with all of the contemporary models of leadership, communication plays an essential role in this model. Bormann (1983) argues that "communication is a necessary but not a sufficient condition for organizational culture. Other things are required such as material goods, artifacts, tools, and technology, but without communication these components would not result in a culture" (p. 100). Trice and Beyer (1991, 1993) suggest that much of the research on the culture as leadership model focuses on changing an existing culture or starting a new culture (i.e., *the cultural innovation leader),* whereas Yukl (1994) explains that the continued effectiveness of an organization may depend on cultural maintenance, a less sensational form of culture as leadership (i.e., *the cultural maintenance leader).* According to Trice and Beyer (1991) both types of leadership involve many of the same elements. For example, both the cultural innovation leader and the cultural maintenance leader engage in creating an impression of competence, articulating an ideology, communicating strong convictions, communicating high expectations and confidence, serving as a role model, and motivating followers' commitment to the organization's objectives and strategies. In contrast, however, cultural maintenance leaders seek to uphold existing values and traditions while making only incremental changes in organizational strategies; whereas, the cultural innovation leader strives to bring about far-reaching, extensive changes and may therefore need to be skilled in the areas of crisis management, interpersonal communication, change agentry, and conflict negotiation. "In either case the leader needs (1) to be able to analyze the culture in sufficient detail to know which cultural assumptions can aid and which ones will hinder the fulfillment of the organizational mission and (2) to possess the intervention skills to make desired changes happen" (Schein, 1992, p. 378).

According to Schein (1992) there are five basic mechanisms through which a leader might embed cultural characteristics into an organization.

1. *To what or whom leaders pay attention.* The things that leaders ask about measures and control communicate priorities, values, and concerns. Praise, criticism, and even the absence of a response each carry a specific message.

2. *How leaders react to crises.* The decisions, actions, and reactions made by a leader while experiencing the pressure and emotionality of a crisis can signal the importance or lack of importance associated with key organizational values and assumptions.

3. *Role modeling.* Leaders demonstrate the importance of fundamental organizational values and expectations by their own actions.

4. *Criteria used to allocate rewards.* The basis for rewards such as praise, pay increases, promotions, or special ceremonies communicates what is valued by the leader and the organization.

5. *Criteria used to select and dismiss organizational members.* Leaders can influence culture by recruiting or promoting people who have particular values, skills, or traits.

In addition to the information that we have discussed in chapter 7, Schein (1992) identifies five secondary methods for accomplishing and/or supporting the process of embedding culture into an organization.

1. *Design of organizational structure.* The extent to which an organization is centralized, decentralized, or operates by the use of self-managed work teams is largely due to the assumptions held by organizational leaders/management rather than the requirements for effective organizational operations (see chap. 3).

2. *Design of systems and procedures.* The formality or lack of formality associated with items such as budgets, reports, performance reviews, and development programs can not only help to reduce role ambiguity but also reflect organizational values (e.g., order and control).

3. *Design of facilities.* The layout of an office, although not always intentional, may be used to signify organizational values (see chap. 5).

4. *Stories, legends, and myths.* Real stories about people and events often aid in the transmission of important organizational values and assumptions. These stories serve more to reflect an organization's culture (see chap. 7).

5. *Formal statements.* Public statements, written creeds, charters, and philosophies must be reinforced by leader behaviors; otherwise, they are not very important except as a complement to other instruments' (see chap. 4).

Clearly, culturally derived explanations about what an organization is, what it does, how it goes about accomplishing its goals, where it has been, where it is going, and what role organization members play in these activities comprise an organization's culture and are essential elements in the culture as a leadership approach. Leaders play a critical role in this model—"they must perpetually diagnose the particular assumptions of the culture and figure out how to use those assumptions constructively or to change them if they are constraints" (Schein, 1992, p. 381).

Moral Leadership According to Sergiovanni (1992) the purpose of moral leadership is "to expand the value structure underlying the way in which leadership is understood and practiced and to expand the bases of authority for the practice of leadership" (p. xiii). Many other authors, such as Foster (1989), Deal (1986), and Rost (1991), question many of the traditional terms such as logic, order, rational thought, objectivity, detachment, and competition that govern our thinking about leadership. Liberation from traditional thinking allows for a focus on the notions of caring, collaboration, emotion, importance of group membership, morality, self-service, duty, and obligation—the moral dimensions of leadership (Sergiovanni, 1992). Sergiovanni (1992) uses a metaphor of the head, heart, and hand to describe the type of transformation that is necessary to become a moral leader. The hand is the leader's interpersonal style and behaviors. The heart deals with the values, dreams, beliefs, and commitments of an individual—their "personal vision." The head is the leader's ability to practice and reflect on situations. Together the three determine leadership practices and according to Sergiovanni (1992) "the head of leadership is shaped by the heart and drives the hand; in turn, reflections on decisions and actions affirm or reshape the heart and the head" (p. 7).

Additionally, Sergiovanni (1992) indicates that true leadership is replacing the "follow me" approach with substitutes for leadership as outlined in Table 11.5.

Moral leadership, with its expanded theoretical and operational formulation for leadership, gives balance to the full range of values and bases of

Table 11.5 Substitutes for Leadership

1. Motivation	Any action, in order to be moral, must be taken in the belief and because of the belief that it is right—from duty, not because of personal inclination, gain, or love (p. 20).
2. Community norms and professional ideal	Involving learning communities (p. 46) and enhancing competence ... and virtue (p. 52).
3. State of flow	The state in which people are so involved in an activity that nothing else seems to matter; the experience itself is so enjoyable that people will do it even at great cost, for the sheer sake of doing it (p. 61).
4. Collegiality as a professional virtue	Fulfillment of obligations, professional obligations, and mutual respect (pp. 90–91).
5. Followership first, then leadership	Followers are people committed to purpose, a cause, a vision ... values and standards to which they adhere, and conviction ... emotional commitment to a set of ideas (p. 71).
6. Virtuous school	Transforming from an organization to a covenantal community ... changing the basis of authority from bureaucratic and psychological to moral (p. 102).
7. Leadership as stewardship	Purposing and empowerment (p. 129).

Source: Sergiovanni, 1992.

authority. Or, as Zaleznik (1990) argues, "Leadership is based on a compact that binds those who lead with those who follow into the same moral, intellectual, and emotional commitment" (p. 12).

Motivation

In organizations, leaders or managers are judged by the accomplishments of their team, group, subordinates, or projects. In order to succeed, they must motivate others. For the sake of clarity, we confine ourselves to work motivation, which is the "set of forces that causes people to engage in one behavior rather than some alternative behavior" (Moorehead & Griffin, 1998, p. 118). This task is confounded by the fact that "more Americans are dissatisfied with their jobs now than 5 years ago" ("Job dissatisfaction," 2000). As a matter of fact, only 50% are satisfied, down from nearly 60% in 1995 ("U.S. Job Satisfaction," 2005) and only 14% say they are very satisfied ("U.S. Job

Satisfaction," 2005). We have already endorsed empowerment and transformational leadership as means for engaging organizational members.

One common motivational error is to assume that what motivates us will motivate others. A second is to believe that successful coaches or athletic heroes have the answers. A surprising number of organizational members quote these individuals when they try to motivate. Professional athletic coaches (e.g., the NBA's Pat Riley, college coaches Lou Holtz and Mike Krzyzewski, and Rick Pitino, who has coached at the college and professional level) are paid up to $100,000 for speeches telling corporate leaders how to motivate employees (Horovitz, 2000; NYT, 2006). Mike Ditka, former NFL coach, however, "doesn't pretend his words can change much. 'Motivation is an overused word,' Ditka says. 'Motivation comes from within. It's called heart, desire, and guts. That's nothing I give someone else'" (Horovitz, 2000, p. 2B). The willingness to spend these sums of money shows an all-too-frequent desire to find a quick answer. One corporate psychologist concluded: "The only time you can be in a room with someone for 1 hour and get your $50,000 worth is when that person is a brain surgeon and you're the patient" (Horovitz, 2000, p. 2B). Remember, in sports there are seasons, scores, clearly identified opponents, penalties, fans, coaches with the power to "bench" players, fields or courts with clearly marked boundaries, heroes, second stringers, clear measuring tools for winning or losing, and specific rules. What organizational activity has these attributes? How do leaders appeal to someone on a Thursday afternoon using these concepts? They cannot. Bottom line: there are no quick fixes and no easy answers.

Guiding Principles

There are five guiding principles. First, the major theories consider work motivation to be intentional and multifaceted. People have reasons for everything they do. People do dumb things, but they usually have some reason that made sense to them at the time.

Second, leaders and organizations care about motivation because of its link to individual job performance. Operationally, job performance (P) is a person's ability (A) times their motivation (M), $P = A \times M$. For example, being fired up to provide excellent customer service (e.g., motivated), without the commensurate training (e.g., handling complaints), means an employee may or may not be able to complete the task (e.g., providing customer service). Performance is a criterion for judging individual and group motivation. By examining behavior (e.g., complaints by customers, number of letters written, reduction of waste, attendance, team performance), organizations can draw conclusions concerning the motivation of their employees. But, as the performance criterion moves from individually controlled and well-specified behavior to more ambiguous behaviors (e.g., initiative, enthusiasm, team spirit, creativity), it becomes more difficult to know if the behavior is based on motivation or something else (e.g., natural ability, circumstances, support staff).

So, setting a performance standard for the more abstract demands placed on individuals in an organization is difficult.

Third, motivational theories consider intrinsic and extrinsic factors. Intrinsic, or internal, "motivation arises from a strong emotional interest in an activity and a sense of freedom and autonomy related to it" (Haasen & Shea, 1997, p. 39). Extrinsic motivation arises when people feel driven by an outside factor, such as a promised reward or a threat.

Fourth, attempting to dramatically change others is likely to fail. This runs counter to popular mythology that suggests everyone can be an "A" student, class president, or successful. To their surprise, after extensive surveys and interviews with the 80,000 of the world's greatest managers, Buckingham and Coffman (1999) were forced to conclude: (1) People don't change that much; (2) don't waste time trying to put in what was left out; (3) try to draw out what was left in; and (4) that is hard enough! If this sounds a little pessimistic, remember that their advice is an attempt to direct leadership efforts where they are most likely to succeed.

Fifth, changing organizations require greater insights into motivation. The postmodern corporation is different from the traditional big corporations that served as vehicles for raising funds to acquire and operate expensive assets like steel mills (see chaps. 1 and 3). "In knowledge-intensive companies, most of the value is produced not by capital equipment, but by talent. When the key capital is human, you have to help employees align their best interest with that of the business" (Steward, 2000, p. 188).

Theories of Work Motivation

Motivation theories divide into two broad types—content and process. Both theory types focus on internal (i.e., intrinsic or endogenous theories) and/or external (i.e., extrinsic or exogenous theories) factors. The needs theories concern themselves with the *content*, or what is identifiable, in the motivation "picture," whereas the intentional choice theories concentrate on the *process*, or what goes on between employees and their environment.

Content Theories

One of the most prevalent themes is that people have certain inner needs (i.e., a craving or imbalance) that lead to drives (i.e., tension or drive to satisfy the need). In response to these needs and drives, we take actions or goal-directed behaviors. We then receive feedback indicating the degree to which we have satisfied the need. If we satisfy the need, we repeat the behavior. If we experience frustration, we try another approach. What are the needs?

Maslow's Need Hierarchy

Anyone completing a basic psychology or public speaking course is familiar with Maslow's Hierarchy (1954). He contended that people are goal-seeking throughout their lives and have internal motives for taking action. We are motivated (i.e., driven) to satisfy certain needs. These needs occur in a hierarchy of preeminence so the lower level needs must be satisfied before we can address a higher level need. A second conclusion is a relatively satisfied need no longer is a motivator of behavior, and the next higher level comes into play. The first three are considered *deficiency* needs and the remaining two are *growth* needs.

Physiological includes the biological needs that are related directly to self-preservation. These include food, oxygen, rest, exercise, sex, drink, and sleep. *Safety and security* include our desire for security, stability, protection, and freedom from fear is a major motivator. In addition, we prefer a safe, predictable environment, creating a need for structure and order. *Belongingness and love* refers to the need people have to love and to be loved. *Esteem* includes our self-evaluation regarding how useful, competent, and important we feel. *Self actualization* occurs as we try to reach the top of our own personal best. We are striving to achieve our full potential, and to become more of what we are capable of being.

Because this approach is intuitively appealing, straightforward, simple, and presented in practically every training seminar or college class, many individuals believe in it. In fact, there is little research to demonstrate its validity (McShane & Von Glinow, 2000). For one thing, "it has been impossible to demonstrate that everyone has the same need hierarchy" (DuBrin, Ireland, & Williams, 1989, p. 362). People are inherently different. Some individuals, such as mountain climbers, forego safety for glory or self-actualization. In third world countries, people work under extremely dangerous conditions for money or to support their families (Bernstein, 1999).

Herzberg's Motivator-Hygiene Theory

Studying how individuals react to their job experiences, Herzberg (1966) made an important finding. *Motivators*, the job experiences, or factors that related to a good feeling on the job were related most often to the job content. *Hygiene* factors, the ones leading to negative feelings, most often related to the surrounding or peripheral aspects of the job. His research further delineated content factors—satisfiers and the context factors—dissatisfiers. Examples of the *satisfiers* include achievement, recognition, work itself, responsibility, and growth; examples of the *dissatifiers* include company policy, supervision, salary, interpersonal relations, working conditions, status, job security, and personal life function.

The insight offered by Hertzberg is removing all the dissatisfiers simply means employees will no longer be dissatisfied. However, *they will not be motivated.* So, simply responding to environmental factors alone does not motivate performance. Employees who are no longer unhappy are, well, no longer unhappy. In addition to this insight, he also emphasized the importance of job content. For the practicing leader or manager, this approach explains why medical and dental benefits do little to motivate employees. Likewise, the role of money in motivating individuals to maintain and improve performance is worth examining. Many experts point to the top companies to show that other factors such as recognition or interesting and challenging work serve as better motivators than money (Cummings & Worley, 2005; Levering & Moskowitz, 2006; Morris, 2006). When money is offered based on the control of a superior or a specific organizational guideline, it is an extrinsic motivator. In other words, regardless of an individual's actions, someone else controls the actual reward. On the other hand, when monetary rewards are tied to an individual's specific needs and the consequences of an individual's performance, the reward becomes intrinsic or controlled by the employee's internal motivation. Money, as a motivator, seems to work best when any of the following conditions exist: (1) you need it badly; (2) it can change your lifestyle; and/or (3) compensation is related to your performance (DuBrin, 2000). Put in context, money can be important as an indication of status and recognition, but its ability to motivate someone on a Thursday afternoon because of a raise 3 months before is in question.

Acquired Needs Theory

McClelland (1962) proposed that certain needs are learned and acquired from our culture. When a need is strong enough, it prompts a person to engage in work activities to satisfy that need. Because the needs are learned, dramatic changes should be possible by encouraging the growth of certain needs in individuals by leaders. The three needs he identified are achievement, power, and affiliation.

The need for achievement includes individuals who examine how to do a job better or how to accomplish something unusual. Monetary rewards are a type of feedback about how well they are doing. They seek responsibility and take calculated risks. People who are high achievers prefer to set their own performance goals (McClelland, 1953). These individuals prefer immediate and efficient feedback on their performance and wish to grapple with moderate goals that are achievable. Driven by these moderate goals (as opposed to easy or difficult ones), they enjoy the responsibility of solving problems. High-achievement managers are characterized by candor, openness, sensitivity, receptivity, participative leadership style, and work satisfaction. Low-achievement managers are more secretive, insensitive, and separated from their work (Mitchell, 1984, p. 14).

The need for power is the second category. McClelland originally thought the need for achievement was the most important source of managerial motivation. His later research indicated that the need for power is the primary motivator of successful managers. The power motive is demonstrated through a desire to control, influence, and be responsible for other people's behavior (McClelland,

1975). Power also has a socialized dimension. When leaders take the responsibility for others, they use their power to benefit people or groups within the organization. Effective leaders have high-power motives (Kotter, 1988).

The need for affiliation is a desire to establish and maintain friendly and warm relationships with others. These individuals seek approval for their work, avoid conflicts, and conform their wishes to the expectations of others. Clearly, in jobs requiring a great deal of social interaction, this is an important motive (e.g., customer service). Because many leadership positions require a certain amount of assertiveness, someone with a high need for affiliation probably will avoid some managerial work.

Analysis of Need Theories

Little research exists to support the successful application of need theories in organizations for increasing motivation (McShane & Von Glinow, 2000). On a broader, philosophical scale, the needs approaches can be useful. First, the folly of making broad generalizations regarding why individuals are motivated becomes apparent—not everyone is alike. For managers, the needs approach opens the window to appreciating the major differences and complexities in motivating individuals. Employees do things for their reasons, not the manager's. Second, the difference between relieving employees from the stress of dissatisfiers and using motivational factors clarifies the difficulties in trying to "buy motivation." There are some practical training applications for McClelland's acquired need theory for individual growth in the achievement need area (McClelland, 1961). Perhaps more useful, his approach explains why many individuals are more interested in power and affiliation. Contrary to a commonly held belief, not everyone wants to be a manager. Earlier (see chap. 1), we explained the differences between the various generations now working. Gen Y, or the GenNexters, have fundamentally different motivational perspectives and needs (Zemke, Raines, & Filipczak, 2000).

Process Theories

They presume that "people are practical, reasoning beings who have anticipations and expectations about their future in the organization" (Sample, 1984, p. 257). Essentially, people can make conscious choices among outcomes according to their estimated probabilities of occurrence and the personal values attached to them" (Casio, 1982, p. 283). Put in behavioral terms, individual behavior is energized through the anticipation of reward. The value we place on various outcomes gives direction to our behavior.

Expectancy Theory

People will work if they have the expectation that the organization will provide the things that they need and want. With this premise, expectancy theory assumes that people (a) are rational, (b) think about what they must do to be rewarded, and (c) determine how much the reward means to them. Motivation is a product of three intervening factors (Vroom, 1964). First, the expectancy, or anticipation of what will occur influences the individual. What is the estimate of the probability that a certain action or effort (e.g., studying) will lead to achieving the desired end or performance (e.g., better grades)? Second, the anticipated satisfaction, or how much someone wants something, provides the valence. A final term is instrumentality, which is the probability assigned by the individual that the performance will lead to certain outcomes. In sum, expectancy is a subjective hunch that increased effort will lead to the desired performance.

So, assume you are trying to get a raise and that you place a high valence on this outcome. If you also can place a high instrumentality (e.g., a certain performance will lead to the reward) that visiting more customers for your organization will lead to being considered for the raise, you probably will pursue this behavior. You make this choice by examining possible alternative activities (e.g., make larger sales to fewer customers, departmental meetings, bring the boss a present) and deciding the best route to pursue. Individuals will make deliberate choices to engage in certain activities in order to obtain predetermined outcomes, according to expectancy theory. There is a clear economic tone because it is assumed that people try to maximize their payoffs by looking at various alternatives. If you believe that cutting class will provide more benefits than going, you are likely to cut class. This approach is appealing because it is straightforward. The leader can alter the follower's belief that they can do the task successfully (effort to performance); the performance will lead to the desired outcomes; or the anticipated satisfaction from doing the task (Nadler & Lawler, 1983). To succeed, the expectancy must be realistic and explicit. If the goal of higher education is for students to achieve excellent grades, we would have to examine the valence of this goal to each student (good chance for some variation here). Then we would have to see if students could be made to believe that certain behaviors (e.g., papers, research groups, test performance) were realistic means to the end. If so, then the students' expectancy could be utilized to motivate them to achieve better grades.

Research indicates that the key issue is the value employees place on the performance outcomes (Fox, Scott, & Donohoe, 1993). Without excellent communication, leaders are likely to impose outcomes important to them or the organization, which begs the key issue for many employees—WIIFM (what's in it for me?). If a leader offers a possible promotion for working overtime, the employee might not see the value. "People are working the equivalent of more than a month more each year than they did a decade ago" which suggests that for some employees this would not be an incentive (Colin, 1999, p. 153). The leader must also determine if the rewards offered can overcome other possible rewards.

Equity Theory

The power of social comparison is the basis for equity theory. Although you may not gather all the necessary information in order to maximize your decisions (e.g., expectancy), equity theory argues that you will be motivated to choose a behavior when there seems to be a fair exchange to be made. We have a type of internal balance sheet that helps us figure out what to do. As with expectancy theory, we compare the overall favorableness of different behaviors. Unlike expectancy theory, no attempt is made to decide the probability between actions and outcomes.

When applied to organizations, this theory concludes that if you perceive a discrepancy between what you are receiving and what others are receiving, you will feel an inequity (Blau, 1994). These comparisons are based on what we get out of our jobs (e.g., outcomes) and what we contribute to our jobs (e.g., inputs). Different outcomes (e.g., pay, promotion, recognition, praise, status) can appear fair or unfair in comparison to other people's inputs (e.g., background, education, training, effort, time). The theory further proposes that people compare their outcomes with that of specific reference persons whose inputs to the organizations are comparable to their own. These comparisons result in three different conditions. The first, underpayment inequity, means we feel we are getting less out of the job than other people are. The second, overpayment inequity, means that in comparing our input/outcome formulation, we are getting more out of the job than other individuals. Finally, if we feel the contributions we make give us the same gain as our comparison group, we experience equity.

The most harmful comparison state is underpayment inequity. Employees who feel that they are under rewarded can reduce their efforts (e.g., become demotivated), increase their efforts (e.g., take a proactive means for establishing equity), or change their means of determining equity (e.g., reexamine inputs and/or outputs). Unless the leader can outline the positive behaviors needed, counterproductive activities can occur in an attempt to restore some semblance of equity (e.g., absenteeism, theft, lowered quality, hounding for raises). Inequities are not difficult to find, such as gender pay. Because examples of unfair treatment are not difficult to find, this approach has a great deal of intuitive appeal. The majority of equity theory studies have focused on pay levels, so it is difficult to measure the other, less tangible, forms of payment. Even with pay, the theory is complex. For example, "salary is listed as number four of five on a list of why people stay at their jobs" (Steele-Pucci, 2006, p. 1) with only 40% of men and 37% of women staying at their jobs because of good pay (Oleck, 1999).

So, how can an organization or leader know the employee's equity perceptions? Even if the inequity is identified, should it be mitigated? Different individuals probably do deserve different rewards based on their contributions.

Pay is an excellent means of communicating with employees if it has a link to the performance and this leads to an additional question (Treacy & Wiersema, 1995). If mitigated, how can this prevent other employees from seeing an inequity? These, and many other questions, make the application of equity theory difficult. One possible alternative is to make the person's job more goal-oriented so individual and group accomplishments are relatively simple to measure, which leads to the third approach.

Goal Setting

Goal setting is widely accepted as a means for motivating employees (Locke & Latham, 1990; Shikdar & Das, 1995). It involves using goals, the objectives that employees are trying to accomplish, to clarify their behaviors. Ample evidence exists that goal setting does affect work performance (Tubbs & Ekeberg, 1991). To be effective, goals must be very specific (e.g., finish seven books by Friday), rather than general (e.g., read as many books as you can). In addition, goals must be realistic, relevant to the organization, and to the person. Finally, difficult goals lead to better performance than easy goals.

Goals need to be connected to the overall mission of the organization. Jan Carizon, president of Scandinavian Airlines (SAS), is fond of the story of two stone cutters who were chipping square blocks out of granite. A visitor asked them what they were doing. The first stone cutter grumbled, "I'm cutting this damned stone into a block." The second, who looked pleased with his work, replied, "I'm on a team that's building a cathedral." Workers who can envision the whole cathedral and who has been given responsibility for constructing their portion of it are far more satisfied and productive than workers who only see the granite before them.

Current Practices

Content and process theories provide excellent backgrounds for leadership behaviors that successfully enhance motivation.

Positive Reinforcement

In the past, managers have tried to manage performance by telling other people what to do or not to do. These are called *antecedents* (Daniels, 1994). Rules, threats, and restrictions work temporarily but a person does not enter an organization as a *tabula rasa*, or clean slate. Old habits will resurface because the control was externally set. Rather than just ask people to accomplish some task based on certain guidelines, we can also provide recognition, reward, or praise. These actions after the behavior are called *consequences*. Antecedents get the behavior started and consequences sustain or stop the behavior. If this is unclear, consider the following examples.

Have you ever gone over the speed limit? The antecedent is markedly clear. "Red-light running causes an estimated 260,000 crashes a year" (Halladay,

2001, p. 13A), with an estimated 1,855 fatalities and 354,000 injuries ("Panto-graph," 2005).

Fifty-two percent of drivers polled nationwide admitted to running a light turning red and 40% admitted to speeding on an interstate in excess of 10 mph ("Risky," 1999). Finally, "each year in the U.S., about 1,800 children under age 14 die in motor vehicles crashes, and more than 274,000 are injured" ("States fail," 2001, p. 3D). The chief culprit is inadequate state laws requiring child restraints even though the importance of child restraints is widely accepted. Now, if you continually receive a traffic ticket (consequence) you would be more likely to discontinue this behavior. If you received some type of positive reward, such as a "thank you" from a passenger noting your renewed interest in safety, you would be enjoying a consequence.

If consequences can be positive or negative, what is wrong with negative? First, negative reinforcement, such as punishment for not following the rules, is only as useful as the enforcement possibility. Remember the traffic examples? If you are told to be at work at 8 a.m., but nothing happens when you arrive at 8:15 a.m. every morning, the threat of punishment loses it power. Second, punishment encourages us to respond just to the extent necessary to avoid the consequences. The familiar phrase "after nine you're mine," refer-ring to the tendency of police officers to allow 9 miles over the speed limit before issuing a ticket makes the point. At work, we will work only to the level necessary to avoid punishment. The familiar question in a college classroom regarding the necessary length of a paper is a good example. Does this mean negative consequences cannot work? Negative consequences can assist in pre-dicting the outcome of behavior. A farmer, who got sick of people ignoring the "No Trespassing" signs, replaced them with "Don't cross this field unless you can do it in 9.9 seconds. The bull can do it in 10" (Haim, 1999). Most individu-als have completed a task, such as a paper or reading a textbook because of an imposed deadline with the commensurate threat of failing.

Positive reinforcement shows people what to do, allows them to learn and develop, and encourages people to perform to the full potential. Too often, leaders assume that "way to go," "attagirl," "attaboy," pats on the back, or pub-lic recognition is the key. To be effective, recognition must relate specifically to behaviors involved by referring to the specific actions using qualitative or quantitative measures. "All organizations should make extensive use of posi-tive reinforcement to encourage good performance. ... The most positive rein-forces are immediate, individualized, contingent on the behavior, and occur frequently" (Boyett & Boyett, 1998, p. 289).

To be fully effective, this process needs to be pushed down into the organi-zation by creating high-performance organizations, using self-directed work groups, and developing empowerment (Daniels, 1994). However, "Employees indicted that they favor recognition from managers and supervisors by a mar-gin of 2–1 over recognition from coworkers or other sources. And nearly 7 out of 10 (69%) employees say nonmonetary forms of recognition provide the best motivation" ("Recognition," 1999, p. 5).

To this point, we have focused on the relationship between the superior and the subordinate. The content theories, although popular because of their intuitive appeal, have not enjoyed much success in organizations. The process theories have been more successful, but the universality of application is open to question. An additional limitation involves the cross-cultural application of these approaches (Adler, 1997; Elizur, Borg, & Beck, 1991). Many of these theories have been developed based on Western cultural values. This brings us to organizational practices as motivators.

Organizational and Cultural Approaches

Once you enter the world of work at 18 or 23, you will spend more time working than engaging in any other single activity. As we prepare to go to our jobs, we can think in terms of a relatively positive upcoming experience or one we dread. Some organizations consistently have fewer turnover, performance, or leadership problems. Earlier, we pointed to *Fortune*'s 100 best companies to work for as examples of excellent cultures. These companies consistently outperform other organizations in almost every category.

What characterizes these companies? In reviewing the 2000 list of the 100 best places to work, the authors asked, "How do these companies maintain an edge in such an environment? One word: culture" (Levering & Moskowitz, 2001, p. 149). Often, we assume the best companies also have the best salaries. "But here's the part that may surprise you: Nobody mentioned money. That is not because the 100 best companies necessarily pay better than their peers. Rather, it's that—pay being equal—most humans seem to need a better reason to get up in the morning" (Fisher, 1998a, p. 70). The 100 best companies in America have nearly twice the employment applications of other companies and retain valued employees more successfully. They offer more health and well-being benefits than other companies, such as 80% more maternity leave. They are more likely to help employees manage the quality of their work lives, including stress-reduction programs, on-site fitness facilities, and prenatal and well-baby programs. In the area of rewards and recognition, the 100 best are more likely to share success with employees. The 100 best also treat all employees equally when it comes to learning and development and invest more time and money in training all employee groups than do other companies ("100 Best," 1999). Table 11.6 provides a summary of the employee-oriented benefits and a list of some examples.

Another study of the 100 best-managed companies concluded that these companies "can't make it without paying attention to the hearts, minds, and lives of their employees" (Caudron, 1998, p. 98). They recognize that "the only way companies can stay ahead is by unleashing the full creative power of people at all levels of the company" (Caudron, 1998, p. 99). Education and train-

Table 11.6 The "100 Best" Common Threads

Family friendly, commitment to diversity, money-making/retirement opportunities (401K, stock options, bonuses), visible executives, stress reduction programs, child care facilities, health care facilities, education benefits, and health risk assessments are common.

26 offer on-site day care

29 offer concierge services, like dry cleaning pick-up

47 offer domestic-partner benefits to same-sex couples

31 offer fully paid sabbaticals

83 offer bounties for employees recommending new hires

Unusual Perks—Specific Examples

Born Information Services	$250 clothing allowance
International Data Group	20 years of service earns an all-expense-paid trip anywhere in the world
Cisco Systems	Web cameras in child care to relieve parents' concerns
MBNA	Medical hotline and adoption support
Amgen	On-site car rental and airport shuttle service
Plante & Moran	Parking spots reserved for expectant moms
Men's Wearhouse	Free consultations with company psychologist
Eli Lilly	Adoption support up to $10,000
Timberland	Canoes, snowshoes, and kayaks available on loan
Acxiom	Pet insurance for dogs and cats
Capital One	$80 per employee per quarter for group activities
American Cast Iron Pipe	Free on-site medical and dental care for current and retired employees
Land's End & Amgen	Clubs for chess, genealogy, gardening, model airplanes, public speaking, tennis, charity
Gould Evans Goodman	3 "spent tents" to rest/sleep at the office
Eli Lilly	Gives newlyweds a week's paid leave
EMC	Summer camp programs for employee's kids
SRA International	On-site medical services
Kingston Technology	Free lunches
American Skandia	Take-home meals
Whole Foods Markets	Acupuncture coverage
Microsoft	Can wear shorts and T-shirts
Ernst & Young	Casual dress everyday
SEI Investments	Open rooms, no cubicles
David Weekley Homes	Celebrations and parties to increase camaraderie
Intel	Culture of learning —Intel University offers 5,000 courses
W.L. Gore & Associates	No titles, pay based on associates' ranking

Sources: Branch, 1999; Fisher, 1998a; Levering & Moskowitz, 2001; Levering & Moskowitz, 2000.

Table 11.7 Nonmonetary Rewards

Functional dress codes
    Informal first-name relationships
        Unifying titles & terminology
            Common entrances to site/building
              Common dining facilities
First-come, first-served parking
    Uniform reward system
        Shared recreational activities/facilities
            Uniform ID badges—prominent first name
              Operator control of work systems
Self-managed work teams
    Operators diagnose/solve problems
        Joint worker/management training
            Operators/managers co-trainers
              Operator–customer interaction
Names, not titles, at all work stations
    Open-door/open-floor practices
        Common coffee bars, rest areas
            Common restrooms, locker rooms
              Functional office size/location
Functional office furnishings
    Peer-group disciplinary processes
        Cross-functional/level networking
            Reprisal-free whistle-blowing
Right of appeal

ing, a sense of ownership, empowerment, and work–family programs are the key initiatives. Table 11.7 summarizes many of the nonmonetary rewards.

Without leadership, organizations will not develop these approaches. In the end, making work a place where people do not mind spending time, and in many cases enjoying it, is a key leadership characteristic.

Conclusion

Leadership is a critical organizational communication issue. We began by defining leadership and providing seven concepts—vision, willing followers, influence, emotional intelligence, seeking information, situational adaptability, and communication—as the generally agreed-on keys.

Management and leadership were compared to draw attention to the important leadership activities. Different perspectives guide these two activities. The use of power resulting in powerlessness or empowerment provided a clear example.

Trait theories, including general characteristics, personality, charisma, and gender, were examined. Being a born leader was discounted, but other traits seem to be important.

Process theories were presented as an additional means for understanding leadership. This will include two-dimensional models, the Blake–Mouton leadership grid, contingency and situational approaches including Fiedler's contingency theory, Vroom Yetton, and situational leadership. Each of these has been tested with varying success. They also remind us of the numerous explanations available for effective leadership. Recent leadership examinations have encouraged the move from transactional to transformational leadership. Remember, "Leaders aren't born—at least not full blown. Neither are they made like instant coffee. Instead, they are slow-brewed" (Boyett & Boyett, p. 43).

Leaders are judged by the accomplishments of their followers. Motivation is a key factor. Five guiding principles were presented. The content and process motivation theories were examined. Content theories, including Maslow, Herzberg, and McClelland were discounted as highly useful. The key process theories—expectancy, equity, and goal setting—are more available for experimentation and verification and show greater promise. Finally, positive reinforcement was examined.

Leadership is about change and it does not occur in a vacuum. The chapter ends with a discussion of organizational and cultural approaches.

An age-old vision of leadership, from Lao Tsu, offers appropriate closure:
The wicked leader is the one who the people despise.
The good leader is the one the people revere.
The great leader is the one the people say, "We did it ourselves."

Study Questions

1. Provide and justify your definition of leadership.
2. Identify and describe the major attributes of leadership?
3. Discuss the positives and negatives of charismatic leadership.
4. What are the major differences between management and leadership?
5. Develop an analysis of power including the best approach for a leader. Include a discussion of the traditional concept of power as opposed to the feminist concept of power.
6. Explain the differences between contingency and situational leadership approaches.
7. What is the difference between transactional and transformational leadership?
8. Identify and describe the contemporary leadership theories.
9. Explain the role of motivation in effective leadership.

12
New Communication Technology

The impact of technology has been discussed throughout this text beginning with an analysis of the digital age (see chap. 1). Networks, the way we connect, "have reshaped our world over the past two centuries—railroads, highways, airports, oil and gas pipelines, TV broadcasting, the electric power grid, and, of course, global telecommunications." "The IT [information technology] revolution was funded by the Pentagon, which sought to create a fast system of communication that the Russians could not access—the Internet" (Issak, 2005, p. 6). "What emerged in the late 20th century was the 'virtual organization': a collective learning network that can almost simultaneously produce and deliver products and services at any time, in any place, and in any variety in order to provide customer satisfaction" (Issak, 2005, p. 90). In many places, a new kind of workplace that is dispersed, flexible, and people-centered is emerging as a result of new communication technologies. "By mastering speed, the virtual corporation creates processes so functionally specific and user-friendly that they are irresistible. These organizations are fast, targeted, knock-quality. The future is your future, and made to order: You can see it, taste it, touch it, buy it" (Issak, 2005, p. 90). Companies are installing chief information officers (CIO) who ensure that organizations use information technology in ways that help its workforce develop the best competitive advantages (Gates, 1999). "The second-generation Internet technologies—combined with the Web itself and e-mail—are drastically reducing the cost of communicating, finding things, and distributing and receiving services online" (Lohr, 2006, p. E1). Globally, expertise can travel digitally so the experts do not have to. "Procter & Gamble uses online networks to get in touch with thousands of experts worldwide" (Hamm, 2006, p. 72). For example, a professor in Bologna, Italy, invented a method for printing edible images onto food, which P&G used to create Pringles potato chips with jokes and pictures printed on them. The digital collaboration boosted Pringles' growth into the double digits whereas similar collaborations have helped P&G to produce 100 new products in the past 2 years (Hamm, 2006).

College students have become highly connected, with nearly 92% of them arriving at school with their own computer or laptop ("Survey Finds College Students," 2005) and chatting on instant messenger an average of 10.5 hours per week (D. Anderson, 2006). This massive increase in technology usage is reflected at home where three fourths of all U.S. homes will be wired for Internet access by 2006 (Tracy, 2004). In fact, "the typical family will spend $595 on communications services ... to surf the Internet, use a wireless phone, or page someone—up from $175 in 1995" (Superville, 2001, p. 9A). "The willingness to use the Internet crosses generational gaps. In 2005, 65% of the U.S. population from 50–64 used the Internet whereas in 1998, only 31% did so" (Stockey, & Laird, p. 1A). Since 1995, more than "200 million people have plugged computers into the Net, by far the fastest spread of a new communications technology ever" (Schlender, 2000, p. 90). At the same time, people do not automatically shop or bank online. "Even the tech-savvy Generation Y prefers handling the merchandise before closing the deal. When asked where they shop, most (73.8%) say they prefer stores compared with 21.9% who would rather shop online" reports the Texas Tech University Institute for Internet Buyer Behavior ("Is Gen Y," 2001, p. 16). Likewise, college students represent more than $175 billion in consumer spending (Odell, 2005), yet only 32% of them will buy back-to-school supplies online (Hull, 2005).

As we move through the 21st century, these technologies will shape our organizations. The remainder of this chapter examines four facets of technology. First, we analyze the relationship between organizations and technology. Second, we provide an overview of the new communication technologies. Third, we examine six information systems. Perhaps the most important issue leads to the chapter's summary. What are the implications of the new technology?

This analysis covers the following key concepts:

- Organizations and technology
- Mechanization, automation, and technology
- New information technologies
- Types of systems
- Implications: Benefits and challenges

Organizations and Technology

Three claims place the impact of new technology on organizations in context. First, technology always has a major impact on organizations. Technology is a cornerstone of organizational activity ranging from equipment for mass production to delivery systems (e.g., trucks, planes) to digital processes. The new communication and information technologies (e.g., e-mail, teleconferencing, computer conferencing, personal computers and local area networks [LAN], interactive cable television, videotext and teletext, satellite communications), computer networks, computer-aided manufacturing (e.g., CAM; robotics) and computer-assisted design (CAD) shift from physically moving things to processing information. Information technologies are driving economic wealth (Katz, 1997). The performance of technology (ability to produce more effectively or efficiently) doubles every 18 months at the same cost for operation (Hollis, 1996). Compare that speed of change with building a high-way or installing a system. Table 12.1 provides a short summary of the major technological connecting processes in organizations.

Second, we are in the middle of massive changes and turbulent times (see chap. 1). For organizations, "computer networking ... may be the most important development in the management of organizations since DuPont, General Motors, and others invented the modern corporation" (Stewart, 1994, p. 44). With cybernetworks, traditional organizational sources of information such as file cabinets, memos, minutes, and face-to-face meetings will diminish in importance as they are replaced by advances in communication technology. This increased connectivity means organizational members can find a "single point of access to all the information they need to get their jobs done" (Koulopoulos, 1997, p. 223).

Third, organizations and individuals must move from using the technologies simply as a means for improving current activities (e.g., better collecting and storing of data; word processing replaces typing; e-mail replaces memos; cell phones replace land lines) to developing improved information gathering and utilizing procedures. When we improve, make easier, or replace a current process, we are automating. We move from *automate* to *informate* when we replace data-crunching with analysis and diagnosis (Zuboff, 1989). This calls for a new type of organization—one based on information (Drucker, 1998). This will require "flexible, learning organizations that continuously change and solve problems through interconnected coordinated self-organizing processes" (Daft & Lewin, 1993, p. 1). "Think of the Intranet as a living, evolving organism that feeds on information. With the proper nourishment, it can grow into a knowledge network" (Cohen, 1998, p. 56). To gain the full advantages of the new communication technologies, we must understand them.

Mechanization, Automation, and Technology

The early applications of technology included mechanization and automation. The original assembly line operations used machines to replace the physical actions of individuals, which is *mechanization*. With mechanization, employees either facilitate the machine's operation (e.g., operators, maintenance) or coordinate the people–machine process (e.g., managers, supervisors). The greater the technological complexity, the lower the human input.

The development of more sophisticated technology led to *automation*, where machines are capable of self-regulation and act as substitutes for an employees' sensory mechanisms. People changed from merely being an extension of the machine to managing the machines. In some cases, the machines relieved individuals of laborious tasks (e.g., repetitive functions—peeling potatoes; meticulous detail work—finding bad potatoes). In other cases, machines have taken over because they do a better job (e.g., finding defective

Table 12.1 Terminology

Internet	The Net is a global mesh of computer networks sharing a common software standard called TCP/IP. Its backbones are high-speed fiber trunk-lines owned by telephone companies.
Intranet	Used to distribute information and speed data among offices. Secure "firewalls" usually protect the intranet from unauthorized users. An intranet can use the Internet to reach multiple business locations.
Extranet	When selected business partners are granted access to a company's intranet. Authorized users (e.g., suppliers, distributors, customers) can view data the company makes available.
Local area network (LAN)	A data network, typically set up within a building, which transmits data in small chunks, called packets, allowing many computers to use the network at the same time.
Wide area network (WAN)	A computer network that covers a wide geographical area, such as a state or country.
Audioconferencing	Conference calls allowing three or more sites to interact in voice only.
Videoconferencing	Conferencing that allows participants to both see and hear each other. The term includes two-way and multipoint conferencing between rooms and desktops.
Desktop videoconferencing (DVC)	Videoconferencing from a personal computer or dedicated system located on an individual's desk.
Multipoint conference unit (MCU)	The bridge linking three or more videoconferencing locations.
World Wide Web (WWW)	Comprises an area of the Internet using graphics and hypertexts to communicate information.
Wireless application protocol (WAP)	Standard for linking the Internet to mobile phones.
Short message service (SMS)	The ability to send and receive text messages on mobile phones.
Global system for mobile (GSM)	The de facto digital phone standard in use around the world.

parts, printers for computers, detail work). *Robotics* is a melding of mechanization and automation. This technology ranges in sophistication from simple, repetitive assembly line operation where the steps are stored in the robot's program to machines capable of making decisions regarding the production.

The New Information Technologies

Information is a competitive tool that can be used effectively through information technologies. For example, communication technologies are used by more than 1,500 organizations to connect their geographically dispersed members (Scott, 1999). E-mail usage is on the rise. In 2002, 31 billion e-mail messages were sent daily—that number is expected to increase to 60 billion in 2006 (Levitt & Mahowald, 2002). Internets, Intranets, videoconferencing, and other technology are used by companies to share information at a hyper-fast speed to remain competitive (Meyers & Davis, 1998). Computers and microchips allow information to be found, stored, retrieved, and utilized in a myriad of ways (Markus, 1994). Computers extend the mind by offering assistance in completing numerous mental functions (e.g., keeping track of finances, spelling checks, research). For researchers, inventors, and designers, computers allow simulations of complex events heretofore requiring years of investigation.

New technologies tend to push older ones aside (e.g., manual typewriters, open-stack library research, handwritten letters). One powerful example is the telephone. The telephone extended the ear's hearing range, developed new patterns of interaction and connectedness, and significantly altered the ways people approach communication. For organizations, the telephone "made it possible for managers to leave the factory floor, for salespeople to change orders in quick response to client demands, for customers to order products directly, [and] for companies to establish branch offices" (Kiesler, 1986, p. 47). It also allowed for the creation of a single corporate headquarters.

The public telephone was a mainstay for salespeople, college students, and, according to the movies and television, blackmailers, drug dealers, and gangsters like Tony Soprano. Superman dressed in a telephone booth, Tippi Hedren used it for a refuge in *The Birds*, and Robert Redford had a lifeline when he was on the run from killers in *Three Days of the Condor*. Pay phones are still important to low-income American households that do not have traditional landlines. However, since cell phones have been introduced, more than 1 million pay phones have been removed (more than 300,000 were removed between the years 1998–2001; more than 700,000 were removed between the years 2000–2004; Hampson, 2001; Mallozzi, 2006). Cell phones have become ubiquitous. In June 2000, there were 97 million users (Koch, 2006). In 2001, around 188 million Americans had cell phones—this is nearly four times the number in 1995, with 54% of the 105 million U.S. households having at least one cell phone (Hampson, 2001; Superville, 2001). By 2006, there were 202.8 million U.S. cell phone users (Koch, 2006) and more than 2 billion worldwide (Hewak, 2005).

Not all media are created equal and the differences determine the potential for adoption.

Media Richness

Media are considered rich when there is a sense of social presence. Leaner media do not carry all types of information simultaneously (Harris & Sherblom, 2005). "The speed of feedback permitted by the medium, the number and types of sensory channels utilized by the medium, the perceived personalness of the source when communicating over the medium, and the richness of language used with the medium" determine media richness (Komsky, 1991, p. 314). Interpersonal communication is very rich because there are ongoing verbal and nonverbal transactions. Annual corporate reports, bank statements, or other financial documents rank very low in media richness. Newsletters are a little better because they carry some information that might involve the reader. E-mail, telephone, and videoconferences complete the path from financial statements (leanest) to interpersonal (richest).

To be effective, we must select the most appropriate communication media for the task (Rice, 1992). Ambiguous situations, such as a newly forming team or an unresolved conflict, require rich media. Studies of product development teams show the importance of working at one location rather than using information technologies (i.e., e-mail) because of the impact of media richness on the development process (Madhavan & Grover, 1998). A clear example of the impact of media richness is found in shopping behaviors. Online shopping still constitutes less than 10% of American retail, and experts do not expect online shopping to pass one fourth of consumers' spending for decades (C. Anderson, 2006). People enjoy doing things, such as shopping, with other people (C. Anderson, 2006). However, as we become more involved in certain types of computer-mediated communication activities such as teams, we learn to develop relationships that can be very interpersonally rewarding. In some cases, the "slower relationship development through a leaner medium may even be an asset to the growth of greater depths in personal intimacy, trust, co-orientation, and affection among group members" (Harris & Sherblom, 2005, p. 327; Walther, 1996).

An important distinction is between *synchronous* and *asynchronous* systems. When there is simultaneous communication (e.g., verbal, nonverbal, ongoing feedback) as in interpersonal transactions, the medium is synchronous. If there is one-way communication as with e-mail, the medium is asynchronous. Videoconferencing is synchronous whereas voice mail is not. This distinction explains the difficulty some organizational members have in adapting to new technologies that might diminish the synchronous nature of a relationship. "The most surprising result (of a Fortune 500 internal survey) was that each individual had one preferred method that he or she used almost exclusively. Almost half preferred written materials, whereas 20% wanted the reassurance of one-to-one conversations. Some had made the switch to high-tech resources and the remainder said that regardless of what other methods were available they would continue to rely on their coworkers" (Rupp, 1996, p. 17). More than 35% of 400 managers polled by the American Management Association said they used e-mail the most over the telephone (26%) and face-to-face meetings (15%). However, "despite the high use of electronic messaging, 36% admit they still prefer the in-person talks" (Armour, 1998, p. 1A).

The concept of richness is important because predictions are that people enjoy greater communication satisfaction with a richer media as we just learned. "E-mails and phone calls, however efficient, cannot substitute for face time. ... There are certain chemical reactions between individuals when we go face to face that can't happen in a virtual organization" (Dahl, 2005, p. 44). Studies also show that as we become more familiar with certain media (e.g., e-mail and the use of emoticons such as :-(for unhappy or <:-) for dumb question), we learn to adjust our expectations and find additional means for creating a sense of personalness. What types of systems are organizations utilizing?

Types of Systems

There are five types of information systems: communication, operational, control, decision support, and interorganizational. The dynamics of a living organizational system guarantees a great deal of overlap, but the categories offer a clearer picture of the various components.

Communication Systems

Communication systems are designed to augment human communication; computer-mediated communication systems (CMCS) "have become a cornerstone to the activities of knowledge workers in the information age and the office of the future" (Compton, White, & DeWine, 1991, p. 23). CMCS change the type of information people receive, overcome temporal and geographical barriers for the information exchange, and break down hierarchical and departmental barriers, standard operating procedures, and organizational norms.

Voice messaging, e-mail, videoconferences, and integrated systems are all examples of CMCS. E-mail has extended our ideas of what we define as active communication. It is remarkably popular because we can write, edit, store and send on our own timetable. Because it is *asynchronous*, meaning the messages can be sent and received at different times, no coordination of face-to-face communication is needed. It works well when the messages are well defined, such as giving instructions, and it increases the likelihood for upward communication. Likewise, "blogs, collaborative databases (called *wikis*) and open-source software development all use the Net to handle much of the coordination among people rather than relying on top-down command and control" (Mandel, 2005, p. 62).

Sharing ideas without physical presence is one of the clear benefits of CMCS. Online forums, connected knowledge bases, electronic bulletin boards, libraries, and virtual conference rooms all facilitate exchanges between employees, allow researchers and problem solvers to exchange proposals, presentations, spreadsheets, technical specs, and swap ideas. The *law of telecoms* states that distances will shrink and eventually become irrelevant and the web of computer networks expand (J. S. Brown, 1998). To utilize the full benefits of these opportunities, organizations must alter traditional information control processes. "A realization that organizations using Intranets have accepted is that to remain competitive in the future, organizations will need to abandon their ideas of information hoarding and embrace knowledge-sharing" (Greengard, 1998, p. 82).

Meetings can be dramatically altered. Absent participants can eavesdrop and add information electronically. Meeting notes can be available to all interested parties instantaneously. Chase Manhattan, Merrill Lynch, and IBM are using software to create *chat rooms* where discussions can be held in real-time (Row, 1998). Discussions with customers, colleagues, or distant experts can occur without leaving your PC.

This electronically created trail also raises a limitation because it might inhibit participants from even using the electronic channels that act as a permanent record. Information, such as deleted e-mail messages, reside in the company's computer system just waiting for a data specialist to retrieve it (E. Brown, 1998). There are other limitations to e-mail. Some individuals react quickly to situations with emotional responses called *flaming*. Because we can post our messages instantly, we might send the emotionally charged message before we have calmed down, presenting a significant issue for organizations (Kennedy, 1997).

Telecommuting or teleworking is the ability to work at locations away from the traditional office with an electronic (e.g., computer, telecommunication connection) connection. In 2000, an estimated 25 million people telecommuted all or part time, an increase from 11 million in 1995. By the end of 2005, the number of people worldwide who work from home at least 1 day a month reached 82.5 million and is predicted to grow to more than 100 million by the end of 2008 (Cable News Network, 2006). "Productivity gains of 10% to 40% and cost savings of $6,000 to $12,000 per year are common for employers" who allow telecommuting ("Virtual offices," 2000, p. 9). Eighteen companies on *Fortune*'s "100 Best Companies to Work For" offer telecommuting (Levering & Moskowitz, 2000). High-tech, information processing, or knowledge-driven industries are the most likely users. Telecommuting can place the employee close to a customer or client. Any organization can use telecommuting if a job requires more time on the computer or phone than in face-to-face meetings. Currently, 87% of the executives polled by Robert Holt International indicated that there would be an increase in telecommuting in the coming decade (Cable News Network, 2006). "According to the recent *Fortune* magazine's survey of the 100 best U.S. companies, 79 allow employees to telecommute at least 20% of their time. In one of the chosen organizations, 60% of the employees work from home!" (*"Can I Work at Home,"* 2006). "At Hewlett Packard, 70% of the U.S. employees have the flexibility to telecommute on a full time, regular, or occasional basis" (Frauenheim, 2005, p. 12).

Distance is its biggest drawback. Employees are disconnected from the culture, rarely participate in information problem-solving, and fail to develop important interpersonal relationships. When political issues arise, the telecommuter is at a distinct advantage and may fail to be adequately considered for additional opportunities or promotions. Careful training needs to be undertaken to assist the telecommuters and managers in making the process successful (Deeprose, 1999; Maruca, 1998; Tergesen, 1998). IBM requires regular visits to office at least once a week.

Mobile, or cell phones, are creating a revolution in how organizational members connect. By the end of 2005 there were 2 billion cell phones worldwide (Hewak, 2005) more than double the number of cell phones reported in 2001 (Baig, 2001). Most organizations have abandoned traditional communication systems (e.g., walkie-talkies, landlines) for the convenience and 24/7 (24 hrs/7 days) features of cell phones.

Operational Systems

Operational systems help with the structural aspects of work. As the name implies, routine activities can be examined to see where inefficiencies are occurring. Because procedures are standardized, a great deal of time and effort can be eliminated. "Computers and information technologies link previously semi-independent aspects of the production system more closely" (Osterman, 1989, p. 7). An overdependence on these systems, however, leads to a significant amount of depersonalization in the organization (Robey, 1991).

A useful example of the speed gained, and the personal influence lost, is with the credit approval process for a Visa charge. When a Visa card is used for a purchase, the elapsed time between the moment the clerk passes the card through a credit verification terminal and the approval code is 15 seconds (Verity, Coy, & Rothfeder, 1990). The approval path begins with National Data Corp.'s (NDC) computers in Cherry Hill, New Jersey. The request transfers to NDC headquarters in Atlanta for acceptance. If the amount is more than $50, the Visa microcomputers send the query to the mainframes in McLean, Virginia, or San Mateo, California. The mainframe verifies the card and checks with the individual issuing bank to see if the money is available. The approval, or denial, is back—in 15 seconds. Your ATM card is an additional example.

Swipe cards have replaced time clocks, bar codes trace deliveries (e.g., UPS, FedEx), and prepayment cards are used for meals at universities and organizations. The data developed can be used to understand how people interact.

Control Systems

Control systems, using data collection and entry, monitor and evaluate organizational performance. These systems allow organizations to obtain "up-to-the-second views of inventories, receivables, and market demand at businesses ranging from fast food to industrial chemicals to toy retailing. For many companies, networks have become essential means of production—their very nervous system" (Verity et al., 1990, p. 143).

Computer checkouts at supermarkets, Wal-Marts, and other stores allow the control of inventories and a rapid response to changes in customer demand. Manufactures, like Saturn, use SCADA (supervisory control and data acquisition) to run their complexes. At Saturn, the system became highly effective when all employees were given easy-to-use graphical computers. Employees have been able to spot problems with brakes, air-bag deployments, power-train controls, and so on (Gates, 1999). Office Depot links its trucks on the 22,000 delivery routes through a wireless system that plans routes and keeps track of deliveries. The system has cut the time spent on filing and searching for delivery paperwork by 50% (Kessler, 2001). Aramark, a Philadelphia snack-supply company, keeps tracks of sales via a wireless handheld computer carried by delivery truck drivers.

Earlier, we discussed electronic monitoring. "Search engines make it possible for employers to scour all manner of digital dirt to vet employees" (Conlin, 2006, p. 53). The American Management Association's *2001 Survey on Workplace Monitoring & Surveillance* found that "more than three quarters of major U. S. companies now check employees' e-mail, Internet, or telephone conversations, or videotape employees at work," which is more than double the 53.3% in 1997 ("Employee surveillance," 2001, pp. 8–9). Twenty-seven percent have fired employees for misuse of office e-mail or Internet connections and 65% have taken some disciplinary actions. "Your online reputation may precede you during a job search" ("Digital dirt," 2006, p. 1D). "More than three fourths of executive recruiters said they routinely use search engines like Goggle and Yahoo to learn more about candidates. Even more significant, 35% said they have eliminated a candidate from consideration based on information discovered online" ("Digital dirt," 2006, p. 1D).

Decision Support Systems

Decision support systems (DDS) operate as extensions of the planning and decision-making processes. Many management information systems (MIS) provide important information to managers to enhance the decision-making process. These systems range from relatively simple data support systems to complex forms of expert systems.

Group support systems (GSS) are various types of groupware used to enhance the team process. The eight general categories are electronic mail/messaging, calendaring/scheduling, group document handling, work-group utilities and development tools, group decision systems and meeting support, information sharing/conferencing products, workflow management, and business process design. Through a combination of computer technology, decision-making techniques, and group meeting procedures, these processes can facilitate problem solving and decision-making (Miranda, 1994). In addition, a commitment to full participation, consideration of diverse views, and vigilance in the information processing seem to be better than in face-to-face situations (Bordia, 1996). These systems take longer than face-to-face groups (Scott, 1999).

Regardless of the decision making system, leaving the final decision to the user has proven to be more successful than letting the system replace the user (Turnage, 1990). Earlier we discussed the use of information (see chap. 10) and indicated the depth of decision-making quality possessed by many organizational members. In many cases, the familiarity of an individual with specific situations means the best decision cannot simply be digitized (Groleau & Taylor, 1996). The entire process of empowerment assumes individual choices in making decisions and over control by DDS could become counterproductive.

Interorganizational Systems

Interorganizational systems link different organizations. Organizations have been able to increase their competitive advantage by cooperating in the design and use of interorganizational systems (Johnston & Vitale, 1988). All the previous communication technologies are used to link organizations to each other.

Implications

There are extensive arguments concerning the impact of new technology. We examine some of these arguments as they relate to the following three groups: organizations, leaders, and organizational members. At this point, many of the issues related to these three areas have been discussed in this chapter and earlier in the text. We focus on the benefits and challenges related to each of the three groups.

Implications for Organizations

Organizational Benefits

Improves Coordination and Productivity   New communication technology "has been associated with improvements in planning, promoting timely and complete feedback, controlling organizational activities, managing time, initiating action plans, responding to the environment, planning flexible work schedules, eliminating manual labor, composing documents, and preparing written documents" (Compton et al., 1991). GE expects to save $18 million a year by going to a paperless office. It is removing almost any machine (e.g., fax machines, desktop printers, copiers) that "spits out paper and isn't shared by a group of workers" (Moore, 2001, p. 10).

At Boeing, the time needed to complete a wide range of projects has been cut by 91% through groupware. Ford Motor Company uses an Intranet to link design centers in Asia, Europe, and the United States, and to develop speedier engineering designs. General Electric is saving $240,000 a year in printing costs by using its Intranet to publish a dictionary of company information that is always up to date. FedEx allows customers to click their way through Internet web pages to track their parcels themselves, which saves $2 million a year (Motz, 1998).

Flattens the Organization At practically every juncture in this text, we have pointed to the virtues of increased contact within organizations over functional boundaries. In addition, empowering employees is fundamental to success. Increased amounts of participation, less centralized leadership, and more egalitarian participation occur with e-mail (Hollingshead, McGrath, & O'Connor, 1993). "It is now possible to have the economic benefits of very small organizations: freedom, motivation, creativity, and innovation" (Malone, 2006, p. 103). Because digital communication flattens organizations by removing access to information, people have the information to make decisions themselves instead of taking orders from someone above them. This creates a 'collective intelligence' where thousands of people and numerous computers solve problems in 'as intelligent a way as possible'" (Malone, 2006, p. 103). Examples include Google, Wikipedia (world's biggest and perhaps best encyclopedia), and InnoCenter, an Eli Lilly creation, which uses the world as a research and development lab.

Organizational Challenges

Organizational Structures Must Change Outdated management schemes stand in the way of successful utilization of the new communication technologies. "Communications in the network are absolutely incompatible with a strict, parochial hierarchy" (Stewart, 1995, p. 50). Superiors must learn to empower, develop teams, and get out of the way. As organizations flatten and become wired, teams will need to create electronic meeting places, share files, develop message boards, and provide access to data if the potential savings are to be realized. If the current practices of using electronic monitoring and control continue, the potential benefits could be lost. "In theory these networks should empower people to become better employees. In practice these knowledge-management networks create brave new infrastructures that effectively enforce employee compliance with organizational norms" (Schrage, 1999, p. 198).

Implications for Leaders
Leader Benefits

Increases Influence   In contrast to our earlier discussions of how technology works to flatten organizations and to decrease the amount of top-down influence in decision-making, it also has the power to increase a leader's influence and visibility throughout multiple levels within the organization. New technology provides leaders with a variety of options with which to broadcast their messages. Many of these options have been discussed earlier in this chapter. Along with the increase in options comes the ability to follow up and reinforce messages like never before. Because technology has allowed for ease of messages transfer, middle managers can give feet to the leader's vision. As such, technology enables managers to tie operational goals into larger organizational strategies further enhancing the leader's influence at all levels.

Increases Accessibility   Based on the *equalization hypothesis* (Dubrovsky, Kiesler, & Sethna, 1991; Hollingshead, 1996), communication through the use of new technologies may promote the development of what we call *electronic confidence* or *on-screen confidence*. This e-confidence not only encourages equal participation in decision-making within the organization, but also it can increase the flow of upward communication. E-mail and videoconferencing are just two ways in which organizational members who are in remote locations (or just down the hallway) can communicate regularly with each other and more importantly with the leadership of the organization. Leaders who, in the past, have found themselves losing touch with ground-level operations, may now have more insight into and more input from team members at all levels within the organization.

Leader Challenges

Greater Accountability   The benefit of increased accessibility brings with it the challenge of greater accountability. This challenge works on two levels. First, technological advances allow leaders to more easily follow-up with subordinates regarding operational goals. Second, subordinates may also hold leaders to higher standards of follow-through when it comes to communicating organizational outcomes and effectiveness.

Competency Development   Keeping pace with new technologies can be a daunting and expensive task. Organizations spend millions of dollars each year just to support computer-based technologies (Rains, 2005). Similarly, leaders will need to develop and maintain a level of technological competence to instill confidence in their ability to lead in the new world of virtual organizations. It is, however, a delicate balance. Leaders who are too tech-savvy may come across as too involved and/or dependent on technology and thus lacking the human element involved in effective leadership (see chap. 11).

Implications for Organizational Members

Organizational Member Benefits

Improves Communication   Electronic transmissions increase communication velocity, support collaborative work, and sustain both strong and weak ties among communication (Wellman et al., 1996). When the amount of participation is enhanced, the quality of ideas improves (Wellman et al., 1996). Communication with customers can be improved dramatically. The workforce is more connected—20% of U.S. workers are mobile at any one time and new communication technologies allow them to stay in contact with one another (Kessler, 2001). "Intranets are causing a systematic rethinking about the nature of employee-to-corporation and employee-to-employee relationships where every employee has instant ability to communicate work, thoughts, gripes, experiences, and solutions to every other employee. This new and expanded power of the employee will also create a set of responsibilities for all members in the organization" (Motz, 1998, p. 16).

Increases Participation   If used correctly, e-mail and other technologies can document an employee's workload and involvement in organizational projects—giving them an opportunity to be recognized for outstanding contributions. Additionally, technology-driven group support systems (GSSs) "minimize barriers to interaction and make it possible for all members to potentially influence group processes (Rains, 2005, p. 194). "[O]rganizational members are less aware of status differences and feel less inhibited about contributing information and sharing ideas ... [likewise] the opportunity for simultaneous input, or parallelism, makes it easier for all members to contribute" (Rains, 2005, p. 195).

Organizational Member Challenges

Decreases Personal Knowledge Confidence   [A] human being's sense of confidence in using personal knowledge is forgotten in the absorption of Internet surfing, computer games, and derivative work on the computer. People seek knowledge in sorting through information that exists, rather than creating knowledge through personal experimentation and experience" (Issak, 2005, p. 90). But, technology is not the only means through which knowledge is obtained. "We have some experiences. We think through them. We develop a theory. And then we put two and two together. That's the way learning works" (Gladwell, 2005, p. 9). Therefore, in contrast to access to new technology and information overload, we must also have confidence in our "adaptive unconscious" (Gladwell, 2005, p. 11). "The mind operates most efficiently by relegating a good deal of high-level, sophisticated thinking to the unconscious … The adaptive unconscious does an excellent job of sizing up the world … setting goals … and initiating action … " (Wilson, 2002).

Difficult to Escape Work   We have moved from 9-to-5 to 24/7. Beepers, cell phones, and laptops make it difficult to leave the work behind. At work, many say "e-mail, voice mail, and other technologies have lengthened their work-day ("More Tech," 199, p. 4). For example, *information overload* can occur. In 2001, workers spent an average of 49 minutes a day on e-mail, which is 30% to 35% more time than they did in 2000. In 2002, management-level workers were predicted to spend 4 hours a day on e-mail according to Ferris Research (Swartz, 2001). And, by 2005, employees were so overwhelmed by e-mail, they had to invent ways to conceal the time they spent online from their employers (Spears, 2005).

Part of the overload problem stems from a lack of training. "While e-mail and voice mail have become the corporate way of life, only 15% of companies say they have trained their employees to use these tools" (Rupp, 1996, p.17).

Not all communication technologies create an overload. Internet- and intranet-based messages can be controlled because we do not have to download the information. Of executives worldwide, 61% who were in the United States indicated that the Internet with the control feature is reducing information overload and only 19% claimed it was making matter worse ("New Age," 1998).

As we examine the benefits and challenges, we are confronted by the fundamental questions for any change. Will organizations, leaders, and organizational members make the appropriate adjustments to allow the potential power to develop? Ironically, with new communication technologies there is little doubt but that organizations will have to learn to utilize the potential power.

Conclusion

The new communication technologies are having a major impact on organizations and society. Mechanization, automation, and information technology represent the phases in the introduction of technology into organizations. Media richness explains how communication processes differ.

There are five types of information systems: communication, operational, control, decision support, and interorganizational. Each of these provides an organization with important opportunities for growth.

The benefits and challenges posed by the new communication technologies bring us back to the content of this text. Change is inevitable. How we respond to the change is the critical issue.

Study Questions

1. What are the three major impacts of communication technologies on organizations?
2. Differentiate between mechanization, automation, and the new technologies.
3. Provide examples of how technology has changed your life.
4. What are the differences between the five types of systems? Which ones have you observed?
5. Explain the benefits and challenges posed by the new communication technology as they relate to organizations, leaders, and organizational members.

References

Chapter 1

Adler, R. B., & Towne, N. (2003). *Looking out/Looking in* (10th ed.). U.S.: Thomson Wadsworth.

Argyris, C. (1991, May–June). Teaching smart people how to learn. *Harvard Business Review*, 99–109.

Armour, S. (1998, September 30). Failure to communicate costly for companies. *USA Today*, p. 1B.

Associated Press. (1999, September 3). Demographics will challenge employers and government. *The Tuscaloosa News*, p. 5B.

Bateson, G. (1972*). Steps to an ecology of the mind*. New York: Ballentine.

Bennis, W., & Goldsmith, J. (1997). *Learning to lead: A workbook on becoming a leader*. Reading, MA: Perseus.

Berlo, D. K. (1960). *The process of communication*. New York: Holt, Rinehart, & Winston.

Bertlanffy, L. V. (1968). *General systems theory*. New York: Braziller.

Bios Group. (2000, November 27). Simplifying complexity. *Fortune*, pp. 232P–232T.

Bolman, L. G., & Deal, T. E. (2003). *Reframing organizations: Artistry, choice, and leadership* (3rd ed.). San Francisco: Jossey-Bass.

Boulding, K. E. (1977). The universe as a general system. *Behavioral Science, 22*, 299–306.

Boyett, J., & Boyett, J. (1998). *The guru guide: The best ideas of top management thinkers*. New York: Wiley.

Branche, A. P., & Rummer, G. A. (1997, February). Managing an organization as a system. *Training*, pp. 68–74.

Carty, S. S. (2006, August 24). Ford Motor considers going private. *USA Today*, p. 1B.

The challenges facing workers in the future. (1999, August). *HRFocus*, p. 6.

Charan, R., & Tichy, N. M. (1998). *Every business is a growth business*. New York: Times Business.

Colvin, G. (1997, November 24). The changing art of becoming unbeatable. *Fortune*, pp. 299–300.

Colvin, G. (2005, July 25). America isn't ready: Here's what to do about it. *Fortune*, pp. 70–82.

Colvin, G. (2006, January 23). The 100 best companies to work for 2006. *Fortune*, pp. 71–128.

Conlin, M. (2006, June 19). Champions of innovation. *Business Week*, pp. 17–29.

Coovert, M. D., Craiger, J. P., & Cannon-Bowers, J. A. (1995). Innovations in modeling and stimulating team performance: Implications for decision making. In R. A. Guzzo, E. Salas, and Associates (Eds.), *Team effectiveness and decision-making in organizations* (pp. 149–203). San Francisco: Jossey-Bass.

Corder, L. (1999, February). Selling change: HR or PR's job? *HRFocus*, p. 13.

Covey, S. R. (1991). *Principle-centered leadership*. New York: Fireside.

Cummings, T. G., & Worley, C. G. (2005). *Organizational development and change* (8th ed.). U.S.: Thompson South-Western.

de Janasz, S. C., Dowd, K. O., & Schneider, B. Z. (2002). *Interpersonal skills in organizations*. Boston: McGraw Hill.

Demos, T. (2006, January 23). Cloudy with a chance of chaos. *Fortune*, pp. 134–145.

Denisi, A. S., & Griffin, R. W. (2005). *Human resource management* (2nd ed.). Boston: Houghton Mifflin.

Diversity boosts performance. (1999, May). *HRFocus*, p. 5.

Dychtwald, K., Erickson, T. J., & Morison, R. (2006). *Workforce crisis: How to beat the coming shortage of skills and talent*. Cambridge, MA: Harvard Business School.

Elliott, L. P. (1999, February 21). Office workers rush to keep up with changing roles. *The Tuscaloosa News*, p. 17A.

Epstein, J., & Axtell, R. (1996). *Growing artificial societies*. Cambridge, MA: MIT Press.

Fairlamb, D. (2001, July 2). Ready, set, Euros! *Business Week*, pp. 48–50.

Farace, R. V., Monge, P. R., & Russell, H. M. (1977). *Communicating and organizing*. Reading, MA: Addison-Wesley.

Farrell, C. (1999, August 9). Women in the workplace: Is parity in sight? *Business Week*, p. 35.

Farrell, C. (2005, October 3). The overworked, networked family. *Business Week*, pp. 68ff.

Fisher, A. (2006, August 21). Have you outgrown your job? *Fortune*, pp. 46–56.

Flannery, T. (2005). *The weather makers: How man is changing the climate and what it means for life on Earth*. New York: Atlantic Monthly Press.

Friedman, T. L. (2005). *The world is flat: A brief history of the twenty-first century*. New York: Farrar, Straus, & Giroux.

Gardner, H. (1995). *Leading minds: An anatomy of leadership*. New York: Basic Books.

Gates, B. (1999). *Business @ the speed of thought: Using a digital nervous system*. New York: Warner.

Griffin, R. W. (2005). *Management*. Boston: Houghton Mifflin.

Grossman, L. (2005, January 24). Grow up? Not so fast. *Time*, pp. 42 ff.

Hamm, S. (2005, March 27). Speed demons. *Business Week*, pp. 70–76.

Hansen, J. (2005). Earth's energy imbalance: Confirmation and implications. *Science308*, 134–345.

Harrell, T. W., & Harrell, M. S. (1984). *Stanford MBA careers: A 20-year longitudinal study* (Research Paper No. 723). Stanford, CA: Stanford University, Graduate School of Business.

Harris, T. E., & Sherblom, J. C. (2005). *Small group and team communication* (3rd. ed.). Boston: Allyn & Bacon.

Hisrich, R. D. (1990). Entrepreneurship/intrapreneurship. *American Psychologist, 45*(2), 209–222.

Hunter, M. (1999, May–June). Work, work, work, work! *Modern Maturity*, pp. 36–49.

International Data Corporation. (2000, January 3). Y2K price tag. *USA Today*, p. 1B.

Issak, R. A. (2005). *The globalization gap: How the rich get richer and the poor get left behind*. Upper Saddle River, NJ: Pearson Education.

James, G. (1996). *Business wisdom of the electronic elite*. New York: Random House.

Jayson, S. (2006, June 29). The 'millennials' come of age. *USA Today*, pp. 1D–2D.

Johnson, R. S. (1998, August 3). The 50 best companies for Blacks & Hispanics. *Fortune*, pp. 94–96.

Jones, E., Watson, B., Gardner, J., & Gallios, C. (2004, December). Organizational communication: Challenges for the new century. *Journal of Communication*, 772–750.

Kasindorf, M., & El Nasser, H. (2001, March 13). Impact of census data debated. *USA Today*, pp. 1A–2A.

Katz, D., & Kahn, R. (1978). *The social psychology of organizations* (2nd ed.). New York: Wiley.

Katz, M. (1997). *Technology forecast 1997.* Menlo Park, CA: Pricewaterhouse World Technology Center.

Kim, D. H. (1993, Fall). The link between individual and organizational learning. *Sloan Management Review*, 37–50.

Kinnick, K. N., & Parton, S. R. (2005). Workplace communication: What the Apprentice teaches about communication skills. *Business Communication Quarterly*, 68(4), 429–456.

Kirk, P. (1999/2000, December/January). Corporate evolution and the chaos advantage. *The Systems Thinker*, 10(10), 1–5.

Landro, L. (2005, November 16). Making it OK to challenge surgeons. *The Wall Street Journal*, pp. D1, D4.

Larkin, T. J., & Larkin, S. (1996, May–June). Reaching and changing frontline employees. *Harvard Business Review*, 95–104.

Leonhardt, L. (2006, March 5). The economics of Henry Ford may be passé. *The New York Times*, pp. C1, C12.

Linden, E. (2006). *The winds of change.* New York: Simon & Schuster.

Lohr, S. (2006, February 21). A cyberfueled growth spurt. *The New York Times*, pp. E1, E10.

Mandel, M. (2005, October 3). The real reasons you're working so hard … and what you can do about it. *Business Week*, pp. 59–67.

Maney, K. (2000, January 3). Now that it's behind us. *USA Today*, pp. 1B–2B.

McClenahen, J. S. (1998, August 17). A world of (top-line) difference. *Industry Week*, pp. 92–102.

McGregor, J. (2006, April 24). The world's most innovative companies. *Business Week*, pp. 63–74.

McKenna, R. (1997). *Real time: Preparing for the age of the never satisfied customer.* Boston, MA: Harvard Business School.

Mullins, M. E. (2003, February 18). Most employers are small. *USA Today*, p. 5B.

O'Toole, J. (1996). *Leading change: The argument for value-based leadership.* New York: Ballantine.

Pepper, G. L., & Larson, G. S. (2006, February). Cultural identity tensions in a post-acquisition organization. *Journal of Applied Communication Research, 34*(1), 49–71.

Peters, T., & Austin, N. (1985). *Passion for excellence: The leadership difference.* New York: Random House.

Pomeroy, A. (2004, July). Great places, inspired employees. *HR Magazine*, pp. 46–54.

Porter, E. (2006, March 2). Stretched to the limit, women still march to work. *The New York Times*, pp. A1, C2.

Reece, B. L., & Brandt, R. (2005). *Effective human relations: Personal and organizational applications* (9th ed.). Boston: Houghton Mifflin.

Reinsch, N. L, Jr., & Shelby, A. N. (1997, December). What communication abilities do practitioners need? Evidence from MBA students. *Business Communication Quarterly, 60*, 7–24.

Rothman, M. A. (1972). *The cybernetic revolution.* New York: Franklin Watts.

Rothwell, W. J., Prescott, R. K., & Taylor, M. (1999, March). Transforming HR into a global powerhouse. *HRFocus*, pp. 7–8.

Sancton, T. (1998, November 8). Betting on the new euro. *Time*, p. 82.

Schein, E. H. (1985). *Organizational culture and leadership.* San Francisco: Jossey-Bass.

Schein, E. H. (1990, February). Organizational culture. *American Psychologist*, 109–119.

Schein, E. H. (1999). *The corporate culture survival guide: Sense and nonsense about culture change.* San Francisco: Jossey-Bass.

Schwartz, J. (2004, September 4). At work and anxious: Employees' health is suffering. *The New York Times*, p. 16A.

Senge, P. M. (1990, Fall). The leader's new work: Building learning organizations. *Sloan Management Review*, 7–23.

Senge, P. (1991). *The fifth discipline: The art and practice of learning organizations.* New York: Doubleday/Currency.

Senge, P., Kleiner, A., Roberts, C., Ross, R., Roth, G., & Smith, B. (1999). *The dance of change: The challenges of sustaining momentum in learning organizations.* New York: Doubleday/Currency.

Senge, P., Roberts, C., Ross, R. B., Smith, B. J., & Kleiner, A. (1994). *The fifth discipline fieldbook: Strategies and tools for building a learning organization.* New York: Doubleday/Currency.

Senn, L. (1986). Corporate cultures: Does your corporate culture stimulate innovation or foster apathy? *Management World, 15*, 16–17.

Spear, G. (2000, October 9). Enter here. *Fortune*, p. 90.

Stata, R. (1989, Spring). Organizational learning—The key to management innovation. *Sloan Management Review, 30*, 63–74.

Stewart, T. A. (1993, December 13). Welcome to the revolution. *Fortune*, pp. 66–80.

Survey: GE campaigns to boost execs' job satisfaction. (1984, March). *World of Work Report*, p. 1.

Sypher, B. D., Applegate, J. L., & Sypher, H. E. (1985). *Culture and communication in organizational processes.* Beverly Hills, CA: Sage.

Toffler, A. (2006, April 1). Futurist Alvin Toffler on the economy of tomorrow. *Bottom Line Personal*, pp. 7–9.

The trouble with MBAs. (2007, April 30). *Fortune*, pp. 49–50.

Ussem, J. (1999, 20th Anniversary Issue). Entrepreneur of the century. *Inc.*, pp. 159–174.

Waldrop, M. M. (1993). *Complexity.* New York: Simon & Schuster.

Watzlawick, P., Beavin, J. B., & Jackson, D. D. (1967). *Pragmatics of human communication: A study of interactional patterns, pathologies, and paradoxes.* New York: Norton.

The website is the business. (2001, Winter). *Fortune Technology Guide*, pp. 144–148.

Weick, K. E. (1979). *The social psychology of organizing* (2nd ed.). New York: Addison-Wesley.

Weick, K. (1995). *Sensemaking in organizations.* Newbury Park, CA: Sage.

Weise, E. (2005, December 19). The Google side of your brain. *USA Today*, pp. 1D–2D.

Wenger, E. (1991, Fall). Communities of practice: Where learning happens. *Benchmark*, pp. 6–8.

Wheatley, M. J. (1992). *Leadership and the new science*. San Francisco, CA: Berrett-Koehler.

Willoughby, D. (2006, May 17). Older workers an elusive asset. *Montgomery Advertiser*, p. 1.

Yen, H. (2001, November 4). Ripple effects from attacks take toll on companies. *The Tuscaloosa News*, p. 3D.

Zemke, R., Raines, C., & Filipczak, B. (2000). *Generations at work: Managing the clash of veterans, boomers, xers, and nexters in your workplace*. New York: AMACOM.

Chapter 2

Adler, R. B., & Towne, N. (2003). *Looking out/Looking in* (10th ed.). U.S.: Thomson Wadsworth.

American Health. (1991, October). Reported by the Associated Press, *Birmingham Post-Herald*, (1991, September 24), p. A2.

Beamer, L., & Varner, I. (2003). *Intercultural communication in the global workplace*. Homewood, IL: Irwin.

Big wheels. (2006, August 26). *The Tuscaloosa News*, p. 1D.

Bishop, J. E. (1994, November 23). Studies conclude doctors' manner, not ability, results in more lawsuits. *The Wall Street Journal*, p. B6.

Bolman, L. G., & Deal, T. E. (2003). *Reframing organizations: Artistry, choice, and leadership* (3rd ed.). San Francisco: Jossey-Bass.

Cialdini, R. B. (1988). *Influence: Science and practice*. New York: HarperCollins.

Carey, A. R., & Laird, B. (1999, February 23). Lingua franca? *USA Today*, p. 1A.

Choi, Y. B. (1993). *Paradigms and conventions: Uncertainty, decision making, and entrepreneurship*. Ann Arbor: The University of Michigan Press.

Dobkin, B. A., & Pace, R. C. (2006). *Communication in a changing world*. New York: McGraw-Hill.

DuBrin, A. J. (2000). *Applying psychology: Individual & organizational effectiveness* (5th ed.). Upper Saddle River, NJ: Prentice Hall.

Elliott, L. P. (1998, April 19). Twenty-eighth annual survey of high achievers' views on education, drugs, social, and sexual issues. *The Tuscaloosa News*, p. 8A.

Fackelmann, K. (2002, November 26). Mistrust of doctors widespread across USA. *USA Today*, p. 9D.

Franklin, D. (2005, September 27). In heeding health warning, memory can be tricky. *The New York Times*, p. D5.

Gibb, J. R. (1961). Defensive communication. *Journal of Communication, 11*, 141–148.

Hamilton, C. (2005). *Communicating for results: A guide for business and the professions* (7th ed). U. S.: Thomson Wadsworth.

Haralson, D., & Tian, Q. (2003, September 30). Views differ on performance reviews. *USA Today*, p. 1B.

Himelstein, L. (1994, October 10). That sure is one devil of a logo. *Business Week*, p. 8.

Hindo, B. (2006, June 19). Satisfaction not guaranteed. *Business Week*, pp. 32–36.

Klyukanov, I. E. (2005). *Principles of intercultural communication*. Boston: Pearson.

Kreps, G. L. (1990). *Organizational communication: Theory and practice* (2nd ed.). New York: Longman.

Kuhn, R. L. (2006, April 24). A problem of perception: Why China and the U.S. aren't on the same page. *Business Week*, p. 33.

Kuhn, T. S. (1962). *The structure of scientific revolutions*. Chicago: University of Chicago Press.

Landro, L. (2005, November 16). Making it OK to challenge surgeons. *The Wall Street Journal*, pp. D1, D4.

Levy, D. (1997, February 19). Good bedside manner can fend off malpractice suits. *USA Today*, p. 10.

Lustig, M. W., & Koester, J. (2003). *Intercultural competence: Interpersonal communication across cultures* (4th ed.). Boston: Allyn & Bacon.

Lynch, D. (2006, February 9). U.S. firms become tongue-tied. *USA Today*, p. 6B.

Marklein, M. B. (2003, February 4). Is there any truth to today's resumes? *USA Today*, pp. 1D–2D.

Mattimore, B. W. (1994). *99% inspiration: Tips, tales, & techniques for liberating your business creativity*. New York: AMACOM.

McShane, S. L., & Von Glinow, M. A. (2000). *Organizational behavior: Emerging realities for the workplace revolution*. Boston: Irwin McGraw-Hill.

McLuhan, M., & Fiore, Q. (1967). *The medium is the massage*. New York: Bantam.

Mehring, J. (2004, August 2). Health care: Trust issues. *Business Week*, p. 28.

Merritt, J. (2002, December 9). You mean cheating is wrong? *Business Week*, p. 8.

Merx, K. (2005, May 18). Workers' unhealthy habits could mean costlier insurance. *The Birmingham News*, p. 3D.

Morrison, A. M., & Von Glinow, M. A. (1990). Women and minorities in management. *American Psychologist, 45*, 200–208.

Mulford, W. R. (1978). Young/old woman: A perception experiment. In J. W. Pheiffer & J. Jones (Eds.), *The 1978 annual handbook for group facilitators* (pp. 40–45). La Jolla, CA: University Associates.

Myers, M. S. (1991). *Every employee a manager*. San Diego: University Associates.

Neuliep, J. W. (2000). *Intercultural communication: A contextual approach*. Boston: Houghton Mifflin.

Osburn, J. D., Moran, L., Musselwhite, E., & Zenger, J. H. (1990). *Self-directed work teams: The new American challenge*. Homewood, IL: Business One Irwin.

Payer, L. (1988). *Medicine & culture: Varieties of treatment in the United States, England, West Germany, and France*. New York: Henry Holt and Company.

Peter, L. J., & Hull, R. (1969). *The Peter principle: Why things always go wrong*. New York: Morrow.

Peters, T., & Austin, N. (1985). *Passion for excellence: The leadership difference*. New York: Random House.

Platt, J. (1970). *Perception and change*. Ann Arbor: University of Michigan Press.

Pollar, O., & Gonzalez, R. (1994). *Dynamics of diversity*. Menlo Park, CA: Crisp.

Reece, B. L., & Brandt, R. (2005). *Effective human relations: Personal and organizational applications* (9th ed.). Boston: Houghton Mifflin.

Stohl, C. (2001). Globalizing organizational communication. In F. M. Jablin & L. L. Putnam (Eds.), *The new handbook of organizational communication* (pp. 323–275). Thousand Oaks, CA: Sage.

Weise, E. (2005, October 7). French mechanics and English cooks may be just fine, study finds. *USA Today*, p. 9A.

Whiteley, R. C. (1991). *The customer driven company: Moving from talk to action.* Reading, MA: Addison-Wesley.

Zelizer, G. L. (2003, November 20). Break cheating patterns early. *USA Today*, p. 15A.

Chapter 3

Albanese, R. (1988). *Management.* Cincinnati: South-Western.

Argyris, C. (1957). *Personality and organization.* New York: Harper & Row.

Argyris, C. (1976). *Increasing leadership effectiveness.* New York: Wiley-Interscience.

Argyris, C., & Schon, D. A. (1974). *Theory in practice: Increasing professional effectiveness.* San Francisco: Jossey-Bass.

Armand-Delille, J. (2006). Managing and communicating cultural diversity. In T. L. Gillis (Ed.), *The IABC handbook of organizational communication* (pp. 179–191). San Francisco: Jossey Bass.

Baker, E. L. (1980, July). Managing organizational culture. *Management Review*, pp. 8–13.

Barker, R. T., & Camarata, M. R. (1998). The role of communication in creating and maintaining a learning organization: Preconditions, indicators, and disciplines. *The Journal of Business Communication, 35*(4), 443–467.

Barker, J. R., & Cheney, G. (1994). The concept and practices of discipline in contemporary organizational life. *Communication Monographs, 61*, 19–43.

Bolman, L. G., & Deal, T. E. (1984). *Modern approaches to understanding and managing organizations.* San Francisco: Jossey-Bass.

Bolman, L. G., & Deal, T. E. (2003). *Reframing organizations: Artistry, choice, and leadership* (3rd ed.). San Francisco: Jossey-Bass.

Bormann, E. G. (1983). Symbolic convergence: Organizational communication and culture. In L. L. Putnam & M. E. Pacanowsky (Eds.), *Communication and organizations: An interpretive approach* (pp. 99–122). Beverly Hills, CA: Sage.

Branch, S. (1999, January 11). The 100 best companies to work for in America. *Fortune*, pp. 119–142.

Brown, E. (1999, March 1). America's most admired companies. *Fortune*, pp. 68–73.

Burrell, G., & Morgan, G. (1979). *Sociological paradigms and organizational analysis.* London: Heinemann.

Carey, A. (1967). The Hawthorne studies: A radical criticism. *American Sociological Review, 32*, 403–416.

Caudron, S. (1998, August 17). The only way to stay ahead. *Industry Week*, pp. 98–102.

Clancy, J. J. (1989). *The invisible powers: The language of business.* Lexington, MA: Lexington.

Collins, J. C., & Porras, J. I. (1994). *Built to last: Successful habits of visionary companies.* New York: HarperBusiness.

Colvin, G. (2005, July 25). America isn't ready: Here's what to do about it. *Fortune*, pp. 70–82.

Colvin, G. (2006, January 23). The 100 best companies to work for 2006. *Fortune*, pp. 71–128.

Conner, D. R. (1998). *Leading at the edge of chaos: How to create the nimble organization.* New York: Wiley.

Conquergood, D. (1991). Rethinking ethnography: Towards a critical cultural politics. *Communication Monographs, 58*, 179–194.

Conrad, C. (1983). Organizational power: Faces and symbolic forms. In L. L. Putnam & M. E. Pacanowsky (Eds.), *Communication and organizations* (pp. 173–194). Beverly Hills, CA: Sage.

Courtright, J. A., Fairhurst, G. T., & Rogers, L. E. (1989). Interaction patterns in organic and mechanistic systems. *Academy of Management Journal, 32*, 273–802.

Deal, T. E., & Kennedy, A. A. (1982). *Corporate cultures: The rites and rituals of corporate life*. Reading, MA: Addison–Wesley.

Deetz, S., & Kersten, S. (1983). Critical models of interpretive research. In L. L. Putnam & M. E. Pacanowsky (Eds.), *Communication and organizations* (pp. 147–171). Beverly Hills, CA: Sage.

Drucker, P. F. (1993). *The post-capitalist society*. New York: Harper Business.

Drucker, P. F. (1999). *Management challenges for the 21st century*. New York: Harper Business.

Fayol, H. (1949). *General and industrial management*. New York: Pittman.

Fiedler, R. E. (1967). *A theory of leadership effectiveness*. New York: McGraw-Hill.

Fiedler, R. E., Chemers, M. N., & Mahar, L. (1978). *Improving leadership effectiveness*. New York: Wiley.

Fischer, F. (1990). *Technology and the politics of expertise*. Newbury Park, CA: Sage.

Fisher, A. (1998, January 12). The 100 best companies to work for in America. *Fortune*, pp. 69–95.

Franke, R., & Karl, J. (1978). The Hawthorne experiments: First statistical interpretations. *American Sociological Review, 43*, 623–643.

Gamson, W. A. (1968). *Power and discontent*. Homewood, IL: Dorsey.

Gates, B. (1999). *Business @ the speed of thought: Using a digital nervous system*. New York: Warner.

Giddens, A. (1979). *Central problems in social theory*. London: Hutchinson.

Goffee, R., & Jones, G. (1998). *The character of a corporation: How your company's culture can make or break your business*. New York: HarperBusiness.

Grates, G. F. (1994). The subtlety and power of communications in corporate renewal initiatives. *Public Relations Quarterly, 39* (1), 40–44.

Griffin, R. W. (2005). *Management*. Boston: Houghton Mifflin.

Gunter, M. (2006, August 7). The green machine. *Fortune*, pp. 42ff.

Habermas, J. (1987). *The theory of communication action: Vol. 2: Lifeworld and system* (T. McCarthy, Trans.). Boston: Beacon.

Hall, J. (1965). *Management's changing theory*. Conroe, TX: Telemetrics International.

Hamm, S. (2006, March 27). Speed demons. *Business Week*, pp. 68–76.

Hammonds, K. H., Zellner, W., & Melcher, R. (1996, March 11). Writing a new social contract. *Business Week*, pp. 60–61.

Harris, T. E. (1990). Organizational culture: An examination of the role of communication. In S. Thomas & W. A. Evans (Eds.), *Communication and culture: language, performance, technology, and media* (pp. 143–155). Norwood, NJ: Ablex.

Healey, J. R., & Kiley, D. (2001, March 6). Chrysler moves to improve its image. *USA Today*, p. 3B.

Hertzberg, F. (1968). One more time, how do you motivate employees? *Harvard Business Review, 46*(1), 53–62.

Hickman, C. G., & Silva, M. A. (1987). *The future 500: Creating tomorrow's organizations today.* New York: New American Library.

Jasinowski, J., & Hamrin, R. (1995). *Making it in America: Proven paths of success from 50 top companies.* New York: Simon & Schuster.

Jelinek, P. (2006, February 5). U.S. Army teaching troops how to pick the right spouse. *The Tuscaloosa News*, p. 11A.

Jesitus, J. (1997, January 6). Cashing in on corporate culture. *Industry Week*, pp. 16–19.

Jones, D. (1998, April 27). Balancing ethics and technology. *USA Today*, p. 1A.

Kanter, R. (1977). *Men and women of the corporations.* New York: Basic.

Kanter, R. M., Stein, B. A.; & Jick, T. D. (1992). *The challenge of organizational change: How companies experience it and leaders guide it.* New York: The Free Press.

Kast, F., & Rosenzweig, J. (1984). *The nature of management.* Chicago: Science Research Associates.

Klimley, A. W. (1999, June 21). Diversity today. *Fortune*, pp. S1–S26.

Kotter, J. P. (1990). *A force for change: How leadership differs from management.* New York: The Free Press.

Labrich, K. (1994, November 14). Why companies fail. *Fortune*, pp. 52–68.

Larkin, T. J., & Larkin, S. (1996, May–June). Reaching and changing frontline employees. *Harvard Business Review*, pp. 95–104.

Lawler, E. E. (1996, November 21). Competencies: A poor performance for the new pay. *Compensation and Benefits Review*, 12–18.

Levering, R., & Moskowitz, M. (2006, January 23). The 2006 list. *Fortune*, pp. 89–113.

Liker, J. K., & Meier, D. (2006). *The Toyota way fieldbook.* New York: McGraw-Hill.

Likert, R. (1961). *New patterns of management.* New York: McGraw-Hill.

Likert, R. (1967). *The human organization.* New York: McGraw-Hill.

Mandel, M. (2005, October 3). The real reasons you're working so hard … and what you can do about it. *Business Week*, pp. 59–67.

Maslow, A. H. (1970). *Motivation and personality* (2nd ed.). New York: Harper & Row.

McGregor, D. M. (1960). *The human side of enterprise.* New York: McGraw-Hill.

Mumby, D. (1988). *Communication and power in the organization: Discourse, ideology, and domination.* Norwood, NJ: Ablex.

Ostaff, F. (1999). *The horizontal organization.* New York: Oxford University Press.

Ouchi, W. G. (1981). *Theory Z: How American business can meet the Japanese challenge.* New York: Avon.

Pacanowsky, R. T., & O'Donnell-Trujillo, N. (1983). Organizational communication as cultural performance. *Communication Monographs, 50*, 126–147.

Pascale, R. T. (1990). *Managing on the edge: Companies that use conflict to stay ahead.* New York: Avon.

Pascale, R. T., & Anthos, A. G. (1981). *The art of Japanese management.* New York: Warner.

Pearlstine, N. (1998, December 7). Big wheels turning. *Time*, pp. 70–72.

Peters, T. J., & Waterman, R. H., Jr. (1982). *In search of excellence: Lessons from America's best-run companies.* New York: Harper & Row.

Pomeroy, A. (2004, July). Great places, inspired employees. *HR Magazine*, pp. 46–54.

Putnam, L. L. (1982). Paradigms for organizational communication research: An overview and synthesis. *Western Journal of Speech Communication, 46*, 192–206.

Roethisberger, F. L., & Dickson, W. (1939). *Management and the worker.* Cambridge, MA: Harvard University Press.

Rosen, R. H. (1991). *The healthy company: Eight strategies to develop people, productivity, and profits.* New York: Tarcher/Putnam.

Rothwell, W. J., Sullivan, R., & McLean, G. N. (1995). *Practicing organizational development: A guide for consultants.* San Diego: Pfeiffer.

Rush, H. M. F. (1972). The work of work and the behavioral sciences: A perspective and overview. In F. Luthers (Ed.), *Contemporary readings in organizational behavior* (pp. 11–28). New York: McGraw-Hill.

Schein, E. H. (1985). *Organizational culture and leadership.* San Francisco: Jossey-Bass.

Schein, E. H. (1990). Organizational culture. *American Psychologist, 45,* 109–119.

Schlosser, E. (2002). *Fast food nation.* New York: Perennial.

Shani, A. B., & Lau, J. B. (1996). *Behavior in organizations: An experiential approach.* Chicago: Irwin.

Smircich, L. (1983). Implications for management theory. In L. L. Putnam & M. E. Pacanowsky (Eds.), *Communication and organizations: An interpretative approach* (pp. 221–242). Beverly Hills, CA: Sage.

Smith, A. (1937), *The wealth of nations.* New York: Modern Library. (Original work published 1776).

Spain, P. J., & J. R. Talbot (Eds.). (1996). *Hoover's handbook of American business 1997.* Austin, TX: Reference Press.

Stewart, T. A. (1998, March 2). America's most admired companies. *Fortune,* pp. 70–82.

Stewart, T. A. (1999, March 29). The all-time greatest hits of managing. *Fortune,* p. 192.

Stuckey, D., & Mullins, M. E. (2005, November 29). U.S. population nears 300M. *USA Today,* p. 1A.

Taylor, F. W. (1911). *The principles of scientific management.* New York: Harper & Row.

Weber, M. (1947). *The theory of social and economic organizations.* (A. M. Henderson and T. Parsons, Trans.). New York: Free Press.

Weick, K. E. (1969). *The social psychology of organizations.* Reading, MA: Addison-Wesley.

Who's excellent now? (1984, November 4). *Business Week,* p. 21.

Wind, Y. M., & Main, J. (1998). *Driving change: How the best companies are preparing for the 21st century.* New York: The Free Press.

Winter, G. (2000, July 18). Theft by employees gets bigger and bolder. *USA Today,* p. 4D.

Chapter 4

Armour, S. (1998, July 2–5). E-mail 'a blessing' for business. *USA Today,* p. 1A.

Bacon, J. (1999, April 7). Mr. nice guy. *USA Today,* p. 8A.

Barton, G. M. (1990, January). Communication: Manage words effectively. *Personnel Journal,* pp. 32–36.

Bateson, G. (1972). *Steps to an ecology of the mind.* New York: Ballentine.

Bennis, W., & Townsend, R. (1995). Reinventing leadership: Strategies to empower the organization. New York: William Morrow.

Blake, L. (1987). Communicate with clarity: Manage meaning. *Personnel Journal, 66,* 43–45.

Blank, W. (1995). *The nine natural laws of leadership.* New York: AMACOM.

Blumenfeld, W. S. (1986). Business communication versus the ubiquitous, but insidious, oxymoron: A semantic gotcha. *The Bulletin, 44*, 33–36.

Blumenfeld, W. S. (1989). *Pretty ugly.* New York: Perigee.

Bolman, L. G., & Deal, T. E. (1984). *Modern approaches to understanding and managing organizations.* San Francisco: Jossey-Bass.

Bolman, L. G., & Deal, T. E. (2003). *Reframing organizations: Artistry, choice and leadership* (3rd ed.). San Francisco: Jossey-Bass.

Bowman, J. P., & Targowski, A. S. (1987). Modeling the communication process: The map is not the territory. *The Journal of Business Communication, 24*, 21–34.

Buckley, R. (1999, October). When you have to put it to them. *Across the Board,* pp. 44–48.

Burke, K. (1969). *A grammar of motives.* Berkeley: University of California Press.

Byers, P. Y. (1997). *Organizational communication: Theory and behavior.* Boston: Allyn & Bacon.

Calloway-Thomas, C., Cooper, P. J., & Blake, C. (1999). *Intercultural communication: Roots and routes.* Boston: Allyn & Bacon.

Carey, A. R., & Laird, B. (1999, February 23). Lingua franca? *USA Today,* p. 1A.

Clancy, J. J. (1989). *The invisible powers: The language of business.* Lexington, MA: Lexington.

Cleary, C., & Packard, T. (1992). The use of metaphor in organizational assessment and change. *Group & Organization Management, 17*(3), 229–313.

Collins, J. C., & Porras, J. I. (1996, September–October). Building your company's vision. *Harvard Business Review,* pp. 68–74.

Condon, J. C., Jr. (1975). Semantics and communication (2nd ed.). New York: Macmillan.

Conductors to keep magic word. (1999, March 31). *The Tuscaloosa News,* p. 1A.

Conrad, C. (1985). *Strategic organizational communication.* New York: Holt, Rinehart, and Winston.

Craig, J. (1997, Winter). Similarity and semantics. *Etc: A Review of General Semantics, 58*(4), pp. 412–414.

Deal, T. E., & Kennedy, A. A. (1982). *Corporate cultures: The rites and rituals of corporate life.* Reading, MA: Addison-Wesley.

Deetz, S. (2001). Conceptual foundations. In F. M. Jablin, & L.L. Putnam (Eds.), *The new handbook of organizational communication: Advances in theory, research, and methods* (pp. 3–46). Thousand Oaks, CA: Sage.

DeVito, J. A. (2004). *The interpersonal communication book* (10th ed.). Boston: Pearson.

Dobkin, B. A., & Pace, R. C. (2006). *Communication in a changing world.* New York: McGraw-Hill.

Drucker, P. (1993). *The post-capitalist society.* New York: The Free Press.

Duncan, W. J., & Feisal, J. P. (1989). No laughing matter: Patterns of humor in the workplace. *Organizational Dynamics, 17*(4), 18–30.

Dwyer, T. (1991). Humor, power, and change in organizations. *Human Relations, 44*(1), 1–19.

Eisenberg, E. M. (1984). Ambiguity as a strategy in organizational communication. *Communication Monographs, 51*, 227–242.

Farace, R. V., Monge, P. R., & Russell, H. M. (1977). *Communicating and organizing.* Reading, MA: Addison-Wesley.

Feller, N. (2005, December 16). 11 million U.S. adults not literate in English. *The Tuscaloosa News,* p. 3A.

Ferrell, O. C., & Fraedrich, J. (1994). *Business ethics: Ethical decision making and cases* (2nd ed.). New York: Houghton-Mifflin.

Fritz, S., Brown, F. W., Lunde, J. P., & Banset, E. A. (1999). *Interpersonal skills for leadership*. Upper Saddle River, NJ: Prentice Hall.

Gardner, H. (1995). *Leading minds: A anatomy of leadership*. New York: Basic Books.

Gass, R. H., & Seiter, J. S. (1999). *Persuasion, social influence, and compliance gaining*. Boston: Allyn & Bacon.

Gibson, J. L., Ivancevich, J. M., & Donnelly, J. H., Jr. (1991). *Organizations*. Homewood, IL: Irwin.

Gilsdorf, J. W. (1983). Executive and managerial attitudes toward business slang: A fortune-list survey. *The Journal of Business Communication, 24*, 36–37.

Gould, D. (1996, Fall). Fads and friction. *Future*, pp. 14–17.

Griffin, R. W. (2005). *Management* (8th ed.). Boston: Houghton Mifflin.

Haney, W. V. (1967). *Communication and organizational behavior: Text and cases* (rev. ed.), Homewood, IL: Irwin.

Harragan, B. L. (1997). *Games mother never taught you: Corporate gamesmanship for women*. New York: Warner.

Harris, T. E., & Sherblom, J. C. (2005). *Small group and team communication* (3rd ed.). Boston: Allyn & Bacon.

Hoover, J. D., & Howard, L. A. (1995). The political correctness controversy revisited. *American Behavioral Scientist, 38*(7), 963–975.

Hubert, C. (2006, July 12). Before you 'send,' realize anybody might see that e-mail. *The Birmingham News*, pp. 1G, 8G.

Jaroslovsky, R. (1988, July/August). What's on your mind, America? *Psychology Today*, p. 56.

Johnson, C. E., & Hackman, M. Z. (1995). *Creative communication*. Prospect Heights, IL: Waveland.

Kehrer, D. (1989). *Doing business boldly*. New York: Simon & Schuster.

Kotter, J. P. (1990). *A force for change: How leadership differs from management*. New York: The Free Press.

Kunerth, J. (1983, September 13). Behind the jargon: How the language of our work works. *Chicago Tribune*, p. 1.

Lewis, R. (1996). *When cultures collide: Managing successfully across cultures*. London: Nicholas Brealey.

Lippitt, G. (1982). Humor: A laugh a day keeps the incongruities at bay. *Training and Development Journal, 36*, 98–100.

Lipton, E. (2006, July 12). Terror database flawed, says report. *The Birmingham News*, p. 4A.

Locker, K. O. (1992). *Business and administrative communication* (7th ed.). Homewood, IL: Irwin.

Lubin, J. (1991, October 9). Thomas battles spotlights harassment. *Wall Street Journal*, pp. B1, B4.

Lynch, D. (2006, February 9). U.S. firms becoming tongue-tied. *The Tuscaloosa News*, p. 6B.

March, J. G., & Olsen, J. P. (1976). *Ambiguity and change in organizations*. Bergen, Norway: Universitetsforlaget.

Marklein, M. B. (1987, November 24). Wayward ways with words. *USA Today*, p. D1.

McClane, W. E., & Singer, D. D. (1991). The effective use of humor in organizational development. *Organizational Development Journal, 9*(1), 67–72.

McCormick, J. (1987, August 17). Decisions. *Newsweek*, p. 62.

Morris, C. (1971). *Writing on the general theory of signs.* The Hague, Netherlands: Mouton.

Multilingualism. (2005, April 24). *The Tuscaloosa News*, p. 1D.

Mumby, D. K., & Clair, R. P. (1997). Organizational discourse. In T. A. Van Dijk (Ed.), *Discourse as social interaction* (Vol. 2, pp. 181–205). London: Sage.

Nora, J. J., Rogers, C. R., & Stramy, R. J. (1986). *Transforming the workplace.* Princeton, NJ: Princeton Research Press.

Offstein, E. H., & Neck, C. P. (2003, December). From "acing the test" to "touching base": The sports metaphor in the classroom. *Business Communication Journal, 66*, 33–35.

O'Mara, J. (1994). *Diversity activities and training designs.* San Diego, CA: Pfeiffer.

Pell, A. R. (1995). *Idiot's guide to managing people.* New York: Alpha.

Peters, T. J., & Waterman, R. H., Jr. (1982). *In search of excellence: Lessons from America's best-run companies.* New York: Harper & Row.

Putnam, L. L., & Fairhurst, G. T. (2001). Discourse analysis in organizations: Issues and concerns. In F. M. Jablin & L. L. Putnam (Eds.), *The new handbook of organizational communication* (pp. 78–136). Thousand Oaks, CA: Sage.

Redding, W. C. (1984). *The corporate manager's guide to better communication.* Glenview, IL: Scott, Foresman.

Rentz, K. C., & Debs, M. B. (1987). Language and corporate values: Teaching ethics in business writing courses. *The Journal of Business Communication, 24*, 27–48.

Rizzo, A. M., & Mendez, C. (1990). *The integration of women in management: A guide for human resources and management development specialists.* New York: Quorum.

Robey, D. (1991). *Designing organizations* (3rd ed.). Homewood, IL: Irwin.

Rothwell, W. J., Sullivan, R., & McLean, G. N. (1995). *Practicing organizational development: A guide for consultants.* San Diego: Pfeiffer.

Schein, E. H. (1985). *Organizational culture and leadership.* San Francisco: Jossey-Bass.

Schemo, D. J. (2006, September 3). Some high school graduates not ready for college. *The Tuscaloosa News*, p. 8A.

Scott, C., & Bain, T. (1987). How arbitrators interpret ambiguous contract language. *Personnel Journal, 64*, 10–14.

Sellers, P. (2006, September 4). MySpace cowboys. *Fortune*, pp. 66–74.

Stewart, L. P., Cooper, P. J., Stewart, A. D., & Friedley, S. A. (2003). *Communication and gender* (4th ed.). Boston: Allyn & Bacon.

Sweeney, P. D., & McFarlin, D. B. (2002). *Organizational behavior: Solutions for management.* Boston: McGraw-Hill Irwin.

Taylor, N. M. (2006, July 31). Language barrier complicates police work. *The Tuscaloosa News*, p. 3B.

Toppo, G. (2005, December 16). One in 20 U.S. adults lack basic English skills. *USA Today*, p. 1A.

Verderber, K. S., & Verderber, R. F. (2001). *Inter-act: Interpersonal communication concepts, skills, and contexts* (9th ed.). U.S.: Wadsworth.

Ward, S., & Snider, J. (2000, October 19). A world bursting with information. *USA Today*, p. 10D.

Watzlawick, P., Beavin, J. B., & Jackson, D. D. (1967). *Pragmatics of human communication: A study of interactional patterns, pathologies, and paradoxes.* New York Norton.

Weick, K. E. (1987). Theorizing about organizational communication. In F. M. Jablin, L. L. Putnam, K. H. Roberts, & L. W. Porter (Eds.), *Handbook of organizational communication* (pp. 97–122). Newbury Park, CA: Sage.

Weil, E. (1998, June/July). Every leader tells a story. *Fast Company*, pp. 38, 40.

Weise, E. (2006, July 20). Demand surges for translators at medical facilities. *USA Today*, p. 7D.

Whiteley, R. C. (1991). *The customer-driven company: Moving from talk to action.* Reading, MA: Addison-Wesley.

Wind, J. Y., & Main, J. (1998). *Driving change: How the best companies are preparing for the 21st century.* New York: The Free Press.

Witten, M. (1993). Narrative and the culture of obedience at the workplace. In D. K. Mumby (Ed.), *Narrative and social control: Critical perspectives* (pp. 97–118). Newbury Park, CA: Sage.

Yang, J., & Lewis, A. (2005, June 28). Habla usted espanol? *USA Today*, p. 1B.

Chapter 5

Adler, R. B., & Towne, N. (2003). *Looking out/looking in* (10th ed.). U.S.: Thomson Wadsworth.

Anderson, P. A. (1999). *Nonverbal communication: forms and functioning.* Mountain View, CA: Mayfield.

Armour, S. (2000, June 27). Companies rethink casual clothes. *USA Today*, pp. 1A–2A.

Armour, S. (2005, October 26). Dust off those ties and pumps: Dress codes gussy up. *USA Today*, 1B.

Associated Press. (1999, April 19). Hitachi workers told to relax. *Montgomery Advertiser*, p. 6B.

Axtell, R. E. (1991). *Gestures: The do's and taboos of body language around the world.* New York: Wiley.

Barro, R. J. (1998, March 16). So you want to hire the beautiful. Well, why not? *Business Week*, p. 18.

Beamer, L., & Varner, I. (2001). *Intercultural communication in the global workplace* (2nd. Ed.). Boston: McGraw-Hill Irwin.

Bencivenga, D. (1998). A humanistic approach to space. *HR Magazine, 43*(4), pp. 72–77.

Bennis, W. (1990). *Why leaders can't lead: The unconscious conspiracy continues.* San Francisco: Jossey-Bass.

Berger, J. (1995, February 5). IBM sheds white shirts. *The Tuscaloosa News*, p. 1E.

Berry, M. (1987, October 26). How mini is too mini? At work you still can't cut it too short. *The Evansville Courier and Press*, p. D1.

Birdwhistell, R. L. (1970). *Kinesics and context: Essays on body motion communication.* Philadelphia: University of Pennsylvania Press.

Blanchard, K., & Johnson, S. (1982). *The one-minute manager.* New York: Morrow.

Blum, D. (1998, October). Face it! *Psychology Today*, pp. 32–39, 66.

Bonuso, C. (1979). *Phi Delta Kappan, 64.* Cited in *Psychology Today, 17,* 17.

Boyanowsky, E. O., & Griffiths, C. T. (1982). Weapons and eye contact as instigators or inhibitors of aggressive arousal in police–citizen interaction. *Journal of Applied Social Psychology, 12,* 398–407.

Bruneau, T. J. (1973). Communicative silences: Forms and functions. *Journal of Communication, 23,* 17–46.

Burgoon, J. K., Birk, T., & Pfau, M. (1990). Nonverbal behaviors, persuasion, and credibility. *Human Communication Research, 17,* 140–169.

Burgoon, J. K., Buller, D. B., & Woodall, W. G. (1996). *Nonverbal communication: The unspoken dialogue.* New York: McGraw-Hill.

Burgoon, J. K., & Dillman, L. (1995). Gender, immediacy, and nonverbal communication. In P. J. Kalbfleisch & M. J. Cody (Eds.), *Gender, power, and communication in human relationships* (pp. 63–82). Hillsdale, NJ: Erlbaum.

Burgoon, J. K., & Saine, T. (1978). *The unspoken dialogue.* Dallas: Houghton Mifflin.

Butler, A. (1987, December 29). It's a crying shame if it is at the office. *The Sunday Courier,* p. F9.

Caggiano, C. (1997, December). Does anyone still wear a power tie? *Inc.,* p. 148.

Calloway-Thomas, C., Cooper, P. J., & Blake, C. (1999). *Intercultural communication: Roots and routes.* Boston: Allyn & Bacon.

Carey, A. R., & Mullins, M. E. (1998, March 4). On the "Dilbert" scale. *USA Today,* p. B1.

Carns, A. (1997, May 7). Office workers rub elbows as more workplaces shrink. *The Wall Street Journal,* p. B1.

Case, J. (1987). The sounds of silence: Why aren't there any good business tapes? *INC., 9*(10), p. 22.

Cash, T. F., Winstead, B. A., & Janda, L. H. (1986). The great American shape-up. *Psychology Today, 20,* 30–37.

Chung, W. V. (1997). Auditing the organizational culture for diversity: A conceptual framework. In C. D. Brown, C. Snedeker, & Beate Sykes (Eds.), *Conflict and diversity.* Cresskill, NJ: Hampton.

Crick, J. (2005, June 13). Hand jive. *Fortune,* pp. 40–41.

Colvin, G. (2006, January 23). The best places to work. *Fortune,* pp. 71–78.

Conlin, M. (2006, July 3). Square feet. Oh, how square. *Business Week,* pp. 101–102.

Cope, L. (1987, August 3). Study shows patients like doctors to look traditional. *The Evansville Courier,* p. 7.

DeVito, J. A. (2004). *The interpersonal communication book* (10th ed.). Boston: Pearson.

Dressing smartly. (2003, September 14). *The Tuscaloosa News,* p. 1D.

Droney, J. M., & Brooks, C. I. (1993). Attributes of self-esteem as a function of duration of eye contact. *Journal of Social Psychology, 133,* 715–718.

Dubrin, A. J. (1999). *Human relations for career and personal success* (5th ed.). Upper Saddle River, NJ: Prentice Hall.

Dubrin, A. J. (2000). *Applying psychology: Individual and organizational effectiveness* (5th ed.). Upper Saddle River, NJ: Prentice Hall.

Duncan, S., Jr. (1975). Interaction units during speaking turns in dyadic, face-to-face conversations. In A. Kendon, R. Harris, & M. Kay (Eds.), *Organization of behavior in face-to-face interaction* (pp. 199–213). The Hague: Mouton.

Dunkin, A. (1995, April 17). Taking care of business—without leaving the house. *Business Week,* pp. 106–107.

Dunung, S. (1998). *Doing business in Asia: The complete guide.* San Francisco: Jossey-Bass.

Edelman, K. A. (1997). Take down the walls, *Across the Board, 34*(3), 32–38.

Edelson, H. (1987, August 25). Too many tears can dampen your career. *USA Today,* p. D4.

Egalitarian rules in Japanese plants. (1987, December 28). *The Evansville Courier,* p. B5.

Ekman, P., & Friesen, W. V. (1987, October 28). Universal facial expressions. *USA Today,* p. D8.

Fischman, J. (1988). Service with a smile. *Psychology Today, 22,* p. 17.

Forbes, C. (1990, April 12). Firm handshake more important than buttering a role, etiquette expert says. *Birmingham Post-Herald,* p. C10.

Fortune, M., Francis, B. C., Gallera, P., Miller, R. J., Stemler, G. J., & Whitman, K. M. (1995, May). Dress code: How are CPA firms handling the trend toward more casual dress at work? An informal survey gives some answers. *Journal of Accountancy, 179,* 39–42.

Gaines, S. (1987, October 11). Employers wake up to worker well being. *Chicago Tribune,* Sec. 7, p. 1.

Gardenswartz, L., & Rowe, A. (1993). *Managing diversity: A complete desk reference and planning guide.* Chicago: Irwin.

Galin, A. (1990). Does the way you dress affect your performance rating? *Personnel, 67,* 49–53.

Gass, R. H., & Seiter, J. S. (1999). *Persuasion, social influence, and compliance gaining.* Boston: Allyn & Bacon.

Goffman, E. (1959). *The presentation of self in everyday life.* Garden City, NY: Anchor.

Goffman, E. (1963). *Stigma: Notes on the management of spoiled identity.* Englewood Cliffs, NJ: Prentice Hall.

Goodall, H. L., Jr., & Goodall, S. (2006). *Communicating in professional contexts: Skills, ethics, and technologies* (2nd ed.). U.S.: Thomson Wadsworth.

Gordon, N. (1998). Workers in today's fishbowl are fish out of water. *National Catholic Reporter, 34*(14), p. 18.

Gordon, W. I., Tengler, C. D., & Infante, D. A. (1982). Women's clothing predispositions as predictors of dress at work, job satisfaction, and career advancement. *The Southern Speech Communication Journal, 47*(4), 422–434.

Gray, J. G., Jr. (1983). *Image impact: The business and professional man's personal packaging program.* Bethesda, MD: Media Impact.

Greenberg, J. (1988, November). Equity and workplace status: A field experiment. *Journal of Applied Psychology, 73,* 606–610.

Gunn, R., & Burroughs, M. (1996). Workplaces that work: Designing high-performance offices. *Futurist, 30*(2), 19–24.

Hackman, M. Z., & Johnson, C. E. (2000). *Leadership: A communication perspective* (3rd ed.). Prospect Heights, IL: Waveland.

Hall, E. T. (1959). *The silent language.* Garden City, NY: Doubleday.

Hall, E. T. (1966). *The hidden dimension.* Garden City, NY: Doubleday.

Hall, E. T. (1972). Proxemics: the study of man's spatial relations. In L. A. Somovar & R. E. Porter (Eds.), *Intercultural communication: A reader* (pp. 210–217). Belmont, CA: Wadsworth.

Hall, E. T. (1985). Social time: The heartbeat of culture. *Psychology Today, 19,* 33.

Hamilton, J. (1996, April 29). The new workplace. *Business Week,* pp. 106–117.

Harper, R. G., Wiens, A. N., & Matarazzo, J. D. (1978). *Nonverbal communication: The state of the art.* New York: Wiley.

Hayes, C. (1996). How to dress when moving up the ladder. *Black Enterprise, 27,* 131–133.

Hecht, M. A., & LaFrance, M. (1998, December). License or obligation to smile: The effect of power and sex on amount and type of smiling. *Personality & Social Psychology Bulletin, 24*(12), 1343.

Heller, R. (1998). *Motivating people.* New York: DK Publishing.

Hellmich, N. (1988, September 23). Career women's code of conduct for the office. *USA Today,* p. D1.

Hendricks, M. (1995, August). More than words. *Entrepreneur, 23*(8), 54–57.

Hendricks, M. (1996, January). Informal wear: Does dressing down send productivity up?" *Entrepreneur, 24*(1), 79–82

Henley, N. M. (1977). *Body politics: Power, sex, and nonverbal communication.* New Jersey: Prentice Hall.

Henley, N. (1995). Body politics revisited: What do we know today? In P. Kalbfleisch & M. Cody (Eds.), *Gender, power, and communication in human relations.* Hillsdale, NJ: Erlbaum.

Hensley, W. E. (1981). The effects of attire, location, and sex on aiding behavior: A similarity explanation. *Journal of Nonverbal Behavior, 6,* 3–11.

Hickson, M. L., & Stacks, D. W. (1985). *Nonverbal communication: Studies and applications.* Dubuque, IA: Wm. C. Brown.

Hindo, B. (2004, November 8). Branding battles. *Business Week,* p. 11.

Ianzito, C. (1995, July/August). Gut reactions. *Psychology Today,* p. 18.

Jones, B. (1996, July). Unsuitable for the job? *Management Review, 85*(7), 51.

Jones, D. (2006, April 14). CEOs vouch for Waiter Rule: Watch how people treat staff. *USA Today,* pp. 1B–2B.

Kearney, K. G., & White, T. I. (1994). *Men & women at work.* Hawthorne, NJ: Career Press.

Knapp, M. L. (1972). *Nonverbal communication in human interaction.* New York: Holt, Rinehart, and Winston.

Knapp, M. L. (1978). *Nonverbal communication in human interaction* (2nd ed.). New York: Holt, Rinehart, and Winston.

Korda, M. (1975). *Power! How to get it, how to use it.* New York: Ballantine.

Korda, M. (1986). Symbols of power. In P. J. Frost, W. F. Mitchell & W. R. Nord (Eds.), *Organizational reality: Reports from the firing line* (3rd ed., pp. 145–156). Glenview, IL: Scott, Foresman.

Krohe, J. (1993). What makes an office work? *Across the Board, 30*(4), 16–23.

Lawrence, S., & Watson, M. (1991). Getting others to help: The effectiveness of professional uniforms in charitable fund raising. *Journal of Applied Communication Research, 19,* 170–185.

Levering, R., & Moskowitz, M. (2006, January 23). The 2006 list: And the winners are. *Fortune,* pp. 89–113.

Levine, R. (1987). Waiting is a power game. *Psychology Today, 21,* 26.

Lieber, R. B. (1996, November). Cool offices, *Fortune,* pp. 134–138.

Liss, B., Walker, M., Hazelton, V., & Cupach, W. D. (1993, February). *Mutual gaze and smiling as correlates to compliance-gaining success.* Paper presented at the annual meeting of the Western States Communication Association, Albuquerque, NM.

Lustig, M. W. & Koester, J. (2003). *Intercultural competence: Interpersonal communication across cultures* (4th ed.). Boston: Allyn & Bacon.

Mack, D. (1990). Female applicant's grooming and personnel selection. *Journal of Social Behavior and Personality, 5,* 399–407.

Mackay, M., & Maxwell, G. (1997). Future shop. *People and Management, 3*(20), 44–47.

Management Recruiters International Inc., (1999, March). Executives believe suit and tie will soon be obsolete. *HRFocus,* p. 4

Mannix, M. (1997, August 4). Casual Friday, five days a week. *U.S. News and World Report,* p. 60.

Marlandro, L. A., & Barker, L. (1983). *Nonverbal communication.* Reading, MA: Addison-Wesley.

McGinley, H., LeFevre, R., & McGinley, P. (1965). The influence of a communicator's body position in opinion change in others. *Journal of Personality and Social Psychology, 31,* 686–690.

Mehrabian, A. (1981). Silent messages: Implicit communication of emotions and attitudes (2nd ed.). Belmont, CA: Wadsworth.

Meyer, H. (1997). Tearing down the walls. *Journal of Business Strategy, 18*(6), 24–29.

Mitchell, W. (1991, January 13). Do not forget why you were invited. *Parade Magazine,* p. 23.

Molloy, J. T. (1975). *Dress for success.* New York: Warner.

Molloy, J. T. (1977). *The woman's dress for success book.* Chicago: Folett.

Molloy, J. T. (1988). *John T. Molloy's new dress for success.* New York: Warner.

Monk, R. (1997). The impact of open-plan offices on organizational performance. *International Journal of Management, 14*(3), 345–349.

Morris, D. (1977). *Manwatching: A field guide to human behavior.* New York: Harry N. Abrams.

Nathan, S. (1999, May 18). Business meetings no longer time to booze it up. *USA Today,* p. 12E.

Neale, M. A., & Norcraft, G. B. (1990). *Organizational behavior: A management challenge.* Chicago: The Dryden Press.

Nelson, A. (2004). *You don't say: Navigating nonverbal communication between the sexes.* New York: The Berkeley Publishing Group.

Newman, H. M. (1982). The sounds of silence in communicative encounters. *Communication Quarterly, 30,* 142–149.

O'Connell, L. (1991, June 30). Experts wary of expressing emotions at work. *The Birmingham News,* p. 9E.

Olson, T. E., & Frieze, I. H. (1987, February 4). Survey: Tall men get big raises. *USA Today,* p. 6B.

Ouchi, W. C. (1981). *Theory Z: How American business can meet the Japanese challenge.* New York: Avon.

Patterson, M. (1968). Spatial factors in social interaction. *Human Factors, 2,* 351–361.

Peak, M. H. (1994, August). Dress-down daze. *Management Review,* pp. 30–32.

Pearce, W. B., & Brommel, N. J. (1972). Vocalic communication in persuasion. *Quarterly Journal of Speech, 58,* 298–306.

Pearce, W. B., & Conklin, F. (1971). Nonverbal vocalic communication and perception of speaker. *Speech Monographs, 38,* 235–241.

People. (1987, August 11). *USA Today,* p. 4D.

Peterson, T. (1991, December 30). O.K. button up—and button down. *Business Week*, p. 48.

Plas, J. M., & Hoover-Dempsey, K. V. (1989). *Working up a storm*. New York: W. W. Norton.

Prasso, S. (2001, March 19). Casual dress: Dot-com casualty? *Business Week*, p. 8.

Raiford, R. (1998, December). Interior design and space planning. *Buildings, 92*(12), 46–48.

Raudsepp, E. (1983). The politics of promotion. *Office Administration, 44*, 28–32.

Ray, R. G. (1999). *The facilitative leader: Behaviors that enable success*. Upper Saddle River, NJ: Prentice Hall.

Re-engineering. (1995). *The Economist, 337*, 91.

Remland, M. S. (2000). *Nonverbal communication in everyday life*. Boston: Houghton Mifflin.

Remland, M. S. (2003). *Nonverbal communication in everyday life* (2nd ed.). Boston: Houghton Mifflin.

Richmond, V. P., McCroskey, J. C., & Payne, S. K. (1987). *Nonverbal behavior in interpersonal relations*. Englewood Cliffs, NJ: Prentice Hall.

Rucker, J., & Sellers, J. A. (1998, February). Changes in business etiquette. *Business Education Forum*, pp. 42–44.

Sabath, A. M. (1990, September). A quiz on business meals. *Communication Briefings, 8*, 4.

Schein, E. H. (1992). *Organizational culture and leadership* (2nd ed.). San Francisco: Jossey-Bass.

Seiler, J. A. (1984). Architecture at work. *Harvard Business Review, 62*(1), 111–120.

Seitz, V. A. (2000). *Your executive image*. Avon, MA: Adams Media.

Shaich, R. (2006, July 10). Not by bread alone. *Fortune*, p. 126.

Shaw, R. (1994, September). Uniforms foster pride and professionalism. *American School and University, 67*, 22–26.

Siegel, S. M., Friedlander, M. L., & Heatherington, L. (1992). Nonverbal relational control in family communication. *Journal of Nonverbal Behavior, 16*, 117–139.

Solomon, J. (1996, September 30). Why worry about pleat pull and sloppy socks? Corporate casual gets complicated. *Newsweek*, p. 51.

Solomon, M. R. (1986). Dress for effect. *Psychology Today, 20*, 32.

Solomon, M. (1987). Standard issue. *Psychology Today, 21*, 31.

Sommer, R. (1969). *Personal space: The behavioral basis for design*. Englewood Cliffs, NJ: Prentice Hall.

Speer, T. L. (1999, March 16). Avoid gift giving and cultural blunders in Asian locales. *USA Today*, p. 3E.

Sprout, A. L. (1994, May 2). Moving into the virtual office. *Fortune*, p. 103.

Stewart, T. A. (1997, January 31). Get with the new power game. *Fortune*, pp. 58–62.

Stone, P. J., & Luchetti, R. (1985). Your office is where you are. *Harvard Business Review, 63*, 103–106.

Street, R. L., & Brady, R. M. (1982). Speech rate acceptance ranges as a function of evaluative domain, listener speech rate, and communication context. *Communication Monographs, 49*, 290–308.

Swartz, J. (2006, January 23). The shoe-in. *Fortune*, pp. 116–117.

Terazono, E. (1995, August). 'Fridaywear' comes to Japan. *World Press Review*, p. 34.

Thourlby, W. W. (1978). *You are what you wear*. New York: New American Library.

Tilsner, J. (1993, July 19). But will they get their own water coolers? *Business Week*, p. 32.

Tomkins, S. S. (1962). *Affect, imagery, consciousness*. New York: Springer.

Tresch, R., Sr., Pearson, P., Munter, M., Wyld, L. D., & Waltman, J. L. (1986). Nonverbal communication. In S. P. Golen (Ed.). *Methods of teaching selected topics in business communication* (pp. 75–80). Urbana, IL: The Association for Business Communication.

Tsai, M. (2002, August 11). There is no tie in teamwear. *The Tuscaloosa News*, pp. 1D, 9D.

VDTs: Fitting the job to the person. (1991, January/February). *Labor Relations Today, 6*. Washington, DC: U.S. Department of Labor.

Visser, M. (1991). *The rituals of dinner*. New York: Penguin.

Weight discrimination. (1999, November 7). It's all too common. *The Tuscaloosa News*, p. D1.

Weiser, J. (1996, February 26). Denim downsize. *The New Republic*, pp. 10–11.

Weiss, E. (1995). Suiting up for success. *Working Women*, pp. 19–20.

Chapter 6

Agenti, P., & Forman, J. (2002). *The power of corporate communication: Crafting the voice and image of your business*. New York: McGraw-Hill.

Allbritton, C. (1198, September 8). It's a small world wide web, after all. *The Tuscaloosa News*, p. 1A.

Allerton, H. E. (2000, July). They're back! *Training & Development*, p. 80.

Aluja, M. K., & Carley, K. M. (1998). Network structure in virtual organizations. *Journal of Computer-Mediated Communication, 3*(4).

Andreeva, N. (1998, August 17). Do the math—it is a small world. *Business Week*, pp. 54–55.

Armour, S. (2000, March 20). Corporate intranets help bring employees into the loop. *USA Today*, p. 3B.

Armour, S. (2001, January 18). Employers prop up morale in light of layoffs, rumors. *USA Today*, p. 1B.

Bad news. (2005, October 2). *Tuscaloosa News*, p. 1D.

Bell, A. H., & Smith, D. M. (1999). *Management communication*. New York: Wiley.

Benton, D. A. (1995). *Applied human relations: An organizational approach* (5th ed.). Englewood Cliffs, NJ: Prentice Hall.

Berner, R. (2006, May 29). I sold it through the grapevine. *Business Week*, pp. 32, 34.

Berry, L. L. (1999). *Discovering the soul of service*. New York: Free Press.

Blaken, R. L., & Liff, A. (1999). *Embracing the future: An action guide for association leaders*. Washington, DC: ASAE.

Blau, J. R., & Alba, R. D. (1982). Empowering nets of participation. *Administrative Science Quarterly, 27*, 363–379.

Bolman, L. G., & Deal, T. E. (2003). *Reframing organizations: Artistry, choice, and leadership* (3rd ed.). San Francisco: Jossey-Bass.

Boyett, J., & Boyett, J. (1998). *The guru guide: The best ideas of the top management thinkers*. New York: Wiley.

Branch, S. (1999, January 11). The 100 best companies to work for in America. *Fortune*, pp. 118–144.

Bridgestone and Ford settle dispute over defective tires. (2005, October 13). *New York Times*, p. C5.

Brunvard, J. M. (1990). *Curses, broiled again: The hottest urban legends going.* New York: W. W. Norton.

Building world class suggestion systems. (1998, April). Center for Suggestion System Development, pp. 1–4.

Capers, R. S., & Lipton, E. (1993). Hubble error: Time, money, and millionths of an inch. *Academy of Management Executive, 7*(4), 41–57.

Carey, A. R., & Mullins, M. E. (2000, June 6). Taking work home. *USA Today,* p. 1B.

Carvell, T. (2000, March 6). Lockheed raises a stink over 'skunkworks.' *Fortune,* p. 80.

Chae, B. P., Paradice, D., Koch, H., & Huy, Vo Van. (2005). *The Journal of Computer Information Systems, 45*(4), 62–74.

Chen, Z., & Lawson, R. B. (1996, Fall). Groupthink: Deciding with the leader and the devil. *Psychological Record, 46*(4), pp. 581–592.

Company still fighting Satan rumor. (1988, November 11). *The Evansville Courier,* p. 6.

Cummings, T. G., & Worley, C. G. (2005). *Organizational development and change* (8th ed.). U.S.: Thomson South-Western.

Daniels, T. D., & Spiker, B. K. (1991). *Perspectives on organizational communication* (2nd ed.). Dubuque, IA: Brown.

Dansereau, F., & Markham, S. E. (1987). Superior–subordinate communication: Multiple levels of analysis. In F. M. Jablin, L. L. Putnam, K. H. Roberts, & L. W. Porter (Eds.), *Handbook of organizational communication* (pp. 343–388). Newbury Park, CA: Sage.

Davis, K. (1953). Management communication and the grapevine. *Harvard Business Review,* 31, 43–49.

Davis, K. (1973, July). The care and cultivation of the corporate grapevine. *Dun's Review,* pp. 44–47.

Deetz, S. A., Tracy, S. J., & Simpson, J. L. (2000). *Leading organizations through transition.* Thousand Oaks, CA: Sage.

Denisi, A. S., & Griffin, R. W. (2005). *Human resource management* (2nd ed.). Boston: Houghton Mifflin.

Donnelly, J. H., Jr. (1991). *Organizations.* Homewood, IL: Irwin.

DuBrin, A. J. (1999). *Human relations for career and personal success* (5th ed.). Upper Saddle River, NJ: Prentice Hall.

Dwyer, P., Carney, D., & Muller, J. (2000, October 2). Did Ford mislead Congress? *Business Week,* pp. 50, 52.

Eldridge, E., & Armour, S. (2000, February 4). Ford employees to get computers. *USA Today,* p. 1B.

Fisher, A. (2005, December 12). Psst! Rumors can help at work. *Fortune,* p. 202.

France, M. (2001, January 29). The litigation machine. *Business Week,* pp. 114–124.

Gates, B. (1999). *Business @ the speed of thought.* New York: Warner.

Gibson, J. L., Ivancevich, J. M., & Donnelly, J. H. (1991). *Organizations* (7th ed.). Homewood, IL: Irwin.

Gillins, P. (1982, February). Must be true—It happened to. *The Chicago Tribune,* p. 20.

Glassman, R. B. (1973). Persistence and loose coupling in living systems. *Behavioral Science, 18,* 83–98.

Glazer, M., P., & Glazer, P. M. (1986, August). Whistleblowing. *Psychology Today,* pp. 36–43.

Goldhaber, G. M. (1993). *Organizational communication* (5th ed.). Madison, WI: Brown and Benchmark.

Gouran, D. S., Hirokawa, R. Y., & Martz, A. E. (1986). A critical analysis of factors related to decisional processes involved in the Challenger disaster. *Central States Speech Journal, 37,* 119–135.

Greenberg, J. (1983). Communication in organizations. In R. A. Baron (Ed.), *Behavior in organizations* (pp. 87–94). Boston: Allyn & Bacon.

Greco, S. (1999, 20th Anniversary Issue). It takes a coffee klatch. *Inc.,* p. 42.

Griffin, R. W. (2005). *Management* (8th ed.). Boston: Houghton Mifflin.

Hamilton, J. (1991, June 3). Blowing the whistle without paying the piper. *Business Week,* pp. 138–139.

Healey, J. R., & Nathan, S. (2000, September 21). Further scrutiny puts Ford in the hot seat. *USA Today,* p. 1B.

Henry, D. (2006, April 24). Creativity pays. Here's how much. *Business Week,* p. 76.

Herman, T. (1994, August 17). News briefs. *Wall Street Journal,* p. A1.

Hiam, A. (1999). *Motivating & rewarding employees.* Holbrook MA: Adams Media.

Hickey, J. V., & Casner-Lotto, J. (1998). How to get true employee participation. *Training and Development, 52*(2), 58–61.

Holtz, S. (1996). Intranets: What's all the excitement? *Communication World,* 13, 54–58.

Hoversten, P. (1999, October 1). Bad math added to doomed Mars craft. *USA Today,* p. 4A.

Huber, G. P., & Daft, R. L. (1987). The information environments of organizations. In F. M. Jablin, L. L. Putnam, K. H. Roberts, & L. W. Porter (Eds.), *Handbook of organizational communication* (pp. 130–164). Newbury Park, CA: Sage.

Ideas. (1999, July 1). *Bottom Line Personal,* 20.

Janis, I. L. (1972). *Victims of groupthink.* Boston: Houghton Mifflin.

Johns, G. (1988). *Organizational behavior: Understanding life at work* (2nd ed.). Glenview, IL: Scott, Foresman.

Jones, D. (1999, February 19). Reengineering and rescuing a legacy's distorted image. *USA Today,* p. 12B.

Katz, D., & Kahn, R. (1966). *The social psychology of organizations.* New York: Wiley.

Katz, D., & Lazarfeld, P. F. (1965). *Personal influence.* New York: Free Press.

Kerwin, K., Burrows, P., & Foust, D. (2000, February 21). Workers of the world, log on. *Business Week,* p. 52.

Kotter, J. P. (1982). *The general managers.* New York: Free Press.

Kruglanski, A. W. (1986, August). Freezethink and the Challenger. *Psychology Today,* pp. 48–49.

Labbs, J. (1999, January). Overload. *Workforce,* pp. 30–33.

Lardner, Jr., G. (1998, July 27). Violence at work is largely unreported. *Washington Post,* p. A2.

Lee, C. (1999, December). So long 20th century. *Training,* pp. 30–48.

Levering, R., & Moskowitz, M. (2000, January 10). The 100 best companies to work for. *Fortune,* p. 82ff.

Light, L., & Landler, M. (1990, December 24). Killing a rumor before it kills a company. *Business Week,* p. 23.

Lussier, R. N. (1999). *Human relations in organizations* (4th ed.). Boston: McGraw-Hill.

Mathis, R. L., & Jackson, J. (1994). *Human resources management.* Minneapolis: West.

McLagan, P. A. (199, December). As the HRD world churns: Trends, forces, and the cusp. Training & Development, pp. 20–30.

McShane, S. L., & Von Glinow, M. A. (2000). *Organizational behavior.* Boston: Irwin.

Milgram, S. (1965). Some conditions of obedience and disobedience to authority. *Human Relations, 18,* 57–75.

Mohrman, S. A., Cohen, S. G., & Mohrman, A. (1995). *Designing team-based organizations: New forms of knowledge application.* San Francisco: Jossey-Bass.

Monge, P. R., & Contractor, N. (2003). *Theories of networks.* New York: Oxford University Press.

Moorehead, G., & Griffin, R. W. (1998). *Organizational behavior: Managing people and organizations.* Boston: Houghton Mifflin.

Mueller, R. K. (1986). *Corporate networking: Building channels for information and influence.* New York. Free Press.

Myers, D. W. (1998). *1999 U.S. master human resources guide.* Chicago: CCH, Inc.

New technologies take time. (1999, April 19). *Business Week,* p. 8.

Newton, B. D. (2001, January 20). Little praise for job appraisals. *Tuscaloosa News,* p. 5B.

Nohria, N. (1998). Is a network perspective a useful way of studying organizations? In G. H. Hickman (Ed.), *Leading organizations: Perspectives for a new era* (pp. 287–301). Thousand Oaks, CA: Sage.

O'Donnell, J. (2005, November 29). Online rumor mill dogs companies. *USA Today,* p. 3B.

O'Reilly, B. (1997, March 3). Secrets of the most admired corporations: New ideas and new products. *Fortune,* pp. 60–64.

Osburn, J. D., Moral, L., Musselwhite, W., & Zenger, J. H. (1990). *Self-directed work units: The new American challenge.* Homewood, IL: Business One Irwin.

Ostaff, F. (1999). *The horizontal organization.* New York: Oxford University Press.

P&G logo changed. (1991, July 11). *Birmingham Post-Herald,* p. B10.

Pasmore, W. (1996). *Creating strategic change: Designing the flexible high-performing organization.* New York: Wiley.

Pearce, J. W., II, & David, F. R. (1983). A social network approach to organizational design-performance. *Academy of Management Review, 8,* 436–444.

Penzias, A. (1989). *Ideas and information: Managing in a high-tech world.* New York: Norton.

Peters, T. (1987). *Thriving on chaos: Handbook for a management revolution.* New York: Knopf.

Peters, T., & Austin, N. (1985). *A passion for excellence: The leadership difference.* New York: Random House.

Preventing sexual harassment: A fact sheet for employees. (1999). Washington, DC: BNA.

Ragins, B. R. (1997). Diversified mentoring relationships in organizations: A power perspective. *Academy of Management Review, 22,* 482–521.

Reece, B. L., & Brandt, R. (2005). Effective *human relations: Personal and organizational applications* (9th ed.). Boston: Houghton Mifflin.

Rees, F. (1991). *How to lead work teams.* San Diego: Pfeiffer.

Risser, R. (1999, August). Sexual harassment training: Truth and consequences. *Training & Development,* pp. 21–23.

Roberts, K. H. (1984). *Communicating in organizations.* Chicago: Science Research Associates.

Rogers, E. M. (1983). *Diffusion of innovations.* New York: Free Press.

Rogers, E. M., & Agarwala-Rogers, R. (1976). *Communication in organizations.* New York: Free Press.

Rowe, M. P., & Baker, M. (1984). Are you hearing enough employee concerns? *Harvard Business Review, 62*, 120–128.

Salopek, J. J. (2000, March). Analyze this. Training & Development, p. 14.

Scheider, A., & Davis, C. (2000, February 13). Intranet architecture. CIR Online. Retrieved from http://intrack.com/Intranet/

Schonfeld, E. (1999, February 15). The exchange economy. *Fortune*, pp. 67–68.

Shani, A. B., & Lau, J. B. (2000). *Behavior in organizations: An experiential approach.* Boston: McGraw-Hill.

Sharpe, S. B. (2000, September 18). Work at home? First, get real. *Newsweek*, pp. 112, 116.

Smart, T., & Schine, E. (1991, January 21). The 1863 law that's haunting business. *Business Week*, p. 68.

Stein, B. A., & Kanter, R. M. (1993). Why good people do bad things: A retrospective on the Hubble fiasco. *Academy of Management Executive, 7*(4), 58–62.

Thurm, S. (2000, June 1). Microsoft's behavior is helping Cisco learn how to avoid trouble. *Wall Street Journal*, p. A1.

Tichy, N. M. (1981). Networks in organizations. In P. C. Nystrom & W. H. Starbuck (Eds.), *Handbook of organizational design* (Vol. 2, pp. 225–249). London: Oxford University Press.

Tichy, N. M., Tushman, M. L., & Fombrun, C. (1979). Social network analysis for organizations. *Academy of Management Review, 4*, 507–519.

Timm, P. R., & DeTienne, K. B. (1995). *Managerial communication: A finger on the pulse.* Englewood Cliffs, NJ: Prentice Hall.

Tietelbaum, R. (1997, June 9). How to harness gray matter. *Fortune*, p. 168.

Tjosvold, D. (1995). Cooperation theory, constructive controversy, and effectiveness: Learning from crisis. In R. A. Guzzo, E. Salas, and Associates (Eds.), *Team effectiveness and decision making in organizations* (pp. 79–112). San Francisco: Jossey-Bass.

Tully, S. (2000, March 20). The B2B tool that is changing the world. *Fortune*, pp. 132–145.

Trujillo, N., & Toth, E. L. (1987). Organizational perspectives for public relations research and practice. *Management Communication Quarterly, 1*, 218–224.

Van de Vliet, A. (1997, November). ESOP's fable becomes a reality. *Management Today*, pp. 112–115.

Van Maanen, J. W., & Barley, S. R. (1984). Occupational communities: Culture and control in organizations. In B. M. Shaw & L. K. Cummings (Eds.), *Research in organizational behavior* (Vol. 6, pp. 82–99). Greenwich, CT: JAI.

Venette, S. J., Sellnow, T. L., & Lang, P. A. (2003). Metanarration's role in restructuring perceptions of crisis: NSTSA's failure in the Ford–Firestone crisis. *Journal of Business Communication, 40*(3), 219–236,

Vickery, H. B., III. (1984, January). Tapping into the employee grapevine. *Association Management*, pp. 59–62.

Virtual offices pose risks to your company. (2000, August). HRfocus, p. 9.

Wagman, R. (1991, July 9). Not everything went as planned in Persian Gulf War. *Birmingham Post-Herald*, p. A5.

Walker Information. (2000). *Halfway out the door: The Walker Information and Hudson Institute National Employee Relationship Report.* Indianapolis, IN: Hudson Institute.

Waterman, R. H., Jr. (1987). *The renewal factor.* New York: Bantam.

Weick, K. E. (1976). Educational organizations as loosely coupled systems. *Administrative Science Quarterly, 21,* 1–16.

Wenger, E. C., & Snyder, W. M. (2000, January–February). Communities of practice: The organizational frontier. *Harvard Business Review,* 139–145.

Whistle blower due $2.7 million windfall. (1990, July 11). *Tuscaloosa News,* p. 4.

Whitworth, B. (2006). Internal communication. In T. L. Gillis (Ed.), *The IABC handbook of organizational communication: A guide to internal communication, public relations, marketing, and leadership* (pp. 205–214). San Francisco: Jossey-Bass.

Wind, J. Y., & Main, J. (1998). *Driving change: How the best companies are preparing for the 21st century.* New York: Free Press.

Wyatt, S. (2000, September 23). Doctored photo highlights need to diversify. *Tuscaloosa News,* p. 5A.

Wurman, R. S. (1987). *Information anxiety.* New York: Doubleday.

Yang, J., & Gelles, K. (2006, March 22). Mentoring's impact. *USA Today,* p. 1B.

Yang, J., & Merrill, D. (2006, March 1). HR executives split on telecommuting, *USA Today,* p. 1A.

Chapter 7

Albrecht, K. (1988). *At America's service.* Homewood, IL: Doe Jones-Irwin.

Albrecht, K. (1994). *The northbound train: Finding the purpose, seeing the direction, sharpening the destiny for your organization.* New York: AMACOM.

Anderson, J. A., & Englehardt, E. E. (2001). *The organizational self and ethical conduct.* Fort Worth, TX: Harcourt College.

Appleby, J., & Davis, R. (2001, March 1). Teamwork used to be a money saver, now it's a lifesaver. *USA Today,* pp. 1B–2B.

Associated Press. (2005, February 28), Red Cross was warned of disaster relief pitfalls. *The Tuscaloosa News,* p. 3A.

Beware the bad ethics program. (1999, July). *HRFocus,* p. 5.

Blumer, H. (1969). *Symbolic interactionism: Perspective and method.* Berkeley: University of California Press.

Boje, D. (1995). Stories of the storytelling organization: A postmodern analysis of Disney in "Tamara-land." *Academy of Management Journal, 38,* 997–1035.

Boulding, K. E. (1961). *The image: Knowledge and life in society.* Ann Arbor: University of Michigan Press.

Boyett, J., & Boyett, J. (1998). *The guru guide: The best ideas of the top management thinkers.* New York: Wiley.

Brown, M. H. (1986). Sense-making and narrative forms: Reality construction in organizations. In L. Thayer (Ed.), *Organization–communication: Emerging perspectives I* (pp. 68–78). Norwood, NJ: Ablex.

Burke, K. (1969). *The grammar of motives and the rhetoric of motives.* Berkeley: University of California Press.

Burrell, B. (1997). *Words we live by: The creeds, mottoes, and pledges that have shaped America.* New York: Free Press.

Cameron, K. (1980, Autumn). Critical questions in assessing organizational effectiveness. *Organizational Dynamics,* pp. 66–75.

Carey, A. R., & Jerding, G. (1998, May 11). Ethics lapses in workplace. *USA Today,* p. B1.

Carroll, J. (2002, July). Heart of a good team. *Spirit,* pp. 42–46.

Caudill, D. W., Durden, K. A., & Lambert, R. P. (1985). The image management puzzle. *Supervisory Management, 30*, 22–26.

Chandler, S. (1998, February 15). Sears' system of rewards has ups and downs. *Chicago Tribune*, p. C1.

Cheney, G., & Christensen, L. T. (2000). Identity at issue: Linkages between "internal" and "external" organizational communication. In F. M. Jablin & L. L. Putnam (Eds.), *New handbook of organizational communication* (pp. 231–269). Thousand Oaks, CA: Sage.

Clancy, J. J. (1989). *The invisible powers: The language of business*. Lexington, MA: Lexington.

Collins, J. C., & Porras, J. I. (1994). *Built to last: Successful habits of visionary companies*. New York: HarperBusiness.

Colvin, G. (2000, March 6). Managing in the info era. *Fortune*, pp. F6–9.

Cone, J. (1989). The empowered employee. *Training and Development Journal, 43*, 96, 98.

Conquergood, D. (1991). Rethinking ethnography: Toward a critical cultural politics. *Communication Monographs, 58*, 179–187.

Conrad, C. (1985). *Strategic organizational communication: cultures, situations, and adaptation*. New York: Holt, Rinehart, & Winston.

Cooper, M., & Nothstine, W. L. (1992). *Power persuasion: Moving an ancient art into the media age*. Greenwood, IN: Educational Video Group.

Dalziel, M. M., & Schoonover, S. C. (1988). *Changing ways: A practical tool for implementing change within organizations*. New York: AMACOM.

Deal, T. E., & Kennedy, A. A. (1982). *Corporate cultures: The rites and rituals of corporate life*. Reading, MA: Addison-Wesley.

Deetz, S. A. (1982). Critical interpretive research in organizational communication. *Western Journal of Speech Communication, 46*, 131–149.

Deetz, S. A. (1995). *Transforming communication, transforming business: Building responsive and responsible workplaces*. Cresskill, NJ: Hampton.

Deetz, S. A., Tracy, S. J., & Simpson, J. L. (2000). *Leading organizations through transition*. Thousand Oaks, CA: Sage.

Diamond, S. J. (1991, February 17). Endless changes fail to breath life into ailing Sears. *The Birmingham News*, pp. 1D, 6D.

Dresang, J. (1986, December 9). Companies get serious about ethics. *USA Today*, pp. B1–B2.

Dressler, C. (1995, December 28). Please no! No meetings! *The Tuscaloosa News*, p. 6B.

Duncan, H. D. (1962). *Communication and social order*. London: Oxford University Press.

Duncan, H. D. (1968). *Symbols in society*. New York: Oxford University Press.

Duncan, W. J. (1989). Organizational culture: Getting a fix on an elusive concept. *The Academy of Management Executives, 3*, 229–235.

Eisenberg, E. M. (1984). Ambiguity as strategy in organizational communication. *Communication Monographs, 51*, 227–242.

Eisenberg, E. M., & Riley, P. (1988). Organizational symbols and sense-making. In G. M. Goldhaber & G. A. Barnett (Eds.), *Handbook of organizational communication* (pp. 131–150). Norwood, NJ: Ablex.

Faircloth, A. (1998, August 3). Guess who's coming to Denny's. *Fortune*, pp. 108–110.

Faules, D. F., & Alexander, D. C. (1978). *Communication and social behavior: A symbolic interaction perspective*. Reading, MA: Addison-Wesley.

Folger, J. P., & Poole, M. S. (1984). *Working through conflict: A communication perspective.* Glenview, IL: Scott, Foresman.

Frank, A. D., & Brownell, J. L. (1989). *Organizational communication and behavior: Communicating to improve performance (2 + 2 = 5).* New York: Holt, Rinehart & Winston.

Gabriel, Y., Fineman, S., & Sims, D. (2000). *Organizing and organizations* (2nd ed.). London: Sage.

Galpin, T. (1996, March). Connecting culture to organizational change. *HRMagazine,* pp. 84–90.

Gardner, H. (1995). *Leading minds: An anatomy of leadership.* New York: Basic Books.

Gardenswartz, L., & Rowe, A. (1993). *Managing diversity: A complete desk reference and planning guide.* Chicago: Irwin.

Giddens, A. (1984). *The constitution of reality.* Berkeley: University of California Press.

Gimein, M. (2001, January 8). Smart is not enough. *Fortune,* pp. 124–133.

Goffman, E. (1959). *The presentation of self in everyday life.* Garden City, NY: Anchor Doubleday.

Goffman, E. (1974). *Frame analysis: An essay on the organization of experience.* New York: Harper & Row.

Gutek, B. A. (1995). *The dynamics of service: Reflections on the changing nature of customer/provider interactions.* San Francisco, CA: Jossey-Bass.

Hackman, M. Z., & Johnson, C. E. (2000). *Leadership: A communication perspective* (3rd ed.). Prospect Heights, IL: Waveland.

Hall, C., & Tian, Q. (1999, February 15). Workplace ethics dilemma. *USA Today,* p. B1.

Harris, T. E. (1984). The "faux pas" in interpersonal communication. In S. Thomas (Ed.), *Communication theory and interpersonal attraction* (Vol. 2, pp. 53–61). Norwood, NJ: Ablex.

Harris, T. E. (1990). Organizational cultures: An examination of the role of communication. In S. Thomas & W. A. Evans (Eds.), *Communication and culture: Language, performance, technology, and media* (Vol. 4, pp. 143–155). Norwood, NJ: Ablex.

Harris, T. E. (1997). Diversity: Importance, ironies, and pathways. In C. D. Brown, C. Snedeker, & B. Sykes (Eds.). *Conflict and diversity* (pp. 17–34). Cresskill, NJ: Hampton.

Healey, J. R., & Nathan, S. (2000, September 21). Further scrutiny puts Ford in the hot seat. *USA Today,* p. 1B.

Hof, R. D. (1998, December 14). Amazon.com the world of e-commerce. *Business Week,* pp. 108–119.

Johannesen, R. L. (1996). *Ethics in human communication* (4th ed.). Prospect Heights, IL: Waveland.

Johnson, K. (1998, November 11). Survey: Women muscled out by bias, harassment. *USA Today,* pp. 1A–2A.

Jonas, H. S., III, Fry, R. E., & Srivastva, S. (1989). The person of the CEO: Understanding the executive experience. *The Academy of Management Executive, 3*(3), 205–215.

Kelly, K. (1990, November 12). At Sears, the more things change. *Business Week,* pp. 66–68.

Kerr, J., & Slocum, J. W. (1987). Managing corporate culture through reward systems *The Academy of Management Executive, 1*(2), 99–107.

Keyton, J. (2005). *Communication & organizational culture: A key to understanding work performances.* Thousand Oaks: CA: Sage.

Kotter, J. P. (1988). *The leadership factor.* New York: Free Press.

Kotter, J. P. (1996). *Leading change.* Boston, MA: Harvard Business School Press.

Labich, K. (1999, September 6). No more crude at Texaco. *Fortune,* pp. 205–212.

Landro, L. (2005, November 16). Making it OK to challenge surgeons. *The Wall Street Journal,* pp. D1, D4.

Levering, R., Moshowitz, M., & Katz, M. (1985). *The 100 best companies to work for in America.* New York: New American Library.

Liden, R. C., & Mitchell, T. R. (1988). Ingratiatory behaviors in organizational settings. *The Academy of Management Review, 13*(4), 572–587.

Lord, R. G., & Maher, K. J. (1991). *Leadership and information processing: Linking perceptions and performance.* Boston: Unwin Hyman.

McShane, S. L., & Von Glinow, M. A. (2000). *Organizational behavior.* Boston: McGraw-Hill.

Meredith, N. (1984, May). Attacking the roots of police violence. *Psychology Today,* pp. 21–26.

Mills, C. (2002). The hidden dimension of blue-collar sense-making about workplace communication. *The Journal of Business Communication, 39*(1), 288–313.

Mitzberg, H. (1991, Winter). The effective organization: Forces and forms. *Sloan Management Review,* pp. 54–67.

Moorhead, G., & Griffin, R. W. (1998). *Organizational behavior: Managing people and organizations.* Boston: Houghton Mifflin.

Mosvick, R. K., & Nelson, R. B. (1987). *We've got to start meeting like this.* Gleview, IL: Scott, Foresman.

Mumby, D. (1988). *Communication and power in organizations: Discourse, ideology, and domination.* Norwood, NJ: Ablex.

Munk, N. (1999, April 12). How Levi's trashed a great American brand. *Fortune,* pp. 83–90.

Pacanowsky, M., & O'Donnell-Trujillo, N. (1983). Organizational communication as cultural performance. *Communication Monographs, 50,* 126–147.

Palus, C. J., & Horth, D. M. (1998). Leading creatively. *Leadership in Action,* 18(2), 1–8.

Pepper, G. L., & Larson, G. S. (2006, February). Cultural identity tensions in a post-acquisition organization. *Journal of Applied Communication Research, 34(1),* pp. 49–71.

Peters, T. (1989). Making it happen. *Journal of Quality and Participation, 12,* 1–7.

Peters, T., & Austin, N. (1985). *A passion for excellence: The leadership difference.* New York: Random House.

Petrelle, J. L., Slaughter, G. Z., & Jorgensen, J. D. (1988). New explorations in organizational relationships: An expectancy model of human symbolic activity. *The Southern Speech Communication Journal, 53,* 279–296.

Pfeffer, J. (1981). Management as symbolic action: The creation and maintenance of organizational paradigms. In L. O. Cummings & B. M. Shaw (Eds.), *Research in organizational behavior* (Vol. 3, p. 1–52). Greenwich, CT: JAI.

Pfeffer, J. (2000). Seven practices of successful organizations. In W. L. French, C. H. Bell, Jr., & R. A. Zawacki (Eds.), *Organizational development and transformation* (pp. 494–514). Boston: McGraw-Hill.

Pine, B. J., II, & Gilmore, J. H. (1999). *The experience economy: Work is theatre & every business a stage.* Boston: Harvard Business School Press.

Poole, M. C., & Van De Ven, A. H. (1989). Using paradox to build management and organizational theories. *Academy of Management Review, 14,* 562–578.

Putnam, L. L. (1983). The interpretive perspective: An alternative to functionalism. In L. L. Putnam & M. E. Pacanowsky (Eds.), *Communication and organizations: An interpretive approach* (pp. 31–54). Beverly Hills, CA: Sage.

Putnam, L., Phillips, N., & Chapman, P. (1996). Metaphors for communication and organization. In S. Clegg, C. Hardy, & W. Nord (Eds.), *Handbook of organizational studies* (pp. 375–408). London: Sage.

Remland, M. S. (2000). *Nonverbal communication in everyday life.* Boston: Houghton Mifflin.

Robbins, S. (1980). *The administrative process.* Englewood Cliffs, NJ: Prentice Hall.

Roberts, B. (1998). *Roberts vs. Texaco.* New York: Avon.

Sanchez, P. (2006). Organizational culture. In T. L. Gillis (Ed.), *The IABC handbook of organizational communication* (pp. 31–43). San Francisco: Jossey-Bass.

Schein, E. H. (1985). *Organizational culture and leadership.* San Francisco: Jossey-Bass.

Schein, E. (1994, May 19). *Organizational and managerial culture as a facilitator or inhibitor of organizational learning* [Organizational Learning Network Working Paper No. 10.004]. Cambridge, MA: MIT.

Stamps, D. (1999, December). Best mission statement, *Training,* pp. 45–47.

Strasser, S., & Loebs, S. F. (1985). Viewpoint: Have our shirts become too starched? *Health Care Management Review, 10,* 81–90.

Ting-Toomey, S. (1985). Toward a theory of conflict and culture. In W. B. Gutnecht, L. T. Stewart, & S. Ting-Toomey (Eds.), *Communication, culture, and organizational processes* (pp. 71–86). Beverly Hills, CA: Sage.

Tompkins, P. K. (1987). Translating organizational theory: Symbolism over substance. In F. M. Jablin, L. L. Putnam, K. H. Roberts, & L. W. Porter (Eds.), *Handbook of organizational communication* (pp. 70–96). Newbury Park, CA: Sage.

Tompkins, P. K., & Cheney, G. (1983). Account analysis of organizations: Decision making and identification. In L. L. Putnam & M. E. Pacanowsky (Eds.), *Communication in organizations: An interpretive approach* (pp. 123–146). Beverly Hills, CA: Sage.

Trice, H. M., & Beyer, J. M. (1985). Six organizational rites to change culture. In R. H. Killman, M. J. Saxton, R. Serpa, & Associates (Eds.), *Gaining control of the corporate culture* (pp. 368–379). San Francisco: Jossey-Bass.

Turner, V. (1980). Social dramas and stories about them. *Critical Inquiry, 7,* 141–168.

Waldron, V. R., & Krone, K. J. (1991). The experience and expression of emotion in the workplace: A study of corrections organizations. *Management Communication Quarterly, 4,* 287–309.

Waterman, R. H., Jr. (1987). *The renewal factor.* New York: Bantam.

Weick, K. E. (1979). *The social psychology of organizing* (2nd ed.). New York: Addison-Wesley.

Weick, K. E. (1988). Organizational cultures as a source of high reliability. In J. L. Gibson, J. M. Ivancevick, & J. M. Donnelly, Jr. (Eds.), *Organizations close-up: A book of readings* (6th ed., pp. 22–38). Plano, TX: Business Publications.

Weick, K. (1995). *Sensemaking in organizations.* Thousand Oaks, CA: Sage.

Wentling, R. M., & Palma-Rivas, N. (1998). Current status and future trends in diversity initiatives in the workplace: Diversity experts' perspective. *Human Resource Development Quarterly, 9*(1), 235–253.

Whitford, D. (2001, January 8). A human place to work. *Fortune*, pp. 108–113.

Wilkins, A. A., & Dyer, W. G., Jr. (1988). Toward culturally sensitive theories of culture change. *The Academy of Management Review, 13*(4), 522–533.

Wilson, G. L., Goodall, H. L., Jr., & Waagen, C. L. (1986). *Organizational communication*. New York: Harper & Row.

Wind, J. Y., & Main, J. (1998). *Driving change: How the best companies are preparing for the 21st century*. New York: Free Press.

Women of color doubt diversity commitment. (1999, May). *HRFocus*, p. 5.

Wood, J. T. (1999). *Relational communication: Continuity and change in personal relationships* (2nd ed.). Belmont, CA: Wadsworth.

Wood, J. T. (2004). *Communication mosaics: An introduction to the field of communication* (3rd ed.). U.S.: Thomson Wadsworth.

Yang, J., & Gonzalez, A. (2005, November 29). Corporate culture penetration. *USA Today*, p. 1B.

Zaleznik, A. (1989, November 26). Freud and organizations. *The New York Times*, Sec. 4, p. 14.

Zemke, R., Raines, C., & Filipczak, B. (2000). *Generations at work: Managing the clash of veterans, boomers, xers, and nexters in your workplace*. New York: AMACOM.

Chapter 8

Albrecht, K. (1988). *At America's service*. Homewood, IL: Dow Jones-Irwin.

Benton, D. A. (1995). *Applied human relations: An organizational approach* (5th ed.). Englewood Cliffs, NJ: Prentice Hall.

Berko, R. M., Wolvin, A. D., & Wolvin, D., R. (1996). *Communicating: A social and career focus* (6th ed.). Boston: Houghton Mifflin.

Blair, G. (1999, February 5). *Starting to manage: The essential skills*. Chartwell-Bratt, USA: Institute of Electrical and Electronics Engineers.

Bone, D. (1988). *The business of listening*. Los Altos, CA: Crisp.

Bormann, E. G., Howell, W. S., Nichols, R. G., & Shapiro, G. L. (1980). *Interpersonal communication in the modern organization*. Engelwood Cliffs, NJ: Prentice Hall.

Boyle, R. C. (1999). A manager's guide to effective listening. *Manage, 51*(1), 6–7.

Brownell, J. (2002). *Listening: Attitudes, principles, and skills* (2nd ed.). Boston: Allyn & Bacon.

Buckingham, M., & Coffman, C. (1999). *First, break all the rules: What the world's greatest managers do differently*. New York: Simon & Schuster.

Burley-Allen, M. (2001, November). Listen up. *HR Magazine*, pp. 115–120.

Callerman, W. G., & McCartney, W. W. (1985). Identifying and overcoming listening problems. *Supervisory Management, 28*, 39–40.

Caudron, S. (1998, August 17). Wake-up call. *Industry Week*, p. 102.

Cohen, A. R., & Fink, S. L. (2001). *Effective behavior in organizations: Cases, concepts, and student experiences* (7th ed.). New York: McGraw-Hill.

Collins, J. C., & Porras, J. I. (1994). *Built to last: Successful habits of visionary companies*. New York: HarperBusiness.

Colvin, G. (2000, March 6). Managing in the info era. *Fortune*, pp. F-6–F-9.

Cooper, L. O. (1997). Listening competency in the workplace: A model for training. *Business Communication Quarterly, 60*(4), 75–85.

Covey, S. R. (1989). *The seven habits of highly effective people.* New York: Simon & Schuster.

Covey, S. R. (1991*). Principle-centered leadership.* New York: Fireside.

Curtis, D. B., Winsor, J. L., & Stephens, R. D. (1989). National preferences in business and communication education. *Communication Education,* 38, 6–14.

Deal, T., & Kennedy, A. (1999). *The new corporate cultures: Revitalizing the workplace after downsizing, mergers, and reengineering.* Reading, MA: Perseus.

Decker, C. L. (1998*). Winning with the P&G 99.* New York: Pocket Books.

DeVito, J. A. (2004). *The interpersonal communication book* (10th ed.). Boston: Pearson.

DiSalvo, V. S., Larsen, D. C., & Seiler, W. J. (1976). Communication skills needed by persons in business organizations. *Communication Education,* 25, 269–275.

Donaldson, M. C., & Donaldson, M. (1996). *Negotiating for dummies.* Foster City, CA: IDG Books Worldwide.

DuBrin, A. J. (1999). *Human relations for career and personal success.* Upper Saddle River, NJ: Prentice Hall.

Fisher, R., & Ertel, D. (1995). *Getting ready to negotiate.* New York: Penguin.

Floyd, J. J. (1985). *Listening: A practical approach.* Glenview, IL: Scott, Foresman.

Fuller, G. (1991). *The negotiator's handbook.* Englewood Cliffs, NJ: Prentice Hall.

Gibb, J. R. (1961). Defensive communication. *Journal of Communication,* 11, 141–148.

Gibbs, M., Hewing, P., Hulbert, J. E., Ramsey, D., & Smith, A. (1985, June). How to teach effective listening skills in a basic business communication class. *The Bulletin of the Association for Business Communication,* 48, 29–32.

Goby, J., & Lewis, H. (2000). The key role of listening in business: A study of the Singapore insurance industry. *Business Communication Quarterly,* 63(2), 290–298.

Gordon, R. D. (1988). The difference between feeling defensive and feeling understood. *The Journal of Business Communication,* 25, 53–64.

Hackman, M. Z., & Johnson, C. E. (2000). *Leadership: A communication perspective* (3rd ed.). Prospect Heights, IL: Waveland.

Hamilton, C. (2005). *Communicating for results: A guide for business and professionals* (7th ed.). U.S.: Thomson Wadsworth.

Harris, R. M. (1997, July). Turn listening into a powerful presence. *Training and Development,* pp. 9–11.

Hart, L. (1998, June 12). Leaders thrive on practical listening. *Atlanta Business Chronicle,* p. 49A.

Hollingshead, A. B., & McGrath, J. E. (1995). Computer-assisted groups: A critical review of the empirical research. In R. A. Guzzo, E. Salas, & Associates (Eds.), *Team-effectiveness and decision making in organizations* (pp. 46–78). San Francisco: Jossey-Bass.

Howell, W. S. (1982). *The empathic communication.* Belmont, CA: Wadsworth.

Hudson Institute. (2000). *Halfway out the door.* Indianapolis: Walker Information.

Hunt, G. T., & Cusella, G. T. (1983). A field study of listening needs in organizations. *Communication Education,* 32, 387–395.

Johnson, D. (1996). Helpful listening and responding. In K. M. Galvin, & P. J. Cooper (Eds.), *Making connections: Readings in relational communication* (pp. 27–44). Roxbury, MA: Roxbury.

Karp, H. (1987). The lost art of feedback. In J. W. Pfeiffer (Ed.), *The 1987 annual: Developing human resources* (pp. 237–246). San Diego: University Associates.

Koehler, J. W., Anatol, K. W. E., & Applebaum, R. L. (1981*). Organizational communi- cation: Behavioral perspectives* (2nd ed.). New York: Holt, Rinehart, & Winston.

Kolata, G. (2005, November 30). When the doctor is in, but you wish he wasn't. *The New York Times,* pp. A1, A16.

Kreitner, R. (2005). *Foundations of management: Basics and best practices.* Boston: Houghton Mifflin.

Levinson, H. (1987, September 28). Congratulations! You've made a mistake. *Behav- ioral Sciences Newsletter,* p. 3.

Lewis, M. J., & Reinsch, N. L., Jr. (1988). Listening in organizational environments. *The Journal of Business Communication, 25,* 49–67.

Maes, J. D., Weldy, T. G., & Icenogle, M. L. (1996). A managerial perspective: Oral communication competency is most important for business students in work- place. *Journal of Business Communication, 33*(4), 67–80.

McIntyre, R. M., & Salas, E. (1995). Measuring and managing for team performance: Emerging principles from complex environments. In R. A. Guzzo, E. Salas, & Associates (Eds.), *Team effectiveness and decision making in organizations.* San Francisco: Jossey-Bass.

Morgan, P., & Bake, H. K. (1985). Building a professional image: Improving listening behavior. *Supervisory Management, 28,* 34–38.

Nichols, R. G., (1962). Listening is good business. *Management of Personnel Quarterly,* 1, 2–9.

Nyquist, M. (1996). Learning to listen. In K. M. Galvin, & P. J. Cooper (Eds.), *Making connections: Readings in relational communication.* Roxbury, MA: Roxbury.

Osborn, M., & Osborn, S. (1994). *Public speaking* (3rd ed.). Boston: Houghton Mifflin.

O'Toole, J. (1996). *Leading change: The argument for value-based leadership.* New York: Ballantine.

Peters, T. (1987). *Thriving on chaos.* New York: Knopf.

Peters, T. (1992). *Liberation management.* New York: Knopf.

Purdy, M. (1996). What is listening? In M. Purdy & D. Borisoff (Eds.), *Listening in everyday life: A personal and professional approach* (2nd ed.). (pp. 1–20). New York: University Press of America.

Ray, R. G. (1999). *The facilitative leader.* Upper Saddle River, NJ: Prentice Hall.

Recognition plus performance measurement equals happy workers. (1999, April*). HRFocus,* p. 5.

Salopek, J. J. (1999, November). Survey says. *Training & Development,* p. 16.

Smeltzer, L. R., & Watson, K. W. (1985). A test of instructional strategies for listening improvement in a simulated business setting. *The Journal of Business Commu- nication, 22,* 33–42.

Survey says that trust is the basis for employee retention. (2001, February). *HRFocus,* p. 8.

Sweeney, P. D., & McFarlin, D. B. (2002). *Organizational behavior: Solutions for man- agement.* Boston: McGraw-Hill.

Tannen, D. (1990). *You just don't understand: Women and men in conversation.* New York: Morrow.

Timm, P. R., & DeTienne, K. B. (1995). *Managerial communication: A finger on the pulse* (3rd ed.). Englewood Cliffs, NJ: Prentice Hall.

Tracey, W. R. (1988). *Critical skills: The guide to top performance for human resource managers.* New York: AMACOM.

Van Slyke, E. J. (1999). *Listening to conflict: Finding constructive solutions to workplace disputes.* New York: AMACOM.

Verderber, K. S., & Verderber, R. F. (2001). *Inter-act: Interpersonal communication concepts, skills, and contexts* (9th ed.). U.S.: Wdsworth.

Wakin, L. (1984, February). The business of listening. *Today's Office,* p. 46.

Wheelan, S. A. (1999). Creating effective teams. Thousand Oaks, CA: Sage.

Whetten, D. A., & Cameron, K. S. (1991). *Developing management skills* (2nd ed.). New York: HarperCollins.

Wilson, G. L., Hantz, A. M., & Hanna, M. S. (1989). *Interpersonal growth through communication* (2nd ed.). Dubuque, IA: Brown.

Windsor, J., Curtis, D., & Stephens, R. (1997). National preferences in business and communication education: An update. *Journal of the Association for Communication Administration, 3,* 170–179.

Wolvin, A. D., & Coakley, C. G. (1996). *Listening* (6th ed.). Dubuque, IA: Brown.

Wood, J. T. (2000). *Relational communication: Continuity and change in personal relationships* (2nd ed.). Belmont, CA: Wadsworth.

Yukl, G. A. (1994). *Leadership in organizations* (3rd ed.). Englewood Cliffs, NJ: Prentice Hall.

Zuboff, S. (1988). *In the age of the smart machine.* New York: Basic.

Chapter 9

Abundis, J., & Lynn, C. (2000, January 1). Gambling on retirement. *USA Today,* p. A1.

Amason, A. C. (1996). Distinguishing between the effects of functional and dysfunctional conflict on strategic decision making: Resolving a paradox for top management teams. *Academy of Management Journal, 39,* 123–148.

Amason, A. C., & Sapienza, H. J. (1997). The effects of top management team size and interaction norms on cognitive and affective conflict. *Journal of Management, 6*(4), 495–528.

Anderson, P. A. (1999). *Nonverbal communication: Forms and functions.* Mountain View, CA: Mayfield.

Ashby, W. R. (1964). *An introduction to cybernetics.* London: University Paperbacks.

Axtell, R. E. (1991). *Gestures: The do's and taboos of body language around the world.* New York: Wiley.

Bartlett, S. (1979, May). Two plus two equals four, except. *Psychology Today,* p. 44.

Bateson, G. (1972). *Steps to an ecology of the mind.* New York: Ballantine.

Benton, D. A. (1995). *Applied human relations: An organizational approach.* Englewood Cliffs, NJ: Prentice Hall.

Berger, C. R., Gardner, R. R., Parks, M. R., & Miller, G. R. (1976). Interpersonal epistemology and interpersonal communication. In G. R. Miller (Ed.), *Explorations in interpersonal communication* (pp. 149–171). Beverly Hills, CA: Sage.

Berlo, D. K. (1960). *The process of communication.* New York: Holt, Rinehart, & Winston.

Bolman, L. G., & Deal, T. E. (1991). *Reframing organizations: Artistry, choice, and leadership.* San Francisco: Jossey-Bass.

Briggs, K. C., & Myers, I. B. (1976). *Myers-Briggs type indicator.* Palo Alto, CA: Consulting Psychologists Press.

Bruneau, T. (1989). Empathy and listening: A conceptual review and theoretical directions. *Journal of International Listening Association, 3,* 1–2.

Byrum, B. (1986). A primer on social styles. In J. W. Pfeiffer & L. D. Goodstein (Eds.), *The 1986 annual: Developing human resources* (pp. 213–228). San Diego: University Associates.

Chambers, H. E. (1998). *The bad attitude survival guide.* Reading, MA: Addison-Wesley Longman.

Ciabattari, J. (1999, February 14). We met at the office. *Parade*, p. 25.

Cohen, A. R., Fink, S. L., Gadon, H., & Willits, R. D. (2001). *Effective behavior in organizations* (7th ed.). Boston: McGraw-Hill Irwin.

Covey, S. R. (1989). *The 7 habits of highly effective people.* New York: Simon & Schuster.

Curtis, D. B., Winsor, J. L., & Stephens, R. D. (1989). National preferences in business and communication education. *Communication Education, 38,* 6–14.

Dahle, C. (1998, June/July). Your first 60 days. *Fast Company*, pp. 183–184.

Dance, F. (1967). Toward a theory of human communication. In F. Dance (Ed.), *Human communication theory* (pp. 18–32). New York: Holt, Rinehart, & Winston.

DeVito, J. A. (1989). *The interpersonal communication handbook* (5th ed.). New York: Harper & Row.

Dillard, J. P., Hale, C., & Segrin, C. (1994). Close relationships in task environments: Perceptions of relational types, illicitness, and power. *Management & Communication Quarterly, 7,* 227–255.

Dillard, J. P., & Miller, K. (1988). Intimate relationships in task environments: In S. Duck (Ed.), *Handbook of personal relationships* (pp. 449–465). New York: Wiley.

Dillard, J. P., Segrin, C., & Segrin, C. (1994). Close relationships in task environments: Perceptions of relational types, illicitness, and power. *Management Communication Quarterly, 7,* 227–255.

Dubrin, A. J., Ireland, R. D., & Williams, J. C. (1989). *Management & organization.* Cincinnati: South-Western.

Eisenberg, E. M., Monge, P. R., & Farace, R. V. (1984). Coorientation of communication roles in managerial dyads. *Human Communication Research, 10,* 258–267.

Elliott, L. P. (1999, February 21). Office workers rush to keep up with changing rules. *The Tuscaloosa News*, p. 17A.

Fisher, A. (1998, June 22). Don't blow your new job. *Fortune*, pp. 159–162.

Fitzgerald, C., & Kirby, L. K. (1997). *Developing leaders: Research and applications in psychological types and leadership development.* New York: Davies Black.

Frank, A., & Brownell, J. (1989). *Organizational communication and behavior.* New York: Holt, Rinehart, & Winston.

Folger, J. P., & Poole, M. S. (1984). *Working through conflict.* Glenview, IL: Scott, Foresman.

Goleman, D. (1996). *Emotional intelligence.* London: Bloomsbury.

Goodall, H. L., Jr. (1990). *Small group communication in organizations* (2nd ed.). Dubuque, IA: Brown.

Greenspan, S. I. (1997). *The growth of the mind.* Reading, MA: Addison-Wesley.

Groder, M. G. (1989). *Business games: How to recognize the players and deal with them.* Springfield, NJ: Boardroom Classics.

Haworth, D. A., & Savage, G. T. (1989). A channel-ratio model of intercultural communication: The trains won't sell, fix them please. *The Journal of Business Communication, 26,* 231–254.

Hocker, J. L., & Wilmot, W. W. (1985). *Interpersonal conflicts* (2nd ed.). Dubuque, IA: Brown.

Huber, G. P. (1990). A theory of the effects of advanced information technologies on organizational design, intelligence, and decision making. *Academy of Management Review, 15,* 47–71.

Hudson Institute. (2000). *Halfway out the door.* Indianapolis, IN: Walker Information.

Hunsaker, P. J., & Alessandra, P. L. (1982). *The art of managing people.* Englewood Cliffs, NJ: Prentice Hall.

Jablin, F. M. (1990). Organizational communication. In G. L. Dahnke & G. W. Clatterbuck (Eds.), *Human communication theory and research* (pp. 156–182). Belmont, CA: Wadsworth.

Johns, G. (1988). *Organizational behavior: Understanding life at work* (2nd ed.). Glenview, IL: Scott, Foresman.

Jung, C. J. (1923). *Psychological types.* New York: Harcourt, Brace.

Kidder, T. (1981). *The soul of a new machine.* New York: Avon.

Killman, R., & Thomas, K. (1977). Developing a forced-choice measure of conflict handling behavior: The "MODE" instrument. *Educational and Psychological Measurement, 37,* 309–325.

Kindler, H. S. (1996, July). Tools for managing disagreement. *Training and Development,* p. 11.

Kreps, G. L. (1990). *Organizational communication* (2nd ed.). New York: Longman.

Learning International. (1986, November 19). Logic's O.K., gut feeling is better. *USA Today,* p. 5B.

Levine, S. (1998). *Getting to resolution: Turning conflict into collaboration.* San Francisco: Berrett-Koehler.

Lord, R. G., & Maher, K. J. (1990). Alternative information-processing models and their implications for theory, research, and practice. *Academy of Management Journal, 15,* 9–28.

Lowndes, L. (1993). Dangerous office liaisons. *Legal Assistant Today,* pp. 64–70.

Lussier, R. N. (1999). *Human relations in organizations.* Boston: McGraw-Hill.

Maes, J. D., Weldly, T. G., & Icenogle, M. L. (1997). A managerial perspective: Oral communication competency is most important for business students in the workplace. *The Journal of Business Communication, 34*(1), 67–80.

Managing employee conflicts. (1996, September). *HR Magazine,* p. 16.

Matejka, K. (1989). *Management solutions.* New York: American Management Association.

Merrill, D. W., & Reid, R. H. (1981). *Personal style and effective performance.* Radnor, PA: Chilton.

Miller, F. R. (1990). Interpersonal communication. In G. L. Dahnke & C. W. Clatterbuck (Eds.), *Human communication theory and research* (pp. 91–122). Belmont, CA: Wadsworth.

Moorehead, G., & Griffin, R. W. (1998). *Organizational behavior: Managing people and organizations* (5th ed.). Boston: Houghton Mifflin.

Naisbitt, J., & Aburdene, P. (1985). *Re-inventing the corporation.* New York: Warner.

Nirenberg, J. (1989). *The American management association executive appointment book.* New York: AMACOM.

Ohbuchi, K., Fukushima, O., & Tedeschi, J. T. (1999). Cultural values in conflict management. *Journal of Cross-Cultural Psychology, 30*(1), 51.

Pace, R. W., & Faules, D. F. (1994). *Organizational communication* (3rd ed.). Englewood Cliffs, NJ: Prentice Hall.

Patterson, K., Grenny J., McMillan, R., & Switzler, A. (2002) *Crucial conversations: Tools for talking when the stakes are high.* New York, NY: McGraw-Hill.

Personnel problems. (1990, March 18). *Parade Magazine,* p. 13.

Pincus, J. D. (1985, November). Study links communication and job performance. *IABC Communication World,* pp. 27–30.

Pinnacle Group. (1987, July 21). It takes guts for executives to make the tough decision. *USA Today,* p. 7B.

Redding, W. C. (1972). *Communication within the organization: An interpretive review of theory and research.* New York: Industrial Communication Council.

Redmond, M. V. (1989). The functions of empathy (decentering) in human relations. *Human Relations,* 42, 593–605.

Redmond, M. V. (2000). *Communication: Theories and applications.* Boston: Houghton Mifflin.

Relocation adjustment time: 8 months. (1987, May 19). *USA Today,* p. 5B.

Rothfeder, J., & Bartimo, J. (1990, July 2). How software in making food sales a piece of cake. *Business Week,* p. 55.

Shannon, C. E., & Weaver, W. C. (1949). *The mathematical theory of communication.* Urbana: University of Illinois Press.

Shani, A. B., & Lau, J. B. (2000). *Behavior in organizations: An experimental approach* (7th ed.). Boston: Irwin McGraw-Hill.

Sharpe, R. (2000, November 20). As leaders, women rule. *Business Week,* pp. 75–84.

Shellenbarger, S. (2000, January 12). An overlooked toll of job upheavals: Valuable friendships. *The Wall Street Journal,* p. 1.

Simon, H. A. (1955). A behavioral model of rational choice. *Quarterly Journal of Economics,* 69, 99–118.

Simon, H. A. (1987). Making management decisions: The role of intuition and emotion. *Academy of Management Executive,* 1, 57–64.

Smith, D. R., & Williamson, L. K. (1985). *Interpersonal communication: Roles, rules, strategies, and games* (3rd ed.). Dubuque, IA: Brown.

Snavely, W. B. (1981). The impact of social styles upon person perception in primary relationships. *Communication Quarterly,* 29, 132–142.

U.S. Department of Labor (1989). *The challenge of new technology to labor–management relations (BMLR Publication No. 135–1989).* Washington, DC: U.S. Government Printing Office.

Ward, A. C. (1998, July–August). Another look at how Toyota integrates product development. *Harvard Business Review,* pp. 36–49.

Ward, S., & Snider, J. (2000, October 19). A world bursting with information. *USA Today,* p. 10D.

Watzlawick, P., Beavin, J. B., & Jackson, D. D. (1967). *The pragmatics of human communication.* New York: Norton.

Weider-Hatfield, D., & Hatfield, J. D. (1995). Relationships among conflict management styles, levels of conflict, and reactions to work. *Journal of Social Psychology,* 135(6), 687.

Weider-Hatfield, D., & Hatfield, J. D. (1996). Superiors' conflict management strategies and subordinate outcomes. *Management Communication Quarterly,* 10(2), 183–199.

Wilmot, W. W. (1979). *Dyadic communication* (2nd ed.). Reading, MA: Addison-Wesley.

Wood, J. T. (2000). *Relational communication: Continuity and change in personal relationships* (2nd ed.). Belmont, CA: Wadsworth.

Yeung, L. (1997). Confrontation or resolution management: Discourse strategies for dealing with conflict in participative decision making. *Journal of Applied Management Studies*, 6 (1), 60–73.

Zipkin, A. (2000, May 31). Nice bosses finish first. *The Tuscaloosa News*, pp. 1A, 4A.

Zorn, T. (1995). Bosses and buddies: Constructing and performing simultaneously hierarchical and close friendship relationships. In J. T. Wood & S. W. Duck (Eds.), *Understanding relationship processes, 6: Understudied relationships: Off the beaten track* (pp. 122–147). Thousand Oaks, CA: Sage.

Zuboff, S. (1988). *In the age of the smart machine.* New York: Basic.

Zuboff, S. (1989). Learning in the age of the smart machine. *Labor Relations Today*, 4, 4.

Chapter 10

Abbott, J. R. (1990). New approaches to collective bargaining and workplace relations: Do they work? Washington, DC: Bureau of Labor-Management Relations & Cooperative Approaches.

Albrecht, K. (1994). *The northbound train: Finding the purpose, setting the direction, shaping the destiny of your organization.* New York: AMACOM.

Aldage, R. J., & Riggs-Fuller, S. R. (1993). Beyond fiasco: A reappraisal of the groupthink phenomena and a new mode of group decision processes. *Psychological Bulletin*, 113(3), 533–552.

Applebaum, E., & Batt, R. (1993). *High-performance work systems: American models of workplace transformation.* Washington, DC: Economic Policy Institute.

Appleby, J. & Davis, R. (2001, March 1). Teamwork used to be a money saver, now it's a lifesaver. *USA Today*, pp. 1B–2B.

Bales, R. F. (1970). *Personality and interpersonal behavior.* New York: Holt, Rinehart, & Winston.

Baron, R. A. (1983). *Behavior in organizations: Understanding and managing the human side of work.* Boston: Allyn & Bacon.

Bennis, W. (1994). *On becoming a leader.* New York: Addison-Wesley.

Bennis, W., & Biederman, P. (1997). *Organizing genius: The secrets of creative collaboration.* Reading, MA: Addison-Wesley.

Berko, R. (1996). Education matters. *Spectra*, p. 8.

Beyerlein, M. (1993). Why do teams work? *Self-Managed Work Teams Newsletter*, 3(1), p. 2.

Beyond quality at Xerox. (1992, August). *At work: Stories of tomorrow's workplaces*, I(2), pp. 1, 24.

Blank, W. (1995). *The nine natural laws of leadership.* New York: AMACOM.

Bolman, L. G., & Deal, T. E. (1991). *Reframing organizations: Artistry, choice, and leadership.* San Francisco: Jossey-Bass.

Bolman, L. G., & Deal, T. E. (1992). What makes a team work? *Organizational Dynamics*, 21(2), 34–44.

Bolman, L. G., & Deal, T. E. (2003). *Reframing organizations: Artistry, choice, and leadership* (3rd ed.). San Francisco: Jossey-Bass.

Bormann, E. G. (1975). *Discussion and group methods* (2nd ed.). New York: Harper & Row.

Boyett, J., & Boyett, J. (1998). *The guru guide.* New York: Wiley.

Brown-Johnson, N. (2004). *The driving force: Lessons in teamwork from Saturn and other leading companies.* Kantonah, NY: Xephor Press.

By the numbers. (1995, August 13*). The Tuscaloosa News*, p. 1E.

Cannon-Bowers, J. A., Tannenbaum, S. I., Salas, E., & Volpe, C. E. (1995). In R. Guzzo, E. Salas & Associates (Eds.). *Team effectiveness and decision making in organizations* (pp. 333–380). San Francisco: Jossey-Bass.

Cohen, A. R., & Fink, S. L. (2001). *Effective behavior in organizations* (7th ed.). Boston: McGraw-Hill.

Cole, D. (1989, May). Meetings that make sense. *Psychology Today*, pp. 12–14.

Colorado governor staff "rough it" in a team effort. (1987, July 13). *USA Today*, p. 2A.

Corporate snooping refined to fine art. (1990, April 29). *The Tuscaloosa News*, P. 7E.

Coser, L. A. (1956). *The functions of social conflict.* New York: Free Press.

Crabtree, S. (2004). Getting personal in the workplace. *The Gallup Management Journal*, pp. 7–8.

Cragan, J. F., & Wright, D. W. (1991). *Communication in small group discussions: An integrated approach* (3rd ed.). St. Paul, MN: West.

Crocker, O., Charney, C., & Chui, S. L. (1984). *Quality circles: A guide to participation and productivity.* Toronto: Methuen.

Cross, W. (1999). *Dictionary of business terms.* Paramus, NJ: Prentice Hall.

Cummings, T. G., & Worley, C. G. (2005). *Organizational development and change* (8th ed.). U.S.: Thomson Southwestern.

Dalziel, M. M., & Schoonover, S. C. (1988). *Changing ways: A practical tool for implementing change within organizations.* New York: AMACOM.

Daniels, T. D., & Spiker, T. D. (1991). *Perspectives on organizational communication* (2nd ed.). Dubuque, IA: Brown.

Deetz, S. A., Tracey, S. J., & Simpson, J. L. (2000). *Leading organizations through transition.* Thousand Oaks, CA: Sage.

DuBrin, A. J., Ireland, R. D., & Williams, J. C. (1989). *Management & organization.* Cincinnati: South-Western.

Dumaine, B. (1994, September 5). The trouble with teams. *Fortune*, pp. 86–92.

Egan, G. (1988). *Change agent skills: A: Assessing and designing excellence.* San Diego: University Associates.

Elgin, B. (2001, May 21). Yahoo! Inside. *Business Week*, pp. 114–123.

Employee involvement in America. (1989). Washington, DC: General Accounting Office.

Farnum, A. (1997, March 17). Getting the best from your smartest people. *Fortune*, p. 150.

FBI's repeat offenses. (2001, May 14). *USA Today*, p. 14A.

Fisher, B. A. (1970). Decision emergence: Phases in group decision-making. *Speech Monographs*, 37(1), 53–66.

Frank, A. D., & Brownell, J. L. (1989). *Organizational communication and behavior.* New York: Holt, Rinehart, & Winston.

Freiberg, K. (1996). *Nuts! Southwest airlines' crazy recipe for business and personal success.* Austin, TX: Bard Books.

Gabriel, Y., Fineman, S., & Sims, D. (2000). *Organizing & organizations* (2nd ed.). London: Sage.

Gass, R. H., & Seiter, J. S. (1999). *Persuasion, social influence, and compliance gaining.* Boston: Allyn & Bacon.

General Accounting Office. (1989, June). Miles to go...Or unity to last. *Journal of Quality and Participation*, pp. 60–67.

Gersick, C. J. G. (1988). Time and transition in work teams: Toward a new model of group development. *Academy of Management Journal*, 31, 9–41.

Gersick, C. J. G. (1989). Marketing time: Predictable transitions in task groups. *Academy of Management Journal*, 32, 274–309.

Gersick, C. J. G. (1990). The students. In J. R. Hackman (Ed.), *Groups that work (and those that don't): Creating conditions for effective teamwork* (pp. 146–153). San Francisco: Jossey-Bass.

Golightly, R. (1993, March). Communicating empowerment at Federal Express *Commitment Plus*, 8, pp. 1–4.

Goodall, H. L., Jr. (1990). *Small group communication in organizations* (2nd ed.). Dubuque, IA: Brown.

Harris, T. E. (1990). Organizational cultures: An examination of the role of communication. In S. Thomas & W. A. Evans (Eds.), *Communication and culture: Language, performance, and media* (pp. 143–155). Norwood, NJ: Ablex.

Harris, T. E., & Sherblom, J. C. (2005). *Small group and team communication* (3rd ed.). Boston: Allyn & Bacon.

Hicks, R. (1990, April 10). Retreat firm molds executives into team. *Birmingham Post-Herald*, p. B6.

Hope, J., & Hope, T. (1997). *Competing in the third wave*. Boston, MA: Harvard Business School.

How to build good teams (May 17, 2006). *The New Zealand Herald*, p. 20.

Huber, G. P. (1986). *Human behavior in organizations* (3rd ed.). Cincinnati: South-Western.

Hudson Institute. (2000). *Halfway out the door*. Indianapolis, IN: Walker Information.

Hultman, K. E. (1998, February). The 10 commandments of team leadership. *Training & Development*, pp. 12–13.

Ilgen, D. R., Major, D. A., Hollenbeck, J. R., & Sego, D. J. (1995). Raising an individual decision-making model to the team level: A new research model and paradigm. In R. A. Guzzo, E. Salas, & Associates (Eds.), *Team effectiveness and decision making in organizations* (pp. 113–148). San Francisco: Jossey-Bass.

Industry Report. (1995, October). *Training Magazine*, p. 72.

Jablin, F. M. (1987). Organizational entry, assimilation, and exit. In F. M. Jablin, L. L. Putnam, & L. W. Porter (Eds.), *Handbook of organizational communication* (pp. 679–740). Newbury Park, CA: Sage.

Jablin, F. M., & Sussman, L. (1983). Organizational group communication: A review of the literature and model of the process. In H. Greenbaum, R. Falcone, & S. Hellweg (Eds.), *Organizational communication: Abstract, analysis, and overview* (Vol. 8, pp. 1–28). Newbury Park, CA: Sage.

Jackall, R. (1983). Moral mazes: Bureaucracy and managerial work. *Harvard Business Review*, 61, 118–130.

Jacobs, N. A. (1982). Quality circles alone can't hike productivity. *Industry Week*, 212(3), 28–29.

Janis, I. (1972). *Victims of groupthink*. Boston, MA: Houghton Mifflin.

Johns, G. (1988). *Organizational behavior: Understanding life at work* (2nd ed.). Glenview, IL: Scott, Foresman.

Johnson, K. (2001, May 14). Bureau suffers another black eye. *USA Today*, p. 3A.

Kanter, R. M. (1983). *Change masters: Innovation for productivity in the American corporation*. New York: Simon & Schuster.

Karp, H. B. (1983). A look at quality circles. In L. D. Goodstein & J. W. Pfeiffer (Eds.). *The 1983 annual for facilitators, trainers, and consultants* (pp. 157–163). San Diego: University Associates.

Katzenback, J. R., Beckett, F., Dichter, S., Feigen, M., Gagnon, C., Hope, Q., et al. (1995). *Real change leaders*. New York: Times Business.

Katzenbach, J. R., & Smith, D. K. (1993). *The wisdom of teams*. Boston: Harvard Business School.

Klein, J. A. (1984). Why supervisors resist employee involvement. *Harvard Business Review*, 62, 87–95.

Lavelle, L. (2001, November 26). The case of the corporate spy. *Business Week*, pp. 56–57.

Lawler, E. E., III, & Mohrman, S. A. (1985). Quality circles after the fad. *Harvard Business Review*, 63, 65–71.

Lefton, R. E. (1988). The eight barriers to teamwork. *Personnel Journal*, 67, 18–21.

Lewis, J. P. (1998). *Team-based project management*. New York: AMACOM.

Manz, C., & Sims, H. P. (1993). *Business without bosses*. New York: Wiley.

Marks, M. L. (1986, March). The question of quality circles. *Psychology Today*, pp. 36–44.

McClenahen, J. S. (2006). Leadership training, crm top change strategies. *Industry Week*, 255 (5), 16.

McGrath, J. E. (1984). *Groups: Interactions and performance*. Englewood Cliffs, NJ: Prentice Hall.

McIntyre, R. M., & Salas, E. (1995). Measuring and managing for team performance: Emerging principles from complex environments. In R. Guzzo, E. Salas, & Associates (Eds.). *Team effectiveness and decision making in organizations* (pp. 9–45). San Francisco: Jossey-Bass.

McShane, S. L., & McFarlin, D. B. (2002). *Organizational behavior: Solutions for management*. Boston: McGraw-Hill Irwin.

McShane, S. L., & Von Glinow, M. A. (2000). *Organizational behavior*. Boston: Irwin McGraw-Hill.

Meyer, G. W., & Stott, G. R. (1985). Quality circles: Panacea or Pandora's box. *Organizational Dynamics*, 13, 34–50.

Miller, G. R. (1990). Interpersonal communication. In G. L. Dahnke & G. W. Clatterbuck (Eds.), *Human communication: Theory and research* (pp. 91–122). Belmont, CA: Wadsworth.

Moorehead, G., & Griffin, R. W. (1998). *Organizational behavior: Managing people and organizations*. Boston: Houghton Mifflin.

Moran, L., Musselwhite, E., & Zenger, J. (1996). *Keeping teams on track*. Chicago: Irwin Professional Publishing.

Naisbitt, J., & Aburdene, P. (1985). *Re-inventing the corporation*. New York: Warner.

Neuborne, E. (1997, February 25). Companies save, but workers pay. *USA Today*, pp. 1B–2B.

Nora, J. J., Rogers, C. R., & Stramy, R. J. (1986). *Transforming the workplace*. Princeton, NJ: Princeton Research Press.

Offerman, L. R., & Gowing, M. K. (1990). Organizations of the future: Changes and challenges. *American Psychologist*, 45, 95–108.

Olsavky, M. A. (Ed.). (1990). *The new work systems network: A compendium of selected work innovation cases* (BLMR Report No. 136). Washington, DC: U.S. Government Printing Office.

Osborn, J. D., Moran, L., Musselwhite, E., & Zenger, J. H. (1990). *Self-directed work teams: The new American challenge.* Homewood, NJ: Business One Irwin.

The plane truth about Lucent. (2001, June 11). *Fortune,* p. 252.

Pomeroy, A. (2004, July). Great places, inspired employees. *HR Magazine,* 46–54.

Poole, M. S. (1983). Decision development in small groups, II: A study of multiple sequences in group development. *Communication Monographs, 50,* 206–232.

Putnam, L. L., & Poole, M. S. (1987). Conflict and negotiations. In F. M. Jablin, L. L. Putnam, K. H. Roberts, L. W. Porter (Eds.), *Handbook of organizational communication* (pp. 549–599). Newbury Park, CA: Sage.

Rees, F. (1991). *How to lead work teams: Facilitation skills.* San Diego: Pfeiffer.

Roberts, P. (1999, April). *Total teamwork: The Mayo Clinic. Fast Company,* pp. 149–162.

Safety risk and cost debated. (1989, May 14). *The Sunday Courier,* p. B1.

Schein, E. H. (1969). *Process consultation: Its role in organizational development.* Reading, MA: Addison-Wesley.

Scholtes, P. R., Joiner, B. L., & Streibel, B. J. (1996). *The team handbook* (2nd ed.). Madison, WI: Joiner Associates.

School burned over cookbook. (1988, November 9). *The Evansville Courier,* p. 3A.

Street, M. D. (1997). Groupthink: An examination of theoretical issues, implications, and future research. *Small Group Research, 28*(1), 72–93.

Sundstrom, E., De Meuse, K. P., & Futrell, D. (1990). Work teams: Applications and effectiveness. *American Psychologist, 45,* 120–133.

Sweeney, P., & McFarlin, D. (2002). *International management: Strategic opportunities and cultural challenges* (2nd ed.). Boston: Houghton Mifflin Company.

These teams made business history. How did they do it? (May 31, 2006). *Fortune,* pp. 26–27.

Torres, C., & Spiegel, J. (1990). *Self-directed work teams: A primer.* San Diego: University Associates.

Tuckman, B. (1965). Development sequence in small groups. *Psychological Bulletin, 63,* 384–399.

Tuckman, B. W. (1977). Stages in small-group development revisited. *Group and Organizational Studies, 2,* 419–427.

Waterman, R. H., Jr. (1987). *The renewal factor: How the best get and keep the competitive edge.* New York: Bantam.

Wellins, R. S., Byham, W. C., & Wilson, J. M. (1991). *Empowered teams: Creating self-directed work groups that improve quality, productivity, and participation.* San Francisco: Jossey-Bass.

Wheelan, S. A. (1999). *Creating effective teams.* Thousand Oaks, CA: Sage.

Whyte, G. (1989). Groupthink reconsidered. *Academy of Management Review, 14,* 40–56.

Wilmot, W. W. (1987). *Dyadic communication* (3rd ed.). New York: Random House.

Wood, R., Hull, F., & Azumi, K. (1983). Evaluating quality circles: The American application. *California Management Review, 1,* 37–51.

Woods, J. A. (1997). *10 minute guide to teams and teamwork.* New York: Alpha Books.

Woodyard, C. (1998, May 1). University takes pain out of parking passes. *USA Today*, p. 4B.

Woodyard, C. (2001, May 9). Teams of employees search and destroy work bottlenecks. *USA Today*, p. 3B.

Work incentives: Bonus busting. (1994, January/February). *Psychology Today*, pp. 20–21.

Yang, D. J., & Buderi, R. (1990, August 13). Step by step with Nike. *Business Week*, pp. 115–116.

Zemke, R., Raines, C., & Filipczak, B. (2000). *Generations at work: Managing the clash of veterans, boomers, xers, and nexters in your workplace.* New York: AMACOM.

Chapter 11

Adler, N. J. (1997). *International dimensions of organizational behavior* (3rd ed.). Cincinnati, OH: South-Western.

Albrecht, K. (1994). *The northbound train: Finding the purpose, setting the direction, shaping the destiny of your organization.* New York: AMACOM.

Anderson, L. S. A., & Anderson, D. (2001). *The change leader's roadmap.* San Francisco: Jossey-Bass/Pfeiffer.

Anderson, J. A., & Englehardt, E. E. (2001). *The organizational self and ethical conduct.* Fort Worth: Harcourt College.

Avolio, B. J., & Bass, B. M. (1990). The implications of transactional and transformational leadership for individual, team, and organizational development. In W. Pasmore & R. W. Woodman (Eds.), *Research in organizational change and development* (vol. 4; pp. 231–272). Greenwich, CT: JAI Press.

Barnard, J. (1999). The empowerment of problem-solving teams: Is it an effective management tool? *Journal of Applied Management Studies*, 8(1), 73–84.

Barrier, M. (1999, January). Leadership skills employees respect. *Nation's Business*, pp. 28–30.

Bass, B. M. (1985). *Leadership and performance beyond expectations.* New York: Free Press.

Bass, B. M. (1990). *Bass and Stogdill's handbook of leadership* (3rd ed.). New York: Free Press.

Bass, B. M., & Avolio, B. J. (1994). *Improving organizational effectiveness through transformational leadership.* Thousand Oaks, CA: Sage.

Belasco, J. A., & Stayer, R. C. (1994). *Flight of the buffalo: Souring to excellence, learning to let employees lead.* New York: Warner Books.

Bell, E., Denton, T., & Nkomo, S. (1993). Women of color in management: Toward an inclusive analysis. In E. Fagenson (Ed.), *Women in management* (pp. 105–130).

Bennis, W. (1994). On becoming a leader. New York: Addison-Wesley.

Bennis, W. (1997). *Managing people is like herding cats.* Provo, UT: Executive Excellence Publishing.

Bennis, W., & Nanus, B. (1995). *Leaders: Strategies for taking charge* (2nd ed.). New York: HarperBusiness.

Bennis, W., & Nanus, G. (1997). Toward the new millennium. In G. R. Hickman (Ed.), *Leading organizations: Perspectives for a new era* (pp. 5–7). Thousand Oaks, CA: Sage.

Bernstein, A. (1999, November 8). Sweatshops: No more excuses. *Business Week*, pp. 104, 106.

Blake, R. R., & McCanse, A. A. (1991). *Leaders: The strategies for taking charge*. New York: Harper & Row.

Blake, R. R., & Mouton, J. S. (1985). *The managerial grid III: The key to leadership excellence*. Houston: Gulf.

Blank, W. (1995). *The nine natural laws of leadership*. New York: AMACOM.

Blau, G. (1994). Testing the effect of level and importance of pay referents on pay level satisfaction. *Human Relations, 47,* 1251–1268.

Bolman, L. G., & Deal, T. E. (1991). *Reframing organizations: Artistry, choice, and leadership*. San Francisco: Jossey-Bass.

Bormann, E. G., (1985). Symbolic convergence: Organizational communication and culture. In L. Putnam & M. Pacanowsky, (Eds.), *Communication and organizations: An interpretive approach* (pp. 99–122). Beverly Hills, CA: Sage.

Boyett, J., & Boyett, J. (1998). *The guru guide: The best ideas of the top management thinkers*. New York: Wiley.

Branch, S. (1999, January 11). The 100 best companies to work for in America. *Fortune*, pp. 118–144.

Buckingham, M., & Coffman, C. (1999). *First, break all the rules: What the world's greatest managers do differently*. New York: Simon & Schuster.

Burns, J. M. (1978). *Leadership*. New York: Harper & Row.

Casio, W. F. (1982). *Applied psychology in personnel management*. Reston, VA: Reston.

Caudron, S. (1998, August 17). The only way to stay ahead. *Industry Week*, pp. 98–102.

Chambers, H. E. (1998). *The bad attitude survival guide*. Reading, MA: Addison-Wesley Longman.

Clark, K. E., & Clark, M. B. (1990). *Measures of leadership*. West Orange, NJ: Leadership Library of America.

Clemes, J. K., & Mayer, D. F. (1987). *The classic touch: Lessons in leadership from Homer to Hemingway*. Homewood, IL: Dow Jones Irwin.

Colin, M. (1999, November 1). Religion in the workplace, *Business Week*, pp. 150–154.

Conger, J. A. (1989). *The charismatic leader: Behind the mystique of exceptional leadership*. San Francisco, CA: Jossey-Bass.

Conger, J., & Kanungo, R. (1998). *Charismatic leadership in organizations*. Thousand Oaks, CA: Sage.

Conger, J. A., Kanungo, R. N., & Associates (1988). *Charismatic leadership: The elusive factor in organizational effectiveness*. San Francisco: Jossey-Bass.

Conner, D. R. (1998*). Leading at the edge of chaos*. New York: Wiley.

Cummings, T. G., & Worley, C. G. (2005). *Organizational development and change* (8th ed.). U.S.: Thomson Southwestern.

Cybert, R. M. (1990). Defining leadership and explicating the process. *Nonprofit Management and Leadership, 1*(1), 29–38.

Daniels, A. C. (1994). *Bringing out the best in people: How to apply the astonishing power of positive reinforcement*. New York: McGraw-Hill.

Deal, T. E. (1986). New images of organizations and leadership. *Peabody Journal of Education, 63,* (3), 1–8.

DePree, M. (1993). *Leadership jazz: The art of conducting business through leadership, followership, teamwork, touch, voice*. New York: Dell.

Domerer, D. (1998). Building and maintaining employee motivation. *Women in Business*, 50(6), 32–33.

Downton, J. V. (1973). *Rebel leadership: Commitment and charisma in a revolutionary process*. New York: Free Press.

Drucker, P. F. (1998). *Peter Drucker on the profession of management*. Boston, MA: Harvard Business School Press.

DuBrin, A. J. (2000). *Applied psychology: Individual and organizational effectiveness* (5th ed.). Upper Saddle River, NJ: Prentice Hall.

DuBrin, A. J., Ireland, R. D., & Williams, J. C. (1989). *Management & organization*. Cincinnati: SouthWestern.

Dunlap, D., & Goldman, P. (1991). Rethinking power in schools, *Educational Administration Quarterly*, 27, pp. 5–29.

Eagly, A. H., Karau, S. J., & Makhijani, M. G. (1995). Gender and the effectiveness of leaders: A meta-analysis. *Psychological Bulletin*, 117, 125–145.

Elizur, D., Borg, I., Hunt, R., & Beck, I. M. (1991). The structure of work values: A cross-cultural comparison. *Journal of Organizational Behavior*, 12, 21–38.

Equal pay, top jobs still elude women. (1999, February). *HRFocus*, p. 16.

Fiedler, F. E. (1972). How do you make leaders more effective? New answers to an old puzzle. Leadership effectiveness. *American Behavioral Scientist*, 24, 630–631.

Fisher, A. (1998a, May 11). Texaco: A series of racial horror stories. *Fortune*, p. 186.

Fisher, A. (1998b, January 12). The 100 best companies to work for in America. *Fortune*, pp. 69–70.

Fisher, J. R., Jr. (1999). How a culture of contribution gives your company a grow-up call. *Journal for Quality and Participation*, 22(4), 6–13.

Foster, W. (1989). Toward a critical practice of leadership. In J. Smyth (Ed.), *Critical perspectives on educational leadership* (pp. 39–92). New York: Falmer Press.

Fox, J. B., Scott, K. D., & Donohoe, J. M. (1993). An investigation into pay valence and performance in pay-for-performance field setting. *Journal of Organizational Behavior*, 14, 687–693.

French, J. R., & Raven, B. (1959). The bases of social power. In D. Cartwright (Ed.), *Studies in social power* (pp. 150–167). Ann Arbor: University of Michigan Press.

French, W. L., Bell, C. H., Jr., & Zawacki, R. A. (2000). *Organization development and transformation: Managing effective change*. Boston: Irwin McGraw-Hill.

Gabriel, Y., Fineman, S., & Sims, D. (2000). *Organizing and organizations* (2nd ed.). London: Sage.

Gardner, H. (1995). *Leading minds: An anatomy of leadership*. New York: Basic Books.

Gardner, W. L., & Avolio, B. J. (1998). The charismatic relationship: A dramaturgical perspective. *Academy of Management Journal*, 41(4), 387–409.

Gardner, W. L., & Martinko, M. J. (1996). Using the Myers-Briggs Type Indicator to study managers: A literature review and research agenda. *Journal of Management*, 22, 45–83.

Gentile, M. (1996). *Managerial excellence through diversity*. Prospect Heights, IL: Waveland.

Gilley, A. M. (2005). *The manager as change leader*. Westport, Conn.: Praeger Publishers.

Goleman, D., Boyatzis, R., & McKee, A. (2002). *Primal leadership realizing the power of emotional intelligence*. Boston, MA: Harvard Business School Press.

Haasen, A., & Shea, G. F. (1997). *Better place to work*. New York: American Management Association.

Hackman, M. Z., & Johnson, C. E. (2000). *Leadership: A communication perspective.* Prospect Heights, IL: Waveland.

Haim, A. (1999). *Motivating & rewarding employees: New and better ways to inspire your people.* Holbrook, MA: Adams Media.

Halladay, J. (2001, February 28). Red-light scofflaws run but can't hide. *USA Today,* p. 13A.

Hardy, C., & Leiba-O'Sullivan, S. (1998). The power behind empowerment: Implications for research and practice. *Human Relations,* 51(4), 451–483.

Harris, T. E. (1990). Organizational cultures: An examination of the role of communication. In S. Thomas & W. A. Evans (Eds.), *Communication and culture: Language, performance, and media* (pp. 143–155). Norwood, NJ: Ablex.

Hart, W. L., Heskett, J. L., & Sasser, W. E. (1990–1991, Winter). Soothing the savage customer. *Best of Business,* pp. 12–20.

Heifetz, R., & Laurie, D. (1997, January/February). The work of leadership. *Harvard Business Review,* pp. 124–134.

Heilman, M. E., & Block, C. J. (1995). Sex stereotypes: do they influence perceptions of managers? *Journal of Social Behavior & Personality,* 10, 237–252.

Hersey, P. (1984). *The situational leader.* Escondido, CA: Center for Leadership Studies.

Hershey, P., & Blanchard, K. H. (1977). *Management of organizational behavior: Utilizing human resources* (3rd ed.). Englewood Cliffs, NJ: Prentice Hall.

Herzberg, R. (1966). *Work and the nature of man.* Cleveland: World Publishing.

Hocker, J. L., & Wilmot, W. W. (1985). *Interpersonal conflict* (2nd ed.). Dubuque, IA: Brown.

Hogan, R., Raskin, R., & Fazzini, D. (1990). The dark side of charisma. In K. E. Clark & M. B. Clark (Eds.), *Measures of leadership* (pp. 343–354). West Orange, NJ: Leadership Library of America.

Hollander, E. P., & Offerman, L. R. (1990). Power and leadership in organizations: Relationships in transition. *American Psychologist,* 45(2), 179–189.

Horovitz, B. (2000, March 14). Coaches calling business plays. *USA Today,* pp. 1B–2B.

House, R. J., & Mitchell, T. R. (1974). Path-goal theory of leadership. *Journal of Contemporary Business,* 3, 81–97.

How can you be a great leader? (2001, April). *Success,* pp. 28–39.

Hughes, R. L., Ginnett, R. C., & Curphy, G. J. (1998). Contingency theories of leadership. In G. R. Hickman (Ed.), *Leading organizations: Perspectives for a new era* (pp. 141–157). Thousand Oaks, CA: Sage.

Jasinowski, J., & Hamrin, R. (1995). *Making it in America: Proven paths to success from 50 top companies.* New York: Simon & Schuster.

Job dissatisfaction is growing despite the booming economy. (2000, December). *HRFocus,* p. 8.

Jones, M. (2000, March). Work as practice and vocation. *Leverage: New ideas for the organizational leader,* pp. 1–2.

Katz, D., Macoby, N., & Morse, N. C. (1950). *Productivity, supervision, and morale in an office setting.* Ann Arbor: University of Michigan, Institute for Social Research.

Konnert, M., & Angenstein, J. (1990). *The superintendency in the nineties.* Lancaster, PA: Technomic Publication Co.

Kotter, J. P. (1988). *The leadership factor.* New York: Free Press.

Kotter, J. P. (1990). *A force for change: How leadership differs from management.* New York: Free Press.

Kotter, J. (1995, March/April). Leading change: Why transformation efforts fail. *Harvard Business Review,* pp. 59–67.

Kouzes, J. M., & Posner, B. Z. (1987). *The leadership challenge: How to get extraordinary things done in organizations.* San Francisco: Jossey-Bass.

Labich, K. (1999, September 6). No more crude at Texaco. *Fortune,* pp. 205–210.

Lambert, C. (1995, March–April). Leadership in a new key. *Harvard Magazine,* pp. 28–33.

Levering, R., & Moskowitz, M. (2000, January 10). The 100 best companies to work for. *Fortune,* pp. 82–110.

Levering, R., & Moskowitz, M. (2001, January 8). The 100 best companies to work for. *Fortune,* pp. 148–168.

Liden, R. C., & Arad, S. (1996). A power perspective of empowerment and work groups: Implications for human resource management research. *Research in Personnel and Human Resource Management, 14,* 205–251.

Lovely, S. (2006). *Setting leadership priorities: what's necessary, what's nice. And what's got to go.* Thousand Oaks, CA: Corwin Press.

Locke, E. A., & Latham, G. P. (1990). *A theory of goal setting and task performance.* Englewood Cliffs, NJ: Prentice Hall.

Madzar, S. (2001). Subordinates' information inquiry: Exploring the effect of perceived leadership style and individual differences. *Journal of Occupational and Organizational Psychology, 74,* 2, 221–232.

Maier, M., Ferguson, K., & Shirvastava, P. (1992). Organizational dysfunction as gendered practice: The case of the NASA space shuttle Challenger disaster. In M. Maier (Ed.), *A major malfunction: the story behind the space shuttle Challenger disaster.* Albany, NY: Research Foundation of the State University of New York.

Maslow, A. H. (1954). *Motivation and personality.* New York: Harper & Row.

McClelland, D. C. (1953). *The achievement motive.* New York: Appleton-Century-Crofts.

McClelland, D. C. (1961). *Achieving society.* Princeton, NJ: Van Nostrand.

McClelland, D. C. (1962). Business drive and national achievement. *Harvard Business Review, 40,* 99–112.

McClelland, D. C. (1975). *Power: The inner experience.* New York: Irvington.

McClenahan, J. S. (1998, August 17). 100 best-managed companies: A world of (topline) difference. *Industry Week,* pp. 92–102.

McKee, R., & Carlson, B. (1999). *The power to change.* Austin, TX: Grid International.

McShane, S. L., & Von Glinow, M. A. (2000). *Organizational behavior.* Boston: Irwin McGraw-Hill.

Miller, W. (1997, August 18). Leadership's common denominator. *Industry Week,* pp. 96–100.

Mitchell, T. R. (1984). *Motivation and performance.* Chicago: Science Research Associates.

Moorehead, G., & Griffin, R. W. (1998). *Organizational behavior: Managing people and organizations.* Boston: Houghton Mifflin.

Mull, R. F., Bayless, K. G., & Jamieson, L. M. (2005). *Recreational sports management.* Champaign, IL: Human Kinetics.

Nadler, D. A., & Lawler, E. E. (1983). Motivation: A diagnostic approach. In J. R. Hackman, E. E. Lawler, III, & L. W. Porter (Eds.), *Perspectives on behavior in organizations* (2nd ed., pp. 36–44). New York: McGraw-Hill.

Neuborne, E. (1996, October 14). Survey: Women fare the best. *USA Today*, p. 3B.

Northhouse, P. G. (2004). *Leadership theory and practice* (3rd ed.). Thousand Oaks, CA: Sage.

Oleck, J. (1999, September 6). Footnotes. *Business Week*, p. 8.

100 best companies do have an edge. (1999, June). *HRFocus*, p. 4.

O'Toole, J. (1996). *Leading change: The argument for values-based leadership*. New York: Ballantine.

Peters, T. (1987). *Thriving on chaos*. New York: Knopf.

Peters, T. J., & Austin, N. (1985). *Passion for excellence: the leadership difference*. New York: Random House.

Pfeffer, J. (1997). *New directions in organizational theory*. New York: Oxford University Press.

Ragins, B., Townsend, B. & Mattis, M. (1998). Gender gap in the executive suite: CEOs and female executives report on breaking the glass ceiling. *Academy of Management Executive*, 12(1), 28–42.

Recognition plus performance measurement equals happy workers. (1999, April). *HRFocus*, p. 5.

Risky business on roads. (1999, March 29). *USA Today*, p. 1A.

Rosener, J. B. (1990, November/December). Ways women lead. *Harvard Business Review*, pp. 119–125.

Rost, J. (1991). *Leadership for the twenty-first century*. New York: Praeger.

Rost, J. C. (1998). Leadership and management. In G. R. Hickman (Ed.), *Leading organizations: Perspectives for a new era* (pp. 97–114). Thousand Oaks, CA: Sage.

Sample, J. A. (1984). The expectancy theory of motivation: Implications for training and development. In J. W. Pfeiffer & L. D. Goodstein (Eds.), *The 1984 annual: Developing human resources* (pp. 257–261). San Diego: University Associates.

Schein, E. H. (1992). *Organizational culture and leadership* (2nd ed.). San Francisco, CA: Jossey-Bass.

Schwartz, N. D. (2001, June 25). Starbucks. *Fortune*, pp. 130–131.

Sellers, P. (1996, January 15). What exactly is charisma? *Fortune*, pp. 68–71.

Senge, P. M. (1990). *The fifth discipline: The art and practice of the learning organization*. New York: Doubleday Currency.

Sergiovanni, T. J. (1992). *Moral leadership*. San Francisco, CA: Jossey-Bass.

Shamir, B., House, R. J., & Arthur, M. B. (1993). The motivational effects of charismatic leadership: A self-concept based theory. *Organization Science*, 4(4), 577–594.

Sharpe, R. (2000, November 20). As leaders, women rule. *Business Week*, pp. 75ff.

Shikdar, A. A., & Das, B. (1995, February). A field study of worker productivity improvements. *Applied Economics*, 26, 21–27.

Shipper, F., & Manz, C. C. (1992, Winter). Employee self-management without formally designated teams: an alternative road to empowerment? *Organizational Dynamics*, 48–61.

Sigford, Jane L. (2006). *The effective school leader's guide to management*. Thousand Oaks, CA: Corwin Press.

Smith, D. M. (1997). Women and leadership. In P. G. Northouse (Ed.), *Leadership: Theory and practice* (pp. 204–238). Thousand Oaks, CA: Sage.

Sokolove, M. (2006, February 5). Follow me. *New York Times*, (sec. 6; p. 96).

States fail to protect children in vehicles. (2001, February 8). *The Tuscaloosa News*, p. 3D.

Steele-Pucci, C. (2006, February). Career-intelligence.com.

Steward, T. A. (2000, January 10). How Teradyne solved the innovator's dilemma. *Fortune*, pp. 188, 190.

Stodgill, R. M. (1974). *Handbook of leadership: A survey of theory and research*. New York: Free Press.

Stodgill, R. M., & Coons, A. E. (1957). *Leader behavior: Its description and measurement*. Columbus: Ohio State University, Bureau of Business Research.

Sergiovanni, T. J. (1992). *Moral leadership*. San Francisco, CA: Jossey-Bass.

Thorlakson, A. J. H., & Murray, R. P. (1996). An empirical study of empowerment in the workplace. *Group & Organizational Management*, 21(1), 67–85.

Treacy, M., & Wiersema, F. (1995). *The discipline of market leaders*. Reading, MA: Addison-Wesley.

Trice, H. M., & Beyer, J. M. (1991). Cultural leadership in organizations. *Organization Science*, 2, 149–169.

Trice, H. M., & Beyer, J. M. (1993). *The cultures of work organizations*. Englewood Cliffs, NJ: Prentice Hall.

Tubbs, M. E., & Ekeberg, S. E. (1991). The role of intentions in work motivation: Implications for goal-setting theory and research. *Academy of Management Review*, 16, 180–199.

U.S. job satisfaction keeps falling. (2005, February 28). Conference-board.org.

Vesespej, M. (1998). Bringing out the best. *Industry Week*, 246(12), p. 18.

Vroom, V. H. (1964). *Work and motivation*. New York: Wiley.

Vroom, V. H., & Jago, A. G. (1988). *The new leadership: Managing participation in organizations*. Englewood Cliffs, NJ: Prentice Hall.

Waldroop, J., & Butler, T. (1998, November 23). Eight failings that bedevil the best. *Fortune*, pp. 293–294.

We need to get serious about running red lights. (2005, August 29). *The Pantagraph*.

Wheatley, M. J. (1994). *Leadership and the new science: Learning about organizations from an orderly universe*. San Francisco: Bennett-Koehler.

Williams, D. (2005). *Real leadership: helping people and organizations face their toughest challenges*. San Francisco: Berrett-Koehler.

Witherspoon, P. D. (1997). *Communicating leadership: An organizational perspective*. Boston: Allyn & Bacon.

Yearout, S., Miles, G., & Koonce, R. (2000, March). Wanted: Leader-builders. *Training & Development*, pp. 34–42.

Yukl, G. A. (1989). *Leadership in organizations* (2nd ed.). Englewood Cliffs, NJ: Prentice Hall.

Yukl, G. A. (1994). *Leadership in organizations* (3rd ed.). Englewood Cliffs, NJ: Prentice Hall.

Zaleznik, A. (1989). *The managerial mystique: Restoring leadership in business*. New York: Harper & Row.

Zemke, R. (1992, April). Second thoughts about the MBTI. *Training*, pp. 42–47.

Zemke, R., Raines, C., & Filipczak, R. (2000). *Generations at work: Managing the clash between veterans, boomers, Xers, and nexters in your workplace*. New York: AMACOM.

Chapter 12

Anderson, C. (2006). *The long tail: Why the future of business is selling less of more*. New York: Hyperion.

Anderson, D. (2006, January 13). Our waning attention span. *Daily Evergreen.* Retrieved February 19, 2006, from http://www.Lexis-Nexis.com

Armour, S. (1998, July 2–5). E-mail 'a blessing' for business. *USA Today,* p. 1A.

Baig, E. C. (2001, June 26). The era of living wirelessly. *USA Today,* pp. 1E–2E.

Bordia, P. (1996). Face-to-face versus computer-mediated communication: A synthesis of the experimental literature. *The Journal of Business Communication, 33*(4), 99–120.

Brown, E. (1998, December 7). You've got mail. *Fortune,* pp. 36–37.

Brown, J. S. (1998, May–June). Seeing differently: A role for pioneering research. *Research Technology Management, 42,* 24–33.

Cable News Network. (2006, March 3). Making the case for telecommuting. *CNN.com.* Retrieved February 20, 2006, from http://www.Lexis-Nexis.com

Can I work at home? (2006, January 16). *Business Line.* Retrieved February 19, 2006, from http://www.Lexis-Nexis.com

Cohen S. (1998, January). Knowledge management's killer app. *Training & Development,* pp. 50–57.

Compton, D. C., White, K., & DeWine, S. (1991). Techno-sense: Making sense of computer-mediated communication systems. *The Journal of Business Communication, 28,* 23–43.

Conlin, M. (2006, March 27). You are what you post. *Business Week,* pp. 52–53.

Daft, R. L., & Lewin, A. Y. (1993). Where are the theories for the "new" organizational form? An editorial essay. *Organization Science, 4,* i–vi.

Dahl, D. (2005, December). Office optional. *Inc. Magazine,* pp. 42, 44.

Deeprose, D. (1999, October). When implementing telecommuting leave nothing to chance. *HRFocus,* pp. 13–15.

Digital dirt. (2006, July 9). *The Tuscaloosa News,* p. 1D.

Drucker, P. F. (1998). *Peter Drucker on the profession of management.* Boston, MA: Harvard Business School Press.

Dubrovsky, V. J., Kiesler, S., & Sethna, B. N. (1991). The equalization phenomenon: Status effects in computer-mediated and face-to-face decision-making groups. *Human–Computer Interaction, 6,* 119–146.

Employee surveillance is still souring, reports AMA survey. (2001, June). *HRFocus,* pp. 8–9.

Frauenheim, E. (2006, November 21). Workplaces in the fast lane of commuting. *Workforce Management,* p. 12.

Gates, B. (1999). *Business @ the speed of thought.* New York: Warner.

Gladwell, M. (2005). *Blink: The power of thinking without thinking.* New York: Little, Brown, and Company.

Green, H. (1999, July 16). The information gold mine. *Business Week E. Biz,* p. EB 17.

Greengard, S. (1998, October). Storing, shaping and sharing collective wisdom. *Workforce, 77,* pp. 82–87.

Groleau, C., & Taylor, J. (1996). Toward a subject-oriented worldview of information. *Canadian Journal of Communication, 21,* 243–265.

Hamm, S. (2006, March 27). Speed demons. *Business Week,* pp. 68–76.

Hampson, R. (2001, February 8). Pay phones vanishing as cellphones take over. *USA Today,* pp. 1A–2A.

Harris, T. E., & Sherblom, J. C. (2005). *Small group and team communication* (3rd ed.). Boston: Allyn & Bacon.

Hewak, J. (2005, November 30). Cell phones offer more than just talk; music, video, photos, distinct ring tones up the ante. *The Hamilton Spectator*. Retrieved February 20, 2006, from http://www.Lexis-Nexis.com

Hollingshead, A. B. (1996). Information suppression and status persistence in group decision making: The effects of communication media. *Human Communication Research, 23*, 193–219.

Hollingshead, A. B., McGrath, J. E., & O'Connor, K. M. (1993, August). Group task performance and communication technology: A longitudinal study of computer-mediated versus face-to-face groups. *Small Group Research, 24*(3), 307–333.

Hollis, D. R. (1996, June). The shape of things to come: The role of IT. *Management Review*, pp. 61–64.

Horowitz, B. (1999, August 19). Wired on campus e-life. *USA Today*, pp. 1B–2B.

Hull, P. (2005, August 23). College students to spend $35B on back-to-school items. *The Island Packet*. Retrieved February 20, 2006, from http://www.Lexis-Nexis.com

Is Gen Y shopping online? (2001, June 11). *Business Week*, p. 16.

Issak, R. A. (2005). *The globalization gap: How the rich get richer and the poor get left behind*. Upper Saddle River, NJ: Pearson Education.

Johnston, H. R., & Vitale, M. R. (1988). Creating competitive advantage with interorganizational information systems. *MIS Quarterly, 12*, 153–166.

Katz, M. (1997). *Technology Forecast 1997*. Menlo Park, CA: Pricewaterhouse World Technology Center.

Kiesler, S. (1986, January–February). The hidden messages in computer networks. *Harvard Business Review, 64*, 46–59.

Kennedy, S. (1997, June 5). The burning issue of electronic hate mail. *Computer Weekly*, p. 22.

Kessler, M. (2001, June 26). Gadgets give workers on the run a leg up. *USA Today*, p. 5E.

Koch, W. (2006, February 7). Businesses putting lid on chatterboxes. *USA Today*, p. 3A.

Komsky, S. H. (1991). A profile of users of electronic mail in a university. *Management Communication Quarterly, 4*, 310–340.

Koulopoulos, T. M. (1997). *Smart companies, smart tools*. New York: Von Nostrand Rheinhold.

Levering, R., & Moskowitz, M. (2000, January 10). The 100 best companies to work for. *Fortune*, pp. 83–110.

Levitt, M. & Mahowald, R. P. (2002, September). Worldwide e-mail usage forecast, 2002–2006: Know what's coming your way [IDC #27975].

Lohr, S. (2006, February 21). A cyberfueled growth spurt. *The New York Times*, pp. E1, E6.

Madhavan, R., & Grover, R. (1998, October). From embedded knowledge to embodied knowledge: New product development as knowledge management. *Journal of Marketing, 62*, 1–12.

Mallozzi, V. M. (2006, February 19). Hey Superman, good luck finding a place to change. *New York Times*. Retrieved on February 20, 2006, from http://www.Lexis-Nexis.com

Malone, T. (2006, July 10). A virtual roundtable. *Fortune*, p. 103.

Mandel, M. (2005, October 3). The real reasons you're working so hard … and what you can do about it. *Business Week*, pp. 59–67.

Markus, M. L. (1994). Finding a happy medium: Explaining the negative effects of electronic communication of social life at work. *ACM Journal*, 199–246.

Maruca, R. F. (1998, July–August). How do you manage an off-site team? *Harvard Business Review*, pp. 22–35.

Meyers, C., & Davis, S. (1998). *Blur: The speed of change in the connected economy.* Reading, MA: Addison-Wesley.

Minsky, B. D., & Marin, D. B. (1999). Why faculty members use e-mail: The role of individual differences in channel choice. *The Journal of Business Communication, 36*(2), 194–217.

Miranda, S. M. (1994). Avoidance of groupthink: Meeting management using group support systems. *Small Group Research, 25*(1), 105–136.

Moore, P. L. (2001, June 25). GE embraces the paperless office. *Business Week*, p. 10.

More tech, less time. (1999, March). *HRFocus*, p. 4.

Motz, A. A. (1998, July). Intranets—an opportunity for records managers. *Records Management Quarterly, 32*, pp. 14–16.

New age heralds end of information overload. (1998, December 8). *Financial News*.

Odell, P. (2005, September 1). Shopping 101. *Promo Magazine*. Retrieved February 20, 2006, from http://www.Lexis-Nexis.com

Osterman, P. (1989). New technology and the organization of work: A review of issues. In D. C. Mowery & B. E. Henderson (Eds.), *The challenge of new technology to labor-management relations* (pp. 5–15). Washington, DC: U.S. Department of Labor.

Rains, S. (2005). Leveling the organizational playing field—virtually. *Communication Research, 32*, 193–234.

Rice, R. E. (1992). Task analyzability, use of new media, and effectiveness: A multi-site exploration of media richness. *Organization Science, 3*, 475–500.

Robey, D. (1991). *Designing organizations* (3rd ed.). Homewood, IL: Irwin.

Row, H. (1998, June). It's (real) time to talk. *Fast Company*, pp. 12–14.

Rupp, D. (1996, November). Tech versus touch. *HR Focus, 73*, 16–18.

Schlender, B. (2000, October 9). Enter here. *Fortune*, p. 90.

Schrage, M. (1999, March). The nightmare of networks. *Fortune,* p. 63–69.

Scott, C. R. (1999). Communication technology and group communication. In L. R. Frey, D. S. Gouran, & M. S. Poole (Eds.), *The handbook of group communication & research* (pp. 432–472). Thousand Oaks, CA: Sage.

Spears, T. (2005, August 25). Office e-mail undermines productivity, study finds: Workers forced to "hide" to avoid barrage of messages, researcher says. *The Vancouver Sun*. Retrieved February 20, 2006, from http://www.Lexis-Nexis.com

Stepanek, M., & Hamm, S. (1998, June 8). When the devil is in the e-mails. *Business Week*, pp. 72, 74.

Stewart, T. A. (1994, July 11). Managing in a wired company. *Fortune*, pp. 44–56.

Stockey, L. L., & Laird, M. E. (2006, March 8). Internet use. *USA Today*, p. 1.

Superville, D. (2001, July 7). Wireless way of life. *The Tuscaloosa News*, p. 8A.

Survey finds college students "make the grade" on smart banking practices. (2005, November 30). *Business Wire*. Retrieved February 19, 2006, from http://www.Lexis-Nexis.com

Swartz, J. (2001, June 26). E-mail overload taxed workers and companies. *USA Today*, p. 1A.

Tergesen, A. (1998, October 12). Making stay-at-homes feel welcome. *Business Week*, pp. 155–156.

Tracy, P. (2004, March 15). *A closer look at the retail consumer electronics industry*. Retrieved February 20, 2006, from http://www.StreetAuthority.com

Turnage, J. (1990). The challenge of new workplace technology for psychology. *American Psychologist, 45*, 171–178.

Verity, J. W., Coy, P., & Rothfeder, J. (1990, October 8). Taming the wild network. *Business Week*, pp. 142–146, 148.

Virtual offices pose risks to your company. (2000, August). *HRFocus*, p. 9.

Walther, J. B. (1996). Computer-mediated communication: Impersonal, interpersonal, and hyperpersonal interaction. *Communication Research, 23*(1), 3–43.

Wellman, B., Salaff, J., Dimitrova, D., Garton, L., Gulia, M., & Haythornthwaite, C. (1996). Computer networks as social networks: Collaborative work, telework, and virtual community. *Annual Review of Sociology, 22*, 213–329.

Wilson, T. (2002). *Strangers to ourselves: Discovering the adaptive unconscious*. Cambridge, MA: Harvard University Press.

Zuboff, S. (1988). *In the age of the smart machine: The future of work and power*. New York: Basic.

Author Index

Subject Index